ATLS®

Advanced Trauma Life Support®

Student Course Manual

THE
COMMITTEE
ON **TRAUMA**

AMERICAN COLLEGE OF SURGEONS
Inspiring Quality:
Highest Standards, Better Outcomes

100+*years*

Chair of Committee on Trauma: Ronald M. Stewart, MD, FACS
Medical Director of Trauma Program: Michael F. Rotondo, MD, FACS
ATLS Committee Chair: Sharon M. Henry, MD, FACS
ATLS Program Manager: Monique Drago, MA, EdD
Executive Editor: Claire Merrick
Project Manager: Danielle S. Haskin
Development Editor: Nancy Peterson
Media Services: Steve Kidd and Alex Menendez, Delve Productions
Designer: Rainer Flor
Production Services: Joy Garcia
Artist: Dragonfly Media Group

Tenth Edition

Advanced Trauma Life Support® Student Course Manual
Library of Congress Control Number: 2017907997
ISBN 78-0-9968262-3-5

DEDICATION

We dedicate the Tenth Edition of ATLS to the memory of Dr. Norman E. McSwain Jr. His dynamic, positive, warm, friendly, and uplifting approach to getting things done through his life's work is a constant inspiration to those whose lives he touched. His tenure with the American College of Surgeons Committee on Trauma (COT) spanned almost exactly the same 40 years of the ATLS course.

Dr. McSwain's time with the COT led him down a path where, without a doubt, he became the most important surgical advocate for prehospital patient care. He first worked to develop, and then led and championed, the Prehospital Trauma Life Support Course (PHTLS) as a vital and integral complement to ATLS. Combined, these two courses have taught more than 2 million students across the globe.

Dr. McSwain received every honor the COT could bestow, and as a last tribute, we are pleased to dedicate this edition of ATLS to his memory. The creators of this Tenth Edition have diligently worked to answer Dr. McSwain's most common greeting: "What have you done for the good of mankind today?" by providing you with the Advanced Trauma Life Support Course, 10th Edition, along with our fervent hope that you will continue to use it to do good for all humankind. Thank you, Dr. McSwain.

Sharon Henry, MD
Karen Brasel, MD
Ronald M. Stewart, MD, FACS

FOREWORD

My first exposure to Advanced Trauma Life Support® (ATLS®) was in San Diego in 1980 while I was a resident. The instructor course was conducted by Paul E. "Skip" Collicott, MD, FACS, and fellow students included a young surgeon in San Diego, A. Brent Eastman, MD, FACS, and one from San Francisco, Donald D. Trunkey, MD, FACS. Over the next year or two, we trained everyone in San Diego, and that work became the language and glue for the San Diego Trauma System. The experience was enlightening, inspiring, and deeply personal. In a weekend, I was educated and had my confidence established: I was adept and skilled in something that had previously been a cause of anxiety and confusion. For the first time, I had been introduced to an "organized course," standards for quality, validated education and skills training, and verification of these skills. It was a life-transforming experience, and I chose a career in trauma in part as a result. During that weekend, I also was introduced to the American College of Surgeons—at its very best.

The Tenth Edition of ATLS continues a tradition of innovation. It takes advantage of electronic delivery and by offering two forms of courses (traditional and electronic) to increase the reach and effectiveness of this landmark course. Just about to celebrate its 40th anniversary and currently used in over 60 countries, the ATLS program and its delivery through the Tenth Edition will continue to foster safe trauma practices for the world at large.

Under the leadership of Sharon Henry, MD, FACS, the ATLS Committee Chair, and Monique Drago, MA, EdD, the Trauma Education Program Manager, along with excellent college staff, we have been able to evolve the program, building on the foundation laid in the Ninth Edition by Karen Brasel, MD, FACS, and Will Chapleau, EMT-P, RN, TNS. The Tenth Edition of the ATLS program takes the finest achievements of the American College of Surgeons and its Fellows to the next level, and ultimately patient care is the greatest beneficiary.

David B. Hoyt, MD, FACS
Executive Director
American College of Surgeons
Chicago, Illinois
United States

The year 1976 was key for improving the care of the injured patient. In that year, orthopedic surgeon Dr. James Styner and his family were tragically involved in a plane crash in a Nebraska cornfield. The largely unprepared medical response by those caring for Dr. Styner and his family subsequently compelled him to action. Dr. Styner joined forces with his colleague, Dr. Paul "Skip" Collicott MD, FACS, and began a course entitled Advanced Trauma Life Support (ATLS). Today this initially small course has become a global movement. ATLS was quickly adopted and aggressively promulgated by the Committee on Trauma. The first course was held in 1980, and since that time ATLS has been diligently refined and improved year after year, decade after decade. More than a million students have been taught in more than 75 countries. From Nebraska to Haiti, more than 60% of ATLS courses are now taught outside North America.

It was also in 1976 that Don Trunkey, MD, FACS and the Committee on Trauma (COT) published *Optimal Hospital Resources for Care of the Injured*, the first document aimed at defining and developing trauma centers and trauma systems. This document led directly to the COT's Verification Review and Consultation (VRC) program and its 450 verified trauma centers across the United States. These two programs have transformed the care of injured patients across the globe, resulting in hundreds of thousands of lives saved. In an interesting twist, ATLS was intended as an educational program, and the VRC was intended to be a set of standards. But in real ways, ATLS standardized the care of trauma patients, and the VRC educated the trauma community on how to provide optimal care for trauma patients.

Thus 1976 heralded radical and positive change in the care of trauma patients. The Tenth Edition of ATLS is the most innovative and creative update since the inception of the ATLS course. I believe this edition is a fitting testament to the memory of those pioneers who, in their mind's eye, could see a path to a better future for the care of the injured. I congratulate the modern pioneers of this Tenth Edition. The development of this edition was led by a team with a similar commitment, zeal, and passion to improve. My hope is that all those taking and teaching ATLS will boldly continue this search to improve the care of the injured. In so doing, we may appropriately honor those pioneers of 1976.

Ronald M. Stewart, MD, FACS
Chair of the ACS Committee on Trauma

PREFACE

ROLE OF THE AMERICAN COLLEGE OF SURGEONS COMMITTEE ON TRAUMA

The American College of Surgeons (ACS) was founded to improve the care of surgical patients, and it has long been a leader in establishing and maintaining the high quality of surgical practice in North America. In accordance with that role, the ACS Committee on Trauma (COT) has worked to establish guidelines for the care of injured patients.

Accordingly, the COT sponsors and contributes to continued development of the Advanced Trauma Life Support (ATLS) program. The ATLS Student Course does not present new concepts in the field of trauma care; rather, it teaches established treatment methods. A systematic, concise approach to the early care of trauma patients is the hallmark of the ATLS Program.

This Tenth Edition was developed for the ACS by members of the ATLS Committee and the ACS COT, other individual Fellows of the College, members of the international ATLS community, and nonsurgical consultants to the Committee who were selected for their special competence in trauma care and their expertise in medical education. (The Preface and Acknowledgments sections of this book contain the names and affiliations of these individuals.) The COT believes that the people who are responsible for caring for injured patients will find the information extremely valuable. The principles of patient care presented in this manual may also be beneficial to people engaged in the care of patients with nontrauma-related diseases.

Injured patients present a wide range of complex problems. The ATLS Student Course is a concise approach to assessing and managing multiply injured patients. The course supplies providers with comprehensive knowledge and techniques that are easily adapted to fit their needs. Students using this manual will learn one safe way to perform each technique. The ACS recognizes that there are other acceptable approaches. However, the knowledge and skills taught in the course are easily adapted to all venues for the care of these patients.

The ATLS Program is revised by the ATLS Committee approximately every four years to respond to changes in available knowledge and incorporate newer and perhaps even safer skills. ATLS Committees in other countries and regions where the program has been introduced have participated in the revision process, and the ATLS Committee appreciates their outstanding contributions.

NEW TO THIS EDITION

This Tenth Edition of the Advanced Trauma Life Support Student Course Manual reflects several changes designed to enhance the educational content and its visual presentation.

CONTENT UPDATES

All chapters were rewritten and revised to ensure clear coverage of the most up-to-date scientific content, which is also represented in updated references. New to this edition are:

- Completely revised skills stations based on unfolding scenarios

- Emphasis on the trauma team, including a new Teamwork section at the end of each chapter and a new appendix focusing on Team Resource Management in ATLS

- Expanded Pitfalls features in each chapter to identify correlating preventive measures meant to avoid the pitfalls

- Additional skills in local hemorrhage control, including wound packing and tourniquet application

- Addition of the new Glasgow Coma Scale (GCS)

- An update of terminology regarding spinal immobilization to emphasize restriction of spinal motion

- Many new photographs and medical illustrations, as well as updated management algorithms, throughout the manual

MYATLS MOBILE APPLICATION

 The course continues to make use of the MyATLS mobile application with both Universal iOS and Android compatibility. The app is full of useful reference content for retrieval at the hospital bedside and for review at your leisure. Content includes:

- Interactive visuals, such as treatment algorithms and x-ray identification
- Just in Time video segments capturing key skills
- Calculators, such as pediatric burn calculator to determine fluid administration
- Animations, such as airway management and surgical cricothyroidotomy

Students, instructors, coordinators, and educators are encouraged to access and regularly use this important tool.

SKILLS VIDEO

As part of the course, video is provided via the MyATLS.com website to show critical skills that providers should be familiar with before taking the course. Skill Stations during the course will allow providers the opportunity to fine-tune skill performance in preparation for the practical assessment. A review of the demonstrated skills before participating in the skills stations will enhance the learner's experience.

EDITORIAL NOTES

The ACS Committee on Trauma is referred to as the ACS COT or *the Committee*, and the State/Provincial Chair(s) is referred to as *S/P Chair(s)*.

The international nature of this edition of the ATLS Student Manual may necessitate changes in the commonly used terms to facilitate understanding by all students and teachers of the program.

Advanced Trauma Life Support® and ATLS® are proprietary trademarks and service marks owned by the American College of Surgeons and cannot be used by individuals or entities outside the ACS COT organization for their goods and services without ACS approval. Accordingly, any reproduction of either or both marks in direct conjunction with the ACS ATLS Program within the ACS Committee on Trauma organization must be accompanied by the common law symbol of trademark ownership.

AMERICAN COLLEGE OF SURGEONS COMMITTEE ON TRAUMA

Ronald M. Stewart, MD, FACS
Committee on Trauma, Chair
Chair of the American College of Surgeons Committee on Trauma
Witten B. Russ Professor and Chair of the Department of Surgery
UT Health San Antonio
San Antonio, Texas
United States

Michael F. Rotondo, MD, FACS
Trauma Program, Medical Director
CEO, University of Rochester Medical Faculty Group
Vice Dean of Clinical Affairs–School of Medicine
Professor of Surgery–Division of Acute Care Surgery
Vice President of Administration–Strong Memorial Hospital
President-Elect–American Association for the Surgery of Trauma
University of Rochester Medical Center
Rochester, New York
United States

COMMITTEE ON ADVANCED TRAUMA LIFE SUPPORT OF THE AMERICAN COLLEGE OF SURGEONS COMMITTEE ON TRAUMA

Sharon M. Henry, MD, FACS
ATLS Committee Chair
Anne Scalea Professor of Surgery
University of Maryland School of Medicine
University of Maryland Medical Center RA
Cowley Shock Trauma Center
Baltimore, Maryland
United States

Saud A. Al Turki, MD, FACS
Ministry of National Guard Health Affairs, King Abdulaziz Medical City
King Saud Bin Abdulaziz University for Health Sciences

Riyadh
Saudi Arabia

Col. (Ret.) Mark W. Bowyer, MD, FACS
Ben Eiseman Professor of Surgery
Chief, Trauma and Combat Surgery
Surgical Director of Simulation, Department of Surgery
The Uniformed Services University
Walter Reed National Military Medical Center
Bethesda, Maryland
United States

Kimberly A. Davis MD, MBA, FACS, FCCM
Professor of Surgery, Trauma
Vice Chairman for Clinical Affairs
Yale School of Medicine
Chief of General Surgery, Trauma and Surgical Critical Care
Trauma Medical Director
Yale New Haven Hospital
New Haven, Connecticut
United States

Julie A. Dunn, MD, MS, FACS
Medical Director, Trauma Research and Education
UC Health Northern Colorado
Loveland, Colorado
United States

Peter F. Ehrlich, MD, FACS
Professor
C S Mott Children's Hospital
Ann Arbor, Michigan
United States

James R. Ficke, MD, FACS
Professor of Orthopaedic Surgery
Johns Hopkins Hospital
Baltimore, Maryland
United States

Glen A. Franklin, MD FACS
Professor
University of Louisville School of Medicine
Louisville, Kentucky
United States

Maria Fernanda Jimenez, MD, FACS
General Surgeon
Hospital Universitario MEDERI
Bogotá, Distrito Capital
Colombia

Martin S. Keller, MD, FACS, FAAP
Associate Professor of Surgery
St. Louis Children's Hospital
Washington University School of Medicine
St. Louis, Missouri
United States

Gilberto K. K. Leung, MBBS, FRCS, PhD
Clinical Associate Professor
The University of Hong Kong Queen Mary University
Pok Fu Lam
Hong Kong

R. Todd Maxson, MD, FACS
Professor of Surgery
University of Arkansas for Medical Sciences
Trauma Medical Director
Arkansas Children's Hospital
Little Rock, Arkansas
United States

Daniel B. Michael, MD, PhD, FACS, FAANS
Director of Neurosurgical Education
William Beaumont Hospital Royal Oak
Professor of Neurosurgery
Oakland University William Beaumont School of Medicine
Royal Oak, Michigan
United States
Director, Michigan Head and Spine Institute
Southfield, Michigan
United States

Neil G. Parry, MD, FACS, FRCSC
Medical Director, Trauma Program
Associate Professor of Surgery and Critical Care
London Health Sciences Center
Schulich School of Medicine, Western University
London, Ontario
Canada

Bruce Potenza, MD, FACS
Critical Care Surgeon, Trauma
UCSD Medical Center
San Diego, California
United States

Martin A. Schreiber MD, FACS
Professor and Chief, Division of Trauma, Critical Care & Acute Surgery
Oregon Health & Science University
Portland, Oregon
United States

Gary A. Vercruysse, MD, FACS
Director of Burn Services
Associate Professor of Surgery, Division of Trauma, Burns,
Acute Care Surgery and Surgical Critical Care
University of Arizona School of Medicine
Tucson, Arizona
United States

Robert J. Winchell, MD, FACS
Chief, Division of Trauma, Burn, Acute and Critical Care
Director of the Trauma Center
Weill Cornell Medicine
New York–Presbyterian Weill Cornell Medical Center
New York, New York
United States

Lewis E. Jacobson, MD, FACS
Chair, Department of Surgery
Director, Trauma and Surgical Critical Care
St. Vincent Indianapolis Hospital
Indianapolis, Indiana
United States

Newton Djin Mori, MD, PhD, FACS
General and Trauma Surgeon
Hospital das Clinicas–University of São Paulo
São Paulo, São Paulo
Brazil

John P. Sutyak, EdM, MD, FACS
Director, Southern Illinois Trauma Center
Associate Professor of Surgery
Southern Illinois University School of Medicine
Springfield, Illinois
United States

ASSOCIATE MEMBERS TO THE COMMITTEE ON ADVANCED TRAUMA LIFE SUPPORT OF THE AMERICAN COLLEGE OF SURGEONS COMMITTEE ON TRAUMA

Mary-Margaret Brandt, MD, MHSA, FACS
Trauma Director
St. Joseph Mercy Health System
Ann Arbor, Michigan
United States

Megan L. Brenner, MD FACS
Assistant Professor of Surgery
University of Maryland Medical Center
Baltimore, Maryland
United States

Frederic J. Cole, Jr., MD, FACS
Associate Medical Director, Trauma Clinic and Patient
Outcomes
Legacy Emanuel Medical Center
Portland, Oregon
United States

Oscar D. Guillamondegui, MD, MPH, FACS
Professor of Surgery
Trauma Medical Director
Vanderbilt University Medical Center
Nashville, Tennessee
United States

LIAISONS TO THE COMMITTEE ON ADVANCED TRAUMA LIFE SUPPORT OF THE AMERICAN COLLEGE OF SURGEONS COMMITTEE ON TRAUMA

Michael Murray, MD
General Surgery
Banner Churchill Community Hospital
Sparks, Nevada
United States

Clark West, MD FACR
Co-Course Director
The University of Texas Health Science
Houston Medical School
Houston, Texas
United States

INTERNATIONAL LIAISON TO THE COMMITTEE ON ADVANCED TRAUMA LIFE SUPPORT OF THE AMERICAN COLLEGE OF SURGEONS COMMITTEE ON TRAUMA

Karen J. Brasel, MD, FACS
Professor and Program Director
Oregon Health and Science University
Portland, Oregon
United States

AMERICAN SOCIETY OF ANESTHESIOLOGISTS LIAISON TO THE COMMITTEE ON ADVANCED TRAUMA LIFE SUPPORT OF THE AMERICAN COLLEGE OF SURGEONS COMMITTEE ON TRAUMA

Richard P. Dutton, MD, MBA

Michael Murray, MD
General Surgery
Banner Churchill Community Hospital
Sparks, Nevada
United States

ADVANCED TRAUMA CARE FOR NURSES LIAISON TO THE COMMITTEE ON ADVANCED TRAUMA LIFE SUPPORT OF THE AMERICAN COLLEGE OF SURGEONS COMMITTEE ON TRAUMA

Jan Howard, MSN, RN, Chair, ATCN Committee
South Bend, Indiana
United States

AMERICAN COLLEGE OF EMERGENCY PHYSICIANS LIAISONS TO THE COMMITTEE ON ADVANCED TRAUMA LIFE SUPPORT OF THE AMERICAN COLLEGE OF SURGEONS COMMITTEE ON TRAUMA

Christopher Cribari, MD
Medical Director, Acute Care Surgery, Medical Center of the Rockies, University of Colorado Health
Loveland, CO
United States

Christopher S. Kang, MD, FACEP
Attending Physician, Emergency Medicine, Madigan Army Medicine Center
Tacoma, Washington
United States

ADVANCED TRAUMA LIFE SUPPORT SENIOR EDUCATOR ADVISORY BOARD

Debbie Paltridge, MHlthSc (ED)
Senior Educator Advisory Board, Chair
Principal Educator
Royal Australasian College of Surgeons
Melbourne, Victoria
Australia

Joe Acker, EMT-P, MPH
Executive Director, Birmingham Regional EMS System
University of Alabama at Birmingham
Birmingham, Alabama
United States

Wesam Abuznadah, MD, MEd, FRCS(C), FACS, RPVI
Assistant Professor, Consultant Vascular and Endovascular Surgery
Associate Dean, Academic and Student Affairs, College of Medicine
King Saud Bin Abdulaziz University for Health Sciences
Jeddah
Saudi Arabia

Jacqueline Bustraan, MSc
Educational Advisor, Trainer and Researcher
Leiden University Medical Center/BOAT (Bustraan
Organisation, Advice and Training)
Leiden
The Netherlands

Marzellus Hofmann, MD, MME
Dean of Medical Education and Student Affairs
Witten/Herdecke University, Faculty of Health
Witten, NRW
Germany

Elizabeth Vallejo de Solezio
National Education, COT Ecuador
Quito
Ecuador

Claus Dieter Stobaus, ME, ED
Postgraduate Program in Education
Pontifical Catholic University of Rio Grande do Sul
Porto Alegre, Rio Grande do Sul
Brazil

John P. Sutyak, EdM, MD, FACS
Director, Southern Illinois Trauma Center
Associate Professor of Surgery
Southern Illinois University School of Medicine
Springfield, Illinois
United States

Prof. Heba Youssef Mohamed Sayed, MD
Professor and Head of Forensic Medicine and Clinical
Toxicology Department
Port Said University
Port Said, Egypt
Arab Republic of Egypt

Kum Ying Tham, MBBS, FRCSE, EDD
Senior Consultant
Tan Tock Seng Hospital
Singapore

ADVANCED TRAUMA LIFE SUPPORT COORDINATOR COMMITTEE

Lesley Dunstall, RN
ATLS Coordinator Committee, Chair
National Coordinator, EMST/ATLS Australasia
Royal Australasian College of Surgeons
North Adelaide, South Australia
Australia

Catherine Wilson, MSN, ACNP-BC, CEN
ATLS Coordinator Committee, Vice Chair
Trauma Outreach Coordinator
Vanderbilt University Medical Center
Nashville, Tennessee
United States

Mary Asselstine, RN
Sunnybrook Health Sciences Centre
Toronto, Ontario
Canada

Ryan Bales, RN
ATLS Coordinator
CNIII Trauma Program
Sacramento, California
United States

Vilma Cabading
Trauma Courses Office, Deanship of Postgraduate Education
King Saud Bin Abdulaziz University for Health Sciences
Riyadh
Saudi Arabia

Sally Campbell, RN, BA
ATLS Course Coordinator
Kaiser Medical Center, Vacaville, California
David Grant Medical Center, Travis Air Force Base,
California
United States

Cristiane de Alencar Domingues, RN, MSN, PhD
Professor
Faculdade das Américas (FAM)
São Paulo, São Paulo
Brazil

Agienszka Gizzi
Regional and International Programmes Coordinator
The Royal College of Surgeons of England
London
United Kingdom

Betty Jean Hancock, MD, FRCSC, FACS
Associate Professor, Pediatric Surgery and Critical Care
University of Manitoba
Children's Hospital of Winnipeg/Health Sciences Centre
Winnipeg, Manitoba
Canada

Sherri Marley, BSN, RN, CEN, TCRN
Clinical Educator for Trauma Services
Eskenazi Health
Indianapolis, Indiana
United States

Martha Romero
ATLS Coordinator
AMDA-Bolivia
Santa Cruz de la Sierra
Bolivia

ACKNOWLEDGMENTS

It is clear that many people are responsible for development of the Tenth Edition, but the outstanding staff in the ATLS Program Office deserves special mention. Their dedication and hard work not only produced the new edition while ensuring that each one is better than the last but also facilitates its use in hundreds of courses around the world each year.

Monique Drago, MA, EdD
Trauma Education Programs Manager
The American College of Surgeons
Chicago, Illinois
United States

Ryan Hieronymus, MBA, PMP
Trauma Education Projects Manager
The American College of Surgeons
Chicago, Illinois
United States

Pascale Leblanc
Trauma Education Projects Manager
The American College of Surgeons
Chicago, Illinois
United States

Kathryn Strong
Program Manager, Trauma Education Programs (LMS)
The American College of Surgeons
Chicago, Illinois
United States

Autumn Zarlengo
Program Manager, Trauma Education Programs (CME/CE)
The American College of Surgeons
Chicago, Illinois
United States

Emily Ladislas
Program Coordinator, Trauma Education Programs (CME/CE)
The American College of Surgeons
Chicago, Illinois
United States

Marlena Libman
Trauma Education Program Coordinator
The American College of Surgeons
Chicago, Illinois
United States

Freddie Scruggs
Trauma Education Program Coordinator
The American College of Surgeons
Chicago, Illinois
United States

Germaine Suiza
Program Coordinator, Trauma Education Programs (LMS)
The American College of Surgeons
Chicago, Illinois
United States

CONTRIBUTORS

While developing this revision, we received a great deal of assistance from many individuals—whether they were reviewing information at meetings, submitting images, or evaluating research. ATLS thanks the following contributors for their time and effort in development of the Tenth Edition.

Wesam Abuznadah, MD, MEd, FRCS(C), FACS, RPVI
Assistant Professor, Consultant Vascular and Endovascular Surgery; Associate Dean, Academic and Student Affairs, College of Medicine
King Saud Bin Abdulaziz University for Health Sciences
Jeddah
Saudi Arabia

Joe Acker, EMT-P, MPH
Executive Director, Birmingham Regional EMS System
University of Alabama at Birmingham
Birmingham, Alabama
United States

Suresh Agarwal, MD, FACS
Professor of Surgery
University of Wisconsin
Madison, Wisconsin
United States

Jameel Ali, MD, MMedEd, FRCSC, FACS
Professor of Surgery
University of Toronto
Toronto, Ontario
Canada

Hayley Allan, BA(hons), Dip Ed, MEd, MRes
National Educator, ATLS UK
The Royal College of Surgeons of England
London
England

Saud Al Turki, MD, FACS
Ministry of National Guard Health Affairs, King Abdulaziz Medical City
King Saud Bin Abdulaziz University for Health Sciences
Riyadh
Kingdom of Saudi Arabia

Mary Asselstine, RN
Sunnybrook Health Sciences Centre
Toronto, Ontario
Canada

Mahmood Ayyaz, MBBS, FCPS, FRCS, FACS
Professor of Surgery, Services Institute of Medical Sciences; Councillor and Director, National Residency Programme; National Course Director, ATLS Pakistan
Services Hospital
College of Physicians and Surgeons Pakistan
Lehore
Pakistan

Mark Bagnall, BMedSc(Hons), MBChB(Hons), MSc, PhD, MRCS(Eng)
Specialist Registrar in General Surgery; General Surgery Representative ATLS UK
Steering Group
United Kingdom

Andrew Baker, MBChB, FRCS(Orth), FCS(Orth), SA
Senior Consultant
Entabeni Hospital
Durban
South Africa

Ryan Bales, RN
ATLS Coordinator
CNIII Trauma Program
Sacramento, California
United States

Raphael Bonvin, MD, MME
Head of Educational Unit
Faculty of Biology and Medicine
Lausanne
Switzerland

Bertil Bouillon, MD
Professor and Chairman Department of Trauma and Orthopaedic Surgery
University of Witten/Herdecke, Cologne Merheim Medical Center
Cologne
Germany

Mark W. Bowyer, MD, FACS
ATLS Board Member Germany Col. (Ret.)
Ben Eiseman Professor of Surgery; Chief, Trauma and Combat Surgery; Surgical Director of Simulation Department of Surgery
The Uniformed Services University; Walter Reed National Military Medical Center
Bethesda, Maryland
United States

Mary-Margaret Brandt, MD, MHSA, FACS
Trauma Director
St. Joseph Mercy Health System
Ann Arbor, Michigan
United States

Frank Branicki, MB, BS, DM, FRCS, FRCS(Glasg), FRACS, FCSHK, FHKAM, FCSECSA, FACS
Professor and Chair, Department of Surgery
United Arab Emirates University
Al Ain
United Arab Emirates

Susan Briggs, MD, MPH, FACS
Director, International Trauma and Disaster Institute
Massachusetts General Hospital
Boston, Massachusetts
United States

George Brighton, MBBS, BSc Honors, MSc, PGCE Med Ed.
Clinical Entrepreneur Fellow NHS England
Royal Devon and Exeter NHS Foundation Trust
Exeter
England

Bertil Bouillon, MD
Professor and Chairman Department of Trauma and Orthopaedic Surgery
University of Witten/Herdecke, Cologne Merheim Medical Center
Cologne
Germany

Guy Brisseau, MD, MEd, FACS
Director, Pediatric Trauma; Director, Surgical Education
Sidra Medical and Research Center
Doha
Qatar

Troy Browne, MBChB, FCA(SA), FANZCA, FCICM
Medical Leader—Anaesthesia, Radiology and Surgical Services; Director of Intensive Care/High Dependency Unit
Bay of Plenty District Health Board
Tauranga
New Zealand

Shane Brun, MD, M.Trauma, M.Ed, FFSEM(UK), FACRRM, FRACGP
Associate Professor
James Cook University
Queensland
Australia

Stephen Bush, MA(Oxon), FRCS, FRCEM
Consultant in Emergency Medicine
Leeds Teaching Hospitals
Trust Leeds, West Yorkshire
United Kingdom

Jacqueline Bustraan, MSc
Educational Advisor, Trainer, and Researcher
Leiden University Medical Center/BOAT (Bustraan Organisation, Advice and Training)
Leiden
The Netherlands

Vilma Cabading
Trauma Courses Office, Deanship of Postgraduate Education
King Saud Bin Abdulaziz University for Health Sciences
Riyadh
Kingdom of Saudi Arabia

Sally Campbell, RN, BA
ATLS Course Director
Kaiser Medical Center/David Grant Medical Center
Vacaville/Travis Air Force Base, California
United States

Juan Carlos Puyana, MD, FACS
Professor of Surgery, Critical Care Medicine and Clinical Translational Medicine
University of Pittsburgh
Pittsburgh, Pennsylvania
United States

Narain Chotirosniramit, MD, FACS, FICS, FRCST
Chief, Trauma and Critical Care Unit; Department of Surgery, Faculty of Medicine
Chiangmai University
Chiangmai
Thailand

Ian Civil, MBChB, FRACS, FACS
Director of Trauma Services
Auckland City Hospital
Auckland
New Zealand

Keith Clancy, MD, MBA, FACS
Trauma Medical Director
Geisinger Wyoming Valley Medical Center
Wilkes-Barre, Pennsylvania
United States

Peter Clements

Frederic J. Cole, Jr., MD, FACS
Legacy Emanuel Medical Center
Portland, Oregon
United States

Jaime Cortes-Ojeda, MD, FACS
Chief Department of Surgery
Hospital Nacional de Niños "Dr. Carlos Sáenz Herrera"
San José
Costa Rica

Renn J. Crichlow, MD MBA
Orthopaedic Trauma Surgeon
St. Vincent Indianapolis Trauma Center
OrthoIndy Hospital
Indianapolis, Indiana
United States

Scott D'Amours, MD, FRCS(C), FRACS, FRCS(Glasg)
Trauma Surgeon, Director of Trauma
Liverpool Hospital
Sydney, New South Wales
Australia

Marc DeMoya, MD, FACS
Associate Professor of Surgery
Massachusetts General Hospital/Harvard Medical School
Boston, Massachusetts
United States

Newton Djin Mori, MD, PhD, FACS
General and Trauma Surgeon
Hospital das Clinicas–University of São Paulo
São Paulo, São Paulo
Brazil

Cristiane de Alencar Domingues, RN, MSN, PhD
Professor
Faculdade das Américas (FAM)
São Paulo, São Paulo
Brazil

Jay Doucet, MD, FRCSC, FACS
Professor of Surgery
University of California, San Diego
San Diego, California
United States

Julia A. Dunn, MD, MS, FACS
Medical Director, Trauma Research and Education
UC Health Northern Colorado
Loveland, Colorado
United States

Lesley Dunstall, RN
National Coordinator; EMST/ATLS Australasia
Royal Australasian College of Surgeons
North Adelaide, South Australia
Australia

David Efron, MD, FACS
Professor of Surgery; Chief, Division of Acute Care Surgery; Director of Adult Trauma
The Johns Hopkins University School of Medicine
Baltimore, Maryland
United States

Froilan Fernandez, MD, FACS
Chair, ACS-COT Chile; Associate Senior Surgical Staff
Hospital Del Trabajador
Santiago
Chile

John Fildes, MD, FACS
Foundation Professor; Chair, Surgery; Chief, Division of Acute Care Surgery; Program Director, Acute Care Surgery Fellowship
University of Nevada, Reno School of Medicine
Las Vegas, Nevada
United States

Esteban Foianini, MD, FACS
Medical Director
Clinica Foianini
Santa Cruz de la Sierra
Bolivia

Adam Fox, DPM, DO, FACS
Assistant Professor of Surgery and Section Chief, Trauma Division of Trauma Surgery and Critical Care, Rutgers NJMS; Associate Trauma Medical Director, NJ Trauma Center
Newark, New Jersey
United States

Robert Michael Galler, DO, FACS, FACOS
Associate Professor, Neurosurgery and Orthopedics; Co-Director, Comprehensive Spine Center, Institute for Advanced Neurosciences
Stony Brook University Medical Center
Long Island, New York
United States

Raj Gandi, MD
Trauma Medical Director
JPS Health Network
Fort Worth, Texas
United States

Naisan Garraway, CD, FRCSC, FACS
Medical Director, Trauma Program
Vancouver General Hospital
Vancouver, British Columbia
Canada

Subash Gautam, MB, FRCS(Eng, Edn, and Glasg), FACS
Head of Department
Fujairah Hospital
Fujairah
United Arab Emirates

Julie Gebhart, PA-C
Lead Orthopedic Trauma Physician; Assistant Manager, Orthopedic Advanced Practice Providers
OrthoIndy Hospital
Indianapolis, Indiana
United States

Agienszka Gizzi
Regional and International Programmes Coordinator
The Royal College of Surgeons of England
London
United Kingdom

Oscar Guillamondegui, MD, MPH, FACS
Professor of Surgery, Trauma Medical Director
Vanderbilt University Medical Center
Nashville, Tennessee
United States

Betty Jean (B. J.) Hancock, MD, FRCSC, FACS
Associate Professor, Pediatric Surgery and Critical Care
University of Manitoba; Children's Hospital of Winnipeg/Health Sciences Centre
Winnipeg, Manitoba
Canada

Paul Harrison, MD, FACS
Trauma Medical Director HCA Continental Division; Associate Medical Director, Clinical Professor of Surgery
Wesley Medical Center/KU School of Medicine
Wichita, Kansas
United States

Col. (Ret.) Walter Henny, MD
University Hospital and Medical School
Rotterdam
The Netherlands

Sharon M. Henry, MD, FACS
Anne Scalea Professor of Surgery
University of Maryland School of Medicine; University of Maryland Medical Center RA Cowley Shock Trauma Center
Baltimore, Maryland
United States

Fergal Hickey, FRCS, FRCSEd, DA(UK), FRCEM, FIFEM
National Director, ATLS Ireland; Consultant in Emergency Medicine
Sligo University Hospital
Sligo
Ireland

Marzellus Hofmann, MD, MME
Dean of Medical Education and Student Affairs
Witten/Herdecke University, Faculty of Health
Witten, NRW
Germany

Annette Holian
Clinical Director-Surgery and Perioperative Services
Royal Australian Air Force

Roxolana Horbowyj, MD, MSChE, FACS
Assistant Professor of Surgery, Department of Surgery
Uniformed Services University of the Health Sciences/Walter Reed National Military Medical Center
Bethesda, Maryland
United States

David B. Hoyt, MD, FACS
Executive Director
American College of Surgeons
Chicago, Illinois
United States

Eliesa Ing, MD
Staff Ophthalmologist, Portland VA HSC
Assistant Professor, Casey Eye Institute/OHSU
Portland, Oregon
United States

Lewis Jacobson, MD, FACS
Chair, Department of Surgery; Director, Trauma and Surgical Critical Care
St. Vincent Indianapolis Hospital
Indianapolis, Indiana
United States

Randeep Jawa, MD, FACS
Clinical Professor of Surgery
Stony Brook University School of Medicine
Stony Brook, New York
United States

Maria Fernanda Jimenez, MD, FACS
General Surgeon
Hospital Universitario MEDERI
Bogotá, Distrito Capital
Colombia

Aaron Joffe, DO, FCCM
Associate Professor of Anesthesiology
University of Washington, Harborview Medical Center
Seattle, Washington
United States

Kimberly Joseph, MD, FACS, FCCM
Division Chair, Trauma Critical Care and Prevention Department, Department of Trauma and Burns
John H. Stoger Hospital of Cook County
Chicago, Illinois
United States

Haytham Kaafarani, MD, MPH, FACS
Patient Safety and Quality Director; Director of Clinical Research, Trauma, Emergency Surgery and Surgical Critical Care
Massachusetts General Hospital and Harvard Medical School
Boston, Massachusetts
United States

Martin Keller, MD, FACS, FAAP
Associate Professor of Surgery
St. Louis Children's Hospital; Washington University School of Medicine
St. Louis, Missouri
United States

John Kortbeek, MD, FRCSC, FACS
Professor, Department of Surgery, Critical Care and Anaesthesia
Cumming School of Medicine, University of Calgary
Calgary, Alberta
Canada

Deborah A. Kuhls, MD, FACS
Professor of Surgery
University of Nevada School of Medicine
Las Vegas, Nevada
United States

Sunir Kumar, MD
Cleveland Clinic
Cleveland, Ohio
United States

Eric Kuncir, MD, MS, FACS
Chief, Division of Emergency General Surgery; Clinical Professor of Surgery
University of California, Irvine
Orange, California
United States

Claus Falck Larsen, DMSc,MPA
consultant,
Clinic at TraumaCentre
Rigshospitalet
University of Southern Denmark
Copenhagen
Denmark

Gilberto K. K. Leung, MBBS, FRCS, PhD
Clinical Associate Professor
The University of Hong Kong Queen Mary University
Pok Fu Lam
Hong Kong

Sarvesh Logsetty, MD, FACS, FRCS(C)
Associate Professor, Director, Manitoba Firefighters Burn Unit
University of Manitoba
Winnipeg, Manitoba
Canada

Siew Kheong Lum, MBBS, FRCSEd, FACS, FRACS (Hon), FAMM, FAMS
Professor of Surgery and ATLS Program Director
Sungai Buloh Hospital
Kuala Lumpur
Malaysia

Patrizio Mao, MD, FACS
Azienda Ospedaliero–Universitaria
San Luigi Gonzaga
Orbassano, Torino
Italy

Sherri Marley, BSN, RN, CEN, TCRN
Clinical Educator for Trauma Services
Eskenazi Hospital
Indianapolis, Indiana
United States

Katherine Martin, MBBS, FRACS
Trauma Surgeon
Alfred Hospital
Melbourne, Victoria
Australia

Sean P. McCully, MD, MS
Surgical Critical Care Fellow
Department of Surgery
Oregon Health and Science University
Portland, Oregon
United States

Chad McIntyre, BS, NRP, FP-C
Manager, Trauma and Flight Services
UF Health Jacksonville
Jacksonville, Florida
United States

Daniel B. Michael, MD, PhD, FACS, FAANS
Director of Neurosurgical Education
William Beaumont Hospital Royal Oak
Professor of Neurosurgery
Oakland University William Beaumont School of Medicine
Royal Oak, Michigan
United States
Director, Michigan Head and Spine Institute
Southfield, Michigan
United States

Mahesh Misra, MD, FACS
Director
All India Institute of Medical Sciences
New Delhi
India

Soledad Monton
Médico en Servicio Navarro de Salud
Servicio Navarro de Salud
Pamplona
Spain

Hunter Moore, MD
Trauma Research Fellow
University of Colorado
Denver, Colorado
United States

John Ng, MD, MS, FACS
Chief, Division of Oculofacial Plastics, Orbital and Reconstructive Surgery; Professor, Departments of Ophthalmology and Otolaryngology/Head and Neck Surgery
Casey Eye Institute–Oregon Health and Science University
Portland, Oregon
United States

Nnamdi Nwauwa, MSCEM, MPH, MBBS
Director, Training and Clinical Services
Emergency Response International
Port Harcourt, Nigeria

James V. O'Connor MD, FACS
Professor of Surgery, University of Maryland School of Medicine
Chief, Thoracic and Vascular Trauma
R Adams Cowley Shock Trauma Center
Baltimore, Maryland
United States

Roddy O'Donnell, MBBS, MA, PhD, FRCPCH, MRCP, FFICM
Consultant Paediatrician and Director of PICU
Addenbrookes Hospital
Cambridge
United Kingdom

Giorgio Olivero, MD, FACS
ATLS Program Director; Professor of Surgery
Department of Surgical Sciences, University of Torino
Torino
Italy

Debbie Paltridge, MHlthSc (ED)
Principal Educator
Royal Australasian College of Surgeons
Melbourne, Victoria
Australia

Neil Parry, MD, FACS, FRCSC
Medical Director, Trauma Program; Associate Professor of Surgery and Critical Care
London Health Sciences Center; Schulich School of Medicine, Western University
London, Ontario
Canada

Albert Pierce

Hermanus Jacobus Christoffel Du Plessis, MB, ChB, MMed(Surg), FCS(SA), FACS

Travis Polk, MD, FACS
Commander, Medical Corps, U.S. Navy; Surgical Director, Healthcare Simulation and Bioskills Training Center
Naval Medical Center Portsmouth
Portsmouth, Virginia
United States

Bruce Potenza, MD, FACS
Critical Care Surgeon, Trauma
UCSD Medical Center
San Diego, California
United States

Tarek Razek, MD, FRCSC, FACS
Chief, Division of Trauma Surgery
McGill University Health Centre
Montreal, Quebec
Canada

Martin Richardson, MBBS, MS, FRACS
Associate Clinical Dean
Epworth Hospital, University of Melbourne
Melbourne, Victoria
Australia

Avraham Rivkind, MD, FACS
Head, Division of Emergency Medicine and Shock Trauma Unit
Hadassah Medical Center
Jerusalem
Israel

Rosalind Roden, BA(Cambridge), FRCEM
Consultant in Emergency Medicine
Leeds Teaching Hospitals
Trust Leeds, West Yorkshire
United Kingdom

Jakob Roed, MD, MPA, DLS
Chief Anesthetist, Department of Anesthesiology and Intensive Care
Zealand University Hospital
Roskilde
Denmark

Dan Rutigliano, DO
Assistant Professor of Surgery
Stony Brook University School of Medicine
Stony Brook, New York
United States

Kennith Sartorelli, MD, FACS
Department of Surgery
University of Vermont College of Medicine
Burlington, Vermont
United States

Patrick Schoettker, MD
Professor of Anesthesiology
University Hospital CHUV
Lausanne, VD
Switzerland

David Schultz, MD, FACS
Thedacare Regional Medical Center Neenah
Neenah, Wisconsin
United States

Kristen C. Sihler, MD, MS, FACS
Maine Medical Center
Portland, Maine
United States

Preecha Siritongtaworn, FRCST,FACS.
Department of Surgery
Faculty of Medicine
Siriraj Hospital
Bangkok, Thailand

David Skarupa, MD, FACS
Assistant Professor of Surgery, Department of Surgery/ Division of Acute Care Surgery
University of Florida College of Medicine–Jacksonville
Jacksonville, Florida
United States

Elizabeth Vallejo de Solezio
National Education, Committee on Trauma Ecuador
Quito, Ecuador

Ronald Stewart, MD, FACS
Chair, American College of Surgeons Committee on Trauma
Witten B. Russ Professor and Chair of the Department of Surgery
UT Health San Antonio
San Antonio, Texas
United States

Claus Stobaus, ME, ED
Postgraduate Program in Education
Pontifical Catholic University of Rio Grande do Sul
Porto Alegre, Rio Grande do Sul
Brazil

John Sutyak, EdM, MD, FACS
Director, Southern Illinois Trauma Center
Associate Professor of Surgery
Southern Illinois University School of Medicine
Springfield, Illinois
United States

Gonzalo Tamayo

Kum-Ying Tham, MBBS, FRCSE, EDD
Senior Consultant
Tan Tock Seng Hospital
Singapore

Phil Truskett
Surgeon at SESIH
SESIH
Sydney, Australia

Gary Vercruysse, MD, FACS
Director of Burns Services; Associate Professor of Surgery, Division of Trauma, Burns, Acute Care Surgery and Surgical Critical Care
University of Arizona School of Medicine
Tucson, Arizona
United States

Eric Voiglio, MD, FACS
Emergency Surgery Unit
University Hospitals of Lyon
Pierre-Bénite
France

James Vosswinkel, MD, FACS
Chief, Division of Trauma
Stony Brook University School of Medicine
Stony Brook, New York
United States

Bob Yellowe, MD, MSc Sport Medicine
Consultant Orthopedic and Trauma Surgeon
University of Port Harcourt Teaching Hospital
Port Harcourt
Nigeria

Dany Westerband, MD, FACS
Medical Director of Trauma Services; Chief, Section of Trauma and Emergency Surgery; Chairman, Department of Surgery
Suburban Hospital–Johns Hopkins Medicine
Bethesda, Maryland
United States

Garry Wilkes, MBBS, FACEM
Director, Emergency Medicine
Monash Medical Centre
Melbourne, Victoria
Australia

Catherine Wilson, MSN, ACNP-BC, CEN
Trauma Outreach Coordinator
Vanderbilt University Medical Center
Nashville, Tennessee
United States

Robert Winchell, MD, FACS
Chief, Division of Trauma, Burn, Acute Care and Critical Care, Director of Trauma Center
Weill Cornell Medicine; New York–Presbyterian Weill Cornell Medical Center
New York, New York
United States

Bob Winter, FRCP, FRCA, FFICM, DM
Medical Director, East Midlands Ambulance Services
Horizon Place
Nottingham
United Kingdom

Christoph Wöelfl, MD, PhD
Head of Departement, Departement of Orthopedic and Trauma Surgery
Krankenhaus Hetzelstift
Neustadt a. d. Weinstrasse
Germany

Jay A. Yelon, DO, FACS, FCCM
Professor of Surgery; Medical Director of Surgical Services
Hofstra Northwell School of Medicine; Southside Hospital/Northwell Health
Bay Shore, New York
United States

Heba Youssef Mohamed Sayed, MD
Professor and Head of Forensic Medicine and Clinical Toxicology Department
Faculty of Medicine–Port Said University
Port Said
Arab Republic of Egypt

Laura Zibners, MD
Honorary Consultant, Pediatric Emergency Medicine
Imperial College, St. Mary's Hospital
London
United Kingdom

HONOR ROLL

Over the past 30 years, ATLS has grown from a local course training of Nebraska doctors to care for trauma patients to a family of trauma specialists from more than 60 countries who volunteer their time to ensure that our materials reflect the most current research and that our course is designed to improve patient outcomes. The Tenth Edition of ATLS reflects the efforts of the individuals who contributed to the first nine editions, and we honor them here:

Georges Abi Saad
Sabas F. Abuabara, MD, FACS
Joe E. Acker, II, MS, MPH, EMT
Fatimah Albarracin, RN
Celia Aldana
Raymond H. Alexander, MD, FACS
Omar Al Ghanimi
Abdullah Al-Harthy
Jameel Ali, MD, MMed Ed, FRCS(C), FACS
Saud Al-Turki, MD, FRCS, ODTS, FACA, FACS
Donna Allerton, RN
Heri Aminuddin, MD
John A. Androulakis, MD, FACS
Charles Aprahamian, MD, FACS
Guillermo Arana, MD, FACS
Marjorie J. Arca, MD, FACS
Ana Luisa Argomedo Manrique
John H. Armstrong, MD, FACS
John L.D. Atkinson, MD, FACS
Ivar Austlid
Gonzalo Avilés
Mahmood Ayyaz, MD

Richard Baillot, MD

Andrew Baker, MD

Barbara A. Barlow, MA, MD, FACS

James Barone, MD, FACS

John Barrett, MD, FACS

Pierre Beaumont, MD

Margareta Behrbohm Fallsberg, PhD, BSc

Richard M. Bell, MD, FACS

Eugene E. Berg, MD, FACS

Richard Bergeron, MD

François Bertrand, MD

Renato Bessa de Melo, MD

Mike Betzner, MD

Emidio Bianco, MD, JD

David P. Blake, MD, FACS

Ken Boffard, MB BCh, FRCS, FRCS(Ed), FACS

Mark W. Bowyer, MD, FACS, DMCC

Don E. Boyle, MD, FACS

Marianne Brandt

Mary-Margaret Brandt, MD, FACS

Frank J. Branicki, MBBS, DM, FRCS, FRACS, FCS(HK), FHKAM(Surg)

Karen Brasel, MPH, MD, FACS

Fred Brenneman, MD, FRCSC, FACS

George Brighton, MD

Åse Brinchmann-Hansen, PhD

Peter Brink, MD, PhD

Karim Brohi, MD

James Brown, MA

Rea Brown, MD, FACS

Allen F. Browne, MD, FACS

Laura Bruna, RN

Gerry Bunting, MD

Andrew R. Burgess, MD, FACS

Richard E. Burney, MD, FACS

David Burris, MD, FACS

Reginald A. Burton, MD, FACS

Jacqueline Bustraan, MSc

Vilma Cabading

Sylvia Campbell, MD, FACS

C. James Carrico, MD, FACS

Carlos Carvajal Hafemann, MD, FACS

Gustavo H. Castagneto, MD, FACS

Candice L. Castro, MD, FACS

C. Gene Cayten, MD, FACS

June Sau-Hung Chan

Zafar Ullah Chaudhry, MD, FRCS, FCPS, FACS

Peggy Chehardy, EdD, CHES

Regina Sutton Chennault, MD, FACS

Robert A. Cherry, MD, FACS

Diane Chetty

Wei Chong Chua, MD

Emmanuel Chrysos, MD, PhD, FACS

Chin-Hung Chung, MB BS, FACS

David E. Clark, MD, FACS

Raul Coimbra, MD, PhD, FACS

Francisco Collet e Silva, MD, FACS, PhD(Med)

Paul E. Collicott, MD, FACS

Arthur Cooper, MD, FACS

Jaime Cortes Ojeda, MD

Clay Cothren Burlew, MD, FACS

Ronald D. Craig, MD

Doug Davey, MD

Kimberly A. Davis, MD, FACS

Cristiane de Alencar Domingues, RN, MSN, PhD

Subrato J. Deb, MD

Alejandro De Gracia, MD, FACS, MAAC

Laura Lee Demmons, RN, MBA

Ronald Denis, MD

Elizabeth de Solezio, PhD

Jesus Díaz Portocarrero, MD, FACS

Mauricio Di Silvio-Lopez, MD, FACS

Frank X. Doto, MS

Jay J. Doucet, MD, FACS

Anne-Michéle Droux

Julia A. Dunn, MD, FACS

Hermanus Jacobus Christoffel Du Plessis, MB, ChB, MMed(Surg), FCS(SA), FACS

Marguerite Dupré, MD

Candida Durão

Ruth Dyson, BA(Hons)

Martin Eason, MD, JD

A. Brent Eastman, MD, FACS

Frank E. Ehrlich, MD, FACS

Martin R. Eichelberger, MD, FACS

Abdelhakim Talaat Elkholy, MBBCh

David Eduardo Eskenazi, MD, FACS

Vagn Norgaard Eskesen, MD

Denis Evoy, MCH, FRCSI

William F. Fallon, Jr., MD, FACS

David V. Feliciano, MD, FACS

Froilan Fernandez, MD

Carlos Fernandez-Bueno, MD

John Fildes, MD, FACS

Ronald P. Fischer, MD, FACS

Stevenson Flanigan, MD, FACS

Lewis M. Flint, Jr, MD, FACS

Cornelia Rita Maria Getruda Fluit, MD, MedSci

Joan Foerster

Esteban Foianini, MD, FACS

Jorge E. Foianini, MD, FACS

Heidi Frankel, MD, FACS

Knut Fredriksen, MD, PhD

Susanne Fristeen, RN

Richard Fuehling, MD

Christine Gaarder, MD

Sylvain Gagnon, MD

Richard Gamelli, MD, FACS

Subash C. Gautam, MD, MBBS, FRCS, FACS

Paul Gebhard

James A. Geiling, MD, FCCP
Thomas A. Gennarelli, MD, FACS
John H. George, MD
Aggelos Geranios, MD
Michael Gerazounis, MD
Roger Gilbertson, MD
Robert W. Gillespie, MD, FACS
Marc Giroux, MD
Gerardo A. Gomez, MD, FACS
Hugo Alfredo Gomez Fernandez, MD, FACS
Khalid Masood Gondal
Javier González-Uriarte, MD, PhD, EBSQ, FSpCS
John Greenwood
Russell L. Gruen, MBBS, PhD, FRACS
Niels Gudmundsen-Vestre
Oscar D. Guillamondegui, MD, FACS
Enrique A. Guzman Cottallat, MD, FACS
J. Alex Haller, Jr., MD, FACS
Betty Jean (B. J.) Hancock, MD, FACS
Burton H. Harris, MD, FACS
Michael L. Hawkins, MD, FACS
Ian Haywood, FRCS(Eng), MRCS, LRCP
James D. Heckman, MD, FACS
June E. Heilman, MD, FACS
David M. Heimbach, MD, FACS
Richard Henn, RN, BSN, M.ED
Walter Henny, MD
Sharon M. Henry, MD, FACS
David N. Herndon, MD, FACS
Grace Herrera-Fernandez
Fergal Hickey, FRCS, FRCS Ed(A&E), DA(UK), FCEM
Erwin F. Hirsch, MD, FACS
Francisco Holguin, MD
Michael Hollands, MB BS, FRACS, FACS
Scott Holmes
Roxolana Horbowyj, MD, FACS
David B. Hoyt, MD, FACS
Arthur Hsieh, MA, NREMT-P
Irvene K. Hughes, RN
Christopher M. Hults, MD, FACS, CDR, USN
Richard C. Hunt, MD, FACEP
John E. Hutton, Jr, MD, FACS
Miles H. Irving, FRCS(Ed), FRCS(Eng)
Randeep S. Jawa, MD, FACS
José María Jover Navalon, MD, FACS
Richard Judd, PhD, EMSI
Gregory J. Jurkovich, MD, FACS
Aage W. Karlsen
Christoph R. Kaufmann, MD, FACS
Howard B. Keith, MD, FACS
James F. Kellam, MD, FRCS, FACS
Steven J. Kilkenny, MD, FACS
Darren Kilroy, FRCS(Ed), FCEM, M.Ed
Lena Klarin, RN
Peggy Knudson, MD, FACS

Amy Koestner, RN, MSN
Radko Komadina, MD, PhD
Digna R. Kool, MD
John B. Kortbeek, MD, FACS
Roman Kosir, MD
Brent Krantz, MD, FACS
Jon R. Krohmer, MD, FACEP
Eric J. Kuncir, MD, FACS
Roslyn Ladner
Ada Lai Yin Kwok
Maria Lampi, BSc, RN
Katherine Lane, PhD
Francis G. Lapiana, MD, FACS
Pedro Larios Aznar
Claus Falck Larsen, MD, PhD(Med), MPA, FACS
Anna M. Ledgerwood, MD, FACS
Dennis G. Leland, MD, FACS
Frank Lewis, MD, FACS
Wilson Li, MD
Helen Livanios, RN
Chong-Jeh Lo, MD, FACS
Sarvesh Logsetty, MD, FACS
Nur Rachmat Lubis, MD
Edward B. Lucci, MD, FACEP
Eduardo Luck, MD, FACS
Thomas G. Luerssen, MD, FACS
Ka Ka Lui
J.S.K. Luitse, MD
Siew-Kheong Lum
Douglas W. Lundy, MD, FACS
Arnold Luterman, MD, FACS
Fernando Machado, MD
Fernando Magallanes Negrete, MD
Jaime Manzano, MD, FACS
Patrizio Mao, MD, FACS
Donald W. Marion, MD, FACS
Michael R. Marohn, DO, FACS
Barry D. Martin, MD
Salvador Martín Mandujano, MD, FACS
Kimball I. Maull, MD, FACS
R. Todd Maxson, MD, FACS
Mary C. McCarthy, MD, FACS
Gerald McCullough, MD, FACS
John E. McDermott, MD, FACS
James A. McGehee, DVM, MS
Chad McIntyre, NREMT-P, FP-C
William F. McManus, MD, FACS
Norman E. McSwain, Jr., MD, FACS
Philip S. Metz, MD, FACS
Cynthia L. Meyer, MD
Daniel B. Michael, MD, PhD, FACS
Salvijus Milasˇius, MD
Frank B. Miller, MD, FACS
Sidney F. Miller, MD, FACS

LEO Pien Ming, MBBS, MRCS (Edin), M.Med (Orthopaedics)
Mahesh C. Misra, MD, FACS
Soledad Monton, MD
Ernest E. Moore, MD, FACS
Forrest O. Moore, MD, FACS
Newton Djin Mori, MD
Johanne Morin, MD
Charles E. Morrow, Jr., MD, FACS
David Mulder, MD, FACS
Stephen G. Murphy, MD
Kimberly K. Nagy, MD, FACS
Raj K. Narayan, MD, FACS
James B. Nichols, DVM, MS
Nicolaos Nicolau, MD, FACS
Martín Odriozola, MD, FACS
Han Boon Oh
Giorgio Olivero, MD, FACS
Franklin C. Olson, EdD
Steve A. Olson, MD, FACS
Osama Ali Omari, MD
Hock Soo Ong, MD, FACS
Gonzalo Ostria P., MD, FACS
Arthur Pagé, MD
José Paiz Tejada
Rattaplee Pak-Art, MD
Fatima Pardo, MD
Steven N. Parks, MD, FACS
BiPinchandra R. Patel, MD, FACS
Chester (Chet) Paul, MD
Jasmeet S. Paul, MD
Andrew Pearce, BScHons, MBBS, FACEM PG Cert Aeromed retrieval
Mark D. Pearlman, MD
Andrew B. Peitzman, MD, FACS
Nicolas Peloponissios, MD
Jean Péloquin, MD
Philip W. Perdue, MD, FACS
Pedro Moniz Pereira, MD
Neil G. Perry, MD, FRCSC, FACS
J.W. Rodney Peyton, FRCS(Ed), MRCP
Lawrence H. Pitts, MD, FACS
Renato Sergio Poggetti, MD, FACS
Alex Poole, MD, FACS
Galen V. Poole, MD, FACS
Danielle Poretti, RN
Ernest Prégent, MD
Raymond R. Price, MD, FACS
Richard R. Price, MD, FACS
Sonia Primeau
Herbert Proctor, MD, FACS
Jacques Provost, MD
Paul Pudimat, MD
Cristina Quintana
Max L. Ramenofsky, MD, FACS

Jesper Ravn, MD
Tarek S. A. Razek, MD, FACS
Marcelo Recalde Hidrobo, MD, FACS
John Reed, MD
Marleta Reynolds, MD, FACS
Stuart A. Reynolds, MD, FACS
Peter Rhee, MD, MPH, FACS, FCCM, DMCC
Bo Richter
Bernard Riley, FFARCS
Charles Rinker, MD, FACS
Avraham Rivkind, MD
Rosalind Roden, FFAEM
Diego Rodriguez, MD
Vicente Rodriguez, MD
Jakob Roed, MD
Olav Røise, MD, PhD
Martha Romero
Ronald E. Rosenthal, MD, FACS
Michael F. Rotondo, MD, FACS
Grace Rozycki, MD, FACS
Daniel Ruiz, MD, FACS
J. Octavio Ruiz Speare, MD, MS, FACS
James M. Ryan, MCh, FRCS(Eng), RAMC
Majid Sabahi, MD
James M. Salander, MD, FACS
Gueider Salas, MD
Jeffrey P. Salomone, MD, FACS
Rocio Sanchez-Aedo Linares, RN
Mårtin Sandberg, MD, PhD
Thomas G. Saul, MD, FACS
Nicole Schaapveld, RN
Domenic Scharplatz, MD, FACS
William P. Schecter, MD, FACS
Inger B. Schipper, MD, PhD, FACS
Patrick Schoettker, MD, M.E.R.
Martin A. Schreiber, MD, FACS
Kari Schrøder Hansen, MD
Thomas E. Scott, MD, FACS
Stuart R. Seiff, MD, FACS
Estrellita C. Serafico
Bolivar Serrano, MD, FACS
Juan Carlos Serrano, MD, FACS
Steven R. Shackford, MD, FACS
Marc J. Shapiro, MD, FACS
Thomas E. Shaver, MD, FACS
Mark Sheridan, MBBS, MMedSc, FRACS
Brian Siegel, MD, FACS
Richard C. Simmonds, DVM, MS
Richard K. Simons, MB, BChir, FRCS, FRCSC, FACS
Preecha Siritongtaworn, MD, FACS
Diana Skaff
Nils Oddvar Skaga, MD
David V. Skinner, FRCS(Ed), FRCS(Eng)
Peter Skippen, MBBS, FRCPC, FJFICM, MHA
Arnold Sladen, MD, FACS

Tone Slåke
R. Stephen Smith, MD, RDMS, FACS
Birgitte Soehus
Ricardo Sonneborn, MD, FACS
Anne Sorvari
Michael Stavropoulos, MD, FACS
Spyridon Stergiopoulos, MD
Gerald O. Strauch, MD, FACS
Luther M. Strayer, III, MD
James K. Styner, MD
LAM Suk-Ching, BN, MHM
Paul-Martin Sutter, MD
John Sutyak, MD, FACS
Lars Bo Svendsen, MD, DMSci
Vasso Tagkalakis
Wael S. Taha, MD
Kathryn Tchorz, MD, FACS
Joseph J. Tepas, III, MD, FACS
Stéphane Tétraeault, MD
Gregory A. Timberlake, MD, FACS
Wei Ting Lee
Gustavo Tisminetzky, MD, FACS, MAAC
Peter G. Trafton, MD, FACS
Stanley Trooksin, MD, FACS
Julio L. Trostchansky, MD, FACS
Philip Truskett, MB BS, FRACS
David Tuggle, MD, FACS
Wolfgang Ummenhofer, MD, DEAA
Jeffrey Upperman, MD, FACS
Jay Upright
Yvonne van den Ende
Armand Robert van Kanten, MD

Endre Varga, MD, PhD
Edina Várkonyi
Panteleimon Vassiliu, MD, PhD
Eugenia Vassilopoulou, MD
Antigoni Vavarouta
Allan Vennike
Antonio Vera Bolea
Alan Verdant, MD
Tore Vikström, MD, PhD
J. Leonel Villavicencio, MD, FACS
Eric Voiglio, MD, PhD, FACS, FRCS
Franklin C. Wagner, MD, FACS
Raymond L. Warpeha, MD, FACS
Clark Watts, MD, FACS
John A. Weigelt, MD, FACS
Leonard J. Weireter Jr., MD, FACS
John West, MD, FACS
Nicholas M. Wetjen, MD
Robert J. White, MD, FACS
Richard L. Wigle, MD, FACS
Stephen Wilkinson, MBBS, MD, FRACS
Daryl Williams, MBBS, FANZCA,GDipBusAd, GdipCR
Robert J. Winchell, MD, FACS
Robert Winter, FRCP, FRCA, DM
Fremont P. Wirth, MD, FACS
Bradley D. Wong, MD, FACS
Nopadol Wora-Urai, MD, FACS
Peter H. Worlock, DM, FRCS(Ed), FRCS(Eng)
Jay A. Yelon, MD, FACS
Bang Wai-Key Yuen, MB BS, FRCS, FRACS, FACS
Ahmad M. Zarour, MD, FACS

COURSE OVERVIEW: PURPOSE, HISTORY, AND CONCEPTS OF THE ATLS PROGRAM

PROGRAM GOALS

The Advanced Trauma Life Support (ATLS) course supplies its participants with a safe and reliable method for the immediate treatment of injured patients and the basic knowledge necessary to:

1. Assess a patient's condition rapidly and accurately.
2. Resuscitate and stabilize patients according to priority.
3. Determine whether a patient's needs exceed the resources of a facility and/or the capability of a provider.
4. Arrange appropriately for a patient's interhospital or intrahospital transfer.
5. Ensure that optimal care is provided and that the level of care does not deteriorate at any point during the evaluation, resuscitation, or transfer process.

COURSE OBJECTIVES

The content and skills presented in this course are designed to assist doctors in providing emergency care for trauma patients. The concept of the "golden hour" emphasizes the urgency necessary for successful treatment of injured patients and is not intended to represent a fixed time period of 60 minutes. Rather, it is the window of opportunity during which doctors can have a positive impact on the morbidity and mortality associated with injury. The ATLS course provides the essential information and skills for doctors to identify and treat life-threatening and potentially life-threatening injuries under the extreme pressures associated with the care of these patients in the fast-paced environment and anxiety of a trauma room. The ATLS course is applicable to clinicians in a variety of situations. It is just as relevant to providers in a large teaching facility in North America or Europe as it is in a developing nation with rudimentary facilities.

Upon completing the ATLS student course, the participant will be able to:

1. Demonstrate the concepts and principles of the primary and secondary patient assessments.
2. Establish management priorities in a trauma situation.
3. Initiate primary and secondary management necessary for the emergency management of acute life-threatening conditions in a timely manner.
4. In a given simulation, demonstrate the following skills, which are often required during initial assessment and treatment of patients with multiple injuries:

   a. Primary and secondary assessment of a patient with simulated, multiple injuries
   b. Establishment of a patent airway and initiation of assisted ventilations
   c. Orotracheal intubation on adult and infant manikins
   d. Pulse oximetry and carbon dioxide detection in exhaled gas
   e. Cricothyroidotomy
   f. Assessment and treatment of a patient in shock, particularly recognition of life-threatening hemorrhage
   g. Intraosseous access
   h. Pleural decompression via needle or finger and chest tube insertion
   i. Recognition of cardiac tamponade and appropriate treatment
   j. Clinical and radiographic identification of thoracic injuries
   k. Use of peritoneal lavage, ultrasound (FAST), and computed tomography (CT) in abdominal evaluation
   l. Evaluation and treatment of a patient with brain injury, including use of the new Glasgow Coma Scale score and CT of the brain

m. Protection of the spinal cord and radiographic and clinical evaluation of spine injuries

n. Musculoskeletal trauma assessment and management

THE NEED

According to the most current information from the World Health Organization (WHO) and the Centers for Disease Control (CDC), more than nine people die every minute from injuries or violence, and 5.8 million people of all ages and economic groups die every year from unintentional injuries and violence (■ FIGURE 1). The burden of injury is even more significant, accounting for 18% of the world's total diseases. Motor vehicle crashes (referred to as road traffic injuries in ■ FIGURE 2) alone cause more than 1 million deaths annually and an estimated 20 million to 50 million significant injuries; they are the leading cause of death due to injury worldwide. Improvements in injury control efforts are having an impact in most developed countries, where trauma remains the leading cause of death in persons 1 through 44 years of age. Significantly, more than 90% of motor vehicle crashes occur in the developing world. Injury-related deaths are expected to rise dramatically by 2020, and deaths due to motor vehicle crashes are projected to increase by 80% from current rates in low- and middle-income countries.

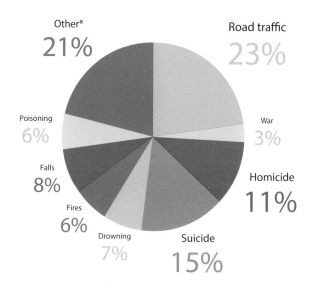

■ FIGURE 2 Distribution of global injury mortality by cause. "Other" category includes smothering, asphyxiation, choking, animal and venomous bites, hypothermia, and hyperthermia as well as natural disasters. Data from *Global Burden of Disease*, 2004. Reproduced with permission from *Injuries and Violence: The Facts*. Geneva: World Health Organization Department of Injuries and Violence Prevention; 2010.

TRIMODAL DEATH DISTRIBUTION

First described in 1982, the trimodal distribution of deaths implies that death due to injury occurs in one of three periods, or peaks. *The first peak* occurs within

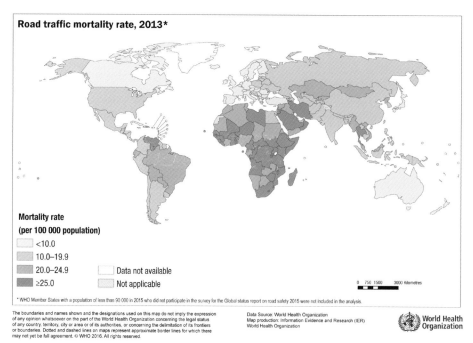

■ FIGURE 1 Road traffic mortality rate, 2013. Reproduced with permission from *Global Health Observatory Map Gallery*. Geneva: World Health Organization Department of Injuries and Violence Prevention; 2016.

seconds to minutes of injury. During this early period, deaths generally result from apnea due to severe brain or high spinal cord injury or rupture of the heart, aorta, or other large blood vessels. Very few of these patients can be saved because of the severity of their injuries. Only prevention can significantly reduce this peak of trauma-related deaths.

The *second peak* occurs within minutes to several hours following injury. Deaths that occur during this period are usually due to subdural and epidural hematomas, hemopneumothorax, ruptured spleen, lacerations of the liver, pelvic fractures, and/or multiple other injuries associated with significant blood loss. The golden hour of care after injury is characterized by the need for rapid assessment and resuscitation, which are the fundamental principles of Advanced Trauma Life Support.

The *third peak*, which occurs several days to weeks after the initial injury, is most often due to sepsis and multiple organ system dysfunctions. Care provided during each of the preceding periods affects outcomes during this stage. The first and every subsequent person to care for the injured patient has a direct effect on long-term outcome.

The temporal distribution of deaths reflects local advances and capabilities of trauma systems. The development of standardized trauma training, better prehospital care, and trauma centers with dedicated trauma teams and established protocols to care for injured patients has altered the picture. ■ FIGURE 3 shows

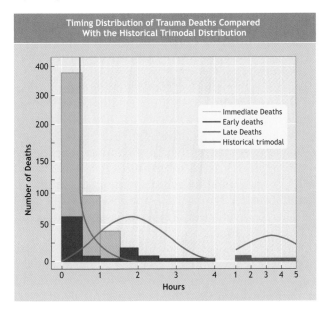

■ **FIGURE 3** Timing distribution of trauma deaths compared with the historical trimodal distribution. The black line represents the historical trimodal distribution, and the bars represent 2010 study data. Reprinted with permission from Gunst M, Ghaemmaghami V, Gruszecki A, et al. Changing epidemiology of trauma deaths leads to a bimodal distribution. *Proc (Baylor Univ Med Cent)*, 2010;23(4):349–354.

the timing distribution of trauma deaths compared with the historical trimodal distribution.

HISTORY

The delivery of trauma care in the United States before 1980 was at best inconsistent. In February 1976, tragedy occurred that changed trauma care in the "first hour" for injured patients in the United States and in much of the rest of the world. An orthopedic surgeon was piloting his plane and crashed in a rural Nebraska cornfield. The surgeon sustained serious injuries, three of his children sustained critical injuries, and one child sustained minor injuries. His wife was killed instantly. The care that he and his family subsequently received was inadequate by the day's standards. The surgeon, recognizing how inadequate their treatment was, stated: "When I can provide better care in the field with limited resources than what my children and I received at the primary care facility, there is something wrong with the system, and the system has to be changed."

A group of private-practice surgeons and doctors in Nebraska, the Lincoln Medical Education Foundation, and the Lincoln area Mobile Heart Team Nurses, with the help of the University of Nebraska Medical Center, the Nebraska State Committee on Trauma (COT) of the American College of Surgeons (ACS), and the Southeast Nebraska Emergency Medical Services identified the need for training in advanced trauma life support. A combined educational format of lectures, lifesaving skill demonstrations, and practical laboratory experiences formed the prototype ATLS course.

A new approach to providing care for individuals who suffer major life-threatening injury premiered in 1978, the year of the first ATLS course. This prototype ATLS course was field-tested in conjunction with the Southeast Nebraska Emergency Medical Services. One year later, the ACS COT, recognizing trauma as a surgical disease, enthusiastically adopted the course under the imprimatur of the College and incorporated it as an educational program.

This course was based on the assumption that appropriate and timely care could significantly improve the outcome of injured patients. The original intent of the ATLS Program was to train doctors who do not manage major trauma on a daily basis, and the primary audience for the course has not changed. However, today the ATLS method is accepted as a standard for the "first hour" of trauma care by many who provide care for the injured, whether the patient is treated in an isolated rural area or a state-of the-art trauma center.

▶ ATLS AND TRAUMA SYSTEMS

As mentioned earlier, Advanced Trauma Life Support (ATLS) was developed in 1976 following a plane crash in which several children were critically injured. They received injury care, but the resources and expertise they needed were not available. This was, unfortunately, typical of the way injury care was provided in most areas of the country. The creators of ATLS had seen how the coordinated efforts of well-trained providers improved survival of the seriously injured on the battlefields of Vietnam and at inner-city hospitals. Since then, ATLS-trained providers have been instrumental in the ongoing development of trauma systems. ATLS has played a major role in bringing together a core group of providers that are trained and focused on injury care. This core group has provided the leadership and the front-line clinical care that have enabled the growth and maturation of coordinated regional trauma systems.

Before the second half of the 20th century, trauma centers did not exist. Injury was thought to be unpredictable instead of something that could be anticipated and include treatment plans to care for injuries. Some large public hospitals, especially those located in areas with high rates of poverty and urban violence, began to demonstrate that focused experience and expertise—among providers as well as facilities—led to better outcomes after injury. Outside of these centers, injury care remained haphazard; it was provided by the closest facility and by practitioners who happened to be available. As a result, the quality of injury care received was largely a matter of chance. However, clear and objective data now show improved outcomes in designated trauma centers. The importance of trauma centers has been a core element of ATLS from its inception, and the dissemination of ATLS principles has contributed significantly to the general acceptance of this concept.

At about the same time, sweeping changes were also occurring in the emergency medical services (EMS) system. Before the 1960s, there were few standards regarding ambulance equipment or training of attendants. The ambulance was seen as a means of transporting patients, not an opportunity for practitioners to initiate care. Aided by the passage of the 1973 Emergency Medical Services Act, which established guidelines and provided funding for regional EMS development, EMS systems rapidly developed and matured over the next 25 years. The wartime experiences of Korea and Vietnam clearly demonstrated the advantages of rapid evacuation and early definitive treatment of casualties, and it became increasingly apparent how crucial it was to coordinate field treatment and transportation to ensure that injured patients arrived at a capable trauma care facility. The notion of a trauma system began to take shape.

Initially, the conception of a trauma system focused on the large urban trauma centers. Drawing on the experience at Cook County Hospital in Chicago, the State of Illinois passed legislation establishing a statewide coordinated network of trauma centers in 1971. When the Maryland Institute for Emergency Medicine was established in 1973, it was the first operational statewide trauma system. Maryland's small size allowed for a system design in which all severely injured patients within the state were transported to a single dedicated trauma facility. Other regions used this model to establish cooperative networks of trauma centers that were connected by a coordinated EMS system and linked by shared quality improvement processes.

These efforts were driven by the finding that a large proportion of deaths after injury in nontrauma hospitals were due to injuries that could have been better managed and controlled. The implementation of such systems led to dramatic decreases in what was termed "preventable death," as well as overall improvements in postinjury outcome that were duplicated in widely varying geographic settings. Following the models established in Illinois and Maryland, these regional systems were founded on the premise that all critically injured patients should be transported to a trauma center and that other acute care facilities in a region would not have a role in the care of the injured. This pattern fit well with the core ATLS paradigm of the small, poorly resourced facility seeking to stabilize and transfer patients. Based on the "exclusion" of undesignated hospitals from the care of the injured, this approach is frequently referred to as the exclusive model of trauma system design.

The exclusive model works well in urban and suburban settings, where there are a sufficient number of trauma centers. Although often described as a regional system, it does not use the resources of all healthcare facilities in a region. This focuses patient volume and experience at the high-level centers, but it leads to attenuation of skills in undesignated centers and results in loss of flexibility and surge capacity. The only way to increase the depth of coverage in an exclusive system is to recruit or build additional trauma centers in areas of need. This theory has largely proven impossible in practice, due to the high startup costs for new trauma centers as well as a widely varying motivation and commitment to injury care across the spectrum of healthcare facilities. The limitations of the exclusive model, and the difficulties in deploying the model on a large scale, were experienced throughout the 1990s. Despite clear evidence of the benefit of trauma systems, very few states and regions were able to establish a system as a matter of governmental policy, and fewer still were able to fulfill a set of eight criteria that had been proposed as cornerstones of exclusive system design. Consequently, inclusive models began to be implemented.

The inclusive model, as the name suggests, proposes that all healthcare facilities in a region be involved with the care of injured patients, at a level commensurate with their commitment, capabilities, and resources. Ideally, through its regulations, rules, and interactions with EMS, the system functions to efficiently match an individual patient's needs with the most appropriate facility, based on resources and proximity. Based on this paradigm, the most severely injured would be either transported directly or expeditiously transferred to the top-level trauma care facilities. At the same time, there would be sufficient local resources and expertise to manage the less severely injured, thus avoiding the risks and resource utilization incurred for transportation to a high-level facility. The notion that personnel highly skilled in trauma care would ever exist outside of the trauma center was not envisioned at the time that ATLS was created. Largely due to the success of ATLS, relatively sophisticated trauma capability is now commonly found outside of a traditional large urban center. This changing landscape has led to modifications in the content and focus of the ATLS course and its target audience. The inclusive system model has been the primary guiding framework for systems development over the last 10 years.

Despite its relatively universal acceptance at the theoretical level, the inclusive model is often misconstrued and misapplied in practice: it is viewed as a *voluntary* system in which all hospitals that wish to participate are *included* at whatever level of participation they choose. This approach fails to fulfill the primary mission of an inclusive trauma system: to ensure that the needs of the patient are the primary driver of resource utilization. An inclusive system ensures that all hospitals participate in the system and are prepared to care for injured patients at a level commensurate with their resources, capabilities, and capacity; but it does not mean that hospitals are free to determine their level of participation based on their own perceived best interest. The needs of the patient population served—objectively assessed—are the parameters that should determine the apportionment and utilization of system resources, including the level and geographic distribution of trauma centers within the system. When this rule is forgotten, the optimal function of systems suffers, and problems of either inadequate access or overutilization may develop.

The model of the inclusive trauma system has been well developed. There is substantial evidence to show the efficacy of these systems in improving outcomes after injury, but inclusive systems are undeniably difficult to develop, finance, maintain, and operate.

The system has a scale and function that places it in the realm of essential public services, yet it operates within the largely market-driven world of healthcare delivery. In most areas, the public health dimensions of the trauma system are not well recognized and not well funded by states or regions. Lacking a federal mandate or federal funding, the responsibility to develop trauma systems has fallen to state and local governments, and progress highly depends on the interest and engagement of public leadership at that level. As a result, some states have well-organized and well-funded systems whereas others have made little success beyond a level of coordination that has developed through individual interactions between front-line providers. Though there is general agreement about the necessary elements and the structure of a trauma system, as well as significant evidence to demonstrate that coordination of these individual elements into a comprehensive system of trauma care leads to improved outcomes after injury, this data has not led to a broad implementation of trauma systems across the country.

From an international perspective, trauma system implementation varies to an even higher degree due to the broad range of social structures and economic development in countries across the globe. Further, many of the cultural and economic forces that have driven trauma systems development in the United States are unique, especially those related to high rates of interpersonal violence and the various ways of financing health care. As a result, approaches to trauma system development are very different.

In many higher-income nations, especially those where health care is already an integral part of the social support network, the benefits of focusing trauma care expertise within trauma centers have been more easily recognized. Moreover, there are fewer economic barriers to the direction of patient flow based on injury severity. Combined with the relatively smaller size of many European nations and the resultant shorter transport times to a specialty center, these benefits have facilitated the functional development of trauma systems following an exclusive model.

By contrast, most low- and middle-income countries have severely limited infrastructure for patient transportation and definitive care. These nations face severe challenges in providing adequate care for the injured, and in providing health care across the board. These challenges are clearly demonstrated by the disproportionately high rates of death related to injury seen in such countries. In these settings, ATLS has had perhaps its greatest impact on systems development, bringing knowledge and basic pathways of trauma care to directly to the providers, independent of the healthcare infrastructure. In addition, ATLS at its core brings forward many of the primary elements of a systematized approach to care, including the concept of transferring patients to more capable facilities as dictated by injury severity, and the importance of communication between providers at various levels of care. In many low- and middle-income countries, ATLS provides both the impetus to improve trauma care and the basic tools to begin to construct a system.

The broad success of ATLS, and the building of a large population of providers who understand the principles and approach to injury care, both in the United States and internationally, continues to be instrumental in furthering the implementation of trauma systems. The wide dissemination of knowledge regarding injury care and the importance of making the correct early decisions has established a common set of principles and a common language that serve to initiate changes in trauma care and act as a cohesive force bringing the various components of a system together. This group of providers committed to the care of the trauma patient, the far-flung ATLS family, is ultimately the source of the overall vision and cohesion necessary to drive improvements in systems of trauma care. They bind the many separate elements of an inclusive system into a functioning whole.

COURSE DEVELOPMENT AND DISSEMINATION

The ATLS course was conducted nationally for the first time under the auspices of the American College of Surgeons in January 1980. International promulgation of the course began in 1980.

The program has grown each year in the number of courses and participants. To date, the course has trained more than 1.5 million participants in more than 75,000 courses around the world. Currently, an average of 50,000 clinicians are trained each year in over 3,000 courses. The greatest growth in recent years has been in the international community, and this group currently represents more than half of all ATLS activity.

The text for the course is revised approximately every 4 years to incorporate new methods of evaluation and treatment that have become accepted parts of the community of doctors who treat trauma patients. Course revisions incorporate suggestions from members of the Subcommittee on ATLS; members of the ACS COT; members of the international ATLS family; representatives to the ATLS Subcommittee from the American College of Emergency Physicians and the American College of Anesthesiologists; and course instructors, coordinators, educators, and participants. Changes to the program reflect accepted, verified practice patterns, not unproven technology

or experimental methods. The international nature of the program mandates that the course be adaptable to a variety of geographic, economic, social, and medical practice situations. To retain current status in the ATLS Program, an individual must reverify training with the latest edition of the materials.

In parallel with the ATLS course is the Prehospital Trauma Life Support (PHTLS) course, sponsored by the National Association of Emergency Medical Technicians (NAEMT). The PHTLS course, developed in cooperation with the ACS COT, is based on the concepts of the ACS ATLS Program and is conducted for emergency medical technicians, paramedics, and nurses who are providers of prehospital trauma care.

Other courses have been developed with similar concepts and philosophies. For example, the Society of Trauma Nurses offers the Advanced Trauma Care for Nurses (ATCN), which is also developed in cooperation with the ACS COT. The ATCN and ATLS courses are conducted parallel to each other; the nurses audit the ATLS lectures and then participate in skill stations separate from the ATLS skill stations conducted for doctors. The benefits of having both prehospital and in-hospital trauma personnel speaking the same "language" are apparent.

INTERNATIONAL DISSEMINATION

As a pilot project, the ATLS Program was exported outside of North America in 1986 to the Republic of Trinidad and Tobago. The ACS Board of Regents gave permission in 1987 for promulgation of the ATLS Program in other countries. The ATLS Program may be requested by a recognized surgical organization or ACS Chapter in another country by corresponding with the ATLS Subcommittee Chairperson, care of the ACS ATLS Program Office, Chicago, Illinois. At the time of publication, the following 78 countries were actively providing the ATLS course to their trauma providers:

1. Argentina (Asociación Argentina de Cirugía)
2. Australia (Royal Australasian College of Surgeons)
3. Bahrain (Kingdom of Saudi Arabia ACS Chapter and Committee on Trauma)
4. Belize (College of Physicians and Surgeons of Costa Rica)
5. Bolivia (AMDA Bolivia)
6. Brazil (The Brazilian Committee on Trauma)
7. Canada (ACS Chapters and Provincial Committees on Trauma)

8. Chile (ACS Chapter and Committee on Trauma)

9. Colombia (ACS Chapter and Committee on Trauma)

10. Costa Rica (College of Physicians and Surgeons of Costa Rica)

11. Cuba (Brazilian Committee on Trauma)

12. Curaçao (ACS Chapter and Committee on Trauma)

13. Cyprus (Cyprus Surgical Society)

14. Czech Republic (Czech Trauma Society)

15. Denmark (ATLS Denmark Fond)

16. Ecuador (ACS Chapter and Committee on Trauma)

17. Egypt (Egyptian Society of Plastic and Reconstructive Surgeons)

18. Estonia (Estonia Surgical Association)

19. Fiji and the nations of the Southwest Pacific (Royal Australasian College of Surgeons)

20. France (Société Française de Chirurgie d'Urgence)

21. Georgia (Georgian Association of Surgeons)

22. Germany (German Society for Trauma Surgery and Task Force for Early Trauma Care)

23. Ghana (Ghana College of Physicians and Surgeons)

24. Greece (ACS Chapter and Committee on Trauma)

25. Grenada (Society of Surgeons of Trinidad and Tobago)

26. Haiti (Partnership with Region 14)

27. Honduras (Asociacion Quirurgica de Honduras)

28. Hong Kong (ACS Chapter and Committee on Trauma)

29. Hungary (Hungarian Trauma Society)

30. India (Association for Trauma Care of India)

31. Indonesia (Indonesian Surgeons Association)

32. Iran (Persian Orthopedic and Trauma Association)

33. Ireland (Royal College of Surgeons in Ireland)

34. Israel (Israel Surgical Society)

35. Italy (ACS Chapter and Committee on Trauma)

36. Jamaica (ACS Chapter and Committee on Trauma)

37. Jordan (Royal Medical Services/NEMSGC)

38. Kenya (Surgical Society of Kenya)

39. Kingdom of Saudi Arabia (ACS Chapter and Committee on Trauma)

40. Kuwait (Kingdom of Saudi Arabia ACS Chapter and Committee on Trauma)

41. Lebanon (Lebanese Chapter of the American College of Surgeons)

42. Lithuania (Lithuanian Society of Traumatology and Orthopaedics)

43. Malaysia (College of Surgeons, Malaysia)

44. Mexico (ACS Chapter and Committee on Trauma)

45. Moldova (Association of Traumatologists and Orthopedics of Republic of Moldova - ATORM)

46. Mongolia (Mongolian Orthopedic Association and National Trauma and Orthopedic Referral Center of Mongolia)

47. Myanmar (Australasian College of Emergency Medicine, International Federation for Emergency Medicine and Royal Australasian College Of Surgeons. The local stakeholders included the Myanmar Department of Health and Department of Medical Science).

48. Netherlands, The (Dutch Trauma Society)

49. New Zealand (Royal Australasian College of Surgeons)

50. Nigeria (Nigerian Orthopaedic Association)

51. Norway (Norwegian Surgical Society)

52. Oman (Oman Surgical Society)

53. Pakistan (College of Physicians and Surgeons Pakistan)

54. Panama (ACS Chapter and Committee on Trauma)

55. Papua New Guinea (Royal Australasian College of Surgeons)

56. Paraguay (Sociedad Paraguaya de Cirugía)

57. Peru (ACS Chapter and Committee on Trauma)

58. Philippines (Philippine College of Surgeons)

59. Portugal (Portuguese Society of Surgeons)

60. Qatar (Kingdom of Saudi Arabia ACS Chapter and Committee on Trauma)

61. Republic of China, Taiwan (Surgical Association of the Republic of China, Taiwan)

62. Republic of Singapore (Chapter of Surgeons, Academy of Medicine)

63. Slovenia (Slovenian Society of Trauma Surgeons)

64. Republic of South Africa (South African Trauma Society)

65. Somoa (Royal Australasian College of Surgeons)

66. Spain (Spanish Society of Surgeons)

67. Sri Lanka (College of Surgeons, Sri Lanka)

68. Sweden (Swedish Society of Surgeons)

69. Switzerland (Swiss Society of Surgeons)

70. Syria (Center for Continuing Medical and Health Education)

71. Taiwan (Taiwan Surgical Association)

72. Thailand (Royal College of Surgeons of Thailand)

73. Trinidad and Tobago (Society of Surgeons of Trinidad and Tobago)

74. United Arab Emirates (Surgical Advisory Committee)

75. United Kingdom (Royal College of Surgeons of England)

76. United States, U.S. territories (ACS Chapters and State Committees on Trauma)

77. Uruguay (Uruguay Society of Surgery)

78. Venezuela (ACS Chapter and Committee on Trauma)

THE CONCEPT

The concept behind the ATLS course has remained simple. Historically, the approach to treating injured patients, as taught in medical schools, was the same as that for patients with a previously undiagnosed medical condition: an extensive history including past medical history, a physical examination starting at the top of the head and progressing down the body, the development of a differential diagnosis, and a list of adjuncts to confirm the diagnosis. Although this approach was adequate for a patient with diabetes mellitus and many acute surgical illnesses, it did not satisfy the needs of patients suffering life-threatening injuries. The approach required change.

Three underlying concepts of the ATLS Program were initially difficult to accept:

1. Treat the greatest threat to life first.
2. Never allow the lack of definitive diagnosis to impede the application of an indicated treatment.
3. A detailed history is not essential to begin the evaluation of a patient with acute injuries.

The result was the development of the ABCDE approach to evaluating and treating injured patients. These concepts also align with the observation that the care of injured patients in many circumstances is a team effort that allows medical personnel with special skills and expertise to provide care simultaneously with surgical leadership of the process.

The ATLS course emphasizes that injury kills in certain reproducible time frames. For example, the loss of an airway kills more quickly than does loss of the ability to breathe. The latter kills more quickly than loss of circulating blood volume. The presence of an expanding intracranial mass lesion is the next most lethal problem. Thus, the mnemonic ABCDE defines the specific, ordered evaluations and interventions that should be followed in all injured patients:

Airway with restriction of cervical spine motion

Breathing

Circulation, stop the bleeding

Disability or neurologic status

Exposure (undress) and **E**nvironment (temperature control)

THE COURSE

The ATLS course emphasizes the rapid initial assessment and primary treatment of injured patients, starting at the time of injury and continuing through initial assessment, lifesaving intervention, reevaluation, stabilization, and, when needed, transfer to a trauma center. The course consists of precourse and postcourse tests, core content, interactive discussions, scenario-driven skill stations, lectures, interactive case presentations, discussions, development of lifesaving skills, practical laboratory experiences, and a final performance proficiency evaluation. Upon completing the course, participants should feel confident in implementing the skills taught in the ATLS course.

THE IMPACT

ATLS training in a developing country has resulted in a decrease in injury mortality. Lower per capita rates of deaths from injuries are observed in areas where providers have ATLS training. In one study, a small trauma team led by a doctor with ATLS experience had equivalent patient survival when compared with a larger team with more doctors in an urban setting. In addition, there were more unexpected survivors than fatalities.

There is abundant evidence that ATLS training improves the knowledge base, the psychomotor skills and their use in resuscitation, and the confidence and performance of doctors who have taken part in the program. The organization and procedural skills taught in the course are retained by course participants for at least 6 years, which may be the most significant impact of all.

ACKNOWLEDGMENTS

The COT of the ACS and the ATLS Subcommittee gratefully acknowledge the following organizations for their time and efforts in developing and field-testing the Advanced Trauma Life Support concept: The Lincoln Medical Education Foundation, Southeast Nebraska Emergency Medical Services, the University of Nebraska College of Medicine, and the Nebraska State Committee on Trauma of the ACS. The committee also is indebted to the Nebraska doctors who supported the development of this course and to the Lincoln Area Mobile Heart Team Nurses who shared their time and ideas to help build it. Appreciation is extended to the organizations identified previously in this overview for their support of the worldwide promulgation of the course. Special recognition is given to the spouses, significant others, children, and practice partners of the ATLS instructors and students. The time that providers spend away from their homes and practices and the effort afforded to this voluntary program are essential components of ATLS Program existence and success.

SUMMARY

The ATLS course provides an easily remembered approach to evaluating and treating injured patients for any doctor, irrespective of practice specialty, even under the stress, anxiety, and intensity that accompanies the resuscitation process. In addition, the program provides a common language for all providers who care for injured patients. The ATLS course offers a foundation for evaluation, treatment, education, and quality assurance—in short, a system of trauma care that is measurable, reproducible, and comprehensive.

The ATLS Program has had a positive impact on the care of injured patients worldwide. This effect is a result of the improved skills and knowledge of the doctors and other healthcare providers who have been course participants. The ATLS course establishes an organized, systematic approach for evaluation and treatment of patients, promotes minimum standards of care, and recognizes injury as a world healthcare issue. Morbidity and mortality have been reduced, but the need to eradicate injury remains. The ATLS Program has changed and will continue to change as advances occur in medicine and the needs and expectations of our societies change.

BIBLIOGRAPHY

1. American College of Emergency Physicians. Clinical and Practice Management Resources. Trauma in the Obstetric Patient: A Bedside Tool. http://www.acepnow.com/article/trauma-obstetric-patient-bedside-tool/. Accessed April 18, 2017.

2. American College of Radiology. ACR–SPR Practice parameter for imaging pregnant or potentially pregnant adolescents and women with ionizing radiation. http://www.acr.org/~/media/9e2e d55531fc4b4fa53ef3b6d3b25df8.pdf. Accessed April 18, 2017.

3. American College of Surgeons Committee on Trauma, American College of Emergency Physicians, American Academy of Pediatrics, et al. Policy statement—equipment for ambulances. *Pediatrics* 2009; 124(1): e166–e171.

4. American College of Surgeons, Committee on Trauma, National Trauma Data Bank (NTDB). http://www.facs.org/trauma/ntdb. Accessed May 12, 2016.

5. American College of Surgeons Committee on Trauma, American College of Emergency Physicians, Pediatric Emergency Medicine Committee, et al. Withholding termination of resuscitation in pediatric out-of-hospital traumatic cardiopulmonary arrest. *Pediatrics* 2014;133:e1104–e1116.

6. Badjatia N, Carney N, Crocco TJ. Guidelines for prehospital management of traumatic brain injury 2nd edition. *Prehospital Emergency Care* January/March 2004;12(Suppl 1).

7. Ball CG, Jafri SM, Kirkpatrick AW, et al. Traumatic urethral injuries: does the digital rectal examination really help us? *Injury* 2009 Sep;40(9):984–986.

8. Barquist E, Pizzutiello M, Tian L, et al. Effect of trauma system maturation on mortality rates in patients with blunt injuries in the Finger Lakes Region of New York State. *J Trauma* 2000;49:63–69; discussion 9-70.

9. Baumann Kreuziger LM, Keenan JC, Morton CT, et al. Management of the bleeding patient receiving new oral anticoagulants: a role for prothrombin complex concentrates. *Biomed Res Int* 2014;2014:583–794.

10. Baxter CR. Volume and electrolyte changes in the early post-burn period. *Clin Plast Surg* 1974;4:693–709.

11. Bazzoli GJ, Madura KJ, Cooper GF, et al.. Progress in the development of trauma systems in the

United States. Results of a national survey. *JAMA* 1995;273:395–401.

12. Berg MD, Schexnayder SM, Chameides L, et al. Part 13: pediatric basic life support: 2010 American Heart Association Guidelines for Cardiopulmonary Resuscitation and Emergency Cardiovascular Care. *Circulation* 2010 Nov 2;122(18 Suppl 3):S862–875.

13. Biffl WL, Moore EE, Elliott JP, et al. Blunt cerebrovascular injuries. *Curr Probl Surg* 1999;36:505–599.

14. Borst GM, Davies SW, Waibel BH et al. When birds can't fly: an analysis of interfacility ground transport using advanced life support when helicopter emergency medical service is unavailable. *J Trauma* 77(2):331–336.

15. Boulanger BR, Milzman D, Mitchell K, et al. Body habitus as a predictor of injury pattern after blunt trauma. *J Trauma* 1992;33:228–232.

16. Boyd DR, Dunea MM, Flashner BA. The Illinois plan for a statewide system of trauma centers. *J Trauma* 1973;13:24–31.

17. Boyle A, Santarius L, Maimaris C. Evaluation of the impact of the Canadian CT head rule on British practice. *Emerg Med J* 2004;21(4): 426–428.

18. Braver ER, Trempel RE. Are older drivers actually at higher risk of involvement in collisions resulting in deaths or nonfatal injuries among their passengers and other road users? *Inj Prev* 2004;10:27–29.

19. Bromberg WJ, Collier BC, Diebel LN, et al. Blunt cerebrovascular injury practice management guidelines: the Eastern Association for the Surgery of Trauma. *J Trauma* 2010;68: 471– 477.

20. Brown JB, Stassen NA, Bankey PE et al. Helicopters improve survival in seriously injured patients requiring interfacility transfer for definitive care. *J Trauma* 70(2):310–314.

21. Bruen KJ, Ballard JR, Morris SE, et al. Reduction of the incidence of amputation in frostbite injury with thrombolytic therapy. *Arch Surg* 2007 Jun;142(6):546–551; discussion 551–553.

22. Bulger EM, Arenson MA, Mock CN, et al. Rib fractures in the elderly. *J Trauma* 2000;48:1040–1046.

23. Bulger EM, Snyder D, Schoelles C, et al. An evidence-based prehospital guideline for external hemorrhage control: American College of Surgeons Committee on Trauma. *Prehospital Emerg Care* 2014;18:163–173.

24. Cales RH. Trauma mortality in Orange County: the effect of implementation of a regional trauma system. *Ann Emerg Med* 1984;13:1–10.

25. Cancio L. Airway management and smoke inhalation injury in the burn patient. *Clin Plast Surg* 2009 Oct;36(4):555–567.

26. Cancio LC. Initial assessment and fluid resuscitation of burn patients. *Surg Clin North Am* 2014 Aug;94(4):741–754.

27. Cancio LC, Lundy JB, Sheridan RL. Evolving changes in the management of burns and environmental injuries. *Surg Clin North Am* 2012 Aug;92(4):959–986, ix.

28. Capizzani AR, Drognonowski R, Ehrlich PF. Assessment of termination of trauma resuscitation guidelines: are children small adults? *J Pediatr Surg* 2010;45:903–907.

29. Carcillo JA. Intravenous fluid choices in critically ill children. *Curr Opin Crit Care* 2014;20:396–401.

30. Carney N, Ghajar J, Jagoda A, et al. Concussion guidelines step 1: systematic review of prevalent indicators. *Neurosurg* 2014 Sep;75(Suppl 1):S3–S15.

31. Carney N, Totten AM, O'Reilly C, et. al. Guidelines for the Management of Severe Traumatic Brain Injury, Fourth Edition. *Neurosurg* 2017;80(1):6–15.

32. Carta T, Gawaziuk J, Liu S, et al. Use of mineral oil Fleet enema for the removal of a large tar burn: a case report, *J Burns* 2015 Mar;41(2):e11–14.

33. Celso B, Tepas J, Langland-Orban B, et al. A systematic review and meta-analysis comparing outcome of severely injured patients treated in trauma centers following the establishment of trauma systems. *J Trauma* 2006;60:371–78; discussion 8.

34. Chames MC, Perlman MD. Trauma during pregnancy: outcomes and clinical management. *Clin Obstet Gynecol* 2008;51:398.

35. Chidester SJ, Williams N, Wang W, et al. A pediatric massive transfusion protocol. *J Trauma* 2012;73(5):1273–1277.

36. Clancy K, Velopulos C, Bilaniuk JW, et al. Screening for blunt cardiac injury: an Eastern Association for the Surgery of Trauma practice management guideline. *J Trauma* 2012 Nov;73(5 Suppl 4):S301–306.

37. Cohen DB, Rinker C, Wilberger JE. Traumatic brain injury in anticoagulated patients. *J Trauma* 2006;60(3):553–557.

38. Como JJ, Bokhari F, Chiu WC, et al. Practice management guidelines for selective nonoperative management of penetrating abdominal trauma. *J Trauma* 2010 Mar;68(3):721–733.

39. Compton J, Copeland K, Flanders S, et al. Implementing SBAR across a large multihospital health system. *Joint Commission J Quality and Patient Safety* 2012;38:261–268.

40. Cothren CC, Osborn PM, Moore EE, et al. Preperitoneal pelvic packing for hemodynamically

unstable pelvic fracture: a paradigm shift. *J Trauma* 2007;2(4):834–842.

41. CRASH-2 collaborators. The importance of early treatment with tranexamic acid in bleeding trauma patients: an exploratory analysis of the CRASH-2 randomized controlled trial. *Lancet* 2011;377(9771):1096–1101.

42. Davidson G, Rivara F, Mack C, et al. Validation of prehospital trauma triage criteria for motor vehicle collisions. *J Trauma* 2014; 76:755–766.6.

43. Dehmer JJ, Adamson WT. Massive transfusion and blood product use in the pediatric trauma patient. *Semin Pediatr Surg* 2010;19(4):286–291.

44. Demetriades D, Kimbrell B, Salim A, et al. Trauma deaths in a mature urban trauma system: is trimodal distribution a valid concept? *JACS* 2005;201(3):343–48.

45. Diaz JJ, Cullinane DC, Altman DT, et al. Practice Management Guidelines for the screening of thoracolumbar spine fracture. *J Trauma* 2007; 63(3):709–718.

46. Ditillo M, Pandit V, Rhee P, et al. Morbid obesity predisposes trauma patients to worse outcomes: a National Trauma Data Bank analysis. *J Trauma* 2014 Jan;76(1):176–179.

47. Doucet J, Bulger E, Sanddal N, et al.; endorsed by the National Association of EMS Physicians (NAEMSP). Appropriate use of helicopter emergency medical services for transport of trauma patients: guidelines from the Emergency Medical System Subcommittee, Committee on Trauma, American College of Surgeons. *J Trauma* 2013 Oct;75(4):734–741.

48. Dressler AM, Finck CM, Carroll CL, et al. Use of a massive transfusion protocol with hemostatic resuscitation for severe intraoperative bleeding in a child. *J Pediatr Surg* 2010;45(7):1530–1533.

49. Eastman AB. Wherever the dart lands: toward the ideal trauma system. *JACS* 2010 Aug;211(2):153–68.

50. Eastridge BJ, Wade CE, Spott MA, et al. Utilizing a trauma systems approach to benchmark and improve combat casualty care. *J Trauma* 2010;69 Suppl 1:S5–S9.

51. Edwards C, Woodard, E. SBAR for maternal transports: going the extra mile. *Nursing for Women's Health* 2009;12:516–520.

52. Esposito TJ, Ingraham A, Luchette FA, et al. Reasons to omit digital rectal exam in trauma patients: no fingers, no rectum, no useful additional information. *J Trauma* 2005 Dec;59(6):1314–1319.

53. Esposito TJ, Sanddal TL, Reynolds SA, et al. Effect of a voluntary trauma system on preventable death and inappropriate care in a rural state. *J Trauma* 2003;54:663–69; discussion 9-70.

54. Estroff JM, Foglia RP, Fuchs JR. A comparison of accidental and nonaccidental trauma: it is worse than you think. *J Emerg Med* 2015;48:274–279.

55. Faul M, Xu L, Wald MM, et al. *Traumatic Brain Injury in the United States: Emergency Department Visits, Hospitalizations, and Deaths.* Atlanta, GA: Centers for Disease Control and Prevention, National Center for Injury Prevention and Control; 2010.

56. Felder S, Margel D, Murrell Z, et al. Usefulness of bowel sound auscultation: a prospective evaluation. *J Surg Educ* 2014;71(5):768–773.

57. German Trauma Society. Prehospital (section 1). Emergency room, extremities (subsection 2.10). In: *S3—Guideline on Treatment of Patients with Severe and Multiple Injuries.* (English version AWMF-Registry No. 012/019). Berlin: German Trauma Society (DGU).

58. Global Burden of Diseases Pediatric Collaboration. Global and national burden of diseases and injuries among children and adolescents between 1990 and 2013: findings from the Global Burden of Disease 2013 Study. *JAMA Peds* 2016;170(3): 267–287.

59. Gonzaga T, Jenabzadeh K, Anderson CP, et al. Use of intra-arterial thrombolytic therapy for acute treatment of frostbite in 62 patients with review of thrombolytic therapy in frostbite. *J Burn Care Res* 2016 Jul–Aug;37(4):e323–324.

60. Guidelines for field triage of injured patients: recommendations of the National Expert Panel on Field Triage, 2011. *MMWR Morb Mortal Wkly Rep* 2012;61:1–21.

61. Guidelines for the Management of Acute Cervical Spine and Spinal Cord Injuries. *Neurosurgery* 2013; 72(Suppl 2):1–259.

62. Gunst M, Ghaemmaghami V, Gruszecki A, et al. Changing epidemiology of trauma deaths leads to abimodal distribution. *Proc (Bayl Univ Med Cent)* 2010;23(4):349–54.

63. Hadley MN, Walters BC, Aarabi B, et al. Clinical assessment following acute cervical spinal cord injury. *Neurosurg* 2013;72(Suppl 2):40–53.

64. Harrington DT, Connolly M, Biffl WL, et al. Transfer times to definitive care facilities are too long: a consequence of an immature trauma system. *Ann Surg* 241(6):961–968.

65. Harvey A, Towner E, Peden M, et al. Injury prevention and the attainment of child and adolescent health. *Bull World Health Organ* 2009;87(5):390–394.

66. Hendrickson JE, Shaz BH, Pereira G, et al. Coagulopathy is prevalent and associated with adverse outcomes in transfused pediatric trauma patients. *J Pediatr* 2012;160(2):204–209.

67. Hendrickson JE, Shaz BH, Pereira G, et al. Implementation of a pediatric trauma massive transfusion protocol: one institution's experience. *Transfusion* 2012;52(6):1228–1236.

68. Hoffman M, Monroe DM. Reversing targeted oral anticoagulants. *ASH Education Book* 2014;1:518–523.

69. Holcomb JB, del Junco DJ, Fox EE, et al. The prospective, observational, multicenter, major trauma transfusion (PROMMTT) study: comparative effectiveness of a time-varying treatment with competing risks. *JAMA Surg* 2013;148(2):127–136.

70. HRSA(Health Resources and Services Administration.) Model trauma care system plan. In: *Administration*. Rockville, MD: U.S Department of Health and Human Services; 1992.

71. HRSA. *Model trauma systems planning and evaluation*. Rockville, MD: U.S. Department of Health and Human Services; 2006.

72. Hurlbert J, Hadley MN, Walters BC, et al. Pharmacological therapy for acute spinal cord injury. *Neurosurg* 2013;72(Suppl 2):93–105.

73. Inaba K, Lustenberger T, Recinos G, et al. Does size matter? A prospective analysis of 28-32 versus 36-40 French chest tube size in trauma. *J Trauma* 2012;72(2):422–427.

74. Inaba K, Nosanov L, Menaker J, et al. Prospective derivation of a clinical decision rule for thoracolumbar spine evaluation after blunt trauma: An American Association for the Surgery of Trauma Multi-Institutional Trials Group Study. *J Trauma* 2015;78(3):459–465.

75. Inaba K, Siboni S, Resnick S, et al. Tourniquet use for civilian extremity trauma. *J Trauma* 2015;79(2):232–237.

76. Intimate Partner Violence Facts. www.who.int/violence_injury_prevention/violence/world_report/factsheets/en/ipvfacts.pdf. Accessed April 18, 2017.

77. Jain V, Chari R, Maslovitz S, et al. Guidelines for the management of a pregnant trauma patient. *J Obstet Gynaecol Can* 2015;37(6):553–571.

78. Johnson MH, Chang A, Brandes SB. The value of digital rectal examination in assessing for pelvic fracture-associated urethral injury: what defines a high-riding or non-palpable prostate? *J Trauma* 2013 Nov;75(5):913–915.

79. Kappel DA, Rossi DC, Polack EP, et al. Does the rural Trauma Team development course shorten the interval from trauma patient arrival to decision to transfer? *J Trauma* 2011;70:315–319.

80. Kassam-Adams N, Marsac ML, Hildenbrand A, et al. Posttraumatic stress following pediatric injury: update on diagnosis, risk factors, and intervention. *JAMA Peds* 2013;167:1158–1165.

81. Kharbanda AB, Flood A, Blumberg K, et al. Analysis of radiation exposure among pediatric patients at national trauma centers. *J Trauma* 2013;74:907–911.

82. Kirshblum S, Waring W 3rd. Updates for the International Standards for Neurological Classification of Spinal Cord Injury. *Phys Med Rehabil Clin N Am* 2014;25(3):505–517.

83. Knegt CD, Meylaerts SA, Leenen LP. Applicability of the trimodal distribution of trauma deaths in a Level I trauma centre in the Netherlands with a population of mainly blunt trauma Injury, *Int. J. Care Injured* 2008;39:993—1000.

84. Kobbe P, Micansky F, Lichte P, et al. Increased morbidity and mortality after bilateral femoral shaft fractures: myth or reality in the era of damage control? *Injury* 2013 Feb;44(2):221–225.

85. Kochanek PM, Carney N, Adelson PD, et al. Guidelines for the acute medical management of severe traumatic brain injury in infants, children, and adolescents—second edition. *Pediatr Crit Med* 2012;13(Suppl 1):S1–82.

86. Konda SR, Davidovich RI, Egol KA. Computed tomography scan to detect traumatic arthrotomies and identify periarticular wounds not requiring surgical intervention: an improvement over the saline load test. *J Trauma* 2013;27(9):498–504.

87. Lai A, Davidson N, Galloway SW, et al. Perioperative management of patients on new oral anticoagulants. *Br J Surg* 2014 Jun;101(7):742–749.

88. Lansink KW, Leenen LP. Do designated trauma systems improve outcome? *Curr Opin Crit Care* 2007;13:686–90.

89. Latenser BA. Critical care of the burn patient: the first 48 hours. *Crit Care Med* 2009 Oct;37(10):2819–2826.

90. Lee C, Bernard A, Fryman L, et al. Imaging may delay transfer of rural trauma victims: a survey of referring physicians. *J Trauma* 2009;65:1359–1363.

91. Lee TH, Ouellet JF, Cook M, et al. Pericardiocentesis in trauma: a systematic review. *J Trauma* 2013;75(4):543–549.

92. Lee PM, Lee C, Rattner P, et al. Intraosseous versus central venous catheter utilization and performance during inpatient medical emergencies. *Crit Care Med* 2015 Jun;43(6):1233–1238.

93. Leeper WR, Leeper TJ, Yogt K, et al. The role of trauma team leaders in missed injuries: does specialty matter? *J Trauma* 2013;75(3):387–390.

94. Lewis P, Wright C. Saving the critically injured trauma patient: a retrospective analysis of

1000 uses of intraosseous access. *Emerg Med J* 2015Jun;32(6):463–467.

95. Ley E, Clond M, Srour M, et al. Emergency department crystalloid resuscitation of 1.5 L or more is associated with increased mortality in elderly and nonelderly trauma patients. *J Trauma* 2011;70(2):398–400.

96. Li C, Friedman B, Conwell Y, et al. Validity of the Patient Health Questionnaire-2 (PHQ-2) in identifying major depression in older people. *J Am Geriatr Soc* 2007 April;55(4):596–602.

97. Liu T, Chen JJ, Bai XJ, et al. The effect of obesity on outcomes in trauma patients: a meta-analysis. *Injury* 2013 Sep;44(9):1145–1152.

98. MacKenzie EJ, Rivara FP, Jurkovich GJ, et al. A national evaluation of the effect of trauma-center care on mortality. *New Engl J Med* 2006;354:366–78.

99. MacKenzie EJ, Weir S, Rivara FP, et al. The value of trauma center care. *J Trauma* 2010;69:1–10.

100. Mathen R, Inaba K, Munera F, et al. Prospective evaluation of multislice computed tomography versus plain radiographic cervical spine clearance in trauma patients. *J Trauma* 2007 Jun;62(6):1427.

101. McCrum ML, McKee J, Lai M, et al. ATLS adherence in the transfer of rural trauma patients to a level I facility. *Injury* 44(9):1241–1245.

102. McKee JL, Roberts DJ, van Wijngaarden-Stephens MH, et al. The right treatment at the right time in the right place: a population-based, before-and-after study of outcomes associated with implementation of an all-inclusive trauma system in a large Canadian province. *Ann Surg* 2015;261:558–564.

103. Medina O, Arom GA, Yeranosian MG, et al. Vascular and nerve injury after knee dislocation: a systematic review. *Clin Orthop Relat Res* 2014 Oct;472(1):2984–2990.

104. Mills WJ, Barei DP, McNair P. The value of the ankle-brachial index for diagnosing arterial injury after knee dislocation: a prospective study. *J Trauma* 2004;56:1261–1265.

105. Milzman DP, Rothenhaus TC. Resuscitation of the geriatric patient. *Emerg Med Clin NA* 1996;14:233–244.

106. Min L, Burruss S, Morley E, et al. A simple clinical risk nomogram to predict mortality-associated geriatric complications in severely injured geriatric patients. *J Trauma* 74(4): 1125–1132.

107. Morrissey BE, Delaney RA, Johnstone AJ, et al.. Do trauma systems work? A comparison of major trauma outcomes between Aberdeen Royal Infirmary and Massachusetts General Hospital. *Injury* 2015;46:150–155.

108. Morshed S, Knops S, Jurkovich GJ, et al.. The impact of trauma-center care on mortality and function following pelvic ring and acetabular injuries. *J Bone Joint Surg Am* 2015;97:265–272.

109. Murphy JT, Jaiswal K, Sabella J, et al. Prehospital cardiopulmonary resuscitation in the pediatric trauma patient. *J Pediatr Surg* 2010 Jul;45(7):1413–1419.

110. Mutschler Amy, Nienaber U, Brockampa T, et al. A critical reappraisal of the ATLS classification of hypovolaemic shock: does it really reflect clinical reality? *Resuscitation* 2013;84: 309–313.

111. Nathens AB, Jurkovich GJ, Rivara FP, et al. Effectiveness of state trauma systems in reducing injury-related mortality: a national evaluation. *J Trauma* 2000;48:25–30; discussion 30-31.

112. National Academy of Sciences. *Accidental Death and Disability: The Neglected Disease of Modern Society*. Washington, DC: National Academies Press; 1966.

113. Natsuhara KM, Yeranosian MG, Cohen JR, et al. What is the frequency of vascular injury after knee dislocation? *Clin Orthop Relat Res* 2014 Sep;472(9):2615–2620.

114. Neff NP, Cannon JW, Morrison JJ, et al. Clearly defining pediatric mass transfusion: cutting through the fog and friction using combat data. *J Trauma* 2015 Jan;78(1):22–28.

115. O'Brien CL, Menon M, Jomha NM. Controversies in the management of open fractures. *Open Orthop J* 2014;8:178–184.

116. O'Malley E, Boyle E, O'Callaghan A, et al. Role of laparoscopy in penetrating abdominal trauma: a systematic review *World J Surg* 2013 Jan;37(1):113–122.

117. O'Toole RV, Lindbloom BJ, Hui E, et al. Are bilateral femoral fractures no longer a marker for death? *J Orthoped Trauma* 2014 Feb;28(2): 77–81.

118. Onzuka J, Worster A, McCreadie B. Is computerized tomography of trauma patients associated with a transfer delay to a regional trauma centre? *CJEM*:10(3):205–208.

119. Osborn PM, Smith WR, Moore EE, et al. Direct retroperitoneal pelvic packing versus pelvic angiography: a comparison of two management protocols for haemodynamically unstable pelvic fractures. *Injury* 2009 Jan;40(1):54–60.

120. Osborne Z, Rowitz B. Moore H, et al. Obesity in trauma: outcomes and disposition trends. *Am J Surg* 2014;207(3):387–392; discussion 391-392.

121. Oyetunji TA, Chang DC, et al. Redefining hypotension in the elderly: normotension is not reassuring. *Arch Surg* 2011 Jul;146(7):865–869.

122. Palusci VJ, Covington TM. Child maltreatment deaths in the U.S. National Child Death Review Case Reporting System. *Child Abuse and Neglect* 2014;28:25–36.

123. Pang JM, Civil I Ng A, Adams D, et al. Is the trimodal pattern of death after trauma a dated concept in the 21st century? Trauma deaths in Auckland 2004. *Injury* 2008;39:102–106.

124. Patregnani JT, Borgman MA, Maegele M, et al. Coagulopathy and shock on admission is associated with mortality for children with traumatic injuries at combat support hospitals. *Pediatr Crit Care Med* 2012;13(3):1–5.

125. Petrone P, Talving P, Browder T, et al. Abdominal injuries in pregnancy: a 155-month study at two level 1 trauma centers. *Injury* 2011;42(1): 47–49.

126. Pham TN, Gibran NS. Thermal and electrical injuries. *Surg Clin North Am* 2007 Feb;87(1):185–206, vii–viii. Review.

127. Post AF, Boro T, Eckland JM. Injury to the brain. In: Mattox KL, Feliciano DV, Moore EE, eds. *Trauma*. 7th ed. New York, NY: McGraw-Hill; 2013:356–376.

128. Pruitt BA. Fluid and electrolyte replacement in the burned patient. *Surg Clin North Am* 1978;58(6):1313–1322.

129. Puntnam-Hornstein E. Report of maltreatment as a risk factor for injury death: a prospective birth cohort. *Child Maltreatment* 2011;16: 163–174.

130. Quick JA, Bartels AN, Coughenour JP, et al. Trauma transfers and definitive imaging: patient benefit but at what cost? *Am Surg* 79(3):301–304.

131. Richardson JD. Trauma centers and trauma surgeons: have we become too specialized? *J Trauma* 2000;48:1-7.

132. Roberts D, Leigh-Smith S, Faris P, et al. Clinical presentation of patients with tension pneumothorax: a systematic review. *Ann Surg* 2015;261(6):1068–1078.

133. Romanowski KS, Barsun A, Pamlieri TL, et al. Frailty score on admission predicts outcomes in elderly burn injury. *J Burn Care Res* 2015;36:1–6.

134. Scaife ER, Rollins MD, Barnhart D, et al. The role of focused abdominal sonography for trauma (FAST) in pediatric trauma evaluation. *J Ped Surg* 2013;48:1377–1383.

135. Schmitt SK, Sexton DJ, Baron EL. Treatment and Prevention of Osteomyelitis Following Trauma in Adults. UpToDate. http://www.uptodate.com/contents/treatment-and-prevention-of-osteomyelitis-following-trauma-in-adults. October 29, 2015.

136. Sheridan RL, Chang P. Acute burn procedures. *Surg Clin North Am* 2014 Aug;94(4):755–764.

137. Shlamovitz GZ, Mower WR, Bergman J, et al. How (un)useful is the pelvic ring stability examination in diagnosing mechanically unstable pelvic fractures in blunt trauma patients? *J Trauma* 2009;66(3):815–820.

138. Shrestha B, Holcomb JB, Camp EA, et al. Damage control resuscitation increases successful nonoperative management rates and survival after severe blunt liver injury. *J Trauma* 2015;78(2):336–341.

139. Snyder D, Tsou A, Schoelles K. *Efficacy of Prehospital Application of Tourniquets and Hemostatic Dressings to Control Traumatic External Hemorrhage*. Washington, DC: National Highway Traffic Safety Administration; 2014, 145.

140. Sosa JL, Baker M, Puente I, et al. Negative laparotomy in abdominal gunshot wounds: potential impact of laparoscopy. *J Trauma* 1995 Feb;38(2):194–197.

141. Steinhausen E, Lefering R, Tjardes T, et al. A risk-adapted approach is beneficial in the management of bilateral femoral shaft fractures in multiple trauma patients: an analysis based on the trauma registry of the German Trauma Society. *J Trauma* 2014;76(5):1288–1293.

142. Stevens JA. Fatalities and injuries from falls among older adults—United States 1993–2003 and 2001–2005. *MMWR Morb Mortal Wkly Rep* 2006;55:1221–1224.

143. Sussman M, DiRusso SM, Sullivan T, et al. Traumatic brain injury in the elderly: increased mortality and worse functional outcome at discharge despite lower injury severity. *J Trauma* 2002;53:219–224.

144. Thomson DP, Thomas SH. Guidelines for air medical dispatch. *Prehosp Emerg Care* 2003 Apr–Jun;7(2):265–271.

145. Tornetta P, Boes MT, Schepsis AA, et al. How effective is a saline arthrogram for wounds around the knee? *Clin Orthop Relat Res* 2008;466:432–435.

146. United Nations, Department of Economic and Social Affairs, Population Division (2015). *World Population Ageing*.

147. United States Bureau of the Census. Population projections of the United States by age, sex, race, and Hispanic origin: 1995 to 2050. http://www.census.gov/prod/1/pop/p25-1130.pdf. Accessed April 18, 2017.

148. Velmahos GC, Demetriades D, Cornwell EE 3rd. Transpelvic gunshot wounds: routine laparotomy or selective management? *World J Surg* 1998 Oct;22(10):1034–1038.

149. Vercruysse GA, Ingram WL, Feliciano DV. The demographics of modern burn care: should most

burns be cared for by the non-burn surgeon? *Am J Surg* 2011;201:91–96.

150. Walls RM, Murphy MF, eds. *The Manual of Emergency Airway Management*. 4th ed. Philadelphia, PA: Lippincott Williams & Wilkins; 2012.

151. Walter J, Doris PE, Shaffer MA. Clinical presentation of patients with acute cervical spine injury. *Ann Emerg Med* 1984;13(7):512–515.

152. Washington CW, Grubb RL Jr. Are routine repeat imaging and intensive care unit admission necessary in mild traumatic brain injury? *J Neurosurg* 2012;116(3):549–557.

153. Weiss M, Dullenkopf A, Fischer JE, et al., European Paediatric Endotracheal Intubation Study Group. Prospective randomized controlled multi-centre trial of cuffed or uncuffed endotracheal tubes in small children. *Br J Anaesth* 2009;103(6):867–873.

154. West JG, Trunkey DD, Lim RC. Systems of trauma care. A study of two counties. *Arch Surg* 1979;114:455–460.

155. Wijdicks EFM, Varelas PN, Gronseth GS, et al. Evidence-based guideline update: determining brain death in adults. Report of the Quality Standards Subcommittee of the American Academy of Neurology. *Neurology* 2010;74:1911–1918.

156. Willett K, Al-Khateeb H, Kotnis R, et al. Risk of mortality: the relationship with associated injuries and fracture. Treatment methods in patients with unilateral or bilateral femoral shaft fractures. *J Trauma* 2010 Aug;69(2):405–410.

157. Yelon JA. Geriatric trauma. In: Moore EE, Feliciano DV, Mattox K, eds. *Trauma*. 7th ed. New York, NY: McGraw Hill, 2012.

BRIEF CONTENTS

DETAILED CONTENTS

CHAPTER 12
TRAUMA IN PREGNANCY AND INTIMATE PARTNER VIOLENCE   226

CHAPTER 13
TRANSFER TO DEFINITIVE CARE   240

APPENDICES   255

ATLS®
Advanced Trauma Life Support®

Student Course Manual

1 INITIAL ASSESSMENT AND MANAGEMENT

Repeat the primary survey frequently to identify any deterioration in the patient's status that indicates the need for additional intervention.

CHAPTER 1 OUTLINE

OBJECTIVES

After reading this chapter and comprehending the knowledge components of the ATLS provider course, you will be able to:

1. Explain the importance of prehospital and hospital preparation to facilitate rapid resuscitation of trauma patients.

2. Identify the correct sequence of priorities for the assessment of injured patients.

3. Explain the principles of the primary survey, as they apply to the assessment of an injured patient.

4. Explain how a patient's medical history and the mechanism of injury contribute to the identification of injuries.

5. Explain the need for immediate resuscitation during the primary survey.

6. Describe the initial assessment of a multiply injured patient, using the correct sequence of priorities.

7. Identify the pitfalls associated with the initial assessment and management of injured patients and describe ways to avoid them.

8. Explain the management techniques employed during the primary assessment and stabilization of a multiply injured patient.

9. Identify the adjuncts to the assessment and management of injured patients as part of the primary survey, and recognize the contraindications to their use.

10. Recognize patients who require transfer to another facility for definitive management.

11. Identify the components of a secondary survey, including adjuncts that may be appropriate during its performance.

12. Discuss the importance of reevaluating a patient who is not responding appropriately to resuscitation and management.

13. Explain the importance of teamwork in the initial assessment of trauma patients.

When treating injured patients, clinicians rapidly assess injuries and institute life-preserving therapy. Because timing is crucial, a systematic approach that can be rapidly and accurately applied is essential. This approach, termed the "initial assessment," includes the following elements:

- Preparation
- Triage
- Primary survey (ABCDEs) with immediate resuscitation of patients with life-threatening injuries
- Adjuncts to the primary survey and resuscitation
- Consideration of the need for patient transfer
- Secondary survey (head-to-toe evaluation and patient history)
- Adjuncts to the secondary survey
- Continued postresuscitation monitoring and reevaluation
- Definitive care

The primary and secondary surveys are repeated frequently to identify any change in the patient's status that indicates the need for additional intervention. The assessment sequence presented in this chapter reflects a linear, or longitudinal, progression of events. In an actual clinical situation, however, many of these activities occur simultaneously. The longitudinal progression of the assessment process allows clinicians an opportunity to mentally review the progress of actual trauma resuscitation.

ATLS® principles guide the assessment and resuscitation of injured patients. Judgment is required to determine which procedures are necessary for individual patients, as they may not require all of them.

PREPARATION

Preparation for trauma patients occurs in two different clinical settings: in the field and in the hospital. First, during the prehospital phase, events are coordinated with the clinicians at the receiving hospital. Second, during the hospital phase, preparations are made to facilitate rapid trauma patient resuscitation.

PREHOSPITAL PHASE

Coordination with prehospital agencies and personnel can greatly expedite treatment in the field (■ FIGURE

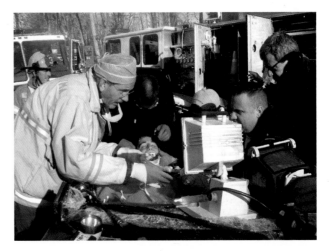

■ FIGURE 1-1 Prehospital Phase. During the prehospital phase, personnel emphasize airway maintenance, control of external bleeding and shock, immobilization of the patient, and immediate transport to the closest appropriate facility, preferably a verified trauma center.

1-1). The prehospital system ideally is set up to notify the receiving hospital before personnel transport the patient from the scene. This allows for mobilization of the hospital's trauma team members so that all necessary personnel and resources are present in the emergency department (ED) at the time of the patient's arrival.

During the prehospital phase, providers emphasize airway maintenance, control of external bleeding and shock, immobilization of the patient, and immediate transport to the closest appropriate facility, preferably a verified trauma center. Prehospital providers must make every effort to minimize scene time, a concept that is supported by the Field Triage Decision Scheme, shown in (■ FIGURE 1-2) and *MyATLS mobile app*.

Emphasis also is placed on obtaining and reporting information needed for triage at the hospital, including time of injury, events related to the injury, and patient history. The mechanisms of injury can suggest the degree of injury as well as specific injuries the patient needs evaluated and treated.

The National Association of Emergency Medical Technicians' Prehospital Trauma Life Support Committee, in cooperation with the Committee on Trauma (COT) of the American College of Surgeons (ACS), has developed the Prehospital Trauma Life Support (PHTLS) course. PHTLS is similar to the ATLS Course in format, although it addresses the prehospital care of injured patients.

The use of prehospital care protocols and the ability to access online medical direction (i.e., direct medical control) can facilitate and improve care initiated in the field. Periodic multidisciplinary review of patient care through a quality improvement process is an essential component of each hospital's trauma program.

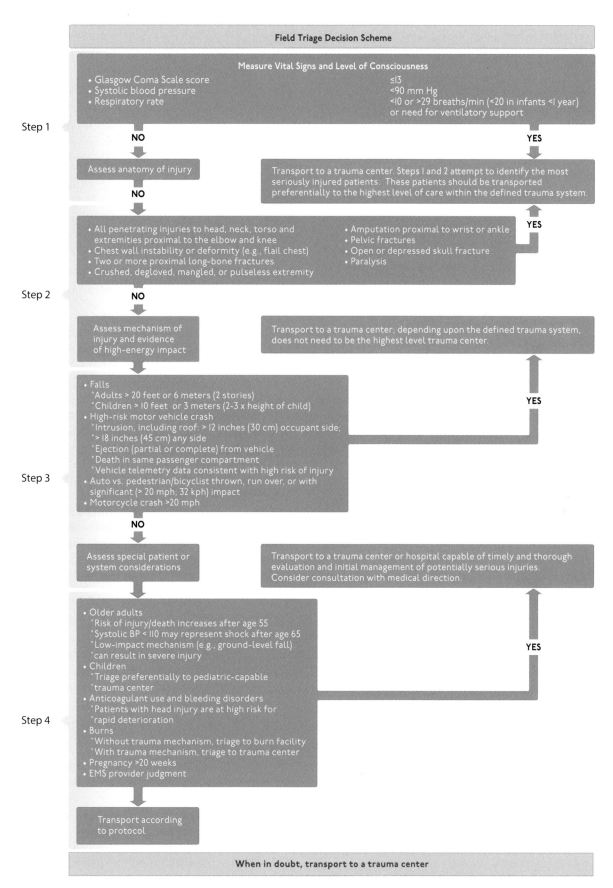

Field Triage Decision Scheme

Measure Vital Signs and Level of Consciousness

- Glasgow Coma Scale score   ≤13
- Systolic blood pressure   <90 mm Hg
- Respiratory rate   <10 or >29 breaths/min (<20 in infants <1 year)
                                              or need for ventilatory support

Step 1   NO   YES

Assess anatomy of injury

Transport to a trauma center. Steps 1 and 2 attempt to identify the most seriously injured patients. These patients should be transported preferentially to the highest level of care within the defined trauma system.

NO   YES

- All penetrating injuries to head, neck, torso and extremities proximal to the elbow and knee
- Chest wall instability or deformity (e.g., flail chest)
- Two or more proximal long-bone fractures
- Crushed, degloved, mangled, or pulseless extremity
- Amputation proximal to wrist or ankle
- Pelvic fractures
- Open or depressed skull fracture
- Paralysis

Step 2   NO

Assess mechanism of injury and evidence of high-energy impact

Transport to a trauma center; depending upon the defined trauma system, does not need to be the highest level trauma center.

YES

- Falls
  °Adults > 20 feet or 6 meters (2 stories)
  °Children > 10 feet or 3 meters (2-3 x height of child)
- High-risk motor vehicle crash
  °Intrusion, including roof: > 12 inches (30 cm) occupant side;
  °> 18 inches (45 cm) any side
  °Ejection (partial or complete) from vehicle
  °Death in same passenger compartment
  °Vehicle telemetry data consistent with high risk of injury
- Auto vs. pedestrian/bicyclist thrown, run over, or with significant (> 20 mph; 32 kph) impact
- Motorcycle crash >20 mph

Step 3   NO

Assess special patient or system considerations

Transport to a trauma center or hospital capable of timely and thorough evaluation and initial management of potentially serious injuries. Consider consultation with medical direction.

YES

- Older adults
  °Risk of injury/death increases after age 55
  °Systolic BP < 110 may represent shock after age 65
  °Low-impact mechanism (e.g., ground-level fall)
  °can result in severe injury
- Children
  °Triage preferentially to pediatric-capable
  °trauma center
- Anticoagulant use and bleeding disorders
  °Patients with head injury are at high risk for
  °rapid deterioration
- Burns
  °Without trauma mechanism, triage to burn facility
  °With trauma mechanism, triage to trauma center
- Pregnancy >20 weeks
- EMS provider judgment

Step 4

Transport according to protocol

When in doubt, transport to a trauma center

■ FIGURE 1-2 Field Triage Decision Scheme

HOSPITAL PHASE

Advance planning for the arrival of trauma patients is essential (see *Pre-alert checklist on the MyATLS mobile app.*) The hand-over between prehospital providers and those at the receiving hospital should be a smooth process, directed by the trauma team leader, ensuring that all important information is available to the entire team. Critical aspects of hospital preparation include the following:

- A resuscitation area is available for trauma patients.

- Properly functioning airway equipment (e.g., laryngoscopes and endotracheal tubes) is organized, tested, and strategically placed to be easily accessible.

- Warmed intravenous crystalloid solutions are immediately available for infusion, as are appropriate monitoring devices.

- A protocol to summon additional medical assistance is in place, as well as a means to ensure prompt responses by laboratory and radiology personnel.

- Transfer agreements with verified trauma centers are established and operational. (See *ACS COT's Resources for Optimal Care of the Injured Patient, 2014*).

Due to concerns about communicable diseases, particularly hepatitis and acquired immunodeficiency syndrome (AIDS), the Centers for Disease Control and Prevention (CDC) and other health agencies strongly recommend the use of standard precautions (e.g., face mask, eye protection, water-impervious gown, and gloves) when coming into contact with body fluids (■ FIGURE 1-3). The ACS COT considers these to be minimum precautions and protection for all healthcare providers. Standard precautions are also an Occupational Safety and Health Administration (OSHA) requirement in the United States.

▸ TRIAGE

Triage involves the sorting of patients based on the resources required for treatment and the resources that are actually available. The order of treatment is based on the ABC priorities (airway with cervical spine protection, breathing, and circulation with hemorrhage control). Other factors that can affect

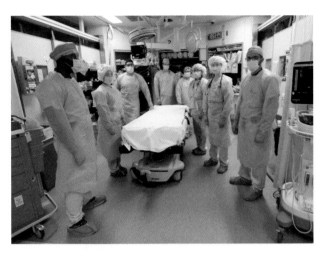

■ FIGURE 1-3 Trauma team members are trained to use standard precautions, including face mask, eye protection, water-impervious gown, and gloves, when coming into contact with body fluids.

triage and treatment priority include the severity of injury, ability to survive, and available resources.

Triage also includes the sorting of patients in the field to help determine the appropriate receiving medical facility. Trauma team activation may be considered for severely injured patients. Prehospital personnel and their medical directors are responsible for ensuring that appropriate patients arrive at appropriate hospitals. For example, delivering a patient who has sustained severe trauma to a hospital other than a trauma center is inappropriate when such a center is available (see ■ FIGURE 1-2). Prehospital trauma scoring is often helpful in identifying severely injured patients who warrant transport to a trauma center. (See *Trauma Scores: Revised and Pediatric.*)

Triage situations are categorized as multiple casualties or mass casualties.

MULTIPLE CASUALTIES

Multiple-casualty incidents are those in which the number of patients and the severity of their injuries *do not* exceed the capability of the facility to render care. In such cases, patients with life-threatening problems and those sustaining multiple-system injuries are treated first.

MASS CASUALTIES

In mass-casualty events, the number of patients and the severity of their injuries *does* exceed the capability of the facility and staff. In such cases, patients having the greatest chance of survival and requiring the least expenditure of time, equipment, supplies, and personnel are treated first. (*See Appendix D: Disaster Management and Emergency Preparedness.*)

PRIMARY SURVEY WITH SIMULTANEOUS RESUSCITATION

Patients are assessed, and their treatment priorities are established, based on their injuries, vital signs, and the injury mechanisms. Logical and sequential treatment priorities are established based on the overall assessment of the patient. The patient's vital functions must be assessed quickly and efficiently. Management consists of a rapid primary survey with simultaneous resuscitation of vital functions, a more detailed secondary survey, and the initiation of definitive care (see *Initial Assessment video on MyATLS mobile app*).

The primary survey encompasses the ABCDEs of trauma care and identifies life-threatening conditions by adhering to this sequence:

- Airway maintenance with restriction of cervical spine motion
- Breathing and ventilation
- Circulation with hemorrhage control
- Disability(assessment of neurologic status)
- Exposure/Environmental control

Clinicians can quickly assess A, B, C, and D in a trauma patient (10-second assessment) by identifying themselves, asking the patient for his or her name, and asking what happened. An appropriate response suggests that there is no major airway compromise (i.e., ability to speak clearly), breathing is not severely compromised (i.e., ability to generate air movement to permit speech), and the level of consciousness is not markedly decreased (i.e., alert enough to describe what happened). Failure to respond to these questions suggests abnormalities in A, B, C, or D that warrant urgent assessment and management.

During the primary survey, life-threatening conditions are identified and treated in a prioritized sequence based on the effects of injuries on the patient's physiology, because at first it may not be possible to identify specific anatomic injuries. For example, airway compromise can occur secondary to head trauma, injuries causing shock, or direct physical trauma to the airway. Regardless of the injury causing airway compromise, the first priority is airway management: clearing the airway, suctioning, administering oxygen, and opening and securing the airway. Because the prioritized sequence is based on the degree of life threat, the abnormality posing the greatest threat to life is addressed first.

Recall that the prioritized assessment and management procedures described in this chapter are presented as sequential steps in order of importance and to ensure clarity; in practice, these steps are frequently accomplished simultaneously by a team of healthcare professionals (see Teamwork, on page 19 and *Appendix E*).

AIRWAY MAINTENANCE WITH RESTRICTION OF CERVICAL SPINE MOTION

Upon initial evaluation of a trauma patient, first assess the airway to ascertain patency. This rapid assessment for signs of airway obstruction includes inspecting for foreign bodies; identifying facial, mandibular, and/or tracheal/laryngeal fractures and other injuries that can result in airway obstruction; and suctioning to clear accumulated blood or secretions that may lead to or be causing airway obstruction. Begin measures to establish a patent airway while restricting cervical spine motion.

If the patient is able to communicate verbally, the airway is not likely to be in immediate jeopardy; however, repeated assessment of airway patency is prudent. In addition, patients with severe head injuries who have an altered level of consciousness or a Glasgow Coma Scale (GCS) score of 8 or lower usually require the placement of a definitive airway (i.e., cuffed, secured tube in the trachea). (The GCS is further explained and demonstrated in *Chapter 6: Head Trauma* and the *MyATLS app*.) Initially, the jaw-thrust or chin-lift maneuver often suffices as an initial intervention. If the patient is unconscious and has no gag reflex, the placement of an oropharyngeal airway can be helpful temporarily. Establish a definitive airway if there is any doubt about the patient's ability to maintain airway integrity.

The finding of nonpurposeful motor responses strongly suggests the need for definitive airway management. Management of the airway in pediatric patients requires knowledge of the unique anatomic features of the position and size of the larynx in children, as well as special equipment (*see Chapter 10: Pediatric Trauma*).

While assessing and managing a patient's airway, take great care to prevent excessive movement of the cervical spine. Based on the mechanism of trauma, assume that a spinal injury exists. Neurologic examination alone does not exclude a diagnosis of cervical spine injury. The spine must be protected from excessive mobility to prevent development of or progression of a deficit. The cervical spine is protected

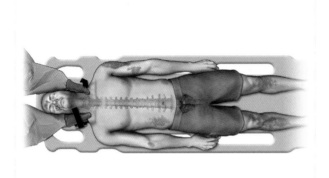

■ **FIGURE 1-4 Cervical spine motion restriction technique.**
When the cervical collar is removed, a member of the trauma team manually stabilizes the patient's head and neck.

PITFALL	PREVENTION
Equipment failure	• Test equipment regularly. • Ensure spare equipment and batteries are readily available.
Unsuccessful intubation	• Identify patients with difficult airway anatomy. • Identify the most experienced/skilled airway manager on your team. • Ensure appropriate equipment is available to rescue the failed airway attempt. • Be prepared to perform a surgical airway.
Progressive airway loss	• Recognize the dynamic status of the airway. • Recognize the injuries that can result in progressive airway loss. • Frequently reassess the patient for signs of deterioration of the airway.

with a cervical collar. When airway management is necessary, the cervical collar is opened, and a team member manually restricts motion of the cervical spine (■ FIGURE 1-4).

While every effort should be made to recognize airway compromise promptly and secure a definitive airway, it is equally important to recognize the potential for progressive airway loss. Frequent reevaluation of airway patency is essential to identify and treat patients who are losing the ability to maintain an adequate airway.

Establish an airway surgically if intubation is contraindicated or cannot be accomplished.

BREATHING AND VENTILATION

Airway patency alone does not ensure adequate ventilation. Adequate gas exchange is required to maximize oxygenation and carbon dioxide elimination. Ventilation requires adequate function of the lungs, chest wall, and diaphragm; therefore, clinicians must rapidly examine and evaluate each component.

To adequately assess jugular venous distention, position of the trachea, and chest wall excursion, expose the patient's neck and chest. Perform auscultation to ensure gas flow in the lungs. Visual inspection and palpation can detect injuries to the chest wall that may be compromising ventilation. Percussion of the thorax can also identify abnormalities, but during a noisy resuscitation this evaluation may be inaccurate.

Injuries that significantly impair ventilation in the short term include tension pneumothorax, massive hemothorax, open pneumothorax, and tracheal or bronchial injuries. These injuries should be identified during the primary survey and often require immediate attention to ensure effective ventilation. Because a tension pneumothorax compromises ventilation and circulation dramatically and acutely, chest decompression should follow immediately when suspected by clinical evaluation.

Every injured patient should receive supplemental oxygen. If the patient is not intubated, oxygen should be delivered by a mask-reservoir device to achieve optimal oxygenation. Use a pulse oximeter to monitor adequacy of hemoglobin oxygen saturation. Simple pneumothorax, simple hemothorax, fractured ribs, flail chest, and pulmonary contusion can compromise ventilation to a lesser degree and are usually identified during the secondary survey. A simple pneumothorax can be converted to a tension pneumothorax when a patient is intubated and positive pressure ventilation is provided before decompressing the pneumothorax with a chest tube.

Airway and ventilatory management are described in further detail in *Chapter 2*.

CIRCULATION WITH HEMORRHAGE CONTROL

Circulatory compromise in trauma patients can result from a variety of injuries. Blood volume, cardiac output, and bleeding are major circulatory issues to consider.

Blood Volume and Cardiac Output

Hemorrhage is the predominant cause of preventable deaths after injury. Identifying, quickly controlling hemorrhage, and initiating resuscitation are therefore crucial steps in assessing and managing such patients. Once tension pneumothorax has been excluded as a cause of shock, consider that hypotension following injury is due to blood loss until proven otherwise. Rapid and accurate assessment of an injured patient's hemodynamic status is essential. The elements of clinical observation that yield important information within seconds are level of consciousness, skin perfusion, and pulse.

- Level of Consciousness—When circulating blood volume is reduced, cerebral perfusion may be critically impaired, resulting in an altered level of consciousness.

- Skin Perfusion—This sign can be helpful in evaluating injured hypovolemic patients. A patient with pink skin, especially in the face and extremities, rarely has critical hypovolemia after injury. Conversely, a patient with hypovolemia may have ashen, gray facial skin and pale extremities.

- Pulse—A rapid, thready pulse is typically a sign of hypovolemia. Assess a central pulse (e.g., femoral or carotid artery) bilaterally for quality, rate, and regularity. Absent central pulses that cannot be attributed to local factors signify the need for immediate resuscitative action.

Bleeding

Identify the source of bleeding as external or internal. External hemorrhage is identified and controlled during the primary survey. Rapid, external blood loss is managed by direct manual pressure on the wound. Tourniquets are effective in massive exsanguination from an extremity but carry a risk of ischemic injury to that extremity. Use a tourniquet only when direct pressure is not effective and the patient's life is threatened. Blind clamping can result in damage to nerves and veins.

The major areas of internal hemorrhage are the chest, abdomen, retroperitoneum, pelvis, and long bones. The source of bleeding is usually identified by physical examination and imaging (e.g., chest x-ray, pelvic x-ray, focused assessment with sonography for trauma [FAST], or diagnostic peritoneal lavage [DPL]). Immediate

management may include chest decompression, and application of a pelvic stabilizing device and/or extremity splints. Definitive management may require surgical or interventional radiologic treatment and pelvic and long-bone stabilization. Initiate surgical consultation or transfer procedures early in these patients.

Definitive bleeding control is essential, along with appropriate replacement of intravascular volume. Vascular access must be established; typically two large-bore peripheral venous catheters are placed to administer fluid, blood, and plasma. Blood samples for baseline hematologic studies are obtained, including a pregnancy test for all females of childbearing age and blood type and cross matching. To assess the presence and degree of shock, blood gases and/or lactate level are obtained. When peripheral sites cannot be accessed, intraosseous infusion, central venous access, or venous cutdown may be used depending on the patient's injuries and the clinician's skill level.

Aggressive and continued volume resuscitation is not a substitute for definitive control of hemorrhage. Shock associated with injury is most often hypovolemic in origin. In such cases, initiate IV fluid therapy with crystalloids. All IV solutions should be warmed either by storage in a warm environment (i.e., 37°C to 40°C, or 98.6°F to 104°F) or administered through fluid-warming devices. A bolus of 1 L of an isotonic solution may be required to achieve an appropriate response in an adult patient. If a patient is unresponsive to initial crystalloid therapy, he or she should receive a blood transfusion. Fluids are administered judiciously, as aggressive resuscitation before control of bleeding has been demonstrated to increase mortality and morbidity.

Severely injured trauma patients are at risk for coagulopathy, which can be further fueled by resuscitative measures. This condition potentially establishes a cycle of ongoing bleeding and further resuscitation, which can be mitigated by use of massive transfusion protocols with blood components administered at predefined low ratios (see Chapter 3: Shock). One study that evaluated trauma patients receiving fluid in the ED found that crystalloid resuscitation of more than 1.5 L independently increased the odds ratio of death. Some severely injured patients arrive with coagulopathy already established, which has led some jurisdictions to administer tranexamic acid preemptively in severely injured patients. European and American military studies demonstrate improved survival when tranexamic acid is administered within 3 hours of injury. When bolused in the field follow up infusion is given over 8 hours in the hospital (see Guidance Document for the Prehospital Use of Tranexamic Acid in Injured Patients).

DISABILITY (NEUROLOGIC EVALUATION)

A rapid neurologic evaluation establishes the patient's level of consciousness and pupillary size and reaction; identifies the presence of lateralizing signs; and determines spinal cord injury level, if present.

The GCS is a quick, simple, and objective method of determining the level of consciousness. The motor score of the GCS correlates with outcome. A decrease in a patient's level of consciousness may indicate decreased cerebral oxygenation and/or perfusion, or it may be caused by direct cerebral injury. An altered level of consciousness indicates the need to immediately reevaluate the patient's oxygenation, ventilation, and perfusion status. Hypoglycemia, alcohol, narcotics, and other drugs can also alter a patient's level of consciousness. Until proven otherwise, always presume that changes in level of consciousness are a result of central nervous system injury. Remember that drug or alcohol intoxication can accompany traumatic brain injury.

Primary brain injury results from the structural effect of the injury to the brain. Prevention of secondary brain injury by maintaining adequate oxygenation and perfusion are the main goals of initial management. Because evidence of brain injury can be absent or minimal at the time of initial evaluation, it is crucial to repeat the examination. Patients with evidence of brain injury should be treated at a facility that has the personnel and resources to anticipate and manage the needs of these patients. When resources to care for these patients are not available arrangements for transfer should begin as soon as this condition is recognized. Similarly, consult a neurosurgeon once a brain injury is recognized.

EXPOSURE AND ENVIRONMENTAL CONTROL

During the primary survey, completely undress the patient, usually by cutting off his or her garments to facilitate a thorough examination and assessment. After completing the assessment, cover the patient with warm blankets or an external warming device to prevent him or her from developing hypothermia in the trauma receiving area. Warm intravenous fluids before infusing them, and maintain a warm environment. Hypothermia can be present when the patient arrives, or it may develop quickly in the ED if the patient is uncovered and undergoes rapid administration of room-temperature fluids or refrigerated blood. Because hypothermia is a potentially lethal complication in injured patients, take aggressive measures to prevent the loss of body heat and restore body temperature

to normal. The patient's body temperature is a higher priority than the comfort of the healthcare providers, and the temperature of the resuscitation area should be increased to minimize the loss of body heat. The use of a high-flow fluid warmer to heat crystalloid fluids to 39°C (102.2°F) is recommended. When fluid warmers are not available, a microwave can be used to warm crystalloid fluids, but it should never be used to warm blood products.

PITFALL	PREVENTION
Hypothermia can be present on admission.	• Ensure a warm environment. • Use warm blankets. • Warm fluids before administering.
Hypothermia may develop after admission.	• Control hemorrhage rapidly. • Warm fluids before administering. • Ensure a warm environment. • Use warm blankets.

ADJUNCTS TO THE PRIMARY SURVEY WITH RESUSCITATION

Adjuncts used during the primary survey include continuous electrocardiography, pulse oximetry, carbon dioxide (CO_2) monitoring, and assessment of ventilatory rate, and arterial blood gas (ABG) measurement. In addition, urinary catheters can be placed to monitor urine output and assess for hematuria. Gastric catheters decompress distention and assess for evidence of blood. Other helpful tests include blood lactate, x-ray examinations (e.g., chest and pelvis), FAST, extended focused assessment with sonography for trauma (eFAST), and DPL.

Physiologic parameters such as pulse rate, blood pressure, pulse pressure, ventilatory rate, ABG levels, body temperature, and urinary output are assessable measures that reflect the adequacy of resuscitation. Values for these parameters should be obtained as soon as is practical during or after completing the primary survey, and reevaluated periodically.

ELECTROCARDIOGRAPHIC MONITORING

Electrocardiographic (ECG) monitoring of all trauma patients is important. Dysrhythmias—including unexplained tachycardia, atrial fibrillation, premature ventricular contractions, and ST segment changes—can indicate blunt cardiac injury. Pulseless electrical activity (PEA) can indicate cardiac tamponade, tension pneumothorax, and/or profound hypovolemia. When bradycardia, aberrant conduction, and premature beats are present, hypoxia and hypoperfusion should be suspected immediately. Extreme hypothermia also produces dysrhythmias.

PULSE OXIMETRY

Pulse oximetry is a valuable adjunct for monitoring oxygenation in injured patients. A small sensor is placed on the finger, toe, earlobe, or another convenient place. Most devices display pulse rate and oxygen saturation continuously. The relative absorption of light by oxyhemoglobin (HbO) and deoxyhemoglobin is assessed by measuring the amount of red and infrared light emerging from tissues traversed by light rays and processed by the device, producing an oxygen saturation level. Pulse oximetry does not measure the partial pressure of oxygen or carbon dioxide. Quantitative measurement of these parameters occurs as soon as is practical and is repeated periodically to establish trends.

In addition, hemoglobin saturation from the pulse oximeter should be compared with the value obtained from the ABG analysis. Inconsistency indicates that one of the two determinations is in error.

VENTILATORY RATE, CAPNOGRAPHY, AND ARTERIAL BLOOD GASES

Ventilatory rate, capnography, and ABG measurements are used to monitor the adequacy of the patient's respirations. Ventilation can be monitored using end tidal carbon dioxide levels. End tidal CO_2 can be detected using colorimetry, capnometry, or capnography—a noninvasive monitoring technique that provides insight into the patient's ventilation, circulation, and metabolism. Because endotracheal tubes can be dislodged whenever a patient is moved, capnography can be used to confirm intubation of the airway (vs the esophagus). However, capnography does not confirm proper position of the tube within the trachea (*see Chapter 2: Airway and Ventilatory Management*). End tidal CO_2 can also be used for tight control of ventilation to avoid hypoventilation and hyperventilation. It reflects cardiac output and is used to predict return of spontaneous circulation(ROSC) during CPR.

In addition to providing information concerning the adequacy of oxygenation and ventilation, ABG values provide acid base information. In the trauma setting, low pH and base excess levels indicate shock; therefore, trending these values can reflect improvements with resuscitation.

URINARY AND GASTRIC CATHETERS

The placement of urinary and gastric catheters occurs during or following the primary survey.

Urinary Catheters

Urinary output is a sensitive indicator of the patient's volume status and reflects renal perfusion. Monitoring of urinary output is best accomplished by insertion of an indwelling bladder catheter. In addition, a urine specimen should be submitted for routine laboratory analysis. Transurethral bladder catheterization is contraindicated for patients who may have urethral injury. Suspect a urethral injury in the presence of either blood at the urethral meatus or perineal ecchymosis.

Accordingly, do not insert a urinary catheter before examining the perineum and genitalia. When urethral injury is suspected, confirm urethral integrity by performing a retrograde urethrogram before the catheter is inserted.

At times anatomic abnormalities (e.g., urethral stricture or prostatic hypertrophy) preclude placement of indwelling bladder catheters, despite appropriate technique. Nonspecialists should avoid excessive manipulation of the urethra and the use of specialized instrumentation. Consult a urologist early.

Gastric Catheters

A gastric tube is indicated to decompress stomach distention, decrease the risk of aspiration, and check for upper gastrointestinal hemorrhage from trauma. Decompression of the stomach reduces the risk of aspiration, but does not prevent it entirely. Thick and semisolid gastric contents will not return through the tube, and placing the tube can induce vomiting. The tube is effective only if it is properly positioned and attached to appropriate suction.

Blood in the gastric aspirate may indicate oropharyngeal (i.e., swallowed) blood, traumatic insertion, or actual injury to the upper digestive tract. If a fracture of the cribriform plate is known or suspected, insert the gastric tube orally to prevent intracranial passage. In this situation, any nasopharyngeal instrumentation is potentially dangerous, and an oral route is recommended.

PITFALL	PREVENTION
Gastric catheter placement can induce vomiting.	• Be prepared to logroll the patient. • Ensure suction is immediately available.
Pulse oximeter findings can be inaccurate.	• Ensure placement of the pulse oximeter is above the BP cuff. • Confirm findings with ABG values.

X-RAY EXAMINATIONS AND DIAGNOSTIC STUDIES

Use x-ray examination judiciously, and do not delay patient resuscitation or transfer to definitive care in patients who require a higher level of care. Anteroposterior (AP) chest and AP pelvic films often provide information to guide resuscitation efforts of patients with blunt trauma. Chest x-rays can show potentially life-threatening injuries that require treatment or further investigation, and pelvic films can show fractures of the pelvis that may indicate the need for early blood transfusion. These films can be taken in the resuscitation area with a portable x-ray unit, but not when they will interrupt the resuscitation process (■ FIGURE 1-5). Do obtain essential diagnostic x-rays, even in pregnant patients.

FAST, eFAST, and DPL are useful tools for quick detection of intraabdominal blood, pneumothorax, and hemothorax. Their use depends on the clinician's skill and experience. DPL can be challenging to perform in patients who are pregnant, have had prior laparoto-

mies, or are obese. Surgical consultation should be obtained before performing this procedure in most circumstances. Furthermore, obesity and intraluminal bowel gas can compromise the images obtained by FAST. The finding of intraabdominal blood indicates the need for surgical intervention in hemodynamically abnormal patients. The presence of blood on FAST or DPL in the hemodynamically stable patient requires the involvement of a surgeon as a change in patient stability may indicate the need for intervention.

CONSIDER NEED FOR PATIENT TRANSFER

During the primary survey with resuscitation, the evaluating doctor frequently obtains sufficient information to determine the need to transfer the patient to another facility for definitive care. This transfer process may be initiated immediately by administrative personnel at the direction of the trauma team leader while additional evaluation and resuscitative measures are being performed. It is important not to delay transfer to perform an in-depth diagnostic evaluation. Only undertake testing that enhances the ability to resuscitate, stabilize, and ensure the patient's safe transfer. Once the decision to transfer a patient has been made, communication between the referring and receiving doctors is essential. ■ FIGURE 1-6 shows a patient monitored during critical care transport.

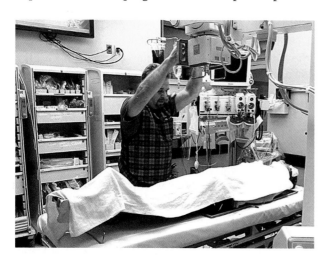

■ **FIGURE 1-5** Radiographic studies are important adjuncts to the primary survey.

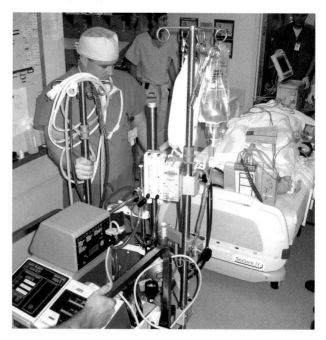

■ **FIGURE 1-6** Vigilant care is also required when transfer takes place within an institution.

SPECIAL POPULATIONS

Patient populations that warrant special consideration during initial assessment are children, pregnant women, older adults, obese patients, and athletes. Priorities for the care of these patients are the same as for all trauma patients, but these individuals may have physiologic responses that do not follow expected patterns and anatomic differences that require special equipment or consideration.

Pediatric patients have unique physiology and anatomy. The quantities of blood, fluids, and medications vary with the size of the child. In addition, the injury patterns and degree and rapidity of heat loss differ. Children typically have abundant physiologic reserve and often have few signs of hypovolemia, even after severe volume depletion. When deterioration does occur, it is precipitous and catastrophic. Specific issues related to pediatric trauma patients are addressed in Chapter 10: Pediatric Trauma.

The anatomic and physiologic changes of pregnancy can modify the patient's response to injury. Early recognition of pregnancy by palpation of the abdomen for a gravid uterus and laboratory testing (e.g., human chorionic gonadotropin [hCG]), as well as early fetal assessment, are important for maternal and fetal survival. Specific issues related to pregnant patients are addressed in Chapter 12: Trauma in Pregnancy and Intimate Partner Violence.

Although cardiovascular disease and cancer are the leading causes of death in older adults, trauma is also an increasing cause of death in this population. Resuscitation of older adults warrants special attention. The aging process diminishes the physiologic reserve of these patients, and chronic cardiac, respiratory, and metabolic diseases can impair their ability to respond to injury in the same manner as younger patients. Comorbidities such as diabetes, congestive heart failure, coronary artery disease, restrictive and obstructive pulmonary disease, coagulopathy, liver disease, and peripheral vascular disease are more common in older patients and may adversely affect outcomes following injury. In addition, the long-term use of medications can alter the usual physiologic response to injury and frequently leads to over-resuscitation or under-resuscitation in this patient population. Despite these facts, most elderly trauma patients recover when they are appropriately treated. Issues specific to older adults with trauma are described in Chapter 11: Geriatric Trauma.

Obese patients pose a particular challenge in the trauma setting, as their anatomy can make procedures such as intubation difficult and hazardous. Diagnostic tests such as FAST, DPL, and CT are also more difficult. In addition, many obese patients have cardiopulmonary disease, which limits their ability to compensate for injury and stress. Rapid fluid resuscitation can exacerbate their underlying comorbidities.

Because of their excellent conditioning, athletes may not manifest early signs of shock, such as tachycardia and tachypnea. They may also have normally low systolic and diastolic blood pressure.

SECONDARY SURVEY

The secondary survey does not begin until the primary survey (ABCDE) is completed, resuscitative efforts are under way, and improvement of the patient's vital functions has been demonstrated. When additional personnel are available, part of the secondary survey may be conducted while the other personnel attend to the primary survey. This method must in no way interfere with the performance of the primary survey, which is the highest priority.

The secondary survey is a head-to-toe evaluation of the trauma patient—that is, a complete history and physical examination, including reassessment of all vital signs. Each region of the body is completely examined. The potential for missing an injury or failing to appreciate the significance of an injury is great, especially in an unresponsive or unstable patient. (See *Secondary Survey video on MyATLS mobile app.*)

HISTORY

Every complete medical assessment includes a history of the mechanism of injury. Often, such a history cannot be obtained from a patient who has sustained trauma; therefore, prehospital personnel and family must furnish this information. The AMPLE history is a useful mnemonic for this purpose:

- Allergies
- Medications currently used
- Past illnesses/Pregnancy
- Last meal
- Events/Environment related to the injury

The patient's condition is greatly influenced by the mechanism of injury. Knowledge of the mechanism of injury can enhance understanding of the patient's physiologic state and provide clues to anticipated injuries. Some injuries can be predicted based on the

TABLE I-I MECHANISMS OF INJURY AND SUSPECTED INJURY PATTERNS

MECHANISM OF INJURY	SUSPECTED INJURY PATTERNS	MECHANISM OF INJURY	SUSPECTED INJURY PATTERNS
BLUNT INJURY			
Frontal impact, automobile collision • Bent steering wheel • Knee imprint, dashboard • Bull's-eye fracture, windscreen	• Cervical spine fracture • Anterior flail chest • Myocardial contusion • Pneumothorax • Traumatic aortic disruption • Fractured spleen or liver • Posterior fracture/dislocation of hip and/or knee • Head injury • Facial fractures	**Rear impact, automobile collision**	• Cervical spine injury • Head injury • Soft tissue injury to neck
		Ejection from vehicle	• Ejection from the vehicle precludes meaningful prediction of injury patterns, but places patient at greater risk for virtually all injury mechanisms.
Side impact, automobile collision	• Contralateral neck sprain • Head injury • Cervical spine fracture • Lateral flail chest • Pneumothorax • Traumatic aortic disruption • Diaphragmatic rupture • Fractured spleen/liver and/or kidney, depending on side of impact • Fractured pelvis or acetabulum	**Motor vehicle impact with pedestrian**	• Head injury • Traumatic aortic disruption • Abdominal visceral injuries • Fractured lower extremities/pelvis
		Fall from height	• Head injury • Axial spine injury • Abdominal visceral injuries • Fractured pelvis or acetabulum • Bilateral lower extremity fractures (including calcaneal fractures)
PENETRATING INJURY		**THERMAL INJURY**	
Stab wounds • Anterior chest	• Cardiac tamponade if within "box" • Hemothorax • Pneumothorax • Hemopneumothorax	**Thermal burns**	• Circumferential eschar on extremity or chest • Occult trauma (mechanism of burn/means of escape)
• Left thoraco-abdominal	• Left diaphragm injury/spleen injury/hemopneumothorax	**Electrical burns**	• Cardiac arrhythmias • Myonecrosis/compartment syndrome
• Abdomen	• Abdominal visceral injury possible if peritoneal penetration	**Inhalational burns**	• Carbon monoxide poisoning • Upper airway swelling • Pulmonary edema
Gunshot wounds (GSW) • Truncal	• High likelihood of injury • Trajectory from GSW/retained projectiles help predict injury		
• Extremity	• Neurovascular injury • Fractures • Compartment syndrome		

direction and amount of energy associated with the mechanism of injury. (■ TABLE 1-1) Injury patterns are also influenced by age groups and activities.

Injuries are divided into two broad categories: blunt and penetrating trauma (see *Biomechanics of Injury*). Other types of injuries for which historical information is important include thermal injuries and those caused by hazardous environments.

Blunt Trauma

Blunt trauma often results from automobile collisions, falls, and other injuries related to transportation, recreation, and occupations. It can also result from interpersonal violence. Important information to obtain about automobile collisions includes seat-belt use, steering wheel deformation, presence and activation of air-bag devices, direction of impact, damage to the automobile in terms of major deformation or intrusion into the passenger compartment, and patient position in the vehicle. Ejection from the vehicle greatly increases the possibility of major injury.

Penetrating Trauma

In penetrating trauma, factors that determine the type and extent of injury and subsequent management include the body region that was injured, organs in the path of the penetrating object, and velocity of the missile. Therefore, in gunshot victims, the velocity, caliber, presumed path of the bullet, and distance from the wea-pon to the wound can provide important clues regarding the extent of injury. (See *Biomechanics of Injury*.)

Thermal Injury

Burns are a significant type of trauma that can occur alone or in conjunction with blunt and/or penetrating trauma resulting from, for example, a burning automobile, explosion, falling debris, or a patient's attempt to escape a fire. Inhalation injury and carbon monoxide poisoning often complicate burn injuries. Information regarding the circumstances of the burn injury can increase the index of suspicion for inhalation injury or toxic exposure from combustion of plastics and chemicals.

Acute or chronic hypothermia without adequate protection against heat loss produces either local or generalized cold injuries. Significant heat loss can occur at moderate temperatures (15°C to 20°C or 59°F to 68°F) if wet clothes, decreased activity, and/or vasodilation caused by alcohol or drugs compromise the patient's ability to conserve heat. Such historical information can be obtained from prehospital personnel. Thermal injuries are addressed in more detail in *Chapter 9: Thermal Injuries* and *Appendix B: Hypothermia and Heat Injuries*.

Hazardous Environment

A history of exposure to chemicals, toxins, and radiation is important to obtain for two main reasons: These agents can produce a variety of pulmonary, cardiac, and internal organ dysfunctions in injured patients, and they can present a hazard to healthcare providers. Frequently, the clinician's only means of preparation for treating a patient with a history of exposure to a hazardous environment is to understand the general principles of management of such conditions and establish immediate contact with a Regional Poison Control Center. *Appendix D: Disaster Management and Emergency Preparedness* provides additional information about hazardous environments.

PHYSICAL EXAMINATION

During the secondary survey, physical examination follows the sequence of head, maxillofacial structures, cervical spine and neck, chest, abdomen and pelvis, perineum/rectum/vagina, musculoskeletal system, and neurological system.

Head

The secondary survey begins with evaluating the head to identify all related neurologic injuries and any other significant injuries. The entire scalp and head should be examined for lacerations, contusions, and evidence of fractures. (*See Chapter 6: Head Trauma*.)

Because edema around the eyes can later preclude an in-depth examination, the eyes should be reevaluated for:

- Visual acuity
- Pupillary size
- Hemorrhage of the conjunctiva and/or fundi
- Penetrating injury
- Contact lenses (remove before edema occurs)
- Dislocation of the lens
- Ocular entrapment

Clinicians can perform a quick visual acuity examination of both eyes by asking the patient to read printed material, such as a handheld Snellen chart or words on a piece of equipment. Ocular mobility should be evaluated to exclude entrapment of extraocular muscles due to orbital fractures. These procedures frequently identify ocular injuries that are not otherwise apparent. Appendix A: Ocular Trauma provides additional detailed information about ocular injuries.

Maxillofacial Structures

Examination of the face should include palpation of all bony structures, assessment of occlusion, intraoral examination, and assessment of soft tissues.

Maxillofacial trauma that is not associated with airway obstruction or major bleeding should be treated only after the patient is stabilized and life-threatening injuries have been managed. At the discretion of appropriate specialists, definitive management may be safely delayed without compromising care. Patients with fractures of the midface may also have a fracture of the cribriform plate. For these patients, gastric intubation should be performed via the oral route. (*See Chapter 6: Head Trauma.*)

PITFALL	PREVENTION
Facial edema in patients with massive facial injury can preclude a complete eye examination.	• Perform ocular examination before edema develops. • Minimize edema development by elevation of the head of bed (reverse Trendelenburg position when spine injuries are suspected).
Some maxillofacial fractures, such as nasal fracture, nondisplaced zygomatic fractures, and orbital rim fractures, can be difficult to identify early in the evaluation process.	• Maintain a high index of suspicion and obtain imaging when necessary. • Reevaluate patients frequently.

Cervical Spine and Neck

Patients with maxillofacial or head trauma should be presumed to have a cervical spine injury (e.g., fracture and/or ligament injury), and cervical spine motion must be restricted. The absence of neurologic deficit does not exclude injury to the cervical spine,

and such injury should be presumed until evaluation of the cervical spine is completed. Evaluation may include radiographic series and/or CT, which should be reviewed by a doctor experienced in detecting cervical spine fractures radiographically. Radiographic evaluation can be avoided in patients who meet The National Emergency X-Radiography Utilization Study (NEXUS) Low-Risk Criteria (NLC) or Canadian C-Spine Rule (CCR). (*See Chapter 7: Spine and Spinal Cord Trauma.*)

Examination of the neck includes inspection, palpation, and auscultation. Cervical spine tenderness, subcutaneous emphysema, tracheal deviation, and laryngeal fracture can be discovered on a detailed examination. The carotid arteries should be palpated and auscultated for bruits. A common sign of potential injury is a seatbelt mark. Most major cervical vascular injuries are the result of penetrating injury; however, blunt force to the neck or traction injury from a shoulder-harness restraint can result in intimal disruption, dissection, and thrombosis. Blunt carotid injury can present with coma or without neurologic finding. CT angiography, angiography, or duplex ultrasonography may be required to exclude the possibility of major cervical vascular injury when the mechanism of injury suggests this possibility.

Protection of a potentially unstable cervical spine injury is imperative for patients who are wearing any type of protective helmet, and extreme care must be taken when removing the helmet. Helmet removal is described in Chapter 2: Airway and Ventilatory Management.

Penetrating injuries to the neck can potentially injure several organ systems. Wounds that extend through the platysma should not be explored manually, probed with instruments, or treated by individuals in the ED who are not trained to manage such injuries. Surgical consultation for their evaluation and management is indicated. The finding of active arterial bleeding, an expanding hematoma, arterial bruit, or airway compromise usually requires operative evaluation. Unexplained or isolated paralysis of an upper extremity should raise the suspicion of a cervical nerve root injury and should be accurately documented.

Chest

Visual evaluation of the chest, both anterior and posterior, can identify conditions such as open pneumothorax and large flail segments. A complete evaluation of the chest wall requires palpation of the entire chest cage, including the clavicles, ribs, and sternum. Sternal pressure can be painful if the sternum is fractured or costochondral separations exist. Contusions and hematomas of the chest wall will alert the clinician to the possibility of occult injury.

Significant chest injury can manifest with pain, dyspnea, and hypoxia. Evaluation includes inspection, palpation, auscultation and percussion, of the chest and a chest x-ray. Auscultation is conducted high on the anterior chest wall for pneumothorax and at the posterior bases for hemothorax. Although auscultatory findings can be difficult to evaluate in a noisy environment, they can be extremely helpful. Distant heart sounds and decreased pulse pressure can indicate cardiac tamponade. In addition, cardiac tamponade and tension pneumothorax are suggested by the presence of distended neck veins, although associated hypovolemia can minimize or eliminate this finding. Percussion of the chest demonstrates hyperresonace. A chest x-ray or eFAST can confirm the presence of a hemothorax or simple pneumothorax. Rib fractures may be present, but they may not be visible on an x-ray. A widened mediastinum and other radiographic signs can suggest an aortic rupture. (*See Chapter 4: Thoracic Trauma.*)

Abdomen and Pelvis

Abdominal injuries must be identified and treated aggressively. Identifying the specific injury is less important than determining whether operative intervention is required. A normal initial examination of the abdomen does not exclude a significant intraabdominal injury. Close observation and frequent reevaluation of the abdomen, preferably by the same observer, are important in managing blunt abdominal trauma, because over time, the patient's abdominal findings can change. Early involvement of a surgeon is essential.

Pelvic fractures can be suspected by the identification of ecchymosis over the iliac wings, pubis, labia, or scrotum. Pain on palpation of the pelvic ring is an important finding in alert patients. In addition, assessment of peripheral pulses can identify vascular injuries.

Patients with a history of unexplained hypotension, neurologic injury, impaired sensorium secondary to alcohol and/or other drugs, and equivocal abdominal findings should be considered candidates for DPL, abdominal ultrasonography, or, if hemodynamic findings are normal, CT of the abdomen. Fractures of the pelvis or lower rib cage also can hinder accurate diagnostic examination of the abdomen, because palpating the abdomen can elicit pain from these areas. (*See Chapter 5: Abdominal and Pelvic Trauma.*)

Perineum, Rectum, and Vagina

The perineum should be examined for contusions, hematomas, lacerations, and urethral bleeding. (*See Chapter 5: Abdominal and Pelvic Trauma.*)

A rectal examination may be performed to assess for the presence of blood within the bowel lumen, integrity of the rectal wall, and quality of sphincter tone.

Vaginal examination should be performed in patients who are at risk of vaginal injury. The clinician should assess for the presence of blood in the vaginal vault and vaginal lacerations. In addition, pregnancy tests should be performed on all females of childbearing age.

Musculoskeletal System

The extremities should be inspected for contusions and deformities. Palpation of the bones and examination

PITFALL	PREVENTION
Pelvic fractures can produce large blood loss.	• Placement of a pelvic binder or sheet can limit blood loss from pelvic fractures. • Do not repeatedly or vigorously manipulate the pelvis in patients with fractures, as clots can become dislodged and increase blood loss.
Extremity fractures and injuries are particularly challenging to diagnose in patients with head or spinal cord injuries.	• Image any areas of suspicion. • Perform frequent reassessments to identify any develop-ing swelling or ecchymosis. • Recognize that subtle findings in patients with head injuries, such as limiting movement of an extremity or response to stimulus of an area, may be the only clues to the presence of an injury.
Compartment syndrome can develop.	• Maintain a high level of suspicion and recognize injuries with a high risk of development of compartment syndrome (e.g., long bone fractures, crush injuries, prolonged ischemia, and circumferential thermal injuries).

for tenderness and abnormal movement aids in the identification of occult fractures.

Significant extremity injuries can exist without fractures being evident on examination or x-rays. Ligament ruptures produce joint instability. Muscle-tendon unit injuries interfere with active motion of the affected structures. Impaired sensation and/or loss of voluntary muscle contraction strength can be caused by nerve injury or ischemia, including that due to compartment syndrome.

The musculoskeletal examination is not complete without an examination of the patient's back. Unless the patient's back is examined, significant injuries can be missed. (*See Chapter 7: Spine and Spinal Cord Trauma, and Chapter 8: Musculoskeletal Trauma.*)

Neurological System

A comprehensive neurologic examination includes motor and sensory evaluation of the extremities, as well as reevaluation of the patient's level of consciousness and pupillary size and response. The GCS score facilitates detection of early changes and trends in the patient's neurological status.

Early consultation with a neurosurgeon is required for patients with head injury. Monitor patients frequently for deterioration in level of consciousness and changes in the neurologic examination, as these findings can reflect worsening of an intracranial injury. If a patient with a head injury deteriorates neurologically, reassess oxygenation, the adequacy of ventilation and perfusion of the brain (i.e., the ABCDEs). Intracranial surgical intervention or measures for reducing intracranial pressure may be necessary. The neurosurgeon will decide whether conditions such as epidural and subdural hematomas require evacuation, and whether depressed skull fractures need operative intervention. (*See Chapter 6: Head Trauma.*)

Thoracic and lumbar spine fractures and/or neurologic injuries must be considered based on physical findings and mechanism of injury. Other injuries can mask the physical findings of spinal injuries, and they can remain undetected unless the clinician obtains the appropriate x-rays. Any evidence of loss of sensation, paralysis, or weakness suggests major injury to the spinal column or peripheral nervous system. Neurologic deficits should be documented when identified, even when transfer to another facility or doctor for specialty care is necessary. Protection of the spinal cord is required at all times until a spine injury is excluded. Early consultation with a neurosurgeon or orthopedic surgeon is necessary if a spinal injury is detected. (*See Chapter 7: Spine and Spinal Cord Trauma.*)

ADJUNCTS TO THE SECONDARY SURVEY

Specialized diagnostic tests may be performed during the secondary survey to identify specific injuries. These include additional x-ray examinations of the spine and extremities; CT scans of the head, chest, abdomen, and spine; contrast urography and angiography; transesophageal ultrasound; bronchoscopy; esophagoscopy; and other diagnostic procedures (■ FIGURE 1-7).

During the secondary survey, complete cervical and thoracolumbar spine imaging may be obtained if the patient's care is not compromised and the mechanism of injury suggests the possibility of spinal injury. Many trauma centers forego plain films and use CT instead for detecting spine injury. Restriction of spinal motion should be maintained until spine injury has been excluded. An AP chest film and additional films pertinent to the site(s) of suspected injury should be obtained. Often these procedures require transportation of the patient to other areas of the hospital, where equipment and personnel to manage life-threatening contingencies may not be immediately available. Therefore, these specialized tests should not be performed until the patient has been carefully examined and his or her hemodynamic status has been normalized. Missed injuries can be minimized by maintaining a high index of suspicion and providing continuous monitoring of the patient's status during performance of additional testing.

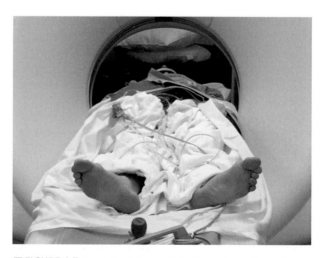

■ FIGURE 1-7 Specialized diagnostic tests may be performed during the secondary survey to identify specific injuries.

REEVALUATION

Trauma patients must be reevaluated constantly to ensure that new findings are not overlooked and to discover any deterioration in previously noted findings. As initial life-threatening injuries are managed, other equally life-threatening problems and less severe injuries may become apparent, which can significantly affect the ultimate prognosis of the patient. A high index of suspicion facilitates early diagnosis and management.

Continuous monitoring of vital signs, oxygen saturation, and urinary output is essential. For adult patients, maintenance of urinary output at 0.5 mL/kg/h is desirable. In pediatric patients who are older than 1 year, an output of 1 mL/kg/h is typically adequate. Periodic ABG analyses and end-tidal CO_2 monitoring are useful in some patients.

The relief of severe pain is an important part of treatment for trauma patients. Many injuries, especially musculoskeletal injuries, produce pain and anxiety in conscious patients. Effective analgesia usually requires the administration of opiates or anxiolytics intravenously (intramuscular injections are to be avoided). These agents are used judiciously and in small doses to achieve the desired level of patient comfort and relief of anxiety while avoiding respiratory status or mental depression, and hemodynamic changes.

DEFINITIVE CARE

Whenever the patient's treatment needs exceed the capability of the receiving institution, transfer is considered. This decision requires a detailed assessment of the patient's injuries and knowledge of the capabilities of the institution, including equipment, resources, and personnel.

Interhospital transfer guidelines will help determine which patients require the highest level of trauma care (see *ACS COT's Resources for Optimal Care of the Injured Patient, 2014*). These guidelines take into account the patient's physiologic status, obvious anatomic injury, mechanisms of injury, concurrent diseases, and other factors that can alter the patient's prognosis. ED and surgical personnel will use these guidelines to determine whether the patient requires transfer to a trauma center or the closest appropriate hospital capable of providing more specialized care. The closest appropriate local facility is chosen, based on its overall capabilities to care for the injured patient. The topic of transfer is described in more detail in Chapter 13: Transfer to Definitive Care.

RECORDS AND LEGAL CONSIDERATIONS

Specific legal considerations, including records, consent for treatment, and forensic evidence, are relevant to ATLS providers.

RECORDS

Meticulous record keeping is crucial during patient assessment and management, including documenting the times of all events. Often more than one clinician cares for an individual patient, and precise records are essential for subsequent practitioners to evaluate the patient's needs and clinical status. Accurate record keeping during resuscitation can be facilitated by assigning a member of the trauma team the primary responsibility to accurately record and collate all patient care information.

Medicolegal problems arise frequently, and precise records are helpful for all individuals concerned. Chronologic reporting with flow sheets helps the attending and consulting doctors quickly assess changes in the patient's condition. See *Sample Trauma Flow Sheet* and *Chapter 13: Transfer to Definitive Care.*

CONSENT FOR TREATMENT

Consent is sought before treatment, if possible. In life-threatening emergencies, it is often not possible to obtain such consent. In these cases, provide treatment first, and obtain formal consent later.

FORENSIC EVIDENCE

If criminal activity is suspected in conjunction with a patient's injury, the personnel caring for the patient must preserve the evidence. All items, such as clothing and bullets, are saved for law enforcement personnel. Laboratory determinations of blood alcohol concentrations and other drugs may be particularly pertinent and have substantial legal implications.

 TEAMWORK

In many centers, trauma patients are assessed by a team whose size and composition varies from institution to institution (■ FIGURE 1-8). The trauma team typically includes a team leader, airway manager, trauma nurse, and trauma technician, as well as various residents and medical students. The specialty of the trauma team leader and airway manager are dependent on local practice, but they should have a strong working knowledge of ATLS principles.

To perform effectively, each trauma team should have one member serving as the team leader. The team leader supervises, checks, and directs the assessment; ideally he or she is not directly involved in the assessment itself. The team leader is not necessarily the most senior person present, although he or she should be trained in ATLS and the basics of medical team management. The team leader supervises the preparation for the arrival of the patient to ensure a smooth transition from the prehospital to hospital environment. He or she assigns roles and tasks to the team members, ensuring that each participant has the necessary training to function in the assigned role. The following are some of the possible roles, depending on the size and composition of the team:

- Assessing the patient, including airway assessment and management
- Undressing and exposing the patient
- Applying monitoring equipment
- Obtaining intravenous access and drawing blood
- Serving as scribe or recorder of resuscitation activity

On arrival of the patient, the team leader supervises the hand-over by EMS personnel, ensuring that no team member begins working on the patient unless immediate life-threatening conditions are obvious (i.e., a "hands-off hand-over"). A useful acronym to manage this step is MIST:

- Mechanism (and time) of injury
- Injuries found and suspected
- Symptoms and Signs
- Treatment initiated

As the ABC assessment proceeds, it is vital that each member knows what the other members have found and/or are doing. This process is facilitated by verbalizing each action and each finding out loud without more than one member speaking at the same time. Requests and orders are not stated in general terms, but instead are directed to an individual, by name. That individual then repeats the request/order and later confirms its completion and, if applicable, its outcome.

The team leader checks the progress of the assessment, periodically summarizes the findings and the patient's condition, and calls for consultants as required. He or she also orders additional examinations and, when appropriate, suggests/directs transfer of the patient.

Throughout the process, all team members are expected to make remarks, ask questions, and offer suggestions, when appropriate. In that case, all other team members should pay attention and then follow the team leader's directions.

When the patient has left the ED, the team leader conducts an "After Action" session. In this session, the team addresses technical and emotional aspects of the resuscitation and identifies opportunities for improvement of team performance.

All subsequent chapters contain a special end-of-chapter feature entitled "Teamwork." This feature highlights specific aspects of the trauma team that relate to the chapter. The topic of teamwork is also explored in detail in *Appendix E: ATLS and Trauma Team Resource Management.*

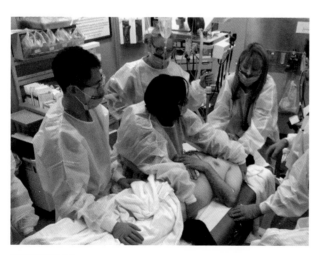

■ FIGURE 1-8 In many centers, trauma patients are assessed by a team. To perform effectively, each team has one member who serves as team leader.

CHAPTER SUMMARY

1. The correct sequence of priorities for assessment of a multiply injured patient is preparation; triage; primary survey with resuscitation; adjuncts to the primary survey and resuscitation; consider need for patient transfer; secondary survey, adjuncts to secondary survey; reevaluation; and definitive care again considering the need for transfer.

2. Principles of the primary and secondary surveys and the guidelines and techniques in the initial resuscitative and definitive care phases of treatment apply to all multiply injured patients.

3. A patient's medical history and the mechanism of injury are critical to identifying injuries.

4. Pitfalls associated with the initial assessment and management of injured patients need to be anticipated and managed to minimize their impact.

5. The primary survey should be repeated frequently, and any abnormalities will prompt a thorough reassessment.

6. Early identification of patients requiring transfer to a higher level of care improves outcomes.

BIBLIOGRAPHY

1. American College of Surgeons Committee on Trauma. *Resources for Optimal Care of the Injured Patient.* Chicago, IL: American College of Surgeons Committee on Trauma; 2006.
2. CRASH-2 collaborators. The importance of early treatment with tranexamic acid in bleeding trauma patients: an exploratory analysis of the CRASH-2 randomised controlled trial. *Lancet* 2011;377(9771):1096–1101.
3. Davidson G, Rivara F, Mack C, et al. Validation of prehospital trauma triage criteria for motor vehicle collisions. *J Trauma* 2014; 76:755–766.6.
4. Esposito TJ, Kuby A, Unfred C, et al. *General Surgeons and the Advanced Trauma Life Support Course.* Chicago, IL: American College of Surgeons, 2008.
5. Fischer, PE, Bulger EM, Perina DG et. al. Guidance document for the prehospital use of Tranexamic Acid in injured patients. *Prehospital Emergency Care*, 2016, 20: 557-59.
6. Guidelines for field triage of injured patients: recommendations of the National Expert Panel on Field Triage, 2011. *Morbidity and Mortality Weekly Report* 2012;61:1–21.
7. Holcomb JB, Dumire RD, Crommett JW, et al. Evaluation of trauma team performance using an advanced human patient simulator for resuscitation training. *J Trauma* 2002; 52:1078–1086.
8. Kappel DA, Rossi DC, Polack EP, et al. Does the rural Trauma Team development course shorten the interval from trauma patient arrival to decision to transfer? *J Trauma* 2011;70: 315–319.
9. Lee C, Bernard A, Fryman L, et al. Imaging may delay transfer of rural trauma victims: a survey of referring physicians. *J Trauma* 2009;65:1359–1363.
10. Leeper WR, Leepr TJ, Yogt K, et al. The role of trauma team leaders in missed injuries: does specialty matter? *J Trauma* 2013;75(3): 387–390.
11. Ley E, Clond M, Srour M, et al. Emergency department crystalloid resuscitation of 1.5 L or more is associated with increased mortality in elderly and nonelderly trauma patients. *J Trauma* 2011;70(2):398–400.
12. Lubbert PH, Kaasschieter EG, Hoorntje LE, et al. Video registration of trauma team performance in the emergency department: the results of a 2-year analysis in a level 1 trauma center. *J Trauma* 2009;67:1412–1420.
13. Manser T. Teamwork and patient safety in dynamic domains of healthcare: a review of the literature. *Acta Anaesthesiol Scand* 2009;53:143–151.
14. McSwain NE Jr., Salomone J, Pons P, et al., eds. *PHTLS: Prehospital Trauma Life Support.* 7th ed. St. Louis, MO: Mosby/Jems; 2011.
15. Nahum AM, Melvin J, eds. *The Biomechanics of Trauma.* Norwalk, CT: Appleton-Century-Crofts; 1985.
16. Neugebauer EAM, Waydhas C, Lendemans S, et al. Clinical practice guideline: the treatment of patients with severe and multiple traumatic injuries. *Dtsch Arztebl Int* 2012;109(6):102–108.
17. Teixeira PG, Inaba K, Hadjizacharia P, et al. Preventable or potentially preventable mortality at a mature trauma center. *J Trauma* 2007;63(6):1338.
18. Wietske H, Schoonhoven L, Schuurmans M, et al. Pressure ulcers from spinal immobilization in trauma patients: a systematic review. *J Trauma* 2014;76:1131–1141.9.

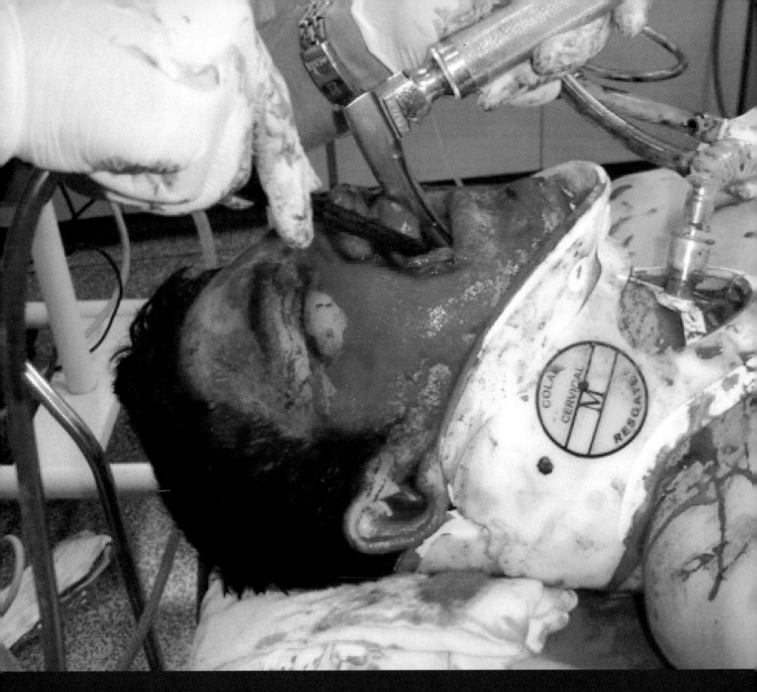

2 AIRWAY AND VENTILATORY MANAGEMENT

The earliest priorities in managing the injured patient are to ensure an intact airway and recognize a compromised airway.

CHAPTER 2 OUTLINE

OBJECTIVES

After reading this chapter and comprehending the knowledge components of the ATLS provider course, you will be able to:

1. Identify the clinical situations in which airway compromise are likely to occur.

2. Recognize the signs and symptoms of acute airway obstruction.

3. Recognize ventilatory compromise and signs of inadequate ventilation.

4. Describe the techniques for maintaining and establishing a patent airway.

5. Describe the techniques for confirming the adequacy of ventilation and oxygenation, including pulse oximetry and end-tidal CO_2 monitoring.

6. Define the term "definitive airway."

7. List the indications for drug-assisted intubation.

8. Outline the steps necessary for maintaining oxygenation before, during, and after establishing a definitive airway.

The inadequate delivery of oxygenated blood to the brain and other vital structures is the quickest killer of injured patients. A protected, unobstructed airway and adequate ventilation are critical to prevent hypoxemia. In fact, securing a compromised airway, delivering oxygen, and supporting ventilation take priority over management of all other conditions. Supplemental oxygen must be administered to all severely injured trauma patients.

Early preventable deaths from airway problems after trauma often result from:

- Failure to adequately assess the airway
- Failure to recognize the need for an airway intervention
- Inability to establish an airway
- Inability to recognize the need for an alternative airway plan in the setting of repeated failed intubation attempts
- Failure to recognize an incorrectly placed airway or to use appropriate techniques to ensure correct tube placement
- Displacement of a previously established airway
- Failure to recognize the need for ventilation

There are many strategies and equipment choices for managing the airway in trauma patients. It is of fundamental importance to take into account the setting in which management of the patient is taking place. The equipment and strategies that have been associated with the highest rate of success are those that are well known and regularly used in the specific setting. Recently developed airway equipment may perform poorly in untrained hands.

AIRWAY

The first steps toward identifying and managing potentially life-threatening airway compromise are to recognize objective signs of airway obstruction and identify any trauma or burn involving the face, neck, and larynx.

PROBLEM RECOGNITION

Airway compromise can be sudden and complete, insidious and partial, and/or progressive and recurrent. Although it is often related to pain or anxiety, or both, tachypnea can be a subtle but early sign of

airway and/or ventilatory compromise. Therefore, initial assessment and frequent reassessment of airway patency and adequacy of ventilation are critical.

During initial airway assessment, a "talking patient" provides momentary reassurance that the airway is patent and not compromised. Therefore, the most important early assessment measure is to talk to the patient and stimulate a verbal response. A positive, appropriate verbal response with a clear voice indicates that the patient's airway is patent, ventilation is intact, and brain perfusion is sufficient. Failure to respond or an inappropriate response suggests an altered level of consciousness that may be a result of airway or ventilatory compromise, or both.

Patients with an altered level of consciousness are at particular risk for airway compromise and often require a definitive airway. A *definitive airway* is defined as a tube placed in the trachea with the cuff inflated below the vocal cords, the tube connected to a form of oxygen-enriched assisted ventilation, and the airway secured in place with an appropriate stabilizing method. Unconscious patients with head injuries, patients who are less responsive due to the use of alcohol and/or other drugs, and patients with thoracic injuries can have compromised ventilatory effort. In these patients, endotracheal intubation serves to provide an airway, deliver supplemental oxygen, support ventilation, and prevent aspiration. Maintaining oxygenation and preventing hypercarbia are critical in managing trauma patients, especially those who have sustained head injuries.

In addition, patients with facial burns and those with potential inhalation injury are at risk for insidious respiratory compromise (■ FIGURE 2-1). For this reason, consider preemptive intubation in burn patients.

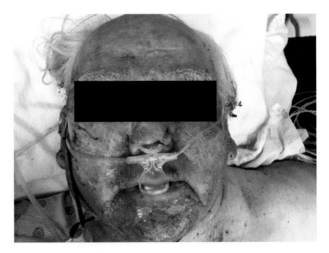

■ **FIGURE 2-1** Patients with facial burns and/or potential inhalation injuries are at risk for insidious respiratory compromise, so consider preemptive intubation.

It is important to anticipate vomiting in all injured patients and be prepared to manage the situation. The presence of gastric contents in the oropharynx presents a significant risk of aspiration with the patient's next breath. In this case, immediately suction and rotate the entire patient to the lateral position while restricting cervical spinal motion.

PITFALL	PREVENTION
Aspiration after vomiting	• Ensure functional suction equipment is available. • Be prepared to rotate the patient laterally while restricting cervical spinal motion when indicated.

Maxillofacial Trauma

Trauma to the face demands aggressive but careful airway management (■ FIGURE 2-2). This type of injury frequently results when an unrestrained passenger is thrown into the windshield or dashboard during a motor vehicle crash. Trauma to the midface can produce fractures and dislocations that compromise the nasopharynx and oropharynx. Facial fractures can be associated with hemorrhage, swelling, increased secretions, and dislodged teeth, which cause additional difficulties in maintaining a patent airway. Fractures of the mandible, especially bilateral body fractures, can cause loss of normal airway structural support, and airway obstruction can result if the patient is in a supine position. Patients who refuse to lie down may be experiencing difficulty in maintaining their airway or handling secretions. Furthermore, providing general anesthesia, sedation,

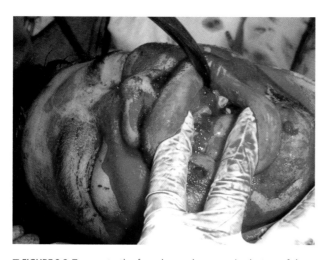

■ FIGURE 2-2 Trauma to the face demands aggressive but careful airway management.

or muscle relaxation can lead to total airway loss due to diminished or absent muscle tone. An understanding of the type of injury is mandatory to providing adequate airway management while anticipating the risks. Endotracheal intubation may be necessary to maintain airway patency.

Neck Trauma

Penetrating injury to the neck can cause vascular injury with significant hematoma, which can result in displacement and obstruction of the airway. It may be necessary to emergently establish a surgical airway if this displacement and obstruction prevent successful endotracheal intubation. Hemorrhage from adjacent vascular injury can be massive, and operative control may be required.

Both blunt and penetrating neck injury can cause disruption of the larynx or trachea, resulting in airway obstruction and/or severe bleeding into the tracheobronchial tree. This situation urgently requires a definitive airway.

Neck injuries involving disruption of the larynx and trachea or compression of the airway from hemorrhage into the soft tissues can cause partial airway obstruction. Initially, patients with this type of serious airway injury may be able to maintain airway patency and ventilation. However, if airway compromise is suspected, a definitive airway is required. To prevent exacerbating an existing airway injury, insert an endotracheal tube cautiously and preferably under direct visualization. Loss of airway patency can be precipitous, and an early surgical airway usually is indicated.

Laryngeal Trauma

Although laryngeal fractures rarely occur, they can present with acute airway obstruction. This injury is indicated by a triad of clinical signs:

1. Hoarseness
2. Subcutaneous emphysema
3. Palpable fracture

Complete obstruction of the airway or severe respiratory distress from partial obstruction warrants an attempt at intubation. Flexible endoscopic intubation may be helpful in this situation, but only if it can be performed promptly. If intubation is unsuccessful, an emergency tracheostomy is indicated, followed by operative repair. However, a tracheostomy is difficult to perform under emergency conditions, can be associated with profuse bleeding, and can be time-consuming. Surgical cricothyroidotomy, although not preferred in this situation, can be a lifesaving option.

Penetrating trauma to the larynx or trachea can be overt and require immediate management. Complete tracheal transection or occlusion of the airway with blood or soft tissue can cause acute airway compromise requiring immediate correction. These injuries are often associated with trauma to the esophagus, carotid artery, or jugular vein, as well as soft tissue destruction or swelling.

Noisy breathing indicates partial airway obstruction that can suddenly become complete, whereas the absence of breathing sounds suggests complete obstruction. When the patient's level of consciousness is depressed, detection of significant airway obstruction is more subtle, and labored breathing may be the only clue to airway obstruction or tracheobronchial injury.

If a fracture of the larynx is suspected, based on the mechanism of injury and subtle physical findings, computed tomography (CT) can help diagnose this injury.

OBJECTIVE SIGNS OF AIRWAY OBSTRUCTION

Patients with objective signs of airway difficulty or limited physiological reserve must be managed with extreme care. This applies, among others, to obese patients, pediatric patients, older adults, and patients who have sustained facial trauma.

The following steps can assist clinicians in identifying objective signs of airway obstruction:

1. Observe the patient to determine whether he or she is agitated (suggesting hypoxia) or obtunded (suggesting hypercarbia). Cyanosis indicates hypoxemia from inadequate oxygenation and is identified by inspecting the nail beds and circumoral skin. However, cyanosis is a late finding of hypoxia, and it may be difficult to detect in pigmented skin. Look for retractions and the use of accessory muscles of ventilation that, when present, offer additional evidence of airway compromise. Pulse oximetry used early in the airway assessment can detect inadequate oxygenation before cyanosis develops.

2. Listen for abnormal sounds. Noisy breathing is obstructed breathing. Snoring, gurgling, and crowing sounds (stridor) can be associated with partial occlusion of the pharynx or larynx. Hoarseness (dysphonia) implies functional laryngeal obstruction.

3. Evaluate the patient's behavior. Abusive and belligerent patients may in fact be hypoxic; do not assume intoxication.

VENTILATION

Ensuring a patent airway is an important step in providing oxygen to patients, but it is only the first step. A patent airway benefits a patient only when ventilation is also adequate. Therefore, clinicians must look for any objective signs of inadequate ventilation.

PROBLEM RECOGNITION

Ventilation can be compromised by airway obstruction, altered ventilatory mechanics, and/or central nervous system (CNS) depression. If clearing the airway does not improve a patient's breathing, other causes of the problem must be identified and managed. Direct trauma to the chest, particularly with rib fractures, causes pain with breathing and leads to rapid, shallow ventilation and hypoxemia. Elderly patients and individuals with preexisting pulmonary dysfunction are at significant risk for ventilatory failure under these circumstances. Pediatric patients may suffer significant thoracic injury without rib fractures.

Intracranial injury can cause abnormal breathing patterns and compromise adequacy of ventilation. Cervical spinal cord injury can result in respiratory muscle paresis or paralysis. The more proximal the injury, the more likely there will be respiratory impairment. Injuries below the C3 level result in maintenance of the diaphragmatic function but loss of the intercostal and abdominal muscle contribution to respiration. Typically these patients display a seesaw pattern of breathing in which the abdomen is pushed out with inspiration, while the lower ribcage is pulled in. This presentation is referred to as "abdominal breathing" or "diaphragmatic breathing." This pattern of respiration is inefficient and results in rapid, shallow breaths that lead to atelectasis and ventilation perfusion mismatching and ultimately respiratory failure.

OBJECTIVE SIGNS OF INADEQUATE VENTILATION

The following steps can assist clinicians in identifying objective signs of inadequate ventilation:

1. Look for symmetrical rise and fall of the chest and adequate chest wall excursion.

Asymmetry suggests splinting of the rib cage, pneumothorax, or a flail chest. Labored breathing may indicate an imminent threat to the patient's ventilation.

2. Listen for movement of air on both sides of the chest. Decreased or absent breath sounds over one or both hemithoraces should alert the examiner to the presence of thoracic injury. (*See Chapter 4: Thoracic Trauma.*) Beware of a rapid respiratory rate, as tachypnea can indicate respiratory distress.

3. Use a pulse oximeter to measure the patient's oxygen saturation and gauge peripheral perfusion. Note, however, that this device does not measure the adequacy of ventilation. Additionally, low oxygen saturation can be an indication of hypoperfusion or shock.

4. Use capnography in spontaneously breathing and intubated patients to assess whether ventilation is adequate. Capnography may also be used in intubated patients to confirm the tube is positioned within the airway.

AIRWAY MANAGEMENT

Clinicians must quickly and accurately assess patients' airway patency and adequacy of ventilation. Pulse oximetry and end-tidal CO_2 measurements are essential. If problems are identified or suspected, take immediate measures to improve oxygenation and reduce the risk of further ventilatory compromise. These measures include airway maintenance techniques, definitive airway measures (including surgical airway), and methods of providing supplemental ventilation. Because all of these actions potentially require neck motion, restriction of cervical spinal motion is necessary in all trauma patients at risk for spinal injury until it has been excluded by appropriate radiographic adjuncts and clinical evaluation.

High-flow oxygen is required both before and immediately after instituting airway management measures. A rigid suction device is essential and should be readily available. Patients with facial injuries can

PITFALL	PREVENTION
Failure to recognize inadequate ventilation	• Monitor the patient's respiratory rate and work of breathing. • Obtain arterial or venous blood gas measurements. • Perform continuous capnography

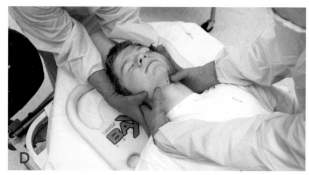
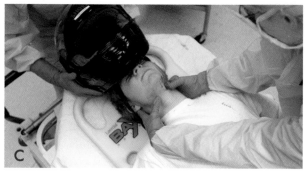

■ **FIGURE 2-3 Helmet Removal.** Removing a helmet properly is a two-person procedure. While one person restricts movement of the cervical spine, (**A**), the second person expands the helmet laterally. The second person then removes the helmet (**B**), while ensuring that the helmet clears the nose and occiput. After the helmet is removed, the first person supports the weight of the patient's head (**C**). and the second person takes over restriction of cervical spine motion (**D**).

have associated cribriform plate fractures, and the insertion of any tube through the nose can result in passage into the cranial vault.

A patient wearing a helmet who requires airway management must have his or her head and neck held in a neutral position while the helmet is remo-ved (■ FIGURE 2-3; also see *Helmet Removal video on MyATLS mobile app*). This is a two-person procedure: One person restricts cervical spinal motion from below while the second person expands the sides of the helmet and removes it from above. Then, clinicians reestablish cervical spinal motion restriction from above and secure the patient's head and neck during airway management. Using a cast cutter to remove the helmet while stabilizing the head and neck can minimize c-spine motion in patients with known c-spine injury.

PREDICTING DIFFICULT AIRWAY MANAGEMENT

Before attempting intubation, assess a patient's airway to predict the difficulty of the maneuver. Factors that indicate potential difficulties with airway maneuvers include:

- C-spine injury
- Severe arthritis of the c-spine
- Significant maxillofacial or mandibular trauma

- Limited mouth opening
- Obesity
- Anatomical variations (e.g., receding chin, overbite, and a short, muscular neck)
- Pediatric patients

When such difficulties are encountered, skilled clinicians should assist.

The mnemonic LEMON is a helpful tool for assessing the potential for a difficult intubation (■ BOX 2-1; also see *LEMON Assessment on MyATLS mobile app*). LEMON has proved useful for preanesthetic evaluation, and several of its components are particularly relevant in trauma (e.g., c-spine injury and limited mouth opening). Look for evidence of a difficult airway (e.g., small mouth or jaw, large overbite, or facial trauma). Any obvious airway obstruction presents an immediate challenge, and the restriction of cervical spinal motion is necessary in most patients following blunt trauma, increases the difficulty of establishing an airway. Rely on clinical judgment and experience in determining whether to proceed immediately with drug-assisted intubation.

AIRWAY DECISION SCHEME

■ FIGURE 2-4 provides a scheme for determining the appropriate route of airway management. This

BOX 2-1 LEMON ASSESSMENT FOR DIFFICULT INTUBATION

L = Look Externally: Look for characteristics that are known to cause difficult intubation or ventilation (e.g., small mouth or jaw, large overbite, or facial trauma).

E = Evaluate the 3-3-2 Rule: To allow for alignment of the pharyngeal, laryngeal, and oral axes and therefore simple intubation, observe the following relationships:

- The distance between the patient's incisor teeth should be at least 3 finger breadths (3)
- The distance between the hyoid bone and chin should be at least 3 finger breadths (3)
- The distance between the thyroid notch and floor of the mouth should be at least 2 finger breadths (2)

M = Mallampati: Ensure that the hypopharynx is adequately visualized. This process has been done traditionally by

assessing the Mallampati classification. In supine patients, the clinician can estimate Mallampati score by asking the patient to open the mouth fully and protrude the tongue; a laryngoscopy light is then shone into the hypopharynx from above to assess the extent of hypopharynx that is visible.

O = Obstruction: Any condition that can cause obstruction of the airway will make laryngoscopy and ventilation difficult.

N = Neck Mobility: This is a vital requirement for successful intubation. In a patient with non-traumatic injuries, clinicians can assess mobility easily by asking the patient to place his or her chin on the chest and then extend the neck so that he or she is looking toward the ceiling. Patients who require cervical spinal motion restriction obviously have no neck movement and are therefore more difficult to intubate.

Continued

BOX 2-1 LEMON ASSESSMENT FOR DIFFICULT INTUBATION *(continued)*

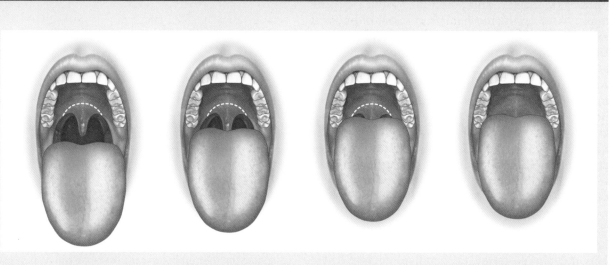

Mallampati Classifications. These classifications are used to visualize the hypopharynx. **Class I**: soft palate, uvula, fauces, pillars entirely visible; **Class II**: soft palate, uvula, fauces partially visible; **Class III**: soft palate, base of uvula visible; **Class IV**: hard palate only visible.

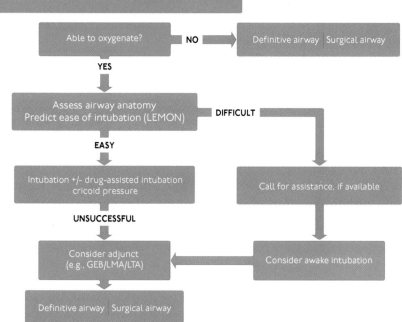

Be Prepared
- -
Equipment:
Suction, O_2, oropharyngeal and nasopharyngeal airways, bag-mask, laryngoscope, gum elastic bougie (GEB), extraglottic devices, surgical or needle cricothyroidotomy kit, endotracheal tubes (various sizes), pulse oximetry, CO_2 detection device, drugs

Restrict cervical spinal motion!

Preoxygenate

O_2 +/– bag-mask +/– oral airway +/– nasal airway

Able to oxygenate? → **NO** → Definitive airway | Surgical airway

YES

Assess airway anatomy
Predict ease of intubation (LEMON) → **DIFFICULT**

EASY

Intubation +/– drug-assisted intubation
cricoid pressure

UNSUCCESSFUL

Call for assistance, if available

Consider adjunct
(e.g., GEB/LMA/LTA) ← Consider awake intubation

Definitive airway | Surgical airway

■ **FIGURE 2-4 Airway Decision Scheme.** Clinicians use this algorithm to determine the appropriate route of airway management. *Note: The ATLS Airway Decision Scheme is a general approach to airway management in trauma. Many centers have developed other detailed airway management algorithms. Be sure to review and learn the standard used by teams in your trauma system.*

algorithm applies only to patients who are in acute respiratory distress or have apnea, are in need of an immediate airway, and potentially have a c-spine injury based on the mechanism of injury or physical examination findings. (Also see functional *Airway Decision Scheme on MyATLS mobile app.*)

The first priority of airway management is to ensure continued oxygenation while restricting cervical spinal motion. Clinicians accomplish this task initially by positioning (i.e., chin-lift or jaw-thrust maneuver) and by using preliminary airway techniques (i.e., nasopharyngeal airway). A team member then passes an endotracheal tube while a second person manually restricts cervical spinal motion. If an endotracheal tube cannot be inserted and the patient's respiratory status is in jeopardy, clinicians may attempt ventilation via a laryngeal mask airway or other extraglottic airway device as a bridge to a definitive airway. If this measure fails, they should perform a cricothyroidotomy. These methods are described in detail in the following sections. (Also see *Airway Management Tips video on MyATLS mobile app.*)

AIRWAY MAINTENANCE TECHNIQUES

In patients who have a decreased level of consciousness, the tongue can fall backward and obstruct the hypopharynx. To readily correct this form of obstruction, healthcare providers use the chin-lift or jaw-thrust maneuvers. The airway can then be maintained with a nasopharyngeal or oropharyngeal airway. Maneuvers used to establish an airway can produce or aggravate c-spine injury, so restriction of cervical spinal motion is mandatory during these procedures.

Chin-Lift Maneuver

The chin-lift maneuver is performed by placing the fingers of one hand under the mandible and then gently lifting it upward to bring the chin anterior. With the thumb of the same hand, lightly depress the lower lip to open the mouth (■ FIGURE 2-5). The thumb also may be placed behind the lower incisors while simultaneously lifting the chin gently. Do not hyperextend the neck while employing the chin-lift maneuver.

Jaw-Thrust Maneuver

To perform a jaw thrust maneuver, grasp the angles of the mandibles with a hand on each side and then

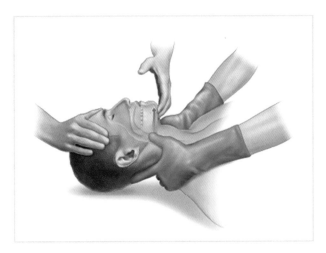

■ FIGURE 2-5 The Chin-Lift Maneuver to Establish an Airway. Providers should avoid hyperextending the neck when using this maneuver.

displace the mandible forward (■ FIGURE 2-6). When used with the facemask of a bag-mask device, this maneuver can result in a good seal and adequate ventilation. As in the chin-lift maneuver, be careful not to extend the patient's neck.

Nasopharyngeal Airway

Nasopharyngeal airways are inserted in one nostril and passed gently into the posterior oropharynx. They should be well lubricated and inserted into the nostril that appears to be unobstructed. If obstruction is encountered during introduction of the airway, stop and try the other nostril. Do not attempt this procedure in patients with suspected or potential cribriform plate fracture. (*See Appendix G: Airway Skills* and *Nasopharyngeal Airway Insertion video on MyATLS mobile app.*)

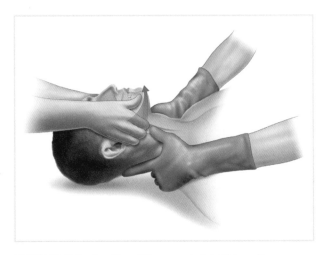

■ FIGURE 2-6 The Jaw-Thrust Maneuver to Establish an Airway. Avoid extending the patient's neck.

Oropharyngeal Airway

Oral airways are inserted into the mouth behind the tongue. The preferred technique is to insert the oral airway upside down, with its curved part directed upward, until it touches the soft palate. At that point, rotate the device 180 degrees, so the curve faces downward, and slip it into place over the tongue (■ FIGURE 2-7; also see *Oropharyngeal Airway Insertion video on MyATLS mobile app*).

Do not use this method in children, because rotating the device can damage the mouth and pharynx. Instead, use a tongue blade to depress the tongue and then insert the device with its curved side down, taking care not to push the tongue backward, which would block the airway.

Both of these techniques can induce gagging, vomiting, and aspiration; therefore, use them with caution in conscious patients. Patients who tolerate an oropharyngeal airway are highly likely to require intubation. (*See Appendix G: Airway Skills*.)

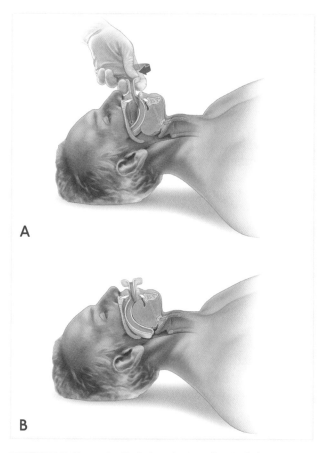

■ FIGURE 2-7 Alternative Technique for Inserting Oral Airway. **A.** In this technique, the oral airway is inserted upside down until the soft palate is encountered. **B.** The device is then rotated 180 degrees and slipped into place over the tongue. Do not use this method in children. *Note: Motion of the cervical spine must be restricted, but that maneuver is not shown in order to emphasize the airway insertion technique.*

Extraglottic and Supraglottic Devices

The following extraglottic, or supraglottic, devices have a role in managing patients who require an advanced airway adjunct, but in whom intubation has failed or is unlikely to succeed. They include laryngeal mask airway, intubating laryngeal mask airway, laryngeal tube airway, intubating laryngeal tube airway, and multilumen esophageal airway.

Laryngeal Mask Airway and Intubating LMA

The laryngeal mask airway (LMA) and intubating laryngeal mask airway (ILMA) have been shown to be effective in the treatment of patients with difficult airways, particularly if attempts at endotracheal intubation or bag-mask ventilation have failed. An example of an LMA appears in (■ FIGURE 2-8). Note that the LMA does not provide a definitive airway, and proper placement of this device is difficult without appropriate training.

The ILMA is an enhancement of the device that allows for intubation through the LMA (see *Laryngeal Mask Airway video on MyATLS mobile app*). When a patient has an LMA or an ILMA in place on arrival in the ED, clinicians must plan for a definitive airway.

Other devices that do not require cuff inflation, such as the i-gel® supraglottic airway device, can be used in place of an LMA if available (■ FIGURE 2-9).

Laryngeal Tube Airway and Intubating LTA

The laryngeal tube airway (LTA) is an extraglottic airway device with capabilities similar to those of the LMA in providing successful patient ventilation (■ FIGURE 2-10). The ILTA is an evolution of the device

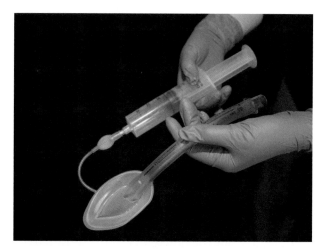

■ FIGURE 2-8 Example of a laryngeal mask airway.

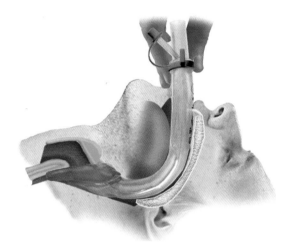

■ **FIGURE 2-9 The i-gel® supraglottic airway.** The tip of the airway should be located into the upper esophageal opening. The cuff should be located against the laryngeal framework, and the incisors should be resting on the integral bite-block.

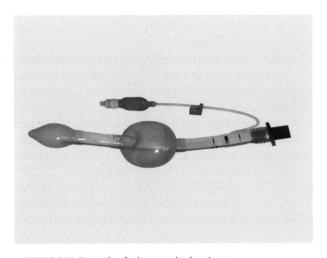

■ **FIGURE 2-10** Example of a laryngeal tube airway.

that allows intubation through the LTA. The LTA is *not* a definitive airway device, so plans to provide a definitive airway are necessary. As with the LMA, the LTA is placed without direct visualization of the glottis and does not require significant manipulation of the head and neck for placement.

Multilumen Esophageal Airway

Some prehospital personnel use multilumen esophageal airway devices to provide oxygenation and ventilation when a definitive airway is not feasible. (■ **FIGURE 2-11**). One of the ports communicates with the esophagus and the other with the airway. Personnel using this device are trained to observe which port occludes the esophagus and which provides air to the trachea. The esophageal port is then occluded with a

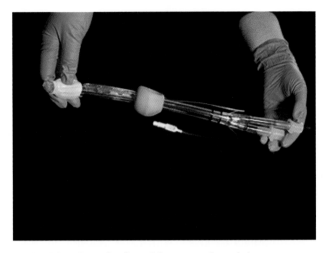

■ **FIGURE 2-11** Example of a multilumen esophageal airway.

balloon, and the other port is ventilated. Using a CO_2 detector provides evidence of airway ventilation. The multilumen esophageal airway device must be removed and/or a definitive airway provided after appropriate assessment. End tidal CO_2 should be monitored, as it provides useful information regarding ventilation and perfusion.

DEFINITIVE AIRWAYS

Recall that a definitive airway requires a tube placed in the trachea with the cuff inflated below the vocal cords, the tube connected to oxygen-enriched assisted ventilation, and the airway secured in place with an appropriate stabilizing method. There are three types of definitive airways: orotracheal tube, nasotracheal tube, and surgical airway (cricothyroidotomy and tracheostomy). The criteria for establishing a definitive airway are based on clinical findings and include:

- A —Inability to maintain a patent airway by other means, with impending or potential airway compromise (e.g., following inhalation injury, facial fractures, or retropharyngeal hematoma)

- B —Inability to maintain adequate oxygenation by facemask oxygen supplementation, or the presence of apnea

- C —Obtundation or combativeness resulting from cerebral hypoperfusion

- D —Obtundation indicating the presence of a head injury and requiring assisted ventilation (Glasgow Coma Scale [GCS] score of 8 or less), sustained seizure activity, and the need to protect the lower airway from aspiration of blood or vomitus

■ TABLE 2-1 outlines the indications for a definitive airway.

The urgency of the patient's condition and the indications for airway intervention dictate the appropriate route and method of airway management to be used. Continued assisted ventilation can be aided by supplemental sedation, analgesics, or muscle relaxants, as indicated. Assessment of the patient's clinical status and the use of a pulse oximeter are helpful in determining the need for a definitive airway, the urgency of the need, and, by inference, the effectiveness of airway placement. The potential for concomitant c-spine injury is a major concern in patients requiring an airway.

Endotracheal Intubation

Although it is important to establish the presence or absence of a c-spine fracture, do not obtain radiological studies, such as CT scan or c-spine x-rays, until after establishing a definitive airway when a patient clearly requires it. Patients with GCS scores of 8 or less require prompt intubation. If there is no immediate need for intubation, obtain radiological evaluation of the c-spine. However, a normal lateral c-spine film does not exclude the possibility of a c-spine injury.

Orotracheal intubation is the preferred route taken to protect the airway. In some specific situations and depending on the clinician's expertise, nasotracheal intubation may be an alternative for spontaneously breathing patients. Both techniques are safe and effective when performed properly, although the orotracheal route is more commonly used and results in fewer complications in the intensive care unit (ICU) (e.g., sinusitis and pressure necrosis). If the patient has apnea, orotracheal intubation is indicated.

Facial, frontal sinus, basilar skull, and cribriform plate fractures are relative contraindications to nasotracheal intubation. Evidence of nasal fracture, raccoon eyes (bilateral ecchymosis in the periorbital region), Battle's sign (postauricular ecchymosis), and possible cerebrospinal fluid (CSF) leaks (rhinorrhea or otorrhea) are all signs of these injuries. As with orotracheal intubation, take precautions to restrict cervical spinal motion.

If clinicians decide to perform orotracheal intubation, the three-person technique with restriction of cervical spinal motion is recommended (see *Advanced Airway video on MyATLS mobile app*).

Cricoid pressure during endotracheal intubation can reduce the risk of aspiration, although it may also reduce the view of the larynx. Laryngeal manipulation by backward, upward, and rightward pressure (BURP) on the thyroid cartilage can aid in visualizing the vocal cords. When the addition of cricoid pressure compromises the view of the larynx, this maneuver should be discontinued or readjusted. Additional hands are required for administering drugs and performing the BURP maneuver.

Over the years, alternative intubation devices have been developed to integrate video and optic imaging techniques. Trauma patients may benefit from their use by experienced providers in specific circumstances. Careful assessment of the situation, equipment, and personnel available is mandatory, and rescue plans must be available.

■ FIGURE 2-12 illustrates intubation through an intubating laryngeal mask. Once the mask is introduced, a dedicated endotracheal tube is inserted, allowing a blind intubation technique.

The Eschmann Tracheal Tube Introducer (ETTI), also known as the gum elastic bougie (GEB), may be used when personnel encounter a problematic airway (■ FIGURE 2-13). Clinicians use the GEB when a patient's vocal cords cannot be visualized on direct laryngoscopy. In fact, using the GEB has allowed for rapid intubation of nearly 80% of prehospital patients in whom direct laryngoscopy was difficult.

TABLE 2-1 INDICATIONS FOR DEFINITIVE AIRWAY

NEED FOR AIRWAY PROTECTION	NEED FOR VENTILATION OR OXYGENATION
Severe maxillofacial fractures • Risk for aspiration from bleeding and/or vomiting	**Inadequate respiratory efforts** • Tachypnea • Hypoxia • Hypercarbia • Cyanosis • Combativeness
Neck injury • Neck hematoma • Laryngeal or tracheal injury • Inhalation injury from burns and facial burns • Stridor • Voice change	• Progressive change • Accessory muscle use • Respiratory muscle paralysis • Abdominal breathing
Head injury • Unconscious • Combative	• Acute neurological deterioration or herniation • Apnea from loss of consciousness or neuromuscular paralysis

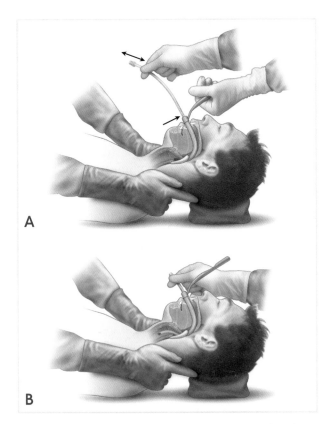

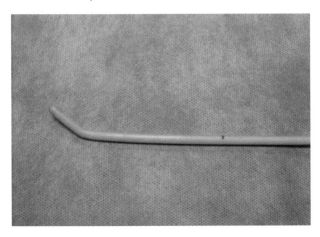

■ **FIGURE 2-12 Intubation through an Intubating Laryngeal Mask.**
A. Once the laryngeal mask is introduced, **B.** a dedicated
endotracheal tube is inserted into it, allowing therefore a "blind"
intubation technique.

■ **FIGURE 2-13 Eschmann Tracheal Tube Introducer (ETTI).** This
device is also known as the gum elastic bougie.

With the laryngoscope in place, pass the GEB blindly
beyond the epiglottis, with the angled tip positioned
anteriorly (see *Gum Elastic Bougie video on MyATLS
mobile app.*) Confirm tracheal position by feeling clicks
as the distal tip rubs along the cartilaginous tracheal
rings (present in 65%–90% of GEB placements); a GEB
inserted into the esophagus will pass its full length
without resistance (■ **FIGURE 2-14**).

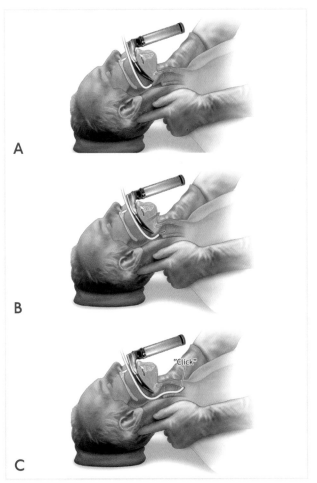

■ **FIGURE 2-14 Insertion of the GEB designed to aid in difficult
intubations. A.** The GEB is lubricated and placed in back of the
epiglottis with the tip angled toward the front of the neck. **B.** It
slides under the epiglottis and is maneuvered in a semiblind or blind
fashion into the trachea. **C.** Placement of the GEB into the trachea
may be detected by the palpable "clicks" as the tip passes over the
cartilaginous rings of the trachea.

After confirming the position of the GEB, pass a
lubricated endotracheal tube over the bougie beyond
the vocal cords. If the endotracheal tube is held up at
the arytenoids or aryepiglottic folds, withdraw the
tube slightly and turn it counter-clockwise 90 degrees
to facilitate advancement beyond the obstruction.
Then, remove the GEB and confirm tube position with
auscultation of breath sounds and capnography.

Following direct laryngoscopy and insertion of an
orotracheal tube, inflate the cuff and institute assisted
ventilation. Proper placement of the tube is suggested—
but not confirmed—by hearing equal breath sounds
bilaterally and detecting no borborygmi (i.e., rumbling
or gurgling noises) in the epigastrium. The presence
of borborygmi in the epigastrium with inspiration
suggests esophageal intubation and warrants removal
of the tube.

A carbon dioxide detector (ideally a capnograph or a colorimetric CO_2 monitoring device) is indicated to help confirm proper intubation of the airway. The presence of CO_2 in exhaled air indicates that the airway has been successfully intubated, but does not ensure the correct position of the endotracheal tube within the trachea (e.g., mainstem intubation is still possible). If CO_2 is not detected, esophageal intubation has occurred. Proper position of the tube within the trachea is best confirmed by chest x-ray, once the possibility of esophageal intubation is excluded. Colorimetric CO_2 indicators are not useful for physiologic monitoring or assessing the adequacy of ventilation, which requires arterial blood gas analysis or continous end-tidal carbon dioxide analysis.

After determining the proper position of the tube, secure it in place. If the patient is moved, reassess tube placement with auscultation of both lateral lung fields for equality of breath sounds and by reassessment for exhaled CO_2.

If orotracheal intubation is unsuccessful on the first attempt or if the cords are difficult to visualize, use a GEB and initiate further preparations for difficult airway management.

PITFALL	PREVENTION
Inability to intubate	• Use rescue airway devices. • Perform needle cricothryotomy followed by surgical airway. • Establish surgical airway.
Equipment failure	• Perform frequent equipment checks. • Ensure backup equipment is available.

Drug-Assisted Intubation

In some cases, intubation is possible and safe without the use of drugs. The use of anesthetic, sedative, and neuromuscular blocking drugs for endotracheal intubation in trauma patients is potentially dangerous. Yet occasionally, the need for an airway justifies the risk of administering these drugs; therefore, it is important to understand their pharmacology, be skilled in the techniques of endotracheal intubation, and be capable of securing a surgical airway if neces-sary. Drug-assisted intubation is indicated in patients who need airway control, but have intact gag reflexes, especially in patients who have sustained head injuries.

The technique for drug-assisted intubation is as follows:

1. Have a plan in the event of failure that includes the possibility of performing a surgical airway. Know where your rescue airway equipment is located.
2. Ensure that suction and the ability to deliver positive pressure ventilation are ready.
3. Preoxygenate the patient with 100% oxygen.
4. Apply pressure over the cricoid cartilage.
5. Administer an induction drug (e.g., etomidate, 0.3 mg/kg) or sedative, according to local protocol.
6. Administer 1 to 2 mg/kg succinylcholine intravenously (usual dose is 100 mg).

After the patient relaxes:

7. Intubate the patient orotracheally.
8. Inflate the cuff and confirm tube placement by auscultating the patient's chest and determining the presence of CO_2 in exhaled air.
9. Release cricoid pressure.
10. Ventilate the patient.

The drug etomidate (Amidate) does not negatively affect blood pressure or intracranial pressure, but it can depress adrenal function and is not universally available. This drug does provide adequate sedation, which is advantageous in these patients. Use etomidate and other sedatives with great care to avoid loss of the airway as the patient becomes sedated. Then administer succinylcholine, which is a short-acting drug. It has a rapid onset of paralysis (<1 minute) and duration of 5 minutes or less.

The most dangerous complication of using sedation and neuromuscular blocking agents is the inability to establish an airway. If endotracheal intubation is unsuccessful, the patient must be ventilated with a bag-mask device until the paralysis resolves; long-acting drugs are not routinely used for RSI for this reason. Because of the potential for severe hyperkalemia, succinylcholine must be used cautiously in patients with severe crush injuries, major burns, and electrical injuries. Extreme caution is warranted in patients with preexisting chronic renal failure, chronic paralysis, and chronic neuromuscular disease.

Induction agents, such as thiopental and sedatives, are potentially dangerous in trauma patients with hypovolemia. Practice patterns, drug preferences, and specific procedures for airway management vary among institutions. The critical principle is that the individual using these techniques needs to be skilled in their use, knowledgeable of the inherent pitfalls associated with RSI, and capable of managing the potential complications.

Surgical Airway

The inability to intubate the trachea is a clear indication for an alternate airway plan, including laryngeal mask airway, laryngeal tube airway, or a surgical airway. A surgical airway (i.e., cricothyroidotomy or tracheostomy) is indicated in the presence of edema of the glottis, fracture of the larynx, severe oropharyngeal hemorrhage that obstructs the airway, or inability to place an endotracheal tube through the vocal cords. A surgical cricothyroidotomy is preferable to a tracheostomy for most patients who require an emergency surgical airway because it is easier to perform, associated with less bleeding, and requires less time to perform than an emergency tracheostomy.

Needle Cricothyroidotomy

Needle cricothyroidotomy involves insertion of a needle through the cricothyroid membrane into the trachea in an emergency situation to provide oxygen on a short-term basis until a definitive airway can be placed. Needle cricothyroidotomy can provide temporary, supplemental oxygenation so that intubation can be accomplished urgently rather than emergently.

The percutaneous transtracheal oxygenation (PTO) technique is performed by placing a large-caliber plastic cannula—12- to 14-gauge for adults, and 16- to 18-gauge in children—through the cricothyroid membrane into the trachea below the level of the obstruction (■ FIGURE 2-15).

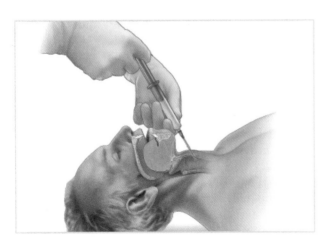

■ FIGURE 2-15 Needle Cricothyroidotomy. This procedure is performed by placing a catheter over a needle or over a wire using the Seldinger technique. *Note: Motion of the cervical spine must be restricted, but that maneuver is not shown in order to emphasize the airway insertion technique.*

The cannula is then connected to oxygen at 15 L/min (50 to 60 psi) with a Y-connector or a side hole cut in the tubing between the oxygen source and the plastic cannula. Intermittent insufflation, 1 second on and 4 seconds off, can then be achieved by placing the thumb over the open end of the Y-connector or the side hole. (See *Cricothyroidotomy video on MyATLS mobile app.*)

The patient may be adequately oxygenated for 30 to 45 minutes using this technique. During the 4 seconds that the oxygen is not being delivered under pressure, some exhalation occurs.

Because of the inadequate exhalation, CO_2 slowly accumulates and thus limits the use of this technique, especially in patients with head injuries.

Use percutaneous transtracheal oxygenation (PTO) with caution when complete foreign-body obstruction of the glottic area is suspected. Significant barotrauma can occur, including pulmonary rupture with tension pneumothorax following PTO. Therefore, careful attention must be paid to effective airflow in and out.

Surgical Cricothyroidotomy

Surgical cricothyroidotomy is performed by making a skin incision that extends through the cricothyroid membrane (■ FIGURE 2-16). Insert a curved hemostat or scalpel handle to dilate the opening, and then insert a small endotracheal or tracheostomy tube (preferably 5 to 7 ID) or tracheostomy tube (preferably 5 to 7 mm OD).

Care must be taken, especially with children, to avoid damage to the cricoid cartilage, which is the only circumferential support for the upper trachea. For this reason, surgical cricothyroidotomy is not recommended for children under 12 years of age. (See *Chapter 10: Pediatric Trauma.*) When an endotracheal tube is used, it must be adequately secured to prevent malpositioning, such as slipping into a bronchus or completely dislodging.

In recent years, percutaneous tracheostomy has been reported as an alternative to open tracheostomy. This procedure is not recommended in the acute trauma situation, because the patient's neck must be hyperextended to properly position the head in order to perform the procedure safely.

MANAGEMENT OF OXYGENATION

Oxygenated inspired air is best provided via a tight-fitting oxygen reservoir face mask with a flow rate of at least 10 L/min. Other methods (e.g., nasal catheter, nasal cannula, and nonrebreather mask) can improve inspired oxygen concentration.

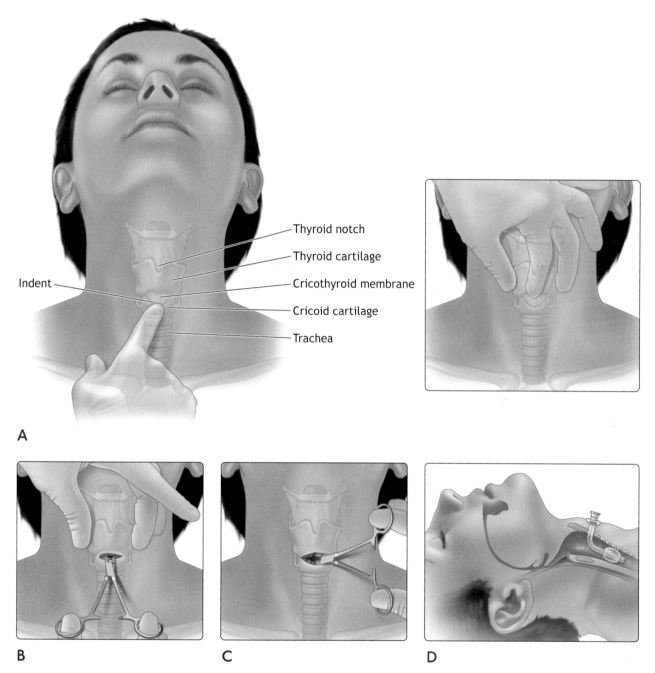

Thyroid notch

Thyroid cartilage

Cricothyroid membrane

Indent

Cricoid cartilage

Trachea

A

B

C

D

■ FIGURE 2-16 Surgical Cricothyroidotomy. **A.** Palpate the thyroid notch, cricothyroid interval, and sternal notch for orientation. **B.** Make a skin incision over the cricothyroid membrane and carefully incise the membrane transversely. **C.** Insert a hemostat or scalpel handle into the incision and rotate it 90 degrees to open the airway. **D.** Insert a properly sized, cuffed endotracheal tube or tracheostomy tube into the cricothyroid membrane incision, directing the tube distally into the trachea.

Because changes in oxygenation occur rapidly and are impossible to detect clinically, pulse oximetry must be used at all times. It is invaluable when difficulties are anticipated in intubation or ventilation, including during transport of critically injured patients. Pulse oximetry is a noninvasive method of continuously measuring the oxygen saturation (O_2 sat) of arterial blood. It does not measure the partial pressure of oxygen (PaO_2) and, depending on the position of the oxyhemoglobin dissociation curve, the PaO_2 can vary widely (■ TABLE 2-2). However, a measured saturation of 95% or greater by pulse oximetry is strong corroborating evidence of adequate peripheral arterial oxygenation (PaO_2 >70 mm Hg, or 9.3 kPa).

Pulse oximetry requires intact peripheral perfusion and cannot distinguish oxyhemoglobin from carboxyhemoglobin or methemoglobin, which limits its usefulness in patients with severe vasoconstriction and those with carbon monoxide poisoning. Profound anemia (hemoglobin <5 g/dL) and hypothermia (<30°C, or <86°F) decrease the reliability of the technique. However, in most trauma patients, pulse oximetry is useful because the continuous monitoring of oxygen saturation provides an immediate assessment of therapeutic interventions.

TABLE 2-2 APPROXIMATE PAO₂ VERSUS O₂ HEMOGLOBIN SATURATION LEVELS

PAO₂ LEVELS	O₂ HEMOGLOBIN SATURATION LEVELS
90 mm Hg	100%
60 mm Hg	90%
30 mm Hg	60%
27 mm Hg	50%

MANAGEMENT OF VENTILATION

Ventilatory assistance may be needed prior to intubation in many trauma patients. Effective ventilation can be achieved by bag-mask techniques. However, one-person ventilation techniques using a bag mask may be less effective than two-person techniques, in which both sets of hands can be used to ensure a good seal. For this reason, bag-mask ventilation should be performed by two people whenever possible. (See *Bag-mask Ventilation video on MyATLS mobile app.*)

Intubation of patients with hypoventilation and/or apnea may not be successful initially and may require multiple attempts. The patient must be ventilated periodically during prolonged efforts to intubate. Every effort should be made to optimize intubation conditions to ensure success on the first attempt.

Upon intubation of the trachea, use positive-pressure breathing techniques to provide assisted ventilation. A volume- or pressure-regulated respirator can be used, depending on equipment availability. Clinicians should be alert to the complications of changes in intrathoracic pressure, which can convert a simple pneumothorax to a tension pneumothorax, or even create a pneumothorax secondary to barotrauma.

Maintain oxygenation and ventilation before, during, and immediately upon completing insertion of the definitive airway. Avoid prolonged periods of inadequate or absent ventilation and oxygenation.

PITFALL	PREVENTION
Poor mask seal in an edentulous patient.	• Pack the space between the cheeks and gum with gauze to improve mask fit.
Loss of airway in low-resourced (rural) center	• Consider the need for transfer early in patients who require definitive airway management. • Frequently reassess patients who are at risk for deterioration.
Loss of airway during transfer	• Frequently reassess the airway before transfer and during transfer. • Discuss the need for airway control with the accepting physician. • Consider the need for early intubation prior to transfer.

TEAMWORK

• Most trauma victims require the individual attention of an airway manager. During the team briefing, before the patient arrives, the team leader should establish the degree of practical expertise of the airway manager. For example, some doctors in training, such as junior residents, may not be comfortable managing a difficult airway such as in a patient who has sustained inhalation burns. The team leader should identify who may be needed to assist the team and how they can be quickly contacted.

- If prehospital information suggests that the patient will require a definitive airway, it may be wise to draw up appropriate drugs for sedation and drug-assisted intubation before the patient arrives. Equipment for managing the difficult airway should also be located within easy access of the resuscitation room.

- The timing of definitive airway management may require discussion with consultants to the trauma team. For example, in patients with head injuries who are not in obvious distress, discussion between the neurosurgical member of the team and the team leader may be helpful.

- Patients may require transfer to the CT scan, operating room, or ICU. Therefore, the team leader should clarify who will be responsible for managing a patient's airway and ventilation after intubation.

CHAPTER SUMMARY

1. Clinical situations in which airway compromise is likely to occur include head trauma, maxillofacial trauma, neck trauma, laryngeal trauma, and airway obstruction due to other reasons.

2. Actual or impending airway obstruction should be suspected in all injured patients. Objective signs of airway obstruction include agitation, cyanosis, abnormal breath sounds, hoarse voice, stridor tracheal displacement, and reduced responsiveness.

3. Recognition of ventilatory compromise and ensuring effective ventilation are of primary importance.

4. Techniques for establishing and maintaining a patent airway include the chin-lift and jaw-thrust maneuvers, oropharyngeal and nasopharyngeal airways, extraglottic and supraglottic devices,

and endotracheal intubation. A surgical airway is indicated whenever an airway is needed and intubation is unsuccessful.

5. With all airway maneuvers, cervical spinal motion must be restricted when injury is present or suspected.

6. The assessment of airway patency and adequacy of ventilation must be performed quickly and accurately. Pulse oximetry and end-tidal CO_2 measurement are essential.

7. A definitive airway requires a tube placed in the trachea with the cuff inflated below the vocal cords, the tube connected to some form of oxygen-enriched assisted ventilation, and the airway secured in place with an appropriate stabilization method. Examples of definitive airways include endotracheal intubation and surgical airways (e.g., surgical cricothyroidotomy). A definitive airway should be established if there is any doubt about the integrity of the patient's airway. A definitive airway should be placed early after the patient has been ventilated with oxygen-enriched air, to prevent prolonged periods of apnea.

8. Drug-assisted intubation may be necessary in patients with an active gag reflex.

9. To maintain a patient's oxygenation, oxygenated inspired air is best provided via a tight-fitting oxygen reservoir face mask with a flow rate of greater than 10 L/min. Other methods (e.g., nasal catheter, nasal cannula, and non-rebreathing mask) can improve inspired oxygen concentration.

BIBLIOGRAPHY

1. Alexander R, Hodgson P, Lomax D, et al. A comparison of the laryngeal mask airway and Guedel airway, bag and facemask for manual ventilation following formal training. *Anaesthesia* 1993;48(3):231–234.

2. Aoi Y, Inagawa G, Hashimoto K, et al. Airway scope laryngoscopy under manual inline stabilization and cervical collar immobilization: a crossover in vivo cinefluoroscopic study. *J Trauma* 2011;71(1):32–36.

3. Aprahamian C, Thompson BM, Finger WA, et al. Experimental cervical spine injury model: evaluation of airway management and splint-

ing techniques. *Ann Emerg Med* 1984;13(8):584–587.

4. Arslan ZI, Yildiz T, Baykara ZN, et al. Tracheal intubation in patients with rigid collar immobilisation of the cervical spine: a comparison of Airtraq and LMA C Trach devices. *Anaesthesia* 2009;64(12):1332–1336. Epub 2009; Oct 22.

5. Asai T, Shingu K. The laryngeal tube. *Br J Anaesth* 2005;95(6):729–736.

6. Bathory I, Frascarolo P, Kern C, et al. Evaluation of the GlideScope for tracheal intubation in patients with cervical spine immobilisation by a semi-rigid collar. *Anaesthesia* 2009;64(12):1337–1341.

7. Bergen JM, Smith DC. A review of etomidate for rapid sequence intubation in the emergency department. *J Emerg Med* 1997;15(2):221–230.

8. Brantigan CO, Grow JB Sr. Cricothyroidotomy: elective use in respiratory problems requiring tracheotomy. *J Thorac Cardiovasc Surg* 1976;71: 72–81.

9. Combes X, Dumerat M, Dhonneur G. Emergency gum elastic bougie-assisted tracheal intubation in four patients with upper airway distortion. *Can J Anaesth* 2004;51(10):1022–1024.

10. Crosby ET, Cooper RM, Douglas MJ, et al. The unanticipated difficult airway with recommendations for management. *Can J Anaesth* 1998;45(8):757–776.

11. Danzl DF, Thomas DM. Nasotracheal intubation in the emergency department. *Crit Care Med* 1980;8(11):667–682.

12. Davies PR, Tighe SQ, Greenslade GL, et al. Laryngeal mask airway and tracheal tube insertion by unskilled personnel. *Lancet* 1990;336 (8721):977–979.

13. Dogra S, Falconer R, Latto IP. Successful difficult intubation. Tracheal tube placement over a gum-elastic bougie. *Anaesthesia* 1990; 45(9):774–776.

14. Dorges V, Ocker H, Wenzel V, et al. Emergency airway management by non-anaesthesia house officers—a comparison of three strategies. *Emerg Med J* 2001;18(2):90–94.

15. El-Orbany MI, Salem MR, Joseph NJ. The Eschmann tracheal tube introducer is not gum, elastic, or a bougie. *Anesthesiology* 2004;101(5);1240; author reply 1242–1244.

16. Frame SB, Simon JM, Kerstein MD, et al. Percutaneous transtracheal catheter ventilation (PTCV) in complete airway obstructions canine model. *J Trauma* 1989;29(6):774–781.

17. Fremstad JD, Martin SH. Lethal complication from insertion of nasogastric tube after severe basilar skull fracture. *J Trauma* 1978; 18:820–822.

18. Gataure PS, Vaughan RS, Latto IP. Simulated difficult intubation: comparison of the gum elastic bougie and the stylet. *Anaesthesia* 1996;1:935–938.

19. Greenberg RS, Brimacombe J, Berry A, et al. A randomized controlled trial comparing the cuffed oropharyngeal airway and the laryngeal mask airway in spontaneously breathing anesthetized adults. *Anesthesiology* 1998;88(4):970–977.

20. Grein AJ, Weiner GM. Laryngeal mask airway versus bag-mask ventilation or endotracheal intubation for neonatal resuscitation. *Cochrane Database Syst Rev* 2005;(2):CD003314.

21. Grmec S, Mally S. Prehospital determination of tracheal tube placement in severe head injury. *Emerg Med J* 2004;21(4):518–520.

22. Guildner CV. Resuscitation—opening the airway: a comparative study of techniques for opening an airway obstructed by the tongue. *J Am Coll Emerg Physicians* 1976;5:588–590.

23. Hagberg C, Bogomolny Y, Gilmore C, et al. An evaluation of the insertion and function of a new supraglottic airway device, the King LT, during spontaneous ventilation. *Anesth Analg* 2006;102(2):621–625.

24. Iserson KV. Blind nasotracheal intubation. *Ann Emerg Med* 1981;10:468.

25. Jabre P, Combes X, Leroux B, et al. Use of the gum elastic bougie for prehospital difficult intubation. *Am J Emerg Med* 2005;23(4):552–555.

26. Jorden RC, Moore EE, Marx JA, et al. A comparison of PTV and endotracheal ventilation in an acute trauma model. *J Trauma* 1985; 25(10):978–983.

27. Kidd JF, Dyson A, Latto IP. Successful difficult intubation. Use of the gum elastic bougie. *Anaesthesia* 1988;43:437–438.

28. Kress TD, Balasubramaniam S. Cricothyroidotomy. *Ann Emerg Med* 1982;11:197–201.

29. Latto IP, Stacey M, Mecklenburgh J, et al. Survey of the use of the gum elastic bougie in clinical practice. *Anaesthesia* 2002;57(4):379–384.

30. Levinson MM, Scuderi PE, Gibson RL, et al. Emergency percutaneous and transtracheal ventilation. *J Am Coll Emerg Physicians* 1979; 8(10):396–400.

31. Levitan R, Ochroch EA. Airway management and direct laryngoscopy. A review and update. *Crit Care Clin* 2000;16(3):373–388, v.

32. Liu EH, Goy RW, Tan BH, et al. Tracheal intubation with videolaryngoscopes in patients with cervical spine immobilization: a

random-ized trial of the Airway Scope and the Glide Scope. *Br J Anaesth* 2009 Sep;103(3):446–451.

33. Macintosh RR. An aid to oral intubation. *BMJ* 1949;1:28.

34. Majernick TG, Bieniek R, Houston JB, et al. Cervical spine movement during orotracheal intubation. *Ann Emerg Med* 1986;15(4):417–420.

35. Morton T, Brady S, Clancy M. Difficult airway equipment in English emergency departments. *Anaesthesia* 2000;55(5):485–488.

36. Nocera A. A flexible solution for emergency intubation difficulties. *Ann Emerg Med* 1996; 27(5):665–667.

37. Noguchi T, Koga K, Shiga Y, et al. The gum elastic bougie eases tracheal intubation while applying cricoid pressure compared to a stylet. *Can J Anaesth* 2003;50(7):712–717.

38. Nolan JP, Wilson ME. An evaluation of the gum elastic bougie. Intubation times and incidence of sore throat. *Anaesthesia* 1992; 47(10):878–881.

39. Nolan JP, Wilson ME. Orotracheal intubation in patients with potential cervical spine injuries. An indication for the gum elastic bougie. *Anaesthesia* 1993;48(7):630–633.

40. Oczenski W, Krenn H, Dahaba AA, et al. Complications following the use of the Combitube, tracheal tube and laryngeal mask airway. *Anaesthesia* 1999;54(12):1161–1165.

41. Pennant JH, Pace NA, Gajraj NM. Role of the laryngeal mask airway in the immobile cervical spine. *J Clin Anesth* 1993;5(3):226–230.

42. Phelan MP. Use of the endotracheal bougie introducer for difficult intubations. *Am J Emerg Med* 2004;22(6):479–482.

43. Reed MJ, Dunn MJ, McKeown DW. Can an airway assessment score predict difficulty at intubation in the emergency department? *Emerg Med J* 2005;22(2):99–102.

44. Reed MJ, Rennie LM, Dunn MJ, et al. Is the "LEMON" method an easily applied emergency airway assessment tool? *Eur J Emerg Med* 2004;11(3);154–157.

45. Russi C, Miller L, Hartley MJ. A comparison of the King- LT to endotracheal intubation and Combitube in a simulated difficult airway. *Prehosp Emerg Care* 2008;12(1):35–41.

46. Seshul MB Sr, Sinn DP, Gerlock AJ Jr. The Andy Gump fracture of the mandible: a cause of respiratory obstruction or distress. *J Trauma* 1978;18:611–612.

47. Silvestri S, Ralls GA, Krauss B, et al. The effectiveness of out-of-hospital use of continuous end-tidal carbon dioxide monitoring on the rate of unrecognized misplaced intubation within a regional emergency medical services system. *Ann Emerg Med* 2005;45(5):497–503.

48. Smith CE, Dejoy SJ. New equipment and techniques for airway management in trauma. *Curr Opin Anaesthesiol* 2001;14(2):197–209.

49. Walls RM, Murphy MF, Luten RC, eds. *The Manual of Emergency Airway Management*. 3rd ed. Philadelphia, PA: Lippincott Williams & Wilkins, 2008.

50. Walter J, Doris PE, Shaffer MA. Clinical presentation of patients with acute cervical spine injury. *Ann Emerg Med* 1984;13(7):512–515.

51. Yeston NS. Noninvasive measurement of blood gases. *Infect Surg* 1990;90:18–24.

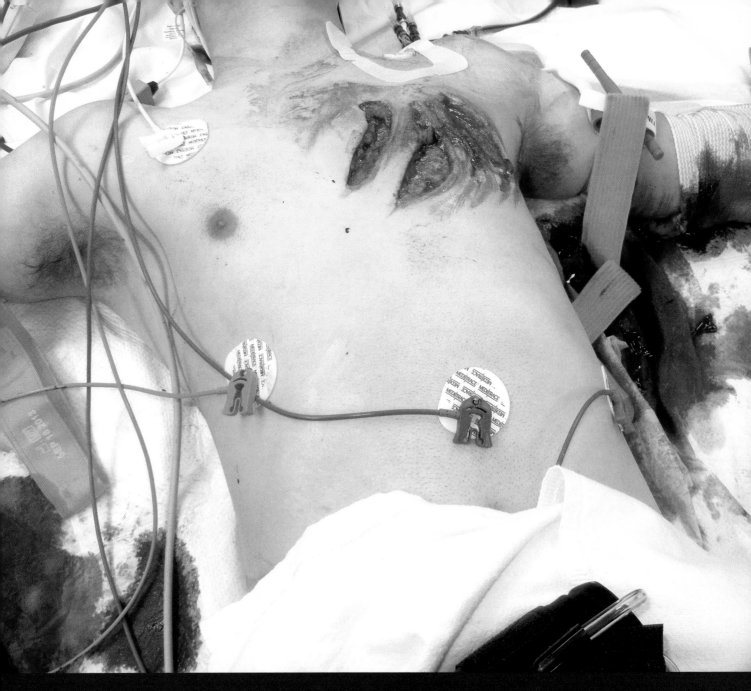

3 SHOCK

The first step in the initial management of shock is to recognize its presence.

CHAPTER 3 OUTLINE

OBJECTIVES

After reading this chapter and comprehending the knowledge components of the ATLS provider course, you will be able to:

1. Define shock.

2. Describe the likely causes of shock in trauma patients.

3. Describe the clinical signs of shock and relate them to the degree of blood loss.

4. Explain the importance of rapidly identifying and controlling the source of hemorrhage in trauma patients.

5. Describe the proper initial management of hemorrhagic shock in trauma patients.

6. Describe the rationale for ongoing evaluation of fluid resuscitation, organ perfusion, and tissue oxygenation in trauma patients.

7. Explain the role of blood replacement in managing shock.

8. Describe special considerations in diagnosing and treating shock related to advanced age, athleticism, pregnancy, medications, hypothermia, and presence of pacemakers and implantable cardioverter-defibrillators.

The first step in managing shock in trauma patients is to recognize its presence. Once shock is identified, initiate treatment based on the probable cause. The definition of shock—an abnormality of the circulatory system that results in inadequate organ perfusion and tissue oxygenation—also guides the trauma team in the diagnosis and treatment. Diagnosing shock in a trauma patient relies on a synthesis of clinical findings and laboratory tests. No single vital sign and no laboratory test, on its own, can definitively diagnose shock. Trauma team members must quickly recognize inadequate tissue perfusion by recognizing the clinical findings that commonly occur in trauma patients.

The second step in managing shock is to identify the probable cause of shock and adjust treatment accordingly. In trauma patients, this process is related to the mechanism of injury. Most injured patients in shock have hypovolemia, but they may suffer from cardiogenic, obstructive, neurogenic, and/or, rarely, septic shock. For example, tension pneumothorax can reduce venous return and produce obstructive shock. Cardiac tamponade also produces obstructive shock, as blood in the pericardial sac inhibits cardiac contractility and cardiac output. Trauma team members should consider these diagnoses in patients with injuries above the diaphragm. Neurogenic shock results from extensive injury to the cervical or upper thoracic spinal cord caused by a loss of sympathetic tone and subsequent vasodilation. Shock does not result from an isolated brain injury unless the brainstem is involved, in which case the prognosis is poor. Patients with spinal cord injury may initially present in shock resulting from both vasodilation

and hypovolemia, especially if there are multiple other injuries. Septic shock is unusual, but must be considered in patients whose arrival at the emergency facility was delayed for many hours. In the elderly, the underlying reason or precipitating cause of traumatic injury may be an unrecognized infection, commonly a urinary tract infection.

Patient management responsibilities begin with recognizing the presence of shock. Initiate treatment immediately and identify the probable cause. The patient's response to initial treatment, coupled with the findings of the primary and secondary surveys, usually provides sufficient information to determine the cause of shock. Hemorrhage is the most common cause of shock in trauma patients.

SHOCK PATHOPHYSIOLOGY

An overview of basic cardiac physiology and blood loss pathophysiology is essential to understanding the shock state.

BASIC CARDIAC PHYSIOLOGY

Cardiac output is defined as the volume of blood pumped by the heart per minute. This value is determined by multiplying the heart rate by the stroke volume (the amount of blood that leaves the heart with each cardiac contraction). Stroke volume is classically determined by preload, myocardial contractility, and afterload (■ FIGURE 3-1).

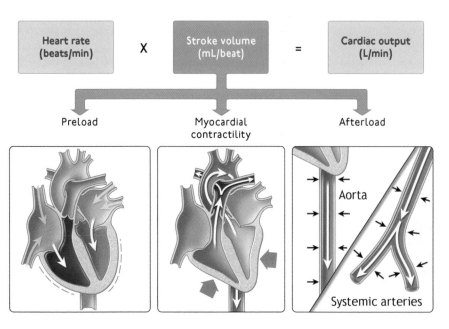

■ FIGURE 3-1 Cardiac output is the volume of blood pumped by the heart per minute, determined by multiplying the heart rate by the stroke volume (i.e., the amount of blood that leaves the heart with each cardiac contraction). Stroke volume is classically determined by preload, myocardial contractility, and afterload.

Preload, the volume of venous blood return to the left and right sides of the heart, is determined by venous capacitance, volume status, and the difference between mean venous systemic pressure and right atrial pressure. This pressure differential determines venous flow. The venous system can be considered a reservoir, or capacitance, system in which the volume of blood is divided into two components:

1. The first component represents the volume of blood that would remain in this capacitance circuit if the pressure in the system were zero. This component does not contribute to the mean systemic venous pressure.

2. The second component represents the venous volume that contributes to the mean systemic venous pressure. Nearly 70% of the body's total blood volume is estimated to be located in the venous circuit. Compliance of the venous system involves a relationship between venous volume and venous pressure. This pressure gradient drives venous flow and therefore the volume of venous return to the heart. Blood loss depletes this component of venous volume and reduces the pressure gradient; consequently, venous return is reduced.

The volume of venous blood returned to the heart determines myocardial muscle fiber length after ventricular filling at the end of diastole. According to Starling's law, muscle fiber length is related to the contractile properties of myocardial muscle. Myocardial contractility is the pump that drives the system.

Afterload, also known as peripheral vascular resistance, is systemic. Simply stated, afterload is resistance to the forward flow of blood.

BLOOD LOSS PATHOPHYSIOLOGY

Early circulatory responses to blood loss are compensatory and include progressive vasoconstriction of cutaneous, muscular, and visceral circulation to preserve blood flow to the kidneys, heart, and brain. The usual response to acute circulating volume depletion is an increase in heart rate in an attempt to preserve cardiac output. In most cases, tachycardia is the earliest measurable circulatory sign of shock. The release of endogenous catecholamines increases peripheral vascular resistance, which in turn increases diastolic blood pressure and reduces pulse pressure. However, this increase in pressure does little to increase organ perfusion and tissue oxygenation.

For patients in early hemorrhagic shock, venous return is preserved to some degree by the compensatory mechanism of contraction of the volume of blood in the venous system. This compensatory mechanism is limited. The most effective method of restoring adequate cardiac output, end-organ perfusion, and tissue oxygenation is to restore venous return to normal by locating and stopping the source of bleeding. Volume repletion will allow recovery from the shock state only when the bleeding has stopped.

At the cellular level, inadequately perfused and poorly oxygenated cells are deprived of essential substrates for normal aerobic metabolism and energy production. Initially, compensation occurs by shifting to anaerobic metabolism, resulting in the formation of lactic acid and development of metabolic acidosis. If shock is prolonged, subsequent end-organ damage and multiple organ dysfunction may result.

Administration of an appropriate quantity of isotonic electrolyte solutions, blood, and blood products helps combat this process. Treatment must focus on reversing the shock state by stopping the bleeding and providing adequate oxygenation, ventilation, and appropriate fluid resuscitation. Rapid intravenous access must be obtained.

Definitive control of hemorrhage and restoration of adequate circulating volume are the goals of treating hemorrhagic shock. Vasopressors are contraindicated as a first-line treatment of hemorrhagic shock because they worsen tissue perfusion. Frequently monitor the patient's indices of perfusion to detect any deterioration in the patient's condition as early as possible so it can be reversed. Monitoring also allows for evaluation of the patient's response to therapy. Reassessment helps clinicians identify patients in compensated shock and those who are unable to mount a compensatory response before cardiovascular collapse occurs.

Most injured patients who are in hemorrhagic shock require early surgical intervention or angioembolization to reverse the shock state. The presence of shock in a trauma patient warrants the immediate involvement of a surgeon. Strongly consider arranging for early transfer of these patients to a trauma center when they present to hospitals that are not equipped to manage their injuries.

INITIAL PATIENT ASSESSMENT

Optimally, clinicians recognize the shock state during the initial patient assessment. To do so, they must be familiar with the clinical differentiation of causes of shock—chiefly, hemorrhagic and non-hemorrhagic shock.

RECOGNITION OF SHOCK

Profound circulatory shock, as evidenced by hemo-dynamic collapse with inadequate perfusion of the skin, kidneys, and central nervous system, is simple to recognize. After ensuring a patent airway and adequate ventilation, trauma team members must carefully evaluate the patient's circulatory status for early manifestations of shock, such as tachycardia and cutaneous vasoconstriction.

Relying solely on systolic blood pressure as an indicator of shock can delay recognition of the condition, as compensatory mechanisms can prevent a measurable fall in systolic pressure until up to 30% of the patient's blood volume is lost. Look closely at pulse rate, pulse character, respiratory rate, skin perfusion, and pulse pressure (i.e., the difference between systolic and diastolic pressure). In most adults, tachycardia and cutaneous vasoconstriction are the typical early physiologic responses to volume loss.

Any injured patient who is cool to the touch and is tachycardic should be considered to be in shock until proven otherwise. Occasionally, a normal heart rate or even bradycardia is associated with an acute reduction of blood volume; other indices of perfusion must be monitored in these situations.

The normal heart rate varies with age. Tachycardia is diagnosed when the heart rate is greater than 160 beats per minute (BPM) in an infant, 140 BPM in a preschool-aged child, 120 BPM in children from school age to puberty, and 100 BPM in adults. Elderly patients may not exhibit tachycardia because of their limited cardiac response to catecholamine stimulation or the concurrent use of medications, such as ß-adrenergic blocking agents. The body's ability to increase the heart rate also may be limited by the presence of a pacemaker. A narrowed pulse pressure suggests significant blood loss and involvement of compensatory mechanisms.

Massive blood loss may produce only a slight decrease in initial hematocrit or hemoglobin concentration. Thus, a very low hematocrit value obtained shortly after injury suggests either massive blood loss or a preexisting anemia, and a normal hematocrit does not exclude significant blood loss. Base deficit and/or lactate levels can be useful in determining the presence and severity of shock. Serial measurements of these parameters to monitor a patient's response to therapy are useful.

CLINICAL DIFFERENTIATION OF CAUSE OF SHOCK

Shock in a trauma patient is classified as hemorrhagic or non-hemorrhagic shock. A patient with injuries above the diaphragm may have evidence of inadequate organ perfusion and tissue oxygenation due to poor cardiac performance from blunt myocardial injury, cardiac tamponade, or a tension pneumothorax that produces inadequate venous return (preload). To recognize and manage all forms of shock, clinicians must maintain a high level of suspicion and carefully observe the patient's response to initial treatment.

Initial determination of the cause of shock requires an appropriate patient history and expeditious, careful physical examination. Selected additional tests, such as chest and pelvic x-rays and focused assessment with sonography for trauma (FAST) examinations, can confirm the cause of shock, but should not delay appropriate resuscitation. (See *FAST video on MyATLS mobile app.*)

Overview of Hemorrhagic Shock

Hemorrhage is the most common cause of shock after injury, and virtually all patients with multiple injuries have some degree of hypovolemia. Therefore, if signs of shock are present, treatment typically is instituted as if the patient were hypovolemic. However, while instituting treatment, it is important to identify the small number of patients whose shock has a different cause (e.g., a secondary condition, such as cardiac tamponade, tension pneumothorax, spinal cord injury, or blunt cardiac injury), which complicates the presentation of hemorrhagic shock.

The treatment of hemorrhagic shock is described later in this chapter, but the primary focus is to promptly identify and stop hemorrhage. Sources of potential blood loss—chest, abdomen, pelvis, retroperitoneum, extremities, and external bleeding—must be quickly assessed by physical examination and appropriate adjunctive studies. Chest x-ray, pelvic x-ray, abdominal

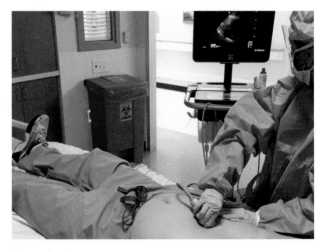

■ **FIGURE 3-2** Using ultrasound (FAST) to search for the cause of shock.

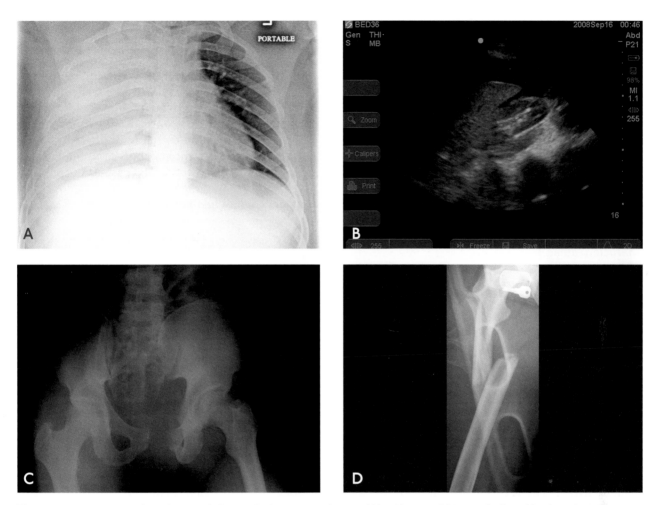

■ FIGURE 3-3 Assessment of circulation includes rapidly determining the site of blood loss. In addition to the floor, blood may be in four other places ("on the floor plus four more"): **A.** the chest; **B.** the abdomen; **C.** the pelvis and retroperitoneum; and **D.** major long bones and soft tissues.

assessment with either FAST or diagnostic peritoneal lavage (DPL), and bladder catheterization may all be necessary to determine the source of blood loss (■ FIGURES 3-2 and 3-3).

Overview of Non-hemorrhagic Shock

The category of non-hemorrhagic shock includes cardiogenic shock, cardiac tamponade, tension pneumothorax, neurogenic shock, and septic shock. Even without blood loss, most non-hemorrhagic shock states transiently improve with volume resuscitation.

Cardiogenic Shock

Myocardial dysfunction can be caused by blunt cardiac injury, cardiac tamponade, an air embolus, or, rarely, myocardial infarction. Suspect a blunt cardiac injury when the mechanism of injury to the thorax involves rapid deceleration. All patients with blunt thoracic trauma need continuous electrocardiographic (ECG) monitoring to detect injury patterns and dysrhythmias. (See *Chapter 4: Thoracic Trauma*.) The shock state may be secondary to myocardial infarction in the elderly and other high-risk patients, such as those with cocaine intoxication. Therefore, cardiac enzyme levels may assist in diagnosing and treating injured patients in the emergency department (ED), as acute myocardial ischemia may be the precipitating event.

Cardiac Tamponade

Although cardiac tamponade is most commonly encountered in patients with penetrating thoracic trauma, it can result from blunt injury to the thorax. Tachycardia, muffled heart sounds, and dilated, engorged neck veins with hypotension and insufficient response to fluid therapy suggest cardiac tamponade.

However, the absence of these classic findings does not exclude the presence of this condition.

Tension pneumothorax can mimic cardiac tamponade, with findings of distended neck veins and hypotension in both. However, absent breath sounds and hyperresonant percussion are not present with tamponade. Echocardiography may be useful in diagnosing tamponade and valve rupture, but it is often not practical or immediately available in the ED. FAST performed in the ED can identify pericardial fluid, which suggests cardiac tamponade as the cause of shock. Cardiac tamponade is best managed by formal operative intervention, as pericardiocentesis is at best only a temporizing maneuver. (See *Chapter 4: Thoracic Trauma.*)

Tension Pneumothorax

Tension pneumothorax is a true surgical emergency that requires immediate diagnosis and treatment. It develops when air enters the pleural space, but a flap-valve mechanism prevents its escape. Intrapleural pressure rises, causing total lung collapse and a shift of the mediastinum to the opposite side, with subsequent impairment of venous return and a fall in cardiac output. Spontaneously breathing patients often manifest extreme tachypnea and air hunger, while mechanically ventilated patients more often manifest hemodynamic collapse. The presence of acute respiratory distress, subcutaneous emphysema, absent unilateral breath sounds, hyperresonance to percussion, and tracheal shift supports the diagnosis of tension pneumothorax and warrants immediate thoracic decompression without waiting for x-ray confirmation of the diagnosis. Needle or finger decompression of tension pneumothorax temporarily relieves this life-threatening condition. Follow this procedure by placing a chest tube using appropriate sterile technique. (See *Appendix G: Breathing Skills* and *Chest Tube video on MyATLS mobile app.*)

Neurogenic Shock

Isolated intracranial injuries do not cause shock, unless the brainstem is injured. Therefore, the presence of shock in patients with head injury necessitates the search for another cause. Cervical and upper thoracic spinal cord injuries can produce hypotension due to loss of sympathetic tone, which compounds the physiologic effects of hypovolemia. In turn, hypovolemia compounds the physiologic effects of sympathetic denervation. The classic presentation of neurogenic shock is hypotension without tachycardia or cutaneous vasoconstriction. A narrowed pulse pressure is not seen in neurogenic shock. Patients who have sustained a spinal cord injury often have concurrent torso trauma; therefore, patients with known or suspected neurogenic shock are treated initially for hypovolemia. The failure of fluid resuscitation to restore organ perfusion and tissue oxygenation suggests either continuing hemorrhage or neurogenic shock. Advanced techniques for monitoring intravascular volume status and cardiac output may be helpful in managing this complex problem. (See *Chapter 7: Spine and Spinal Cord Trauma.*)

Septic Shock

Shock due to infection immediately after injury is uncommon; however, it can occur when a patient's arrival at the ED is delayed for several hours. Septic shock can occur in patients with penetrating abdominal injuries and contamination of the peritoneal cavity by intestinal contents. Patients with sepsis who also have hypotension and are afebrile are clinically difficult to distinguish from those in hypovolemic shock, as patients in both groups can have tachycardia, cutaneous vasoconstriction, impaired urinary output, decreased systolic pressure, and narrow pulse pressure. Patients with early septic shock can have a normal circulating volume, modest tachycardia, warm skin, near normal systolic blood pressure, and a wide pulse pressure.

HEMORRHAGIC SHOCK

Hemorrhage is the most common cause of shock in trauma patients. The trauma patient's response to blood loss is made more complex by fluid shifts among the fluid compartments in the body, particularly in the extracellular fluid compartment. Soft tissue injury, even without severe hemorrhage, can result in shifts of fluid to the extracellular compartment. The response to blood loss must be considered in the context of these fluid shifts. Also consider the changes associated with severe, prolonged shock and the pathophysiologic results of resuscitation and reperfusion.

DEFINITION OF HEMORRHAGE

Hemorrhage is an acute loss of circulating blood volume. Although it can vary considerably, normal adult blood volume is approximately 7% of body weight. For example, a 70-kg male has a circulating blood volume of approximately 5 L. The blood volume of obese adults is estimated based on their ideal body weight, because calculation based on actual weight can result in significant overestimation. The blood volume for a child is calculated as 8% to 9% of body weight (70–80 mL/kg). (See *Chapter 10: Pediatric Trauma*.)

PHYSIOLOGIC CLASSIFICATION

The physiologic effects of hemorrhage are divided into four classes, based on clinical signs, which are useful for estimating the percentage of acute blood loss. The clinical signs represent a continuum of ongoing hemorrhage and serve only to guide initial therapy. Subsequent volume replacement is determined by the patient's response to therapy. The following classification system is useful in emphasizing the early signs and pathophysiology of the shock state:

- Class I hemorrhage is exemplified by the condition of an individual who has donated 1 unit of blood.

- Class II hemorrhage is uncomplicated hemorrhage for which crystalloid fluid resuscitation is required.

- Class III hemorrhage is a complicated hemorrhagic state in which at least crystalloid infusion is required and perhaps also blood replacement.

- Class IV hemorrhage is considered a preterminal event; unless aggressive measures are taken, the patient will die within minutes. Blood transfusion is required.

■ TABLE 3-1 outlines the estimated blood loss and other critical measures for patients in each classification of shock.

Class I Hemorrhage: <15% Blood Volume Loss

The clinical symptoms of volume loss with class I hemorrhage are minimal. In uncomplicated situations, minimal tachycardia occurs. No measurable changes occur in blood pressure, pulse pressure, or respiratory rate. For otherwise healthy patients, this amount of blood loss does not require replacement, because transcapillary refill and other compensatory mechanisms will restore blood volume within 24 hours, usually without the need for blood transfusion.

TABLE 3-1 SIGNS AND SYMPTOMS OF HEMORRHAGE BY CLASS

PARAMETER	CLASS I	CLASS II (MILD)	CLASS III (MODERATE)	CLASS IV (SEVERE)
Approximate blood loss	<15%	15–30%	31–40%	>40%
Heart rate	↔	↔/↑	↑	↑/↑↑
Blood pressure	↔	↔	↔/↓	↓
Pulse pressure	↔	↓	↓	↓
Respiratory rate	↔	↔	↔/↑	↑
Urine output	↔	↔	↓	↓↓
Glasgow Coma Scale score	↔	↔	↓	↓
Base deficit[a]	0 to –2 mEq/L	–2 to –6 mEq/L	–6 to –10 mEq/L	–10 mEq/L or less
Need for blood products	Monitor	Possible	Yes	Massive Transfusion Protocol

[a] Base excess is the quantity of base (HCO_3^-, in mEq/L) that is above or below the normal range in the body. A negative number is called a base deficit and indicates metabolic acidosis.

Data from: Mutschler A, Nienaber U, Brockamp T, et al. A critical reappraisal of the ATLS classification of hypovolaemic shock: does it really reflect clinical reality? *Resuscitation* 2013,84:309–313.

Class II Hemorrhage: 15% to 30% Blood Volume Loss

Clinical signs of class II hemorrhage include tachycardia, tachypnea, and decreased pulse pressure. The latter sign is related primarily to a rise in diastolic blood pressure due to an increase in circulating catecholamines, which produce an increase in peripheral vascular tone and resistance. Systolic pressure changes minimally in early hemorrhagic shock; therefore, it is important to evaluate pulse pressure rather than systolic pressure. Other pertinent clinical findings associated with this amount of blood loss include subtle central nervous system (CNS) changes, such as anxiety, fear, and hostility. Despite the significant blood loss and cardiovascular changes, urinary output is only mildly affected. The measured urine flow is usually 20 to 30 mL/hour in an adult with class II hemorrhage.

Accompanying fluid losses can exaggerate the clinical manifestations of class II hemorrhage. Some patients in this category may eventually require blood transfusion, but most are stabilized initially with crystalloid solutions.

Class III Hemorrhage: 31% to 40% Blood Volume Loss

Patients with class III hemorrhage typically present with the classic signs of inadequate perfusion, including marked tachycardia and tachypnea, significant changes in mental status, and a measurable fall in systolic blood pressure. In an uncomplicated case, this is the least amount of blood loss that consistently causes a drop in systolic blood pressure. The priority of initial management is to stop the hemorrhage, by emergency operation or embolization, if necessary. Most patients in this category will require packed red blood cells (pRBCs) and blood products to reverse the shock state.

Class IV Hemorrhage: >40% Blood Volume Loss

The degree of exsanguination with class IV hemorrhage is immediately life-threatening. Symptoms include marked tachycardia, a significant decrease in systolic blood pressure, and a very narrow pulse pressure or unmeasurable diastolic blood pressure. (Bradycardia may develop preterminally.) Urinary output is negligible, and mental status is markedly depressed. The skin is cold and pale. Patients with class IV hemorrhage frequently require rapid transfusion and immediate surgical intervention. These decisions are based on

PITFALL	PREVENTION
Diagnosis of shock can be missed when only a single parameter is used.	• Use all clinical information, including heart rate, blood pressure, skin perfusion, and mental status. • When available, obtain arterial blood gas measurements of pH, pO_2, PCO_2, oxygen saturation, and base deficit. • Measurement of end-tidal CO_2 and serum lactate can add useful diagnostic information.
Injury in elderly patients may be related to underlying infection.	• Always obtain screening urinalysis. • Look for subtle evidence of infection.

the patient's response to the initial management techniques described in this chapter.

CONFOUNDING FACTORS

The physiologic classification system is helpful, but the following factors may confound and profoundly alter the classic hemodynamic response to the acute loss of circulating blood volume; all individuals involved in the initial assessment and resuscitation of injured patients must promptly recognize them:

- Patient age
- Severity of injury, particularly the type and anatomic location of injury
- Time lapse between injury and initiation of treatment
- Prehospital fluid therapy
- Medications used for chronic conditions

It is dangerous to wait until a trauma patient fits a precise physiologic classification of shock before initiating appropriate volume restoration. Initiate hemorrhage control and balanced fluid resuscitation when early signs and symptoms of blood loss are apparent or suspected—not when the blood pressure is falling or absent. Stop the bleeding.

FLUID CHANGES SECONDARY TO SOFT-TISSUE INJURY

Major soft-tissue injuries and fractures compromise the hemodynamic status of injured patients in two ways: First, blood is lost into the site of injury, particularly in major fractures. For example, a fractured tibia or humerus can result in the loss of up to 750 mL of blood. Twice that amount, 1500 mL, is commonly associated with femur fractures, and several liters of blood can accumulate in a retroperitoneal hematoma associated with a pelvic fracture. Obese patients are at risk for extensive blood loss into soft tissues, even in the absence of fractures. Elderly patients are also at risk because of fragile skin and subcutaneous tissues that injures more readily and tamponades less effectively, in addition to inelastic blood vessels that do not spasm and thrombose when injured or transected.

Second, edema that occurs in injured soft tissues constitutes another source of fluid loss. The degree of this additional volume loss is related to the magnitude of the soft-tissue injury. Tissue injury results in activation of a systemic inflammatory response and production and release of multiple cytokines. Many of these locally active substances have profound effects on the vascular endothelium, resulting in increased permeability. Tissue edema is the result of shifts in fluid primarily from the plasma into the extravascular, or extracellular, space as a result of alterations in endothelial permeability. Such shifts produce an additional depletion in intravascular volume.

PITFALL	PREVENTION
Blood loss can be underestimated from soft-tissue injury, particularly in obese and elderly individuals.	• Evaluate and dress wounds early to control bleeding with direct pressure and temporary closure. • Reassess wounds and wash and close them definitively once the patient has stabilized.

INITIAL MANAGEMENT OF HEMORRHAGIC SHOCK

The diagnosis and treatment of shock must occur almost simultaneously. For most trauma patients, clinicians begin treatment as if the patient has hemorrhagic shock, unless a different cause of shock is clearly evident. The basic management principle is to stop the bleeding and replace the volume loss.

PHYSICAL EXAMINATION

The physical examination is focused on diagnosing immediately life-threatening injuries and assessing the ABCDEs. Baseline observations are important to assess the patient's response to therapy, and repeated measurements of vital signs, urinary output, and level of consciousness are essential. A more detailed examination of the patient follows as the situation permits.

Airway and Breathing

Establishing a patent airway with adequate ventilation and oxygenation is the first priority. Provide supplementary oxygen to maintain oxygen saturation at greater than 95%.

Circulation: Hemorrhage Control

Priorities for managing circulation include controlling obvious hemorrhage, obtaining adequate intravenous access, and assessing tissue perfusion. Bleeding from external wounds in the extremities usually can be controlled by direct pressure to the bleeding site, although massive blood loss from an extremity may require a tourniquet. A sheet or pelvic binder may be used to control bleeding from pelvic fractures. (See *Pelvic Binder video on MyATLS mobile app.*) Surgical or angioembolization may be required to control internal hemorrhage. The priority is to stop the bleeding, not to calculate the volume of fluid lost.

Disability: Neurological Examination

A brief neurological examination will determine the patient's level of consciousness, which is useful in assessing cerebral perfusion. Alterations in CNS function in patients who have hypovolemic shock do not necessarily imply direct intracranial injury and may reflect inadequate perfusion. Repeat neurological evaluation after restoring perfusion and oxygenation. (See *Chapter 6: Head Trauma.*)

Exposure: Complete Examination

After addressing lifesaving priorities, completely undress the patient and carefully examine him or her from head to toe to search for additional injuries. When exposing a patient, it is essential to prevent hypothermia, a condition that can exacerbate blood loss by contributing to coagulopathy and worsening acidosis. To prevent hypothermia, always use fluid warmers and external passive and active warming techniques.

Gastric Dilation: Decompression

Gastric dilation often occurs in trauma patients, especially in children. This condition can cause unexplained hypotension or cardiac dysrhythmia, usually bradycardia from excessive vagal stimulation. In unconscious patients, gastric distention increases the risk of aspiration of gastric contents, a potentially fatal complication. Consider decompressing the stomach by inserting a nasal or oral tube and attaching it to suction. Be aware that proper positioning of the tube does not eliminate the risk of aspiration.

Urinary Catheterization

Bladder catheterization allows clinicians to assess the urine for hematuria, which can identify the genitourinary system as a source of blood loss. Monitoring urine output also allows for continuous evaluation of renal perfusion. Blood at the urethral meatus or perineal hematoma/bruising may indicate urethral injury and contraindicates the insertion of a transurethral catheter before radiographic confirmation of an intact urethra. (See *Chapter 5: Abdominal and Pelvic Trauma*.)

VASCULAR ACCESS

Obtain access to the vascular system promptly. This measure is best accomplished by inserting two large-caliber (minimum of 18-gauge in an adult) peripheral intravenous catheters. The rate of flow is proportional to the fourth power of the radius of the cannula and inversely related to its length, as described in Poiseuille's law. Hence, short, large-caliber peripheral intravenous lines are preferred for the rapid infusion of fluid, rather than longer, thinner catheters. Use fluid warmers and rapid infusion pumps in the presence of massive hemorrhage and severe hypotension.

The most desirable sites for peripheral, percutaneous intravenous lines in adults are the forearms and antecubital veins. This can be challenging in the young, very old, obese patients, and intravenous drug users. If peripheral access cannot be obtained, consider placement of an intraosseous needle for temporary access. If circumstances prevent the use of peripheral veins, clinicians may initiate large-caliber, central venous (i.e., femoral, jugular, or subclavian vein) access. (See *Appendix G: Circulation Skills* and *Intraosseous*

Puncture video on MyATLS mobile app.) The clinician's experience and skill are critical determinants in selecting the most appropriate procedure or route for establishing vascular access. Intraosseous access with specially designed equipment is possible in all *age groups*. This access may be used in the hospital until intravenous access is obtained and is discontinued when it is no longer necessary.

As intravenous lines are started, draw blood samples for type and crossmatch, appropriate laboratory analyses, toxicology studies, and pregnancy testing for all females of childbearing age. Blood gas analysis also may be performed at this time. A chest x-ray must be obtained after attempts at inserting a subclavian or internal jugular line to document the position of the line and evaluate for a pneumothorax or hemothorax. In emergency situations, central venous access is frequently not accomplished under tightly controlled or completely sterile conditions. Therefore, these lines should be changed in a more controlled environment as soon as the patient's condition permits.

INITIAL FLUID THERAPY

The amount of fluid and blood required for resuscitation is difficult to predict on initial evaluation of a patient. Administer an initial, warmed fluid bolus of isotonic fluid. The usual dose is 1 liter for adults and 20 mL/kg for pediatric patients weighing less than 40 kilograms. Absolute volumes of resuscitation fluid should be based on patient response to fluid administration, keeping in mind that this initial fluid amount includes any fluid given in the prehospital setting. Assess the patient's response to fluid resuscitation and identify evidence of adequate end-organ perfusion and tissue oxygenation. Observe the patient's response during this initial fluid administration and base further therapeutic and diagnostic decisions on this response. Persistent infusion of large volumes of fluid and blood in an attempt to achieve a normal blood pressure is not a substitute for definitive control of bleeding.

■ TABLE 3-2 outlines general guidelines for establishing the amount of fluid and blood likely required during resuscitation. If the amount of fluid required to restore or maintain adequate organ perfusion and tissue oxygenation greatly exceeds these estimates, carefully reassess the situation and search for unrecognized injuries and other causes of shock.

The goal of resuscitation is to restore organ perfusion and tissue oxygenation, which is accomplished with administering crystalloid solution and blood products to replace lost intravascular volume. However, if the patient's blood pressure increases rapidly before the hemorrhage has been definitively

TABLE 3-2 RESPONSES TO INITIAL FLUID RESUSCITATION[a]

	RAPID RESPONSE	TRANSIENT RESPONSE	MINIMAL OR NO RESPONSE
Vital signs	Return to normal	Transient improvement, recurrence of decreased blood pressure and increased heart rate	Remain abnormal
Estimated blood loss	Minimal (<15 %)	Moderate and ongoing (15%–40%)	Severe (>40%)
Need for blood	Low	Moderate to high	Immediate
Blood preparation	Type and crossmatch	Type-specific	Emergency blood release
Need for operative intervention	Possibly	Likely	Highly likely
Early presence of surgeon	Yes	Yes	Yes

[a] Isotonic crystalloid solution, up to 1000 mL in adults; 20 mL/kg in children

PITFALL	PREVENTION
Shock does not respond to initial crystalloid fluid bolus.	• Look for a source of ongoing blood loss: "floor and four more (abdomen/ pelvis, retroperitoneum, thorax, and extremities). • Consider a non-hemorrhagic source of shock. • Begin blood and blood component replacement. • Obtain surgical consultation for definitive hemorrhage control.

controlled, more bleeding can occur. For this reason, administering excessive crystalloid solution can be harmful.

Fluid resuscitation and avoidance of hypotension are important principles in the initial management of patients with blunt trauma, particularly those with traumatic brain injury. In penetrating trauma with hemorrhage, delaying aggressive fluid resuscitation until definitive control of hemorrhage is achieved may prevent additional bleeding; a careful, balanced approach with frequent reevaluation is required. Balancing the goal of organ perfusion and tissue oxygenation with the avoidance of rebleeding by accepting a lower-than-normal blood pressure has been termed "controlled resuscitation," "balanced resuscitation," "hypotensive resuscitation," and "permissive hypotension." Such a resuscitation strategy may be a bridge to, but is not a substitute for, definitive surgical control of bleeding.

Early resuscitation with blood and blood products must be considered in patients with evidence of class III and IV hemorrhage. Early administration of blood products at a low ratio of packed red blood cells to plasma and platelets can prevent the development of coagulopathy and thrombocytopenia.

Measuring Patient Response to Fluid Therapy

The same signs and symptoms of inadequate perfusion that are used to diagnose shock help determine the patient's response to therapy. The return of normal blood pressure, pulse pressure, and pulse rate are signs that perfusion is returning to normal, however, these observations do not provide information regarding organ perfusion and tissue oxygenation. Improvement in the intravascular volume status is important evidence of enhanced perfusion, but it is difficult to quantitate. The volume of urinary output is a reasonably sensitive indicator of renal perfusion; normal urine volumes generally imply adequate renal blood flow, if not modified by underlying kidney injury, marked hyperglycemia or the administration of diuretic agents. For this reason, urinary output is one of the prime indicators of resuscitation and patient response.

Within certain limits, urinary output is used to monitor renal blood flow. Adequate volume replacement during resuscitation should produce a urinary output of approximately 0.5 mL/kg/hr in adults, whereas 1 mL/kg/hr is adequate urinary output for pediatric patients. For children under 1 year of age, 2 mL/kg/hr should be maintained. The inability to obtain urinary output at these levels or a decreasing urinary output with an increasing specific gravity suggests inadequate resuscitation. This situation should stimulate further volume replacement and continued diagnostic investigation for the cause.

Patients in early hypovolemic shock have respiratory alkalosis from tachypnea, which is frequently followed by mild metabolic acidosis and does not require treatment. However, severe metabolic acidosis can develop from long-standing or severe shock. Metabolic acidosis is caused by anaerobic metabolism, as a result of inadequate tissue perfusion and the production of lactic acid. Persistent acidosis is usually caused by inadequate resuscitation or ongoing blood loss. In patients in shock, treat metabolic acidosis with fluids, blood, and interventions to control hemorrhage. Base deficit and/or lactate values can be useful in determining the presence and severity of shock, and then serial measurement of these parameters can be used to monitor the response to therapy. Do not use sodium bicarbonate to treat metabolic acidosis from hypovolemic shock.

Patterns of Patient Response

The patient's response to initial fluid resuscitation is the key to determining subsequent therapy. Having established a preliminary diagnosis and treatment plan based on the initial assessment, the clinician modifies the plan based on the patient's response. Observing the response to the initial resuscitation can identify patients whose blood loss was greater than estimated and those with ongoing bleeding who require operative control of internal hemorrhage.

The potential patterns of response to initial fluid administration can be divided into three groups: rapid response, transient response, and minimal or no response. Vital signs and management guidelines for patients in each of these categories were outlined earlier (see Table 3-2).

Rapid Response

Patients in this group, referred to as "rapid responders," quickly respond to the initial fluid bolus and become hemodynamically normal, without signs of inadequate tissue perfusion and oxygenation. Once this occurs, clinicians can slow the fluids to maintenance rates. These patients typically have lost less than 15% of their blood volume (class I hemorrhage), and no further fluid bolus or immediate blood administration is indicated. However, typed and crossmatched blood should be kept available. Surgical consultation and evaluation are necessary during initial assessment and treatment of rapid responders, as operative intervention could still be necessary.

Transient Response

Patients in the second group, "transient responders," respond to the initial fluid bolus. However, they begin to show deterioration of perfusion indices as the initial fluids are slowed to maintenance levels, indicating either an ongoing blood loss or inadequate resuscitation. Most of these patients initially have lost an estimated 15% to 40% of their blood volume (class II and III hemorrhage). Transfusion of blood and blood products is indicated, but even more important is recognizing that such patients require operative or angiographic control of hemorrhage. A transient response to blood administration identifies patients who are still bleeding and require rapid surgical intervention. Also consider initiating a massive transfusion protocol (MTP).

Minimal or No Response

Failure to respond to crystalloid and blood administration in the ED dictates the need for immediate, definitive intervention (i.e., operation or angioembolization) to control exsanguinating hemorrhage. On very rare occasions, failure to respond to fluid resuscitation is due to pump failure as a result of blunt cardiac injury, cardiac tamponade, or tension pneumothorax. Non-hemorrhagic shock always should be considered as a diagnosis in this group of patients (class IV hemorrhage). Advanced monitoring techniques such as cardiac ultrasonography are useful to identify the cause of shock. MTP should be initiated in these patients (■ FIGURE 3-4).

BLOOD REPLACEMENT

The decision to initiate blood transfusion is based on the patient's response, as described in the previous section. Patients who are transient responders or nonresponders require pRBCs, plasma and platelets as an early part of their resuscitation.

■ FIGURE 3-4 Massive transfusion of blood products in a trauma patient.

CROSSMATCHED, TYPE-SPECIFIC, AND TYPE O BLOOD

The main purpose of blood transfusion is to restore the oxygen-carrying capacity of the intravascular volume. Fully crossmatched pRBCs are preferable for this purpose, but the complete crossmatching process requires approximately 1 hour in most blood banks. For patients who stabilize rapidly, crossmatched pRBCs should be obtained and made available for transfusion when indicated.

If crossmatched blood is unavailable, type O pRBCs are indicated for patients with exsanguinating hemorrhage. AB plasma is given when uncrossmatched plasma is needed. To avoid sensitization and future complications, Rh-negative pRBCs are preferred for females of childbearing age. As soon as it is available, the use of unmatched, type-specific pRBCs is preferred over type O pRBCs. An exception to this rule is when multiple, unidentified casualties are being treated simultaneously, and the risk of inadvertently administering the wrong unit of blood to a patient is increased.

PREVENT HYPOTHERMIA

Hypothermia must be prevented and reversed if a patient is hypothermic on arrival to the hospital. The use of blood warmers in the ED is critical, even if cumbersome. The most efficient way to prevent hypothermia in any patient receiving massive resuscitation of crystalloid and blood is to heat the fluid to 39°C (102.2°F) before infusing it. This can be accomplished by storing crystalloids in a warmer or infusing them through intravenous fluid warmers. Blood products cannot be stored in a warmer, but they can be heated by passage through intravenous fluid warmers.

AUTOTRANSFUSION

Adaptations of standard tube thoracostomy collection devices are commercially available, allowing for sterile collection, anticoagulation (generally with sodium citrate solutions rather than heparin), and transfusion of shed blood. Consider collection of shed blood for autotransfusion in patients with massive hemothorax. This blood generally has only low levels of coagulation factors, so plasma and platelets may still be needed.

MASSIVE TRANSFUSION

A small subset of patients with shock will require massive transfusion, most often defined as > 10 units of pRBCs within the first 24 hours of admission or more than 4 units in 1 hour. Early administration of pRBCs, plasma, and platelets in a balanced ratio to minimize excessive crystalloid administration may improve patient survival. This approach has been termed "balanced," "hemostatic," or "damage-control" resuscitation. Simultaneous efforts to rapidly control bleeding and reduce the detrimental effects of coagulopathy, hypothermia, and acidosis in these patients are extremely important. A MTP that includes the immediate availability of all blood components should be in place to provide optimal resuscitation for these patients, because extensive resources are required to provide these large quantities of blood. Appropriate administration of blood products has been shown to improve outcome in this patient population. Identification of the small subset of patients that benefit from this can be a challenge and several scores have been developed to assist the clinician in making the decision to initiate the MTP. None have been shown to be completely accurate. (See *Trauma Scores: Revised and Pediatric* and *ACS TQIP Massive Transfusion in Trauma Guidelines*.)

COAGULOPATHY

Severe injury and hemorrhage result in the consumption of coagulation factors and early coagulopathy. Such coagulopathy is present in up to 30% of severely injured patients on admission, in the absence of preexisting anticoagulant use. Massive fluid resuscitation with the resultant dilution of platelets and clotting factors, as well as the adverse effect of hypothermia on platelet aggregation and the clotting cascade, contributes to coagulopathy in injured patients.

Prothrombin time, partial thromboplastin time, and platelet count are valuable baseline studies to obtain in the first hour, especially in patients with a history of coagulation disorders or who take medications that alter coagulation (also see Anticoagulation Reversal table in *Chapter 6: Head Trauma*). These studies may also be useful in caring for patients whose bleeding history is unavailable. Point-of-care testing is available in many EDs. Thromboelastography (TEG) and rotational thromboelastometry (ROTEM) can be helpful in determining the clotting deficiency and appropriate blood components to correct the deficiency.

Some jurisdictions administer tranexamic acid in the prehospital setting to severely injured patients in response to recent studies that demonstrated improved survival when this drug is administered within 3 hours of injury. The first dose is usually given over 10 minutes and is administered in the field; the follow-up dose of 1 gram is given over 8 hours. (See *Guidance Document Regarding the Pre-Hospital Use of Tranexamic Acid for Injured Patients*.)

In patients who do not require massive transfusion, the use of platelets, cryoprecipitate, and fresh-frozen plasma should be guided by coagulation studies, along with fibrinogen levels and balanced resuscitation principles. Of note, many newer anticoagulant and antiplatelet agents cannot be detected by conventional testing of PT, PTT, INR, and platelet count. Some of the oral anticoagulants have no reversal agents.

Patients with major brain injury are particularly prone to coagulation abnormalities. Coagulation parameters need to be closely monitored in these patients; early administration of plasma or clotting factors and/or platelets improves survival if they are on known anticoagulants or antiplatelet agents.

CALCIUM ADMINISTRATION

Most patients receiving blood transfusions do not need calcium supplements. When necessary, calcium administration should be guided by measurement of ionized calcium. Excessive, supplemental calcium can be harmful.

► SPECIAL CONSIDERATIONS

Special considerations in diagnosing and treating shock include the mistaken use of blood pressure as a direct measure of cardiac output. The response of elderly patients, athletes, pregnant patients, patients on

PITFALL	PREVENTION
Uncontrolled blood loss can occur in patients taking antiplatelet or anticoagulant medications.	• Obtain medication list as soon as possible. • Administer reversal agents as soon as possible. • Where available, monitor coagulation with thromboelastography (TEG) or rotational thromboelastometry (ROTEM). • Consider administering platelet transfusion, even with normal platelet count.
Thromboembolic complications can occur from agents given to reverse anticoagulant and antiplatelet medications.	• Weigh the risk of bleeding with the risk of thromboembolic complications. • Where available, monitor coagulation with TEG or ROTEM.

medications, hypothermic patients, and patients with pacemakers or implantable cardioverter-defibrillators (ICDs) may differ from the expected.

EQUATING BLOOD PRESSURE TO CARDIAC OUTPUT

Treatment of hemorrhagic shock requires correction of inadequate organ perfusion by increasing organ blood flow and tissue oxygenation. Increasing blood flow requires an increase in cardiac output. Ohm's law ($V = I \times R$) applied to cardiovascular physiology states that blood pressure (V) is proportional to cardiac output (I) and systemic vascular resistance (R; afterload). An increase in blood pressure should not be equated with a concomitant increase in cardiac output or recovery from shock. For example, an increase in peripheral resistance with vasopressor therapy, with no change in cardiac output, results in increased blood pressure but no improvement in tissue perfusion or oxygenation.

ADVANCED AGE

In the cardiovascular system, the aging process produces a relative decrease in sympathetic activity.

This is thought to result from a deficit in the receptor response to catecholamines, rather than reduced production of catecholamines. Cardiac compliance decreases with age, and unlike younger patients, older patients are unable to increase their heart rate or the efficiency of myocardial contraction when stressed by blood volume loss.

Atherosclerotic vascular occlusive disease makes many vital organs extremely sensitive to even the slightest reduction in blood flow. In addition, many elderly patients have preexisting volume depletion resulting from long-term diuretic use or subtle malnutrition. For these reasons, elderly trauma patients exhibit poor tolerance to hypotension secondary to blood loss. For example, a systolic blood pressure of 100 mm Hg may represent shock in an elderly patient. ß-adrenergic blockade can mask tachycardia as an early indicator of shock, and other medications can adversely affect the stress response to injury or block it completely. Because the therapeutic range for volume resuscitation is relatively narrow in elderly patients, consider using early advanced monitoring to avoid excessive or inadequate volume restoration.

Reduced pulmonary compliance, decreased diffusion capacity, and general weakness of the muscles of respiration limit elderly patients' ability to meet increased demands for gas exchange imposed by injury. This compounds the cellular hypoxia already produced by a reduction in local oxygen delivery. Glomerular and tubular senescence in the kidney reduces elderly patients' ability to preserve volume in response to the release of stress hormones such as aldosterone, catecholamines, vasopressin, and cortisol. The kidney is also more susceptible to the effects of reduced blood flow, and nephrotoxic agents such as drugs, contrast agents, and the toxic products of cellular destruction can further decrease renal function.

For all of these reasons, the mortality and morbidity rates increase directly with age. Despite adverse effects of the aging process, comorbidities from preexisting disease, and general reduction in the "physiologic reserve" of geriatric patients, most of these patients may recover and return to their preinjury status. Treatment begins with prompt, aggressive resuscitation and careful monitoring. (See *Chapter 11: Geriatric Trauma*.)

ATHLETES

Rigorous athletic training routines change the cardiovascular dynamics of this group of patients. Blood volume may increase 15% to 20%, cardiac output can increase 6-fold, stroke volume can increase 50%, and the resting pulse can average 50 BPM. Highly trained athletes' bodies have a remarkable ability to compensate for blood loss, and they may not manifest the usual responses to hypovolemia, even with significant blood loss.

PREGNANCY

The normal hypervolemia that occurs with pregnancy means that it takes a greater amount of blood loss to manifest perfusion abnormalities in the mother, which also may be reflected in decreased fetal perfusion. (See *Chapter 12: Trauma in Pregnancy and Intimate Partner Violence*.)

MEDICATIONS

Specific medications can affect a patient's response to shock. For example, ß-adrenergic receptor blockers and calcium channel blockers can significantly alter a patient's hemodynamic response to hemorrhage. Insulin overdosing may be responsible for hypoglycemia and may have contributed to the injury-producing event. Long-term diuretic therapy may explain unexpected hypokalemia, and nonsteroidal anti-inflammatory drugs (NSAIDs) may adversely affect platelet function and increase bleeding.

HYPOTHERMIA

Patients suffering from hypothermia and hemorrhagic shock do not respond as expected to the administration of blood products and fluid resuscitation. In hypothermia, coagulopathy may develop or worsen. Body temperature is an important vital sign to monitor during the initial assessment phase. Esophageal or bladder temperature is an accurate clinical measurement of the core temperature. A trauma victim under the influence of alcohol and exposed to cold temperatures is more likely to have hypothermia as a result of vasodilation. Rapid rewarming in an environment with appropriate external warming devices, heat lamps, thermal caps, heated respiratory gases, and warmed intravenous fluids and blood will generally correct hypotension and mild to moderate hypothermia. Core rewarming techniques includes irrigation of the peritoneal or thoracic cavity with crystalloid solutions warmed to 39°C (102.2°F); for severe hypothermia, extracorporeal bypass is indicated. Hypothermia is best treated by prevention. (See *Appendix B: Hypothermia and Heat Injuries*.)

PRESENCE OF PACEMAKER OR IMPLANTABLE CARDIOVERTER-DEFIBRILLATOR

Patients with pacemakers or ICDs with pacemakers are unable to respond to blood loss as expected, because cardiac output is directly related to heart rate. Heart rate may remain at the device's set rate regardless of volume status in these patients. In a significant number of patients with myocardial conduction defects who have such devices in place, additional monitoring may be required to guide fluid therapy. Many devices can be adjusted to increase heart rate if clinically indicated.

REASSESSING PATIENT RESPONSE AND AVOIDING COMPLICATIONS

Inadequate volume replacement is the most common complication of hemorrhagic shock. Patients in shock need immediate, appropriate, and aggressive therapy that restores organ perfusion.

CONTINUED HEMORRHAGE

An undiagnosed source of bleeding is the most common cause of poor response to fluid therapy. These patients, also classed as transient responders, require persistent investigation to identify the source of blood loss. Immediate surgical intervention may be necessary.

MONITORING

The goal of resuscitation is to restore organ perfusion and tissue oxygenation. This state is identified by appropriate urinary output, CNS function, skin color, and return of pulse and blood pressure toward normal. Monitoring the response to resuscitation is best accomplished for some patients in an environment where sophisticated techniques are used. For elderly patients and patients with non-hemorrhagic causes of shock, consider early transfer to an intensive care unit or trauma center.

RECOGNITION OF OTHER PROBLEMS

When a patient fails to respond to therapy, causes may include one or more of the following: undiagnosed bleeding, cardiac tamponade, tension pneumothorax, ventilatory problems, unrecognized fluid loss, acute gastric distention, myocardial infarction, diabetic acidosis, hypoadrenalism, or neurogenic shock. Constant reevaluation, especially when a patient's condition deviates from expected patterns, is the key to recognizing and treating such problems as early as possible.

TEAMWORK

One of the most challenging situations a trauma team faces is managing a trauma victim who arrives in profound shock. The team leader must direct the team decisively and calmly, using ATLS principles.

Identifying and controlling the site of hemorrhage with simultaneous resuscitation involves coordinating multiple efforts. The team leader must ensure that rapid intravenous access is obtained even in challenging patients. The decision to activate the massive transfusion protocol should be made early to avoid the lethal triad of coagulopathy, hypothermia, and acidosis. The team must be aware of the amount of fluid and blood products administered, as well as the patient's physiological response, and make necessary adjustments.

The team leader ensures that the areas of external hemorrhage are controlled and determines when to perform adjuncts such as chest x-ray, pelvic x-ray, FAST, and/or diagnostic peritoneal lavage (DPL). Decisions regarding surgery or angioembolization should be made as quickly as possible and the necessary consultants involved. When required services are unavailable, the trauma team arranges for rapid, safe transfer to definitive care.

CHAPTER SUMMARY

1. Shock is an abnormality of the circulatory system that results in inadequate organ perfusion and tissue oxygenation.

2. Hemorrhage is the cause of shock in most trauma patients. Treatment of these patients requires immediate hemorrhage control and fluid or blood replacement. Stop the bleeding.

3. Diagnosis and treatment of shock must occur almost simultaneously.

4. Initial assessment of a patient in shock requires careful physical examination, looking for signs of

tension pneumothorax, cardiac tamponade, and other causes of shock.

5. Management of hemorrhagic shock includes rapid hemostasis and balanced resuscitation with crystalloids and blood.

6. The classes of hemorrhage and response to interventions serve as a guide to resuscitation.

7. Special considerations in diagnosis and treatment of shock include differences in the response to shock in extremes of age, athleticism, pregnancy, hypothermia, and presence of some medications and pacemakers/ICDs. Avoid the pitfall of equating blood pressure with cardiac output.

ADDITIONAL RESOURCES

The STOP the Bleeding Campaign
Rossaint et al. *Critical Care* 2013;17(2):136
http://ccforum.com/content/17/2/136

ACS TQIP Massive Transfusion in Trauma Guidelines
https://www.facs.org/~/media/files/quality%20
programs/trauma/tqip/massive%20transfusion%20
in%20trauma%20guildelines.ashx

Management of Bleeding and Coagulopathy Following Major Trauma: An Updated European Guideline
Spahn et al. *Critical Care* 2013;17(2):R76
http://ccforum.com/content/17/2/R76

BIBLIOGRAPHY

1. Abou-Khalil B, Scalea TM, Trooskin SZ, et al. Hemodynamic responses to shock in young trauma patients: need for invasive monitoring. *Crit Care Med* 1994;22(4):633–639.
2. Alam HB, Rhee P. New developments in fluid resuscitation. *Surg Clin North Am* 2007;87(1): 55–72.
3. Asensio JA, Murray J, Demetriades D, et al. Penetrating cardiac injuries: a prospective study of variables predicting outcomes. *J Am Coll Surg* 1998;186(1):24–34.
4. Baumann Kreuziger LM, Keenan JC, Morton CT, et al. Management of the bleeding patient receiving new oral anticoagulants: a role for prothrombin complex concentrates. *Biomed Res Int* 2014; 2014:583794.
5. Bickell WH, Wall MJ, Pepe PE, et al. Immediate versus delayed fluid resuscitation for hypotensive patients with penetrating torso injuries. *N Engl J Med* 1994;331(17):1105–1109.
6. Brohi K, Cohen MJ, Ganter MT, et al. Acute coagulopathy of trauma: hypoperfusion induces systemic anticoagulation and hyperfibrinolysis. *J Trauma* 2008;64(5):1211–1217.
7. Bruns B, Lindsey M, Rowe K, et al. Hemoglobin drops within minutes of injuries and predicts need for an intervention to stop hemorrhage. *J Trauma* 2007Aug;63(2):312–315.
8. Bunn F, Roberts I, Tasker R, et al. Hypertonic versus near isotonic crystalloid for fluid resuscitation in critically ill patients. *Cochrane Database Syst Rev* 2004;3:CD002045.
9. Burris D, Rhee P, Kaufmann C, et al. Controlled resuscitation for uncontrolled hemorrhagic shock. *J Trauma* 1999;46(2):216–223.
10. Carrico CJ, Canizaro PC, Shires GT. Fluid resuscitation following injury: rationale for the use of balanced salt solutions. *Crit Care Med* 1976;4(2):46–54.
11. Chernow B, Rainey TG, Lake CR. Endogenous and exogenous catecholamines in critical care medicine. *Crit Care Med* 1982;10:409.
12. Cogbill TH, Blintz M, Johnson JA, et al. Acute gastric dilatation after trauma. *J Trauma* 1987;27(10):1113–1117.
13. Cook RE, Keating JF, Gillespie I. The role of angiography in the management of haemorrhage from major fractures of the pelvis. *J Bone Joint Surg Br* 2002;84(2):178–182.
14. Cooper DJ, Walley KR, Wiggs BR, et al. Bicarbonate does not improve hemodynamics in critically ill patients who have lactic acidosis. *Ann Intern Med* 1990;112:492.
15. Cotton BA, Au BK, Nunez TC, et al. Predefined massive transfusion protocols are associated with a reduction in organ failure and postinjury complications. *J Trauma* 2009;66:41–49.
16. Cotton BA, Dossett LA, Au BK, et al. Room for (performance) improvement: provider-related factors associated with poor outcomes in massive transfusion. *J Trauma* 2009;67(5):1004–1012.
17. Davis JW, Kaups KL, Parks SN. Base deficit is superior to pH in evaluating clearance of acidosis after traumatic shock. *J Trauma* 1998 Jan;44(1):114–118.
18. Davis JW, Parks SN, Kaups KL, et al. Admission base deficit predicts transfusion requirements and risk of complications. *J Trauma* 1997Mar; 42(3):571–573.
19. Dent D, Alsabrook G, Erickson BA, et al. Blunt splenic injuries: high nonoperative management

rate can be achieved with selective embolization. *J Trauma* 2004;56(5):1063–1067.

20. Dutton RP, Mackenzie CF, Scalea TM. Hypotensive resuscitation during active hemorrhage: impact on in-hospital mortality. *J Trauma* 2002;52(6):1141–1146.

21. Eastridge BJ, Salinas J, McManus JG, et al. Hypotension begins at 110 mm Hg: redefining "hypo-tension" with data. *J Trauma* 2007Aug;63(2):291–299.

22. Fangio P, Asehnoune K, Edouard A, et al. Early embolization and vasopressor administration for management of life-threatening hemorrhage from pelvic fracture. *J Trauma* 2005;58(5):978–984; discussion 984.

23. Ferrara A, MacArthur JD, Wright HK, et al. Hypothermia and acidosis worsen coagulopathy in patients requiring massive transfusion. *Am J Surg* 1990;160(5):515.

24. Glover JL, Broadie TA. Intraoperative auto-transfusion. *World J Surg* 1987;11(1):60–64.

25. Granger DN. Role of xanthine oxidase and granulocytes in ischemia-reperfusion injury. *Heart Circ Physiol* 1988;255(6):H1269–H1275.

26. Greaves I, Porter KM, Revell MP. Fluid resuscitation in pre-hospital trauma care: a consensus view. *J R Coll Surg Edinb* 2002;47(2):451–457.

27. Hak DJ. The role of pelvic angiography in evaluation and management of pelvic trauma. *Orthop Clin North Am* 2004;35(4):439–443, v.

28. Hampton DA, Fabricant LJ, Differding J, et al. Prehospital intravenous fluid is associated with increased survival in trauma patients. *J Trauma* 2013;75(1):S9.

29. Harrigan C, Lucas CE, Ledgerwood AM, et al. Serial changes in primary hemostasis after massive transfusion. *Surgery* 1985;98(4):836–844.

30. Hoffman M, Monroe DM. Reversing targeted oral anticoagulants. *ASH Education Book* 2014;1:518–523.

31. Holcomb JB, del Junco DJ, Fox EE, et al. The prospective, observational, multicenter, major trauma transfusion (PROMMTT) study: comparative effectiveness of a time-varying treatment with competing risks. *JAMA Surg* 2013;148(2):127–136.

32. Holcomb JB, Wade CE, Michalek JE, et al. Increased plasma and platelet to red blood cell ratios improves outcome in 466 massively transfused civilian trauma patients. *Ann Surg* 2008Sep;248(3):447–458.

33. Hoyt DB. Fluid resuscitation: the target from an analysis of trauma systems and patient survival. *J Trauma* 2003;54(5):S31–S35.

34. Jurkovich GJ, Greiser WB, Luterman A, et al. Hypothermia in trauma victims: an ominous predictor of survival. *J Trauma* 1987;Sep 1;27(9):1019–1024.

35. Kaplan LJ, Kellum JA. Initial pH, base deficit, lactate, anion gap, strong ion difference, and strong ion gap predict outcome from major vascular injury. *Crit Care Med* 2004;32(5):1120–1124.

36. Karmy-Jones R, Nathens A, Jurkovich GJ, et al. Urgent and emergent thoracotomy for penetrating chest trauma. *J Trauma* 2004;56(3):664–668; discussion 668–669.

37. Knudson MM, Maull KI. Nonoperative management of solid organ injuries: past, present, and future. *Surg Clin North Am* 1999;79(6):1357–1371.

38. Kragh JF Jr, Walters TJ, Baer DG, et al. Survival with emergency tourniquet use to stop bleeding in major limb trauma. *Ann Surg* 2009Jan;249(1):1–7.

39. Kruse JA, Vyskocil JJ, Haupt MT. Intraosseous: a flexible option for the adult or child with delayed, difficult, or impossible conventional vascular access. *Crit Care Med* 2015Jun;22(50):728–729.

40. Lai A, Davidson N, Galloway SW, et al. Perioperative management of patients on new oral anticoagulants. *Br J Surg* 2014Jun;101 (7):742–749.

41. Lee PM, Lee C, Rattner P, et al. Intraosseous versus central venous catheter utilization and performance during inpatient medical emergencies. *Crit Care Med* 2015Jun;43(6):1233–1238.

42. Lewis P, Wright C. Saving the critically injured trauma patient: a retrospective analysis of 1000 uses of intraosseous access. *Emerg Med J* 2015Jun;32(6):463–467.

43. Lucas CE, Ledgerwood AM. Cardiovascular and renal response to hemorrhagic and septic shock. In: Clowes GHA Jr, ed. *Trauma, Sepsis and Shock: The Physiological Basis of Therapy.* New York, NY: Marcel Dekker; 1988:187–215.

44. Mandal AK, Sanusi M. Penetrating chest wounds: 24 years' experience. *World J Surg* 2001;25(9):1145–1149.

45. Martin MJ, Fitz Sullivan E, Salim A, et al. Discordance between lactate and base deficit in the surgical intensive care unit: which one do you trust? *Am J Surg* 2006;191(5):625–630.

46. McManus J, Yershov AL, Ludwig D, et al. Radial pulse character relationships to systolic blood pressure and trauma outcomes. *Prehosp Emerg Care* 2005;9(4):423–428.

47. Mizushima Y, Tohira H, Mizobata Y, et al. Fluid resuscitation of trauma patients: how fast is the optimal rate? *Am J Emerg Med* 2005;23(7):833–837.

48. Novak L, Shackford SR, Bourguignon P, et al. Comparison of standard and alternative prehospital resuscitation in uncontrolled hemorrhagic shock and head injury. *J Trauma* 1999;47(5):834–844.

49. Nunez TC, Young PP, Holcomb JB, et al. Creation, implementation, and maturation of a massive transfusion protocol for the exsanguinating trauma patient. *J Trauma* 2010Jun;68(6):1498–1505.

50. Peck KR, Altieri M. Intraosseous infusions: an old technique with modern applications. *Pediatr Nurs* 1988;14(4):296.

51. Revell M, Greaves I, Porter K. Endpoints for fluid resuscitation in hemorrhagic shock. *J Trauma* 2003;54(5):S63–S67.

52. Riskin DJ, Tsai TC, Riskin L, et al. Massive transfusion protocols: the role of aggressive resuscitation versus product ratio in mortality reduction. *J Am Coll Surg* 2009;209(2):198–205.

53. Roback JD, Caldwell S, Carson J, et al. Evidence-based practice guidelines for plasma transfusion. *Transfusion* 2010 Jun;50(6):1227–1239.

54. Rohrer MJ, Natale AM. Effect of hypothermia on the coagulation cascade. *Crit Care Med* 1992;20(10):1402–1405.

55. Rotondo MF, Schwab CW, McGonigal MD, et al. "Damage control": an approach for improved survival in exsanguinating penetrating abdominal injury. *J Trauma* 1993;35(3):375–382.

56. Sarnoff SJ. Myocardial contractility as described by ventricular function curves: observations on Starling's law of the heart. *Physiol Rev* 1955;35(1):107–122.

57. Scalea TM, Hartnett RW, Duncan AO, et al. Central venous oxygen saturation: a useful clinical tool in trauma patients. *J Trauma* 1990;30(12): 1539–1543.

58. Shrestha B, Holcomb JB, Camp EA, et al. Damage-control resuscitation increases successful nonoperative management rates and survival after severe blunt liver injury. *J Trauma* 2015;78(2):336–341.

59. Snyder D, Tsou A, Schoelles K. Efficacy of prehospital application of tourniquets and hemostatic dressings to control traumatic external hemorrhage. Washington, DC: National Highway Traffic Safety Administration. 2014, 145.

60. Thourani VH, Feliciano DV, Cooper WA, et al. Penetrating cardiac trauma at an urban trauma center: a 22-year perspective. *Am Surg* 1999;65(9):811–816.

61. Tyburski JG, Astra L, Wilson RF, et al. Factors affecting prognosis with penetrating wounds of the heart. *J Trauma* 2000;48(4):587–590; discussion 590–591.

62. Williams JF, Seneff MG, Friedman BC, et al. Use of femoral venous catheters in critically ill adults: prospective study. *Crit Care Med* 1991;19:550–553.

63. York J, Arrilaga A, Graham R, et al. Fluid resuscitation of patients with multiple injuries and severe closed head injury: experience with an aggressive fluid resuscitation strategy. *J Trauma* 2000;48(3):376–379.

64. Mutschler A, Nienaber U, Brockamp T, et al. A critical reappraisal of the ATLS classification of hypovolaemic shock: does it really reflect clinical reality? *Resuscitation* 2013,84:309–313.

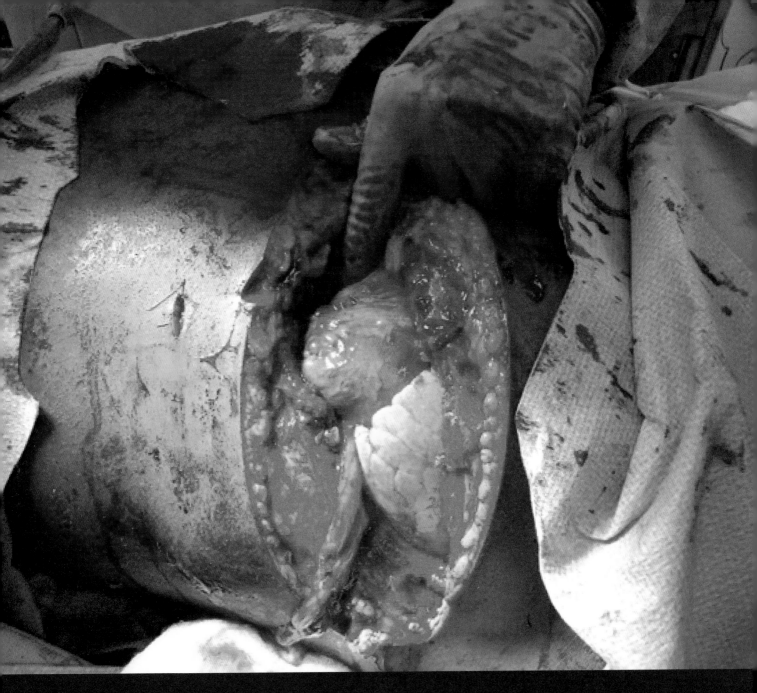

4 THORACIC TRAUMA

Thoracic injury is common in polytrauma patients and can be life-threatening, especially if not promptly identified and treated during the primary survey.

CHAPTER 4 OUTLINE

OBJECTIVES

After reading this chapter and comprehending the knowledge components of the ATLS provider course, you will be able to:

1. Identify and describe treatment of the following life-threatening injuries during the primary survey: airway obstruction, tracheobronchial tree injury, tension pneumothorax, open pneumothorax, massive hemothorax, and cardiac tamponade.

2. Identify and describe treatment of the following potentially life-threatening injuries during the secondary survey: simple pneumothorax, hemothorax, flail chest, pulmonary contusion, blunt cardiac injury, traumatic aortic disruption, traumatic diaphragmatic injury, and blunt esophageal rupture.

3. Describe the significance and treatment of subcutaneous emphysema, thoracic crush injuries, and sternal, rib, and clavicular fractures.

Thoracic trauma is a significant cause of mortality; in fact, many patients with thoracic trauma die after reaching the hospital. However, many of these deaths can be prevented with prompt diagnosis and treatment. Less than 10% of blunt chest injuries and only 15% to 30% of penetrating chest injuries require operative intervention. Most patients who sustain thoracic trauma can be treated by technical procedures within the capabilities of clinicians trained in ATLS. Many of the principles outlined in this chapter also apply to iatrogenic thoracic injuries, such as hemothorax or pneumothorax from central line placement and esophageal injury during endoscopy.

The physiologic consequences of thoracic trauma are hypoxia, hypercarbia, and acidosis. Contusion, hematoma, and alveolar collapse, or changes in intrathoracic pressure relationships (e.g., tension pneumothorax and open pneumothorax) cause hypoxia and lead to metabolic acidosis. Hypercarbia causes respiratory acidosis and most often follows inadequate ventilation caused by changes in intrathoracic pressure relationships and depressed level of consciousness.

Initial assessment and treatment of patients with thoracic trauma consists of the primary survey with resuscitation of vital functions, detailed secondary survey, and definitive care. Because hypoxia is the most serious consequence of chest injury, the goal of early intervention is to prevent or correct hypoxia.

Injuries that are an immediate threat to life are treated as quickly and simply as possible. Most life-threatening thoracic injuries can be treated with airway control or decompression of the chest with a needle, finger, or tube. The secondary survey is influenced by the history of the injury and a high index of suspicion for specific injuries.

PRIMARY SURVEY: LIFE-THREATENING INJURIES

As in all trauma patients, the primary survey of patients with thoracic injuries begins with the airway, followed by breathing and then circulation. Major problems should be corrected as they are identified.

AIRWAY PROBLEMS

It is critical to recognize and address major injuries affecting the airway during the primary survey.

Airway Obstruction

Airway obstruction results from swelling, bleeding, or vomitus that is aspirated into the airway, interfering with gas exchange. Several injury mechanisms can produce this type of problem. Laryngeal injury can accompany major thoracic trauma or result from a direct blow to the neck or a shoulder restraint that is misplaced across the neck. Posterior dislocation of the clavicular head occasionally leads to airway obstruction. Alternatively, penetrating trauma involving the neck or chest can result in injury and bleeding, which produces obstruction. Although the clinical presentation is occasionally subtle, acute airway obstruction from laryngeal trauma is a life-threatening injury. (See *Chapter 2: Airway and Ventilatory Management*.)

During the primary survey, look for evidence of air hunger, such as intercostal and supraclavicular muscle retractions. Inspect the oropharynx for foreign body obstruction. Listen for air movement at the patient's nose, mouth, and lung fields. Listen for evidence of partial upper airway obstruction (stridor) or a marked change in the expected voice quality in patients who are able to speak. Feel for crepitus over the anterior neck.

Patients with airway obstruction may be treated with clearance of the blood or vomitus from the airway by suctioning. This maneuver is frequently only temporizing, and placement of a definitive airway is necessary. Palpate for a defect in the region of the sternoclavicular joint. Reduce a posterior dislocation or fracture of the clavicle by extending the patient's shoulders or grasping the clavicle with a penetrating towel clamp, which may alleviate the obstruction. The reduction is typically stable when the patient remains in the supine position.

Tracheobronchial Tree Injury

Injury to the trachea or a major bronchus is an unusual but potentially fatal condition. The majority of tracheobronchial tree injuries occur within 1 inch (2.54 cm) of the carina. These injuries can be severe, and the majority of patients die at the scene. Those who reach the hospital alive have a high mortality rate from associated injuries, inadequate airway, or development of a tension pneumothorax or tension pneumopericardium.

Rapid deceleration following blunt trauma produces injury where a point of attachment meets an area of mobility. Blast injuries commonly produce severe injury at air-fluid interfaces. Penetrating trauma produces injury through direct laceration, tearing, or transfer of kinetic injury with cavitation. Intubation can potentially cause or worsen an injury to the trachea or proximal bronchi.

Patients typically present with hemoptysis, cervical subcutaneous emphysema, tension pneumothorax, and/or cyanosis. Incomplete expansion of the lung and continued large air leak after placement of a chest tube suggests a tracheobronchial injury, and placement of more than one chest tube may be necessary to overcome the significant air leak. (See *Chest Tube animation on MyATLS mobile app.*) Bronchoscopy confirms the diagnosis. If tracheobronchial injury is suspected, obtain immediate surgical consultation.

Immediate treatment may require placement of a definitive airway. Intubation of patients with tracheobronchial injuries is frequently difficult because of anatomic distortion from paratracheal hematoma, associated oropharyngeal injuries, and/or the tracheobronchial injury itself. Advanced airway skills, such as fiber-optically assisted endotracheal tube placement past the tear site or selective intubation of the unaffected bronchus, may be required. For such patients, immediate operative intervention is indicated. In more stable patients, operative treatment of tracheobronchial injuries may be delayed until the acute inflammation and edema resolve.

BREATHING PROBLEMS

Completely expose the patient's chest and neck to allow for assessment of neck veins and breathing. This may require temporarily releasing the front of the cervical collar; in this case, actively restrict cervical motion by holding the patient's head while the collar is loosened. Look at the chest wall to assess movement and determine whether it is equal. Assess the adequacy of respirations. Listen to the chest to evaluate for equal breath sounds and identify any extra sounds that may indicate effusion or contusion. Palpate to determine if there are areas of tenderness, crepitus, or defects.

Significant, yet often subtle, signs of chest injury and/or hypoxia include increased respiratory rate and changes in the patient's breathing pattern, which are often manifested by progressively shallow respirations. Recall that cyanosis is a late sign of hypoxia in trauma patients and can be difficult to perceive in darkly pigmented skin; its absence does not necessarily indicate adequate tissue oxygenation or an adequate airway.

Tension pneumothorax, open pneumothorax (sucking chest wound), and massive hemothorax are the major thoracic injuries that affect breathing. It is imperative for clinicians to recognize and manage these injuries during the primary survey.

Tension Pneumothorax

Tension pneumothorax develops when a "one-way valve" air leak occurs from the lung or through the chest wall (■ FIGURE 4-1). Air is forced into the pleural space with no means of escape, eventually collapsing the affected lung. The mediastinum is displaced to the opposite side, decreasing venous return and compressing the opposite lung. Shock (often classified as obstructive

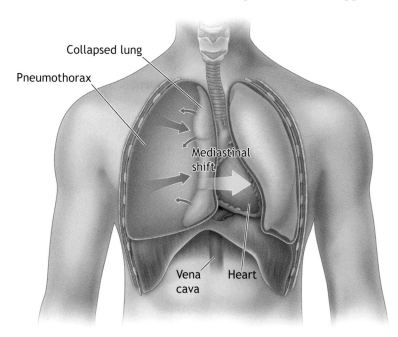

■ FIGURE 4-1 **Tension Pneumothorax.** A "one-way valve" air leak occurs from the lung or through the chest wall, and air is forced into the thoracic cavity, eventually collapsing the affected lung.

shock) results from marked decrease in venous return, causing a reduction in cardiac output.

The most common cause of tension pneumothorax is mechanical positive-pressure ventilation in patients with visceral pleural injury. Tension pneumothorax also can complicate a simple pneumothorax following penetrating or blunt chest trauma in which a parenchymal lung injury fails to seal, or after attempted subclavian or internal jugular venous catheter insertion. Occasionally, traumatic defects in the chest wall cause a tension pneumothorax when occlusive dressings are secured on four sides or the defect itself constitutes a flap-valve mechanism. Rarely, tension pneumothorax occurs from markedly displaced thoracic spine fractures. Tension pneumothorax is a clinical diagnosis reflecting air under pressure in the affected pleural space. Do not delay treatment to obtain radiologic confirmation.

Patients who are spontaneously breathing often manifest extreme tachypnea and air hunger, whereas patients who are mechanically ventilated manifest hemodynamic collapse. Tension pneumothorax is characterized by some or all of the following signs and symptoms:

- Chest pain

- Air hunger

- Tachypnea

- Respiratory distress

- Tachycardia

- Hypotension

- Tracheal deviation away from the side of the injury

- Unilateral absence of breath sounds

- Elevated hemithorax without respiratory movement

- Neck vein distention

- Cyanosis (late manifestation)

Perform a breathing assessment, as described above. A hyperresonant note on percussion, deviated trachea, distended neck veins, and absent breath sounds are signs of tension pneumothorax. Arterial saturation should be assessed using a pulse oximeter and will be decreased when tension pneumothorax is present. When ultrasound is available, tension pneumothorax can be diagnosed using an extended FAST (eFAST) examination.

Tension pneumothorax requires immediate decompression and may be managed initially by rapidly inserting a large over-the-needle catheter into the

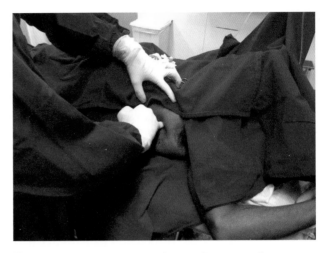

■ **FIGURE 4-2 Finger Decompression.** Tension pneumothorax can be managed initially by rapidly applying the finger decompression technique.

pleural space. Due to the variable thickness of the chest wall, kinking of the catheter, and other technical or anatomic complications, needle decompression may not be successful. In this case, finger thoracostomy is an alternative approach (■ FIGURE 4-2; also see *Appendix G: Breathing Skills*.)

Chest wall thickness influences the likelihood of success with needle decompression. Evidence suggests that a 5-cm over-the-needle catheter will reach the pleural space >50% of the time, whereas an 8-cm over-the-needle catheter will reach the pleural space >90% of the time. Studies have also demonstrated that over-the-needle catheter placement in the field into the anterior chest wall by paramedics was too medial in 44% of patients. Recent evidence supports placing the large, over-the-needle catheter at the fifth interspace, slightly anterior to the midaxillary line. However, even with an over-the-needle catheter of the appropriate size, the maneuver will not always be successful.

Successful needle decompression converts tension pneumothorax to a simple pneumothorax. However, there is a possibility of subsequent pneumothorax as a result of the maneuver, so continual reassessment of the patient is necessary. Tube thoracostomy is mandatory after needle or finger decompression of the chest.

Open Pneumothorax

Large injuries to the chest wall that remain open can result in an open pneumothorax, also known as a sucking chest wound (■ FIGURE 4-3). Equilibration between intrathoracic pressure and atmospheric pressure is immediate. Because air tends to follow the path of least resistance, when the opening in the chest wall is approximately two-thirds the diameter of the trachea

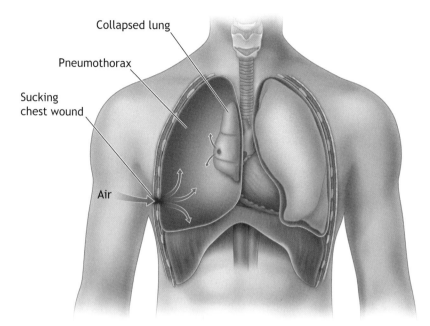

Collapsed lung

Pneumothorax

Sucking
chest wound

Air

■ FIGURE 4-3 Open Pneumothorax. Large defects of the chest wall that remain open can result in an open pneumothorax, or sucking chest wound.

or greater, air passes preferentially through the chest wall defect with each inspiration. Effective ventilation is thereby impaired, leading to hypoxia and hypercarbia.

Open pneumothorax is commonly found and treated at the scene by prehospital personnel. The clinical signs and symptoms are pain, difficulty breathing, tachypnea, decreased breath sounds on the affected side, and noisy movement of air through the chest wall injury.

For initial management of an open pneumothorax, promptly close the defect with a sterile dressing large enough to overlap the wound's edges. Any occlusive dressing (e.g. plastic wrap or petrolatum gauze) may be used as temporary measure to enable rapid assessment to continue. Tape it securely on *only* three sides to provide a flutter-valve effect (■ FIGURE 4-4). As the patient breathes in, the dressing occludes the wound, preventing air from entering. During exhalation, the open end of the dressing allows air to escape from the pleural space. Taping all four edges of the dressing can cause air to accumulate in the thoracic cavity, resulting in a tension pneumothorax unless a chest tube is in place. Place a chest tube remote from the wound as soon as possible. Subsequent definitive surgical closure of the wound is frequently required. (See *Appendix G: Breathing Skills*.)

Massive Hemothorax

The accumulation of >1500 ml of blood in one side of the chest with a massive hemothorax can significantly

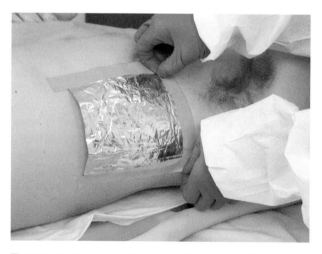

■ FIGURE 4-4 Dressing for Treatment of Open Pneumothorax. Promptly close the defect with a sterile occlusive dressing that is large enough to overlap the wound's edges. Tape it securely on three sides to provide a flutter-valve effect.

PITFALL	PREVENTION
Tension pneumothorax develops after placing dressing over open chest wound.	• Ensure the occlusive dressing is secured only on three sides. • Treat pneumothorax with placement of chest tube through intact skin.

compromise respiratory efforts by compressing the lung and preventing adequate oxygenation and ventilation. Insert a chest tube to improve ventilation and oxygenation, request emergent surgical consultation, and begin appropriate resuscitation. Massive acute accumulation of blood produces hypotension and shock and will be discussed further in the section below.

■ TABLE 4-1 outlines the different presentations of tension pneumothorax and massive hemothorax.

CIRCULATION PROBLEMS

Major thoracic injuries that affect circulation and should be recognized and addressed during the primary survey are massive hemothorax, cardiac tamponade, and traumatic circulatory arrest.

Pulseless electrical activity (PEA) is manifested by an electrocardiogram (ECG) that shows a rhythm while the patient has no identifiable pulse. This dysrhythmia can be present with cardiac tamponade, tension pneumothorax, or profound hypovolemia. Severe blunt injury can result in blunt rupture of the atria or the ventricles, and the only manifestation may be PEA arrest. Other causes of PEA arrest include hypovolemia, hypoxia, hydrogen ion (acidosis), hypokalemia/ hyperkalemia, hypoglycemia, hypothermia, toxins, cardiac tamponade, tension pneumothorax, and thrombosis (coronary or pulmonary).

Inspect the skin for mottling, cyanosis, and pallor. Neck veins should be assessed for distention, although they may not be distended in patients with concomitant hypovolemia. Listen for the regularity and quality of the heartbeat. Assess a central pulse for quality, rate, and regularity. In patients with hypovolemia, the distal pulses may be absent because of volume depletion. Palpate the skin to assess its temperature and determine whether it is dry or sweaty.

Measure blood pressure and pulse pressure, and monitor the patient with electrocardiography and pulse oximetry. Patients with blunt chest injury are at risk for myocardial dysfunction, which is increased by the presence of hypoxia and acidosis. Dysrhythmias should be managed according to standard protocols.

Massive Hemothorax

Massive hemothorax results from the rapid accumulation of more than 1500 mL of blood or one-third or more of the patient's blood volume in the chest cavity (■ FIGURE 4-5). It is most commonly caused by a penetrating wound that disrupts the systemic or hilar vessels, although massive hemothorax can also result from blunt trauma.

In patients with massive hemothorax, the neck veins may be flat due to severe hypovolemia, or they may be distended if there is an associated tension pneumothorax. Rarely will the mechanical effects of massive intrathoracic blood shift the mediastinum enough to cause distended neck veins. A massive hemothorax is suggested when shock is associated with the absence of breath sounds or dullness to percussion on one side of the chest.

Massive hemothorax is initially managed by simultaneously restoring blood volume and decompressing the chest cavity. Establish large-caliber intravenous lines, infuse crystalloid, and begin transfusion of uncrossmatched or type-specific blood as soon as possible. When appropriate, blood from the chest tube can be collected in a device suitable for autotransfusion. A single chest tube (28-32 French) is inserted, usually at the fifth intercostal space, just anterior to the midaxillary line, and rapid restoration of volume continues as decompression of the chest cavity is completed. The immediate return of 1500 mL or more of blood generally indicates the need for urgent thoracotomy.

TABLE 4-I DIFFERENTIATING TENSION PNEUMOTHORAX AND MASSIVE HEMOTHORAX

CONDITION	PHYSICAL SIGNS				
	BREATH SOUNDS	PERCUSSION	TRACHEAL POSITION	NECK VEINS	CHEST MOVEMENT
Tension pneumothorax	Decreased or absent	Hyperresonant	Deviated away	Distended	Expanded immobile
Massive hemothorax	Decreased	Dull	Midline	Collapsed	Mobile

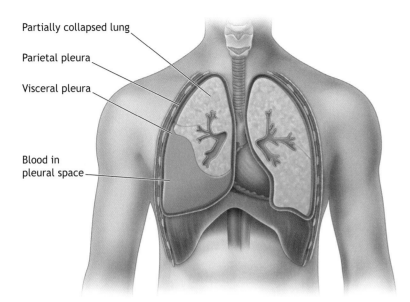

Partially collapsed lung

Parietal pleura

Visceral pleura

Blood in
pleural space

■ FIGURE 4-5 Massive Hemothorax. This condition results from the rapid accumulation of more than 1500 mL of blood or one-third or more of the patient's blood volume in the chest cavity.

Patients who have an initial output of less than 1500 mL of fluid, but continue to bleed, may also require thoracotomy. This decision is based on the rate of continuing blood loss (200 mL/hr for 2 to 4 hours), as well as the patient's physiologic status and whether the chest is completely evacuated of blood. Again, the persistent need for blood transfusion is an indication for thoracotomy. During patient resuscitation, the volume of blood initially drained from the chest tube and the rate of continuing blood loss must be factored into the resuscitation required. Color of the blood (indicating an arterial or venous source) is a poor indicator of the necessity for thoracotomy.

Penetrating anterior chest wounds medial to the nipple line and posterior wounds medial to the scapula (the mediastinal "box") should alert the practitioner to the possible need for thoracotomy because of potential damage to the great vessels, hilar structures, and the heart, with the associated potential for cardiac tamponade. Do not perform thoracotomy unless a surgeon, qualified by training and experience, is present.

Cardiac Tamponade

Cardiac tamponade is compression of the heart by an accumulation of fluid in the pericardial sac. This results in decreased cardiac output due to decreased inflow to the heart. The human pericardial sac is a fixed fibrous structure, and a relatively small amount of blood can restrict cardiac activity and interfere with cardiac filling. Cardiac tamponade most commonly results from penetrating injuries, although blunt injury also can cause the pericardium to fill with

blood from the heart, great vessels, or epicardial vessels (■ FIGURE 4-6).

Cardiac tamponade can develop slowly, allowing for a less urgent evaluation, or rapidly, requiring rapid diagnosis and treatment. The classic clinical triad of muffled heart sounds, hypotension, and distended veins is not uniformly present with cardiac tamponade. Muffled heart tones are difficult to assess in the noisy resuscitation room, and distended neck veins may be absent due to hypovolemia. Kussmaul's sign (i.e., a rise in venous pressure with inspiration when breathing spontaneously) is a true paradoxical venous pressure abnormality that is associated with tamponade. PEA is suggestive of cardiac tamponade but can have other causes, as explained earlier.

Tension pneumothorax, particularly on the left side, can mimic cardiac tamponade. Because of the similarity in their signs, tension pneumothorax can initially be confused with cardiac tamponade. The presence of hyperresonance on percussion indicates tension pneumothorax, whereas the presence of bilateral breath sounds indicates cardiac tamponade.

Focused assessment with sonography for trauma (FAST) is a rapid and accurate method of imaging the heart and pericardium that can effectively identify cardiac tamponade.

FAST is 90–95% accurate in identifying the presence of pericardial fluid for the experienced operator (see *FAST video on MyATLS mobile app*). Concomitant hemothorax may account for both false positive and false negative exams. Remember that tamponade can develop at any time during the resuscitation phase, and repeat FAST exams may be necessary. Providers experienced in ultrasonography may also be able to assess myocardial dysfunction and ventricular filling.

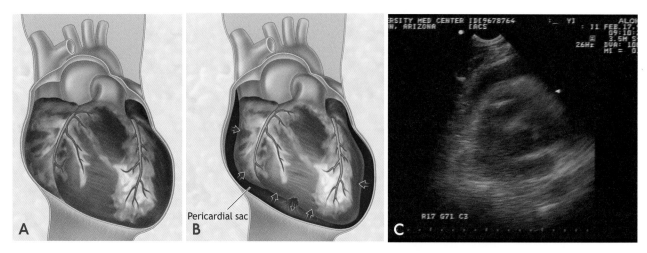

■ FIGURE 4-6 Cardiac Tamponade. A. Normal heart. B. Cardiac tamponade can result from penetrating or blunt injuries that cause the pericardium to fill with blood from the heart, great vessels, or pericardial vessels. C. Ultrasound image showing cardiac tamponade.

Additional methods of diagnosing cardiac tamponade include echocardiography and/or pericardial window, which may be particularly useful when FAST is unavailable or equivocal.

When pericardial fluid or tamponade is diagnosed, emergency thoracotomy or sternotomy should be performed by a qualified surgeon as soon as possible. Administration of intravenous fluid will raise the patient's venous pressure and improve cardiac output transiently while preparations are made for surgery. If surgical intervention is not possible, pericardiocentesis can be therapeutic, but it does not constitute definitive treatment for cardiac tamponade.

When subxiphoid pericardiocentesis is used as a temporizing maneuver, the use of a large, over-the-needle catheter or the Seldinger technique for insertion of a flexible catheter is ideal, but the urgent priority is to aspirate blood from the pericardial sac. Because complications are common with blind insertion techniques, pericardiocentesis should represent a lifesaving measure of last resort in a setting where no qualified surgeon is available to perform a thoracotomy or sternotomy. Ultrasound guidance can facilitate accurate insertion of the large, over-the-needle catheter into the pericardial space.

Traumatic Circulatory Arrest

Trauma patients who are unconscious and have no pulse, including PEA (as observed in extreme hypovolemia), ventricular fibrillation, and asystole (true cardiac arrest) are considered to be in circulatory arrest. Causes of traumatic circulatory arrest include severe hypoxia, tension pneumothorax, profound hypovolemia, cardiac tamponade, cardiac herniation, and severe myocardial contusion. An important con-

sideration is that a cardiac event may have preceded the traumatic event.

Circulatory arrest is diagnosed according to clinical findings (unconscious and no pulse) and requires immediate action. Every second counts, and there should be no delay for ECG monitoring or echocardiography. Recent evidence shows that some patients in traumatic circulatory arrest can survive (1.9%) if closed cardiopulmonary resuscitation (CPR) and appropriate resuscitation are performed. In centers proficient with resuscitative thoracotomy, 10% survival and higher has been reported with circulatory arrest following penetrating and blunt trauma.

Start closed CPR simultaneously with ABC management. Secure a definitive airway with orotracheal intubation (without rapid sequence induction). Administer mechanical ventilation with 100% oxygen. To alleviate a potential tension pneumothorax, perform bilateral finger or tube thoracostomies. No local anesthesia is necessary, as the patient is unconscious. Continuously monitor ECG and oxygen saturation, and begin rapid fluid resuscitation through large-bore IV lines or intraosseous needles. Administer epinephrine (1 mg) and, if ventricular fibrillation is present, treat it according to Advanced Cardiac Life Support (ACLS) protocols.

According to local policy and the availability of a surgical team skilled in repair of such injuries, a resuscitative thoracotomy may be required if there is no return of spontaneous circulation (ROSC). If no surgeon is available to perform the thoracotomy and cardiac tamponade has been diagnosed or is highly suspected, a decompressive needle pericardiocentesis may be performed, preferably under ultrasound guidance.

■ FIGURE 4-7 presents an algorithm for management of traumatic circulatory arrest.

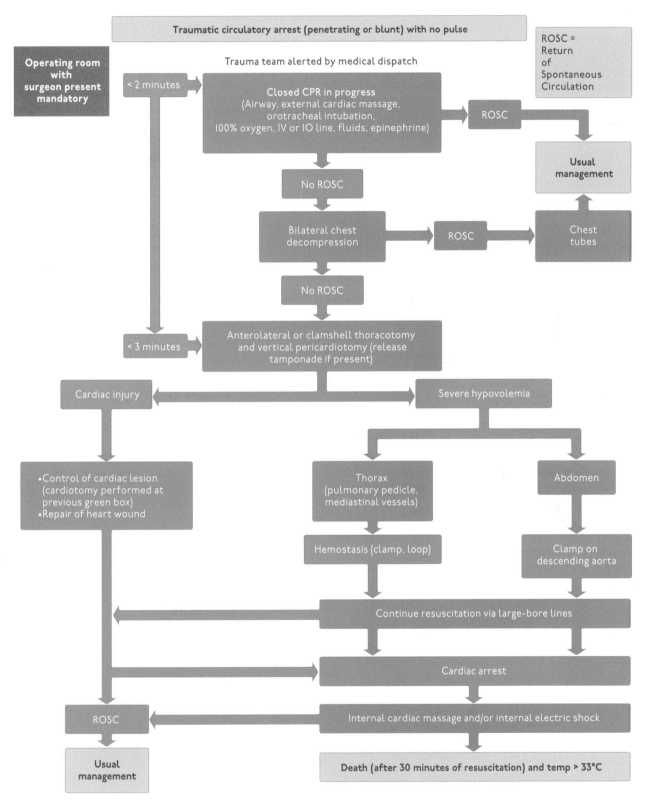

■ **FIGURE 4-7 Algorithm for management of traumatic circulatory arrest.** ECM = external cardiac massage; OTI = orotracheal intubation; IVL = intravenous line; IOL = intraosseous line.

SECONDARY SURVEY

The secondary survey of patients with thoracic trauma involves further, in-depth physical examination, ongoing ECG and pulse oximetry monitoring, arterial blood gas (ABG) measurements, upright chest x-ray in patients without suspected spinal column instability, and chest computed tomography (CT) scan in selected patients with suspected aortic or spinal injury. In addition to lung expansion and the presence of fluid, the chest film should be reviewed for widening of the mediastinum, a shift of the midline, and loss of anatomic detail. Multiple rib fractures and fractures of the first or second rib(s) suggest that a significant force was delivered to the chest and underlying tissues. Extended FAST (eFAST) has been used to detect both pneumothoraces and hemothoraces. However, other potentially life-threatening injuries are not well visualized on ultrasound, making the chest radiograph a necessary part of any evaluation after traumatic injury (see *Appendix G: Breathing Skills*).

POTENTIALLY LIFE-THREATENING INJURIES

Unlike immediately life-threatening conditions that are recognized during the primary survey, other potentially lethal injuries are often not obvious on initial physical examination. Diagnosis requires a high index of suspicion and appropriate use of adjunctive studies. If overlooked, these injuries can lead to increased complications or death.

The following eight potentially lethal injuries should be identified and managed during the secondary survey:

- Simple pneumothorax
- Hemothorax
- Flail chest
- Pulmonary contusion
- Blunt cardiac injury
- Traumatic aortic disruption
- Traumatic diaphragmatic injury
- Blunt esophageal rupture

Simple Pneumothorax

Pneumothorax results from air entering the potential space between the visceral and parietal pleura (■ FIGURE 4-8). The thorax is typically completely filled by the lungs, which are held to the chest wall by surface tension between the pleural surfaces. Air in the pleural space disrupts the cohesive forces between the visceral and parietal pleura, allowing the lung to collapse. A ventilation-perfusion defect occurs because the blood that perfuses the nonventilated area is not oxygenated.

Both penetrating and nonpenetrating trauma can cause this injury. Lung laceration with air leakage is the most common cause of pneumothorax from blunt trauma.

Perform a comprehensive physical examination of the chest, including inspection for bruising, lacerations, and contusions. Assess movement of the chest wall and assess and compare breath sounds bilaterally. When a pneumothorax is present, breath sounds are often decreased on the affected side. Percussion may demonstrate hyperresonance, although

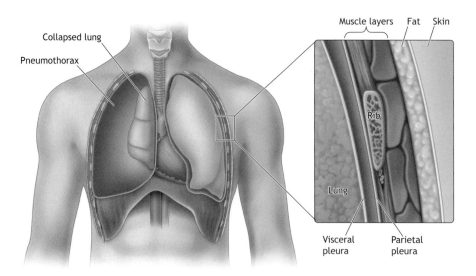

■ FIGURE 4-8 Simple Pneumothorax. Pneumothorax results from air entering the potential space between the visceral and parietal pleura.

this finding is extremely difficult to hear in a noisy resuscitation bay.

An upright expiratory chest x-ray aids in the diagnosis. Patients with blunt polytrauma are not candidates for this evaluation, although patients with penetrating chest trauma may be.

Any pneumothorax is best treated with a chest tube placed in the fifth intercostal space, just anterior to the midaxillary line. Observation and aspiration of a small, asymptomatic pneumothorax may be appropriate, but a qualified doctor should make this treatment decision. After inserting a chest tube and connecting it to an underwater seal apparatus with or without suction, a chest x-ray examination is done to confirm appropriate placement and reexpansion of the lung. Ideally, a patient with a known pneumothorax should not undergo general anesthesia or receive positive pressure ventilation without having a chest tube inserted. In selected circumstances, such as when a "subclinical pneumothorax" (i.e., occult) has been diagnosed, the trauma team may decide to carefully observe the patient for signs that the pneumothorax is expanding. The safest approach is to place a chest tube before a tension pneumothorax can develop.

A patient with a pneumothorax should also undergo chest decompression before transport via air ambulance due to the potential risk of expansion of the pneumothorax at altitude, even in a pressurized cabin.

Hemothorax

A hemothorax is a type of pleural effusion in which blood (<1500 mL) accumulates in the pleural cavity. The primary cause of hemothorax is laceration of the lung, great vessels, an intercostal vessel, or an internal mammary artery from penetrating or blunt trauma. Thoracic spine fractures may also be associated with a hemothorax. Bleeding is usually self-limited and does not require operative intervention.

Expose the chest and cervical areas, and observe the movement of the chest wall. Look for any penetrating chest wall injuries, including the posterior thorax. Assess and compare breath sounds in both hemithoraces. Typically, dullness to percussion is heard on the affected side. Obtain a chest x-ray with the patient in the supine position. A small amount of blood will be identified as a homogeneous opacity on the affected side.

An acute hemothorax that is large enough to appear on a chest x-ray may be treated with a 28-32 French chest tube. The chest tube evacuates blood, reduces the risk of a clotted hemothorax, and, allows for continuous monitoring of blood loss.

Evacuation of blood and fluid also enables clinicians to more completely assess the patient for potential diaphragmatic injury.

Although many factors are involved in the decision to operate on a patient with a hemothorax, the patient's physiologic status and the volume of blood drainage from the chest tube are important considerations. Greater than 1500 mL of blood obtained immediately through the chest tube indicates a massive hemothorax that may require operative intervention. Also, if drainage of more than 200 mL/hr for 2 to 4 hours occurs, or if blood transfusion is required, the trauma team should consider operative exploration. The ultimate decision for operative intervention is based on the patient's hemodynamic status.

PITFALL	PREVENTION
Retained hemothorax	• Ensure appropriate placement of chest tube. • Obtain surgical consultation.

Flail Chest and Pulmonary Contusion

A flail chest occurs when a segment of the chest wall does not have bony continuity with the rest of the thoracic cage. This condition usually results from trauma associated with multiple rib fractures (i.e., two or more adjacent ribs fractured in two or more places), although it can also occur when there is a costochondral separation of a single rib from the thorax (■ FIGURE 4-9).

A pulmonary contusion is a bruise of the lung, caused by thoracic trauma. Blood and other fluids accumulate in the lung tissue, interfering with ventilation and potentially leading to hypoxia. Pulmonary contusion can occur without rib fractures or flail chest, particularly in young patients without completely ossified ribs. Children have far more compliant chest walls than adults and may suffer contusions and other internal chest injury without overlying rib fractures.

In adults, pulmonary contusion is most often encountered with concomitant rib fractures, and it is the most common potentially lethal chest injury. The resultant respiratory failure can be subtle, developing over time rather than occurring instantaneously. Limited ventilatory reserve may predispose older adult patients to early respiratory failure.

A flail segment may not be apparent by physical examination, particularly soon after injury. Decreased

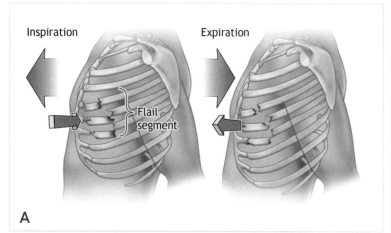

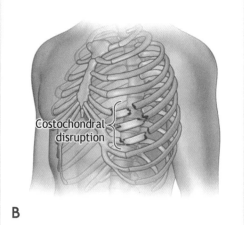

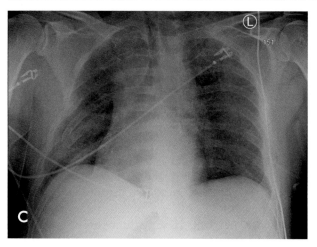

■ **FIGURE 4-9 Flail Chest.** The presence of a flail chest segment results in disruption of normal chest wall movement. **A.** Flail chest from multiple rib fractures. **B.** Flail chest from costochondral separation. **C.** Plain x-ray showing thoracic trauma associated with multiple rib fractures. A segment of the chest wall does not have bony continuity with the rest of the thoracic cage.

respiratory effort, combined with contusion and atelectasis, may limit movement of the chest wall. Thick chest wall musculature may also limit visualization of abnormal chest movement. If the injury results in significant underlying pulmonary contusion, serious hypoxia can result. Restricted chest wall movement associated with pain and underlying lung contusion can lead to respiratory failure.

Observation of abnormal respiratory motion and palpation of crepitus from rib or cartilage fractures can aid the diagnosis. A chest x-ray may suggest multiple rib fractures but may not show costochondral separation.

Initial treatment of flail chest and pulmonary contusion includes administration of humidified oxygen, adequate ventilation, and cautious fluid resuscitation. In the absence of systemic hypotension, the administration of crystalloid intravenous solutions should be carefully controlled to prevent volume overload, which can further compromise the patient's respiratory status.

Patients with significant hypoxia (i.e., $PaO_2 < 60$ mm Hg [8.6 kPa] or $SaO_2 < 90\%$) on room air may require intubation and ventilation within the first hour after injury. Associated medical conditions, such as chronic obstructive pulmonary disease and renal failure, increase the likelihood of requiring early intubation and mechanical ventilation.

Definitive treatment of flail chest and pulmonary contusion involves ensuring adequate oxygenation, administering fluids judiciously, and providing analgesia to improve ventilation. The plan for definitive management may change with time and patient response, warranting careful monitoring and reevaluation of the patient.

Analgesia can be achieved with intravenous narcotics or local anesthetic administration, which avoids the potential respiratory depression common with systemic narcotics. Options for administering local anesthetics include intermittent intercostal nerve block(s) and transcutaneous intrapleural, extrapleural, or epidural anesthesia. When used properly, local anesthetic agents can provide excellent analgesia and prevent the need for intubation. However, prevention of hypoxia is of paramount importance for trauma patients, and a short period of intubation and ventilation may be necessary until clinicians have diagnosed the entire injury pattern. Careful assessment of the patient's respiratory rate, arterial oxygen saturation, and work of breathing

PITFALL	PREVENTION
Underestimating effect of pulmonary contusion	• Monitor arterial saturation. • Monitor end-tidal CO_2. • Correlate with ABG measurements. • Monitor breathing. • Intubate when necessary. • Provide crystalloid fluid judiciously.

will indicate appropriate timing for intubation and ventilation, should it be necessary.

Blunt Cardiac Injury

Recent literature review demonstrates 50% of blunt cardiac injury (BCI) was related to motor vehicle crash (MVC), followed by pedestrian struck by vehicles, motorcycle crashes, and then falls from heights greater than 20 feet (6 meters). Blunt cardiac injury can result in myocardial muscle contusion, cardiac chamber rupture, coronary artery dissection and/or thrombosis, and valvular disruption. Cardiac rupture typically presents with cardiac tamponade and should be recognized during the primary survey. However, occasionally the signs and symptoms of tamponade are slow to develop with an atrial rupture. Early use of FAST can facilitate diagnosis.

Trauma team members must consider the importance of BCI due to trauma. Patients with blunt myocardial injury may report chest discomfort, but this symptom is often attributed to chest wall contusion or fractures of the sternum and/or ribs. The true diagnosis of blunt myocardial injury can be established only by direct inspection of the injured myocardium. Clinically significant sequelae are hypotension, dysrhythmias, and/or wall-motion abnormality on two-dimensional echocardiography. The electrocardiographic changes are variable and may even indicate frank myocardial infarction. Multiple premature ventricular contractions, unexplained sinus tachycardia, atrial fibrillation, bundle-branch block (usually right), and ST segment changes are the most common ECG findings. Elevated central venous pressure with no obvious cause may indicate right ventricular dysfunction secondary to contusion. Clinicians must also remember that the traumatic event may have been precipitated by a myocardial ischemic episode.

The presence of cardiac troponins can be diagnostic of myocardial infarction. However, their use in diagnosing blunt cardiac injury is inconclusive and offers no additional information beyond that available from ECG. Patients with a blunt injury to the heart diagnosed by conduction abnormalities (an abnormal ECG) are at risk for sudden dysrhythmias and should be monitored for the first 24 hours. After this interval, the risk of a dysrhythmia appears to decrease substantially. Patients without ECG abnormalities do not require further monitoring.

Traumatic Aortic Disruption

Traumatic aortic rupture is a common cause of sudden death after a vehicle collision or fall from a great height. Survivors of these injuries frequently recover if aortic rupture is promptly identified and treated expeditiously. Those patients with the best possibility of surviving tend to have an incomplete laceration near the ligamentum arteriosum of the aorta. Continuity is maintained by an intact adventitial layer or contained mediastinal hematoma, preventing immediate exsanguination and death (■ FIGURE 4-10).

Blood may escape into the mediastinum, but one characteristic shared by all survivors is that they have a contained hematoma. Persistent or recurrent hypotension is usually due to a separate, unidentified bleeding site. Although free rupture of a transected aorta into the left chest does occur and can cause hypotension, it usually is fatal unless the trauma team can repair it within a few minutes.

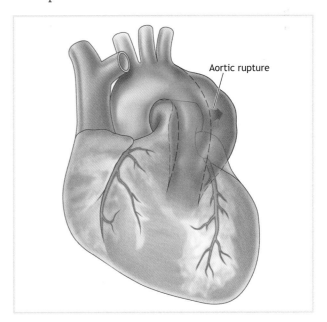

Aortic rupture

■ FIGURE 4-10 Aortic Rupture. Traumatic aortic rupture is a common cause of sudden death after a vehicle collision or fall from a great height. Maintain a high index of suspicion prompted by a history of decelerating force and characteristic findings on chest x-ray films.

Specific signs and symptoms of traumatic aortic disruption are frequently absent. Maintain a high index of suspicion prompted by a history of decelerating force and its characteristic findings on chest x-ray, and evaluate the patient further. Other radiographic signs of blunt aortic injury include:

- Widened mediastinum
- Obliteration of the aortic knob
- Deviation of the trachea to the right
- Depression of the left mainstem bronchus
- Elevation of the right mainstem bronchus
- Obliteration of the space between the pulmonary artery and the aorta (obscuration of the aortopulmonary window)
- Deviation of the esophagus (nasogastric tube) to the right
- Widened paratracheal stripe
- Widened paraspinal interfaces
- Presence of a pleural or apical cap
- Left hemothorax
- Fractures of the first or second rib or scapula

False positive and false negative findings can occur with each x-ray sign, and, infrequently (1%–13%), no mediastinal or initial chest x-ray abnormality is present in patients with great-vessel injury. Even a slight suspicion of aortic injury warrants evaluation of the patient at a facility capable of repairing the injury.

Helical contrast-enhanced computed tomography (CT) of the chest has proven to be an accurate screening method for patients with suspected blunt aortic injury. CT scanning should be performed liberally, because the findings on chest x-ray, especially the supine view, are unreliable. If results are equivocal, aortography should be performed. In general, patients who are hemodynamically abnormal should not be placed in a CT scanner. The sensitivity and specificity of helical contrast-enhanced CT have been shown to be close to 100%, but this result is technology dependent. If this test is negative for mediastinal hematoma and aortic rupture, no further diagnostic imaging of the aorta is likely necessary, although the surgical consultant will dictate the need for further imaging. Transesophageal echocardiography (TEE) appears to be a useful, less invasive diagnostic tool. The trauma surgeon caring for the patient is in the best position to determine which, if any, other diagnostic tests are warranted.

Heart rate and blood pressure control can decrease the likelihood of rupture. Pain should first be controlled with analgesics. If no contraindications exist, heart rate control with a short-acting beta blocker to a goal heart rate of less than 80 beats per minute (BPM) and blood pressure control with a goal mean arterial pressure of 60 to 70 mm Hg is recommended. When beta blockade with esmolol is not sufficient or contraindicated, a calcium channel blocker (nicardipine) can be used; if that fails, nitroglycerin or nitroprusside can be carefully added. Hypotension is an obvious contraindication to these medications.

A qualified surgeon should treat patients with blunt traumatic aortic injury and assist in the diagnosis. Open repair involves resection and repair of the torn segment or, infrequently, primary repair. Endovascular repair is the most common option for managing aortic injury and has excellent short-term outcomes. Close post-discharge follow-up is necessary to identify long-term complications.

Low-resourced facilities should not delay transfer by performing extensive evaluations of a wide mediastinum, because free rupture of the contained hematoma and rapid death from exsanguination may occur. All patients with a mechanism of injury and simple chest x-ray findings suggestive of aortic disruption should be transferred to a facility capable of rapid, definitive diagnosis and treatment of this potentially lethal injury.

Traumatic Diaphragmatic Injury

Traumatic diaphragmatic ruptures are more commonly diagnosed on the left side, perhaps because the liver obliterates the defect or protects it on the right side, whereas the appearance of displaced bowel, stomach, and/or nasogastric (NG) tube is more easily detected in the left chest. Blunt trauma produces large radial tears that lead to herniation (■ FIGURE 4-11), whereas penetrating trauma produces small perforations that can remain asymptomatic for years.

Diaphragmatic injuries are frequently missed initially when the chest film is misinterpreted as showing an elevated diaphragm, acute gastric dilation, loculated hemopneumothorax, or subpulmonic hematoma. Appearance of an elevated right diaphragm on a chest x-ray may be the only finding of a right-sided injury. If a laceration of the left diaphragm is suspected, a gastric tube can be inserted; if the gastric tube appears in the thoracic cavity on the chest film, the need for special contrast studies is eliminated. Occasionally, the condition is not identified on the initial x-ray film or subsequent CT scan, in which case an upper gastrointestinal contrast study should be performed. The appearance of peritoneal lavage fluid in the chest tube drainage also confirms the diagnosis in

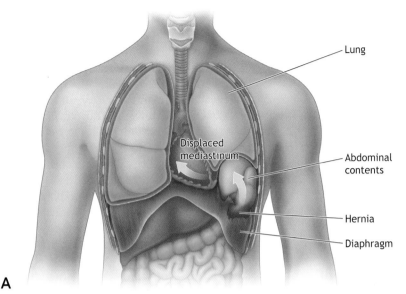

A

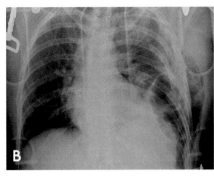

■ FIGURE 4-11 Diaphragmatic Rupture. A. Blunt trauma produces large radial tears that lead to herniation, whereas penetrating trauma produces small perforations that can take time—sometimes even years—to develop into diaphragmatic hernias. B. Radiograph view.

patients who have undergone diagnostic peritoneal lavage. Minimally invasive endoscopic procedures (e.g., laparoscopy and thoracoscopy) may be helpful in evaluating the diaphragm in indeterminate cases.

Operation for other abdominal injuries often reveals a diaphragmatic tear. Treatment is by direct repair. Care must be taken when placing a chest tube in patients with suspected diaphragm injury, as tubes can inadvertently injure the abdominal contents that have become displaced into the chest cavity.

Blunt Esophageal Rupture

Esophageal trauma most commonly results from penetrating injury. Although rare, blunt esophageal trauma, caused by the forceful expulsion of gastric contents into the esophagus from a severe blow to the upper abdomen, can be lethal if unrecognized. This forceful ejection produces a linear tear in the lower esophagus, allowing leakage into the mediastinum. The resulting mediastinitis and immediate or delayed rupture into the pleural space causes empyema.

The clinical picture of patients with blunt esophageal rupture is identical to that of post-emetic esophageal rupture. The clinical setting of esophageal injury is typically a patient with a left pneumothorax or hemothorax without a rib fracture who has received a severe blow to the lower sternum or epigastrium and is in pain or shock out of proportion to the apparent injury. Particulate matter may drain from the chest tube after the blood begins to clear. The presence of mediastinal air also suggests the diagnosis, which often can be confirmed by contrast studies and/or esophagoscopy.

Treatment of esophageal rupture consists of wide drainage of the pleural space and mediastinum with direct repair of the injury. Repairs performed within a few hours of injury improve the patient's prognosis.

OTHER MANIFESTATIONS OF CHEST INJURIES

During the secondary survey, the trauma team should look for other significant thoracic injuries including subcutaneous emphysema; crushing injury (traumatic asphyxia); and rib, sternum, and scapular fractures. Although these injuries may not be immediately life-threatening, they can potentially cause significant morbidity.

Subcutaneous Emphysema

Subcutaneous emphysema can result from airway injury, lung injury, or, rarely, blast injury. Although this condition does not require treatment, clinicians must recognize the underlying injury and treat it. If positive-pressure ventilation is required, consider performing tube thoracostomy on the side of the subcutaneous emphysema in case a tension pneumothorax develops.

Crushing Injury to the Chest

Findings associated with a crush injury to the chest, or traumatic asphyxia, include upper torso, facial, and arm plethora with petechiae secondary to acute, temporary compression of the superior vena cava. Massive swelling and even cerebral edema may be present. Associated injuries must be treated.

Rib, Sternum, and Scapular Fractures

The ribs are the most commonly injured component of the thoracic cage, and injuries to the ribs are often significant. Pain on motion typically results in splinting of the thorax, which impairs ventilation, oxygenation, and effective coughing. The incidence of atelectasis and pneumonia rises significantly with preexisting lung disease.

The scapula, humerus, and clavicle, along with their muscular attachments, provide a barrier to injury to the upper ribs (1 to 3). Fractures of the scapula, first or second rib, or the sternum suggest a magnitude of injury that places the head, neck, spinal cord, lungs, and great vessels at risk for serious associated injury. Due to the severity of the associated injuries, mortality can be as high as 35%.

Sternal and scapular fractures generally result from a direct blow. Pulmonary contusion may accompany sternal fractures, and blunt cardiac injury should be considered with all such fractures. Operative repair of sternal and scapular fractures occasionally is indicated. Rarely, posterior sternoclavicular dislocation results in mediastinal displacement of the clavicular heads with accompanying superior vena caval obstruction. Immediate reduction is required.

The middle ribs (4 to 9) sustain most of the effects of blunt trauma. Anteroposterior compression of the thoracic cage will bow the ribs outward and cause midshaft fractures. Direct force applied to the ribs tends to fracture them and drive the ends of the bones into the thorax, increasing the potential for intrathoracic injury, such as a pneumothorax or hemothorax.

In general, a young patient with a more flexible chest wall is less likely to sustain rib fractures. Therefore, the presence of multiple rib fractures in young patients implies a greater transfer of force than in older patients.

Osteopenia is common in older adults; therefore, multiple bony injuries, including rib fractures, may occur with reports of only minor trauma. This population may experience the delayed development of clinical hemothorax and may warrant close follow-up. The presence of rib fractures in the elderly should raise significant concern, as the incidence of pneumonia and mortality is double that in younger patients. (See *Chapter 11: Geriatric Trauma*.)

Fractures of the lower ribs (10 to 12) should increase suspicion for hepatosplenic injury. Localized pain, tenderness on palpation, and crepitation are present in patients with rib injury. A palpable or visible deformity suggests rib fractures. In these patients, obtain a chest x-ray primarily to exclude other intrathoracic injuries and not simply to identify rib fractures. Fractures of anterior cartilages or separation of costochondral junctions have the same significance as rib fractures, but they are not visible on the x-ray examinations. Special techniques for rib x-rays are not considered useful, because they may not detect all rib injuries and do not aid treatment decisions; further, they are expensive and require painful positioning of the patient.

Taping, rib belts, and external splints are contraindicated. Relief of pain is important to enable adequate ventilation. Intercostal block, epidural anesthesia, and systemic analgesics are effective and may be necessary. Early and aggressive pain control, including the use of systemic narcotics and topical, local or regional anesthesia, improves outcome in patients with rib, sternum, or scapular fractures.

Increased use of CT has resulted in the identification of injuries not previously known or diagnosed, such as minimal aortic injuries and occult or subclinical pneumothoraces and hemothoraces. Clinicians should discuss appropriate treatment of these occult injuries with the proper specialty consultant.

TEAMWORK

The team leader must:

- Quickly establish the competencies of team members in performing needle decompression and chest drainage techniques.

- Consider the potential need for bilateral chest drains and assess team resources accordingly.

- Recognize patients who have undergone prehospital intervention, such as needle decompression or open chest drainage, assess the patient's response, and determine the need for additional timely interventions.

- Recognize when open thoracotomy will benefit the patient and ensure that the capability exists for safe transport without delay to a skilled surgical facility.

CHAPTER SUMMARY

1. Thoracic injury is common in the polytrauma patient and can pose life-threatening problems

if not promptly identified and treated during the primary survey. These patients can usually be treated or their conditions temporarily relieved by relatively simple measures, such as intubation, ventilation, tube thoracostomy, and fluid resuscitation. Clinicians with the ability to recognize these important injuries and the skill to perform the necessary procedures can save lives. The primary survey includes management of airway obstruction, laryngeal injury, upper chest injury, tracheobronchial tree injury, tension pneumothorax, open pneumothorax, massive hemothorax, cardiac tamponade, and traumatic circulatory arrest.

2. The secondary survey includes identification, using adjunctive studies such as x-rays, laboratory tests, and ECG, and initial treatment of the following potentially life-threatening injuries: simple pneumothorax, hemothorax, pulmonary contusion, flail chest, blunt cardiac injury, traumatic aortic disruption, traumatic diaphragmatic injury, and blunt esophageal rupture.

3. Several manifestations of thoracic trauma may indicate a greater risk of associated injuries, including subcutaneous emphysema, crush injuries of the chest, and injuries to the ribs, scapula, and sternum.

BIBLIOGRAPHY

1. Ball CG, Williams BH, Wyrzykowski AD, et al. A caveat to the performance of pericardial ultrasound in patients with penetrating cardiac wounds. *J Trauma* 2009;67(5):1123–1124.
2. Brasel KJ, Stafford RE, Weigelt JA, et al. Treatment of occult pneumothoraces from blunt trauma. *J Trauma* 1999;46(6):987–990; discussion 990–991.
3. Bulger EM, Edwards T, Klotz P, et al. Epidural analgesia improves outcome after multiple rib fractures. *Surgery* 2004;136(2):426–430.
4. Callaham M. Pericardiocentesis in traumatic and nontraumatic cardiac tamponade. *Ann Emerg Med* 1984;13(10):924–945.
5. Clancy K, Velopulos C,, Bilaniuk JW, et al. Screening for blunt cardiac injury: an Eastern Association for the Surgery of Trauma practice management guideline. *J Trauma* 2012;73(5 Suppl 4):S301–S306.
6. Cook J, Salerno C, Krishnadasan B, et al. The effect of changing presentation and management on the outcome of blunt rupture of the thoracic aorta. *J Thorac Cardiovasc Surg* 2006;131(3):594–600.
7. Demetriades D, Velmahos GC, Scalea TM, et al. Diagnosis and treatment of blunt aortic injuries: changing perspectives. *J Trauma* 2008;64:1415–1419.
8. Demetriades D, Velmahos GC, Scalea TM, et al. Operative repair or endovascular stent graft in blunt traumatic thoracic aortic injuries: results of an American Association for the Surgery of Trauma multicenter study. *J Trauma* 2008;64:561–571.
9. Dulchavsky SA, Schwarz KL, Kirkpatrick AW, et al. Prospective evaluation of thoracic ultrasound in the detection of pneumothorax. *J Trauma* 2001;(50):201–205.
10. Dunham CM, Barraco RD, Clark DE, et al. Guidelines for emergency tracheal intubation immediately following traumatic injury: an EAST Practice Management Guidelines Workgroup. *J Trauma* 2003;55:162–179.
11. Dyer DS, Moore EE, Ilke DN, et al. Thoracic aortic injury: how predictive is mechanism and is chest computed tomography a reliable screening tool? A prospective study of 1,561 patients. *J Trauma* 2000;48(4):673–82; discussion 682–683.
12. Ekeh AP, Peterson W, Woods RJ, et al. Is chest x-ray an adequate screening tool for the diagnosis of blunt thoracic aortic injury? *J Trauma* 2008;65:1088–1092.
13. Flagel B, Luchette FA, Reed RL, et al. Half a dozen ribs: the breakpoint for mortality. *Surgery* 2005;138:717–725.
14. Harcke HT, Pearse LA, Levy AD, et al. Chest wall thickness in military personnel: implications for needle thoracentesis in tension pneumothorax. *Mil Med* 2007;172(120):1260–1263.
15. Heniford BT, Carrillo EG, Spain DA, et al. The role of thoracoscopy in the management of retained thoracic collections after trauma. *Ann Thorac Surg* 1997;63(4):940–943.
16. Hershberger RC, Bernadette A, Murphy M, et al. Endovascular grafts for treatment of traumatic injury to the aortic arch and great vessels. *J Trauma* 2009;67(3):660–671.
17. Hopson LR, Hirsh E, Delgado J, et al. Guidelines for withholding or termination of resuscitation in prehospital traumatic cardiopulmonary arrest: a joint position paper from the National Association of EMS Physicians Standards and Clinical Practice Committee and the American College of Surgeons Committee on Trauma. *Prehosp Emerg Care* 2003;7(1):141–146.

18. Hopson LR, Hirsh E, Delgado J, et al. Guidelines for withholding or termination of resuscitation in prehospital traumatic cardiopulmonary arrest. *J Am Coll Surg* 2003;196(3),475–481.

19. Hunt PA, Greaves I, Owens WA. Emergency thoracotomy in thoracic trauma—a review. *Injury* 2006;37(1):1–19.

20. Inaba K, Branco BC, Eckstein M, et al. Optimal positioning for emergent needle thoracostomy: a cadaver-based study. *J Trauma* 2011;71:1099–1103.

21. Inaba K, Lustenberger T, Recinos G, et al. Does size matter? A prospective analysis of 28-32 versus 36-40 French chest tube size in trauma. *J Trauma* 2012;72(2):422–427.

22. Karalis DG, Victor MF, Davis GA, et al. The role of echocardiography in blunt chest trauma: a transthoracic and transesophageal echocardiography study. *J Trauma* 1994;36(1):53–58.

23. Karmy-Jones R, Jurkovich GJ, Nathens AB, et al. Timing of urgent thoracotomy for hemorrhage after trauma: a multicenter study. *Archives of Surgery* 2001;136(5):513–518.

24. Lang-Lazdunski L, Mourox J, Pons F, et al. Role of videothoracoscopy in chest trauma. *Ann Thorac Surg* 1997;63(2):327–333.

25. Lee TH1, Ouellet JF, Cook M, et al. Pericardiocentesis in trauma: a systematic review. *J Trauma* 2013;75(4):543–549.

26. Lockey D, Crewdson K, Davies G. Traumatic cardiac arrest: who are the survivors? *Ann Emerg Med* 2006;48(3):240–244.

27. Marnocha KE, Maglinte DDT, Woods J, et al. Blunt chest trauma and suspected aortic rupture: reliability of chest radiograph findings. *Ann Emerg Med* 1985;14(7):644–649.

28. Meyer DM, Jessen ME, Wait MA. Early evacuation of traumatic retained hemothoraces using thoracoscopy: a prospective randomized trial. *Ann Thorac Surg* 1997;64(5):1396–1400.

29. Mirvis SE, Shanmugantham K, Buell J, et al. Use of spiral computed tomography for the assessment of blunt trauma patients with potential aortic injury. *J Trauma* 1999;45:922–930.

30. Moon MR, Luchette FA, Gibson SW, et al. Prospective, randomized comparison of epidural versus parenteral opioid analgesia in thoracic trauma. *Ann Surg* 1999;229:684–692.

31. Powell DW, Moore EE, Cothren CC, et al. Is emergency department resuscitative thoracotomy futile care for the critically injured patient requiring prehospital cardiopulmonary resuscitation? *J Am Coll Surg* 2004;199(2):211–215.

32. Ramzy AI, Rodriguez A, Turney SZ. Management of major tracheobronchial ruptures in patients with multiple system trauma. *J Trauma* 1988;28:914–920.

33. Reed AB, Thompson JK, Crafton CJ, et al. Timing of endovascular repair of blunt traumatic thoracic aortic transections. *J Vasc Surg* 2006;43(4):684–688.

34. Rhee PM, Acosta J, Bridgeman A, et al. Survival after emergency department thoracotomy: review of published data from the past 25 years. *J Am Coll Surg* 2000;190(3):288–298.

35. Richardson JD, Adams L, Flint LM. Selective management of flail chest and pulmonary contusion. *Ann Surg* 1982;196(4):481–487.

36. Roberts D, Leigh-Smith S, Faris P, et al. Clinical presentation of patients with tension pneumothorax: a systematic review. *Ann Surg* 2015;261(6):1068–1078.

37. Rosato RM, Shapiro MJ, Keegan MJ, et al. Cardiac injury complicating traumatic asphyxia. *J Trauma* 1991;31(10):1387–1389.

38. Rozycki GS, Feliciano DV, Oschner MG, et al. The role of ultrasound in patients with possible penetrating cardiac wounds: a prospective multicenter study. *J Trauma* 1999;46(4):542–551.

39. Simon B, Cushman J, Barraco R, et al. Pain management in blunt thoracic trauma: an EAST Practice Management Guidelines Workgroup. *J Trauma* 2005;59:1256–1267.

40. Sisley AC, Rozyycki GS, Ballard RB, et al. Rapid detection of traumatic effusion using surgeon-performed ultrasonography. *J Trauma* 1998;44:291–297.

41. Smith MD, Cassidy JM, Souther S, et al. Transesophageal echocardiography in the diagnosis of traumatic rupture of the aorta. *N Engl J Med* 1995;332:356–362.

42. Søreide K, Søiland H, Lossius HM, et al. Resuscitative emergency thoracotomy in a Scandinavian trauma hospital—is it justified? *Injury* 2007;38(1):34–42.

43. Stafford RE, Linn J, Washington L. Incidence and management of occult hemothoraces. *Am J Surg* 2006;192(6):722–726.

44. Swaaenburg JC, Klaase JM, DeJongste MJ, et al. Troponin I, troponin T, CKMB-activity and CKMG-mass as markers for the detection of myocardial contusion in patients who experienced blunt trauma. *Clin Chim Acta* 1998;272(2):171–181.

45. Tehrani HY, Peterson BG, Katariya K, et al. Endovascular repair of thoracic aortic tears. *Ann Thorac Surg* 2006;82(3):873–877.

46. Weiss RL, Brier JA, O'Connor W, et al. The usefulness of transesophageal echocardiography in diagnosing cardiac contusions. *Chest* 1996;109(1):73–77.

47. Wilkerson RG, Stone MB. Sensitivity of bedside ultrasound and supine anteroposterior chest radiographs for the identification of pneumothorax after blunt trauma. [Review] [24 refs] *Acad Emerg Med* 2010;17(1):11–17.

48. Woodring JH. A normal mediastinum in blunt trauma rupture of the thoracic aorta and brachiocephalic arteries. *J Emerg Med* 1990;8:467–476.

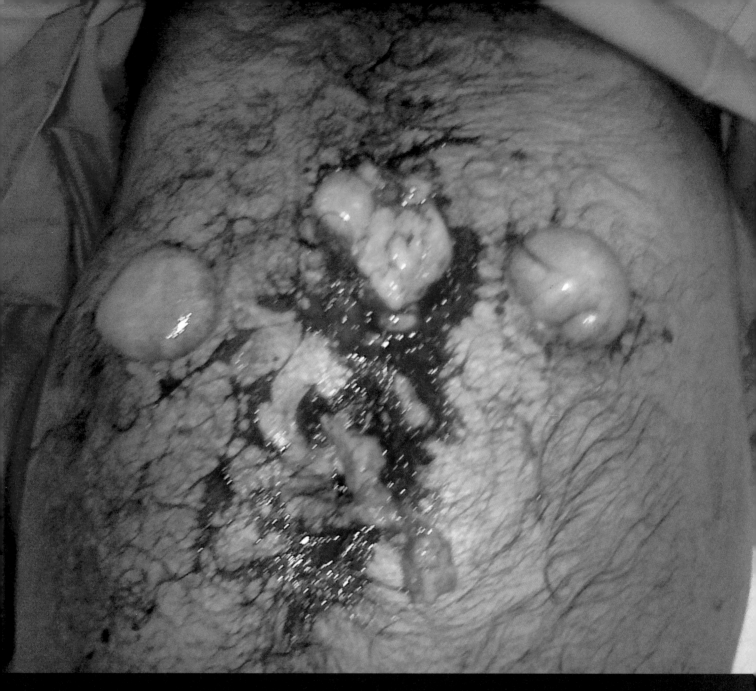

5 ABDOMINAL AND PELVIC TRAUMA

When uncontrolled or unrecognized, blood loss from abdominal and pelvic injuries can result in preventable death.

CHAPTER 5 OUTLINE

OBJECTIVES

After reading this chapter and comprehending the knowledge components of the ATLS provider course, you will be able to:

1. Identify the anatomic regions of the abdomen that are critical in assessing and managing trauma patients.

2. Recognize a patient who is at risk for abdominal and pelvic injuries based on the mechanism of injury.

3. Identify patients who require surgical consultation and possible surgical and/or catheter-based intervention.

4. Use the appropriate diagnostic procedures to determine if a patient has ongoing hemorrhage and/or other injuries that can cause delayed morbidity and mortality.

5. Describe the acute management of abdominal and pelvic injuries.

The assessment of circulation during the primary survey includes early evaluation for possible intra-abdominal and/or pelvic hemorrhage in patients who have sustained blunt trauma. Penetrating torso wounds between the nipple and perineum must be considered as potential causes of intraperitoneal injury. The mechanism of injury, injury forces, location of injury, and hemodynamic status of the patient determine the priority and best method of abdominal and pelvic assessment.

Unrecognized abdominal and pelvic injuries continue to cause preventable death after truncal trauma. Rupture of a hollow viscus and bleeding from a solid organ or the bony pelvis may not be easily recognized. In addition, patient assessment is often compromised by alcohol intoxication, use of illicit drugs, injury to the brain or spinal cord, and injury to adjacent structures such as the ribs and spine. Significant blood loss can be present in the abdominal cavity without a dramatic change in the external appearance or dimensions of the abdomen and without obvious signs of peritoneal irritation. Any patient who has sustained injury to the torso from a direct blow, deceleration, blast, or penetrating injury must be considered to have an abdominal visceral, vascular, or pelvic injury until proven otherwise.

ANATOMY OF THE ABDOMEN

A review of the anatomy of the abdomen, with emphasis on structures that are critical in assessment and management of trauma patients, is provided in (■ FIGURE 5-1).

The abdomen is partially enclosed by the lower thorax. The *anterior abdomen* is defined as the area between the costal margins superiorly, the inguinal ligaments and symphysis pubis inferiorly, and the anterior axillary lines laterally. Most of the hollow viscera are at risk when there is an injury to the anterior abdomen.

The *thoracoabdomen* is the area inferior to the nipple line anteriorly and the infrascapular line posteriorly, and superior to the costal margins. This area encompasses the diaphragm, liver, spleen, and stomach, and is somewhat protected by the bony thorax. Because the diaphragm rises to the level of the fourth intercostal space during full expiration, fractures of the lower ribs and penetrating wounds below the nipple line can injure the abdominal viscera.

The *flank* is the area between the anterior and posterior axillary lines from the sixth intercostal space to the iliac crest.

The *back* is the area located posterior to the posterior axillary lines from the tip of the scapulae to the iliac crests. This includes the posterior thoracoabdomen. Musculature in the flank, back, and paraspinal region acts as a partial protection from visceral injury.

The flank and back contain the *retroperitoneal space*. This potential space is the area posterior to the peritoneal lining of the abdomen. It contains the abdominal aorta; inferior vena cava; most of the duodenum, pancreas, kidneys, and ureters; the posterior aspects of the ascending colon and descending colon; and the retroperitoneal components of the pelvic cavity. Injuries to the retroperitoneal visceral structures are difficult to recognize because they occur deep within the abdomen and may not initially present with signs or symptoms of peritonitis. In addition, the retroperitoneal space is not sampled by diagnostic peritoneal lavage (DPL) and is poorly visualized with focused assessment with sonography for trauma (FAST).

The *pelvic cavity* is the area surrounded by the pelvic bones, containing the lower part of the retroperitoneal and intraperitoneal spaces. It contains the rectum,

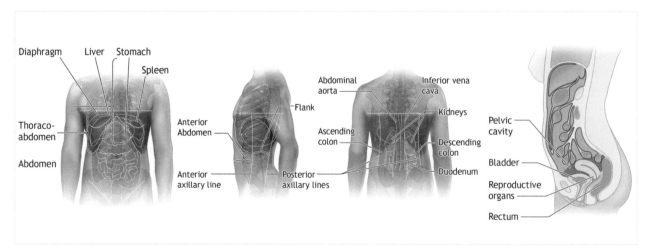

■ FIGURE 5-1 Anatomy of the Abdomen. A. Anterior abdomen and thoraco-abdomen. B. Flank. C. Back. D. Pelvic Cavity.

bladder, iliac vessels, and female internal reproductive organs. Significant blood loss can occur from injuries to organs within the pelvis and/or directly from the bony pelvis.

MECHANISM OF INJURY

Consideration of the mechanism of injury facilitates the early identification of potential injuries, directs which diagnostic studies may be necessary for evaluation, and identifies the potential need for patient transfer. Common injuries from blunt and penetrating trauma are described in this section.

BLUNT

A *direct blow*, such as contact with the lower rim of a steering wheel, bicycle or motorcycle handlebars, or an intruded door in a motor vehicle crash, can cause compression and crushing injuries to abdominopelvic viscera and pelvic bones. Such forces deform solid and hollow organs and can cause rupture with secondary hemorrhage and contamination by visceral contents, leading to associated peritonitis.

Shearing injuries are a form of crush injury that can result when a restraint device is worn inappropriately (■ FIGURE 5-2A). Patients injured in motor vehicle crashes and who fall from significant heights may sustain *deceleration injuries*, in which there is a differential movement of fixed and mobile parts of the body. Examples include lacerations of the liver and spleen, both movable organs that are fixed at the sites of their supporting ligaments. Bucket handle injuries to the small bowel are also examples of deceleration injuries (■ FIGURE 5-2B).

In patients who sustain blunt trauma, the organs most frequently injured are the spleen (40% to 55%), liver (35% to 45%), and small bowel (5% to 10%). Additionally, there is a 15% incidence of retroperitoneal hematoma in patients who undergo laparotomy for blunt trauma. Although restraint devices reduce the incidence of many more major injuries, they are associated with specific patterns of injury, as shown in ■ TABLE 5-1. Air-bag deployment does not preclude abdominal injury.

PENETRATING

Stab wounds and low-energy gunshot wounds cause tissue damage by lacerating and tearing. High-energy gunshot wounds transfer more kinetic energy, causing

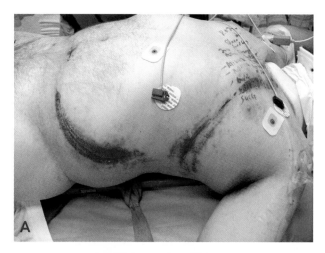

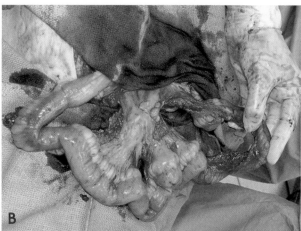

■ FIGURE 5-2 Lap Belt and Bucket Handle Injuries. A. Injuries may be more likely when a restraint device is not in the optimal position. B. Small bowel "bucket handle" injury.

increased damage surrounding the track of the missile due to temporary cavitation.

Stab wounds traverse adjacent abdominal structures and most commonly involve the liver (40%), small bowel (30%), diaphragm (20%), and colon (15%) (■ FIGURE 5-3).

Gunshot wounds can cause additional intra-abdominal injuries based on the trajectory, cavitation effect, and possible bullet fragmentation. Gunshot wounds most commonly injure the small bowel (50%), colon (40%), liver (30%), and abdominal vascular structures (25%). The type of weapon, the muzzle velocity, and type of ammunition are important determinants of degree of tissue injury. In the case of shotguns, the distance between the shotgun and the patient determines the severity of injuries incurred.

BLAST

Blast injury from explosive devices occurs through several mechanisms, including penetrating fragment

TABLE 5-1 INJURIES ASSOCIATED WITH RESTRAINT DEVICES

RESTRAINT DEVICE	INJURY
Lap Seat Belt • Compression • Hyperflexion	• Tear or avulsion of bowel mesentery (bucket handle) • Rupture of small bowel or colon • Thrombosis of iliac artery or abdominal aorta • Chance fracture of lumbar vertebrae • Pancreatic or duodenal injury
Shoulder Harness • Sliding under the seat belt ("submarining") • Compression	• Rupture of upper abdominal viscera • Intimal tear or thrombosis in innominate, carotid, subclavian, or vertebral arteries • Fracture or dislocation of cervical spine • Rib fractures • Pulmonary contusion
Air Bag • Contact • Contact/deceleration • Flexion (unrestrained) • Hyperextension (unrestrained)	• Face and eye abrasions • Cardiac Injuries • Spine fractures

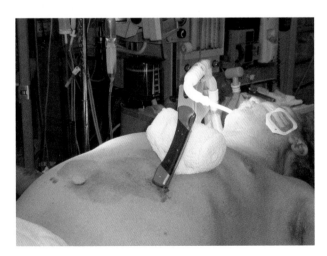

■ **FIGURE 5-3** Stab wounds most commonly injure the liver, small bowel, diaphragm, and colon.

wounds and blunt injuries from the patient being thrown or struck by projectiles. The treating doctor must consider the possibility of combined penetrating and blunt mechanisms in these patients. Patients close to the source of the explosion can incur additional injuries to the tympanic membranes, lungs, and bowel related to blast overpressure. These injuries may have delayed presentation. The potential for overpressure injury following an explosion should not distract the clinician from a systematic approach to identifying and treating blunt and penetrating injuries.

PITFALL	PREVENTION
Missed abdominal injury	• Understand the role that mechanism of injury plays in abdominal injury. Do not underestimate the extent of energy delivered to the abdomen in blunt trauma. • Recognize that small, low-energy wounds (e.g., stab and fragment wounds) can cause visceral and/or vascular injuries. • Perform frequent abdominal reevaluation, as a single examination does not completely eliminate the presence of injury. • High-energy projectiles can produce injuries tangential to the path of the missile. • Missile trajectories can be altered by tumbling or creation of a secondary path after striking bone or fragmenting. This can result in remote injuries (compared with cutaneous wounds).

ASSESSMENT AND MANAGEMENT

In hypotensive patients, the goal is to rapidly identify an abdominal or pelvic injury and determine whether it is the cause of hypotension. The patient history, physical exam, and supplemental diagnostic tools can establish the presence of abdominal and pelvic injuries that require urgent hemorrhage control. Hemodynamically normal patients without signs of peritonitis may undergo a more detailed evaluation to determine the presence of injuries that can cause delayed morbidity and mortality. This evaluation must include repeated physical examinations to identify any signs of bleeding or peritonitis that may develop over time.

HISTORY

When assessing a patient injured in a motor vehicle crash, pertinent historical information includes the vehicle speed, type of collision (e.g., frontal impact, lateral impact, sideswipe, rear impact, or rollover), any intrusion into the passenger compartment, types of restraints, deployment of air bags, patient position in the vehicle, and status of other occupants. For patients injured by falling, the height of the fall is important historical information due to the increased potential for deceleration injury at greater heights. The patient, other vehicle occupants, witnesses, law enforcement, and emergency medical personnel may be able to provide historical information. Prehospital care providers should supply data regarding vital signs, obvious injuries, and patient response to prehospital treatment.

When assessing a patient who has sustained penetrating trauma, pertinent historical information includes the time of injury, type of weapon (e.g., knife, handgun, rifle, or shotgun), distance from the assailant (particularly important with shotgun wounds, as the likelihood of major visceral injuries decreases beyond the 10-foot or 3-meter range), number of stab wounds or gunshots sustained, and the amount of external bleeding noted at the scene. Important additional information to obtain from the patient includes the magnitude and location of abdominal pain.

Explosions can produce visceral overpressure injuries. The risk increases when the patient is in close proximity to the blast and when a blast occurs within a closed space.

PHYSICAL EXAMINATION

The abdominal examination is conducted in a systematic sequence: inspection, auscultation, percussion, and palpation. This is followed by examination of the pelvis and buttocks, as well as; urethral, perineal, and, if indicated, rectal and vaginal exams. The findings, whether positive or negative, should be completely documented in the patient's medical record.

Inspection, Auscultation, Percussion, and Palpation

In most circumstances, the patient must be fully undressed to allow for a thorough inspection. During the inspection, examine the anterior and posterior abdomen, as well as the lower chest and perineum, for abrasions and contusions from restraint devices, lacerations, penetrating wounds, impaled foreign bodies, evisceration of omentum or bowel, and the pregnant state.

Inspect the flank, scrotum, urethral meatus, and perianal area for blood, swelling, and bruising. Laceration of the perineum, vagina, rectum, or buttocks may be associated with an open pelvic fracture in blunt trauma patients. Skin folds in obese patients can mask penetrating injuries and increase the difficulty of assessing the abdomen and pelvis. For a complete back examination, cautiously logroll the patient. (See *Logroll video on MyATLS mobile app.*)

At the conclusion of the rapid physical exam, cover the patient with warmed blankets to help prevent hypothermia.

Although auscultation is necessary, the presence or absence of bowel sounds does not necessarily correlate with injury, and the ability to hear bowels sounds may be compromised in a noisy emergency department.

Percussion causes slight movement of the peritoneum and may elicit signs of peritoneal irritation. When rebound tenderness is present, do not seek additional evidence of irritation, as it may cause the patient further unnecessary pain.

Voluntary guarding by the patient may make the abdominal examination unreliable. In contrast, involuntary muscle guarding is a reliable sign of peritoneal irritation. Palpation may elicit and distinguish superficial (i.e., abdominal wall) and deep tenderness. Determine whether a pregnant uterus is present and, if so, estimate the fetal age.

Pelvic Assessment

Major pelvic hemorrhage can occur rapidly, and clinicians must make the diagnosis quickly so they can initiate appropriate resuscitative treatment. Unexplained hypotension may be the only initial indication of major pelvic disruption. Mechanical instability of the pelvic ring should be assumed in patients who have pelvic fractures with hypotension and no other source of blood loss. Placement of a pelvic binder is a priority and may be lifesaving in this circumstance.

Physical exam findings suggestive of pelvic fracture include evidence of ruptured urethra (scrotal hematoma or blood at the urethral meatus), discrepancy in limb length, and rotational deformity of a leg without obvious fracture. In these patients, avoid manually manipulating the pelvis, as doing so may dislodge an existing blood clot and cause further hemorrhage.

Gentle palpation of the bony pelvis for tenderness may provide useful information about the presence of pelvic fracture. Distraction of the pelvis is not recommended during the early assessment of injuries because it may worsen or cause recurrent pelvic bleeding.

The mechanically unstable hemipelvis migrates cephalad because of muscular forces and rotates outward secondary to the effect of gravity on the unstable hemipelvis. External rotation of the unstable pelvis results in an increased pelvic volume that can accommodate a larger volume of blood. The pelvis can be stabilized with a binder or sheet to limit this expansion. The binder should be centered over the greater trochanters rather than over the iliac crests. The presence of lower-extremity neurologic abnormalities or open wounds in the flank, perineum, vagina, or rectum may be evidence of pelvic-ring instability. An anteroposterior (AP) x-ray of the pelvis is a useful adjunct to identify a pelvic fracture, given the limitations of clinical examination. (See Appendix G: Circulation Skills.)

PITFALL	PREVENTION
Repeated manipulation of a fractured pelvis can aggravate hemorrhage.	• Gentle palpation of the bony pelvis may provide useful information about the presence of pelvic fractures; avoid multiple examinations and distraction of the pelvis. • Apply a pelvic binder correctly and early to limit hemorrhage.
Skin folds in obese patients can mask penetrating injuries and increase the difficulty of abdominal and pelvic assessment.	• Examine skin folds for wounds, foreign bodies, and injuries.
The abdominal examination of pediatric patients may be difficult to interpret.	• Use diagnostic studies (e.g., FAST, CT or other imaging) as needed to assess equivocal findings.

Urethral, Perineal, Rectal, Vaginal, and Gluteal Examination

The presence of blood at the urethral meatus strongly suggests a urethral injury. Ecchymosis or hematoma of the scrotum and perineum is also suggestive of urethral injury, although these signs may be absent immediately after injury. In patients who have sustained blunt trauma, the goals of the rectal examination are to assess sphincter tone and rectal mucosal integrity and to identify any palpable fractures of the pelvis. Palpation of the prostate gland is not a reliable sign of urethral injury. In patients with penetrating wounds, the rectal examination is used to assess sphincter tone and look for gross blood, which may indicate a bowel perforation. Do not place a urinary catheter in a patient with a perineal hematoma or blood at the urethral meatus before a definitive assessment for urethral injury.

Bony fragments from pelvic fracture or penetrating wounds can lacerate the vagina. Perform a vaginal exam when injury is suspected, such as in the presence of complex perineal laceration, pelvic fracture, or trans-pelvic gunshot wound. In unresponsive menstruating women, examine the vagina for the presence of tampons; left in place, they can cause delayed sepsis.

The gluteal region extends from the iliac crests to the gluteal folds. Penetrating injuries to this area are associated with up to a 50% incidence of significant intra-abdominal injuries, including rectal injuries below the peritoneal reflection. These wounds mandate an evaluation for such injuries.

ADJUNCTS TO PHYSICAL EXAMINATION

After diagnosing and treating problems with a patient's airway, breathing, and circulation, clinicians frequently insert gastric tubes and urinary catheters as adjuncts to the primary survey.

Gastric Tubes and Urinary Catheters

The therapeutic goals of a gastric tube placed early in the primary survey include relief of acute gastric dilation and stomach decompression before performing DPL (if needed). Gastric tubes may reduce the incidence of aspiration in these cases. However, they can trigger vomiting in a patient with an active gag reflex. The presence of blood in the gastric contents suggests an injury to the esophagus or upper gastrointestinal tract if nasopharyngeal and/or oropharyngeal sources are excluded. If a patient has severe facial fractures or possible basilar skull fracture, insert the gastric tube through the mouth to prevent passage of the nasal tube through the cribriform plate into the brain.

A urinary catheter placed during resuscitation will relieve retention, identify bleeding, allow for monitoring of urinary output as an index of tissue perfusion, and decompress the bladder before DPL (if performed). A full bladder enhances the pelvic images of the FAST. Therefore, if FAST is being considered, delay placing a urinary catheter until after the test is completed. Gross hematuria is an indication of trauma to the genitourinary tract, including the kidney, ureters, and bladder. The absence of hematuria does not exclude an injury to the genitourinary tract. A retrograde urethrogram is mandatory when the patient is unable to void, requires a pelvic binder, or has blood at the meatus, scrotal hematoma, or perineal ecchymosis. To reduce the risk of increasing the complexity of a urethral injury, confirm an intact urethra before inserting a urinary catheter. A disrupted urethra detected during the primary or secondary survey may require insertion of a suprapubic tube by an experienced doctor.

PITFALL	PREVENTION
In a patient with midface fractures, a nasogastric tube can pass into the sinuses and cranial cavity.	• Avoid a nasogastric tube in patients with midface injury; instead use an orogastric tube.
Pediatric patients have high rates of acute gastric distention following trauma.	• A gastric tube may be beneficial in pediatrics patients to reduce the risks of aspiration and vagal stimulation.
Passage of a gastric tube may be impossible in patients with hiatal hernias (more common in older adults).	• To avoid iatrogenic injury, do not continue to attempt nasogastric tube placement if several attempts are unsuccessful. Eventual placement may require radiologic or other assistance.

Other Studies

With preparation and an organized team approach, the physical examination can be performed very quickly. In patients with hemodynamic abnormalities, rapid exclusion of intra-abdominal hemorrhage is necessary

and can be accomplished with either FAST or DPL. The only contraindication to these studies is an existing indication for laparotomy.

Patients with the following findings require further abdominal evaluation to identify or exclude intra-abdominal injury:

- Altered sensorium
- Altered sensation
- Injury to adjacent structures, such as lower ribs, pelvis, and lumbar spine
- Equivocal physical examination
- Prolonged loss of contact with patient anticipated, such as general anesthesia for extraabdominal injuries or lengthy radiographic studies
- Seat-belt sign with suspicion of bowel injury

When intra-abdominal injury is suspected, a number of studies can provide useful information. However, when indications for patient transfer already exist, do not perform time-consuming tests, including abdominal CT. ■ TABLE 5-2 summarizes the indications, advantages, and disadvantages of using DPL, FAST, and CT in evaluating blunt abdominal trauma.

X-rays for Abdominal Trauma

An AP chest x-ray is recommended for assessing patients with multisystem blunt trauma. Hemodynamically abnormal patients with penetrating abdominal wounds do not require screening x-rays in the emergency department (ED). If the patient is hemodynamically normal and has penetrating trauma above the umbilicus or a suspected thoracoabdominal injury, an upright chest x-ray is useful to exclude an associated hemothorax or pneumothorax, or to determine the presence of intraperitoneal air. With radiopaque markers or clips applied to all entrance and exit wounds, a supine abdominal x-ray may be obtained in hemodynamically normal penetrating trauma patients to demonstrate the path of the missile and determine the presence of retroperitoneal air. Obtaining two views (i.e., AP and lateral) may allow for spatial orientation of foreign bodies. An AP pelvic x-ray may help to establish the source of blood loss in hemodynamically abnormal patients and in patients with pelvic pain or tenderness. An alert, awake patient without pelvic pain or tenderness does not require a pelvic radiograph.

TABLE 5-2 COMPARISON OF DPL, FAST, AND CT IN ABDOMINAL TRAUMA

	DPL	FAST	CT SCAN
Advantages	• Early operative determination • Performed rapidly • Can detect bowel injury • No need for transport from resuscitation area	• Early operative determination • Noninvasive • Performed rapidly • Repeatable • No need for transport from resuscitation area	• Anatomic diagnosis • Noninvasive • Repeatable • Visualizes retroperitoneal structures • Visualizes bony and soft-tissue structures • Visualizes extraluminal air
Disadvantages	• Invasive • Risk of procedure-related injury • Requires gastric and urinary decompression for prevention of complications • Not repeatable • Interferes with interpretation of subsequent CT or FAST • Low specificity • Can miss diaphragm injuries	• Operator-dependent • Bowel gas and subcutaneous air distort images • Can miss diaphragm, bowel, and pancreatic injuries • Does not completely assess retroperitoneal structures • Does not visualize extraluminal air • Body habitus can limit image clarity	• Higher cost and longer time • Radiation and IV contrast exposure • Can miss diaphragm injuries • Can miss some bowel and pancreatic injuries • Requires transport from resuscitation area
Indications	• Abnormal hemodynamics in blunt abdominal trauma • Penetrating abdominal trauma without other indications for immediate laparotomy	• Abnormal hemodynamics in blunt abdominal trauma • Penetrating abdominal trauma without other indications for immediate laparotomy	• Normal hemodynamics in blunt or penetrating abdominal trauma • Penetrating back/flank trauma without other indications for immediate laparotomy

Focused Assessment with Sonography for Trauma

When performed by properly trained individuals, FAST is an accepted, rapid, and reliable study for identifying intraperitoneal fluid (■ FIGURE 5-4). It has the advantage of being repeatable and can also detect pericardial tamponade, one of the nonhypovolemic causes of hypotension.

FAST includes examination of four regions: the pericardial sac, hepatorenal fossa, splenorenal fossa, and pelvis or pouch of Douglas (■ FIGURE 5-5A). After doing an initial scan, clinicians may perform a single or multiple repeat scans to detect progressive hemoperitoneum (■ FIGURE 5-5B). FAST can be performed at the bedside in the resuscitation room at the same time other diagnostic or therapeutic procedures are performed. See *Appendix G: Circulation Skills*, and *FAST video on MyATLS mobile app*.

Diagnostic Peritoneal Lavage

DPL is another rapidly performed study to identify hemorrhage (■ FIGURE 5-6). Because it can significantly alter subsequent examinations of the patient, the surgical team caring for the patient should perform the DPL. Note that DPL requires gastric and urinary decompression for prevention of complications. The technique is most useful in patients who are hemodynamically abnormal with blunt abdominal trauma or in penetrating trauma patients with multiple cavitary or apparent tangential trajectories. Finally,

PITFALL	PREVENTION
False–negative FAST examination	• Recognize that obesity can degrade images obtained with FAST. • Maintain a high index of suspicion. • Use alternative diagnostic testing and/or repeat evaluation(s). • Recognize that FAST is insensitive for the diagnosis of hollow visceral injury.

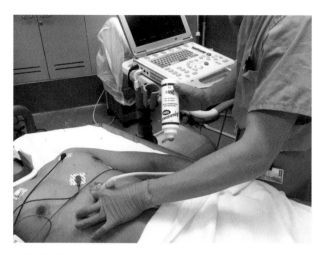

■ FIGURE 5-4 Focused Assessment with Sonography for Trauma (FAST). In FAST, ultrasound technology is used to detect the presence of hemoperitoneum.

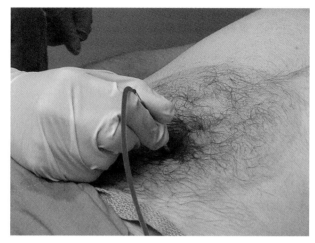

■ FIGURE 5-6 Diagnostic Peritoneal Lavage (DPL). DPL is a rapidly performed, invasive procedure that is sensitive for the detection of intraperitoneal hemorrhage.

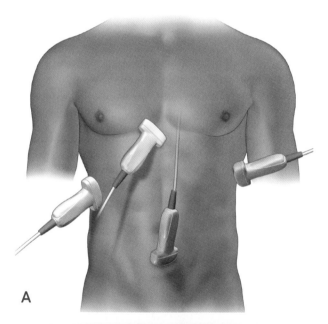

A

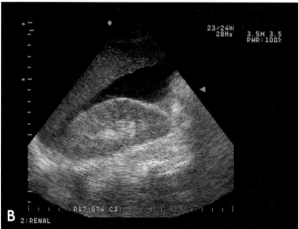

B

■ FIGURE 5-5 A. Probe locations. B. FAST image of the right upper quadrant showing the liver, kidney, and free fluid.

hemodynamically normal patients who require abdominal evaluation in settings where FAST and CT are not available may benefit from the use of DPL. In settings where CT and/or FAST are available, DPL is rarely used because it is invasive and requires surgical expertise.

Relative contraindications to DPL include previous abdominal operations, morbid obesity, advanced cirrhosis, and preexisting coagulopathy. An open, semi-open, or closed (Seldinger) infraumbilical technique is acceptable in the hands of trained clinicians. In patients with pelvic fractures, an open supraumbilical approach is preferred to avoid entering an anterior pre-peritoneal pelvic hematoma. In patients with advanced pregnancy, use an open supraumbilical approach to avoid damaging the enlarged uterus. Aspiration of gastrointestinal contents, vegetable fibers, or bile through the lavage catheter mandates laparotomy. Aspiration of 10 cc or more of blood in hemodynamically abnormal patients requires laparotomy. (See *Appendix G: Circulation Skills*.)

Computed Tomography

CT is a diagnostic procedure that requires transporting the patient to the scanner (i.e., removing the patient from the resuscitation area), administering IV contrast, and radiation exposure. CT is a time-consuming (although less so with modern CT scanners) procedure that should be used only in hemodynamically normal patients in whom there is no apparent indication for an emergency laparotomy. Do not perform CT scanning if it delays transfer of a patient to a higher level of care.

CT scans provide information relative to specific organ injury and extent, and they can diagnose retroperitoneal and pelvic organ injuries that are difficult to assess with a physical examination, FAST, and DPL. Relative contraindications for using CT include a delay until the scanner is available, an uncooperative patient who cannot be safely sedated, and allergy to the contrast agent. CT can miss some gastrointestinal, diaphragmatic, and pancreatic injuries. In the absence of hepatic or splenic injuries, the presence of free fluid in the abdominal cavity suggests an injury to the gastrointestinal tract and/or its mesentery, and many trauma surgeons believe this finding to be an indication for early operative intervention.

Diagnostic Laparoscopy or Thoracoscopy

Diagnostic laparoscopy is an accepted method for evaluating a hemodynamically normal, penetrating trauma patient with potential tangential injury and without indication for laparotomy. Laparoscopy is useful to diagnose diaphragmatic injury and peritoneal penetration. The need for general anesthesia limits its usefulness.

Contrast Studies

Contrast studies can aid in the diagnosis of specifically suspected injuries, but they should not delay the care of hemodynamically abnormal patients. These studies include

- Urethrography
- Cystography
- Intravenous pyelogram
- Gastrointestinal contrast studies

Urethrography should be performed before inserting a urinary catheter when a urethral injury is suspected. The urethrogram is performed with an 8 French urinary catheter secured in the meatus by balloon inflation to 1.5 to 2 mL. Approximately 30 to 35 mL of undiluted contrast material is instilled with gentle pressure. In males, a radiograph is taken with an anterior-posterior projection and with slight stretching of the penis toward one of the patient's shoulders. An adequate study shows reflux of contrast into the bladder.

A *cystogram* or *CT cystography* is the most effective method of diagnosing an intraperitoneal or extra-peritoneal bladder rupture. A syringe barrel is attach-ed to the indwelling bladder catheter and held 40 cm above the patient. Then 350 mL of water-soluble contrast is allowed to flow into the bladder until either the flow

stops, the patient voids spontaneously, or the patient reports discomfort. An additional 50 mL of contrast is instilled to ensure bladder distention. Anterior-posterior pre-drainage, filled, and post-drainage radiographs are essential to definitively exclude bladder injury. CT evaluation of the bladder and pelvis (CT cystogram) is an alternative study that yields additional information about the kidneys and pelvic bones.

Suspected urinary system injuries are best evaluated by contrast-enhanced CT scan. If CT is not available, *intravenous pyelogram (IVP)* provides an alternative. A high-dose, rapid injection of renal contrast ("screening IVP") is performed using 200 mg of iodine/kg body weight. Visualization of the renal calyces on an abdominal radiograph should appear 2 minutes after the injection is completed. Unilateral renal non-visualization occurs with an absent kidney, thrombosis, or avulsion of the renal artery, and massive parenchymal disruption. Non-visualization may warrant further radiologic evaluation.

Isolated injuries to retroperitoneal gastrointestinal structures (e.g., duodenum, ascending or descending colon, rectum, biliary tract, and pancreas) may not

PITFALL	PREVENTION
Delayed recognition of intra-abdominal or pelvic injury, leading to early death from hemorrhage or late death from a visceral injury.	• Recognize mechanisms of injury that can result in intra-abdominal injury. • Recognize the factors that can limit the utility of the physical examination. • Use diagnostic adjuncts such as FAST, DPL, and CT to aid in the diagnosis of injury.
Assessment with physical exam and adjuncts such as ultrasound and x-rays can be compromised in obese patients.	• Maintain a high index of suspicion for abdominal/pelvic injury in obese patients with the potential for abdominal injury, regardless of mechanism. • Recognize the potential limitations of imaging adjuncts.
Seemingly minor abdominal and pelvic injuries can result in severe bleeding in older, frail individuals, as well as individuals receiving anticoagulant therapy.	• Early and aggressive therapy is essential for optimal results. • Make an early deter-mination of the degree of coagulopathy and initiate reversal, when appropriate.

immediately cause peritonitis and may not be detected on DPL or FAST. When injury to one of these structures is suspected, CT with contrast, specific upper and lower gastrointestinal intravenous contrast studies, and pancreaticobiliary imaging studies can be useful. However, the surgeon who ultimately cares for the patient will guide these studies.

EVALUATION OF SPECIFIC PENETRATING INJURIES

The etiology of injury (e.g., stab wound or gunshot), anatomical location (e.g., thoracoabdominal, anterior, posterior, or flank) and available resources influence the evaluation of penetrating abdominal trauma. In anterior abdominal stab wounds, options include serial physical examination, FAST, and DPL. Diagnostic laparoscopy is a reliable study to determine peritoneal and diaphragmatic penetration in thoracoabdominal injuries, in addition to double (PO and IV) and triple (PO, rectal, and IV) contrast CT scans. Double- or triple-contrast CT scans are useful in flank and back injuries. In all cases of penetrating trauma, immediate surgery may be required for diagnosis and treatment.

PITFALL	PREVENTION
Transfer is delayed to perform CT scan of the abdomen.	• When a patient requires transfer to a higher level of care, CT must not delay transfer. • CT should be performed if it will alter care at the referring facility or facilitate stabilization of the patient for transfer.

Most abdominal gunshot wounds are managed by exploratory laparotomy. The incidence of significant intraperitoneal injury approaches 98% when peritoneal penetration is present. Stab wounds to the abdomen may be managed more selectively, but approximately 30% cause intraperitoneal injury. Thus, indications for laparotomy in patients with penetrating abdominal wounds include

- Hemodynamic abnormality
- Gunshot wound with a transperitoneal trajectory
- Signs of peritoneal irritation
- Signs of peritoneal penetration (e.g., evisceration)

PITFALL	PREVENTION
Delayed diagnosis of intra-abdominal injury in a patient with a tangential gunshot wound to the abdomen	• Tangential GSWs may not be truly tangential (e.g., penetrate the peritoneal cavity). • High-velocity penetrating wounds can produce injury without peritoneal penetration but by blast effect; this is most common with explosive or military wounds.

Thoracoabdominal Wounds

Evaluation options for patients without indications for immediate laparotomy, but with possible injuries to the diaphragm and upper abdominal structures include thoracoscopy, laparoscopy, DPL, and CT.

Anterior Abdominal Wounds: Nonoperative Management

Approximately 55% to 60% of all patients with stab wounds that penetrate the anterior peritoneum have hypotension, peritonitis, or evisceration of the omentum or small bowel. These patients require emergency laparotomy. However, nonoperative management can be considered in hemodynamically normal patients without peritoneal signs or evisceration. Less invasive diagnostic options for these patients (who may have pain at the site of the stab wound) include serial physical examinations over a 24-hour period (with or without serial FAST exams), DPL, CT scan, or diagnostic laparoscopy.

Although a positive FAST may be helpful in this situation, a negative FAST does not exclude the possibility of a visceral injury without a large volume of intra-abdominal fluid. Serial physical examinations are labor intensive but have an overall accuracy rate of 94%. CT scan and DPL may allow for earlier diagnosis of injury in relatively asymptomatic patients. Diagnostic laparoscopy can confirm or exclude peritoneal penetration, but it is less useful in identifying specific injuries. The surgeon determines when DPL and laparoscopy are to be used.

Flank and Back Injuries: Nonoperative Management

The thickness of the flank and back muscles protects underlying viscera against injury from many stab wounds and some gunshot wounds. For those who do not demonstrate indications for immediate laparotomy, less invasive diagnostic options include serial physical examinations (with or without serial FAST exams), double- or triple-contrast CT scans, and DPL. In patients with wounds posterior to the anterior axillary line, serial examination for the development of peritonitis is very accurate in detecting retroperitoneal and intraperitoneal injuries.

Double or triple contrast-enhanced CT is a time-consuming study that may more fully evaluate the retroperitoneal colon on the side of the wound. The accuracy is comparable to that of serial physical examinations. However, the CT should allow for earlier diagnosis of injury when it is performed properly.

Rarely, retroperitoneal injuries can be missed by serial examinations and contrast CT. Early outpatient follow-up is mandatory after the 24-hour period of in-hospital observation because of the subtle presentation of certain colonic injuries.

PITFALL	PREVENTION
Concussive and blast injuries can cause intraperitoneal injury without peritoneal penetration.	• Perform evaluation for abdominal/pelvic injury in victims of concussive and blast trauma, even when no exterior wounds are present.
Assessment with physical exam, ultrasound, and x-rays is compromised in the obese patient. Image quality of all radiographs is decreased, and DPL is difficult, if not impossible, in the ED.	• Maintain a high index of suspicion for abdominal/pelvic injury in the obese patient regardless of mechanism. • CT scan may represent the best potential imaging modality. • In some cases, operation may be required for diagnosis.
Delayed exploration of hemodynamically abnormal patient with abdominal stab wound.	• All hemodynamically abnormal patients should undergo laparotomy. • Serial physical examinations are not an option in hemodynamically abnormal patients and those with peritonitis or evisceration. • CT scan, DPL, and FAST are not indicated in hemodynamically abnormal patients or those with peritonitis or evisceration with penetrating abdominal trauma.

DPL also can be used in such patients as an early screening test. A positive DPL is an indication for an urgent laparotomy. However, DPL may not detect retroperitoneal colon injuries.

INDICATIONS FOR LAPAROTOMY

Surgical judgment is required to determine the timing and need for laparotomy (■ FIGURE 5-7). The following indications are commonly used to facilitate the decision-making process in this regard:

- Blunt abdominal trauma with hypotension, with a positive FAST or clinical evidence of intraperitoneal bleeding, or without another source of bleeding
- Hypotension with an abdominal wound that penetrates the anterior fascia
- Gunshot wounds that traverse the peritoneal cavity
- Evisceration
- Bleeding from the stomach, rectum, or genitourinary tract following penetrating trauma
- Peritonitis
- Free air, retroperitoneal air, or rupture of the hemidiaphragm
- Contrast-enhanced CT that demonstrates ruptured gastrointestinal tract, intraperitoneal bladder injury, renal pedicle injury, or severe visceral parenchymal injury after blunt or penetrating trauma

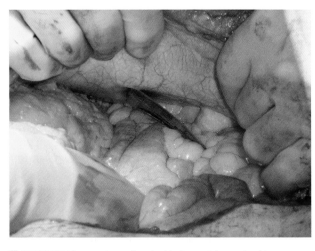

■ FIGURE 5-7 Laparotomy. Surgical judgment is required to determine the timing and need for laparotomy.

- Blunt or penetrating abdominal trauma with aspiration of gastrointestinal contents, vegetable fibers, or bile from DPL, or aspiration of 10 cc or more of blood in hemodynamically abnormal patients

EVALUATION OF OTHER SPECIFIC INJURIES

The liver, spleen, and kidney are the organs predominantly involved following blunt trauma, although the relative incidence of hollow visceral perforation, and lumbar spinal injuries increases with improper seat-belt usage (see Table 5-1). Diagnosis of injuries to the diaphragm, duodenum, pancreas, genitourinary system, and small bowel can be difficult. Most penetrating injuries are diagnosed at laparotomy.

Diaphragm Injuries

Blunt tears can occur in any portion of either diaphragm, although the left hemidiaphragm is most often injured. A common injury is 5 to 10 cm in length and involves the posterolateral left hemidiaphragm. Abnormalities on the initial chest x-ray include elevation or "blurring" of the hemidiaphragm, hemothorax, an abnormal gas shadow that obscures the hemidiaphragm, or a gastric tube positioned in the chest. However, the initial chest x-ray can be normal in a small percentage of patients. Suspect this diagnosis for any penetrating wound of the thoracoabdomen, and confirm it with laparotomy, thoracoscopy, or laparoscopy.

Duodenal Injuries

Duodenal rupture is classically encountered in unrestrained drivers involved in frontal-impact motor vehicle collisions and patients who sustain direct blows to the abdomen, such as from bicycle handlebars. A bloody gastric aspirate or retroperitoneal air on an abdominal radiograph or CT should raise suspicion for this injury. An upper gastrointestinal x-ray series, double-contrast CT, or emergent laparotomy is indicated for high-risk patients.

Pancreatic Injuries

Pancreatic injuries often result from a direct epigastric blow that compresses the pancreas against the vertebral column. An early normal serum amylase level does not exclude major pancreatic trauma.

Conversely, the amylase level can be elevated from nonpancreatic sources. Double-contrast CT may not identify significant pancreatic trauma in the immediate postinjury period (up to 8 hours). It may be repeated, or other pancreatic imaging performed, if injury is suspected. Surgical exploration of the pancreas may be warranted following equivocal diagnostic studies.

Genitourinary Injuries

Contusions, hematomas, and ecchymoses of the back or flank are markers of potential underlying renal injury and warrant an evaluation (CT or IVP) of the urinary tract. Gross hematuria is an indication for imaging the urinary tract. Gross hematuria and microscopic hematuria in patients with an episode of shock are markers for increased risk of renal abdominal injuries. An abdominal CT scan with IV contrast can document the presence and extent of a blunt renal injury, which frequently can be treated nonoperatively. Thrombosis of the renal artery and disruption of the renal pedicle secondary to deceleration are rare injuries in which hematuria may be absent, although the patient can have severe abdominal pain. With either injury, an IVP, CT, or renal arteriogram can be useful in diagnosis.

An anterior pelvic fracture usually is present in patients with urethral injuries. Urethral disruptions are divided into those above (posterior) and below (anterior) the urogenital diaphragm. A posterior urethral injury is usually associated with multisystem injuries and pelvic fractures, whereas an anterior urethral injury results from a straddle impact and can be an isolated injury.

Hollow Viscus Injuries

Blunt injury to the intestines generally results from sudden deceleration with subsequent tearing near a fixed point of attachment, particularly if the patient's seat belt was positioned incorrectly. A transverse, linear ecchymosis on the abdominal wall (seat-belt sign) or lumbar distraction fracture (i.e., Chance fracture) on x-ray should alert clinicians to the possibility of intestinal injury. Although some patients have early abdominal pain and tenderness, the diagnosis of hollow viscus injuries can be difficult since they are not always associated with hemorrhage.

Solid Organ Injuries

Injuries to the liver, spleen, and kidney that result in shock, hemodynamic abnormality, or evidence of continuing hemorrhage are indications for urgent laparotomy. Solid organ injury in hemodynamically normal patients can often be managed nonoperatively. Admit these patients to the hospital for careful observation, and evaluation by a surgeon is essential. Concomitant hollow viscus injury occurs in less than 5% of patients initially diagnosed with isolated solid organ injuries.

PITFALL	PREVENTION
Missed diaphragmatic injury in penetrating thoracoabdominal injury	• Exclude the diagnosis of penetrating diaphragm injury with laparotomy, thoracoscopy, or laparoscopy.
Missed intestinal injury	• Additional assessments (e.g., serial physical examinations, repeat CT, repeat ultrasound, DPL, laparoscopy, and laparotomy) are often indicated when bowel injury is a clinical concern.

Pelvic Fractures and Associated Injuries

Patients with hypotension and pelvic fractures have high mortality. Sound decision making is crucial for optimal patient outcome. Pelvic fractures associated with hemorrhage commonly involve disruption of the posterior osseous ligamentous complex (i.e., sacroiliac, sacrospinous, sacrotuberous, and fibromuscular pelvic floor), evidenced by a sacral fracture, a sacroiliac fracture, and/or dislocation of the sacroiliac joint.

Mechanism of Injury and Classification

Pelvic ring injury can occur following a motor vehicle crash, motorcycle crash, pedestrian–vehicle collision, direct crushing injury, or fall. Pelvic fractures are classified into four types, based on injury force patterns: AP compression, lateral compression, vertical shear, and combined mechanism (■ FIGURE 5-8).

AP compression injury is often associated with a motorcycle or a head-on motor vehicle crash. This mechanism produces external rotation of the hemipelvis with separation of the symphysis pubis and tearing of the posterior ligamentous complex. The disrupted pelvic ring widens, tearing the posterior venous plexus and branches of the internal iliac arterial system. Hemorrhage can be severe and life threatening.

Lateral compression injury, which involves force directed laterally into the pelvis, is the most common mechanism of pelvic fracture in a motor vehicle collision. In contrast to AP compression, the hemipelvis rotates internally during lateral compression, reducing pelvic volume and reducing tension on the pelvic vascular structures. This internal rotation may drive the pubis into the lower genitourinary system, potentially causing injury to the bladder and/or urethra. Hemorrhage and other sequelae from lateral compression injury rarely result in death, but can produce severe and permanent morbidity, and elderly patients can develop significant bleeding from pelvic fractures from this mechanism. When this occurs, these patients require early hemorrhage control techniques such as angioembolization. Frail and elderly patients may bleed significantly following minor trauma from lateral compression fractures.

Vertical displacement of the sacroiliac joint can also disrupt the iliac vasculature and cause severe hemorrhage. In this mechanism, a high-energy shear force occurs along a vertical plane across the anterior and posterior

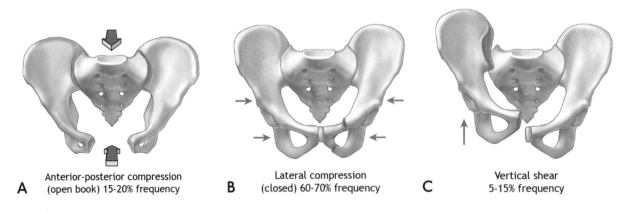

A Anterior-posterior compression (open book) 15-20% frequency	**B** Lateral compression (closed) 60-70% frequency	**C** Vertical shear 5-15% frequency

■ FIGURE 5-8 Pelvic Fractures. **A.** AP Compression fracture. **B.** Lateral compression fracture. **C.** Vertical shear fracture.

aspects of the ring. This *vertical shearing* disrupts the sacrospinous and sacrotuberous ligaments and leads to major pelvic instability. A fall from a height greater than 12 feet commonly results in a vertical shear injury.

Mortality in patients with all types of pelvic fractures is approximately one in six (range 5%–30%). Mortality rises to approximately one in four (range 10%–42%) in patients with closed pelvic fractures and hypotension. In patients with open pelvic fractures, mortality is approximately 50%. Hemorrhage is the major potentially reversible factor contributing to mortality. (See *Appendix G: Circulation Skills*.)

Management

Initial management of hypovolemic shock associated with a major pelvic disruption requires rapid hemorrhage control and fluid resuscitation. Hemorrhage control is achieved through mechanical stabilization of the pelvic ring and external counter pressure. Patients with these injuries may be initially assessed and treated in facilities that do not have the resources to definitively manage the associated hemorrhage. In such cases, trauma team members can use simple techniques to stabilize the pelvis before patient transfer. Because pelvic injuries associated with major hemorrhage externally rotate the hemipelvis, internal rotation of the lower limbs may assist in hemorrhage control by reducing pelvic volume. By applying a support directly to the patient's pelvis, clinicians can splint the disrupted pelvis and further reduce potential pelvic hemorrhage. A sheet, pelvic binder, or other device can produce sufficient temporary fixation for the unstable pelvis when applied at the level of the greater trochanters of the femur (■ FIGURE 5-9). (Also see *Pelvic Binder video on MyATLS mobile app*.) In cases of vertical shear injuries, longitudinal traction applied through the skin or the skeleton can also assist in providing stability. This should be done with the consultation of an orthopedic specialist.

External pelvic binders are a temporary emergency procedure. Proper application is mandatory, and patients with pelvic binders require careful monitoring. Tight binders or those left in position for prolonged

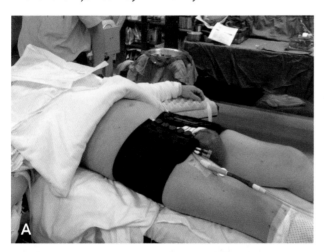
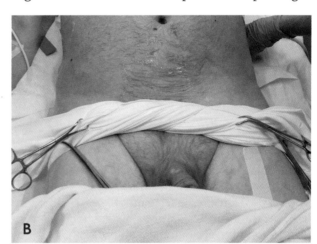
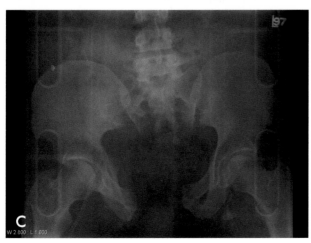
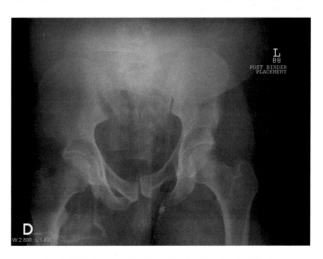

■ **FIGURE 5-9 Pelvic Stabilization. A.** Pelvic binder. **B.** Pelvic stabilization using a sheet. **C.** Before application of pelvic binder. **D.** After application of pelvic binder.

PITFALL	PREVENTION
Delayed treatment of pelvic hemorrhage.	• Achieve hemorrhage control early by applying a pelvic binder, angioembolization, and/ or operative measures.
A patient develops a pressure ulcer over the trochanter after a pelvic binders is left in place for 24 hours.	• Carefully monitor patients with pelvic binders for skin ulceration. • Develop plan for early definitive hemorrhage control.
Unexplained hypotension in elderly patient with history of a fall.	• Look carefully for evidence of subcutaneous bleeding. • Recognize that, in frail patients, low-energy mechanism pelvic fractures can cause bleeding requiring treatment and transfusion.

time periods can cause skin breakdown and ulceration over bony prominences.

Optimal care of patients with hemodynamic abnormalities related to pelvic fracture demands a team effort of trauma surgeons, orthopedic surgeons, and interventional radiologists or vascular surgeons. Angiographic embolization is frequently employed to stop arterial hemorrhage related to pelvic fractures. Preperitoneal packing is an alternative method to control pelvic hemorrhage when angioembolization is delayed or unavailable. Hemorrhage control techniques are not exclusive and more than one technique may be required for successful hemorrhage control. An experienced trauma surgeon should construct the therapeutic plan for a patient with pelvic hemorrhage based on available resources.

Although definitive management of patients with hemorrhagic shock and pelvic fractures varies, one treatment algorithm is shown in (■ FIGURE 5-10). Significant resources are required to care for patients with severe pelvic fractures. Early consideration of transfer to a trauma center is essential. In resource-limited environments, the absence of surgical and/or angiographic resources for hemodynamically abnormal patients with pelvic fractures or hemodynamically normal patients with significant solid organ injury mandates early transfer to a trauma center with these facilities.

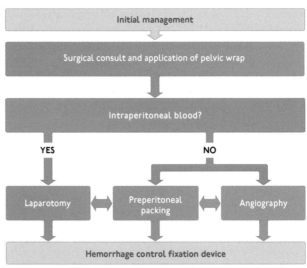

■ FIGURE 5-10 Pelvic Fractures and Hemorrhagic Shock Management Algorithm.

TEAMWORK

• The team must be able to determine the priorities of treatment and identify which of perhaps several simultaneous studies and interventions need to be performed. The team leader must recognize the need to apply a pelvic binder and ensure its correct placement while continuing to evaluate the patient's response to resuscitation.

• Ensure that team members work effectively and swiftly to avoid any delay in the transfer of a patient with abdominal injury to definitive care.

CHAPTER SUMMARY

1. The three distinct regions of the abdomen are the peritoneal cavity, retroperitoneal space, and pelvic cavity. The pelvic cavity contains components of both the peritoneal cavity and retroperitoneal space.

2. Early consultation with a surgeon is necessary for a patient with possible intra-abdominal injuries. Once the patient's vital functions have been restored, evaluation and management varies depending on the mechanism of injury.

3. Hemodynamically abnormal patients with multiple blunt injuries should be rapidly assessed

for intra-abdominal bleeding or contamination from the gastrointestinal tract by performing a FAST or DPL.

4. Patients who require transfer to a higher level of care should be recognized early and stabilized without performing nonessential diagnostic tests.

5. Indications for CT scan in hemodynamically normal patients include the inability to reliably evaluate the abdomen with physical examination, as well as the presence of abdominal pain, abdominal tenderness, or both. The decision to operate is based on the specific organ(s) involved and injury severity.

6. All patients with penetrating wounds of the abdomen and associated hypotension, peritonitis, or evisceration require emergent laparotomy. Patients with gunshot wounds that by physical examination or routine radiographic results obviously traverse the peritoneal cavity or visceral/vascular area of the retroperitoneum also usually require laparotomy. Asymptomatic patients with anterior abdominal stab wounds that penetrate the fascia or peritoneum on local wound exploration require further evaluation; there are several acceptable alternatives.

7. Asymptomatic patients with flank or back stab wounds that are not obviously superficial are evaluated by serial physical examinations or contrast-enhanced CT.

8. Management of blunt and penetrating trauma to the abdomen and pelvis includes

   • Delineating the injury mechanism

   • Reestablishing vital functions and optimizing oxygenation and tissue perfusion

   • Prompt recognition of sources of hemorrhage with efforts at hemorrhage control

   • Meticulous initial physical examination, repeated at regular intervals

   • Pelvic stabilization

   • Laparotomy

   • Angiographic embolization and pre-peritoneal packing

   • Selecting special diagnostic maneuvers as needed, performed with a minimal loss of time

   • Maintaining a high index of suspicion related to occult vascular and retroperitoneal injuries

BIBLIOGRAPHY

1. Agolini SF, Shah K, Jaffe J, et al. Arterial embolization is a rapid and effective technique for controlling pelvic fracture hemorrhage. *J Trauma* 1997;43(3):395–399.
2. Anderson PA, Rivara FP, Maier RV, et al. The epidemiology of seat belt–associated injuries. *J Trauma* 1991;31:60–67.
3. Aquilera PA, Choi T, Durham BH. Ultrasound-aided supra-pubic cystostomy catheter placement in the emergency department. *J Emerg Med* 2004;26(3):319–321.
4. Ball CG, Jafri SM, Kirkpatrick AW, et al. Traumatic urethral injuries: does the digital rectal examination really help us? *Injury* 2009Sep;40(9):984–986.
5. Ballard RB, Rozycki GS, Newman PG, et al. An algorithm to reduce the incidence of false-negative FAST examinations in patients at high risk for occult injury. *J Am Coll Surg* 1999;189(2):145–150.
6. Boulanger BR, Milzman D, Mitchell K, et al.. Body habitus as a predictor of injury pattern after blunt trauma. *J Trauma* 1992;33:228–232.
7. Boyle EM, Maier RV, Salazar JD, et al. Diagnosis of injuries after stab wounds to the back and flank. *J Trauma* 1997;42(2):260–265.
8. Como JJ, Bokhari F, Chiu WC, et al. Practice management guidelines for selective nonoperative management of penetrating abdominal trauma. *J Trauma* 2010Mar;68(3):721–733.
9. Cothren CC, Osborn PM, Moore EE, et al. Preperitoneal pelvic packing for hemodynamically unstable pelvic fracture: a paradigm shift. *J Trauma* 2007;2(4):834–842.
10. Cryer HM, Miller FB, Evers BM, et al. Pelvic fracture classification: correlation with hemorrhage. *J Trauma* 1988;28:973–980.
11. Dalal SA, Burgess AR, Siegel JH, et al. Pelvic fracture in multiple trauma: classification by mechanism is key to pattern of organ injury, resuscitative requirements, and outcome. *J Trauma* 1989;29:981–1002.
12. Demetriades D, Rabinowitz B, Sofianos C, et al. The management of penetrating injuries of the back: a prospective study of 230 patients. *Ann Surg* 1988;207:72–74.
13. Dischinger PC, Cushing BM, Kerns TJ. Injury patterns associated with direction of impact:

drivers admitted to trauma centers. *J Trauma* 1993;35:454–459.

14. Ditillo M, Pandit V, Rhee P, et al. Morbid obesity predisposes trauma patients to worse outcomes: a National Trauma Data Bank analysis. *J Trauma* 2014 Jan;76(1):176–179.

15. Esposito TJ, Ingraham A, Luchette FA, et al. Reasons to omit digital rectal exam in trauma patients: no fingers, no rectum, no useful additional information. *J Trauma* 2005 Dec; 59(6):1314–1319.

16. Fabian TC, Croce MA. Abdominal trauma, including indications for laparotomy. In: Mattox LK, Feliciano DV, Moore EE, eds. *Trauma*. East Norwalk, CT: Appleton & Lange; 2000: 583–602.

17. Felder S, Margel D, Murrell Z, et al. Usefulness of bowel sound auscultation: a prospective evaluation. *J Surg Educ* 2014;71(5):768–773.

18. Holmes JF, Harris D, Battistella FD. Performance of abdominal ultrasonography in blunt trauma patients with out-of-hospital or emergency department hypotension. *Ann Emerg Med* 2004;43(3):354–361.

19. Huizinga WK, Baker LW, Mtshali ZW. Selective management of abdominal and thoracic stab wounds with established peritoneal penetration: the eviscerated omentum. *Am J Surg* 1987;153:564–568.

20. Johnson MH, Chang A, Brandes SB. The value of digital rectal examination in assessing for pelvic fracture-associated urethral injury: what defines a high-riding or non-palpable prostate? *J Trauma* 2013 Nov;75(5):913–915.

21. Knudson MM, McAninch JW, Gomez R. Hematuria as a predictor of abdominal injury after blunt trauma. *Am J Surg* 1992;164(5):482–486.

22. Koraitim MM. Pelvic fracture urethral injuries: the unresolved controversy. *J Urol* 1999;161(5):1433–1441.

23. Liu M, Lee C, Veng F. Prospective comparison of diagnostic peritoneal lavage, computed tomographic scanning, and ultrasonography for the diagnosis of blunt abdominal trauma. *J Trauma* 1993;35:267–270.

24. Liu T, Chen JJ, Bai XJ, et al. The effect of obesity on outcomes in trauma patients: a meta-analysis. *Injury* 2013 Sep;44(9):1145–1152.

25. McCarthy MC, Lowdermilk GA, Canal DF, et al. Prediction of injury caused by penetrating wounds to the abdomen, flank, and back. *Arch Surg* 1991;26:962–966.

26. Mendez C, Gubler KD, Maier RV. Diagnostic accuracy of peritoneal lavage in patients with pelvic fractures. *Arch Surg* 1994;129(5):477–481.

27. Meyer DM, Thal ER, Weigelt JA, et al. The role of abdominal CT in the evaluation of stab wounds to the back. *J Trauma* 1989;29: 1226–1230.

28. Miller KS, McAninch JW. Radiographic assessment of renal trauma: our 15-year experience. *J Urol* 1995;154(2 Pt 1):352–355.

29. O'Malley E, Boyle E, O'Callaghan A, et al. Role of laparoscopy in penetrating abdominal trauma: a systematic review. *World J Surg* 2013 Jan;37(1):113–122.

30. Osborn PM, Smith WR, Moore EE, et al. Direct retroperitoneal pelvic packing versus pelvic angiography: a comparison of two management protocols for haemodynamically unstable pelvic fractures.. *Injury* 2009 Jan;40(1): 54–60.

31. Osborne Z, Rowitz B. Moore H, et al. Obesity in trauma: outcomes and disposition trends. *Am J Surg* 2014 207(3):387–392; discussion 391–392.

32. Phillips T, Sclafani SJA, Goldstein A, et al. Use of the contrast-enhanced CT enema in the management of penetrating trauma to the flank and back. *J Trauma* 1986;26:593–601.

33. Poblemann T, Gasslen A, Hufner T, et al. Extraperitoneal packing at laparotomy. Presented at OTA-AAST Annual meeting Oct 12–14, 2000, San Antonio, Texas.

34. Reid AB, Letts RM, Black GB. Pediatric chance fractures: association with intraabdominal injuries and seat belt use. *J Trauma* 1990;30:384–391.

35. Robin AP, Andrews JR, Lange DA, et al. Selective management of anterior abdominal stab wounds. *J Trauma* 1989;29:1684–1689.

36. Routt ML Jr, Simonian PT, Swiontkowski MF. Stabilization of pelvic ring disruptions. *Orthop Clin North Am* 1997;28(3):369–388.

37. Rozycki GS, Ballard RB, Feliciano DV, et al. Surgeon-performed ultrasound for the assessment of truncal injuries: lessons learned from 1540 patients. *Ann Surg* 1998;228(4):557–565.

38. Rozycki GS. Abdominal ultrasonography in trauma. *Surg Clin North Am* 1995;75:175–191.

39. Shackford SR, Rogers FB, Osler TM, et al. Focused abdominal sonography for trauma: the learning curve of nonradiologist clinicians in detecting hemoperitoneum. *J Trauma* 1999;46(4): 553–562.

40. Shlamovitz GZ, Mower WR, Bergman J, et al. How (un)useful is the pelvic ring stability examination in diagnosing mechanically unstable pelvic fractures in blunt trauma patients? *J Trauma* 2009;66(3):815–820.

41. Sosa JL, Baker M, Puente I, et al. Negative laparotomy in abdominal gunshot wounds:

potential impact of laparoscopy. *J Trauma* 1995 Feb;38(2):194–197.

42. Takishima T, Sugimota K, Hirata M, et al. Serum amylase level on admission in the diagnosis of blunt injury to the pancreas: its significance and limitations. *Ann Surg* 1997;226(1): 70–76.

43. Udobi KF, Rodriguez A, Chiu WC, Scalea TM. Role of ultrasonography in penetrating abdominal trauma: a prospective clinical study. *J Trauma* 2001;50(3):475–479.

44. Ultrasound in the evaluation and management of blunt abdominal trauma. *Ann Emerg Med* 1997;29(3):357–366.

45. Velmahos GC, Demetriades D, Cornwell EE 3rd. Transpelvic gunshot wounds: routine laparotomy or selective management? *World J Surg* 1998 Oct; 22(10):1034–1038.

46. Zantut LF, Ivatury RR, Smith RS, et al. Diagnostic and therapeutic laparoscopy for penetrating abdominal trauma: a multicenter experience. *J Trauma* 1997;42(5):825–829.

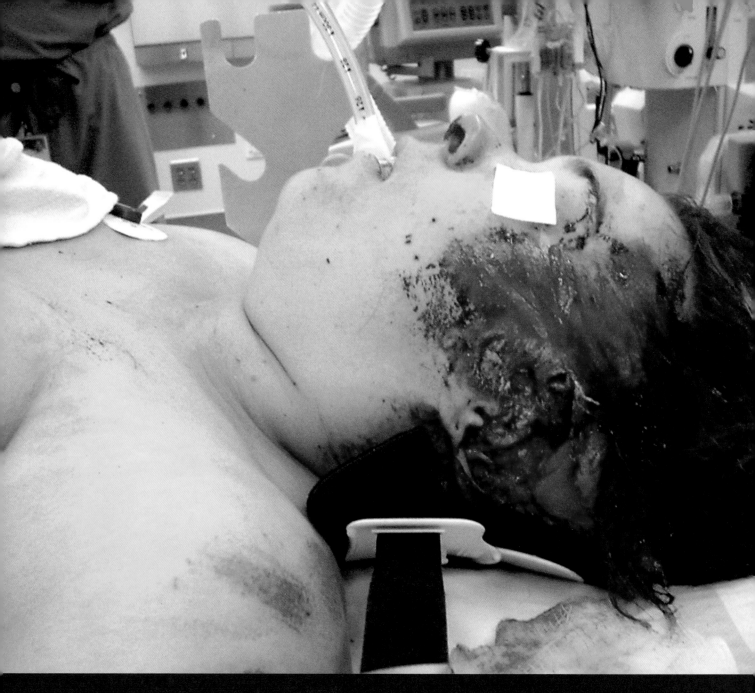

6 HEAD TRAUMA

The primary goal of treatment for patients with suspected traumatic brain injury is to prevent secondary brain injury.

CHAPTER 6 OUTLINE

OBJECTIVES

After reading this chapter and comprehending the knowledge components of the ATLS provider course, you will be able to:

1. Describe basic intracranial anatomy and the physiological principles of intracranial pressure, the Monro–Kellie Doctrine, and cerebral blood flow.

2. Describe the primary survey and resuscitation of patients with head and brain injuries.

3. Describe the components of a focused neurological examination.

4. Explain the role of adequate resuscitation in limiting secondary brain injury.

5. Identify the considerations for patient transfer, admission, consultation, and discharge of patients with head injuries.

Head injuries are among the most common types of trauma encountered in emergency departments (EDs). Many patients with severe brain injuries die before reaching a hospital; in fact, nearly 90% of prehospital trauma-related deaths involve brain injury. Approximately 75% of patients with brain injuries who receive medical attention can be categorized as having mild injuries, 15% as moderate, and 10% as severe. Most recent United States data estimate 1,700,000 traumatic brain injuries (TBIs) occur annually, including 275,000 hospitalizations and 52,000 deaths.

TBI survivors are often left with neuropsychological impairments that result in disabilities affecting work and social activity. Every year, an estimated 80,000 to 90,000 people in the United States experience long-term disability from brain injury. In one average European country (Denmark), approximately 300 individuals per million inhabitants suffer moderate to severe head injuries annually, and more than one-third of these individuals require brain injury rehabilitation. Given these statistics, it is clear that even a small reduction in the mortality and morbidity resulting from brain injury can have a major impact on public health.

The primary goal of treatment for patients with suspected TBI is to prevent secondary brain injury. The most important ways to limit secondary brain damage and thereby improve a patient's outcome are to ensure adequate oxygenation and maintain blood pressure at a level that is sufficient to perfuse the brain. After managing the ABCDEs, patients who are determined by clinical examination to have head trauma and require care at a trauma center should be transferred without delay. If neurosurgical capabilities exist, it is critical to identify any mass lesion that requires surgical evacuation, and this objective is best achieved by rapidly obtaining a computed tomographic (CT) scan of the head. CT scanning should not delay patient transfer to a trauma center that is capable of immediate and definitive neurosurgical intervention.

Triage for a patient with brain injury depends on how severe the injury is and what facilities are available within a particular community. For facilities without neurosurgical coverage, ensure that pre-arranged transfer agreements with higher-level care facilities are in place. Consult with a neurosurgeon early in the course of treatment. ■ BOX 6-1 lists key information to communicate when consulting a neurosurgeon about a patient with TBI.

ANATOMY REVIEW

A review of cranial anatomy includes the scalp, skull, meninges, brain, ventricular system, and intracranial compartments (■ FIGURE 6-1).

SCALP

Because of the scalp's generous blood supply, scalp lacerations can result in major blood loss, hemorrhagic shock, and even death. Patients who are subject to long transport times are at particular risk for these complications.

SKULL

The base of the skull is irregular, and its surface can contribute to injury as the brain moves within the skull during the acceleration and deceleration that occurs during the traumatic event. The anterior fossa houses the frontal lobes, the middle fossa houses the temporal lobes, and the posterior fossa contains the lower brainstem and cerebellum.

MENINGES

The meninges cover the brain and consist of three layers: the dura mater, arachnoid mater, and pia mater (■ FIGURE 6-2). The dura mater is a tough,

---

BOX 6-1 NEUROSURGICAL CONSULTATION FOR PATIENTS WITH TBI

When consulting a neurosurgeon about a patient with TBI, communicate the following information:

- Patient age
- Mechanism and time of injury
- Patient's respiratory and cardiovascular status (particularly blood pressure and oxygen saturation)
- Results of the neurological examination, including the GCS score (particularly the motor response), pupil size, and reaction to light

- Presence of any focal neurological deficits
- Presence of suspected abnormal neuromuscular status
- Presence and type of associated injuries
- Results of diagnostic studies, particularly CT scan (if available)
- Treatment of hypotension or hypoxia
- Use of anticoagulants

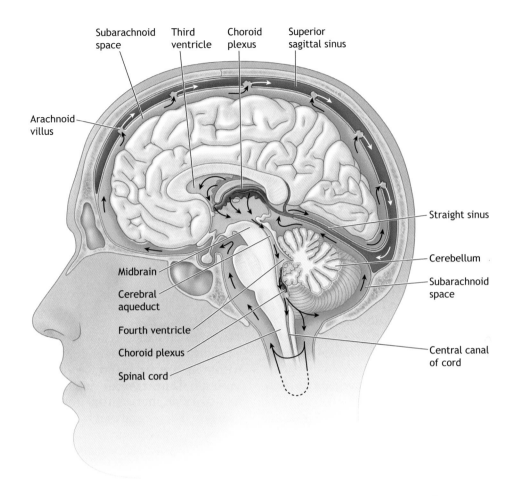

Subarachnoid space
Third ventricle
Choroid plexus
Superior sagittal sinus

Arachnoid villus

Straight sinus

Cerebellum

Subarachnoid space

Midbrain
Cerebral aqueduct
Fourth ventricle
Choroid plexus
Spinal cord

Central canal of cord

■ **FIGURE 6-1** Overview of cranial anatomy. The arrows represent the production, circulation, and resorption of cerebrospinal fluid.

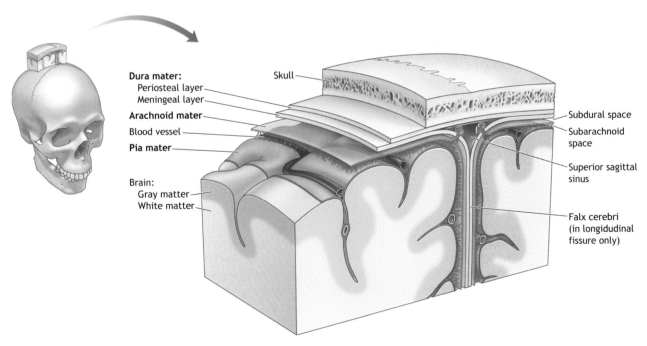

Dura mater:
    Periosteal layer
    Meningeal layer
Arachnoid mater
Blood vessel
Pia mater

Skull

Subdural space
Subarachnoid space
Superior sagittal sinus

Brain:
    Gray matter
    White matter

Falx cerebri (in longidudinal fissure only)

■ **FIGURE 6-2** The three layers of the meninges are the dura mater, arachnoid mater, and pia mater.

fibrous membrane that adheres firmly to the internal surface of the skull. At specific sites, the dura splits into two "leaves" that enclose the large venous sinuses, which provide the major venous drainage from the brain. The midline superior sagittal sinus drains into the bilateral transverse and sigmoid sinuses, which are usually larger on the right side. Laceration of these venous sinuses can result in massive hemorrhage.

Meningeal arteries lie between the dura and the internal surface of the skull in the epidural space. Overlying skull fractures can lacerate these arteries and cause an epidural hematoma. The most commonly injured meningeal vessel is the middle meningeal artery, which is located over the temporal fossa. An expanding hematoma from arterial injury in this location can lead to rapid deterioration and death. Epidural hematomas can also result from injury to the dural sinuses and from skull fractures, which tend to expand slowly and put less pressure on the underlying brain. However, most epidural hematomas constitute life-threatening emergencies that must be evaluated by a neurosurgeon as soon as possible.

Beneath the dura is a second meningeal layer: the thin, transparent arachnoid mater. Because the dura is not attached to the underlying arachnoid membrane, a potential space between these layers exists (the subdural space), into which hemorrhage can occur. In brain injury, bridging veins that travel from the surface of the brain to the venous sinuses within the dura may tear, leading to the formation of a subdural hematoma.

The third layer, the pia mater, is firmly attached to the surface of the brain. Cerebrospinal fluid (CSF) fills the space between the watertight arachnoid mater and the pia mater (the subarachnoid space), cushioning the brain and spinal cord. Hemorrhage into this fluid-filled space (subarachnoid hemorrhage) frequently accompanies brain contusion and injuries to major blood vessels at the base of the brain.

BRAIN

The brain consists of the cerebrum, brainstem, and cerebellum. The cerebrum is composed of the right and left hemispheres, which are separated by the falx cerebri. The left hemisphere contains the language centers in virtually all right-handed people and in more than 85% of left-handed people. The frontal lobe controls executive function, emotions, motor function, and, on the dominant side, expression of speech (motor speech areas). The parietal lobe directs sensory function

and spatial orientation, the temporal lobe regulates certain memory functions, and the occipital lobe is responsible for vision.

The brainstem is composed of the midbrain, pons, and medulla. The midbrain and upper pons contain the reticular activating system, which is responsible for the state of alertness. Vital cardiorespiratory centers reside in the medulla, which extends downward to connect with the spinal cord. Even small lesions in the brainstem can be associated with severe neurological deficits.

The cerebellum, responsible mainly for coordination and balance, projects posteriorly in the posterior fossa and connects to the spinal cord, brainstem, and cerebral hemispheres.

VENTRICULAR SYSTEM

The ventricles are a system of CSF-filled spaces and aqueducts within the brain. CSF is constantly produced within the ventricles and absorbed over the surface of the brain. The presence of blood in the CSF can impair its reabsorption, resulting in increased intracranial pressure. Edema and mass lesions (e.g., hematomas) can cause effacement or shifting of the normally symmetric ventricles, which can readily be identified on brain CT scans.

INTRACRANIAL COMPARTMENTS

Tough meningeal partitions separate the brain into regions. The tentorium cerebelli divides the intracranial cavity into the supratentorial and infratentorial compartments. The midbrain passes through an opening called the tentorial hiatus or notch. The oculomotor nerve (cranial nerve III) runs along the edge of the tentorium and may become compressed against it during temporal lobe herniation. Parasympathetic fibers that constrict the pupils lie on the surface of the third cranial nerve; compression of these superficial fibers during herniation causes pupillary dilation due to un-opposed sympathetic activity, often referred to as a "blown" pupil (■ FIGURE 6-3).

The part of the brain that usually herniates through the tentorial notch is the medial part of the temporal lobe, known as the uncus (■ FIGURE 6-4). Uncal herniation also causes compression of the corticospinal (pyramidal) tract in the midbrain. The motor tract crosses to the opposite side at the foramen magnum, so compression at the level of the midbrain results in weakness of the opposite side of the body (contralateral hemiparesis). Ipsilateral pupillary dilat-

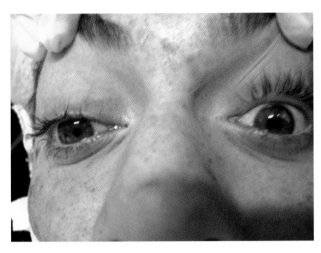

■ **FIGURE 6-3** Unequal pupils: the left is greater than the right.

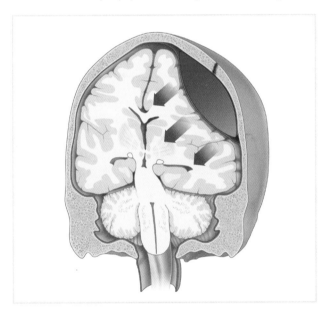

■ **FIGURE 6-4 Lateral (Uncal) Herniation.** A lesion of the middle meningeal artery secondary to a fracture of the temporal bone may cause temporal epidural hematoma. The uncus compresses the upper brain stem, involving the reticular system (decreasing GCS), the oculomotor nerve (pupillary changes), and the corticospinal tract in the midbrain (contralateral hemiparesis).

ion associated with contralateral hemiparesis is the classic sign of uncal herniation. Rarely, the mass lesion pushes the opposite side of the midbrain against the tentorial edge, resulting in hemiparesis and a dilated pupil on the same side as the hematoma.

PHYSIOLOGY REVIEW

Physiological concepts that relate to head trauma include intracranial pressure, the Monro–Kellie Doctrine, and cerebral blood flow.

INTRACRANIAL PRESSURE

Elevation of intracranial pressure (ICP) can reduce cerebral perfusion and cause or exacerbate ischemia. The normal ICP for patients in the resting state is approximately 10 mm Hg. Pressures greater than 22 mm Hg, particularly if sustained and refractory to treatment, are associated with poor outcomes.

MONRO–KELLIE DOCTRINE

The Monro–Kellie Doctrine is a simple, yet vital concept that explains ICP dynamics. The doctrine states that the total volume of the intracranial contents must remain constant, because the cranium is a rigid container incapable of expanding. When the normal intracranial volume is exceeded, ICP rises. Venous blood and CSF can be compressed out of the container, providing a degree of pressure buffering (■ FIGURE 6-5 and ■ FIGURE 6-6). Thus, very early after injury, a mass such as a blood clot can enlarge while the ICP remains normal. However, once the limit of displacement of CSF and intravascular blood has been reached, ICP rapidly increases.

CEREBRAL BLOOD FLOW

TBI that is severe enough to cause coma can markedly reduce cerebral blood flow (CBF) during the first few hours after injury. CBF usually increases over the next 2 to 3 days, but for patients who remain comatose, it

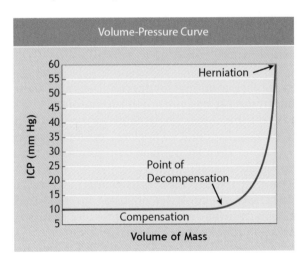

■ **FIGURE 6-5 Volume–Pressure Curve.** The intracranial contents initially can compensate for a new intracranial mass, such as a subdural or epidural hematoma. Once the volume of this mass reaches a critical threshold, a rapid increase in ICP often occurs, which can lead to reduction or cessation of cerebral blood flow.

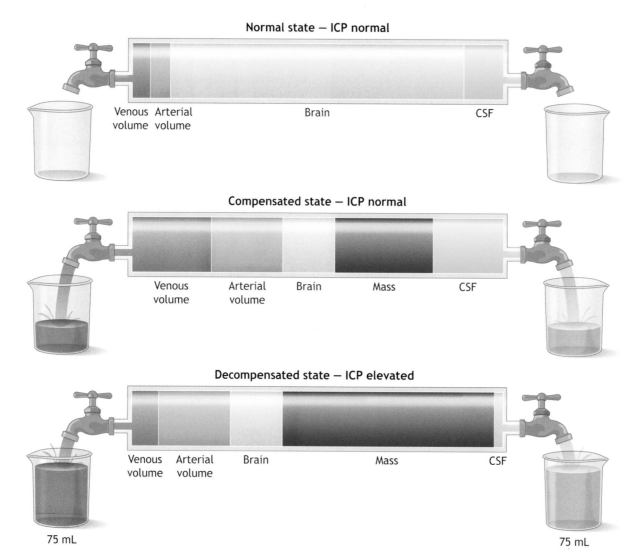

■ **FIGURE 6-6 The Monro–Kellie Doctrine Regarding Intracranial Compensation for Expanding Mass.** The total volume of the intracranial contents remains constant. If the addition of a mass such as a hematoma compresses an equal volume of CSF and venous blood, ICP remains normal. However, when this compensatory mechanism is exhausted, ICP increases exponentially for even a small additional increase in hematoma volume. (Adapted with permission from Narayan RK: Head Injury. In: Grossman RG, Hamilton WJ eds., *Principles of Neurosurgery*. New York, NY: Raven Press, 1991.)

remains below normal for days or weeks after injury. There is increasing evidence that low levels of CBF do not meet the metabolic demands of the brain early after injury. Regional, even global, cerebral ischemia is common after severe head injury for both known and undetermined reasons.

The precapillary cerebral vasculature typically can reflexively constrict or dilate in response to changes in mean arterial blood pressure (MAP). For clinical purposes, cerebral perfusion pressure (CPP) is defined as mean arterial blood pressure minus intracranial pressure (CPP = MAP − ICP). A MAP of 50 to 150 mm Hg is "autoregulated" to maintain a constant CBF (pressure autoregulation). Severe TBI can disrupt pressure autoregulation to the point that the brain cannot adequately compensate for

changes in CPP. In this situation, if the MAP is too low, ischemia and infarction result. If the MAP is too high, marked brain swelling occurs with elevated ICP.

Cerebral blood vessels also constrict or dilate in response to changes in the partial pressure of oxygen (PaO_2) and the partial pressure of carbon dioxide ($PaCO_2$) in the blood (chemical regulation). Therefore, secondary injury can occur from hypotension, hypoxia, hypercapnia, and iatrogenic hypocapnia.

Make every effort to enhance cerebral perfusion and blood flow by reducing elevated ICP, maintaining normal intravascular volume and MAP, and restoring normal oxygenation and ventilation. Hematomas and other lesions that increase intracranial volume should be evacuated early. Maintaining a normal CPP may help improve CBF; however, CPP does not equate with or ensure adequate CBF. Once compensatory mechanisms are exhausted and ICP increases exponentially, brain perfusion is compromised.

CLASSIFICATION OF HEAD INJURIES

Head injuries are classified in several ways. For practical purposes, the severity of injury and morphology are used as classifications in this chapter (■ TABLE 6-1). (Also see *Classifications of Brain Injury on MyATLS mobile app.*)

SEVERITY OF INJURY

The Glasgow Coma Scale (GCS) score is used as an objective clinical measure of the severity of brain injury (■ TABLE 6-2). (Also see *Glasgow Coma Scale tool on MyATLS mobile app.*) A GCS score of 8 or less has become the generally accepted definition of coma or severe brain injury. Patients with a brain injury who have a GCS score of 9 to 12 are categorized as having "moderate injury," and individuals with a GCS score of 13 to 15 are designated as having "mild injury." In assessing the GCS score, when there is right/left or upper/lower asymmetry, be sure to use the best motor response to calculate the score, because it is the most reliable predictor of outcome. However, the actual responses on both sides of the body, face, arm, and leg must still be recorded.

MORPHOLOGY

Head trauma may include skull fractures and intracranial lesions, such as contusions, hematomas, diffuse injuries, and resultant swelling (edema/hyperemia).

Skull Fractures

Skull fractures can occur in the cranial vault or skull base. They may be linear or stellate as well as open or closed. Basilar skull fractures usually require CT scanning with bone-window settings for identification. Clinical signs of a basilar skull fracture include periorbital ecchymosis (raccoon eyes), retroauricular ecchymosis (Battle's sign), CSF leakage from the nose (rhinorrhea) or ear (otorrhea), and dysfunction of cranial nerves VII and VIII (facial paralysis and hearing loss), which may occur immediately or a few days after initial injury. The presence of these signs should increase the index of suspicion and help identify basilar skull fractures. Some fractures traverse the carotid canals and can damage the carotid arteries (dissection, pseudoaneurysm, or

TABLE 6-1 CLASSIFICATIONS OF TRAUMATIC BRAIN INJURY

Severity	• Mild		• GCS Score 13–15
	• Moderate		• GCS Score 9–12
	• Severe		• GCS Score 3–8
Morphology	• Skull fractures	• Vault	• Linear vs. stellate
			• Depressed/nondepressed
		• Basilar	• With/without CSF leak
			• With/without seventh nerve palsy
	• Intracranial lesions	• Focal	• Epidural
			• Subdural
			• Intracerebral
		• Diffuse	• Concussion
			• Multiple contusions
			• Hypoxic/ischemic injury
			• Axonal injury

Source: Adapted with permission from Valadka AB, Narayan RK. Emergency room management of the head-injured patient. In: Narayan RK, Wilberger JE, Povlishock JT, eds. *Neurotrauma*. New York, NY: McGraw-Hill, 1996:120.

TABLE 6-2 GLASGOW COMA SCALE (GCS)

ORIGINAL SCALE	REVISED SCALE	SCORE
Eye Opening (E)	Eye Opening (E)	
Spontaneous	Spontaneous	4
To speech	To sound	3
To pain	To pressure	2
None	None	1
	Non-testable	NT
Verbal Response (V)	Verbal Response (V)	
Oriented	Oriented	5
Confused conversation	Confused	4
Inappropriate words	Words	3
Incomprehensible sounds	Sounds	2
None	None	1
	Non-testable	NT
Best Motor Response (M)	Best Motor Response (M)	
Obeys commands	Obeys commands	6
Localizes pain	Localizing	5
Flexion withdrawal to pain	Normal flexion	4
Abnormal flexion (decorticate)	Abnormal flexion	3
Extension (decerebrate)	Extension	2
None (flaccid)	None	1
	Non-testable	NT

GCS Score = (E[4] + V[5] + M[6]) = Best possible score 15; worst possible score 3.

*If an area cannot be assessed, no numerical score is given for that region, and it is considered "non-testable." *Source:* www.glasgowcomascale.org

thrombosis). In such cases, doctors should consider performing a cerebral arteriography (CT angiography [CT-A] or conventional angiogram).

Open or compound skull fractures provide direct communication between the scalp laceration and the cerebral surface when the dura is torn. Do not underestimate the significance of a skull fracture, because it takes considerable force to fracture the skull. A linear vault fracture in conscious patients increases the likelihood of an intracranial hematoma by approximately 400 times.

Intracranial Lesions

Intracranial lesions are classified as diffuse or focal, although these two forms frequently coexist.

Diffuse Brain Injuries

Diffuse brain injuries range from mild concussions, in which the head CT is normal, to severe hypoxic, ischemic injuries. With a concussion, the patient has a transient, nonfocal neurological disturbance that often includes loss of consciousness. Severe diffuse injuries often result from a hypoxic, ischemic insult to the brain from prolonged shock or apnea occurring immediately after the trauma. In such cases, the CT may initially appear normal, or the brain may appear diffusely swollen, and the normal gray-white distinction is absent. Another diffuse pattern, often seen in high-velocity impact or deceleration injuries, may produce multiple punctate hemorrhages throughout the cerebral hemispheres. These "shearing injuries," often seen in the border between the gray matter and white matter, are referred to as diffuse axonal injury (DAI) and define a clinical syndrome of severe brain injury with variable but often poor outcome.

Focal Brain Injuries

Focal lesions include epidural hematomas, subdural hematomas, contusions, and intracerebral hematomas (■ FIGURE 6-7).

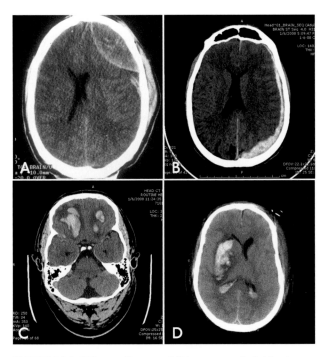

■ **FIGURE 6-7 CT Scans of Intracranial Hematomas. A.** Epidural hematoma. **B.** Subdural hematoma. **C.** Bilateral contusions with hemorrhage. **D.** Right intraparenchymal hemorrhage with right to left midline shift and associated biventricular hemorrhages.

Epidural Hematomas

Epidural hematomas are relatively uncommon, occurring in about 0.5% of patients with brain injuries and 9% of patients with TBI who are comatose. These hematomas typically become biconvex or lenticular in shape as they push the adherent dura away from the inner table of the skull. They are most often located in the temporal or temporoparietal regions and often result from a tear of the middle meningeal artery due to fracture. These clots are classically arterial in origin; however, they also may result from disruption of a major venous sinus or bleeding from a skull fracture. The classic presentation of an epidural hematoma is with a lucid interval between the time of injury and neurological deterioration.

Subdural Hematomas

Subdural hematomas are more common than epidural hematomas, occurring in approximately 30% of patients with severe brain injuries. They often develop from the shearing of small surface or bridging blood vessels of the cerebral cortex. In contrast to the lenticular shape of an epidural hematoma on a CT scan, subdural hematomas often appear to conform to contours of the brain. Damage underlying

an acute subdural hematoma is typically much more severe than that associated with epidural hematomas due to the presence of concomitant parenchymal injury.

Contusions and Intracerebral Hematomas

Cerebral contusions are fairly common; they occur in approximately 20% to 30% of patients with severe brain injuries. Most contusions are in the frontal and temporal lobes, although they may be in any part of the brain. In a period of hours or days, contusions can evolve to form an intracerebral hematoma or a coalescent contusion with enough mass effect to require immediate surgical evacuation. This condition occurs in as many as 20% of patients presenting with contusions on initial CT scan of the head. For this reason, patients with contusions generally undergo repeat CT scanning to evaluate for changes in the pattern of injury within 24 hours of the initial scan.

EVIDENCE-BASED TREATMENT GUIDELINES

Evidence-based guidelines are available for the treatment of TBI. The 4th edition of the Brain Trauma Foundation Guidelines for the Management of Severe Traumatic Brain Injury were e-published in September of 2016, and the print synopsis was published in the *Journal of Neurosurgery* in January of 2017. The new guidelines are different in many ways from the old guidelines. New levels of evidence are labeled from highest quality to lowest: levels I, IIA, IIB, and III.

The first guidelines addressing TBI, *Guidelines for the Management of Severe Traumatic Brain Injury*, were published by the Brain Trauma Foundation in 1995, revised in 2000, and updated most recently in 2016. Additional evidence-based reviews have since been published regarding the prehospital management of TBI; severe TBI in infants, children and adolescents; early prognostic indicators in severe TBI; and combat-related head injury. The Brain Trauma Foundation TBI guidelines, which are referenced in this chapter, can be downloaded from the foundation website: http://www. braintrauma.org. In addition, the American College of Surgeons Trauma Quality Improvement Program (TQIP) published a guideline for managing TBI in 2015. (See *ACS TQIP Best Practices in the Management of Traumatic Brain Injury.*)

Even patients with apparently devastating TBI on presentation can realize significant neurological recovery. Vigorous management and improved understanding of the pathophysiology of severe head injury, especially the role of hypotension, hypoxia, and cerebral perfusion, have significantly affected patient outcomes. ■ TABLE 6-3 is an overview of TBI management.

MANAGEMENT OF MILD BRAIN INJURY (GCS SCORE 13–15)

Mild traumatic brain injury is defined by a post-resuscitation GCS score between 13 and 15. Often

these patients have sustained a concussion, which is a transient loss of neurologic function following a head injury. A patient with mild brain injury who is conscious and talking may relate a history of disorientation, amnesia, or transient loss of consciousness. The history of a brief loss of consciousness can be difficult to confirm, and the clinical picture often is confounded by alcohol or other intoxicants. Never ascribe alterations in mental status to confounding factors until brain injury can be definitively excluded. Management of patients with mild brain injury is described in (■ FIGURE 6-8). (Also see *Management of Mild Brain Injury algorithm on MyATLS mobile app.*)

TABLE 6-3 MANAGEMENT OVERVIEW OF TRAUMATIC BRAIN INJURY

All patients: Perform ABCDEs with special attention to hypoxia and hypotension.

GCS CLASSIFCATION	13–15 MILD TRAUMATIC BRAIN INJURY		9–12 MODERATE TRAUMATIC BRAIN INJURY	3–8 SEVERE TRAUMATIC BRAIN INJURY
Initial Management[a]	AMPLE history and neurological exam: ask particularly about use of anticoagulants		Neurosurgery evaluation or transfer required	Urgent neurosurgery consultation or transfer required
	May discharge if admission criteria not met	Admit for indications below:	*Primary survey and resuscitation	*Primary survey and resuscitation
	Determine mechanism, time of injury, initial GCS, confusion, amnestic interval, seizure, headache severity, etc.

*Secondary survey including focused neurological exam | No CT available, CT abnormal, skull fracture, CSF leak

Focal neurological deficit

GCS does not return to 15 within 2 hours | *Arrange for transfer to definitive neurosurgical evaluation and management

*Focused neurological exam

*Secondary survey and AMPLE history | *Intubation and ventilation for airway protection

*Treat hypotension, hypovolemia, and hypoxia

*Focused neurological exam

*Secondary survey and AMPLE history |
| Diagnostic | *CT scanning as determined by head CT rules (Table 6-3)

*Blood/Urine EtOH and toxicology screens | CT not available, CT abnormal, skull fracture

Significant intoxication (admit or observe) | *CT scan in all cases

*Evaluate carefully for other injuries

*Type and crossmatch, coagulation studies | *CT scan in all cases

*Evaluate carefully for other injuries

*Type and crossmatch, coagulation studies |

[a]Items marked with an asterisk (*) denote action required.

TABLE 6-3 MANAGEMENT OVERVIEW OF TRAUMATIC BRAIN INJURY (CONTINUED)

All patients: Perform ABCDEs with special attention to hypoxia and hypotension.

GCS CLASSIFCATION	13-15 MILD TRAUMATIC BRAIN INJURY		9-12 MODERATE TRAUMATIC BRAIN INJURY	3-8 SEVERE TRAUMATIC BRAIN INJURY
Secondary Management	*Serial exam-inations until GCS is 15 and patient has no perseveration or memory deficit *Rule out indication for CT (Table 6-4)	*Perform serial examinations *Perform follow-up CT scan if first is abnormal or GCS remains less than 15 *Repeat CT (or transfer) if neurological status deteriorates	*Serial exams *Consider follow-up CT in 12–18 hours	*Frequent serial neurological exam-inations with GCS *$PaCO_2$ 35-40 mm Hg *Mannitol, brief hyperventi-lation, no less than 25 mm Hg for deterioration *$PaCO_2$ no less than 25 mm Hg, except with signs of cerebral herniation. Avoid hyperventilation in the first 24 hours after injury when cerebral blood flow can be critically reduced. When hyperventilation is used SjO_2 (jugular venous oxygen saturations) or $PbTO_2$ (brain tissue O_2 partial pressure), measurements are recommended to monitor oxygen delivery. *Address intracranial lesions appropriately
Disposition	*Home if patient does not meet criteria for admission *Discharge with Head Injury Warning Sheet and follow-up arranged	Obtain neuro-surgical evaluation if CT or neurological exam is abnormal or patient status deteriorates *Arrange for medical follow-up and neuropsychological evaluation as required (may be done as outpatient)	*Repeat CT immediately for deterioration and manage as in severe brain injury *Transfer to trauma center	*Transfer as soon as possible to definitive neurosurgical care

aItems marked with an asterisk (*) denote action required.

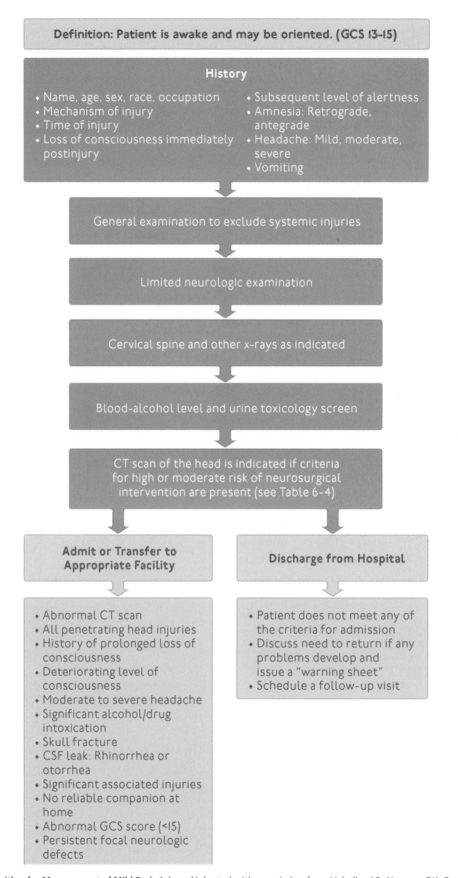

Definition: Patient is awake and may be oriented. (GCS 13-15)

History

- Name, age, sex, race, occupation
- Mechanism of injury
- Time of injury
- Loss of consciousness immediately postinjury

- Subsequent level of alertness
- Amnesia: Retrograde, antegrade
- Headache: Mild, moderate, severe
- Vomiting

General examination to exclude systemic injuries

Limited neurologic examination

Cervical spine and other x-rays as indicated

Blood-alcohol level and urine toxicology screen

CT scan of the head is indicated if criteria for high or moderate risk of neurosurgical intervention are present (see Table 6-4)

Admit or Transfer to Appropriate Facility

- Abnormal CT scan
- All penetrating head injuries
- History of prolonged loss of consciousness
- Deteriorating level of consciousness
- Moderate to severe headache
- Significant alcohol/drug intoxication
- Skull fracture
- CSF leak: Rhinorrhea or otorrhea
- Significant associated injuries
- No reliable companion at home
- Abnormal GCS score (<15)
- Persistent focal neurologic defects

Discharge from Hospital

- Patient does not meet any of the criteria for admission
- Discuss need to return if any problems develop and issue a "warning sheet"
- Schedule a follow-up visit

■ **FIGURE 6-8 Algorithm for Management of Mild Brain Injury.** (Adapted with permission from Valadka AB, Narayan RK, Emergency room management of the head-injured patient. In: Narayan RK, Wilberger JE, Povlishock JT, eds., *Neurotrauma*. New York, NY: McGraw-Hill, 1996.)

PITFALL	PREVENTION
Patient suffers second TBI soon after treatment for initial mild brain injury.	• Even when a patient appears neurologically normal, caution him or her to avoid activities that potentially can lead to a secondary brain injury (e.g., vigorous exercise, contact sports, and other activities that reproduce or cause symptoms). • Reassessment at outpatient follow up will determine timing of return to full activity or the need for referral for rehabilitative/cognitive services.

TABLE 6-4 INDICATIONS FOR CT SCANNING IN PATIENTS WITH MILD TBI

Head CT is required for patients with suspected mild brain trauma (i.e., witnessed loss of consciousness, definite amnesia, or witnessed disorientation in a patient with a GCS score of I3–I5) *and* any one of the following factors:

High risk for neurosurgical intervention:	Moderate risk for brain injury on CT:
• GCS score less than I5 at 2 hours after injury • Suspected open or depressed skull fracture • Any sign of basilar skull fracture (e.g., hemotympanum, raccoon eyes, CSF otorrhea or rhinorrhea, Battle's sign) • Vomiting (more than two episodes) • Age more than 65 years • Anticoagulant use*	• Loss of consciousness (more than 5 minutes) • Amnesia before impact (more than 30 minutes) • Dangerous mechanism (e.g., pedestrian struck by motor vehicle, occupant ejected from motor vehicle, fall from height more than 3 feet or five stairs)

Source: Adapted from Stiell IG, Wells GA, Vandemheen K, et al. The Canadian CT Head Rule for patients with minor head injury. *Lancet* 200I; 357:I294.
*Patients on anticoagulation were excluded from the use of Canadian CT Head Rule.

Most patients with mild brain injury make uneventful recoveries. Approximately 3% unexpectedly deteriorate, potentially resulting in severe neurological dysfunction unless the decline in mental status is detected early.

The secondary survey is particularly important in evaluating patients with mild TBI. Note the mechanism of injury and give particular attention to any loss of consciousness, including the length of time the patient was unresponsive, any seizure activity, and the subsequent level of alertness. Determine the duration of amnesia for events both before (retrograde) and after (antegrade) the traumatic incident. Serial examination and documentation of the GCS score is important in all patients. CT scanning is the preferred method of imaging, although obtaining CT scans should not delay transfer of the patient who requires it.

Obtain a CT scan in all patients with suspected brain injury who have a clinically suspected open skull fracture, any sign of basilar skull fracture, and more than two episodes of vomiting. Also obtain a CT scan in patients who are older than 65 years (■ TABLE 6-4). CT should also be considered if the patient had a loss of consciousness for longer than 5 minutes, retrograde amnesia for longer than 30 minutes, a dangerous mechanism of injury, severe headaches, seizures, short term memory deficit, alcohol or drug intoxication, coagulopathy or a focal neurological deficit attributable to the brain.

When these parameters are applied to patients with a GCS score of 13, approximately 25% will have a CT finding indicative of trauma, and 1.3% will require neurosurgical intervention. For patients with a GCS score of 15, 10% will have CT findings indicative of trauma, and 0.5% will require neurosurgical intervention.

If abnormalities are observed on the CT scan, or if the patient remains symptomatic or continues to have neurological abnormalities, admit the patient to the hospital and consult a neurosurgeon (or transfer to a trauma center).

If patients are asymptomatic, fully awake and alert, and have no neurological abnormalities, they may be observed for several hours, reexamined, and, if still normal, safely discharged. Ideally, the patient is discharged to the care of a companion who can observe the patient continually over the subsequent 24 hours. Provide an instruction sheet that directs both the patient and the companion to continue close observation and to return to the ED if the patient develops headaches or experiences a decline in mental status or focal neurological deficits. In all cases, supply written discharge instructions and carefully review them with the patient and/or companion (■ FIGURE 6-9). If the patient is not alert or oriented enough to clearly understand the written and verbal instructions, reconsider discharging him or her.

Mild Traumatic Brain Injury Warning Discharge Instructions

Patient Name: _____

Date: _____

We have found no evidence to indicate that your head injury was serious. However, new symptoms and unexpected complications can develop hours or even days after the injury. The first 24 hours are the most crucial and you should remain with a reliable companion at least during this period. If any of the following signs develop, call your doctor or come back to the hospital.

1 *Inappropriate drowsiness or increasing difficulty in awakening patient (awaken every 2 hours during period of sleep)*
2 *Nausea or vomiting*
3 *Convulsions or fits*
4 *Bleeding or watery drainage from the nose or ear*
5 *Severe headaches*
6 *Weakness or loss of feeling in the arm or leg*
7 *Confusion or strange behavior*
8 *One pupil (black part of eye) much larger than the other; peculiar movements of the eyes, double vision, or other visual disturbances*
9 *A very slow or very rapid pulse, or an unusual breathing pattern.*

If there is swelling at the site of the injury, apply an ice pack, making sure that there is a cloth or towel between the ice pack and the skin. If swelling increases markedly in spite of the ice pack application, call us or come back to the hospital.

You may eat or drink as usual if you so desire. However, you should NOT drink alcoholic beverages for at least 3 days after your injury.

Do not take any sedatives or any pain relievers stronger than acetaminophen, at least for the first 24 hours. Do not use aspirin-containing medicines.

If you have any further questions, or in case of emergency, we can be reached at: <telephone number>

Physician's Signature _____

■ FIGURE 6-9 Example of Mild TBI Warning Discharge Instructions.

MANAGEMENT OF MODERATE BRAIN INJURY (GCS SCORE 9–12)

Approximately 15% of patients with brain injury who are seen in the ED have a moderate injury. These patients can still follow simple commands, but they usually are confused or somnolent and can have focal neurological deficits such as hemiparesis. Approximately 10% to 20% of these patients deteriorate and lapse into coma. For this reason, serial neurological examinations are critical in the treatment of these patients.

Management of patients with moderate brain injury is described in (■ FIGURE 6-10). (Also see *Management*

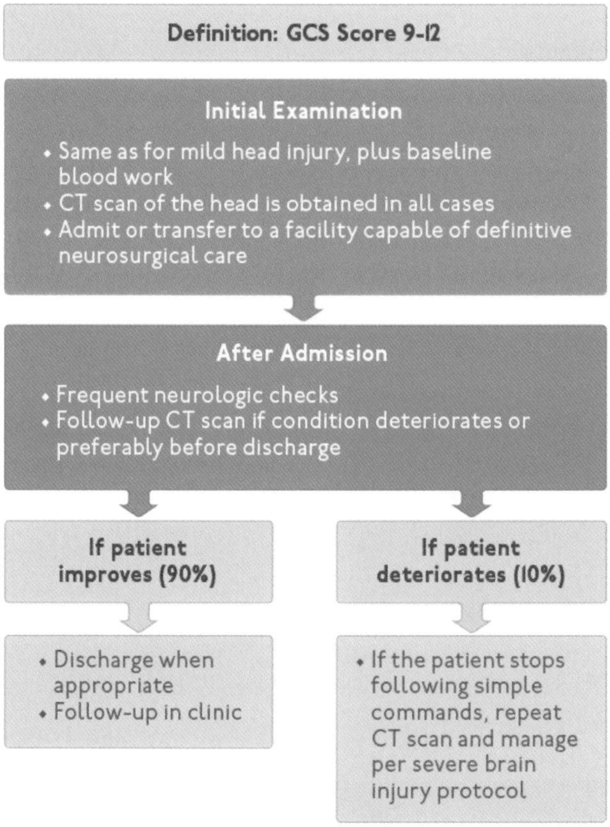

Definition: GCS Score 9-12

Initial Examination
- Same as for mild head injury, plus baseline blood work
- CT scan of the head is obtained in all cases
- Admit or transfer to a facility capable of definitive neurosurgical care

After Admission
- Frequent neurologic checks
- Follow-up CT scan if condition deteriorates or preferably before discharge

If patient improves (90%)
- Discharge when appropriate
- Follow-up in clinic

If patient deteriorates (10%)
- If the patient stops following simple commands, repeat CT scan and manage per severe brain injury protocol

■ **FIGURE 6-10 Algorithm for Management of Moderate Brain Injury.** (Adapted with permission from Valadka AB, Narayan RK, Emergency room management of the head-injured patient. In: Narayan RK, Wilberger JE, Povlishock JT, eds., *Neurotrauma.* New York, NY: McGraw-Hill, 1996.)

of Moderate Brain Injury algorithm on MyATLS mobile app.)

On admission to the ED, obtain a brief history and ensure cardiopulmonary stability before neurological assessment. Obtain a CT scan of the head and contact a neurosurgeon or a trauma center if transfer is necessary. All patients with moderate TBI require admission for

PITFALL	PREVENTION
A patient with a GCS score of 12 deteriorates to a GCS score of 9.	• Reevaluate the patient frequently to detect any decline in mental status. • Use narcotics and sedatives cautiously. • When necessary, use blood gas monitoring or capnography to ensure adequate ventilation. • Intubate the patient when ventilation is inadequate.

observation in unit capable of close nursing observation and frequent neurological reassessment for at least the first 12 to 24 hours. A follow-up CT scan within 24 hours is recommended if the initial CT scan is abnormal or the patient's neurological status deteriorates.

MANAGEMENT OF SEVERE BRAIN INJURY (GCS SCORE 3–8)

Approximately 10% of patients with brain injury who are treated in the ED have a severe injury. Such patients are unable to follow simple commands, even after cardiopulmonary stabilization. Although severe TBI includes a wide spectrum of brain injury, it identifies the patients who are at greatest risk of suffering significant morbidity and mortality. A "wait and see" approach in such patients can be disastrous, and prompt diagnosis and treatment are extremely important. Do not delay patient transfer in order to obtain a CT scan.

The initial management of severe brain injury is outlined in (■ FIGURE 6-11). (Also see *Initial Management of Severe Brain Injury algorithm on MyATLS mobile app.*)

PRIMARY SURVEY AND RESUSCITATION

Brain injury often is adversely affected by secondary insults. The mortality rate for patients with severe brain injury who have hypotension on admission is more than double that of patients who do not have hypotension. The presence of hypoxia in addition to hypotension is associated with an increase in the relative risk of mortality of 75%. It is imperative to rapidly achieve cardiopulmonary stabilization in patients with severe brain injury. ■ BOX 6-2 outlines the priorities of the initial evaluation and triage of patients with severe brain injuries. (Also see *Appendix G: Disability Skills*.)

AIRWAY AND BREATHING

Transient respiratory arrest and hypoxia are common with severe brain injury and can cause secondary brain injury. Perform early endotracheal intubation in comatose patients.

Ventilate the patient with 100% oxygen until blood gas measurements are obtained, and then make appropriate adjustments to the fraction of inspired oxygen (FIO_2). Pulse oximetry is a useful adjunct, and oxygen saturations of > 98% are desirable. Set

Definition: Patient is unable to follow even simple
commands because of impaired consciousness
(GCS Score 3-8)

Assessment and management

- ABCDEs
- Primary survey and resuscitation
- Secondary survey and AMPLE
  history
- Admit or transfer to a facility
  capable of definitive
  neurosurgical care
- Therapeutic agents (usually
  administered after consultation
  with neurosurgeon)
  - Mannitol
  - Avoid hyperventilation in the first 24 hours unless
    signs of herniation
  - Hypertonic saline

- Neurologic reevaluation:
- GCS
  - Eye opening
  - Motor response
  - Verbal response
- Pupillary light response
- Focal neurologic exam

CT scan

■ FIGURE 6-11 Algorithm for Initial Management of Severe Brain Injury. (Adapted with permission from Valadka AB, Narayan RK, Emergency room management of the head-injured patient. In: Narayan RK, Wilberger JE, Povlishock JT, eds., *Neurotrauma.* New York, NY: McGraw-Hill, 1996.)

BOX 6-2 PRIORITIES FOR THE INITIAL EVALUATION AND TRIAGE OF PATIENTS WITH SEVERE BRAIN INJURIES

1. All patients should undergo a primary survey, adhering to the ABCDE priorities. First assess the airway. If the patient requires airway control, perform and document a brief neurological examination before administering drugs for intubation. Assess the adequacy of breathing next, and monitor oxygen saturation.

2. As soon as the patient's blood pressure (BP) is normalized, perform a neurological exam, including GCS score and pupillary reaction. If BP cannot be normalized, continue to perform the neurological examination and record the hypotension.

3. If the patient's systolic BP cannot be raised to > 100 mm Hg, the doctor's first priority is to establish the cause of the hypotension; the neurosurgical evaluation takes second priority. In such cases, the patient should undergo focused assessment with sonography for trauma (FAST) or diagnostic peritoneal lavage (DPL) in the ED and may need to go directly to the OR for a laparotomy. Obtain

CT scans of the head after the laparotomy. If there is clinical evidence of an intracranial mass, diagnostic burr holes or craniotomy may be undertaken in the OR while the celiotomy is being performed.

4. If the patient's systolic BP is > 100 mm Hg after resuscitation and there is clinical evidence of a possible intracranial mass (e.g., unequal pupils or asymmetric results on motor exam), the highest priority is to obtain a CT head scan. A DPL or FAST exam may be performed in the ED, CT area, or OR, but do not delay the patient's neurological evaluation or treatment.

5. In borderline cases—such as when the systolic BP can be temporarily corrected but tends to slowly decrease—make every effort to get a head CT before taking the patient to the OR for a laparotomy or thoracotomy. Such cases call for sound clinical judgment and cooperation between the trauma surgeon and neurosurgeon.

ventilation parameters to maintain a PCO₂ of approximately 35 mm Hg. Reserve hyperventilation acutely in patients with severe brain injury to those with acute neurologic deterioration or signs of herniation. Prolonged hyperventilation with $PCO_2 < 25$ mm Hg is not recommended (Guidelines IIB).

CIRCULATION

Hypotension usually is not due to the brain injury itself, except in the terminal stages when medullary failure supervenes or there is a concomitant spinal cord injury. Intracranial hemorrhage cannot cause hemorrhagic shock. If the patient is hypotensive, establish euvolemia as soon as possible using blood products, or isotonic fluids as needed.

Remember, the neurological examination of patients with hypotension is unreliable. Hypotensive patients who are unresponsive to any form of stimulation can recover and substantially improve soon after normal blood pressure is restored. It is crucial to immediately seek and treat the primary source of the hypotension.

Maintain systolic blood pressure (SBP) at ≥ 100 mm Hg for patients 50 to 69 years or at ≥ 110 mm Hg or higher for patients 15 to 49 years or older than 70 years; this may decrease mortality and improve outcomes (III).

The goals of treatment include clinical, laboratory, and monitoring parameters ■ TABLE 6-5.

NEUROLOGICAL EXAMINATION

As soon as the patient's cardiopulmonary status is managed, perform a rapid, focused neurological examination. This consists primarily of determining the patient's GCS score, pupillary light response, and focal neurological deficit.

It is important to recognize confounding issues in the evaluation of TBI, including the presence of drugs, alcohol/other intoxicants, and other injuries. Do not overlook a severe brain injury because the patient is also intoxicated.

The postictal state after a traumatic seizure will typically worsen the patient's responsiveness for minutes or hours. In a comatose patient, motor responses can be elicited by pinching the trapezius muscle or with nail-bed or supraorbital ridge pressure. When a patient demonstrates variable responses to stimulation, the best motor response elicited is a more accurate prognostic indicator than the worst response. Testing for doll's-eye movements (oculocephalic), the caloric test with ice water (oculovestibular), and testing of corneal responses are deferred to a neurosurgeon. Never attempt doll's-eye testing until a cervical spine injury has been ruled out.

It is important to obtain the GCS score and perform a pupillary examination before sedating or paralyzing the patient, because knowledge of the patient's clinical condition is important for determining subsequent treatment. Do not use long-acting paralytic and sedating agents during the primary survey. Avoid sedation except when a patient's agitated state could present a risk. Use the shortest-acting agents available when pharmacologic paralysis or brief sedation is

TABLE 6-5 GOALS OF TREATMENT OF BRAIN INJURY: CLINICAL, LABORATORY AND MONITORING PARAMETERS

CATEGORY	PARAMETER	NORMAL VALUES
Clinical Parameters	Systolic BP	≥ 100 mm Hg
	Temperature	36–38°C
Laboratory Parameters	Glucose	80–180 mg/dL
	Hemoglobin	≥ 7 g/dl
	International normalized ratio (INR)	≤ 1.4
	Na	135–145 meq/dL
	PaO_2	≥ 100 mm Hg
	$PaCO_2$	35–45 mm Hg
	pH	7.35–7.45
	Platelets	≥ 75 X 10^3/mm³
Monitoring Parameters	CPP	≥ 60 mm Hg*
	Intracranial pressure	5–15 mm Hg*
	$PbtO_2$	≥ 15 mm Hg*
	Pulse oximetry	≥ 95%

*Unlikely to be available in the ED or in low-resource settings
Data from ACS TQIP Best Practices in the Management of Traumatic Brain Injury. ACS Committee on Trauma, January 2015.

PITFALL	SOLUTION
A patient with TBI is noted to be seizing when the long-acting paralytic agent wears off.	• Avoid long-acting paralytic agents, as muscle paralysis confounds the neurologic examination • Use benzodiazepines to acutely manage seizures; muscle relaxants mask rather than control seizures.

necessary for safe endotracheal intubation or obtaining reliable diagnostic studies.

When a patient requires intubation because of airway compromise, perform and document a brief neurological examination before administering any sedatives or paralytics.

ANESTHETICS, ANALGESICS, AND SEDATIVES

Anesthetics, sedation, and analgesic agents should be used cautiously in patients who have suspected or confirmed brain injury. Overuse of these agents can cause a delay in recognizing the progression of a serious brain injury, impair respiration, or result in unnecessary treatment (e.g., endotracheal intubation). Instead, use short-acting, easily reversible agents at the lowest dose needed to effect pain relief and mild sedation. Low doses of IV narcotics may be given for analgesia and reversed with naloxone if needed. Short-acting IV benzodiazapines, such as midazolam (Versed), may be used for sedation and reversed with flumazenil.

Although diprovan (Propofol) is recommended for the control of ICP, it is not recommended for improvement in mortality or 6-month outcomes. Diprovan can produce significant morbidity when used in high-dose (IIB).

SECONDARY SURVEY

Perform serial examinations (note GCS score, lateralizing signs, and pupillary reaction) to detect neurological deterioration as early as possible. A well-known early sign of temporal lobe (uncal) herniation is dilation of the pupil and loss of the pupillary response to light. Direct trauma to the eye can also cause abnormal pupillary response and may make pupil evaluation difficult. However, in the setting of brain trauma, brain injury should be considered first. A complete neurologic examination is performed during the secondary survey. See *Appendix G: Disability Skills.*

DIAGNOSTIC PROCEDURES

For patients with moderate or severe traumatic brain injury, clinicians must obtain a head CT scan as soon as possible after hemodynamic normalization. CT scanning also should be repeated whenever there is a change in the patient's clinical status and routinely within 24 hours of injury for patients with subfrontal/temporal intraparenchymal contusions, patients receiving anticoagulation therapy, patients older than 65 years, and patients who have an intracranial hemorrhage with a volume of >10 mL. See *Appendix G: Skills — Adjuncts.*

CT findings of significance include scalp swelling and subgaleal hematomas at the region of impact. Skull fractures can be seen better with bone windows but are often apparent even on the soft-tissue windows. Crucial CT findings are intracranial blood, contusions, shift of midline structures (mass effect), and obliteration of the basal cisterns (see ■ FIGURE 6-7). A shift of 5 mm or greater often indicates the need for surgery to evacuate the blood clot or contusion causing the shift.

MEDICAL THERAPIES FOR BRAIN INJURY

The primary aim of intensive care protocols is to prevent secondary damage to an already injured brain. The basic principle of TBI treatment is that, if injured neural tissue is given optimal conditions in which to recover, it can regain normal function. Medical therapies for brain injury include intravenous fluids, correction of anticoagulation, temporary hyperventilation, mannitol (Osmitrol), hypertonic saline, barbiturates, and anticonvulsants.

INTRAVENOUS FLUIDS

To resuscitate the patient and maintain normovolemia, trauma team members administer intravenous fluids, blood, and blood products as required. Hypovolemia in patients with TBI is harmful. Clinicians must also take care not to overload the patient with fluids, and avoid using hypotonic fluids. Moreover, using glucose-containing fluids can cause hyperglycemia, which can harm the injured brain. Ringer's lactate solution or normal saline is thus recommended for resuscitation. Carefully monitor serum sodium levels in patients with head injuries. Hyponatremia is associated with brain edema and should be prevented.

CORRECTION OF ANTICOAGULATION

Use caution in assessing and managing patients with TBI who are receiving anticoagulation or anti-platelet therapy. After obtaining the international normalized ratio (INR), clinicians should promptly obtain a CT of these patients when indicated. Rapid normalization of anticoagulation is generally required (■ TABLE 6-6).

HYPERVENTILATION

In most patients, normocarbia is preferred. Hyperventilation acts by reducing $PaCO_2$ and causing cerebral vasoconstriction. Aggressive and prolonged hyperventilation can result in cerebral ischemia in the already injured brain by causing severe cerebral vasoconstriction and thus impaired cerebral perfusion. This risk is particularly high if the $PaCO_2$ is allowed to fall below 30 mm Hg (4.0 kPa). Hypercarbia (PCO_2 > 45 mm Hg) will promote vasodilation and increase intracranial pressure, and should therefore be avoided.

Prophylactic hyperventilation (pCO_2 < 25 mm Hg) is not recommended (IIB).

Use hyperventilation only in moderation and for as limited a period as possible. In general, it is preferable to keep the $PaCO_2$ at approximately 35 mm Hg (4.7 kPa), the low end of the normal range (35 mm Hg to 45 mm Hg). Brief periods of hyperventilation ($PaCO_2$ of 25 to 30 mm Hg [3.3 to 4.7 kPa]) may be necessary to manage acute neurological deterioration while other treatments are initiated. Hyperventilation will lower ICP in a deteriorating patient with expanding intracranial hematoma until doctors can perform emergent craniotomy.

MANNITOL

Mannitol (Osmitrol) is used to reduce elevated ICP. The most common preparation is a 20% solution (20 g of mannitol per 100 ml of solution). Do not give mannitol to patients with hypotension, because mannitol does not lower ICP in patients with hypovolemia and is a potent osmotic diuretic. This effect can further exacerbate hypotension and cerebral ischemia. Acute neurological deterioration—such as when a patient under observation develops a dilated pupil, has hemiparesis, or loses consciousness—is a strong indication for administering mannitol in a euvolemic patient. In this case, give the patient a bolus of mannitol (1 g/kg) rapidly (over 5 minutes) and transport her or him immediately to the CT scanner—or directly to the operating room, if a causative surgical lesion is already identified. If surgical services are not available, transfer the patient for definitive care.

TABLE 6-6 ANTICOAGULATION REVERSAL

ANTICOAGULANT	TREATMENT	COMMENTS
Antiplatelets (e.g., aspirin, plavix)	Platelets	May need to repeat; consider desmopressin acetate (Deamino-Delta-D-Arginine Vasopressin)
Coumadin (warfarin)	FFP, Vitamin K, prothrombin complex concentrate (Kcentra), Factor VIIa	Normalize INR; avoid fluid overload in elderly patients and patients who sustained cardiac injury
Heparin	Protamine sulfate	Monitor PTT
Low molecular weight heparin, e.g., Lovenox (enoxaparin)	Protamine sulfate	N/A
Direct thrombin inhibitors dabigatran etexilate (Pradaxa)	idarucizumab (Praxbind)	May benefit from prothrombin complex concentrate (e.g., Kcentra)
Xarelto (rivaroxaban)	N/A	May benefit from prothrombin complex concentrate (e.g., Kcentra)

FFP: Fresh frozen plasma; INR: International Normalized Ratio; PTT: Partial thromboplastin time.

Use 0.25–1 g/kg to control elevated ICP ; arterial hypotension (systolic blood pressure <90 mm Hg) should be avoided.

Use with ICP monitor, unless evidence of herniation, keep Sosm <320 mOsm, maintain euvolemia, and use bolus rather than continuous drip.

HYPERTONIC SALINE

Hypertonic saline is also used to reduce elevated ICP, in concentrations of 3% to 23.4%; this may be the preferable agent for patients with hypotension, because it does not act as a diuretic. However, there is no difference between mannitol and hypertonic saline in lowering ICP, and neither adequately lowers ICP in hypovolemic patients.

BARBITURATES

Barbiturates are effective in reducing ICP refractory to other measures, although they should not be used in the presence of hypotension or hypovolemia. Furthermore, barbiturates often cause hypotension, so they are not indicated in the acute resuscitative phase. The long half-life of most barbiturates prolongs the time for determining brain death, which is a consideration in patients with devastating and likely nonsurvivable injury.

Barbiturates are not recommended to induce burst suppression measured by EEG to prevent the development of intracranial hypertension. "High-dose barbiturate administration is recommended to control elevated ICP refractory to maximum standard medical and surgical treatment. Hemodynamic stability is essential before and during barbiturate therapy (IIB)."

ANTICONVULSANTS

Posttraumatic epilepsy occurs in approximately 5% of patients admitted to the hospital with closed head injuries and 15% of individuals with severe head injuries. The three main factors linked to a high incidence of late epilepsy are seizures occurring within the first week, an intracranial hematoma, and a depressed skull fracture. Acute seizures can be controlled with anticonvulsants, but early anticonvulsant use does not change long-term traumatic seizure outcome.

Anticonvulsants can inhibit brain recovery, so they should be used only when absolutely necessary. Currently, phenytoin (Dilantin) and fosphenytoin (Cerebyx) are generally used in the acute phase. For adults, the usual loading dose is 1 g of phenytoin intravenously given no faster than 50 mg/min. The usual maintenance dose is 100 mg/8 hours, with the dose titrated to achieve therapeutic serum levels. Valium (Diazepam) or ativan (Lorazepam) is frequently used in addition to phenytoin until the seizure stops. Control of continuous seizures may require general anesthesia. It is imperative to control acute seizures as soon as possible, because prolonged seizures (30 to 60 minutes) can cause secondary brain injury.

Prophylactic use of phenytoin (Dilantin) or valproate (Depakote) is not recommended for preventing late posttraumatic seizures (PTS). Phenytoin is recommended to decrease the incidence of early PTS (within 7 days of injury), when the overall benefit is felt to outweigh the complications associated with such treatment. However, early PTS has not been associated with worse outcomes (IIA).

SURGICAL MANAGEMENT

Surgical management may be necessary for scalp wounds, depressed skull fractures, intracranial mass lesions, and penetrating brain injuries.

SCALP WOUNDS

It is important to clean and inspect the wound thoroughly before suturing. The most common cause of infected scalp wounds is inadequate cleansing and debridement. Blood loss from scalp wounds may be extensive, especially in children and older adults (■ FIGURE 6-12). Control scalp hemorrhage by applying direct pressure and cauterizing or ligating large vessels. Then apply appropriate sutures, clips, or staples. Carefully inspect the wound, using direct vision, for signs of a skull fracture or foreign material. CSF leakage indicates that there is an associated dural tear. Consult a neurosurgeon in all cases of open or depressed skull fractures. Not infrequently, a subgaleal collection of blood can feel like a skull fracture. In such cases, the presence of a fracture can be confirmed or excluded by plain x-ray examination of the region and/or a CT scan.

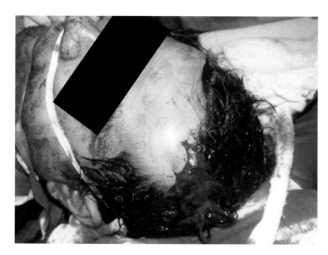

■ **FIGURE 6-12** Blood loss from scalp wounds can be extensive, especially in children.

DEPRESSED SKULL FRACTURES

For patients with depressed skull fractures, a CT scan is valuable in identifying the degree of depression and, importantly, excluding the presence of an intracranial hematoma or contusion. Generally, depressed skull fractures require operative elevation when the degree of depression is greater than the thickness of the adjacent skull, or when they are open and grossly contaminated. Less severe depressed fractures can often be managed with closure of the overlying scalp laceration, if present.

INTRACRANIAL MASS LESIONS

Intracranial mass lesions should be managed by a neurosurgeon. If a neurosurgeon is not available in the facility that initially receives a patient with an intracranial mass lesion, early transfer to a hospital with neurosurgical capabilities is essential. In exceptional circumstances, a rapidly expanding intracranial hematoma can be imminently life-threatening and may not allow time for transfer if neurosurgical care is a considerable distance away, such as in austere or remote areas. Emergency craniotomy in a rapidly deteriorating patient by a non-neurosurgeon should be considered only in extreme circumstances. Surgeons properly trained in the procedure should perform this surgery, but only after discussing the lesion with and obtaining the advice of a neurosurgeon.

There are few indications for a craniotomy performed by a non-neurosurgeon. This procedure is justified only when definitive neurosurgical care is unavailable. The Committee on Trauma strongly recommends that individuals who anticipate the need for this procedure receive proper training from a neurosurgeon.

PENETRATING BRAIN INJURIES

CT scanning of the head is strongly recommended to evaluate patients with penetrating brain injury. Plain radiographs of the head can be helpful in assessing bullet trajectory and fragmentation, as well as the presence of large foreign bodies and intracranial air. However, when CT is available, plain radiographs are not essential. CT and/or conventional angiography are recommended with any penetrating brain injury and when a trajectory passes through or near the skull base or a major dural venous sinus. Substantial subarachnoid hemorrhage or delayed hematoma should also prompt consideration of vascular imaging. Patients with a penetrating injury involving the orbitofacial or pterional regions should undergo angiography to identify a traumatic intracranial aneurysm or arteriovenous (AV) fistula; when an injury of this kind is identified, surgical or endovascular management is recommended. Magnetic resonance imaging (MRI) can play a role in evaluating injuries from penetrating wooden and other nonmagnetic objects. The presence on CT of large contusions, hematomas, and intraventricular hemorrhage is associated with increased mortality, especially when both hemispheres are involved.

Prophylactic broad-spectrum antibiotics are appropriate for patients with penetrating brain injury, open skull fracture, and CSF leak. (*Management of Penetrating Brain Injury guidelines, L3 recommendation*). Early ICP monitoring is recommended when the clinician is unable to assess the neurological examination accurately, the need to evacuate a mass lesion is unclear, or imaging studies suggest elevated ICP.

It is appropriate to treat small bullet entrance wounds to the head with local wound care and closure in patients whose scalp is not devitalized and who have no major intracranial pathology.

Objects that penetrate the intracranial compartment or infratemporal fossa and remain partially exteriorized (e.g., arrows, knives, screwdrivers) must be left in place until possible vascular injury has been evaluated and definitive neurosurgical management established. Disturbing or removing penetrating objects prematurely can lead to fatal vascular injury or intracranial hemorrhage.

Burr hole craniostomy/craniotomy, which involves placing a 10- to 15-mm drill hole in the skull, has been advocated as a method of emergently diagnosing accessible hematomas in patients with rapid neurologic deterioration who are located in austere or remote regions where neurosurgeons and imaging are not readily available. Unfortunately, even in very experienced hands, these drill holes are easily placed incorrectly, and they seldom result in draining enough of the hematoma to make a clinical difference. In patients who need an evacuation, bone flap craniotomy (versus a simple burr hole) is the definitive lifesaving procedure to decompress the brain. Trauma team members should make every attempt to have a practitioner trained and experienced in doing the procedure perform it in a timely fashion.

PROGNOSIS

All patients should be treated aggressively pending consultation with a neurosurgeon. This is particularly true of children, who have a remarkable ability to recover from seemingly devastating injuries.

BRAIN DEATH

A diagnosis of brain death implies that there is no possibility for recovery of brain function. Most experts agree that the diagnosis of brain death requires meeting these criteria:

- Glasgow Coma Scale score = 3
- Nonreactive pupils
- Absent brainstem reflexes (e.g., oculocephalic, corneal, and doll's eyes, and no gag reflex)
- No spontaneous ventilatory effort on formal apnea testing
- Absence of confounding factors such as alcohol or drug intoxication or hypothermia

Ancillary studies that may be used to confirm the diagnosis of brain death include:

- Electroencephalography: No activity at high gain
- CBF studies: No CBF (e.g., isotope studies, Doppler studies, xenon CBF studies)
- Cerebral angiography

Certain reversible conditions, such as hypothermia or barbiturate coma, can mimic brain death; therefore, consider making this diagnosis only after all physiological parameters are normalized and central nervous system function is not potentially affected by medications. Because children are often able to recover from extremely severe brain injuries, carefully consider diagnosing brain death in these patients. If any doubt exists, especially in children, multiple serial exams spaced several hours apart are useful in confirming the initial clinical impression. Notify local organ procurement agencies about all patients with the diagnosis or impending diagnosis of brain death before discontinuing artificial life support measures.

TEAMWORK

The team leader must:

- Ensure that the team is capable of managing a primary brain injury to the best possible outcome by preventing secondary brain injury.
- Recognize the importance of managing the airway to ensure patients with head injuries do not experience unnecessary hypoxia.
- Recognize the need to involve neurosurgical expertise at an appropriate stage and in a timely fashion, particularly when a patient requires surgical intervention.
- Ensure the timely transfer of patients with TBI to a trauma center when it is required.
- However, the team leader must ensure that patients with significant head injuries are transferred to facilities where they can be appropriately monitored and observed closely for signs of deterioration.
- Because some patients require neurosurgical intervention early, be able to prioritize the treatment of brain injury with other life-threatening injuries such as hemorrhage. Manage the discussion between representatives of different surgical specialties to ensure the patient's injuries are treated in the correct sequence. For example, a patient who is exsanguinating from a pelvic fracture requires control of the bleeding before being transferred for a neurosurgical procedure.

CHAPTER SUMMARY

1. Understanding basic intracranial anatomy and physiology is vital to managing head injury.

2. Patients with head and brain injuries must be evaluated efficiently. In a comatose patient, secure and maintain the airway by endotracheal intubation. Perform a neurological examination before paralyzing the patient. Search for associated injuries, and remember that hypotension can affect the neurological examination.

3. Trauma team members should become familiar with the Glasgow Coma Scale (GCS) and practice its use, as well as performance of rapid, focused neurological examinations. Frequently reassess the patient's neurological status.

4. Adequate resuscitation is important in limiting secondary brain injury. Prevent hypovolemia and hypoxemia. Treat shock aggressively and look for its cause. Resuscitate with Ringer's lactate solution, normal saline, or similar isotonic solutions without dextrose. Do not use hypotonic solutions. The goal in resuscitating the patient with brain injuries is to prevent secondary brain injury.

5. Determine the need for transfer, admission, consultation, or discharge. Contact a neurosurgeon as early as possible. If a neurosurgeon is not available at the facility, transfer all patients with moderate or severe head injuries.

BIBLIOGRAPHY

1. Amirjamshidi A, Abbassioun K, Rahmat H. Minimal debridement or simple wound closure as the only surgical treatment in war victims with low-velocity penetrating head injuries. Indications and management protocol based upon more than 8 years' follow-up of 99 cases from Iran–Iraq conflict. *Surg Neurol* 2003;60(2):105–110; discussion 110–111.

2. Andrews BT, Chiles BW, Olsen WL, et al. The effect of intra-cerebral hematoma location on the risk of brainstem compression and on clinical outcome. *J Neurosurg* 1988;69:518–522.

3. Atkinson JLD. The neglected prehospital phase of head injury: apnea and catecholamine surge. *Mayo Clin Proc* 2000;75(1):37–47.

4. Aubry M, Cantu R, Dvorak J, et al. Summary and agreement statement of the first International Conference on Concussion in Sport, Vienna 2001. *Phys Sportsmed* 2002;30:57–62 (copublished in *Br J Sports Med* 2002;36:3–7 and *Clin J Sport Med* 2002;12:6–12).

5. Boyle A, Santarius L, Maimaris C. Evaluation of the impact of the Canadian CT head rule on British practice. *Emerg Med J* 2004;21(4): 426–428.

6. Carney N, Totten AM, O'Reilly C, Ullman JS, et al.: Guidelines for the Management of Severe Traumatic Brain Injury. *Neurosurgery* 2017; 80:1 6-13.

7. Carney N, Ghajar J, Jagoda A, et al. Concussion guidelines step 1: systematic review of prevalent indicators. *Neurosurgery* 2014Sep;75(Suppl 1):S3–S15.

8. Chestnut RM, Marshall LF, Klauber MR, et al. The role of secondary brain injury in determining outcome from severe head injury. *J Trauma* 1993;34:216–222.

9. Chibbaro S, Tacconi L. Orbito-cranial injuries caused by penetrating non-missile foreign bodies. Experience with eighteen patients. *Acta Neurochir* (Wien) 2006;148(9), 937–941; discussion 941–942.

10. Clement CM, Stiell IG, Schull MJ, et al. Clinical features of head injury patients presenting with a Glasgow Coma Scale score of 15 and who require neurosurgical intervention. *Ann Emerg Med* 2006;48(3):245–251.

11. Eisenberg HM, Frankowski RF, Contant CR, et al. High-dose barbiturates control elevated intracranial pressure in patients with severe head injury. *J Neurosurg* 1988;69:15–23.

12. Faul M, Xu L, Wald MM, et al. Traumatic brain injury in the United States: emergency department visits, hospitalizations, and deaths. Atlanta, GA: Centers for Disease Control and Prevention, National Center for Injury Prevention and Control; 2010.

13. Giri BK, Krishnappa IK, Bryan RMJ, et al. Regional cerebral blood flow after cortical impact injury complicated by a secondary insult in rats. *Stroke* 2000;31:961–967.

14. Gonul E, Erdogan E, Tasar M, et al. Penetrating orbitocranial gunshot injuries. *Surg Neurol* 2005;63(1):24–30; discussion 31.

15. Injury Prevention & Control: Traumatic Brain Injury & Concussion. http://www.cdc.gov/traumaticbraininjury/. Accessed May 4, 2012.

16. Johnson U, Nilsson P, Ronne-Engstrom E, et al. Favorable outcome in traumatic brain injury patients with impaired cerebral pressure autoregulation when treated at low cerebral perfusion pressure levels. *Neurosurgery* 2011; 68:714–722.

17. Management of Penetrating Brain Injury *J Trauma* 2001; 51(2) supplement/August.

18. Marion DW, Spiegel TP. Changes in the management of severe traumatic brain injury: 1991–1997. *Crit Care Med* 2000;28:16–18.

19. McCror, P, Johnston K, Meeuwisse W, et al. Summary and agreement statement of the 2nd International Conference on Concussion in Sport, Prague 2004. *Br J Sports Med* 2005;39:196–204.

20. Mower WR, Hoffman JR, Herbert M, et al. Developing a decision instrument to guide computed tomographic imaging of blunt head injury patients. *J Trauma* 2005;59(4):954–959.

21. Muizelaar JP, Marmarou A, Ward JD, et al. Adverse effects of prolonged hyperventilation in patients with severe head injury: a randomized clinical trial. *J Neurosurg* 1991;75:731–739.

22. Part 1: Guidelines for the management of penetrating brain injury. Introduction and methodology. *J Trauma* 2001;51(2 Suppl):S3–S6.

23. Part 2: Prognosis in penetrating brain injury. *J Trauma* 2001;51(2 Suppl):S44–S86.

24. Post AF, Boro T, Eckland JM: Injury to the Brain In: Mattox KL, Feliciano DV, Moore EE, eds. *Trauma*. 7th ed. New York, NY: McGraw-Hill; 2013:356–376.

25. Robertson CS, Valadka AB, Hannay HJ, et al. Prevention of secondary ischemic insults after severe head injury. *Crit Care Med* 1999; 27:2086–2095.

26. Rosengart AJ, Huo D, Tolentino J, et al. Outcome in patients with subarachnoid hemorrhage treated with antiepileptic drugs. *J Neurosurg* 2007;107:253–260.

27. Rosner MJ, Rosner SD, Johnson AH. Cerebral perfusion pressure management protocols and clinical results. *J Neurosurg* 1995;83:949–962.

28. Sakellaridis N, Pavlou E, Karatzas S, et al. Comparison of mannitol and hypertonic saline in the treatment of severe brain injuries. *J Neurosurg* 2011;114:545–548.

29. Smits M, Dippel DW, de Haan GG, et al. External validation of the Canadian CT Head Rule and the New Orleans Criteria for CT scanning in patients with minor head injury. *JAMA* 2005;294(12):1519–1525.

30. Stiell IG, Clement CM, Rowe BH, et al. Comparison of the Canadian CT Head Rule and the New Orleans Criteria in patients with minor head injury. *JAMA* 2005;294(12):1511–1518.

31. Stiell IG, Lesiuk H, Wells GA, et al. Canadian CT head rule study for patients with minor head injury: methodology for phase II (validation and economic analysis). *Ann Emerg Med* 2001;38(3):317–322.

32. Stiell IG, Lesiuk H, Wells GA, et al. The Canadian CT Head Rule Study for patients with minor head injury: rationale, objectives, and methodology for phase I (derivation). *Ann Emerg Med* 2001;38(2):160–169.

33. Stiell IG, Wells GA, Vandemheen K, et al. The Canadian CT Head Rule for patients with minor head injury. *Lancet* 2001;357(9266):1391–1396.

34. Sultan HY, Boyle A, Pereira M, et al. Application of the Canadian CT head rules in managing minor head injuries in a UK emergency department: implications for the implementation of the NICE guidelines. *Emerg Med J* 2004;21(4):420–425.

35. Temkin NR, Dikman SS, Wilensky AJ, et al. A randomized, double-blind study of phenytoin for the prevention of post-traumatic seizures. *N Engl J Med* 1990;323:497–502.

36. Wijdicks EFM, Varelas PN, Gronseth GS, et al. Evidence-based guideline update: Determining brain death in adults. Report of the Quality Standards Subcommittee of the American Academy of Neurology. *Neurology* 2010;74:1911–1918.

37. Valadka AB, Narayan RK. Emergency room management of the head-injured patient. In: Narayan RK, Wilberger JE, Povlishock JT, eds. Neurotrauma. New York, NY: McGraw-Hill, 1996:120.

38. Narayan RK: Head Injury. In: Grossman RG, Hamilton WJ eds., Principles of Neurosurgery. New York, NY: Raven Press, 1991

39. Carney N, Totten AM, O'Reilly C, Ullman JS et. al. Guidelines for the Management of severe Traumatic Brain Injury, Fourth Edition. Neurosurgery 0:1–10, 2016 DOI: 10.1227/NEU.0000000000001432

40. Washington CW, Grubb RL, Jr. Are routine repeat imaging and intensive care unit admission necessary in mild traumatic brain injury? *J Neurosurg.* 2012;116(3):549-557.

41. Cohen DB, Rinker C, Wilberger JE. Traumatic brain injury in anticoagulated patients. *J Trauma.* 2006;60(3):553-557.

42. Prehospital Emergency care supplement to volume 12 (1) Jan/March 2004 Guidelines for prehospital management of traumatic brain injury 2nd edition.

43. www.glasgowcomascale.org

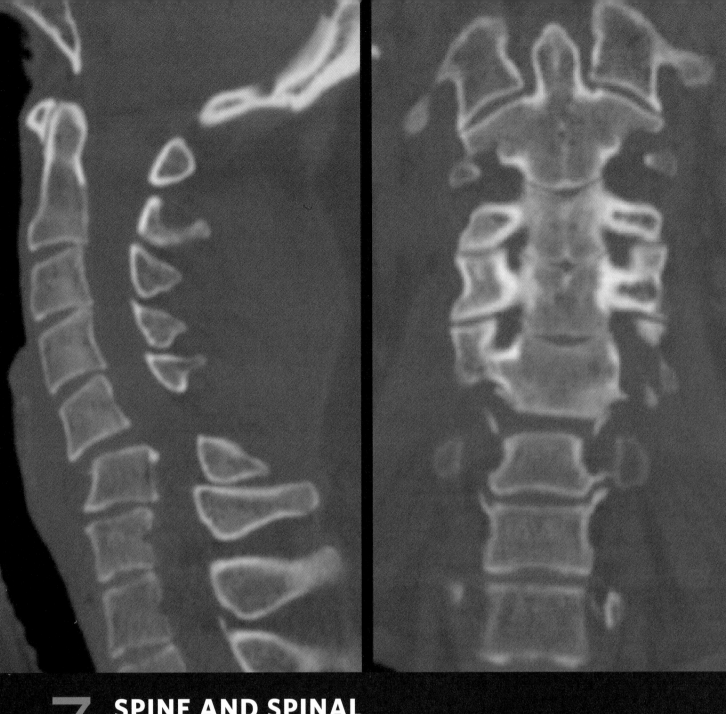

7 SPINE AND SPINAL CORD TRAUMA

Because spine injury can occur with both blunt and penetrating trauma, and with or without neurological deficits, it must be considered in all patients with multiple injuries. These patients require limitation of spinal motion to protect the spine from further damage until spine injury has been ruled out.

CHAPTER 7 OUTLINE

OBJECTIVES

After reading this chapter and comprehending the knowledge components of the ATLS provider course, you will be able to:

1. Describe the basic anatomy and physiology of the spine.

2. Describe the appropriate evaluation of a patient with suspected spinal injury and documentation of injury.

3. Identify the common types of spinal injuries and the x-ray features that help identify them.

4. Describe the appropriate treatment of patients with spinal injuries during the first hours after injury.

5. Determine the appropriate disposition of patients with spine trauma.

Spine injury, with or without neurological deficits, must always be considered in patients with multiple injuries. Approximately 5% of patients with brain injury have an associated spinal injury, whereas 25% of patients with spinal injury have at least a mild brain injury. Approximately 55% of spinal injuries occur in the cervical region, 15% in the thoracic region, 15% at the thoracolumbar junction, and 15% in the lumbosacral area. Up to 10% of patients with a cervical spine fracture have a second, noncontiguous vertebral column fracture.

In patients with potential spine injuries, excessive manipulation and inadequate restriction of spinal motion can cause additional neurological damage and worsen the patient's outcome. At least 5% of patients with spine injury experience the onset of neurological symptoms or a worsening of preexisting symptoms after reaching the emergency department (ED). These complications are typically due to ischemia or progression of spinal cord edema, but they can also result from excessive movement of the spine. If the patient's spine is protected, evaluation of the spine and exclusion of spinal injury can be safely deferred, especially in the presence of systemic instability, such as hypotension and respiratory inadequacy. Spinal protection does not require patients to spend hours on a long spine board; lying supine on a firm surface and utilizing spinal precautions when moving is sufficient.

Excluding the presence of a spinal injury can be straightforward in patients *without* neurological deficit, pain or tenderness along the spine, evidence of intoxication, or additional painful injuries. In this case, the absence of pain or tenderness along the spine virtually excludes the presence of a significant spinal injury. The possibility of cervical spine injuries may be eliminated based on clinical tools, described later in this chapter.

However, in other patients, such as those who are comatose or have a depressed level of consciousness, the process of evaluating for spine injury is more complicated. In this case, the clinician needs to obtain the appropriate radiographic imaging to exclude a spinal injury. If the images are inconclusive, restrict motion of the spine until further testing can be performed. Remember, the presence of a cervical collar and backboard can provide a false sense of security that movement of the spine is restricted. If the patient is not correctly secured to the board and the collar is not properly fitted, motion is still possible.

Although the dangers of excessive spinal motion have been well documented, prolonged positioning of patients on a hard backboard and with a hard cervical collar (c-collar) can also be hazardous. In addition to causing severe discomfort in conscious patients, serious decubitus ulcers can form, and respiratory compromise can result from prolonged use. Therefore, long backboards should be used only during patient transportation, and every effort should be made to remove patients from spine boards as quickly as possible.

ANATOMY AND PHYSIOLOGY

The following review of the anatomy and physiology of the spine and spinal cord includes the spinal column, spinal cord anatomy, dermatomes, myotomes, the differences between neurogenic and spinal shock, and the effects of spine injury on other organ systems.

SPINAL COLUMN

The spinal column consists of 7 cervical, 12 thoracic, and 5 lumbar vertebrae, as well as the sacrum and coccyx (■ FIGURE 7-1). The typical vertebra consists of an anteriorly placed vertebral body, which forms part of the main weight-bearing column. The vertebral bodies are separated by intervertebral disks that are held together anteriorly and posteriorly by the anterior and posterior longitudinal ligaments, respectively. Posterolaterally, two pedicles form the pillars on which the roof of the vertebral canal (i.e., the lamina) rests. The facet joints, interspinous ligaments, and paraspinal muscles all contribute to spine stability.

The cervical spine, because of its mobility and exposure, is the most vulnerable part of the spine to injury. The cervical canal is wide from the foramen magnum to the lower part of C2. Most patients with injuries at this level who survive are neurologically intact on arrival to the hospital. However, approximately one-third of patients with upper cervical spine injuries (i.e., injury above C3) die at the scene from apnea caused by loss of central innervation of the phrenic nerves. Below the level of C3, the spinal canal diameter is much smaller relative to the spinal cord diameter, and vertebral column injuries are much more likely to cause spinal cord injuries.

A child's cervical spine is markedly different from that of an adult's until approximately 8 years of age. These differences include more flexible joint capsules and interspinous ligaments, as well as flat facet joints and vertebral bodies that are wedged anteriorly and tend to slide forward with flexion. The differences decline steadily until approximately age 12, when the cervical spine is more similar to an adult's. (See *Chapter 10: Pediatric Trauma.*)

Thoracic spine mobility is much more restricted than cervical spine mobility, and the thoracic spine has additional support from the rib cage. Hence, the

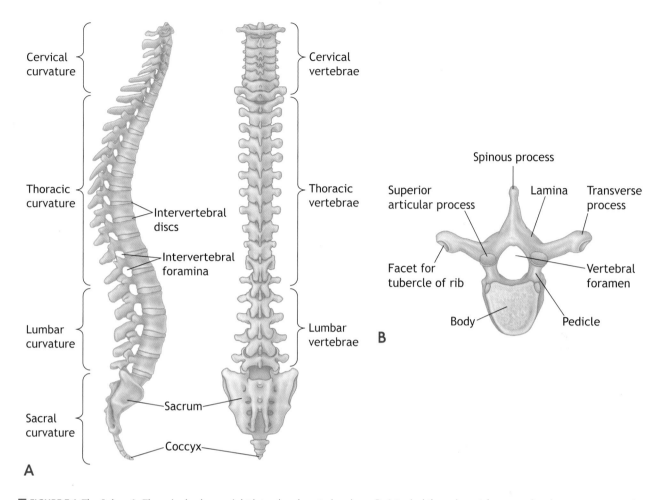

FIGURE 7-1 The Spine. A. The spinal column, right lateral and posterior views. **B.** A typical thoracic vertebra, superior view.

incidence of thoracic fractures is much lower. Most thoracic spine fractures are wedge compression fractures that are not associated with spinal cord injury. However, when a fracture-dislocation in the thoracic spine does occur, it almost always results in a complete spinal cord injury because of the relatively narrow thoracic canal. The thoracolumbar junction is a fulcrum between the inflexible thoracic region and the more mobile lumbar levels. This makes it more vulnerable to injury, and 15% of all spinal injuries occur in this region.

SPINAL CORD ANATOMY

The spinal cord originates at the caudal end of the medulla oblongata at the foramen magnum. In adults, it usually ends near the L1 bony level as the conus medullaris. Below this level is the cauda equina, which is somewhat more resilient to injury. Of the many tracts in the spinal cord, only three can be readily assessed clinically: the lateral corticospinal tract, spinothalamic tract, and dorsal columns. Each is a paired tract that can

be injured on one or both sides of the cord. The location in the spinal cord, function, and method of testing for each tract are outlined in ■ TABLE 7-1.

When a patient has no demonstrable sensory or motor function below a certain level, he or she is said to have a *complete spinal cord injury*. An *incomplete spinal cord injury* is one in which some degree of motor or sensory function remains; in this case, the prognosis for recovery is significantly better than that for complete spinal cord injury.

DERMATOMES

A dermatome is the area of skin innervated by the sensory axons within a particular segmental nerve root. The sensory level is the lowest dermatome with normal sensory function and can often differ on the two sides of the body. For practical purposes, the upper cervical dermatomes (C1 to C4) are somewhat variable in their cutaneous distribution and are not commonly used for localization. However, note that the supraclavicular nerves (C2 through C4) provide sensory

TABLE 7-1 CLINICAL ASSESSMENT OF SPINAL CORD TRACTS

TRACT	LOCATION IN SPINAL CORD	FUNCTION	METHOD OF TESTING
Corticospinal tract	In the anterior and lateral segments of the cord	Controls motor power on the same side of the body	By voluntary muscle contractions or involuntary response to painful stimuli
Spinothalamic tract	In the anterolateral aspect of the cord	Transmits pain and temperature sensation from the opposite side of the body	By pinprick
Dorsal columns	In the posteromedial aspect of the cord	Carries position sense (proprioception), vibration sense, and some light-touch sensation from the same side of the body	By position sense in the toes and fingers or vibration sense using a tuning fork

TABLE 7-2 KEY SPINAL NERVE SEGMENTS AND AREAS OF INNERVATION

SPINAL NERVE SEGMENT	INJURY
C5	Area over the deltoid
C6	Thumb
C7	Middle finger
C8	Little finger
T4	Nipple
T8	Xiphisternum
T10	Umbilicus
T12	Symphysis pubis
L4	Medial aspect of the calf
L5	Web space between the first and second toes
S1	Lateral border of the foot
S3	Ischial tuberosity area
S4 ans S5	Perianal region

innervation to the region overlying the pectoralis muscle (cervical cape). The presence of sensation in this region may confuse examiners when they are trying to determine the sensory level in patients with lower cervical injuries. The key spinal nerve segments and areas of innervation are outlined in ■ TABLE 7-2 and illustrated in ■ FIGURE 7-2 (also see *Dermatomes Guide on MyATLS mobile app*). The International Standards for Neurological Classification of Spinal Cord Injury worksheet, published by the American Spinal Injury Association (ASIA), can be used to document the motor and sensory examination. It provides detailed information on the patient's neurologic examination. Details regarding how to score the motor examination are contained within the document.

MYOTOMES

Each segmental nerve root innervates more than one muscle, and most muscles are innervated by more than one root (usually two). Nevertheless, for simplicity, certain muscles or muscle groups are identified as representing a single spinal nerve segment. The key myotomes are shown in ■ FIGURE 7-3 (also see *Nerve Myotomes Guide on MyATLS mobile app*). The key muscles should be tested for strength on both sides and graded on a 6-point scale (0–5) from normal strength to paralysis (see *Muscle Strength Grading Guide on MyATLS mobile app*). In addition, the external anal sphincter should be tested for voluntary contraction by digital examination.

Early, accurate documentation of a patient's sensation and strength is essential, because it helps to assess

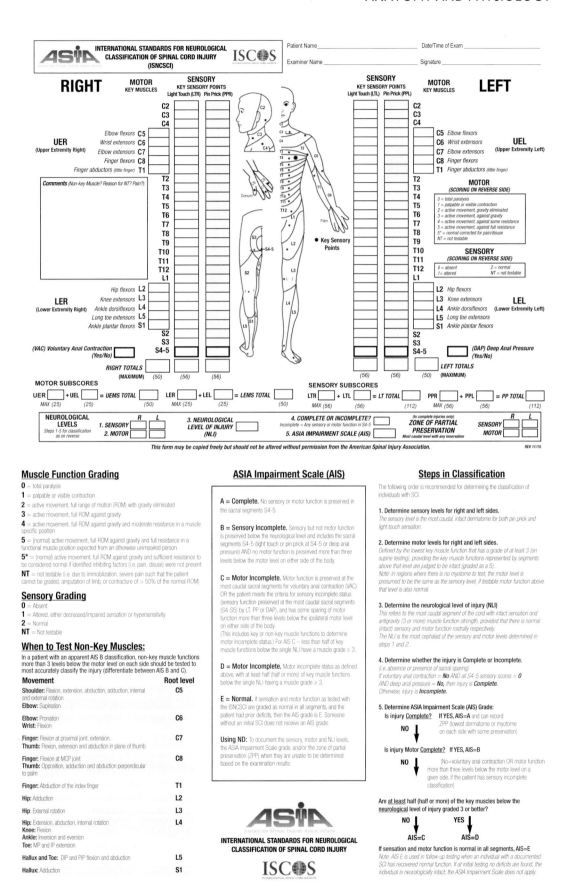

■ FIGURE 7-2 International Standards for Neurological Classification of Spinal Cord Injury. A. Sensory and Motor Evaluation of Spinal Cord. **B.** Clinical Classifications of Spinal Cord Injuries.

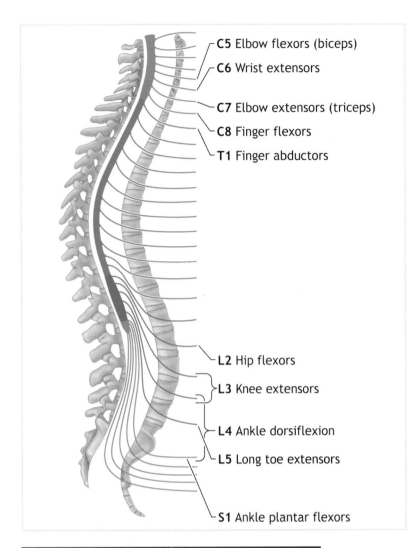

C5 Elbow flexors (biceps)
C6 Wrist extensors
C7 Elbow extensors (triceps)
C8 Finger flexors
T1 Finger abductors

L2 Hip flexors
L3 Knee extensors
L4 Ankle dorsiflexion
L5 Long toe extensors
S1 Ankle plantar flexors

■ **FIGURE 7-3 Key Myotomes.** Myotomes are used to evaluate the level of motor function.

PITFALL	PREVENTION
The sensory and motor examination is confounded by pain.	• When necessary, repeat the exam multiple times.
A patient is able to observe the examination itself, which may alter the findings.	• Attempt to prevent or distract the patient from watching your clinical exam.
A patient's altered level of consciousness limits your ability to perform a defini-tive neurological examination.	• Always presume the presence of an injury, restrict movement of the spine while managing life-threatening injuries, reassess, and perform radiographic evaluation as necessary.

neurological improvement or deterioration on subsequent examinations.

NEUROGENIC SHOCK VERSUS SPINAL SHOCK

Neurogenic shock results in the loss of vasomotor tone and sympathetic innervation to the heart. Injury to the cervical or upper thoracic spinal cord (T6 and above) can cause impairment of the descending sympathetic pathways. The resultant loss of vasomotor tone causes vasodilation of visceral and peripheral blood vessels, pooling of blood, and, consequently, hypotension. Loss of sympathetic innervation to the heart can cause bradycardia or at least the inability to mount a tachycardic response to hypovolemia. However, when shock is present, it is still necessary to rule out other sources because hypovolemic (hemorrhagic) shock is the most common type of shock in trauma patients and can be present in addition to neurogenic shock. The physiologic effects of neurogenic shock are not reversed with fluid resuscitation alone, and massive resuscitation can result in fluid overload and/or pulmonary edema. Judicious use of vasopressors may be required after moderate volume replacement, and atropine may be used to counteract hemodynamically significant bradycardia.

Spinal shock refers to the flaccidity (loss of muscle tone) and loss of reflexes that occur immediately after spinal cord injury. After a period of time, spasticity ensues.

EFFECTS OF SPINE INJURY ON OTHER ORGAN SYSTEMS

When a patient's spine is injured, the primary concern should be potential respiratory failure. Hypoventilation can occur from paralysis of the intercostal muscles (i.e., injury to the lower cervical or upper thoracic spinal cord) or the diaphragm (i.e., injury to C3 to C5).

The inability to perceive pain can mask a potentially serious injury elsewhere in the body, such as the usual signs of acute abdominal or pelvic pain associated with pelvic fracture.

DOCUMENTATION OF SPINAL CORD INJURIES

Spinal cord injuries can be classified according to level, severity of neurological deficit, spinal cord syndromes, and morphology.

LEVEL

The *bony level of injury* refers to the specific vertebral level at which bony damage has occurred. The *neurological level of injury* describes the most caudal segment of the spinal cord that has normal sensory and motor function on both sides of the body. The neurological level of injury is determined primarily by clinical examination. The term *sensory level* is used when referring to the most caudal segment of the spinal cord with normal sensory function. The *motor level* is defined similarly with respect to motor function as the lowest key muscle that has a muscle-strength grade of at least 3 on a 6-point scale. The zone of partial preservation is the area just below the injury level where some impaired sensory and/or motor function is found.

Frequently, there is a discrepancy between the bony and neurological levels of injury because the spinal nerves enter the spinal canal through the foramina and ascend or descend inside the spinal canal before actually entering the spinal cord. Determining the level of injury on both sides is important.

Apart from the initial management to stabilize the bony injury, all subsequent descriptions of injury level are based on the neurological level.

SEVERITY OF NEUROLOGICAL DEFICIT

Spinal cord injury can be categorized as:

- Incomplete or complete paraplegia (thoracic injury)
- Incomplete or complete quadriplegia/tetraplegia (cervical injury)

Any motor or sensory function below the injury level constitutes an incomplete injury and should be documented appropriately. Signs of an incomplete injury include any sensation (including position sense) or voluntary movement in the lower extremities, sacral sparing, voluntary anal sphincter contraction, and voluntary toe flexion. Sacral reflexes, such as the bulbocavernosus reflex or anal wink, do not qualify as sacral sparing.

SPINAL CORD SYNDROMES

Characteristic patterns of neurological injury are encountered in patients with spinal cord injuries, such as central cord syndrome, anterior cord syndrome, and Brown-Séquard syndrome. It is helpful to recognize these patterns, as their prognoses differ from complete and incomplete spinal cord injuries.

Central cord syndrome is characterized by a disproportionately greater loss of motor strength in the upper extremities than in the lower extremities, with varying degrees of sensory loss. This syndrome typically occurs after a hyperextension injury in a patient with preexisting cervical canal stenosis. The mechanism is commonly that of a forward fall resulting in a facial impact. Central cord syndrome can occur with or without cervical spine fracture or dislocation. The prognosis for recovery in central cord injuries is somewhat better than with other incomplete injuries. These injuries are frequently found in patients, especially the elderly, who have underlying spinal stenosis and suffer a ground-level fall.

Anterior cord syndrome results from injury to the motor and sensory pathways in the anterior part of the cord. It is characterized by paraplegia and a bilateral loss of pain and temperature sensation. However, sensation from the intact dorsal column (i.e., position, vibration, and deep pressure sense) is preserved. This syndrome has the poorest prognosis of the incomplete injuries and occurs most commonly following cord ischemia.

Brown-Séquard syndrome results from hemisection of the cord, usually due to a penetrating trauma. In its pure form, the syndrome consists of ipsilateral motor loss (corticospinal tract) and loss of position sense (dorsal column), associated with contralateral loss of pain and temperature sensation beginning one to two levels below the level of injury (spino-thalamic tract). Even when the syndrome is caused by a direct penetrating injury to the cord, some recovery is usually achieved.

MORPHOLOGY

Spinal injuries can be described as fractures, fracture-dislocations, spinal cord injury without radiographic abnormalities (SCIWORA), and penetrating injuries. Each of these categories can be further described as stable or unstable. However, determining the stability of a particular type of injury is not always simple and, indeed, even experts may disagree. Particularly during the initial treatment, all patients with radiographic evidence of injury and all those with neurological deficits should be considered to have an unstable spinal injury. Spinal motion of these patients should be restricted, and turning and/or repositioning requires adequate personnel using logrolling technique until consultation with a specialist, typically a neurosurgeon or orthopedic surgeon.

SPECIFIC TYPES OF SPINAL INJURIES

Spinal injuries of particular concern to clinicians in the trauma setting include cervical spine fractures, thoracic spine fractures, thoracolumbar junction fractures, lumbar fractures, penetrating injuries, and the potential for associated blunt carotid and vertebral vascular injuries.

CERVICAL SPINE FRACTURES

Cervical spine injuries can result from one or a combination of the following mechanisms of injury: axial loading, flexion, extension, rotation, lateral bending, and distraction.

Cervical spine injury in children is a relatively rare event, occurring in less than 1% of cases. Of note, upper cervical spine injuries in children (C1–C4) are almost twice as common as lower cervical spine injuries. Additionally, anatomical differences, emotional distress, and inability to communicate make evaluation of the spine even more challenging in this population. (See *Chapter 10: Pediatric Trauma.*)

Specific types of cervical spine injuries of note to clinicians in the trauma setting are atlanto-occipital dislocation, atlas (C1) fracture, C1 rotary subluxation, and axis (C2) fractures.

Atlanto-Occipital Dislocation

Craniocervical disruption injuries are uncommon and result from severe traumatic flexion and distraction. Most patients with this injury die of brainstem destruction and apnea or have profound neurological impairments (e.g., ventilator dependence and quadriplegia/tetraplegia). Patients may survive if they are promptly resuscitated at the injury scene. Atlanto-occipital dislocation is a common cause of death in cases of shaken baby syndrome.

Atlas (C1) Fracture

The atlas is a thin, bony ring with broad articular surfaces. Fractures of the atlas represent approximately 5% of acute cervical spine fractures, and up to 40% of atlas fractures are associated with fractures of the axis (C2). The most common C1 fracture is a burst fracture (Jefferson fracture). The typical mechanism of injury is axial loading, which occurs when a large load falls vertically on the head or a patient lands on the top of his or her head in a relatively neutral position. Jefferson fractures involve disruption of the anterior and posterior rings of C1 with lateral displacement of the lateral masses. The fracture is best seen on an open-mouth view of the C1 to C2 region and axial computed tomography (CT) scans (■ FIGURE 7-4).

These fractures usually are not associated with spinal cord injuries; however, they are unstable and should be initially treated with a properly sized rigid cervical collar. Unilateral ring or lateral mass fractures are not uncommon and tend to be stable injuries. However, treat all such fractures as unstable until the patient is examined by a specialist, typically a neurosurgeon or orthopedic surgeon.

C1 Rotary Subluxation

The C1 rotary subluxation injury is most often seen in children. It can occur spontaneously, after major or minor trauma, with an upper respiratory infection, or with rheumatoid arthritis. The patient presents with

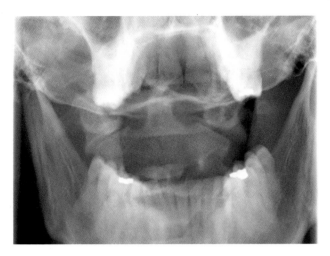

■ FIGURE 7-4 Jefferson Fracture. Open-mouth view radiograph showing a Jefferson fracture. This fracture involves disruption of both the anterior and posterior rings of C1, with lateral displacement of the lateral masses.

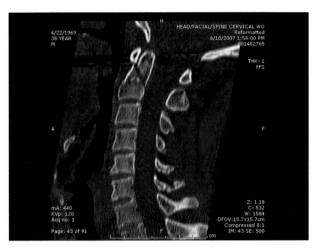

■ FIGURE 7-5 Odontoid Fracture. CT view of a Type II odontoid fracture, which occurs through the base of the dens.

a persistent rotation of the head (torticollis). With this injury, the odontoid is not equidistant from the two lateral masses of C1. Do not force the patient to overcome the rotation, but restrict motion with him or her in the rotated position and refer for further specialized treatment.

Axis (C2) Fractures

The axis is the largest cervical vertebra and the most unusual in shape. Thus it is susceptible to various fractures, depending on the force and direction of the impact. Acute fractures of C2 represent approximately 18% of all cervical spine injuries. Axis fractures of note to trauma care providers include odontoid fractures and posterior element fractures.

Odontoid Fractures

Approximately 60% of C2 fractures involve the odontoid process, a peg-shaped bony protuberance that projects upward and is normally positioned in contact with the anterior arch of C1. The odontoid process is held in place primarily by the transverse ligament. Type I odontoid fractures typically involve the tip of the odontoid and are relatively uncommon. Type II odontoid fractures occur through the base of the dens and are the most common odontoid fracture (■ FIGURE 7-5). In children younger than 6 years of age, the epiphysis may be prominent and resemble a fracture at this level. Type III odontoid fractures occur at the base of the dens and extend obliquely into the body of the axis.

Posterior Element Fractures

A posterior element fracture, or hangman's fracture, involves the posterior elements of C2—the pars interarticularis (■ FIGURE 7-6). This type of fracture is usually caused by an extension-type injury. Ensure that patients with this fracture are maintained in properly sized rigid cervical collar until specialized care is available.

Fractures and Dislocations (C3 through C7)

The area of greatest flexion and extension of the cervical spine occurs at C5–C6 and is thus most vulnerable to injury. In adults, the most common level of cervical vertebral fracture is C5, and the most common level of subluxation is C5 on C6. Other injuries include subluxation of the articular processes (including unilateral or bilateral locked facets) and fractures of the laminae, spinous processes, pedicles, or lateral masses. Rarely, ligamentous disruption occurs without fractures or facet dislocations.

The incidence of neurological injury increases significantly with facet dislocations and is much more severe with bilateral locked facets.

THORACIC SPINE FRACTURES

Thoracic spine fractures may be classified into four broad categories: anterior wedge compression injuries, burst injuries, Chance fractures, and fracture-dislocations.

Axial loading with flexion produces an *anterior wedge compression injury*. The amount of wedging usually is quite minor, and the anterior portion of the vertebral

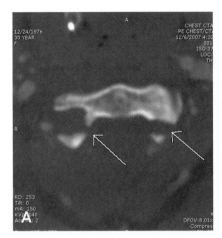
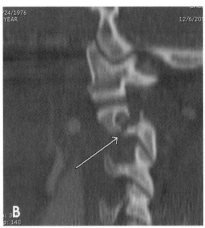
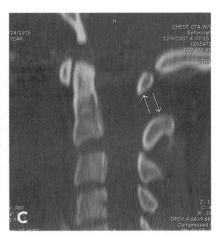

■ **FIGURE 7-6 Hangman's Fracture (arrows).** Demonstrated in CT reconstructions: **A.** axial; **B.** sagittal paramedian; and **C.** sagittal midline. Note the anterior angulation and excessive distance between the spinous processes of C1 and C2 (double arrows).

body rarely is more than 25% shorter than the posterior body. Due to the rigidity of the rib cage, most of these fractures are stable.

Burst injury is caused by vertical-axial compression.

Chance fractures are transverse fractures through the vertebral body (■ **FIGURE 7-7**). They are caused by flexion about an axis anterior to the vertebral column and are most frequently seen following motor vehicle crashes in which the patient was restrained by only an improperly placed lap belt. Chance fractures can be associated with retroperitoneal and abdominal visceral injuries.

Due to the orientation of the facet joints, *fracture-dislocations* are relatively uncommon in the thoracic and lumbar spine. These injuries nearly always result from extreme flexion or severe blunt trauma to the spine, which causes disruption of the posterior elements (pedicles, facets, and lamina) of the vertebra. The thoracic spinal canal is narrow in relation to the spinal cord, so fracture subluxations in

the thoracic spine commonly result in complete neurological deficits.

Simple compression fractures are usually stable and often treated with a rigid brace. Burst fractures, Chance fractures, and fracture-dislocations are extremely unstable and nearly always require internal fixation.

THORACOLUMBAR JUNCTION FRACTURES (T11 THROUGH L1)

Fractures at the level of the thoracolumbar junction are due to the immobility of the thoracic spine compared with the lumbar spine. Because these fractures most often result from a combination of acute hyperflexion and rotation, they are usually unstable. People who fall from a height and restrained drivers who sustain severe flexion with high kinetic energy transfer are at particular risk for this type of injury.

The spinal cord terminates as the conus medullaris at approximately the level of L1, and injury to this part of the cord commonly results in bladder and bowel dysfunction, as well as decreased sensation and strength in the lower extremities. Patients with thoracolumbar fractures are particularly vulnerable to rotational movement, so be extremely careful when logrolling them. (See *Logroll video on MyATLS mobile app.*)

LUMBAR FRACTURES

The radiographic signs associated with a lumbar fracture are similar to those of thoracic and thoracolumbar fractures. However, because only the cauda equina is involved, the probability of a complete neurological deficit is much lower with these injuries.

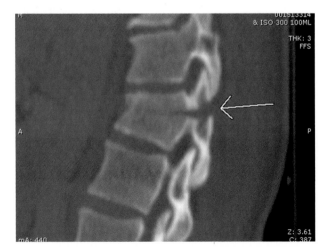

■ **FIGURE 7-7 Chance Fracture.** Radiograph showing a Chance fracture, which is a transverse fracture through the vertebral body.

PENETRATING INJURIES

Penetrating injuries often result in a complete neurological deficit due to the path of the missile involved (most often a bullet or knife). These deficits also can result from the energy transfer associated with a high-velocity missile (e.g., bullet) passing close to the spinal cord rather than through it. Penetrating injuries of the spine usually are stable unless the missile destroys a significant portion of the vertebra.

BLUNT CAROTID AND VERTEBRAL ARTERY INJURIES

Blunt trauma to the neck can result in carotid and vertebral arterial injuries; early recognition and treatment of these injuries may reduce the patient's risk of stroke. Specific spinal indications in screening for these injuries include C1–C3 fractures, cervical spine fracture with subluxation, and fractures involving the foramen transversarium.

▶ RADIOGRAPHIC EVALUATION

Both careful clinical examination and thorough radiographic assessment are critical in identifying significant spine injury.

CERVICAL SPINE

Many trauma patients have a c-collar placed by emergency medical services (EMS) in the field. Current guidelines for spinal motion restriction in the prehospital setting allow for more flexibility in the use of long spine boards and cervical collars. With the use of clinical screening decision tools such as the Canadian C-Spine Rule (CCR; ■ FIGURE 7-8) and the National Emergency X-Radiography Utilization Study (NEXUS; ■ FIGURE 7-9), c-spine collars and blocks may be discontinued in many of these patients without the need for radiologic imaging.

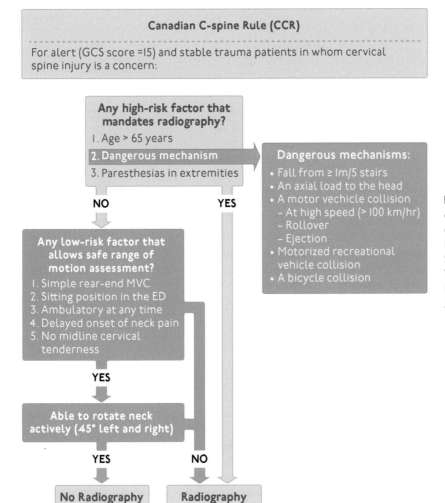

■ FIGURE 7-8 Canadian C-Spine Rule. A clinical decision tool for cervical spine evaluation. MVC = motor vehicle collison; ED = emergency department. Adapted from Stiell IG, Wells GA, Vandemheen KL, et al. The Canadian C-Spine rule of radiography in alert and stable trauma patients. *JAMA* 2001;286:1841–1848.

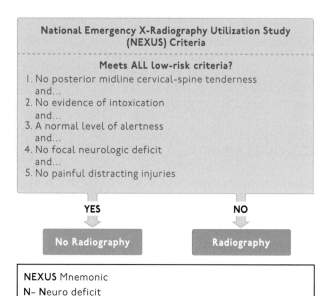

National Emergency X-Radiography Utilization Study (NEXUS) Criteria

Meets ALL low-risk criteria?

1. No posterior midline cervical-spine tenderness
   and...
2. No evidence of intoxication
   and...
3. A normal level of alertness
   and...
4. No focal neurologic deficit
   and...
5. No painful distracting injuries

YES → No Radiography

NO → Radiography

NEXUS Mnemonic

N– **N**euro deficit
E– **E**tOH (alcohol)/intoxication
X– e**X**treme distracting injury(ies)
U– **U**nable to provide history (altered level of consciousness)
S– **S**pinal tenderness (midline)

Explanations:

These are for purposes of clarity only. There are not precise definitions for the individual NEXUS Criteria, which are subject to interpretation by individual physicians.

1. Midline posterior bony cervical spine tenderness is present if the patient complains of pain on palpation of the posterior midline neck from the nuchal ridge to the prominence of the first thoracic vertebra, or if the patient evinces pain with direct palpation of any cervical spinous process.

2. Patients should be considered intoxicated if they have either of the following:
   • A recent history by the patient or an observer of intoxication or intoxicating ingestion
   • Evidence of intoxication on physical examination, such as odor of alcohol, slurred speech, ataxia, dysmetria or other cerebellar findings, or any behavior consistent with intoxication. Patients may also be considered to be intoxicated if tests of bodily secretions are positive for drugs (including but not limited to alcohol) that affect level of alertness.

3. An altered level of alertness can include any of the following:
   • Glasgow Coma Scale score of 14 or less
   • Disorientation to person, place, time, or events
   • Inability to remember 3 objects at 5 minutes
   • Delayed or inappropriate response to external stimuli
   • Other

4. Any focal neurologic complaint (by history) or finding (on motor or sensory examination).

5. No precise definition for distracting painful injury is possible. This includes any condition thought by the clinician to be producing pain sufficient to distract the patient from a second (neck) injury. Examples may include, but are not limited to:
   • Any long bone fracture
   • A visceral injury requiring surgical consultation
   • A large laceration, degloving injury, or crush injury
   • Large burns
   • Any other injury producing acute functional impairment

Physicians may also classify any injury as distracting if it is thought to have the potential to impair the patient's ability to appreciate other injuries.

■ **FIGURE 7-9 National Emergency X-Radiography Utilization Study (NEXUS) Criteria and Mnemonic.** A clinical decision tool for cervical spine evaluation. Adapted from Hoffman JR, Mower WR, Wolfson AB, et al. Validity of a set of clinical criteria to rule out injury to the cervical spine in patients with blunt trauma. National Emergency X-Radiography Utilization Study Group. *N Engl J Med* 2000; 343:94–99.

There are two options for patients who require radiographic evaluation of the cervical spine. In locations with available technology, the primary screening modality is multidetector CT (MDCT) from the occiput to T1 with sagittal and coronal reconstructions. Where this technology is not available, plain radiographic films from the occiput to T1, including lateral, anteroposterior (AP), and open-mouth odontoid views should be obtained.

With plain films, the base of the skull, all seven cervical vertebrae, and the first thoracic vertebra must be visualized on the lateral view. The patient's shoulders may need to be pulled down when obtaining this x-ray to avoid missing an injury in the lower cervical spine. If all seven cervical vertebrae are not visualized on the lateral x-ray film, obtain a swimmer's view of the lower cervical and upper thoracic area.

The open-mouth odontoid view should include the entire odontoid process and the right and left C1 and C2 articulations.

The AP view of the c-spine assists in identifying a unilateral facet dislocation in cases in which little or no dislocation is visible on the lateral film.

When these films are of good quality and are properly interpreted, unstable cervical spine injuries can be detected with a sensitivity of greater than 97%. A doctor qualified to interpret these films must review the complete series of cervical spine radiographs before the spine is considered normal. Do not remove the cervical collar until a neurologic assessment and evaluation of the c-spine, including palpation of the spine with voluntary movement in all planes, have been performed and found to be unconcerning or without injury.

When the lower cervical spine is not adequately visualized on the plain films or areas suspicious for injury are identified, MDCT scans can be obtained. MDCT scans may be used instead of plain images to evaluate the cervical spine.

It is possible for patients to have an isolated ligamentous spine injury that results in instability without an associated fracture and/or subluxation. Patients with neck pain and normal radiography should be evaluated by magnetic resonance imaging (MRI) or flexion-extension x-ray films. Flexion-extension x-rays of the cervical spine can detect occult instability or determine the stability of a known fracture. When patient transfer is planned, spinal imaging can be deferred to the receiving facility while maintaining spinal motion restriction. Under no circumstances should clinicians force the patient's neck into a position that elicits pain. All movements must be voluntary. Obtain these films under the direct supervision and control of a doctor experienced in their interpretation.

In some patients with significant soft-tissue injury, paraspinal muscle spasm may severely limit the degree of flexion and extension that the patient allows. MRI may be the most sensitive tool for identifying soft-tissue injury if performed within 72 hours of injury. However, data regarding correlation of cervical spine instability with positive MRI findings are lacking.

Approximately 10% of patients with a cervical spine fracture have a second, noncontiguous vertebral column fracture. This fact warrants a complete radiographic screening of the entire spine in patients with a cervical spine fracture.

In the presence of neurological deficits, MRI is recommended to detect any soft-tissue compressive lesion that cannot be detected with plain films or MDCT, such as a spinal epidural hematoma or traumatic herniated disk. MRI may also detect spinal cord contusions or disruption, as well as paraspinal ligamentous and soft-tissue injury. However, MRI is frequently not feasible in patients with hemodynamic instability. These specialized studies should be performed at the discretion of a spine surgery consultant.

■ BOX 7-1 presents guidelines for screening trauma patients with suspected spine injury.

THORACIC AND LUMBAR SPINE

The indications for screening radiography of the thoracic and lumbar spine are essentially the same as those for the cervical spine. Where available, MDCT scanning of the thoracic and lumbar spine can be used as the initial screening modality. Reformatted views from the chest/abdomen/pelvis MDCT may be used. If MDCT is unavailable, obtain AP and lateral plain radiographs; however, note that MDCT has superior sensitivity.

On the AP views, observe the vertical alignment of the pedicles and distance between the pedicles of each vertebra. Unstable fractures commonly cause widening of the interpedicular distance. The lateral films detect subluxations, compression fractures, and Chance fractures.

CT scanning is particularly useful for detecting fractures of the posterior elements (pedicles, lamina, and spinous processes) and determining the degree of canal compromise caused by burst fractures. Sagittal and coronal reconstruction of axial CT images should be performed.

As with the cervical spine, a complete series of high-quality radiographs must be properly interpreted as without injury by a qualified doctor before spine precautions are discontinued. However, due to the possibility of pressure ulcers, do *not* wait for final radiographic interpretation before removing the patient from a long board.

PITFALL	PREVENTION
An inadequate secondary assessment results in the failure to recognize a spinal cord injury, particularly an incomplete spinal cord injury.	• Be sure to perform a thorough neurological assessment during the secondary survey or once life-threatening injuries have been managed.
Patients with a diminished level of consciousness and those who arrive in shock are often difficult to assess for the presence of spinal cord injury.	• For these patients, perform a careful repeat assessment after managing initial life-threatening injuries.

GENERAL MANAGEMENT

General management of spine and spinal cord trauma includes restricting spinal motion, intravenous fluids, medications, and transfer, if appropriate. (See *Appendix G: Disability Skills*.)

SPINAL MOTION RESTRICTION

Prehospital care personnel typically restrict the movement of the spine of patients before transporting

BOX 7-1 GUIDELINES FOR SCREENING PATIENTS WITH SUSPECTED SPINE INJURY

Because trauma patients can have unrecognized spinal injuries, be sure to restrict spinal motion until they can undergo appropriate clinical examination and imaging.

SUSPECTED CERVICAL SPINE INJURY

1. The presence of paraplegia or quadriplegia/tetraplegia is presumptive evidence of spinal instability.

2. Use validated clinical decision tools such as the Canadian C-Spine Rule and NEXUS to help determine the need for radiographic evaluation and to clinically clear the c-spine. Patients who are awake, alert, sober, and neurologically normal, with no neck pain, midline tenderness, or a distracting injury, are extremely unlikely to have an acute c-spine fracture or instability. With the patient in a supine position, remove the c-collar and palpate the spine. If there is no significant tenderness, ask the patient to voluntarily move his or her neck from side to side and flex and extend his or her neck. Never force the patient's neck. If there is no pain, c-spine films are not necessary, and the c-collar can be safely removed.

3. Patients who **do** have neck pain or midline tenderness require radiographic imaging. The burden of proof is on the clinician to exclude a spinal injury. When technology is available, all such patients should undergo MDCT from the occiput to T1 with sagittal and coronal reconstructions. When technology is not available, patients should undergo lateral, AP, and open-mouth odontoid x-ray examinations of the c-spine. Suspicious or inadequately visualized areas on the plain films may require MDCT. C-spine films should be assessed for:

   - bony deformity/fracture of the vertebral body or processes
   - loss of alignment of the posterior aspect of the vertebral bodies (anterior extent of the vertebral canal)
   - increased distance between the spinous processes at one level
   - narrowing of the vertebral canal
   - increased prevertebral soft-tissue space

   If these films are normal, the c-collar may be removed to obtain flexion and extension views. A qualified clinician may obtain lateral cervical spine films with the patient voluntarily flexing and extending his or her neck. If the films show no subluxation, the patient's c-spine can be cleared and the c-collar removed. However, if any of these films are suspicious or unclear, replace the collar and consult with a spine specialist.

4. Patients who have an altered level of consciousness or are unable to describe their symptoms require imaging. Ideally, obtain MDCT from the occiput to T1 with sagittal

and coronal reconstructions. When this technology is not available, lateral, AP, and open-mouth odontoid films with CT supplementation through suspicious or poorly visualized areas are sufficient.

   In children, CT supplementation is optional. If the entire c-spine can be visualized and is found to be normal, the collar can be removed after appropriate evaluation by a doctor skilled in evaluating and managing patients with spine injuries. Clearance of the c-spine is particularly important if pulmonary or other management strategies are compromised by the inability to mobilize the patient.

5. When in doubt, leave the collar on.

SUSPECTED THORACOLUMBAR SPINE INJURY

1. The presence of paraplegia or a level of sensory loss on the chest or abdomen is presumptive evidence of spinal instability.

2. Patients who are neurologically normal, awake, alert, and sober, with no significant traumatic mechanism and no midline thoracolumbar back pain or tenderness, are unlikely to have an unstable injury. Thoracolumbar radiographs may not be necessary.

3. Patients who have spine pain or tenderness on palpation, neurological deficits, an altered level of consciousness, or significant mechanism of injury should undergo screening with MDCT. If MDCT is unavailable, obtain AP and lateral radiographs of the entire thoracic and lumbar spine. All images must be of good quality and interpreted as normal by a qualified doctor before discontinuing spine precautions.

4. For all patients in whom a spine injury is detected or suspected, consult with doctors who are skilled in evaluating and managing patients with spine injuries.

5. Quickly evaluate patients with or without neurological deficits (e.g., quadriplegia/tetraplegia or paraplegia) and remove them from the backboard as soon as possible. A patient who is allowed to lie on a hard board for more than 2 hours is at high risk for pressure ulcers.

6. Trauma patients who require emergency surgery before a complete workup of the spine can be accomplished should be transported carefully, assuming that an unstable spine injury is present. Leave the c-collar in place and logroll the patient to and from the operating table. Do not leave the patient on a rigid backboard during surgery. The surgical team should take particular care to protect the neck as much as possible during the operation. The anesthesiologist should be informed of the status of the workup.

them to the ED. Prevent spinal movement of any patient with a suspected spine injury above and below the suspected injury site until a fracture is excluded. This is accomplished simply by laying the patient supine without rotating or bending the spinal column on a firm surface with a properly sized and placed rigid cervical collar. Remember to maintain spinal motion restriction until an injury is excluded. Occasionally patients present to the ED without a c-collar, in which case the treating physician should follow clinical decision-making guidelines to determine the need for cervical spine imaging and rigid collar placement.

Clinicians should not attempt to reduce an obvious deformity. Children may have torticollis, and elderly patients may have severe degenerative spine disease that causes them to have a nontraumatic kyphotic deformity of the spine. Such patients should be left

in a position of comfort, with movement of the spine restricted. Similarly, a cervical collar may not fit obese patients, so use bolsters to support the neck. Supplemental padding is often necessary. Attempts to align the spine to aid restriction of motion on the backboard are not recommended if they cause pain.

A semirigid collar does not ensure complete motion restriction of the cervical spine. Supplementation with bolsters and straps to the long spine board is more effective. However, the use of long spine boards is recommended *for extrication and rapid patient movement* (see *EMS Spinal Precautions and the use of the Long Backboard: Position Statement by the National Association of EMS Physicians and American College of Surgeons Committee on Trauma*).

The logroll maneuver is performed to evaluate the patient's spine and remove the long spine board while limiting spinal movement. (■ FIGURE 7-10; also see

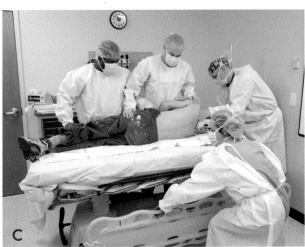
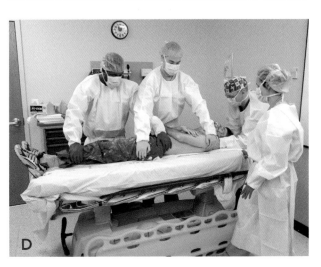
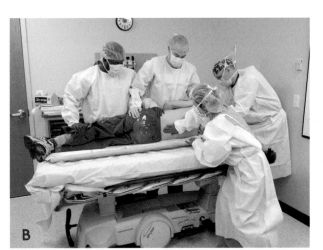
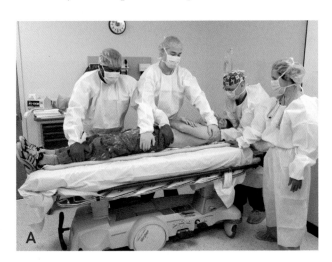

■ FIGURE 7-10 Four-Person Logroll. At least four people are needed for logrolling a patient to remove a spine board and/or examine the back. **A.** One person stands at the patient's head to control the head and c-spine, and two are along the patient's sides to control the body and extremities. **B.** As the patient is rolled, three people maintain alignment of the spine while **C.** the fourth person removes the board and examines the back. **D.** Once the board is removed, three people return the patient to the supine position while maintaining alignment of the spine.

Logroll video on MyATLS mobile app). The team leader determines when in resuscitation and management of the patient this procedure should be performed. One person is assigned to restrict motion of the head and neck. Other individuals positioned on the same side of the patient's torso manually prevent segmental rotation, flexion, extension, lateral bending, or sagging of the chest or abdomen while transferring the patient. Another person is responsible for moving the patient's legs, and a fourth person removes the backboad and examines the back.

INTRAVENOUS FLUIDS

If active hemorrhage is not detected or suspected, persistent hypotension should raise the suspicion of neurogenic shock. Patients with hypovolemic shock usually have tachycardia, whereas those with neurogenic shock classically have bradycardia. If the patient's blood pressure does not improve after a fluid challenge, and no sites of occult hemorrhage are found, the judicious use of vasopressors may be indicated. Phenylephrine hydrochloride, dopamine, or norepinephrine is recommended. Overzealous fluid administration can cause pulmonary edema in patients with neurogenic shock. If the patient's fluid status is uncertain, ultrasound estimation of volume status or invasive monitoring may be helpful. Insert a urinary catheter to monitor urinary output and prevent bladder distention.

MEDICATIONS

There is insufficient evidence to support the use of steroids in spinal cord injury.

TRANSFER

When necessary, patients with spine fractures or neurological deficit should be transferred to a facility capable of providing definitive care. (See *Chapter 13: Transfer to Definitive Care* and *Criteria for Interhospital Transfer on MyATLS mobile app*.) The safest procedure is to transfer the patient after consultation with the accepting trauma team leader and/or a spine specialist. Stabilize the patient and apply the necessary splints, backboard, and/or semirigid cervical collar. Remember, cervical spine injuries above C6 can result in partial or total loss of respiratory function. If there is any concern about the adequacy of ventilation, intubate the patient before transfer. Always avoid unnecessary delay.

TEAMWORK

- The trauma team must ensure adequate spinal motion restriction during the primary and secondary surveys, as well as during transport of patients with proven or suspected spinal injury.

- As long as the patient's spine is protected, a detailed examination can safely be deferred until the patient is stable.

- Although there are often many competing clinical interests, the trauma team must ensure that a complete and adequate examination of the spine is performed. The team leader should decide the appropriate time for this exam.

CHAPTER SUMMARY

1. The spinal column consists of cervical, thoracic, and lumbar vertebrae. The spinal cord contains three important tracts: the corticospinal tract, the spinothalamic tract, and the dorsal columns.

2. Attend to life-threatening injuries first, minimizing movement of the spinal column. Restrict the movement of the patient's spine until vertebral fractures and spinal cord injuries have been excluded. Obtain early consultation with a neurosurgeon and/or orthopedic surgeon whenever a spinal injury is suspected or detected.

3. Document the patient's history and physical examination to establish a baseline for any changes in the patient's neurological status.

4. Obtain images, when indicated, as soon as life-threatening injuries are managed.

5. Spinal cord injuries may be complete or incomplete and may involve any level of the spinal cord.

6. When necessary, transfer patients with vertebral fractures or spinal cord injuries to a facility capable of providing definitive care as quickly and safely as possible.

BIBLIOGRAPHY

1. Biffl WL, Moore EE, Elliott JP, et al. Blunt cerebrovascular injuries. *Curr Probl Surg* 1999;36: 505–599.

2. Bromberg WJ, Collier BC, Diebel LN, et al. Blunt cerebrovascular injury practice management guidelines: the Eastern Association for the Surgery of Trauma. *J Trauma* 2010;68: 471–477.

3. Brown CV, Antevil JL, Sise MJ, et al. Spiral computed tomography for the diagnosis of cervical, thoracic, and lumbar spine fractures: its time has come. *J Trauma* 2005;58(5):890–895; discussion 895–896.

4. Coleman WP, Benzel D, Cahill DW, et al. A critical appraisal of the reporting of the National Acute Spinal Cord Injury Studies (II and III) of methylprednisolone in acute spinal cord injury. *J Spinal Disord* 2000;13(3):185–199.

5. Como JJ, DIav JJ, Dunham CM, et al. Practice management guidelines for identification of cervical spine injuries following trauma: Update from the Eastern Association for the Surgery of Trauma practice management guidelines committee. *J Trauma* 2009;67:651–659.

6. Cooper C, Dunham CM, Rodriguez A. Falls and major injuries are risk factors for thoracolumbar fractures: cognitive impairment and multiple injuries impede the detection of back pain and tenderness. *J Trauma* 1995;38: 692–696.

7. Cothren CC, Moore EE, Ray CE, et al. Cervical spine fracture patterns mandating screening to rule out blunt cerebrovascular injury. *Surgery* 2007;141(1):76–82.

8. Diaz JJ, Cullinane DC, Altman DT, et al. Practice Management Guidelines for the screening of thoracolumbar spine fracture. *J Trauma* 2007; 63(3):709–718.

9. Ghanta MK, Smith LM, Polin RS, et al. An analysis of Eastern Association for the Surgery of Trauma practice guidelines for cervical spine evaluation in a series of patients with multiple imaging techniques. *Am Surg* 2002;68(6):563–567; discussion 567–568.

10. Grogan EL, Morris JA, Dittus RS, et al. Cervical spine evaluation in urban trauma centers: lowering institutional costs and complications through helical CT scan. *J Am Coll Surg* 2005; 200(2):160–165.

11. Guidelines for the Management of Acute Cervical Spine and Spinal Cord Injuries. *Neurosurgery*. 2013;72(Suppl 2):1–259.

12. Guly HR, Bouamra O, Lecky FE. The incidence of neurogenic shock in patients with isolated spinal cord injury in the emergency department. *Resuscitation* 2008;76:57–62.

13. Hadley MN, Walters BC, Aarabi B, et al. Clinical assessment following acute cervical spinal cord injury. *Neurosurgery* 2013;72(Suppl 2): 40–53.

14. Hoffman JR, Mower WR, Wolfson AB, et al. Validity of a set of clinical criteria to rule out injury to the cervical spine in patients with blunt trauma. National Emergency X-Radiography Utilization Study Group. *N Engl J Med* 2000; 343:94–99.

15. Holmes JF, Akkinepalli R. Computed tomography versus plain radiography to screen for cervical spine injury: a meta-analysis. *J Trauma* 2005; 58(5):902–905.

16. Hurlbert RJ. Strategies of medical intervention in the management of acute spinal cord injury. Spine 2006;31(Suppl 11):S16–S21; discussion S36.

17. Hurlbert J, Hadley MN, Walters BC, et al. Pharmacological therapy for acute spinal cord injury. *Neurosurgery* 2013;72(Suppl 2): 93–105.

18. Inaba K, Nosanov L, Menaker J, et al. Prospective derivation of a clinical decision rule for thoracolumbar spine evaluation after blunt trauma: An America Association for the Surgery of Trauma Multi-Institutional Trials Group Study. *J Trauma* 2015;78(3):459–465.

19. Kirshblum S, Waring W 3rd. Updates for the International Standards for Neurological Classification of Spinal Cord Injury. *Phys Med Rehabil Clin N Am* 2014;25(3):505–517.

20. Krassioukov AV, Karlsson AK, Wecht JM, et al. Assessment of autonomic dysfunction following spinal cord injury: Rationale for additions to International Standards for Neurological Assessment. *J Rehabil Res Dev* 2007;44:103–112.

21. Mathen R, Inaba K, Munera F, et al. Prospective evaluation of multislice computed tomography versus plain radiographic cervical spine clearance in trauma patients. *J Trauma* 2007 Jun;62(6):1427.

22. McGuire RA, Neville S, Green BA, et al. Spine instability and the logrolling maneuver. *J Trauma* 1987;27:525–531.

23. Michael DB, Guyot DR, Darmody WR. Coincidence of head and cervical spine injury. *J Neurotrauma* 1989;6:177–189.

24. Panacek EA, Mower WR, Holmes JF, et al. Test performance of the individual NEXUS low-risk clinical screening criteria for cervical spine injury. *Ann Emerg Med* 2001 Jul;38(1):22–25.

25. Patel JC, Tepas JJ, Mollitt DL, et al. Pediatric cervical spine injuries: defining the disease. *J Pediatr Surg* 2001;36:373–376.

26. Pieretti-Vanmarcke R, Velmahos GC, Nance ML, et al. Clinical clearance of the cervical spine in blunt trauma patients younger than 3 years: a multi-center study of the American Association for the Surgery of Trauma. *J Trauma* 2009;67:543–550.

27. Position statement. EMS spinal precautions and the use of the long backboard; National Association of EMS Physicians and American College of Surgeons Committee on Trauma. *Prehospital Emergency Care* 2013;17;392–393.

28. Ryken TC, Hadley MN, Walters BC, et al. Guidelines for the management of acute cervical spine and spinal cord injuries. Chapter 5—Radiographic assessment. *Neurosurgery* 2013;72(3, Suppl 2): 54–72.

29. Sanchez B, Waxman K, Jones T, et al. Cervical spine clearance in blunt trauma: evaluation of a computed tomography-based protocol. *J Trauma* 2005;59(1):179–183.

30. Sayer FT, Kronvall E, Nilsson OG. Methylprednisolone treatment in acute spinal cord injury: the myth challenged through a structured analysis of published literature. *Spine J* 2006;6(3):335–343.

31. Sixta S, Moore FO, Ditillo MF, et al. Screening for thoracolumbar spinal injuries in blunt trauma: An Eastern Association for the Surgery of Trauma practice management guideline. *J Trauma* 2012;73(5, Suppl 4):S326–S332.

32. Stiell IG, Clement CM, Grimshaw J, et al. Implementation of the Canadian C-Spine Rule: prospective 12 centre cluster randomised trial. *BMJ* 2009;339:b4146.

33. Stiell IG, Wells GA, Vandemheen KL, et al. The Canadian C-Spine rule of radiography in alert and stable trauma patients. *JAMA* 2001;286:1841–1848.

34. Vaillancourt C, Stiell IG, Beaudoin T, et al. The out-of-hospital validation of the Canadian C-Spine Rule by paramedics. *Ann Emerg Med* 2009Nov;54(5):663–671.

35. Vicellio P, Simon H, Pressman B, et al. A prospective multicenter study of cervical spine injury in children. *Pediatrics* 2001Aug;108(2):E20.

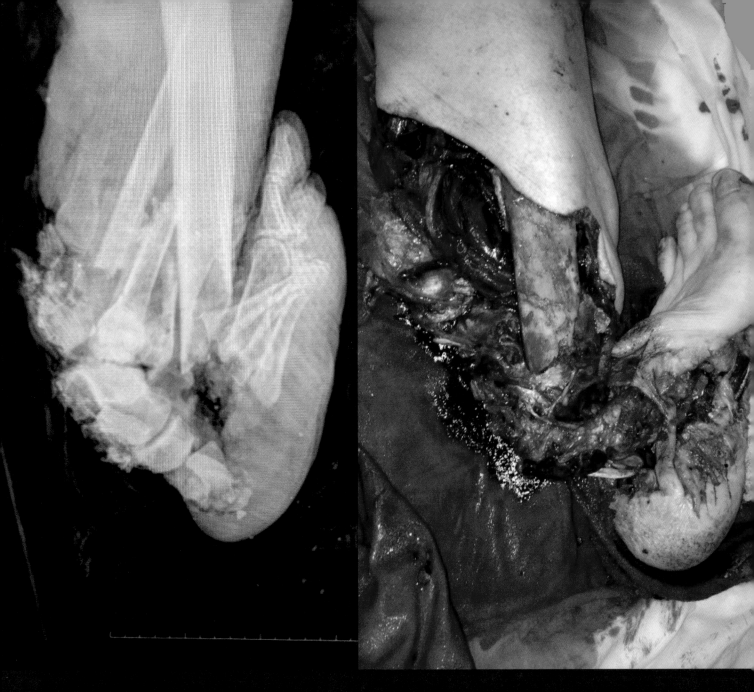

8 MUSCULOSKELETAL TRAUMA

Injuries to the musculoskeletal system are common in trauma patients. The delayed recognition and treatment of these injuries can result in life-threatening hemorrhage or limb loss.

CHAPTER 8 OUTLINE

OBJECTIVES

After reading this chapter and comprehending the knowledge components of the ATLS provider course, you will be able to:

1. Explain the significance of musculoskeletal injuries in patients with multiple injuries.

2. Outline the priorities of the primary survey and resuscitation of patients with extremity injuries, quickly separating the potentially life-threatening injuries from those that are less urgent.

3. Identify the adjuncts needed in the immediate treatment of life-threatening extremity hemorrhage.

4. Describe key elements of the secondary survey of patients with musculoskeletal trauma, including the history and physical examination.

5. Explain the principles of the initial management of limb-threatening musculoskeletal injuries.

6. Describe the appropriate assessment and initial management of patients with contusions, lacerations, joint and ligament injuries, and fractures.

7. Describe the principles of proper immobilization of patients with musculoskeletal injuries.

Many patients who sustain blunt trauma also incur injuries to the musculoskeletal system. These injuries often appear dramatic, but only infrequently cause immediate threat to life or limb. However, musculoskeletal injuries have the potential to distract team members from more urgent resuscitation priorities. First, clinicians need to recognize the presence of life-threatening extremity injuries during the primary survey and understand their association with severe thoracic and abdominal injuries. The provider must also be familiar with extremity anatomy to be able to protect the patient from further disability, and anticipate and prevent complications.

Major musculoskeletal injuries indicate that the body sustained significant forces (■ FIGURE 8-1). For example, a patient with long-bone fractures above and below the diaphragm is at increased risk for associated internal torso injuries. Unstable pelvic fractures and open femur fractures can be accompanied by brisk bleeding. Severe crush injuries cause the release of myoglobin from the muscle, which can precipitate in the renal tubules and result in renal failure. Swelling into an intact musculofascial space can cause an acute compartment syndrome that, if not diagnosed and treated, may lead to lasting impairment and loss of the extremity. Fat embolism, an uncommon but highly lethal complication of long-bone fractures, can lead to pulmonary failure and impaired cerebral function.

Musculoskeletal trauma does not warrant a re-ordering of the ABCDE priorities of resuscitation, but its presence does pose a challenge to clinicians. Musculoskeletal injuries cannot be ignored and treated at a later time; rather, clinicians must treat the whole patient, including musculoskeletal injuries, to ensure an optimal outcome. Despite careful assessment,

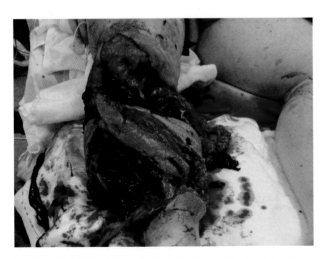

■ FIGURE 8-1 Major injuries indicate that the patient sustained significant forces, and significant blood loss is possible.

fractures and soft tissue injuries may not be initially recognized in patients with multiple injuries.

Continued reevaluation of the patient is necessary to identify all injuries.

PRIMARY SURVEY AND RESUSCITATION OF PATIENTS WITH POTENTIALLY LIFE-THREATENING EXTREMITY INJURIES

During the primary survey, it is imperative to recognize and control hemorrhage from musculoskeletal injuries.

Potentially life-threatening extremity injuries include major arterial hemorrhage, bilateral femoral fractures, and crush syndrome. (Pelvic disruption is described in Chapter 5: Abdominal and Pelvic Trauma.)

Deep soft-tissue lacerations may involve major vessels and lead to exsanguinating hemorrhage. Hemorrhage control is best achieved with direct pressure. Hemorrhage from long-bone fractures can be significant, and femoral fractures in particular often result in significant blood loss into the thigh. Appropriate splinting of fractures can significantly decrease bleeding by reducing motion and enhancing the tamponade effect of the muscle and fascia. If the fracture is open, application of a sterile pressure dressing typically controls hemorrhage. Appropriate fluid resuscitation is an important supplement to these mechanical measures.

PITFALL	PREVENTION
Blood loss from musculoskeletal injuries is not immediately recognized.	• Recognize that femur fractures and any open long-bone fractures with major soft-tissue involvement are potential sites of significant hemorrhage.

MAJOR ARTERIAL HEMORRHAGE AND TRAUMATIC AMPUTATION

Penetrating extremity wounds can result in major arterial vascular injury. Blunt trauma resulting in an extremity fracture or joint dislocation in close proximity to an artery can also disrupt the artery. These injuries may lead to significant hemorrhage through the open wound or into the soft tissues. Patients with traumatic amputation are at particularly high risk of life-threatening hemorrhage and may require application of a tourniquet.

Assessment

Assess injured extremities for external bleeding, loss of a previously palpable pulse, and changes in pulse quality, Doppler tone, and ankle/brachial index. The ankle/brachial index is determined by taking the systolic blood pressure value at the ankle of the injured leg and dividing it by the systolic blood pressure of the uninjured arm. A cold, pale, pulseless extremity indicates an interruption in arterial blood supply. A rapidly expanding hematoma suggests a significant vascular injury.

Management

A stepwise approach to controlling arterial bleeding begins with manual pressure to the wound. (Bleedingcontrol.org provides lay public training in hemorrhage control.) A pressure dressing is then applied, using a stack of gauze held in place by a circumferential elastic bandage to concentrate pressure over the injury. If bleeding persists, apply manual pressure to the artery proximal to the injury. If bleeding continues, consider applying a manual tourniquet (such as a windlass device) or a pneumatic tourniquet applied directly to the skin (■ FIGURE 8-2).

Tighten the tourniquet until bleeding stops. A properly applied tourniquet must occlude arterial inflow, as occluding only the venous system can increase hemorrhage and result in a swollen, cyanotic extremity. A pneumatic tourniquet may require a pressure as high as 250 mm Hg in an upper extremity and 400 mm Hg in a lower extremity. Ensure that the time of tourniquet application is documented. In these cases, immediate surgical consultation is essential, and early transfer to a trauma center should be considered.

If time to operative intervention is longer than 1 hour, a single attempt to deflate the tourniquet may be considered in an otherwise stable patient. The risks of tourniquet use increase with time; if a tourniquet must remain in place for a prolonged period to save a life, the choice of life over limb must be made.

The use of arteriography and other diagnostic tools is indicated only in resuscitated patients who have no hemodynamic abnormalities; other patients with clear vascular injuries require urgent operation. If a major arterial injury exists or is suspected, immediately consult a surgeon skilled in vascular and extremity trauma.

Application of vascular clamps into bleeding open wounds while the patient is in the ED is not advised, unless a superficial vessel is clearly identified. If a fracture is associated with an open hemorrhaging wound, realign and splint it while a second person applies direct pressure to the open wound. Joint dislocations should be reduced, if possible; if the joint cannot be reduced, emergency orthopedic intervention may be required.

Amputation, a severe form of open fracture that results in loss of an extremity, is a traumatic event for the patient, both physically and emotionally. Patients with traumatic amputation may benefit from tourniquet application. They require consultation with and intervention by a surgeon. Certain mangled extremity injuries with prolonged ischemia, nerve injury, and muscle damage may require amputation. Amputation can be lifesaving in a patient with hemodynamic abnormalities resulting from the injured extremity.

Although the potential for replantation should be considered in an upper extremity, it must be considered in conjunction with the patient's other injuries. A patient with multiple injuries who requires intensive resuscitation and/or emergency surgery for extremity or other injuries is not a candidate for replantation. Replantation is usually performed on patients with an isolated extremity injury. For the required decision making and management, transport patients with traumatic amputation of an upper extremity to an appropriate surgical team skilled in replantation procedures.

In such cases, thoroughly wash the amputated part in isotonic solution (e.g., Ringer's lactate) and wrap it in moist sterile gauze. Then wrap the part in a similarly moistened sterile towel, place in a plastic bag, and transport with the patient in an insulated cooling chest with crushed ice. Be careful not to freeze the amputated part.

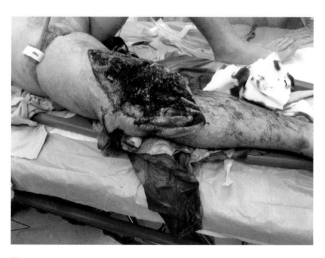

■ FIGURE 8-2 The judicious use of a tourniquet can be lifesaving and/or limb-saving in the presence of ongoing hemorrhage.

BILATERAL FEMUR FRACTURES

Patients who have sustained bilateral femur fractures are at significantly greater risk of complications and death. Such fractures indicate the patient has been subjected to significant force and should alert clinicians to the possibility of associated injuries. Compared with patients with unilateral femur fractures, patients with bilateral femur fractures are at higher risk for significant blood loss, severe associated injuries, pulmonary complications, multiple organ failure, and death. These patients should be assessed and managed in the same way as those with unilateral femur fractures. Consider early transfer to a trauma center.

PITFALL	PREVENTION
Delayed transfer to a trauma center	• Transfer patients with vascular injury and concomitant fracture to a trauma center with vascular and orthopedic surgical capabilities. • Bilateral femur fractures result in a significantly increased risk of complications and death; these patients benefit from early transfer to a trauma center.

CRUSH SYNDROME

Crush syndrome, or traumatic rhabdomyolysis, refers to the clinical effects of injured muscle that, if left untreated, can lead to acute renal failure and shock. This condition is seen in individuals who have sustained a compression injury to significant muscle mass, most often to a thigh or calf. The muscular insult is a combination of direct muscle injury, muscle ischemia, and cell death with release of myoglobin.

Assessment

Myoglobin produces dark amber urine that tests positive for hemoglobin. A myoglobin assay may be requested to confirm its presence. Amber-colored urine in the presence of serum creatine kinase of 10,000 U/L or more is indicative of rhabdomyolysis when urine myoglobin levels are not available. Rhabdomyolysis can lead to metabolic acidosis, hyperkalemia, hypocalcemia, and disseminated intravascular coagulation.

Management

Initiating early and aggressive intravenous fluid therapy during resuscitation is critical to protecting the kidneys and preventing renal failure in patients with rhabdomyolysis. Myoglobin-induced renal failure can be prevented with intravascular fluid expansion, alkalinization of the urine by intravenous administration of bicarbonate, and osmotic diuresis.

ADJUNCTS TO THE PRIMARY SURVEY

Adjuncts to the primary survey of patients with musculoskeletal trauma include fracture immobilization and x-ray examination, when fracture is suspected as a cause of shock.

FRACTURE IMMOBILIZATION

The goal of initial fracture immobilization is to realign the injured extremity in as close to anatomic position as possible and prevent excessive motion at the fracture site. This is accomplished by applying inline traction to realign the extremity and maintaining traction with an immobilization device (■ FIGURE 8-3). Proper application of a splint helps control blood loss, reduces pain, and prevents further neurovascular compromise and soft-tissue injury. If an open fracture is present, pull the exposed bone back into the wound, because open fractures require surgical

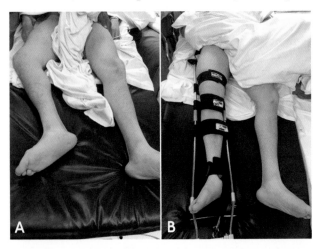

■ FIGURE 8-3 The goal of initial fracture immobilization is to realign the injured extremity in as close to anatomic position as possible and prevent excessive fracture-site motion. **A.** Shortening and external rotation of right leg due to a mid-shaft femur fracture **B.** Application of in-line traction with stabilization of the leg in normal anatomic position.

debridement. Remove gross contamination and particulate matter from the wound, and administer weight-based dosing of antibiotics as early as possible in patients with open fractures. (See *Appendix G: Circulation Skills*.)

Qualified clinicians may attempt reduction of joint dislocations. If a closed reduction successfully relocates the joint, immobilize it in the anatomic position with prefabricated splints, pillows, or plaster to maintain the extremity in its reduced position.

If reduction is unsuccessful, splint the joint in the position in which it was found. Apply splints as soon as possible, because they can control hemorrhage and pain.

However, resuscitation efforts must take priority over splint application. Assess the neurovascular status of the extremity before and after manipulation and splinting.

X-RAY EXAMINATION

Although x-ray examination of most skeletal injuries is appropriate during the secondary survey, it may be undertaken during the primary survey when fracture is suspected as a cause of shock. The decisions regarding which x-ray films to obtain and when to obtain them are based on the patient's initial and obvious clinical findings, the patient's hemodynamic status, and the mechanism of injury.

► SECONDARY SURVEY

Important elements of the secondary survey of patients with musculoskeletal injuries are the history and physical examination.

HISTORY

Key aspects of the patient history are mechanism of injury, environment, preinjury status and predisposing factors, and prehospital observations and care.

Mechanism of Injury

Information obtained from the patient, relatives, prehospital and transport personnel, and bystanders at the scene of the injury should be documented and included as a part of the patient's history. It is particularly important to determine the mechanism of injury, which can help identify injuries that may not be immediately apparent. (See *Biomechanics of Injury*.)

The clinician should mentally reconstruct the injury scene, consider other potential injuries the patient may have sustained, and determine as much of the following information as possible:

1. Where was the patient located before the crash? In a motor vehicle crash, the patient's precrash location (i.e., driver or passenger) can suggest the type of fracture—for example, a lateral compression fracture of the pelvis may result from a side impact collision.

2. Where was the patient located after the crash—inside the vehicle or ejected? Was a seat belt or airbag in use? This information may indicate certain patterns of injury. If the patient was ejected, determine the distance the patient was thrown, as well as the landing conditions. Ejection generally results in unpredictable patterns of injury and more severe injuries.

3. Was the vehicle's exterior damaged, such as having its front end deformed by a head-on collision? This information raises the suspicion of a hip dislocation.

4. Was the vehicle's interior damaged, such as a deformed dashboard? This finding indicates a greater likelihood of lower-extremity injuries.

5. Did the patient fall? If so, what was the distance of the fall, and how did the patient land? This information helps identify the spectrum of injuries.

6. Was the patient crushed by an object? If so, identify the weight of the crushing object, the site of the injury, and duration of weight applied to the site. Depending on whether a subcutaneous bony surface or a muscular area was crushed, different degrees of soft-tissue damage may occur, ranging from a simple contusion to a severe degloving extremity injury with compartment syndrome and tissue loss.

7. Did an explosion occur? If so, what was the magnitude of the blast, and what was the patient's distance from the blast? An individual close to the explosion may sustain primary blast injury from the force of the blast wave. A secondary blast injury may occur from debris and other objects accelerated by the blast (e.g., fragments), leading to penetrating wounds, lacerations, and contusions. The patient may also be violently thrown to the ground or against other objects by the blast effect, leading to blunt musculoskeletal and other injuries (i.e., a tertiary blast injury).

■ FIGURE 8-4 Impact points vary based on vehicle and individual, i.e., height of bumper and patient's age and size.

8. Was the patient involved in a vehicle-pedestrian collision? Musculoskeletal injuries follow predictable patterns based on the patient's size and age (■ FIGURE 8-4).

Environment

When applicable, ask prehospital care personnel for the following information about the post-crash environment:

1. Did the patient sustain an open fracture in a contaminated environment?

2. Was the patient exposed to temperature extremes?

3. Were broken glass fragments, which can also injure the examiner, at the scene?

4. Were there any sources of bacterial contamination, such as dirt, animal feces, and fresh or salt water?

This information can help the clinician anticipate potential problems and determine the initial antibiotic treatment.

Preinjury Status and Predisposing Factors

When possible, determine the patient's baseline condition before injury. This information can enhance understanding of the patient's condition, help determine treatment regimen, and affect outcome. An AMPLE history should be obtained, including information about the patient's exercise tolerance and activity level, ingestion of alcohol and/or other drugs, emotional problems or illnesses, and previous musculoskeletal injuries.

Prehospital Observations and Care

All prehospital observations and care must be reported and documented. Findings at the incident site that may help to identify potential injuries include

- The time of injury, especially if there is ongoing bleeding, an open fracture, and a delay in reaching the hospital

- Position in which the patient was found

- Bleeding or pooling of blood at the scene, including the estimated amount

- Bone or fracture ends that may have been exposed

- Open wounds in proximity to obvious or suspected fractures

- Obvious deformity or dislocation

- Any crushing mechanism that can result in a crush syndrome

- Presence or absence of motor and/or sensory function in each extremity

- Any delays in extrication procedures or transport

- Changes in limb function, perfusion, or neurologic state, especially after immobilization or during transfer to the hospital

- Reduction of fractures or dislocations during extrication or splinting at the scene

- Dressings and splints applied, with special attention to excessive pressure over bony prominences that can result in peripheral nerve compression or compartment syndrome

- Time of tourniquet placement, if applicable

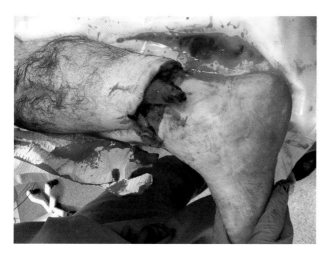

■ **FIGURE 8-6** Example of an open fracture. Open fractures and joint injuries are prone to problems with infection, healing, and function.

necessary. The patient should be adequately resuscitated and, if possible, hemodynamically normal. Wounds may then be operatively debrided, fractures stabilized, and distal pulses confirmed. Tetanus prophylaxis should be administered. (See *Tetanus Immunization.*)

PITFALL	PREVENTION
Failure to give timely antibiotics to patients with open fractures	• Recognize that infection is a significant risk in patients with open fractures. • Administer weight-based doses of appropriate antibiotics as soon as an open fracture is suspected.

the same limb segment as an associated fracture. At no time should the wound be probed.

Documentation of the open wound begins during the prehospital phase with the initial description of the injury and any treatment rendered at the scene. If an open wound exists over or near a joint, it should be assumed that the injury connects with or enters the joint. The presence of an open joint injury may be identified using CT. The presence of intraarticular gas on a CT of the affected extremity is highly sensitive and specific for identifying open joint injury. If CT is not available, consider insertion of saline or dye into the joint to determine whether the joint cavity communicates with the wound. If an open joint is suspected, request consultation by an orthopedic surgeon, as surgical exploration and debridement may be indicated.

Management

Management decisions should be based on a complete history of the incident and assessment of the injury. Treat all patients with open fractures as soon as possible with intravenous antibiotics using weight-based dosing. First-generation cephalosporins are necessary for all patients with open fractures (■ TABLE 8-2). Delay of antibiotic administration beyond three hours is related to an increased risk of infection.

Remove gross contamination and particulates from the wound as soon as possible, and cover it with a moist sterile dressing. Apply appropriate immobilization after accurately describing the wound and determining any associated soft-tissue, circulatory, and neurologic involvement. Prompt surgical consultation is

VASCULAR INJURIES

In patients who manifest vascular insufficiency associated with a history of blunt, crushing, twisting, or penetrating injury or dislocation to an extremity, clinicians should strongly suspect a vascular injury.

Assessment

The limb may initially appear viable because extremities often have some collateral circulation that provides adequate flow. Non-occlusive vascular injury, such as an intimal tear, can cause coolness and prolonged capillary refill in the distal part of the extremity, as well as diminished peripheral pulses and an abnormal ankle/brachial index. Alternatively, the distal extremity may have complete disruption of flow and be cold, pale, and pulseless.

Management

It is crucial to promptly recognize and emergently treat an acutely avascular extremity.

Early operative revascularization is required to restore arterial flow to an ischemic extremity. Muscle necrosis begins when there is a lack of arterial blood flow for more than 6 hours. Nerves may be even more sensitive to an anoxic environment. If there is an associated fracture deformity, correct it by gently pulling the limb out to length, realigning the fracture, and splinting the injured extremity. This maneuver often restores blood flow to an ischemic extremity when the artery is kinked by shortening and deformity at the fracture site.

TABLE 8-2 INTRAVENOUS ANTIBIOTIC WEIGHT-BASED DOSING GUIDELINES

OPEN FRACTURES	FIRST-GENERATION CEPHALOSPORINS (GRAM-POSITIVE COVERAGE) CEFAZOLIN	IF ANAPHYLACTIC PENICILLIN ALLERGY (INSTEAD OF FIRST-GENERATION CEPHALOSPORIN) CLINDAMYCIN	AMINOGLYCOCIDE (GRAM-NEGATIVE COVERAGE) GENTAMICIN	PIPERACILLIN/ TAZOBACTAM (BROAD-SPECTRUM GRAM-POSITIVE AND NEGATIVE COVERAGE)
Wound <1 cm; minimal contamination or soft tissue damage	<50 kg: 1 gm Q 8 hr 50–100 kg: 2 gm Q 8 hr >100 kg: 3 gm Q 8 hr	<80 kg: 600 mg Q 8 hr >80 kg: 900 mg Q 8 hr		
Wound 1–10 cm; moderate soft tissue damage; comminution of fracture	<50 kg: 1 gm Q 8 hr 50–100 kg: 2 gm Q 8 hr >100 kg: 3 gm Q 8 hr	<80 kg: 600 mg Q 8 hr >80 kg: 900 mg Q 8 hr		
Severe soft-tissue damage and substantial contamination with associated vascular injury	<50 kg: 1 gm Q 8 hr 50–100 kg: 2 gm Q 8 hr >100 kg: 3 gm Q 8 hr	<80 kg: 600 mg Q 8 hr >80 kg: 900 mg Q 8 hr	Loading dose in ER: 2.5 mg/kg for child (or <50 kg) 5 mg/kg for adult (i.e., 150-lb pt = 340 mg)	
Farmyard, soil or standing water, irrespective of wound size or severity				3.375 gm Q 6 hr (<100 kg) 4.5 gm Q 6 hr (>100 kg) **If anaphylactic penicillin allergy consult Infectious Disease Department or Pharmacy

Data from: Schmitt SK, Sexton DJ, Baron EL. Treatment and Prevention of Osteomyelitis Following Trauma in Adults. UpToDate. http://www.uptodate.com/contents/treatment-and-prevention-of-osteomyelitis-following-trauma-in-adults. October 29, 2015; O'Brien CL, Menon M, Jomha NM. Controversies in the management of open fractures. *Open Orthop J* 2014;8:178-184.

When an arterial injury is associated with dislocation of a joint, a clinician may attempt gentle reduction maneuvers. Otherwise, the clinician must splint the dislocated joint and obtain emergency surgical consultation. CT angiography may be used to evaluate extremity vascular injuries, but it must not delay reestablishing arterial blood flow and is indicated only after consultation with a surgeon.

The potential for vascular compromise also exists whenever an injured extremity is splinted. It is therefore important to perform and document a careful neurovascular examination of the injured extremity before and after reduction and application of a splint. Vascular compromise can be identified by loss of or change in the distal pulse, but excessive pain after splint application must be investigated. Patients in casts can also have vascular compromise Promptly release splints, casts, and any other circumferential dressings upon any sign of vascular compromise, and then reassess vascular supply.

COMPARTMENT SYNDROME

Compartment syndrome develops when increased pressure within a musculofascial compartment causes ischemia and subsequent necrosis. This increased pressure may be caused by an increase in compartment content (e.g., bleeding into the compartment or swelling after revascularization of an ischemic extremity) or a decrease in the compartment size (e.g., a constrictive dressing). Compartment syndrome can occur wherever muscle is contained within a closed fascial space. Remember, the skin acts as a restricting layer in certain circumstances. Common areas for compartment syndrome include the lower leg, forearm, foot, hand, gluteal region, and thigh (■ FIGURE 8-7).

Delayed recognition and treatment of compartment syndrome is catastrophic and can result in neurologic deficit, muscle necrosis, ischemic contracture, infection, delayed healing of fractures, and possible amputation.

Assessment

Any injury to an extremity can cause compartment syndrome. However, certain injuries or activities are considered high risk, including

- Tibia and forearm fractures

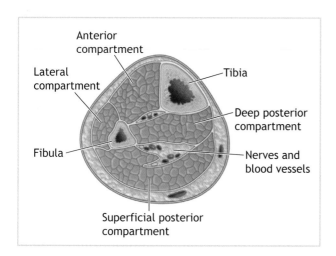

■ FIGURE 8-7 Compartment Syndrome. This condition develops when increased pressure within a compartment causes ischemia and subsequent necrosis. The illustration of a cross section of the lower leg shows the anatomy and relations of the four musculofasical compartments.

- Injuries immobilized in tight dressings or casts
- Severe crush injury to muscle
- Localized, prolonged external pressure to an extremity
- Increased capillary permeability secondary to reperfusion of ischemic muscle
- Burns
- Excessive exercise

■ BOX 8-1 details the signs and symptoms of compartment syndrome. Early diagnosis is the key to successful treatment of acute compartment syndrome. A high degree of awareness is important, especially if the patient has an altered sensorium and is unable to respond appropriately to pain. The absence of a palpable distal pulse is an uncommon or late finding and is not necessary to diagnose compartment syndrome. Capillary refill times are also unreliable for diagnosing compartment syndrome. Weakness or paralysis of the involved muscles in the affected limb is a late sign and indicates nerve or muscle damage. Clinical diagnosis is based on the history of injury and physical signs, coupled with a high index of suspicion. If pulse abnormalities are present, the possibility of a proximal vascular injury must be considered.

Measurement of intracompartmental pressure can be helpful in diagnosing suspected compartment syndrome. Tissue pressures of greater than 30 mm Hg suggest decreased capillary blood flow, which can result in muscle and nerve damage from anoxia. Blood pressure is also important: The lower the systemic pressure, the lower the compartment pressure that causes a compartment syndrome.

Compartment syndrome is a clinical diagnosis. Pressure measurements are only an adjunct to aid in its diagnosis.

BOX 8-1 SIGNS AND SYMPTOMS OF COMPARTMENT SYNDROME

- Pain greater than expected and out of proportion to the stimulus or injury
- Pain on passive stretch of the affected muscle
- Tense swelling of the affected compartment
- Paresthesias or altered sensation distal to the affected compartment

Management

Compartment syndrome is a time- and pressure-dependent condition. The higher the compartment pressure and the longer it remains elevated, the greater the degree of resulting neuromuscular damage and resulting functional deficit. If compartment syndrome is suspected, promptly release all constrictive dressings, casts, and splints applied over the affected extremity and immediately obtain a surgical consultation. The only treatment for a compartment syndrome is a fasciotomy (■ FIGURE 8-8). A delay in performing a fasciotomy may result in myoglobinuria, which may cause decreased renal function. Immediately obtain surgical consultation for suspected or diagnosed compartment syndrome.

NEUROLOGICAL INJURY SECONDARY TO FRACTURE OR DISLOCATION

Fractures and particularly dislocations can cause significant neurologic injury due to the anatomic relationship and proximity of nerves to bones and joints (e.g., sciatic nerve compression from posterior hip dislocation and axillary nerve injury from anterior shoulder dislocation). Optimal functional outcome depends on prompt recognition and treatment of the injury.

PITFALL	PREVENTION
Delayed diagnosis of compartment syndrome.	• Maintain a high index of suspicion for compartment syndrome in any patient with a significant musculoskeletal injury. • Be aware that compartment syndrome can be difficult to recognize in patients with altered mental status. • Frequently reevaluate patients with altered mental status for signs of compartment syndrome.

Assessment

A thorough examination of the neurologic system is essential in patients with musculoskeletal injury. Determination of neurologic impairment is important, and progressive changes must be documented.

Assessment usually demonstrates a deformity of the extremity. Assessment of nerve function typically requires a cooperative patient. For each significant peripheral nerve, voluntary motor function and sensation must be confirmed systematically. ■ TABLE 8-3 and ■ TABLE 8-4 outline peripheral nerve assessment of the upper extremities and lower extremities, respectively. (Also see *Peripheral Nerve Assessment of Upper Extremities* and *Peripheral Nerve Assessment of Lower Extremities* on *MyATLS mobile app.*) Muscle testing must include palpation of the contracting muscle.

In most patients with multiple injuries, it is difficult to initially assess nerve function. However, assessment must be continually repeated, especially after the patient is stabilized. Progression of neurologic findings is indicative of continued nerve compression. The most important aspect of any neurologic assessment is to document the progression of neurologic findings. It is also an important aspect of surgical decision making.

Management

Reduce and splint fracture deformities. Qualified clinicians may attempt to carefully reduce dislocations, after which neurologic function should be reevaluated and the limb splinted. If reduction is successful, the subsequent treating doctor must be notified that the joint was dislocated and successfully reduced.

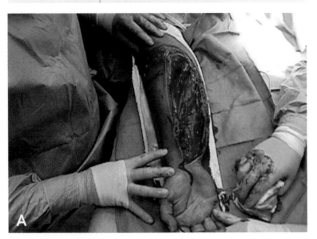
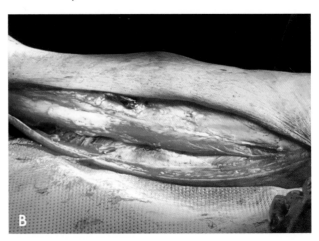

■ FIGURE 8-8 Fasciotomy to Treat Compartment Syndrome. A. Intraoperative photo showing fasciotomy of upper extremity compartment syndrome secondary to crush injury. B. Postsurgical decompression of compartment syndrome of the lower leg, showing medial incision.

OTHER EXTREMITY INJURIES

Other significant extremity injuries include contusions and lacerations, joint injuries, and fractures.

CONTUSIONS AND LACERATIONS

Assess simple contusions and/or lacerations to rule out possible vascular and/or neurologic injuries. In ge-neral, lacerations require debridement and closure. If a laceration extends below the fascial level, it may require operative intervention to more completely debride the wound and assess for damage to underlying structures.

Contusions are usually recognized by pain, localized swelling, and tenderness. If the patient is seen early, contusions are treated by limiting function of the injured part and applying cold packs.

Crushing and internal degloving injuries can be subtle and must be suspected based on the mechanism of injury. With crush injury, devascularization and

TABLE 8-3 PERIPHERAL NERVE ASSESSMENT OF UPPER EXTREMITIES

NERVE	MOTOR	SENSATION	INJURY
Ulnar	Index and little finger abduction	Little finger	Elbow injury
Median distal	Thenar contraction with opposition	Distal tip of index finger	Wrist fracture or dislocation
Median, anterior interosseous	Index tip flexion	None	Supracondylar fracture of humerus (children)
Musculocutaneous	Elbow flexion	Radial forearm	Anterior shoulder dislocation
Radial	Thumb, finger metocarpo-phalangeal extension	First dorsal web space	Distal humeral shaft, anterior shoulder dislocation
Axillary	Deltoid	Lateral shoulder	Anterior shoulder dislocation, proximal humerus fracture

TABLE 8-4 PERIPHERAL NERVE ASSESSMENT OF LOWER EXTREMITIES

NERVE	MOTOR	SENSATION	INJURY
Femoral	Knee extension	Anterior knee	Pubic rami fractures
Obturator	Hip adduction	Medial thigh	Obturator ring fractures
Posterior tibial	Toe flexion	Sole of foot	Knee dislocation
Superficial peroneal	Ankle eversion	Lateral dorsum of foot	Fibular neck fracture, knee dislocation
Deep peroneal	Ankle/toe dorsiflexion	Dorsal first to second web space	Fibular neck fracture, compartment syndrome
Sciatic nerve	Ankle dorsiflexion or plantar flexion	Foot	Posterior hip dislocation
Superior gluteal	Hip abduction	Upper buttocks	Acetabular fracture
Inferior gluteal	Gluteus maximus hip extension	Lower buttocks	Acetabular fracture

necrosis of muscle can occur. Soft-tissue avulsion can shear the skin from the deep fascia, allowing for the significant accumulation of blood in the resulting cavity (i.e., Morel-Lavallée lesion). Alternatively, the skin may be sheared from its blood supply and undergo necrosis over a few days. This area may have overlying abrasions or bruised skin, which are clues to a more severe degree of muscle damage and potential compartment or crush syndromes. These soft-tissue injuries are best evaluated by knowing the mechanism of injury and by palpating the specific component involved. Consider obtaining surgical consultation, as drainage or debridement may be indicated.

The risk of tetanus is increased with wounds that are more than 6 hours old, contused or abraded, more than 1 cm in depth, from high-velocity missiles, due to burns or cold, and significantly contaminated, particularly wounds with denervated or ischemic tissue (See *Tetanus Immunization*.)

JOINT AND LIGAMENT INJURIES

When a joint has sustained significant ligamentous injury but is not dislocated, the injury is not usually limb-threatening. However, prompt diagnosis and treatment are important to optimize limb function.

Assessment

With joint injuries, the patient usually reports abnormal stress to the joint, for example, impact to the anterior tibia that subluxed the knee posteriorly, impact to the lateral aspect of the leg that resulted in a valgus strain to the knee, or a fall onto an outstretched arm that caused hyperextension of the elbow.

Physical examination reveals tenderness throughout the affected joint. A hemarthrosis is usually present unless the joint capsule is disrupted and the bleeding diffuses into the soft tissues. Passive ligamentous testing of the affected joint reveals instability. X-ray examination is usually negative, although some small avulsion fractures from ligamentous insertions or origins may be present radiographically.

Management

Immobilize joint injuries, and serially reassess the vascular and neurologic status of the limb distal to the injury. Knee dislocations frequently return to near anatomic position and may not be obvious at presentation. In a patient with a multi-ligament knee injury, a dislocation may have oc-

curred and placed the limb at risk for neurovascular injury. Surgical consultation is usually required for joint stabilization.

FRACTURES

Fractures are defined as a break in the continuity of the bone cortex. They may be associated with abnormal motion, soft-tissue injury, bony crepitus, and pain. A fracture can be open or closed.

Assessment

Examination of the extremity typically demonstrates pain, swelling, deformity, tenderness, crepitus, and abnormal motion at the fracture site. Evaluation for crepitus and abnormal motion is painful and may increase soft-tissue damage. These maneuvers are seldom necessary to make the diagnosis and must not be done routinely or repetitively. Be sure to periodically reassess the neurovascular status of a fractured limb, particularly if a splint is in place.

X-ray films taken at right angles to one another confirm the history and physical examination findings of fracture (■ FIGURE 8-9). Depending on the patient's hemodynamic status, x-ray examination may need to be delayed until the patient is stabilized. To exclude occult dislocation and concomitant injury, x-ray films must include the joints above and below the suspected fracture site.

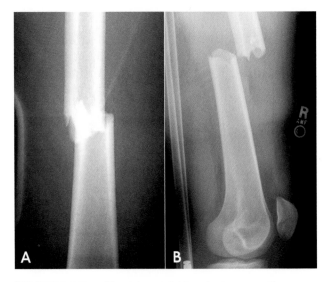

■ FIGURE 8-9 X-ray films taken at right angles to one another confirm the history and physical examination findings of fracture. **A.** AP view of the distal femur. **B.** Lateral view of the distal femur. Satisfactory x-rays of an injured long bone should include two orthogonal views, and the entire bone should be visualized. Thus the images alone would be inadequate.

Management

Immobilization must include the joint above and below the fracture. After splinting, be sure to reassess the neurologic and vascular status of the extremity. Surgical consultation is required for further treatment.

PRINCIPLES OF IMMOBILIZATION

Unless associated with life-threatening injuries, splinting of extremity injuries can typically be accomplished during the secondary survey. However, all such injuries must be splinted before a patient is transported. Assess the limb's neurovascular status before and after applying splints or realigning a fracture.

FEMORAL FRACTURES

Femoral fractures are immobilized temporarily with traction splints (see ■ FIGURE 8-3; also see *Traction Splint video on MyATLS mobile app*). The traction splint's force is applied distally at the ankle. Proximally, the post is pushed into the gluteal crease to apply pressure to the buttocks, perineum, and groin. Excessive traction can cause skin damage to the foot, ankle, and perineum. Because neurovascular compromise can also result from application of a traction splint, clinicians must assess the neurovascular status of the limb before and after applying the splint. Do not apply traction in patients with an ipsilateral tibia shaft fracture. Hip fractures can be similarly immobilized with a traction splint but are more suitably immobilized with skin traction or foam boot traction with the knee in slight flexion. A simple method of splinting is to bind the injured leg to the opposite leg.

KNEE INJURIES

Application of a commercially available knee immobilizer or a posterior long-leg plaster splint is effective in maintaining comfort and stability. Do not immobilize the knee in complete extension, but with approximately 10 degrees of flexion to reduce tension on the neurovascular structures.

TIBIAL FRACTURES

Immobilize tibial fractures to minimize pain and further soft-tissue injury and decrease the risk of compartment syndrome. If readily available, plaster splints immobilizing the lower thigh, knee, and ankle are preferred.

ANKLE FRACTURES

Ankle fractures may be immobilized with a well-padded splint, thereby decreasing pain while avoiding pressure over bony prominences (■ FIGURE 8-10).

PITFALL	PREVENTION
Application of traction to an extremity with a tibia/fibula fracture can result in a neurovascular injury.	• Avoid use of traction in extremities with combined femur and tibia/fibula fractures. • Use a long-leg posterior splint with an additional sugar-tong splint for the lower leg.

UPPER EXTREMITY AND HAND INJURIES

The hand may be temporarily splinted in an anatomic, functional position with the wrist slightly dorsiflexed and the fingers gently flexed 45 degrees at the metacarpophalangeal joints. This position typically is accomplished by gently immobilizing the hand over a large roll of gauze and using a short-arm splint.

The forearm and wrist are immobilized flat on padded or pillow splints. The elbow is typically immobilized in a flexed position, either by using padded splints or by direct immobilization with respect to the body using a sling-and-swath device. The upper arm may be immobilized by splinting it to the body or applying a sling or swath, which can be augmented by a thoracobrachial bandage. Shoulder injuries are managed by a sling-and-swath device or a hook- and-loop type of dressing.

PAIN CONTROL

The appropriate use of splints significantly decreases a patient's discomfort by controlling the amount of motion that occurs at the injured site. If pain is not relieved or recurs, the splint should be removed and the limb further investigated. Analgesics are indicated for patients with joint injuries and fractures. Patients who do not appear to have significant pain

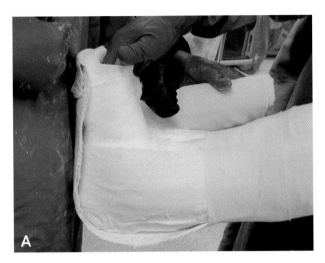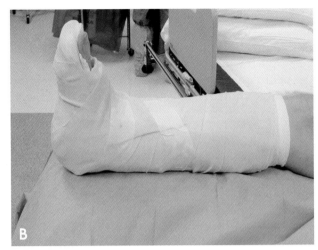

■ **FIGURE 8-10 Splinting of an ankle fracture.** Note extensive use of padding with posterior and sugartong splints. **A.** Posterior and sugartong plaster splints being secured in place with an elastic bandage wrap. **B.** Completed splint.

or discomfort from a major fracture may have other associated injuries which interfere with sensory perception (e.g., intracranial or spinal cord lesions) or be under the influence of alcohol and/or drugs.

Effective pain relief usually requires the administration of narcotics, which should be given in small doses intravenously and repeated as needed. Administer sedatives cautiously in patients with isolated extremity injuries, such as when reducing a dislocation. Whenever analgesics or sedatives are administered to an injured patient, the potential exists for respiratory arrest. Consequently, appropriate resuscitative equipment and naloxone (Narcan) must be immediately available.

Regional nerve blocks play a role in pain relief and the reduction of appropriate fractures. It is essential to assess and document any peripheral nerve injury before administering a nerve block. Always keep the risk of compartment syndrome in mind, as this condition may be masked in a patient who has undergone a nerve block.

▶ ASSOCIATED INJURIES

Because of their common mechanism, certain musculoskeletal injuries are often associated with other injuries that are not immediately apparent or may be missed (■ TABLE 8-5).

Steps to ensure recognition and management of these injuries include:

1. Review the injury history, especially the mechanism of injury, to determine whether another injury is present.

TABLE 8-5 MUSCULOSKELETAL INJURIES: COMMON MISSED OR ASSOCIATED INJURIES

INJURY	MISSED/ASSOCIATED INJURY
• Clavicular fracture • Scapular fracture • Fracture and/or dislocation of shoulder	• Major thoracic injury, especially pulmonary contusion and rib fractures • Scapulothoracic dissociation
• Fracture/dislocation of elbow	• Brachial artery injury • Median, ulnar, and radial nerve injury
• Femur fracture	• Femoral neck fracture • Ligamentous knee injury • Posterior hip dislocation
• Posterior knee dislocation	• Femoral fracture • Posterior hip dislocation
• Knee dislocation • Displaced tibial plateau	• Popliteal artery and nerve injuries
• Calcaneal fracture	• Spine injury or fracture • Fracture-dislocation of talus and calcaneus • Tibial plateau fracture
• Open fracture	• 70% incidence of associated nonskeletal injury

2. Thoroughly reexamine all extremities, with special emphasis on the hands, wrists, feet, and the joints above and below fractures and dislocations.

3. Visually examine the patient's back, including the spine and pelvis.

4. Document open injuries and closed soft-tissue injuries that may indicate an unstable injury.

5. Review the x-rays obtained in the secondary survey to identify subtle injuries that may be associated with more obvious trauma.

OCCULT SKELETAL INJURIES

Not all injuries can be diagnosed during the initial assessment. Joints and bones that are covered or well-padded within muscular areas may contain occult injuries. It can be difficult to identify nondisplaced fractures or joint ligamentous injuries, especially if the patient is unresponsive or has other severe injuries. In fact, injuries are commonly discovered days after the injury incident—for example, when the patient is being mobilized. Therefore, it is crucial to reassess the patient repeatedly and to communicate with other members of the trauma team and the patient's family about the possibility of occult skeletal injuries.

PITFALL	PREVENTION
Occult injuries may not be identified during the primary assessment or secondary survey.	• Logroll the patient and remove all clothing to ensure complete evaluation and avoid missing injuries. • Repeat the head-to-toe examination once the patient has been stabilized to identify occult injuries.

TEAMWORK

- Musculoskeletal injuries, especially open fractures, often appear dramatic and can potentially distract team members from more urgent resuscitation priorities. The team leader must ensure that team members focus on life-threatening injuries first

- Because potentially life-threatening musculoskeletal injuries can be detected during the assessment of circulation, the team leader must rapidly direct the team to control external hemorrhage using sterile pressure dressings, splints, or tourniquets as appropriate. The trauma team's ability to work on different tasks simultaneously is particularly relevant in this scenario.

- More than one team member may be required to apply a traction splint, and the team leader may direct other assistants or specialist team members (e.g., vascular and orthopedic surgeons) to assist the team.

- The team must be able to recognize limb-threatening injuries and report these accurately to the team leader so decisions can be made for managing these injuries in conjunction with life-threatening problems involving airway, breathing, and circulation.

- Ensure that the trauma team performs a complete secondary survey, so injuries are not overlooked. Occult injuries are particularly common in patients with a depressed level of consciousness, and the team leader should ensure timely reevaluation of the limbs to minimize missed injuries.

CHAPTER SUMMARY

1. Musculoskeletal injuries can pose threats to both life and limb.

2. The initial assessment of musculoskeletal trauma is intended to identify those injuries that pose a threat to life and/or limb. Although uncommon, life-threatening musculoskeletal injuries must be promptly assessed and managed. A staged approach to hemorrhage control is utilized by applying direct pressure, splints, and tourniquets.

3. Most extremity injuries are appropriately diagnosed and managed during the secondary survey. A thorough history and careful physical examination, including completely undressing the patient, is essential to identify musculoskeletal injuries.

4. It is essential to recognize and manage arterial injuries, compartment syndrome, open fractures, crush injuries, and dislocations in a timely manner.

5. Knowledge of the mechanism of injury and history of the injury-producing event can guide clinicians to suspect potential associated injuries.

6. Early splinting of fractures and dislocations can prevent serious complications and late sequelae. Careful neurovascular examination must be performed both prior to and after application of a splint or traction device.

Special thanks to Julie Gebhart, PA-C, Lead Orthopedic Physician Assistant, and Renn Crichlow, MD, Orthopedic Trauma Surgeon, OrthoIndy and St. Vincent Trauma Center, for all their help and collaboration with this project, as well as provision of many of the photographs used in the chapter.

BIBLIOGRAPHY

1. Beekley AC, Starnes BW, Sebesta JA. Lessons learned from modern military surgery. *Surg Clin North Am* 2007;87(1):157–184, vii.

2. Brown CV, Rhee P, Chan L, et al. Preventing renal failure in patients with rhabdomyolysis: do bicarbonate and mannitol make a difference? *J Trauma* 2004;56:1191.

3. Bulger EM, Snyder D, Schoelles C, et al. An evidence-based prehospital guideline for external hemorrhage control: American College of Surgeons Committee on Trauma. *Prehospital Emergency Care* 2014;18:163–173.

4. Clifford CC. Treating traumatic bleeding in a combat setting. *Mil Med* 2004;169(12 Suppl): 8–10, 14.

5. Elliot GB, Johnstone AJ. Diagnosing acute compartment syndrome. *J Bone Joint Surg Br* 2003;85:625–630.

6. German Trauma Society. Prehospital (section 1). Emergency room, extremities (subsection 2.10). In: S3—*Guideline on Treatment of Patients with Severe and Multiple Injuries*. (English version AWMF-Registry No. 012/019). Berlin: German Trauma Society (DGU).

7. Gustilo RB, Mendoza RM, Williams DN. Problems in the management of type III (severe) open fractures: a new classification of type III open fractures. *J Trauma* 1985;24:742.

8. Inaba K, Siboni S, Resnick S, et al. Tourniquet use for civilian extremity trauma. *J Trauma* 2015:79(2):232–237.

9. King RB, Filips D, Blitz S, et al. Evaluation of possible tourniquet systems for use in the Canadian Forces. *J Trauma* 2006;60(5):1061–1071.

10. Kobbe P, Micansky F, Lichte P, et al. Increased morbidity and mortality after bilateral femoral shaft fractures: myth or reality in the era of damage control? *Injury* 2013Feb;44(2):221–225.

11. Konda SR, Davidovich RI, Egol KA. Computed tomography scan to detect traumatic arthrotomies and identify periarticular wounds not requiring surgical intervention: an improvement over the saline load test. *J Trauma* 2013;27(9):498–504.

12. Kostler W, Strohm PC, Sudkamp NP. Acute compartment syndrome of the limb. *Injury* 2004;35(12):1221–1227.

13. Lakstein D, Blumenfeld A, Sokolov T, et al. Tourniquets for hemorrhage control on the battlefield: a 4-year accumulated experience. *J Trauma* 2003;54(5 Suppl):S221–S225.

14. Mabry RL. Tourniquet use on the battlefield. *Mil Med* 2006;171(5):352–356.

15. Medina O, Arom GA, Yeranosian MG, et al. Vascular and nerve injury after knee dislocation: a systematic review. *Clin Orthop Relat Res* 2014Oct;472(1):2984–2990.

16. Mills WJ, Barei DP, McNair P. The value of the ankle-brachial index for diagnosing arterial injury after knee dislocation: a prospective study. *J Trauma* 2004;56:1261–1265.

17. Natsuhara KM. Yeranosian MG, Cohen JR, et al. What is the frequency of vascular injury after knee dislocation? *Clin Orthop Relat Res* 2014Sep;472(9):2615–2620.

18. Ododeh M. The role of reperfusion-induced injury in the pathogenesis of the crush syndrome. *N Engl J Med* 1991;324:1417–1421.

19. Okike K, Bhattacharyya T. Trends in the management of open fractures. A critical analysis. *J Bone Joint Surg Am* 2006;88:2739–2748.

20. Olson SA, Glasgow RR. Acute compartment syndrome in lower extremity musculoskeletal trauma. *J Am Acad Orthop Surg* 2005;13(7):436–444.

21. O'Brien CL, Menon M, Jomha NM. Controversies in the management of open fractures. *Open Orthop J* 2014;8:178–184.

22. O'Toole RV, Lindbloom BJ, Hui E, et al. Are bilateral femoral fractures no longer a marker for death? *J Orthoped Trauma* 2014 Feb;28(2): 77–81.

23. Schmitt SK, Sexton DJ, Baron EL. Treatment and Prevention of Osteomyelitis Following Trauma in Adults. UpToDate. http://www.uptodate.com/contents/treatment-and-prevention-of-osteomyelitis-following-trauma-in-adults. October 29, 2015.

24. Steinhausen E, Lefering R, Tjardes T, et al. A risk-adapted approach is beneficial in the management of bilateral femoral shaft fractures

in multiple trauma patients: an analysis based on the trauma registry of the German Trauma Society. *J Trauma* 2014;76(5):1288– 1293.

25. Tornetta P, Boes MT, Schepsis AA, et al. How effective is a saline arthrogram for wounds around the knee? *Clin Orthop Relat Res.* 2008;466:432–435.

26. Ulmer T. The clinical diagnosis of compartment syndrome of the lower leg: are clinical findings predictive of the disorder? *J Orthop Trauma* 2002;16(8):572–577.

27. Walters TJ, Mabry RL. Issues related to the use of tourniquets on the battlefield. *Mil Med* 2005;170(9):770–775.

28. Walters TJ, Wenke JC, Kauvar DS, et al. Effectiveness of self-applied tourniquets in human volunteers. *Prehosp Emerg Care* 2005;9(4):416–422.

29. Welling DR, Burris DG, Hutton JE, et al. A balanced approach to tourniquet use: lessons learned and relearned. *J Am Coll Surg* 2006;203(1):106–115.

30. Willett K, Al-Khateeb H, Kotnis R, et al. Risk of mortality: the relationship with associated injuries and fracture. Treatment methods in patients with unilateral or bilateral femoral shaft fractures. *J Trauma* 2010 Aug;69(2):405–410.

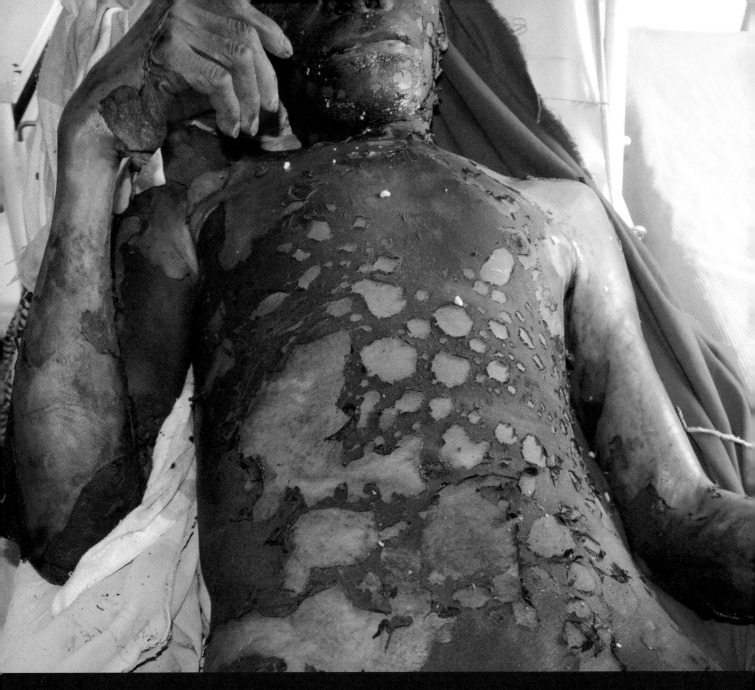

9 THERMAL INJURIES

The most significant difference between burns and other injuries is that the consequences of burn injury are directly linked to the extent of the inflammatory response to the injury.

CHAPTER 9 OUTLINE

OBJECTIVES

After reading this chapter and comprehending the knowledge components of the ATLS provider course, you will be able to:

1. Explain how the unique pathophysiology of burn injury affects the approach to patient management when compared with other traumatic injuries.

2. Identify the unique problems that can be encountered in the initial assessment of patients with burn injuries.

3. Describe how to manage the unique problems that can be encountered in the initial assessment of patients with burn injuries.

4. Estimate the extent of the patient's burn injury, including the size and depth of the burn(s), and develop a prioritized plan for emergency

management of the patient's injuries.

5. Describe the unique characteristics of burn injury that affect the secondary survey.

6. Describe common mechanisms of burn injuries, and explain the impact of specific mechanisms on management of the injured patients.

7. List the criteria for transferring patients with burn injuries to burn centers.

8. Describe the tissue effects of cold injury and the initial treatment of patients with tissue injury from cold exposure.

9. Describe the management of patients with hypothermia, including rewarming risks.

Thermal injuries are major causes of morbidity and mortality, but adherence to the basic principles of initial trauma resuscitation and the timely application of simple emergency measures can help minimize their impact. The major principles of thermal injury management include maintaining a high index of suspicion for the presence of airway compromise following smoke inhalation and secondary to burn edema; identifying and managing associated mechanical injuries; maintaining hemodynamic normality with volume resuscitation; controlling temperature; and removing the patient from the injurious environment. Clinicians also must take measures to prevent and treat the potential complications of specific burn injuries. Examples include rhabdomyolysis and cardiac dysrhythmias, which can be associated with electrical burns; extremity or truncal compartment syndrome, which can occur with large burn resuscitations; and ocular injuries due to flames or explosions.

The most significant difference between burns and other injuries is that the consequences of burn injury are directly linked to the extent of the inflammatory response to the injury. The larger and deeper the burn, the worse the inflammation. Depending on the cause, the energy transfer and resultant edema may not be evident immediately; for example, flame injury is more rapidly evident than most chemical injuries—an important factor in burn injury management. Monitor intravenous lines closely to ensure they do not become dislodged as the patient becomes more edematous. Regularly check ties securing endotracheal and nasogastric tubes to ensure they are not too tight, and check that identification bands are loose or not circumferentially affixed.

Note: Heat injuries, including heat exhaustion and heat stroke, are discussed in *Appendix B: Hypothermia and Heat Injuries*.

PRIMARY SURVEY AND RESUSCITATION OF PATIENTS WITH BURNS

Lifesaving measures for patients with burn injuries include stopping the burning process, ensuring that airway and ventilation are adequate, and managing circulation by gaining intravenous access.

STOP THE BURNING PROCESS

Completely remove the patient's clothing to stop the burning process; however, do not peel off adherent clothing. Synthetic fabrics can ignite, burn rapidly at high temperatures, and melt into hot residue that continues to burn the patient. At the same time, take care to prevent overexposure and hypothermia. Recognize that attempts made at the scene to extinguish the fire (e.g., "stop, drop, and roll"), although appropriate, can lead to contamination of the burn with debris or contaminated water.

Exercise care when removing any clothing that was contaminated by chemicals. Brush any dry chemical powders from the wound. Caregivers also can be injured and should avoid direct contact with the chemical. After removing the powder, decontaminate the burn areas by rinsing with copious amounts of warm saline irrigation or rinsing in a warm shower when the facilities are available and the patient is able.

Once the burning process has been stopped, cover the patient with warm, clean, dry linens to prevent hypothermia.

ESTABLISH AIRWAY CONTROL

The airway can become obstructed not only from direct injury (e.g., inhalation injury) but also from the massive edema resulting from the burn injury. Edema is typically not present immediately, and signs of obstruction may initially be subtle until the patient is in crisis. Early evaluation to determine the need for endotracheal intubation is essential.

Factors that increase the risk for upper airway obstruction are increasing burn size and depth, burns to the head and face, inhalation injury, associated trauma, and burns inside the mouth (■ FIGURE 9-1). Burns localized to the face and mouth cause more localized

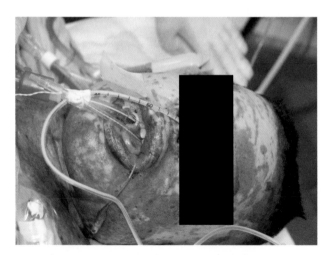

■ FIGURE 9-1 Factors that increase the risk for upper airway obstruction are increasing burn size and depth, burns to the head and face, inhalation injury, associated trauma, and burns inside the mouth.

edema and pose a greater risk for airway compromise. Because their airways are smaller, children with burn injuries are at higher risk for airway problems than their adult counterparts.

A history of confinement in a burning environment or early signs of airway injury on arrival in the emergency department (ED) warrants evaluation of the patient's airway and definitive management. Pharyngeal thermal injuries can produce marked upper airway edema, and early protection of the airway is critical. The clinical manifestations of inhalation injury may be subtle and frequently do not appear in the first 24 hours. If the provider waits for x-ray evidence of pulmonary injury or changes in blood gas determinations, airway edema can preclude intubation, and a surgical airway may be required. When in doubt, examine the patient's oropharynx for signs of inflammation, mucosal injury, soot in the pharynx, and edema, taking care not to injure the area further.

Although the larynx protects the subglottic airway from direct thermal injury, the airway is extremely susceptible to obstruction resulting from exposure to heat.

American Burn Life Support (ABLS) indications for early intubation include:

- Signs of airway obstruction (hoarseness, stridor, accessory respiratory muscle use, sternal retraction)

- Extent of the burn (total body surface area burn > 40%–50%)

- Extensive and deep facial burns

- Burns inside the mouth

- Significant edema or risk for edema

- Difficulty swallowing

- Signs of respiratory compromise: inability to clear secretions, respiratory fatigue, poor oxygenation or ventilation

- Decreased level of consciousness where airway protective reflexes are impaired

- Anticipated patient transfer of large burn with airway issue without qualified personnel to intubate en route

A carboxyhemoglobin level greater than 10% in a patient who was involved in a fire also suggests inhalation injury. Transfer to a burn center is indicated for patients suspected of experiencing inhalation injury; however, if the transport time is prolonged, intubate the patient before transport. Stridor may occur late and indicates the need for immediate endotracheal intubation. Circumferential burns of the neck can lead to swelling of the tissues around the airway; therefore, early intubation is also indicated for full-thickness circumferential neck burns.

PITFALL	PREVENTION
Airway obstruction in a patient with burn injury may not be present immediately.	• Recognize smoke inhalation as a potential cause of airway obstruction from particulate and chemical injury. • Evaluate the patient for circumferential burns of the neck and chest, which can compromise the airway and gas exchange. • Patients with inhalation injury are at risk for bronchial obstruction from secretions and debris, and they may require bronchoscopy. Place an adequately sized airway—preferably a size 8 mm internal diameter (ID) endotracheal tube (minimum 7.5 mm ID in adults).

ENSURE ADEQUATE VENTILATION

Direct thermal injury to the lower airway is very rare and essentially occurs only after exposure to superheated steam or ignition of inhaled flammable gases. Breathing concerns arise from three general causes: hypoxia, carbon monoxide poisoning, and smoke inhalation injury.

Hypoxia may be related to inhalation injury, poor compliance due to circumferential chest burns, or thoracic trauma unrelated to the thermal injury. In these situations, administer supplemental oxygen with or without intubation.

Always assume carbon monoxide (CO) exposure in patients who were burned in enclosed areas. The diagnosis of CO poisoning is made primarily from a history of exposure and direct measurement of carboxyhemoglobin (HbCO). Patients with CO levels of less than 20% usually have no physical symptoms. Higher CO levels can result in:

- headache and nausea (20%–30%)

- confusion (30%–40%)

- coma (40%–60%)

- death (>60%)

Cherry-red skin color in patients with CO exposure is rare, and may only be seen in moribund patients. Due to the increased affinity of hemoglobin for CO—240 times that of oxygen—it displaces oxygen from the hemoglobin molecule and shifts the oxyhemoglobin dissociation curve to the left. CO dissociates very slowly, and its half-life is approximately 4 hours when the patient is breathing room air. Because the half-life of HbCO can be reduced to 40 minutes by breathing 100% oxygen, any patient in whom CO exposure could have occurred should receive high-flow (100%) oxygen via a non-rebreathing mask.

It is important to place an appropriately sized endotracheal tube (ETT), as placing a tube that is too small will make ventilation, clearing of secretions, and bronchoscopy difficult or impossible. Efforts should be made to use endotracheal tubes at least 7.5 mm ID or larger in an adult and size 4.5 mm ID ETT in a child.

Arterial blood gas determinations should be obtained as a baseline for evaluating a patient's pulmonary status. However, measurements of arterial PaO_2 do not reliably predict CO poisoning, because a CO partial pressure of only 1 mm Hg results in an HbCO level of 40% or greater. Therefore, baseline HbCO levels should be obtained, and 100% oxygen should be administered. If a carboxyhemoglobin level is not available and the patient has been involved in a closed-space fire, empiric treatment with 100% oxygen for 4 to 6 hours is reasonable as an effective treatment for CO poisoning and has few disadvantages. An exception is a patient with chronic obstructive lung disease, who should be monitored very closely when 100% oxygen is administered.

Pulse oximetry cannot be relied on to rule out carbon monoxide poisoning, as most oximeters cannot distinguish oxyhemoglobin from carboxyhemoglobin. In a patient with CO poisoning, the oximeter may read 98% to 100% saturation and not reflect the true oxygen saturation of the patient, which must be obtained from the arterial blood gas. A discrepancy between the arterial blood gas and the oximeter may be explained by the presence of carboxyhemoglobin or an inadvertent venous sample.

Cyanide inhalation from the products of combustion is possible in burns occurring in confined spaces, in which case the clinician should consult with a burn or poison control center. A sign of potential cyanide toxicity is persistent profound unexplained metabolic acidosis.

There is no role for hyperbaric oxygen therapy in the primary resuscitation of a patient with critical burn injury. Once the principles of ATLS are followed to stabilize the patient, consult with the local burn center for further guidance regarding whether hyperbaric oxygen would benefit the patient.

Products of combustion, including carbon particles and toxic fumes, are important causes of inhalation injury. Smoke particles settle into the distal bronchioles, leading to damage and death of the mucosal cells. Damage to the airways then leads to an increased inflammatory response, which in turn leads to an increase in capillary leakage, resulting in increased fluid requirements and an oxygen diffusion defect. Furthermore, necrotic cells tend to slough and obstruct the airways. Diminished clearance of the airway produces plugging, which results in an increased risk of pneumonia. Not only is the care of patients with inhalation injury more complex, but their mortality is doubled compared with other burn injured individuals.

The American Burn Association has identified two requirements for the diagnosis of smoke inhalation injury: exposure to a combustible agent and signs of exposure to smoke in the lower airway, below the vocal cords, seen on bronchoscopy. The likelihood of smoke inhalation injury is much higher when the injury occurs within an enclosed place and in cases of prolonged exposure.

As a baseline for evaluating the pulmonary status of a patient with smoke inhalation injury, clinicians should obtain a chest x-ray and arterial blood gas determination. These values may deteriorate over time; normal values on admission do not exclude inhalation injury. The treatment of smoke inhalation injury is supportive. A patient with a high likelihood of smoke inhalation injury associated with a significant burn (i.e., greater than 20% total body surface area [TBSA] in an adult, or greater than 10% TBSA in patients less than 10 or greater than 50 years of age) should be intubated. If the patient's hemodynamic condition permits and spinal injury has been excluded, elevate the patient's head and chest by 30 degrees to help reduce neck and chest wall edema. If a full-thickness burn of the anterior and lateral chest wall leads to severe restriction of chest wall motion, even in the absence of a circumferential burn, chest wall escharotomy may be required.

MANAGE CIRCULATION WITH BURN SHOCK RESUSCITATION

Evaluation of circulating blood volume is often difficult in severely burned patients, who also may have accompanying injuries that contribute to hypovolemic shock and further complicate the clinical picture. Treat shock according to the resuscitation principles outlined in Chapter 3: Shock, with the goal of maintaining end organ perfusion. In contrast to resuscitation for other types of trauma in which fluid deficit is typically secondary to hemorrhagic losses, burn resuscitation is required to replace the *ongoing* losses from capillary leak due to inflammation. Therefore, clinicians should provide burn resuscitation fluids for deep partial and full-thickness burns larger than 20% TBSA, taking care not to over-resuscitate (■ FIGURE 9-2).

After establishing airway patency and identifying and treating life-threatening injuries, immediately establish intravenous access with two large-caliber (at least 18-gauge) intravenous lines in a peripheral vein. If the extent of the burn precludes placing the catheter through unburned skin, place the IV through the burned skin into an accessible vein. The upper extremities are preferable to the lower extremities as a site for venous access because of the increased risk of phlebitis and septic phlebitis when the saphenous veins are used for venous access. If peripheral IVs cannot be obtained, consider central venous access or intraosseous infusion.

Begin infusion with a warmed isotonic crystalloid solution, preferably lactated Ringer's solution. Be aware that resulting edema can dislodge peripheral intravenous lines. Consider placing longer catheters in larger burns.

Blood pressure measurements can be difficult to obtain and may be unreliable in patients with severe burn injuries. Insert an indwelling urinary catheter in all patients receiving burn resuscitation fluids, and monitor urine output to assess perfusion. Osmotic diuresis (e.g., glycosuria or use of mannitol) can interfere with the accuracy of urine output as a marker of perfusion by overestimating perfusion.

The initial fluid rate used for burn resuscitation has been updated by the American Burn Association to reflect concerns about over-resuscitation when

PITFALL	PREVENTION
Intravenous catheters and endotracheal tubes can become dislodged after resuscitation.	• Remember that edema takes time to develop. • Use long IV catheters to account for the inevitable swelling that will occur. • Do not cut endotracheal tubes, and regularly assess their positioning.

using the traditional Parkland formula. The current consensus guidelines state that fluid resuscitation should begin at *2 ml of lactated Ringer's x patient's body weight in kg x % TBSA for second- and third-degree burns.*

The calculated fluid volume is initiated in the following manner: one-half of the total fluid is provided in the first 8 hours after the burn injury (for example, a 100-kg man with 80% TBSA burns requires 2 × 80 × 100 = 16,000 mL in 24 hours). One-half of that volume (8,000 mL) should be provided in the first 8 hours, so the patient should be started at a rate of 1000 mL/hr. The remaining one-half of the total fluid is administered during the subsequent 16 hours.

It is important to understand that formulas provide a starting target rate; subsequently, the amount of fluids provided should be adjusted based on a urine output target of 0.5 mL/kg/hr for adults and 1 mL/kg/hr for children weighing less than 30 kg. In adults, urine output should be maintained between 30 and 50 cc/hr to minimize potential over-resuscitation.

The actual fluid rate that a patient requires depends on the severity of injury, because larger and deeper burns require proportionately more fluid. Inhalation injury also increases the amount of burn resuscitation required. If the initial resuscitation rate fails to produce the target urine output, increase the fluid rate until the urine output goal is met. However, do *not* precipitously decrease the IV rate by one-half at 8 hours; rather, base the reduction in IV fluid rate on urine output and titrate to the lower urine output rate. Fluid boluses should be avoided unless the patient is hypotensive. Low urine output is best treated with titration of the fluid rate.

Resuscitation of pediatric burn patients (■ FIGURE 9-3) should begin at 3 mL/kg/% TBSA; this balances a higher resuscitation volume requirement due to larger surface area per unit body mass with the smaller pediatric intravascular volume, increasing risk for volume overload. Very small children (i.e., < 30 kg), should receive maintenance fluids of D5LR (5% dextrose in Lactated Ringers), in addition to the burn resuscitation fluid. ■ TABLE 9-1 outlines the adjusted fluid rates and target urine output by burn type.

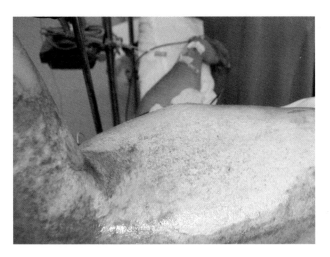

■ FIGURE 9-2 Patients with burns require resuscitation with Ringer's lactate solution starting at 2 mL per kilogram of body weight per percentage BSA of partial-thickness and full-thickness burns during the first 24 hours to maintain adequate perfusion, titrated hourly.

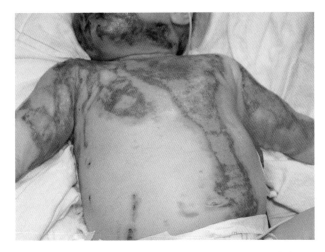

■ **FIGURE 9-3** Resuscitation of pediatric burn patients must balance a higher resuscitation volume requirement due to larger surface area per unit body mass with the smaller pediatric intravascular volume, which increases the risk for volume overload.

It is important to understand that under-resuscitation results in hypoperfusion and end organ injury. Over-resuscitation results in increased edema, which can lead to complications, such as burn depth progression or abdominal and extremity compartment syndrome. The goal of resuscitation is to maintain the fine balance of adequate perfusion as indicated by urine output.

Cardiac dysrhythmias may be the first sign of hypoxia and electrolyte or acid-base abnormalities; therefore, electrocardiography (ECG) should be performed for cardiac rhythm disturbances. Persistent acidemia in patients with burn injuries may be multifactorial,

PITFALL	PREVENTION
Under- or over-resuscitation of burn patients.	• Titrate fluid resuscitation to the patient's physiologic response, adjusting the fluid rate up or down based on urine output. • Recognize factors that affect the volume of resuscitation and urine output, such as inhalation injury, age of patient, renal failure, diuretics, and alcohol. • Tachycardia is a poor marker for resuscitation in the burn patient. Use other parameters to discern physiologic response.

including under-resuscitation or infusion of large volumes of saline for resuscitation.

PATIENT ASSESSMENT

In addition to a detailed AMPLE history, it is important to estimate the size of the body surface area burned and the depth of the burn injury.

TABLE 9-1 BURN RESUSCITATION FLUID RATES AND TARGET URINE OUTPUT BY BURN TYPE AND AGE

CATEGORY OF BURN	AGE AND WEIGHT	ADJUSTED FLUID RATES	URINE OUTPUT
Flame or Scald	Adults and older children (≥14 years old)	2 ml LR x kg x % TBSA	0.5 ml/kg/hr 30–50 ml/hr
	Children (<14 years old)	3 ml LR x kg x % TBSA	1 ml/kg/hr
	Infants and young children (≤30kg)	3 ml LR x kg x % TBSA Plus a sugar-containing solution at maintenance rate	1 ml/kg/hr
Electrical Injury	All ages	4 ml LR x kg x % TBSA until urine clears	1-1.5 ml/kg/hr until urine clears

LR, lactated Ringer's solution; TBSA, total body surface area

HISTORY

The injury history is extremely valuable when treating patients with burns. Burn survivors can sustain associated injuries while attempting to escape a fire, and explosions can result in internal injuries (e.g., central nervous system, myocardial, pulmonary, and abdominal injuries) and fractures. It is essential to establish the time of the burn injury. Burns sustained within an enclosed space suggest the potential for inhalation injury and anoxic brain injury when there is an associated loss of consciousness.

The history, whether obtained from the patient or other individuals, should include a brief survey of preexisting illnesses and drug therapy, as well as any known allergies and/or drug sensitivities. Check the status of the patient's tetanus immunization. Be aware that some individuals attempt suicide through self-immolation. Match the patient history to the burn pattern; if the account of the injury is suspicious, consider the possibility of abuse in both children and adults.

BODY SURFACE AREA

The *rule of nines* is a practical guide for determining the extent of a burn using calculations based on areas of partial- and full-thickness burns (■ FIGURE 9-4). The adult body configuration is divided into anatomic regions

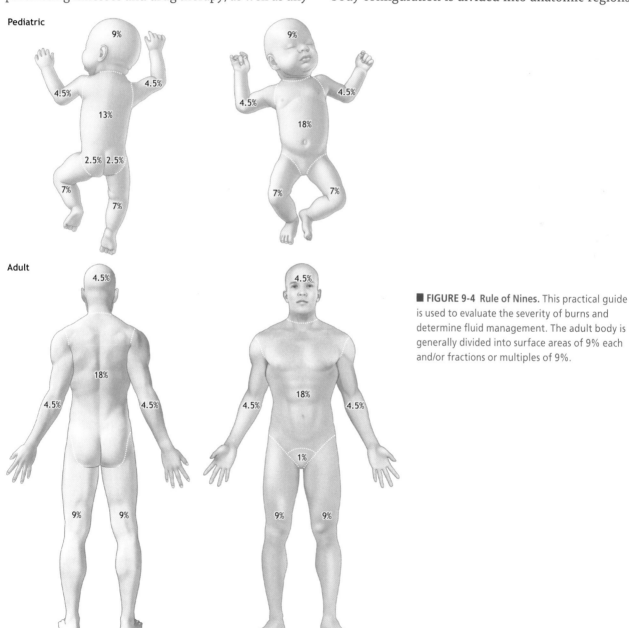

■ **FIGURE 9-4 Rule of Nines.** This practical guide is used to evaluate the severity of burns and determine fluid management. The adult body is generally divided into surface areas of 9% each and/or fractions or multiples of 9%.

that represent multiples of 9%. BSA distribution differs considerably for children, because a young child's head represents a larger proportion of the surface area, and the lower extremities represent a smaller proportion than an adult's. The palmar surface (including the fingers) of the patient's hand represents approximately 1% of the patient's body surface. The rule of nines helps estimate the extent of burns with irregular outlines or distribution and is the preferred tool for calculating and documenting the extent of a burn injury.

PITFALL	PREVENTION
Overestimating or underestimating burn size	• Do not include superficial burns in size estimation. • Use the rule of nines, recognizing that children have a proportionately larger head than adults do. • For irregular or oddly sized burns, use the patient's palm and fingers to represent 1% BSA. • Remember to logroll the patient to assess their posterior aspect.

DEPTH OF BURN

The depth of burn is important in evaluating the severity of a burn, planning for wound care, and predicting functional and cosmetic results.

Superficial (first-degree) burns (e.g., sunburn) are characterized by erythema and pain, and they do not blister. These burns are not life threatening and generally do not require intravenous fluid replacement, because the epidermis remains intact. This type of burn is not discussed further in this chapter and is not included in the assessment of burn size.

Partial-thickness burns are characterized as either superficial partial thickness or deep partial thickness. Superficial partial-thickness burns are moist, painfully hypersensitive (even to air current), potentially blistered, homogenously pink, and blanch to touch (■ FIGURE 9-5 A and B). Deep partial-thickness burns are drier, less painful, potentially blistered, red or mottled in appearance, and do not blanch to touch (■ FIGURE 9-5 C).

Full-thickness burns usually appear leathery (■ FIGURE 9-5 D). The skin may appear translucent or waxy white. The surface is painless to light touch or pinprick and generally dry. Once the epidermis is removed, the underlying dermis may be red initially, but it does not blanch with pressure. This dermis is also usually dry and does not weep. The deeper the burn, the less

pliable and elastic it becomes; therefore these areas may appear to be less swollen.

SECONDARY SURVEY AND RELATED ADJUNCTS

Key aspects of the secondary survey and its related adjuncts include documentation, baseline trauma bloodwork, including carboxyhemoglobin levels, and x-rays, maintenance of peripheral circulation in circumferential extremity burns, gastric tube insertion, narcotic analgesics and sedatives, wound care, and tetanus immunization.

DOCUMENTATION

A flow sheet or other report that outlines the patient's treatment, including the amount of fluid given and a pictorial diagram of the burn area and depth, should be initiated when the patient is admitted to the ED. This flow sheet should accompany the patient when transferred to the burn unit.

BASELINE DETERMINATIONS FOR PATIENTS WITH MAJOR BURNS

Obtain blood samples for a complete blood count (CBC), type and crossmatch/screen, an arterial blood gas with HbCO (carboxyhemoglobin), serum glucose, electrolytes, and pregnancy test in all females of childbearing age. Obtain a chest x-ray in patients who are intubated or suspected of having smoke inhalation injury, and repeat films as necessary. Other x-rays may be indicated for appraisal of associated injuries.

PERIPHERAL CIRCULATION IN CIRCUMFERENTIAL EXTREMITY BURNS

The goal of assessing peripheral circulation in a patient with burns is to rule out compartment syndrome. Compartment syndrome results from an increase in pressure inside a compartment that interferes with perfusion to the structures within that compartment. In burns, this condition results from the combination of decreased skin elasticity and increased edema in the soft tissue. In extremities, the main concern is perfusion to the muscle within the compartment. Although a compartment pressure greater than systolic blood pressure is required to lose a pulse distal

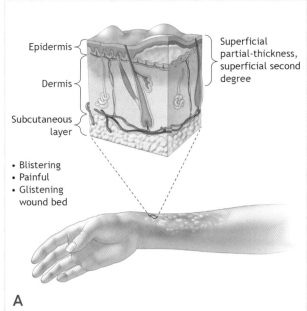

Epidermis
Dermis
Subcutaneous layer

Superficial partial-thickness, superficial second degree

• Blistering
• Painful
• Glistening wound bed

A

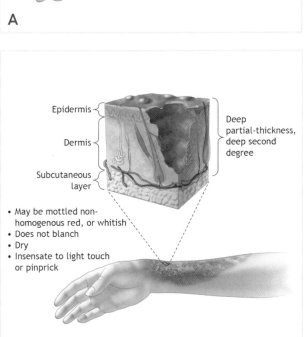

Epidermis
Dermis
Subcutaneous layer

Deep partial-thickness, deep second degree

• May be mottled non-homogenous red, or whitish
• Does not blanch
• Dry
• Insensate to light touch or pinprick

B

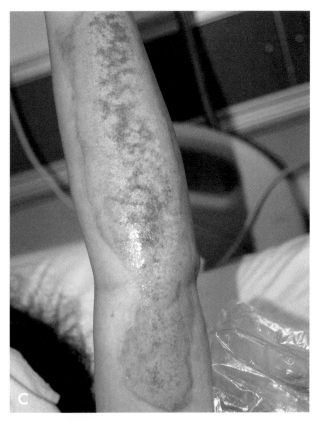

C

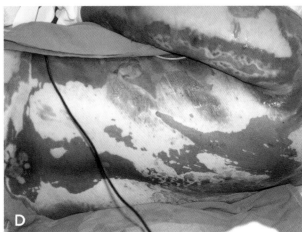

D

■ FIGURE 9-5 Depth of Burns. A. Schematic of superficial partial-thickness burn injury. B. Schematic of deep partial-thickness burn. C. Photograph of deep partial-thickness burn. D. Photograph of full-thickness burn.

to the burn, a pressure of > 30 mm Hg within the compartment can lead to muscle necrosis. Once the pulse is gone, it may be too late to save the muscle. Thus, clinicians must be aware of the signs and symptoms of compartment syndrome:

• Pain greater than expected and out of proportion to the stimulus or injury

• Pain on passive stretch of the affected muscle

• Tense swelling of the affected compartment

• Paresthesias or altered sensation distal to the affected compartment

A high index of suspicion is necessary when patients are unable to cooperate with an exam.

Compartment syndromes may also present with circumferential chest and abdominal burns, leading to increased peak inspiratory pressures or abdominal compartment syndrome. Chest and abdominal escharotomies performed along the anterior axillary lines with a cross-incision at the clavicular line and the junction of the thorax and abdomen usually relieve the problem.

To maintain peripheral circulation in patients with circumferential extremity burns, the clinician should:

- Remove all jewelry and identification or allergy bands on the patient's extremities.

- Assess the status of distal circulation, checking for cyanosis, impaired capillary refill, and progressive neurologic signs such as paresthesia and deep-tissue pain. Assessment of peripheral pulses in patients with burns is best performed with a Doppler ultrasonic flow meter.

- Relieve circulatory compromise in a circumferentially burned limb by escharotomy, always with surgical consultation. Escharotomies usually are not needed within the first 6 hours of a burn injury.

- Although fasciotomy is seldom required, it may be necessary to restore circulation in patients with associated skeletal trauma, crush injury, or high-voltage electrical injury.

- Although standard escharotomy diagrams are generally followed, always attempt to incise the skin through the burned, not the unburned skin (if unburned skin is present), as the burned skin will likely be debrided by the burn center.

GASTRIC TUBE INSERTION

Insert a gastric tube and attach it to a suction setup if the patient experiences nausea, vomiting, or abdominal distention, or when a patient's burns involve more than 20% total BSA. To prevent vomiting and possible aspiration in patients with nausea, vomiting, or abdominal distention, or when a patient's burns involve more than 20% total BSA, insert a gastric tube and ensure it is functioning before transferring the patient.

NARCOTICS, ANALGESICS, AND SEDATIVES

Severely burned patients may be restless and anxious from hypoxemia or hypovolemia rather than pain. Consequently, manage hypoxemia and inadequate fluid resuscitation before administering narcotic analgesics or sedatives, which can mask the signs of hypoxemia and hypovolemia. Narcotic analgesics and sedatives should be administered in small, frequent doses by the intravenous route only. Remember that simply covering the wound will decrease the pain.

WOUND CARE

Partial-thickness burns are painful when air currents pass over the burned surface, so gently covering the burn with clean sheets decreases the pain and deflects air currents. Do not break blisters or apply an antiseptic agent. Remove any previously applied medication before using antibacterial topical agents. Application of cold compresses can cause hypothermia. Do not apply cold water to a patient with extensive burns (i.e., > 10% TBSA). A fresh burn is a clean area that must be protected from contamination. When necessary, clean a dirty wound with sterile saline. Ensure that all individuals who come into contact with the wound wear gloves and a gown, and minimize the number of caregivers within the patient's environment without protective gear.

PITFALL	PREVENTION
Patient develops deep-tissue injury from constricting dressings and ties.	• Remember that edema takes time to develop. • Reassess or avoid circumferential ties and dressings. • Remove constricting rings and clothing early.
Patient develops deep-tissue injury from constricting burn eschar.	• Recognize that burned skin is not elastic. Circumferential burns may require escharotomies.

ANTIBIOTICS

There is no indication for prophylactic antibiotics in the early postburn period. Reserve use of antibiotics for the treatment of infection.

TETANUS

Determination of the patient's tetanus immunization status and initiation of appropriate management is very important. (See *Tetanus Immunization.*)

UNIQUE BURN INJURIES

Although the majority of burn injuries are thermal, there are other causes of burn injury that warrant special consideration, including chemical, electrical, and tar burns, as well as burn patterns that indicate abuse.

CHEMICAL BURNS

Chemical injury can result from exposure to acids, alkalies, and petroleum products. Acidic burns cause a coagulation necrosis of the surrounding tissue, which impedes the penetration of the acid to some extent. Alkali burns are generally more serious than acid burns, as the alkali penetrates more deeply by liquefaction necrosis of the tissue.

Rapid removal of the chemical and immediate attention to wound care are essential. Chemical burns are influenced by the duration of contact, concentration of the chemical, and amount of the agent. If dry powder is still present on the skin, brush it away before irrigating with water. Otherwise, immediately flush away the chemical with large amounts of warmed water, for at least 20 to 30 minutes, using a shower or hose (■ FIGURE 9-6). Alkali burns require longer irrigation. Neutralizing agents offer no advantage over water lavage, because reaction with the neutralizing agent can itself produce heat and cause further tissue damage. Alkali burns to the eye require continuous irrigation during the first 8 hours after the burn. A

PITFALL	PREVENTION
Patient presents with chemical burn and exposure to unfamiliar compound.	• Obtain the manu- facturer's Material Safety Data Sheet or contact a poison center to identify potential toxicities.

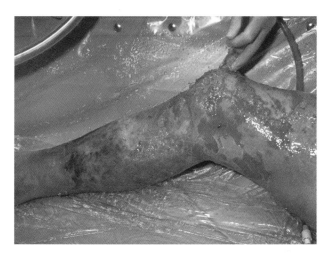

■ **FIGURE 9-6 Chemical Burn.** Immediately flush away the chemical with large amounts of water, continuing for at least 20 to 30 minutes.

small-caliber cannula can be fixed in the palpebral sulcus for irrigation. Certain chemical burns (such as hydrofluoric acid burns) require specialized burn unit consultation. It is important to ascertain the nature of the chemical and if possible obtain a copy of the Material Safety Data Sheet to address any systemic toxicity that may result. Providers must also take care to protect themselves from inadvertent exposure during the decontamination process.

ELECTRICAL BURNS

Electrical burns result when a source of electrical power makes contact with a patient, and current is transmitted through the body. The body can also serve as a volume conductor of electrical energy, and the heat generated results in thermal injury to tissue. Different rates of heat loss from superficial and deep tissues allow for relatively normal overlying skin to coexist with deep-muscle necrosis. Therefore, electrical burns frequently are more serious than they appear on the body surface, and extremities, particularly digits, are especially at risk. In addition, the current travels inside blood vessels and nerves and can cause local thrombosis and nerve injury. Severe electrical injuries usually result in contracture of the affected extremity. A clenched hand with a small electrical entrance wound should alert the clinician that a deep soft-tissue injury is likely much more extensive than is visible to the naked eye (■ FIGURE 9-7). Patients with severe electrical injuries frequently require fasciotomies and should be transferred to burn centers early in their course of treatment.

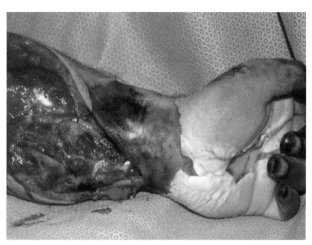

■ **FIGURE 9-7 Electrical Burn.** A clenched hand with a small electrical entrance wound should alert the clinician that a deep soft-tissue injury is likely much more extensive than is visible to the naked eye. This patient has received a volar forearm fasciotomy to decompress the muscle.

Immediate treatment of a patient with a significant electrical burn includes establishing an airway and ensuring adequate oxygenation and ventilation, placing an intravenous line in an uninvolved extremity, ECG monitoring, and placing an indwelling bladder catheter. Electricity can cause cardiac arrhythmias that may produce cardiac arrest. Prolonged monitoring is reserved for patients who demonstrate injury from the burn, loss of consciousness, exposure to high voltage (>1,000 volts) or cardiac rhythm abnormalities or arrhythmias on early evaluation.

Because electricity causes forced contraction of muscles, clinicians need to examine the patient for associated skeletal and muscular damage, including the possibility of fracture of the spine. Rhabdomyolysis from the electricity traveling through muscle results in myoglobin release, which can cause acute renal failure. Do not wait for laboratory confirmation before instituting therapy for myoglobinuria. If the patient's urine is dark red, assume that hemochromogens are in the urine. ABA consensus formula guidelines are to start resuscitation for electrical burn injury at 4 mL/kg/%TBSA to ensure a urinary output of 100 mL/hr in adults and 1–1.5 mL/kg/hr in children weighing less than 30 kg. Once the urine is clear of pigmentation, titrate the IV fluid down to ensure a standard urine output of 0.5cc/kg/hr. Consult a local burn unit before initiating a bicarbonate infusion or using mannitol.

TAR BURNS

In industrial settings, individuals can sustain injuries secondary to hot tar or asphalt. The temperature of molten tar can be very high—up to 450°F (232°C)—if it is fresh from the melting pot. A complicating factor is adherence of the tar to skin and infiltration into clothing, resulting in continued transfer of heat. Treatment includes rapid cooling of the tar and care to avoid further trauma while removing the tar. A number of methods are reported in the literature; the simplest is use of mineral oil to dissolve the tar. The oil is inert, safe on injured skin, and available in large quantities.

BURN PATTERNS INDICATING ABUSE

It is important for clinicians to maintain awareness that intentional burn injury can occur in both children and adults. Patients who are unable to control their environment, such as the very young and the very old, are particularly vulnerable to abuse and neglect. Circular burns and burns with clear edges and unique patterns should arouse suspicion; they may reflect a cigarette or other hot object (e.g., an iron) being held against the patient. Burns on the soles of a child's feet usually suggest that the child was placed into hot water versus having hot water fall on him or her, as contact with a cold bathtub can protect the bottom of the foot. A burn to the posterior aspect of the lower extremities and buttocks may be seen in an abused elder patient who has been placed in a bathtub with hot water in it. Old burn injuries in the setting of a new traumatic injury such as a fracture should also raise suspicion for abuse. Above all, the mechanism and pattern of injury should match the history of the injury.

▶ ## PATIENT TRANSFER

The criteria for transfer of patients to burn centers has been developed by the American Burn Association.

CRITERIA FOR TRANSFER

The following types of burn injuries typically require transfer to a burn center:

1. Partial-thickness burns on greater than 10% TBSA.

2. Burns involving the face, hands, feet, genitalia, perineum, and major joints

3. Third-degree burns in any age group

4. Electrical burns, including lightning injury

PITFALL	PREVENTION
Patient with an electrical burn develops acute renal failure.	• Remember, with electrical burns, that muscle injury can occur with few outward signs of injury. • Test urine for hemochromogen, and administer proper volume to ensure adequate urine output. • Repeatedly assess the patient for the development of compartment syndrome, recognizing that electrical burns may need fasciotomies. • Patients with electrical injuries may develop cardiac arrhythmias and should have a 12-lead ECG and continuous monitoring.

5. Chemical burns

6. Inhalation injury

7. Burn injury in patients with preexisting medical disorders that could complicate management, prolong recovery, or affect mortality (e.g., diabetes, renal failure)

8. Any patient with burns and concomitant trauma (e.g., fractures) in which the burn injury poses the greatest risk of morbidity or mortality. In such cases, if the trauma poses the greater immediate risk, the patient may be initially stabilized in a trauma center before being transferred to a burn unit. Physician judgment is necessary in such situations and should be considered in concert with the regional medical control plan and triage protocols.

9. Burned children in hospitals without qualified personnel or equipment for the care of children

10. Burn injury in patients who will require special social, emotional, or rehabilitative intervention

Because these criteria are so comprehensive, clinicians may elect to consult with a burn center and determine a mutually agreeable plan other than transfer. For example, in the case of a partial-thickness hand or face burn, if adequate wound care can be taught and oral pain control tolerated, follow-up at an outpatient burn clinic can avoid the costs of immediate transfer to a burn center.

TRANSFER PROCEDURES

Transfer of any patient must be coordinated with the burn center staff. All pertinent information regarding test results, vital signs, fluids administered, and urinary output should be documented on the burn/trauma flow sheet that is sent with the patient, along with any other information deemed important by the referring and receiving doctors.

COLD INJURY: LOCAL TISSUE EFFECTS

The severity of cold injury depends on temperature, duration of exposure, environmental conditions, amount of protective clothing, and the patient's general state of health. Lower temperatures, immobilization, prolonged exposure, moisture, the presence of peripheral vascular disease, and open wounds all increase the severity of the injury.

PITFALL	PREVENTION
Patient loses airway during transfer.	• Reassess airway frequently before transfer. • When the patient has risk factors for inhalation injury or has received significant amounts of resuscitation fluid, contact the receiving facility to discuss intubation before transfer.
Patient experiences severe pain with dressing change.	• Provide adequate analgesia before manipulating burns. • Use non-adherent dressings or burn sheets to protect burn from contamination before transfer.
The receiving hospital is unable to discern the burn wound size from the documentation.	• Ensure that appropriate information is relayed by using transfer forms or checklist.
The receiving hospital is unable to discern the amount of fluid resuscitation provided from the documentation.	• Ensure that the flow sheets documenting IV fluids and urinary output are sent with the patient.

TYPES OF COLD INJURY

Two types of cold injury are seen in trauma patients: frostbite and nonfreezing injury.

Frostbite

Damage from frostbite can be due to freezing of tissue, ice crystal formation causing cell membrane injury, microvascular occlusion, and subsequent tissue anoxia (■ FIGURE 9-8). Some of the tissue damage also can result from reperfusion injury that occurs on rewarming. Frostbite is classified into first-degree, second-degree, third-degree, and fourth-degree according to depth of involvement.

1. First-degree frostbite: Hyperemia and edema are present without skin necrosis.

2. Second-degree frostbite: Large, clear vesicle formation accompanies the hyperemia and edema with partial-thickness skin necrosis.

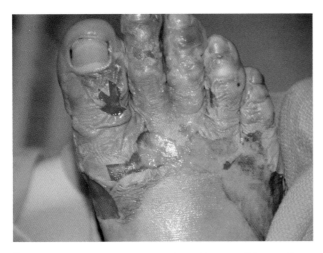

■ **FIGURE 9-8 Frostbite.** Frostbite is due to freezing of tissue with intracellular ice crystal formation, microvascular occlusion, and subsequent tissue anoxia.

3. Third-degree frostbite: Full-thickness and subcutaneous tissue necrosis occurs, commonly with hemorrhagic vesicle formation.

4. Fourth-degree frostbite: Full-thickness skin necrosis occurs, including muscle and bone with later necrosis.

Although the affected body part is typically hard, cold, white, and numb initially, the appearance of the lesion changes during the course of treatment as the area warms up and becomes perfused. The initial treatment regimen applies to all degrees of insult, and the initial classification is often not prognostically accurate. The final surgical management of frostbite depends on the level of demarcation of the perfused tissue. This demarcation may take from weeks to months to reach a final stage.

Nonfreezing Injury

Nonfreezing injury is due to microvascular endothelial damage, stasis, and vascular occlusion. Trench foot or cold immersion foot (or hand) describes a nonfreezing injury of the hands or feet—typically in soldiers, sailors, fishermen, and the homeless—resulting from long-term exposure to wet conditions and temperatures just above freezing (1.6°C to 10°C, or 35°F to 50°F). Although the entire foot can appear black, deep-tissue destruction may not be present. Alternating arterial vasospasm and vasodilation occur, with the affected tissue first cold and numb, and then progress to hyperemia in 24 to 48 hours. With hyperemia comes intense, painful burning and dysesthesia, as well as tissue damage characterized by edema, blistering, redness, ecchymosis, and ulcerations. Complications of

local infection, cellulitis, lymphangitis, and gangrene can occur. Proper attention to foot hygiene can prevent the occurrence of most such complications.

MANAGEMENT OF FROSTBITE AND NONFREEZING COLD INJURIES

Treatment should begin immediately to decrease the duration of tissue freezing. Do not attempt rewarming if there is a risk of refreezing. Replace constricting, damp clothing with warm blankets, and give the patient hot fluids by mouth, if he or she is able to drink. Place the injured part in circulating water at a constant 40°C (104°F) until pink color and perfusion return (usually within 20 to 30 minutes). This treatment is best accomplished in an inpatient setting in a large tank, such as a whirlpool tank, or by placing the injured limb into a bucket with warm water running in. Excessive dry heat can cause a burn injury, as the limb is usually insensate. Do not rub or massage the area. Rewarming can be extremely painful, and adequate analgesics (intravenous narcotics) are essential. Warming of large areas can result in reperfusion syndrome, with acidosis, hyperkalemia, and local swelling; therefore, monitor the patient's cardiac status and peripheral perfusion during rewarming.

Local Wound Care of Frostbite

The goal of wound care for frostbite is to preserve damaged tissue by preventing infection, avoiding opening uninfected vesicles, and elevating the injured area. Protect the affected tissue by a tent or cradle, and avoid pressure to the injured tissue.

When treating hypothermic patients, it is important to recognize the differences between passive and active rewarming. Passive rewarming involves placing the patient in an environment that reduces heat loss (e.g., using dry clothing and blankets), and relies on the patient's intrinsic thermoregulatory mechanism to generate heat and raise body temperature. This method is used for mild hypothermia. Active rewarming involves supplying additional sources of heat energy to the patient (e.g., warmed IV solution, warmed packs to areas of high vascular flow such as the groin and axilla, and initiating circulatory bypass). Active rewarming is used for patients with moderate and severe hypothermia.

Only rarely is fluid loss massive enough to require resuscitation with intravenous fluids, although patients may be dehydrated. Tetanus prophylaxis depends on the patient's tetanus immunization status. Systemic antibiotics are not indicated prophylactically, but are reserved for identified infections. Keep the wounds clean, and leave uninfected nonhemmorhagic blisters intact for 7 to 10 days to provide a sterile biologic dressing to protect underlying epithelialization. Tobacco, nicotine, and other vasoconstrictive agents must be withheld. Instruct the patient to minimize weight bearing until edema is resolved.

Numerous adjuvants have been attempted in an effort to restore blood supply to cold-injured tissue. Unfortunately, most are ineffective. Sympathetic blockade (e.g., sympathectomy or drugs) and vaso-dilating agents have generally not proven helpful in altering the progression of acute cold injury. Heparin and hyperbaric oxygen also have failed to demonstrate substantial treatment benefit. Retrospective case series have suggested that thrombolytic agents may show some promise, but only when thrombolytic therapy was administered within 23 hours of the frostbite injury.

Occasionally patients arrive at the ED several days after suffering frostbite, presenting with black, clearly dead toes, fingers, hands, or feet. In this circumstance, rewarming of the tissue is not necessary.

With all cold injuries, estimations of depth of injury and extent of tissue damage are not usually accurate until demarcation is evident. This often requires several weeks or months of observation. Dress these wounds regularly with a local topical antiseptic to help prevent bacterial colonization, and debride them once demarcation between live and dead tissue has developed. Early surgical debridement or amputation is seldom necessary, unless infection occurs.

COLD INJURY: SYSTEMIC HYPOTHERMIA

Trauma patients are susceptible to hypothermia, and any degree of hypothermia in them can be detrimental. Hypothermia is any core temperature below 36°C (96.8°F), and severe hypothermia is any core temperature below 32°C (89.6°F). Hypothermia is common in severely injured individuals, but further loss of core temperature can be limited by administering only warmed intravenous fluids and blood, judiciously exposing the patient, and maintaining a warm environment. Avoid iatrogenic hypothermia during exposure and fluid administration, as hypothermia can worsen coagulopathy and affect organ function.

The signs of hypothermia and its treatment are explained in more detail in *Appendix B: Hypothermia and Heat Injuries*.

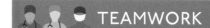

TEAMWORK

The team leader must:

- Ensure that the trauma team recognizes the unique aspects of applying the ATLS principles to treating burn-injured patients.

- Help the team recognize the importance of limiting exposure to minimize hypothermia in the patient and infection of the burn.

- Encourage the trauma team to communicate early and regularly regarding concerns about the challenges of resuscitating a burn-injured patient (e.g., IV access and need for escharotomies).

CHAPTER SUMMARY

1. Burn injuries are unique; burn inflammation/edema may not be immediately evident and requires comprehension of the underlying pathophysiology.

2. Immediate lifesaving measures for patients with burn injury include stopping the burn process, recognizing inhalation injury and assuring an adequate airway, oxygenation and ventilation, and rapidly instituting intravenous fluid therapy.

3. Fluid resuscitation is needed to maintain perfusion in face of the ongoing fluid loss from inflammation. The inflammatory response that drives the circulatory needs is directly related to the size and depth of the burn. Only partial and full thickness burns are included in calculating burn size. The rule of nines is a useful and practical guide to determine the size of the burn, with children having proportionately larger heads.

PITFALL	PREVENTION
Patient becomes hypothermic.	• Remember, thermoregulation is difficult in patients with burn injuries. • If irrigating the burns, use warmed saline. • Warm the ambient temperature. • Use heating lamps and warming blankets to rewarm the patient. • Use warmed IV fluids.

4. Attention must be paid to special problems unique to thermal injuries. Carbon monoxide poisoning should be suspected and identified. Circumferential burns may require escharotomy.

5. Nonthermal causes of burn injury should be recognized and appropriate treatment started. Chemical burns require immediate removal of clothing to prevent further injury, as well as copious irrigation. Electrical burns may be associated with extensive occult injuries. Patients sustaining thermal injury are at risk for hypothermia. Judicious analgesia should not be overlooked.

6. The American Burn Association has identified types of burn injuries that typically require referral to a burn center. Transfer principles are similar to non-burned patients but include an accurate assessment of the patient's burn size and depth.

7. Early management of cold-injured patients includes adhering to the ABCDEs of resuscitation, identifying the type and extent of cold injury, measuring the patient's core temperature, preparing a patient-care flow sheet, and initiating rapid rewarming techniques.

BIBLIOGRAPHY

1. Baxter CR. Volume and electrolyte changes in the early postburn period. *Clin Plast Surg* 1974;4:693–709.

2. Bruen KJ, Ballard JR, Morris SE, et al. Reduction of the incidence of amputation in frostbite injury with thrombolytic therapy. *Arch Surg* 2007 Jun;142(6):546–551; discussion 551–553.

3. Cancio L. Airway management and smoke inhalation injury in the burn patient. *Clin Plast Surg* 2009 Oct;36(4):555–567.

4. Cancio LC. Initial assessment and fluid resuscitation of burn patients. *Surg Clin North Am* 2014 Aug;94(4):741–754.

5. Cancio LC, Lundy JB, Sheridan RL. Evolving changes in the management of burns and environmental injuries. *Surg Clin North Am* 2012 Aug;92(4):959–986, ix.

6. Carta T, Gawaziuk J, Liu S, et al. Use of mineral oil Fleet enema for the removal of a large tar burn: a case report, *J Burns*, 2015 Mar;41(2):e11-4.

7. Gentilello LM, Cobean RA, Offner PJ, et al. Continuous arteriovenous rewarming: rapid reversal of hypothermia in critically ill patients. *J Trauma* 1992;32(3):316–327.

8. Gonzaga T, Jenebzadeh K, Anderson CP, Mohr WJ, Endorf FW, Ahrenholz DH. Use of intraarterial thrombolytic therapy for acute treatment of frostbite in 62 patients with review of thrombolytic therapy in frostbite. *J Burn Care Res*, 2015.

9. Halebian P, Robinson N, Barie P, et al. Whole body oxygen utilization during carbon monoxide poisoning and isocapneic nitrogen hypoxia. *J Trauma* 1986;26:110–117.

10. Jurkovich GJ. Hypothermia in the trauma patient. In: Maull KI, Cleveland HC, Strauch GO, et al., eds. *Advances in Trauma*. Vol. 4. Chicago, IL: Yearbook; 1989:11–140.

11. Jurkovich GJ, Greiser W, Luterman A, et al. Hypothermia in trauma victims: an ominous predictor of survival. *J Trauma* 1987;27:1019–1024.

12. Latenser BA. Critical care of the burn patient: the first 48 hours. *Crit Care Med* 2009 Oct;37(10):2819–2826.

13. Moss J. Accidental severe hypothermia. *Surg Gynecol Obstet* 1986;162:501–513.

14. Mozingo DW, Smith AA, McManus WF, et al. Chemical burns. *J Trauma* 1988;28:642–647.

15. Perry RJ, Moore CA, Morgan BD, et al. Determining the approximate area of burn: an inconsistency investigated and reevaluated. *BMJ* 1996;312:1338.

16. Pham TN, Gibran NS. Thermal and electrical injuries. *Surg Clin North Am* 2007 Feb;87(1):185–206, vii–viii. Review.

17. Pruitt BA. Fluid and electrolyte replacement in the burned patient. *Surg Clin North Am* 1978, 58;6:1313–1322.

18. Reed R, Bracey A, Hudson J, et al. Hypothermia and blood coagulation: dissociation between enzyme activity and clotting factor levels. *Circ Shock* 1990;32:141–152.

19. Saffle JR, Crandall A, Warden GD. Cataracts: a long-term complication of electrical injury. *J Trauma* 1985;25:17–21.

20. Schaller M, Fischer A, Perret C. Hyperkalemia: a prognostic factor during acute severe hypo-thermia. *JAMA* 1990;264:1842–1845.

21. Sheehy TW, Navari RM. Hypothermia. *Ala J Med Sci* 1984;21(4):374–381.

22. Sheridan RL, Chang P. Acute burn procedures. *Surg Clin North Am* 2014 Aug;94(4):755–764.

23. Stratta RJ, Saffle JR, Kravitz M, et al. Management of tar and asphalt injuries. *Am J Surg* 1983;146: 766–769.

24. Vercruysse GA, Ingram WL, Feliciano DV. The demographics of modern burn care: should most burns be cared for by the non-burn surgeon? *Am J Surg* 2011;201:91–96.

10 PEDIATRIC TRAUMA

Injury remains the most common cause of death and disability in childhood. Injury morbidity and mortality surpass all major diseases in children and young adults, making trauma the most serious public health and health care problem in this population.

CHAPTER 10 OUTLINE

OBJECTIVES

After reading this chapter and comprehending the knowledge components of the ATLS provider course, you will be able to:

1. Identify the unique characteristics of children as trauma patients, including common types and patterns of injuries, the anatomic and physiologic differences from adults, and the long-term effects of injury.

2. Describe the primary management of trauma in children, including related issues unique to pediatric patients, the anatomic and physiologic differences that affect resuscitation, and the different equipment needs when compared with adult trauma patients.

3. Identify the injury patterns associated with child maltreatment, and describe the factors that lead to suspicion of child maltreatment.

4. List the ABCDEs of injury prevention.

Injury remains the most common cause of death and disability in childhood. Each year, more than 10 million children—nearly 1 of every 6 children—in the United States require emergency department care for the treatment of injuries. Each year, more than 10,000 children in the United States die from serious injury. Injury morbidity and mortality surpass all major diseases in children and young adults, making trauma the most serious public health and healthcare problem in this population. Globally, road traffic accidents are the leading cause of adolescent deaths. Failure to secure a compromised airway, support breathing, and recognize and respond to intra-abdominal and intracranial hemorrhage are the leading causes of unsuccessful resuscitation in pediatric patients with severe trauma. Therefore, by applying ATLS principles to the care of injured children, trauma team members can significantly affect ultimate survival and long-term outcomes.

TYPES AND PATTERNS OF INJURY

Injuries associated with motor vehicles are the most common cause of death in children of all ages, whether they are occupants, pedestrians, or cyclists. Deaths due to drowning, house fires, homicides, and falls follow in descending order. Child maltreatment accounts for the great majority of homicides in infants (i.e., children younger than 12 months of age), whereas firearm injuries account for most of the homicides in children (over age 1) and adolescents. Falls account for the majority of all pediatric injuries, but infrequently result in death.

Blunt mechanisms of injury and children's unique physical characteristics result in multisystem injury being the rule rather than the exception. Clinicians should presume, therefore, that multiple organ systems may be injured until proven otherwise. ■ TABLE 10-1 outlines common mechanisms of injury and associated patterns of injury in pediatric patients.

The condition of *the majority of* injured children will not deteriorate during treatment, and *most* injured children have no hemodynamic abnormalities. Nevertheless, the condition of *some* children with multisystem injuries will rapidly deteriorate, and serious complications will develop. Therefore, early transfer of pediatric patients to a facility capable of treating children with multisystem injuries is optimal.

The Field Triage Decision Scheme (see Figure 1-2 in *Chapter 1*) and Pediatric Trauma Score ■ TABLE 10-2 are both useful tools for the early identification of pediatric patients with multisystem injuries.

TABLE 10-1 COMMON MECHANISMS OF INJURY AND ASSOCIATED PATTERNS OF INJURY IN PEDIATRIC PATIENTS

MECHANISM OF INJURY	COMMON PATTERNS OF INJURY
Pedestrian struck by motor vehicle	• Low speed: Lower-extremity fractures • High speed: Multiple trauma, head and neck injuries, lower-extremity fractures
Occupant in motor vehicle collision	• Unrestrained: Multiple trauma, head and neck injuries, scalp and facial lacerations • Restrained: Chest and abdominal injuries, lower spine fractures
Fall from a height	• Low: Upper-extremity fractures • Medium: Head and neck injuries, upper- and lower-extremity fractures • High: Multiple trauma, head and neck injuries, upper- and lower-extremity fractures
Fall from a bicycle	• Without helmet: Head and neck lacerations, scalp and facial lacerations, upper-extremity fractures • With helmet: Upper-extremity fractures • Striking handlebar: Internal abdominal injuries

UNIQUE CHARACTERISTICS OF PEDIATRIC PATIENTS

The priorities for assessing and managing pediatric trauma patients are the same as for adults. However, the unique anatomic and physiologic characteristics of this population combine with the common mechanisms of injury to produce distinct injury patterns. For example, most serious pediatric trauma is blunt trauma that involves the brain. As a result, apnea, hypoventilation, and hypoxia occur five times more often than hypovolemia with hypotension in children who have sustained trauma. Therefore, treatment protocols for pediatric trauma patients emphasize aggressive management of the airway and breathing.

TABLE 10-2 PEDIATRIC TRAUMA SCORE

ASSESSMENT COMPONENT	SCORE		
	+2	+1	-1
Weight	>20 kg (>44 lb)	10–20 kg (22–44 lb)	<10 kg (<22 lb)
Airway	Normal	Oral or nasal airway, oxygen	Intubated, cricothyroidotomy, or tracheostomy
Systolic Blood Pressure	>90 mm Hg; good peripheral pulses and perfusion	50–90 mm Hg; carotid/femoral pulses palpable	<50 mm Hg; weak or no pulses
Level of Consciousness	Awake	Obtunded or any loss of consciousness	Coma, unresponsive
Fracture	None seen or suspected	Single, closed	Open or multiple
Cutaneous	None visible	Contusion, abrasion, laceration <7 cm not through fascia	Tissue loss, any gunshot wound or stab wound through fascia
Totals:			

Source: Adapted with permission from Tepas JJ, Mollitt DL, Talbert JL, et al. The pediatric trauma score as a predictor of injury severity in the injured child. *Journal of Pediatric Surgery* 1987; 22(1)15.

SIZE, SHAPE, AND SURFACE AREA

Because children have smaller body mass than adults, the energy imparted from objects such as fenders and bumpers, or from falls, results in greater force being applied per unit of body area. This concentrated energy is transmitted to a body that has less fat, less connective tissue, and a closer proximity of multiple organs than in adults. These factors result in the high frequency of multiple injuries seen in the pediatric population. In addition, a child's head is proportionately larger than an adult's, which results in a higher frequency of blunt brain injuries in this age group.

The ratio of a child's body surface area to body mass is highest at birth and decreases as the child matures. As a result, thermal energy loss is a significant stress factor in children. Hypothermia may develop quickly and complicate the treatment of pediatric patients with hypotension.

SKELETON

A child's skeleton is incompletely calcified, contains multiple active growth centers, and is more pliable than an adult's. Therefore, bone fractures are less likely to occur in children, even when they have sustained internal organ damage. For example, rib fractures in children are uncommon, whereas pulmonary contusion is not. Other soft tissues of the thorax and mediastinum also can sustain significant damage without evidence of bony injury or external trauma. The presence of skull and/or rib fractures in a child suggests the transfer of a massive amount of energy; in this case, underlying organ injuries, such as traumatic brain injury and pulmonary contusion, should be suspected.

PSYCHOLOGICAL STATUS

The potential for significant psychological ramifications should be considered in children who sustain trauma. In young children, emotional instability frequently leads to a regressive psychological behavior when stress, pain, and other perceived threats intervene in the child's environment. Children have a limited ability to interact with unfamiliar individuals in strange and difficult situations, which can make history taking and cooperative manipulation, especially if it is painful, extremely difficult. Clinicians who understand these characteristics and are willing to soothe an injured child are more likely to establish a good rapport, which facilitates a comprehensive assessment of the child's psychological and physical injuries.

The presence of parents or other caregivers during evaluation and treatment, including resuscitation, may assist clinicians by minimizing the injured child's natural fears and anxieties.

LONG-TERM EFFECTS OF INJURY

A major consideration in treating injured children is the effect of that injury on their subsequent growth and development. Unlike adults, children must recover from the traumatic event and then continue the normal process of growth and development. The potential physiologic and psychological effects of injury on this process can be significant, particularly in cases involving long-term function, growth deformity, or subsequent abnormal development. Children who sustain even a minor injury may have prolonged disability in cerebral function, psychological adjustment, or organ system function.

Some evidence suggests that as many as 60% of children who sustain severe multisystem trauma have residual personality changes at one year after hospital discharge, and 50% show cognitive and physical handicaps. Social, affective, and learning disabilities are present in one-half of seriously injured children. In addition, childhood injuries have a significant impact on the family—personality and emotional disturbances are found in two-thirds of uninjured siblings. Frequently, a child's injuries impose a strain on the parents' personal relationship, including possible financial and employment hardships. Trauma may affect not only the child's survival but also the quality of the child's life for years to come.

Bony and solid visceral injuries are cases in point: Injuries through growth centers can cause growth abnormalities of the injured bone. If the injured bone is a femur, a leg length discrepancy may result, causing a lifelong disability in running and walking. If the fracture is through the growth center of one or more thoracic vertebra, the result may be scoliosis, kyphosis, or even gibbus deformity. Another example is massive disruption of a child's spleen, which may require a splenectomy and predisposes the child to a lifelong risk of overwhelming postsplenectomy sepsis and death.

Ionizing radiation, used commonly in evaluation of injured patients may increase the risk of certain malignancies and should be used if the information needed cannot obtained by other means, the information gained will change the clinical management of the patient, obtaining the studies will not delay the transfer of patients who require higher levels of care, and studies are obtained using the lowest possible radiation doses.

Nevertheless, the long-term quality of life for children who have sustained trauma is surprisingly positive, even though in many cases they will experience lifelong physical challenges. Most patients report a good to excellent quality of life and find gainful employment as adults, an outcome justifying aggressive resuscitation attempts even for pediatric patients whose initial physiologic status might suggest otherwise.

EQUIPMENT

Successful assessment and treatment of injured children depends on immediately available equipment of the appropriate size (■ TABLE 10-3; also see *Pediatric Equipment on MyATLS mobile app*). A length-based resuscitation tape, such as the Broselow® Pediatric Emergency Tape, is an ideal adjunct for rapidly determining weight based on length for appropriate fluid volumes, drug doses, and equipment size. By measuring the child's height, clinicians can readily determine his or her 'estimated weight. One side of the tape provides drugs and their recommended doses for pediatric patients based on weight, and the other side identifies equipment needs for pediatric patients based on length (■ FIGURE 10-1). Clinicians should be familiar with length-based resuscitation tapes and their uses.

PITFALL	PREVENTION
Incorrect doses of fluids or medications are administered	• Recognize the need for weight-based dosing, and use a resuscitation tape to estimate weight from length.
Hypothermia rapidly develops	• Recognize the significance of a high body surface area in children, and keep the environment warm and the child covered.

AIRWAY

The "A" of the ABCDEs of initial assessment is the same in the child as for adults. Establishing a patent airway to provide adequate tissue oxygenation is the first objective. The inability to establish and/or maintain a patent airway with the associated lack of oxygenation and ventilation is the most common

TABLE 10-3 PEDIATRIC EQUIPMENT[a]

| AGE AND WEIGHT | AIRWAY AND BREATHING | | | | | | |
	O₂ MASK	ORAL AIRWAY	BAG-VALVE	LARYNGO-SCOPE	ET TUBE	STYLET	SUCTION
Premie 3 kg	Premie, newborn	Infant	Infant	0 straight	2.5–3.0 no cuff	6 Fr	6–8 Fr
0–6 mos 3.5 kg	Newborn	Infant, small	Infant	1 straight	3.0–3.5 no cuff	6 Fr	8 Fr
6–12 mos 7 kg	Pediatric	Small	Pediatric	1 straight	3.5–4.0 cuffed or uncuffed	6 Fr	8-10 Fr
1–3 yrs 10–12 kg	Pediatric	Small	Pediatric	1 straight	4.0–4.5 cuffed or uncuffed	6 Fr	10 Fr
4–7 yrs 16–18 kg	Pediatric	Medium	Pediatric	2 straight or curved	5.0–5.5 no cuff	14 Fr	14 Fr
8–10 yrs 24–30 kg	Adult	Medium, large	Pediatric, adult	2-3 straight or curved	5.5–6.5 cuffed	14 Fr	14 Fr

| AGE AND WEIGHT | CIRCULATION | | SUPPLEMENTAL EQUIPMENT | | | |
	BP CUFF	IV CATHETER[b]	OG/NG TUBE	CHEST TUBE	URINARY CATHETER	CERVICAL COLLAR
Premie 3 kg	Premie, newborn	22–24 ga	8 Fr	10-14 Fr	5 Fr feeding	—
0–6 mos 3.5 kg	Newborn, infant	22 ga	10 Fr	12-18 Fr	6 Fr or 5–8 Fr feeding	—
6–12 mos 7 kg	Infant, child	22 ga	12 Fr	14–20 Fr	8 Fr	Small
1–3 yrs 10–12 kg	Child	20-22 ga	12 Fr	14–24 Fr	10 Fr	Small
4–7 yrs 16–18 kg	Child	20 ga	12 Fr	20-28 Fr	10–12 Fr	Small
8–10 yrs 24–30 kg	Child, adult	18-20 ga	14 Fr	28-32 Fr	12 Fr	Medium

[a]Use of a length-based resuscitation tape, such as a Broselow™ Pediatric Emergency Tape, is preferred.
[b]Use of the largest IV catheter that can readily be inserted with reasonable certainty of success is preferred.

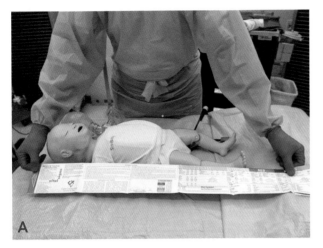

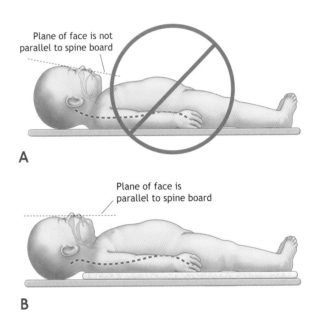

■ **FIGURE 10-1 Resuscitation Tape. A.** A length-based resuscitation tape, such as the Broselow® Pediatric Emergency Tape, is an ideal adjunct to rapidly determine weight based on length for appropriate fluid volumes, drug doses, and equipment size. **B.** Detail, showing recommended drug doses and equipment needs for pediatric patients based on length.

cause of cardiac arrest in children. Therefore, the child's airway is the first priority. (Also see *Chapter 2: Airway and Ventilatory Management*, and *Appendix G: Airway Skills*.)

ANATOMY

The smaller the child, the greater is the disproportion between the size of the cranium and the midface. The large occiput results in passive flexion of the cervical spine, leading to a propensity for the posterior pharynx to buckle anteriorly. To avoid passive flexion of the cervical spine, ensure that the plane of the midface is maintained parallel to the spine board in a neutral position, rather than in the "sniffing position" (■ FIGURE 10-2A). Placement of a 1-inch layer of padding beneath the infant or toddler's entire torso will preserve neutral alignment of the spinal column (■ FIGURE 10-2B).

Several anatomical features of children affect airway assessment and management. The soft tissues of an infant's oropharynx (i.e., the tongue and tonsils) are relatively large compared with the tissues in the oral cavity, which may compromise visualization of the larynx. A child's larynx is funnel shaped, allowing secretions to accumulate in the retropharyngeal area. The larynx and vocal cords are more cephalad and anterior in the neck. The vocal cords are frequently more difficult to visualize when the child's head is in the normal, supine, anatomical position during intubation than when it is in the neutral position required for optimal cervical spine protection.

An infant's trachea is approximately 5 cm long and grows to 7 cm by about 18 months. Failure to appreciate this short length can result in intubation of the right

■ **FIGURE 10-2 Positioning for Airway Maintenance. A.** Improper positioning of a child to maintain a patent airway. The disproportion between the size of the child's cranium and midface leads to a propensity for the posterior pharynx to buckle anteriorly. The large occiput causes passive flexion of the cervical spine. **B.** Proper positioning of a child to maintain a patent airway. Avoid passive flexion of the cervical spine by keeping the plane of the midface parallel to the spine board in a neutral position, rather than in the "sniffing position." Placement of a 1-inch layer of padding beneath the infant's or toddler's entire torso will preserve neutral alignment of the spinal column.

mainstem bronchus, inadequate ventilation, accidental tube dislodgment, and/or mechanical barotrauma. The optimal endotracheal tube (ETT) depth (in centimeters) can be calculated as three times the appropriate tube size. For example, a 4.0 ETT would be properly positioned at 12 cm from the gums.

MANAGEMENT

In a spontaneously breathing child with a partially obstructed airway, optimize the airway by keeping the plane of the face parallel to the plane of the stretcher or gurney while restricting motion of the cervical spine. Use the jaw-thrust maneuver combined with bimanual inline spinal motion restriction to open the airway. After the mouth and oropharynx are cleared of secretions and debris, administer supplemental oxygen. If the patient is unconscious, mechanical methods of maintaining the airway may be necessary. Before attempting to mechanically establish an airway, fully preoxygenate the child.

Oral Airway

An oral airway should be inserted only if a child is unconscious, because vomiting is likely to occur if the gag reflex is intact. The practice of inserting the airway backward and rotating it 180 degrees is not recommended for children, since trauma and hemorrhage into soft-tissue structures of the oropharynx may occur. Insert the oral airway gently and directly into the oropharynx. Using a tongue blade to depress the tongue may be helpful.

Orotracheal Intubation

Orotracheal intubation is indicated for injured children in a variety of situations, including

- a child with severe brain injury who requires controlled ventilation

- a child in whom an airway cannot be maintained

- a child who exhibits signs of ventilatory failure

- a child who has suffered significant hypovolemia and has a depressed sensorium or requires operative intervention

Orotracheal intubation is the most reliable means of establishing an airway and administering ventilation to a child. The smallest area of a young child's airway is at the cricoid ring, which forms a natural seal around an uncuffed ETT, a device that is commonly used in infants because of their anatomic features.

(See *Infant Endotracheal Intubation video on MyATLS mobile app.*) However, the use of cuffed ETTs, even in toddlers and small children, provides the benefit of improving ventilation and CO_2 management, resulting in improved cerebral blood flow. Previous concerns about cuffed endotracheal tubes causing tracheal necrosis are no longer relevant due to improvements in the design of the cuffs. Ideally, cuff pressure should be measured as soon as is feasible, and <30 mm Hg is considered safe.

A simple technique to gauge the ETT size needed for a specific patient is to approximate the diameter of the child's external nares or the tip of the child's smallest finger and use a tube with a similar diameter. Length-based pediatric resuscitation tapes also list appropriate tube sizes. Ensure the ready availability of tubes that are one size larger and one size smaller than the predicted size. If using a stylet to facilitate intubation, ensure that the tip does not extend beyond the end of the tube.

Most trauma centers use a protocol for emergency intubation, referred to as drug-assisted or drug-facilitated intubation, also known as rapid sequence intubation. Clinicians must pay careful attention to the child's weight, vital signs (pulse and blood pressure), and level of consciousness to determine which branch of the Algorithm for Drug-Assisted Intubation (■ FIGURE 10-3) to use. (Also see *Drug-Assisted Intubation in Pediatric Patients on MyATLS mobile app.*)

Preoxygenate children who require an endotracheal tube for airway control. Infants have a more pronounced vagal response to endotracheal intubation than do children and adults, and they may experience

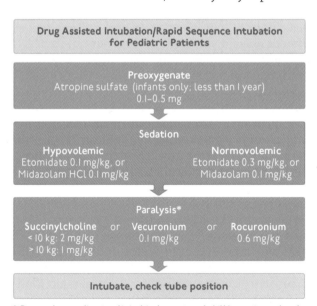

■ FIGURE 10-3 Algorithm for Drug-Assisted Intubation/Rapid Sequence Intubation in Pediatric Patients.

bradycardia with direct laryngeal stimulation. Bradycardia in infants is much more likely to be due to hypoxia. Atropine sulfate pretreatment should be considered for infants requiring drug-assisted intubation, but it is not required for children. Atropine also dries oral secretions, enabling visualization of landmarks for intubation.

After inserting the endotracheal tube, ensure that its position is assessed clinically (see below) and, if correct, the tube carefully secured. If it is not possible to place the ETT after the patient is chemically paralyzed, ventilate the child with 100% oxygen administered with a self-inflating bag-mask device until a definitive airway is secured.

Orotracheal intubation under direct vision with restriction of cervical motion is the preferred method of obtaining definitive airway control. Do not perform nasotracheal intubation in children, as it requires blind passage around a relatively acute angle in the nasopharynx toward the anterosuperiorly located glottis, making intubation by this route difficult. The potential for penetrating the child's cranial vault or damaging the more prominent nasopharyngeal (adenoidal) soft tissues and causing hemorrhage also discourages the use of the nasotracheal route for airway control.

Once the ETT is past the glottic opening, position it 2 to 3 cm below the level of the vocal cords and carefully secure in place. Next, conduct primary confirmation techniques, such as auscultation of both hemithoraces in the axillae, to ensure that right mainstem bronchial intubation has not occurred and that both sides of the chest are being adequately ventilated. Then use a secondary confirmation device, such as a real-time waveform capnograph, a colorimetric end-tidal carbon dioxide detector, or an esophageal detector device, to document tracheal intubation, and obtain a chest x-ray to accurately identify ETT position.

Because young children have short tracheas, any movement of the head can result in displacement of the ETT, inadvertent extubation, right mainstem bronchial intubation, or vigorous coughing due to irritation of the carina by the tip of the tube. These conditions may not be recognized clinically until significant deterioration has occurred. Thus, clinicians should evaluate breath sounds periodically to ensure that the tube remains in the appropriate position and identify the possibility of evolving ventilatory dysfunction.

If there is any doubt about correct placement of the ETT that cannot be resolved expeditiously, remove the tube and replace it immediately. The mnemonic, "Don't be a DOPE" (D for dislodgment, O for obstruction, P for pneumothorax, E for equipment failure) may be a useful reminder of the common causes of deterioration in intubated patients.

Cricothyroidotomy

When airway maintenance and control cannot be accomplished by bag-mask ventilation or orotracheal intubation, a rescue airway with either laryngeal mask airway (LMA), intubating LMA, or needle cricothyroidotomy is necessary. Needle-jet insufflation via the cricothyroid membrane is an appropriate, temporizing technique for oxygenation, but it does not provide adequate ventilation, and progressive hypercarbia will occur. LMAs are appropriate adjunct airways for infants and children, but their placement requires experience, and ventilation may distend the patient's stomach if it is overly vigorous.

Surgical cricothyroidotomy is rarely indicated for infants or small children. It can be performed in older children in whom the cricothyroid membrane is easily palpable (usually by the age of 12 years).

PITFALL	PREVENTION
Patient's oxygen saturation decreases	Use the "Don't be a DOPE" mnemonic as a reminder of the common causes of deterioration in intubated patients: • D—Dislodgment can easily occur, as the trachea of an infant or child is short. Secure the tube well and recognize the situation early if it occurs. Use monitoring equipment, especially during transport, to help alert the provider of this problem. • O—Obstruction with secretions or secondary to kinking can occur, as the diameter of the tubes is small. Suctioning can clear secretions, but tube replacement may be necessary. • P—Pneumothorax. Tension pneumothorax can develop with positive pressure in patients with underlying pneumothorax from traumatic injury or barotrauma related to mechanical ventilation. This conditions warrants decompression. • E—Equipment failure. Ventilators, pulse oximeters, and oxygen delivery devices can malfunction. Ensure that equipment is well maintained and properly functioning, and use backup equipment when necessary.

BREATHING

A key factor in evaluating and managing breathing and ventilation in injured pediatric trauma patients is the recognition of impaired gas exchange. This includes oxygenation and elimination of carbon dioxide resulting from alterations of breathing caused by mechanical issues such as pneumothorax and lung injury from contusion or aspiration. In such cases, apply appropriate countermeasures such as tube thoracostomy and assisted ventilation.

BREATHING AND VENTILATION

The respiratory rate in children decreases with age. An infant breathes 30 to 40 times per minute, whereas an older child breathes 15 to 20 times per minute. Normal, spontaneous tidal volumes vary from 4 to 6 mL/kg for infants and children, although slightly larger tidal volumes of 6 to 8 mL/kg and occasionally as high as 10 mL/kg may be required during assisted ventilation. Although most bag-mask devices used with pediatric patients are designed to limit the pressure exerted manually on the child's airway, excessive volume or pressure during assisted ventilation substantially increases the potential for iatrogenic barotrauma due to the fragile nature of the immature tracheobronchial tree and alveoli. When an adult bag-mask device is used to ventilate a pediatric patient, the risk of barotrauma is significantly increased. Use of a pediatric bag-mask is recommended for children under 30 kg.

Hypoxia is the most common cause of pediatric cardiac arrest. However, before cardiac arrest occurs, hypoventilation causes respiratory acidosis, which is the most common acid-base abnormality encountered during the resuscitation of injured children. With adequate ventilation and perfusion, a child should be able to maintain relatively normal pH. In the absence of adequate ventilation and perfusion, attempting to correct an acidosis with sodium bicarbonate can result in further hypercarbia and worsened acidosis.

NEEDLE AND TUBE THORACOSTOMY

Injuries that disrupt pleural apposition—for example, hemothorax, pneumothorax, and hemopneumothorax, have similar physiologic consequences in children and adults. These injuries are managed with pleural decompression, preceded in the case of tension pneumothorax by needle decompression just over the top of the third rib in the midclavicular line. Take care during this procedure when using 14- to 18-gauge over-the-needle catheters in infants and small children, as the longer needle length may cause rather than cure a tension pneumothorax.

Chest tubes need to be proportionally smaller (see ■ TABLE 10-3) and are placed into the thoracic cavity by tunneling the tube over the rib above the skin incision site and then directing it superiorly and posteriorly along the inside of the chest wall. Tunneling is especially important in children because of their thinner chest wall. The site of chest tube insertion is the same in children as in adults: the fifth intercostal space, just anterior to the midaxillary line. (See *Chapter 4: Thoracic Trauma*, and *Appendix G: Breathing Skills*.)

CIRCULATION AND SHOCK

Key factors in evaluating and managing circulation in pediatric trauma patients include recognizing circulatory compromise, accurately determining the patient's weight and circulatory volume, obtaining venous access, administering resuscitation fluids and/or blood replacement, assessing the adequacy of resuscitation, and achieving thermoregulation.

RECOGNITION OF CIRCULATORY COMPROMISE

Injuries in children can result in significant blood loss. A child's increased physiologic reserve allows for maintenance of systolic blood pressure in the normal range, even in the presence of shock (■ FIGURE 10-4). Up to a 30% decrease in circulating blood volume may be required to manifest a decrease in the child's systolic

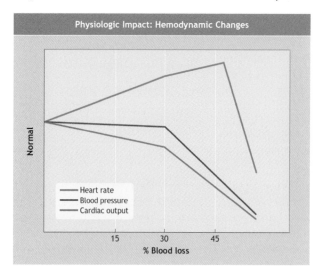

■ FIGURE 10-4 Physiological Impact of Hemodynamic Changes on Pediatric Patients.

blood pressure. This can mislead clinicians who are not familiar with the subtle physiologic changes manifested by children in hypovolemic shock. Tachycardia and poor skin perfusion often are the only keys to early recognition of hypovolemia and the early initiation of appropriate fluid resuscitation. When possible, early assessment by a surgeon is essential to the appropriate treatment of injured children.

Although a child's primary response to hypovolemia is tachycardia, this sign also can be caused by pain, fear, and psychological stress. Other more subtle signs of blood loss in children include progressive weakening of peripheral pulses, a narrowing of pulse pressure to less than 20 mm Hg, skin mottling (which substitutes for clammy skin in infants and young children), cool extremities compared with the torso skin, and a decrease in level of consciousness with a dulled response to pain. A decrease in blood pressure and other indices of inadequate organ perfusion, such as urinary output, should be monitored closely, but generally develop later. Changes in vital organ function by degree of volume loss are outlined in ■ TABLE 10-4.

The mean normal systolic blood pressure for children is 90 mm Hg plus twice the child's age in years. The lower limit of normal systolic blood pressure in children is 70 mm Hg plus twice the child's age in years. The diastolic pressure should be about two-thirds of the systolic blood pressure. (Normal vital functions by age group are listed in ■ TABLE 10-5.) Hypotension in a child represents a state of decompensated shock and indicates severe blood loss of greater than 45% of the circulating blood volume. Tachycardia changing to bradycardia often accompanies this hypotension, and this change may occur suddenly in infants. These physiologic changes must be treated by a rapid infusion of both isotonic crystalloid and blood.

PITFALL	PREVENTION
Failure to recognize and treat shock in a child	• Recognize that tachycardia may be the only physiologic abnormality. • Recognize that children have increased physiologic reserve. • Recognize that normal vital signs vary with the age of the child. • Carefully reassess the patient for mottled skin and a subtle decrease in mentation.

TABLE 10-4 SYSTEMIC RESPONSES TO BLOOD LOSS IN PEDIATRIC PATIENTS

SYSTEM	MILD BLOOD VOLUME LOSS (<30%)	MODERATE BLOOD VOLUME LOSS (30%–45%)	SEVERE BLOOD VOLUME LOSS (>45%)
Cardiovascular	Increased heart rate; weak, thready peripheral pulses; normal systolic blood pressure (80 – 90 + 2 × age in years); normal pulse pressure	Markedly increased heart rate; weak, thready central pulses; absent peripheral pulses; low normal systolic blood pressure (70 – 80 + 2 × age in years); narrowed pulse pressure	Tachycardia followed by bradycardia; very weak or absent central pulses; absent peripheral pulses; hypotension (<70 + 2 × age in years); narrowed pulse pressure (or undetectable diastolic blood pressure)
Central Nervous System	Anxious; irritable; confused	Lethargic; dulled response to pain[a]	Comatose
Skin	Cool, mottled; prolonged capillary refill	Cyanotic; markedly prolonged capillary refill	Pale and cold
Urine Output[b]	Low to very low	Minimal	None

[a] A child's dulled response to pain with moderate blood volume loss may indicate a decreased response to IV catheter insertion.
[b] Monitor urine output after initial decompression by urinary catheter. Low normal is 2 ml/kg/hr (infant), 1.5 ml/kg/hr (younger child), 1 ml/hg/hr (older child), and 0.5 ml/hg/hr (adolescent). IV contrast can falsely elevate urinary output.

TABLE 10-5 NORMAL VITAL FUNCTIONS BY AGE GROUP					
AGE GROUP	WEIGHT RANGE (in kg)	HEART RATE (beats/min)	BLOOD PRESSURE (mm Hg)	RESPIRATORY RATE (breaths/min)	URINARY OUTPUT (mL/kg/hr)
Infant 0–12 months	0–10	<160	>60	<60	2.0
Toddler 1–2 years	10–14	<150	>70	<40	1.5
Preschool 3–5 years	14–18	<140	>75	<35	1.0
School age 6–12 years	18–36	<120	>80	<30	1.0
Adolescent ≥13 years	36–70	<100	>90	<30	0.5

DETERMINATION OF WEIGHT AND CIRCULATING BLOOD VOLUME

It is often difficult for emergency department (ED) personnel to estimate a child's weight, particularly when they do not often treat children. The simplest and quickest method of determining a child's weight in order to accurately calculate fluid volumes and drug dosages is to ask a caregiver. If a caregiver is unavailable, a length-based resuscitation tape is extremely helpful. This tool rapidly provides the child's approximate weight, respiratory rate, fluid resuscitation volume, and a variety of drug dosages. A final method for estimating weight in kilograms is the formula ([2 × age in years] + 10).

The goal of fluid resuscitation is to rapidly replace the circulating volume. An infant's blood volume can be estimated at 80 mL/kg, and a child age 1-3 years at 75 mL/kg, and children over age 3 years at 70 mL/kg.

VENOUS ACCESS

Intravenous access in young children with hypovolemia can be a challenging skill, even in the most experienced hands. Severe hypovolemic shock is typically caused by the disruption of intrathoracic or intra-abdominal organs or blood vessels. A peripheral percutaneous route is preferable to establish venous access. If percutaneous access is unsuccessful after two attempts, consider intraosseous infusion via a bone-marrow needle: 18-gauge in infants, 15-gauge

in young children (■ FIGURE 10-5; also see *Intraosseous Puncture video on MyATLS mobile app.*) or insertion of a femoral venous line of appropriate size using

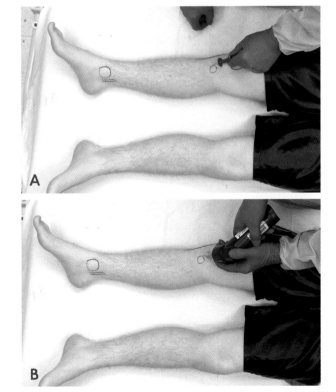

■ FIGURE 10-5 Intraosseous Infusion, A. Distal femur, B. Proximal tibia. If percutaneous access is unsuccessful after two attempts, consider starting intraosseous infusion via a bone-marrow needle (18 gauge in infants, 15 gauge in young children).

the Seldinger technique. If these procedures fail, a physician with skill and expertise can perform direct venous cutdown, but this procedure should be used only as a last resort, since it can rarely be performed in less than 10 minutes, even in experienced hands, whereas even providers with limited skill and expertise can reliably place an intraosseous needle in the bone-marrow cavity in less than 1 minute. (See *Appendix G: Circulation Skills*.)

The preferred sites for venous access in children are

- Percutaneous peripheral (two attempts)—Antecubital fossa(e) or saphenous vein(s) at the ankle

- Intraosseous placement—(1) Anteromedial tibia, (2) distal femur. Complications of this procedure include cellulitis, osteomyelitis, compartment syndrome, and iatrogenic fracture. The preferred site for intraosseous cannulation is the proximal tibia, below the level of the tibial tuberosity. An alternative site is the distal femur, although the contralateral proximal tibia is preferred. Intraosseous cannulation should not be performed in an extremity with a known or suspected fracture.

- Percutaneous placement—Femoral vein(s)

- Percutaneous placement—External or internal jugular or subclavian vein(s) (should be reserved for pediatric experts; do not use if there is airway compromise, or a cervical collar is applied)

- Venous cutdown—Saphenous vein(s) at the ankle

FLUID RESUSCITATION AND BLOOD REPLACEMENT

Fluid resuscitation for injured children is weight-based, with the goal of replacing lost intravascular volume. Evidence of hemorrhage may be evident with the loss of 25% of a child's circulating blood volume. The initial fluid resuscitation strategy for injured children recommended in previous editions of ATLS has consisted of the intravenous administration of warmed isotonic crystalloid solution as an initial 20 mL/kg bolus, followed by one or two additional 20 mL/kg isotonic crystalloid boluses pending the child's physiologic response. If the child demonstrates evidence of ongoing bleeding after the second or third crystalloid bolus, 10 mL/kg of packed red blood cells may be given.

Recent advances in trauma resuscitation in adults with hemorrhagic shock have resulted in a move away from crystalloid resuscitation in favor of "damage control resuscitation," consisting of the restrictive use of crystalloid fluids and early administration of balanced ratios of packed red blood cells, fresh frozen plasma, and platelets. This approach appears to interrupt the lethal triad of hypothermia, acidosis, and trauma-induced coagulopathy, and has been associated with improved outcomes in severely injured adults.

There has been movement in pediatric trauma centers in the United States toward crystalloid restrictive balanced blood product resuscitation strategies in children with evidence of hemorrhagic shock, although published studies supporting this approach are lacking at the time of this publication. The basic tenets of this strategy are an initial 20 mL/kg bolus of isotonic crystalloid followed by weight-based blood product resuscitation with 10-20 mL/kg of packed red blood cells and 10-20 mL/kg of fresh frozen plasma and platelets, typically as part of a pediatric mass transfusion protocol. A limited number of studies have evaluated the use of blood-based massive transfusion protocols for injured children, but researchers have not been able to demonstrate a survival advantage. For facilities without ready access to blood products, crystalloid resuscitation remains an acceptable alternative until transfer to an appropriate facility.

Carefully monitor injured children for response to fluid resuscitation and adequacy of organ perfusion. A return toward hemodynamic normality is indicated by

- Slowing of the heart rate (age appropriate with improvement of other physiologic signs)

- Clearing of the sensorium

- Return of peripheral pulses

- Return of normal skin color

- Increased warmth of extremities

- Increased systolic blood pressure with return to age-appropriate normal

- Increased pulse pressure (>20 mm Hg)

- Urinary output of 1 to 2 mL/kg/hour (age dependent)

Children generally have one of three responses to fluid resuscitation:

1. The condition of most children will be stabilized by using crystalloid fluid only, and blood is not required; these children are considered "responders." Some children respond to

crystalloid and blood resuscitation; these children are also considered responders.

2. Some children have an initial response to crystalloid fluid and blood, but then deterioration occurs; this group is termed "transient responders."

3. Other children do not respond at all to crystalloid fluid and blood infusion; this group is referred to as "nonresponders."

Transient responders and nonresponders are candidates for the prompt infusion of additional blood products, activation of a mass transfusion protocol, and consideration for early operation. Similar to adult resuscitation practices, earlier administration of blood products in refractory patients may be appropriate.

The resuscitation flow diagram is a useful aid in the initial treatment of injured children (■ FIGURE 10-6). (Also see *Resuscitation Flow Diagram for Pediatric Patients with Normal and Abnormal Hemodynamics on MyATLS mobile app.*)

URINE OUTPUT

Urine output varies with age and size: The output goal for infants is 1-2 mL/kg/hr; for children over age one

up to adolescence the goal is 1-1.5 mL/kg/hr; and 0.5 mL/kg/hr for teenagers.

Measurement of urine output and urine specific gravity is a reliable method of determining the adequacy of volume resuscitation. When the circulating blood volume has been restored, urinary output should return to normal. Insertion of a urinary catheter facilitates accurate measurement of a child's urinary output for patients who receive substantial volume resuscitation.

THERMOREGULATION

The high ratio of body surface area to body mass in children increases heat exchange with the environment and directly affects the body's ability to regulate core temperature. A child's increased metabolic rate, thin skin, and lack of substantial subcutaneous tissue also contribute to increased evaporative heat loss and caloric expenditure. Hypothermia can significantly compromise a child's response 'to treatment, prolong coagulation times, and adversely affect central nervous system (CNS) function. While the child is exposed during the initial survey and resuscitation phase, overhead heat lamps, heaters, and/or thermal blankets may be necessary to preserve body heat. Warm the room as well as the intravenous fluids, blood products, and inhaled gases. After examining the child during the initial resuscitation phase, cover his or her body with warm blankets to avoid unnecessary heat loss.

CARDIOPULMONARY RESUSCITATION

Children who undergo cardiopulmonary resuscitation (CPR) in the field with return of spontaneous circulation before arriving in the trauma center have approximately a 50% chance of neurologically intact survival. Children who present to an emergency department still in traumatic cardiopulmonary arrest have a uniformly dismal prognosis. Children who receive CPR for more than 15 minutes before arrival to an ED or have fixed pupils on arrival uniformly are nonsurvivors. For pediatric trauma patients who arrive in the trauma bay with continued CPR of long duration, prolonged resuscitative efforts are not beneficial.

CHEST TRAUMA

Eight percent of all injuries in children involve the chest. Chest injury also serves as a marker

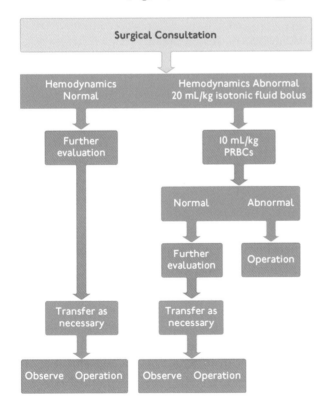

■ FIGURE 10-6 Resuscitation Flow Diagram for Pediatric Patients with normal and abnormal hemodynamics.

for other organ system injury, as more than two-thirds of children with chest injury have multiple injuries. The mechanism of injury and anatomy of a child's chest are responsible for the spectrum of injuries seen.

The vast majority of chest injuries in childhood are due to blunt mechanisms, most commonly caused by motor vehicle injury or falls. The pliability, or compliance, of a child's chest wall allows kinetic energy to be transmitted to the underlying pulmonary parenchyma, causing pulmonary contusion. Rib fractures and mediastinal injuries are not common; if present, they indicate a severe impacting force. Specific injuries caused by thoracic trauma in children are similar to those encountered in adults, although the frequencies of these injuries differ.

The mobility of mediastinal structures makes children more susceptible to tension pneumothorax, the most common immediately life-threatening injury in children. Pneumomediastinum is rare and benign in the overwhelming majority of cases. Diaphragmatic rupture, aortic transection, major tracheobronchial tears, flail chest, and cardiac contusions are also uncommon in pediatric trauma patients. When identified, treatment for these injuries is the same as for adults. Significant injuries in children rarely occur alone and are frequently a component of major multisystem injury.

The incidence of penetrating thoracic injury increases after 10 years of age. Penetrating trauma to the chest in children is managed the same way as for adults.

Unlike in adult patients, most chest injuries in children can be identified with standard screening chest radiographs. Cross-sectional imaging is rarely required in the evaluation of blunt injuries to the chest in children and should be reserved for those whose findings cannot be explained by standard radiographs.

Most pediatric thoracic injuries can be successfully managed using an appropriate combination of supportive care and tube thoracostomy. Thoracotomy is not generally needed in children. (Also see *Chapter 4: Thoracic Trauma*, and *Appendix G: Breathing Skills*.)

ABDOMINAL TRAUMA

Most pediatric abdominal injuries result from blunt trauma that primarily involves motor vehicles and falls. Serious intra-abdominal injuries warrant prompt involvement by a surgeon, and hypotensive children who sustain blunt or penetrating abdominal trauma require prompt operative intervention.

ASSESSMENT

Conscious infants and young children are generally frightened by the traumatic events, which can complicate the abdominal examination. While talking quietly and calmly to the child, ask questions about the presence of abdominal pain and gently assess the tone of the abdominal musculature. Do not apply deep, painful palpation when beginning the examination; this may cause voluntary guarding that can confuse the findings.

Most infants and young children who are stressed and crying will swallow large amounts of air. If the upper abdomen is distended on examination, insert a gastric tube to decompress the stomach as part of the resuscitation phase. Orogastric tube decompression is preferred in infants.

The presence of shoulder- and/or lap-belt marks increases the likelihood that intra-abdominal injuries are present, especially in the presence of lumbar fracture, intraperitoneal fluid, or persistent tachycardia.

Abdominal examination in unconscious patients does not vary greatly with age. Decompression of the urinary bladder facilitates abdominal evaluation. Since gastric dilation and a distended urinary bladder can both cause abdominal tenderness, interpret this finding with caution, unless these organs have been fully decompressed.

DIAGNOSTIC ADJUNCTS

Diagnostic adjuncts for assessing abdominal trauma in children include CT, focused assessment with sonography for trauma (FAST), and diagnostic peritoneal lavage (DPL).

Computed Tomography

Helical CT scanning allows for the rapid and precise identification of injuries. CT scanning is often used to evaluate the abdomens of children who have sustained blunt trauma and have no hemodynamic abnormalities. It should be immediately available and performed early in treatment, although its use must not delay definitive treatment. CT of the abdomen should routinely be performed with IV contrast agents according to local practice.

Identifying intra-abdominal injuries by CT in pediatric patients with no hemodynamic abnormalities can allow for nonoperative management by the surgeon. Early involvement of a surgeon is essential to establish a baseline that allows him or her to determine whether and when operation is indicated. Centers that lack surgical support and where transfer of injured children is planned are justified in forgoing the CT evaluation before transport to definitive care.

Injured children who require CT scanning as an adjunctive study often require sedation to prevent movement during the scanning process. Thus, a clinician skilled in pediatric airway management and pediatric vascular access should accompany an injured child requiring resuscitation or sedation who undergoes CT scan. CT scanning is not without risk. Fatal cancers are predicted to occur in as many as 1 in 1000 patients who undergo CT as children. Thus, the need for accurate diagnosis of internal injury must be balanced against the risk of late malignancy. Every effort should be made to avoid CT scanning before transfer to a definitive trauma center, or to avoid repeat CT upon arrival at a trauma center, unless deemed absolutely necessary. When CT evaluation is necessary, radiation must be kept As Low As Reasonably Achievable (ALARA). To achieve the lowest doses possible, perform CT scans only when medically necessary, scan only when the results will change management, scan only the area of interest, and use the lowest radiation dose possible.

Focused Assessment Sonography in Trauma

Although FAST has been used as a tool for the evaluation abdominal injuries in children since the 1990s, the efficacy of this modality has been the subject of debate resulting from reports of relatively low sensitivity and high false negative rates. However, FAST is widely used as an extension of the abdominal examination in injured children; it offers the advantage that imaging may be repeated throughout resuscitation and avoids ionizing radiation. Some investigators have shown that FAST identifies even small amounts of intra-abdominal blood in pediatric trauma patients, a finding that is unlikely to be associated with significant injury. If large amounts of intra-abdominal blood are found, significant injury is more likely to be present. However, even in these patients, operative management is indicated not by the amount of intraperitoneal blood, but by hemodynamic abnormality and its response to treatment. FAST is incapable of identifying isolated intraparenchymal injuries, which account for up to one-third of solid organ injuries in children. Clinically significant intra-abdominal injuries may also be present in the absence of any free intraperitoneal fluid. In summary, FAST should not be relied upon as the sole diagnostic test to rule out the presence of intra-abdominal injury. If a small amount of intra-abdominal fluid is found and the child is hemodynamically normal, obtain a CT scan.

Diagnostic Peritoneal Lavage

Diagnostic peritoneal lavage (DPL) may be used to detect intra-abdominal bleeding in children who have hemodynamic abnormalities and cannot be safely transported to the CT scanner, and when CT and FAST are not readily available and the presence of blood will lead to immediate operative intervention. This is an uncommon occurrence, as most pediatric patients have self-limited intra-abdominal injuries with no hemodynamic abnormalities. Therefore, blood found by DPL would not mandate operative exploration in a child who is otherwise stable.

Use 10 ml/kg warmed crystalloid solution for the lavage. The delicacy of the child's abdominal wall can lead to uncontrolled penetration of the peritoneal cavity and produce iatrogenic injury, even when an open technique is used. DPL has utility in diagnosing injuries to intra-abdominal viscera only; retroperitoneal organs cannot be evaluated reliably by this technique. Evaluation of the effluent from the DPL is the same in children as it is in adults.

Only the surgeon who will ultimately treat the child should perform the DPL, since this procedure can interfere with subsequent abdominal examinations and imaging upon which the decision to operate may be partially based.

NONOPERATIVE MANAGEMENT

Selective, nonoperative management of solid organ injuries in children who are hemodynamically normal is performed in most trauma centers, especially those with pediatric capabilities. The presence of intraperitoneal blood on CT or FAST, the grade of injury, and/or the presence of a vascular blush does not necessarily mandate a laparotomy. Bleeding from an injured spleen, liver, or kidney generally is self-limited. Therefore, a CT or FAST that is positive for blood alone does not mandate a laparotomy in children who are hemodynamically normal or stabilize rapidly with fluid resuscitation. If the child's hemodynamic condition cannot be normalized and the diagnostic procedure performed is positive for blood, perform a prompt laparotomy to control hemorrhage.

For nonoperative management, children must be treated in a facility with pediatric intensive care capabilities and under the supervision of a qualified surgeon. In resource-limited environments, consider operatively treating abdominal solid organ injuries.

Angioembolization of solid organ injuries in children is a treatment option, but it should be performed only in centers with experience in pediatric interventional procedures and ready access to an operating room. The treating surgeon must make the decision to perform angioembolization.

Nonoperative management of confirmed solid organ injuries is a surgical decision made by surgeons, just as is the decision to operate. Therefore, the surgeon must supervise the treatment of pediatric trauma patients.

SPECIFIC VISCERAL INJURIES

A number of abdominal visceral injuries are more common in children than in adults. Injuries such as those caused by a bicycle handlebar, an elbow striking a child in the right upper quadrant, and lap-belt injuries are common and result when the visceral contents are forcibly compressed between the blow on the anterior abdominal wall and the spine posteriorly. This type of injury also may be caused by child maltreatment.

Blunt pancreatic injuries occur from similar mechanisms, and their treatment is dependent on the extent of injury. Small bowel perforations at or near the ligament of Treitz are more common in children than in adults, as are mesenteric and small bowel avulsion injuries. These particular injuries are often diagnosed late because of the vague early symptoms.

Bladder rupture is also more common in children than in adults, because of the shallow depth of the child's pelvis.

Children who are restrained by a lap belt only are at particular risk for enteric disruption, especially if they have a lap-belt mark on the abdominal wall or sustain a flexion-distraction (Chance) fracture of the lumbar spine. Any patient with this mechanism of injury and these findings should be presumed to have a high likelihood of injury to the gastrointestinal tract, until proven otherwise.

Penetrating injuries of the perineum, or straddle injuries, may occur with falls onto a prominent object and result in intraperitoneal injuries due to the proximity of the peritoneum to the perineum. Rupture of a hollow viscus requires early operative intervention. (Also see *Chapter 5: Abdominal and Pelvic Trauma*.)

HEAD TRAUMA

The information provided in *Chapter 6: Head Trauma* also applies to pediatric patients. This section emphasizes information that is specific to children.

Most head injuries in the pediatric population are the result of motor vehicle crashes, child maltreatment, bicycle crashes, and falls. Data from national pediatric trauma data repositories indicate that an understanding of the interaction between the CNS and extracranial injuries is imperative, because hypotension and hypoxia from associated injuries adversely affect the outcome from intracranial injury. Lack of attention to the ABCDE's and associated injuries can significantly increase mortality from head injury. As in adults, hypotension is infrequently caused by head injury alone, and other explanations for this finding should be investigated aggressively.

A child's brain is anatomically different from that of an adult. It doubles in size in the first 6 months of life and achieves 80% of the adult brain size by 2 years of age. The subarachnoid space is relatively smaller, offering less protection to the brain because there is less buoyancy. Thus, head momentum is more likely to impart parenchymal structural damage. Normal cerebral blood flow increases progressively to nearly twice that of adult levels by the age of 5 years and then decreases. This accounts in part for children's significant susceptibility to cerebral hypoxia and hypercarbia.

ASSESSMENT

Children and adults can differ in their response to head trauma, which influences the evaluation of injured children. Following are the principal differences:

1. The outcome in children who suffer severe brain injury is better than that in adults. However,

PITFALL	PREVENTION
Delay in transfer in order to obtain CT scan	• Recognize that children who will be transferred to a trauma center are not likely to benefit from imaging at the receiving hospital.
Delayed identification of hollow visceral injury	• Recognize that the risk of hollow viscus injury is based on the mechanism of injury. • Perform frequent reassessments to identify changes in clinical exam findings as quickly as possible. • Recognize that early involvement of a surgeon is necessary.
Delayed laparotomy	• Recognize that persistent hemodynamic instability in a child with abdominal injury mandates laparotomy.

the outcome in children younger than 3 years of age is worse than that following a similar injury in an older child. Children are particularly susceptible to the effects of the secondary brain injury that can be produced by hypovolemia with attendant reductions in cerebral perfusion, hypoxia, seizures, and/or hyperthermia. The effect of the combination of hypovolemia and hypoxia on the injured brain is devastating, but hypotension from hypovolemia is the most serious single risk factor. It is critical to ensure adequate and rapid restoration of an appropriate circulating blood volume and avoid hypoxia.

2. Although infrequent, hypotension can occur in infants following significant blood loss into the subgaleal, intraventricular, or epidural spaces, because of the infants' open cranial sutures and fontanelles. In such cases, treatment focuses on appropriate volume restoration.

3. Infants, with their open fontanelles and mobile cranial sutures, have more tolerance for an expanding intracranial mass lesion or brain swelling, and signs of these conditions may be hidden until rapid decompensation occurs. An infant who is not in a coma but who has bulging fontanelles or suture diastases should be assumed to have a more severe injury, and early neurosurgical consultation is essential.

4. Vomiting and amnesia are common after brain injury in children and do not necessarily imply increased intracranial pressure. However, persistent vomiting or vomiting that becomes more frequent is a concern and mandates CT of the head.

5. Impact seizures, or seizures that occur shortly after brain injury, are more common in children and are usually self-limited. All seizure activity requires investigation by CT of the head.

6. Children tend to have fewer focal mass lesions than do adults, but elevated intracranial pressure due to brain swelling is more common. Rapid restoration of normal circulating blood volume is critical to maintain cerebral perfusion pressure (CPP). If hypovolemia is not corrected promptly, the outcome from head injury can be worsened by secondary brain injury. Emergency CT is vital to identify children who require imminent surgery.

7. The Glasgow Coma Scale (GCS) is useful in evaluating pediatric patients, but the verbal score component must be modified for children younger than 4 years (■ TABLE 10-6).

TABLE 10-6 PEDIATRIC VERBAL SCORE

VERBAL RESPONSE	V-SCORE
Appropriate words or social smile, fixes and follows	5
Cries, but consolable	4
Persistently irritable	3
Restless, agitated	2
None	1

8. Because increased intracranial pressure frequently develops in children, neurosurgical consultation to consider intracranial pressure monitoring should be obtained early in the course of resuscitation for children with (a) a GCS score of 8 or less, or motor scores of 1 or 2; (b) multiple injuries associated with brain injury that require major volume resuscitation, immediate lifesaving thoracic or abdominal surgery, or for which stabilization and assessment is prolonged; or (c) a CT scan of the brain that demonstrates evidence of brain hemorrhage, cerebral swelling, or transtentorial or cerebellar herniation. Management of intracranial pressure is integral to optimizing CPP.

9. Medication dosages are determined by the child's size and in consultation with a neurosurgeon. Drugs often used in children with head injuries include 3% hypertonic saline and mannitol to reduce intracranial pressure, and Levetiracetam and Phenytoin for seizures.

Criteria are available to identify patients who are at low risk for head, cervical spine, and abdominal injury and therefore do not require CT (■ FIGURE 10-7).

MANAGEMENT

Management of traumatic brain injury in children involves the rapid, early assessment and management of the ABCDEs, as well as appropriate neurosurgical involvement from the beginning of treatment. Appropriate sequential assessment and management of the brain injury focused on preventing secondary brain injury—that is, hypoxia and hypoperfusion—is also critical. Early endotracheal intubation with adequate

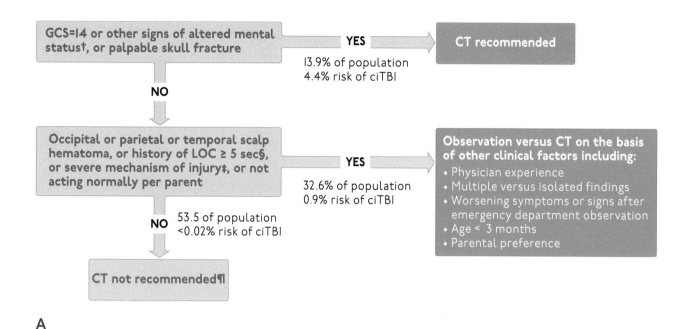

A

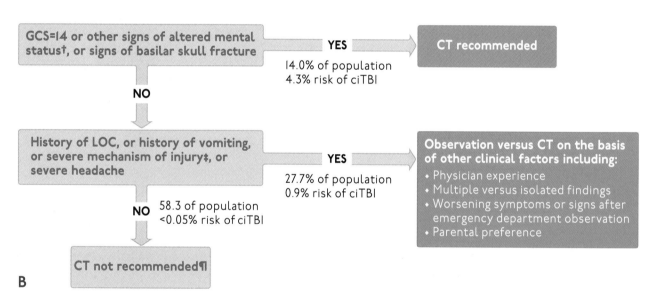

B

■ **FIGURE 10-7 Pediatric Emergency Care Applied Research Network (PECARN) Criteria for Head CT.** Suggested CT algorithm for children younger than 2 years (A) and for those aged 2 years and older (B) with GCS scores of 14-15 after head trauma.*

GCS=Glasgow Coma Scale. ciTBI=clinically-important traumatic brain injury. LOC=loss of consciousness.

*Data are from the combined derivation and validation populations.

†Other signs of altered mental status: agitation, somnolence, repetitive questioning, or slow response to verbal communication.

‡Severe mechanism of injury: motor vehicle crash with patient ejection, death of another passenger, or rollover; pedestrian or bicyclist without helmet struck by a motorized vehicle; falls of more than 0·9 m (3 feet) (or more than 1·5 m [5 feet] for panel B); or head struck by a high-impact object.

§Patients with certain isolated findings (i.e., with no other findings suggestive of traumatic brain injury), such as isolated LOC, isolated headache, isolated vomiting, and certain types of isolated scalp hematomas in infants older than 3 months, have a risk of ciTBI substantially lower than 1%.

¶Risk of ciTBI exceedingly low, generally lower than risk of CT-induced malignancies. Therefore, CT scans are not indicated for most patients in this group.

(Reprinted with permission from Kuperman N, Holmes JF, Dayan PS, et al. Identification of children at very low risk of clinically important brain injuries after head trauma: a prospective cohort study. *Lancet* 374: 2009; 1160–1170.)

oxygenation and ventilation can help avoid progressive CNS damage. Attempts to orally intubate the trachea in an uncooperative child with a brain injury may be difficult and actually increase intracranial pressure. In the hands of clinicians who have considered the risks and benefits of intubating such children, pharmacologic sedation and neuromuscular blockade may be used to facilitate intubation.

Hypertonic saline and mannitol create hyperosmolality and increased sodium levels in the brain, decreasing edema and pressure within the injured cranial vault. These substances have the added benefit of being rheostatic agents that improve blood flow and downregulate the inflammatory response.

As with all trauma patients, it is also essential to continuously reassess all parameters. (Also see *Chapter 6: Head Trauma* and *Appendix G: Disability Skills*.)

SPINAL CORD INJURY

The information provided in Chapter 7: Spine and Spinal Cord Trauma also applies to pediatric patients. This section emphasizes information that is specific to pediatric spinal injury.

Spinal cord injury in children is fortunately uncommon—only 5% of spinal cord injuries occur in the pediatric age group. For children younger than 10 years of age, motor vehicle crashes most commonly produce these injuries. For children aged 10 to 14 years, motor vehicles and sporting activities account for an equal number of spinal injuries.

ANATOMICAL DIFFERENCES

Anatomical differences in children to be considered in treating spinal injury include the following:

- Interspinous ligaments and joint capsules are more flexible.
- Vertebral bodies are wedged anteriorly and tend to slide forward with flexion.
- The facet joints are flat.
- Children have relatively large heads compared with their necks. Therefore, the angular momentum is greater, and the fulcrum exists higher in the cervical spine, which accounts for more injuries at the level of the occiput to C3.
- Growth plates are not closed, and growth centers are not completely formed.

- Forces applied to the upper neck are relatively greater than in the adult.

RADIOLOGICAL CONSIDERATIONS

Pseudosubluxation frequently complicates the radiographic evaluation of a child's cervical spine. Approximately 40% of children younger than 7 years of age show anterior displacement of C2 on C3, and 20% of children up to 16 years exhibit this phenomenon. This radiographic finding is seen less commonly at C3 on C4. Up to 3 mm of movement may be seen when these joints are studied by flexion and extension maneuvers.

When subluxation is seen on a lateral cervical spine x-ray, ascertain whether it is a pseudosubluxation or a true cervical spine injury. Pseudosubluxation of the cervical vertebrae is made more pronounced by the flexion of the cervical spine that occurs when a child lies supine on a hard surface. To correct this radiographic anomaly, ensure the child's head is in a neutral position by placing a 1-inch layer of padding beneath the entire body from shoulders to hips, but not the head, and repeat the x-ray (see Figure 10-2). True subluxation will not disappear with this maneuver and mandates further evaluation. Cervical spine injury usually can be identified from neurological examination findings and by detection of an area of soft-tissue swelling, muscle spasm, or a step-off deformity on careful palpation of the posterior cervical spine.

An increased distance between the dens and the anterior arch of C1 occurs in approximately 20% of young children. Gaps exceeding the upper limit of normal for the adult population are seen frequently.

Skeletal growth centers can resemble fractures. Basilar odontoid synchondrosis appears as a radiolucent area at the base of the dens, especially in children younger than 5 years. Apical odontoid epiphyses appear as separations on the odontoid x-ray and are usually seen between the ages of 5 and 11 years. The growth center of the spinous process can resemble fractures of the tip of the spinous process.

Children sustain *spinal cord injury without radiographic abnormalities* (SCIWORA) more commonly than adults. A normal cervical spine series may be found in up to two-thirds of children who have suffered spinal cord injury. Thus, if spinal cord injury is suspected, based on history or the results of neurological examination, normal spine x-ray examination does not exclude significant spinal cord injury. When in doubt about the integrity of the cervical spine or spinal cord, assume that an unstable injury exists, limit spinal motion and obtain appropriate consultation.

CT and MRI scans should not be used as routine screening modalities for evaluation of the pediatric cervical spine; rather plain radiographs should be performed as the initial imaging tool. Indications for the use of CT or MRI scans include the inability to completely evaluate the cervical spine with plain films, delineating abnormalities seen on plain films, neurologic findings on physical exam, and assessment of the spine in children with traumatic brain injuries CT scan may not detect the ligamentous injuries that are more common in children.

Spinal cord injuries in children are treated in the same way as spinal cord injuries in adults. Consultation with a spine surgeon should be obtained early. (Also see *Chapter 7: Spine and Spinal Cord Trauma* and *Appendix G: Disability Skills*.)

MUSCULOSKELETAL TRAUMA

The initial priorities for managing skeletal trauma in children are similar to those for the adult. Additional concerns involve potential injury to the child's growth plates.

HISTORY

The patient's history is vital in evaluation of musculoskeletal trauma. In younger children, x-ray diagnosis of fractures and dislocations is difficult due to the lack of mineralization around the epiphysis and the presence of a physis (growth plate). Information about the magnitude, mechanism, and time of the injury facilitates better correlation of the physical and x-ray findings. Radiographic evidence of fractures of differing ages should alert clinicians to possible child maltreatment, as should lower-extremity fractures in children who are too young to walk.

BLOOD LOSS

Blood loss associated with longbone and pelvic fractures is proportionately less in children than in adults. Blood loss related to an isolated closed femur fracture that is treated appropriately is associated with an average fall in hematocrit of 4 percentage points, which is not enough to cause shock. Therefore, hemodynamic instability in the presence of an isolated femur fracture should prompt evaluation for other sources of blood loss, which usually will be found within the abdomen.

SPECIAL CONSIDERATIONS OF THE IMMATURE SKELETON

Bones lengthen as new bone is laid down by the physis near the articular surfaces. Injuries to, or adjacent to, this area before the physis has closed can retard normal growth or alter the development of the bone in an abnormal way. Crush injuries to the physis, which are often difficult to recognize radiographically, have the worst prognosis.

The immature, pliable nature of bones in children can lead to "greenstick" fractures, which are incomplete with angulation maintained by cortical splinters on the concave surface. The torus, or "buckle," fracture that is seen in small children involves angulation due to cortical impaction with a radiolucent fracture line. Both types of fractures may suggest maltreatment in patients with vague, inconsistent, or conflicting histories. Supracondylar fractures at the elbow or knee have a high propensity for vascular injury as well as injury to the growth plate.

FRACTURE SPLINTING

Simple splinting of fractured extremities in children usually is sufficient until definitive orthopedic evaluation can be performed. Injured extremities with evidence of vascular compromise require emergency evaluation to prevent the adverse sequelae of ischemia. A single attempt to reduce the fracture to restore blood flow is appropriate, followed by simple splinting or traction splinting of the extremity. (Also see *Chapter 8: Musculoskeletal Trauma* and *Appendix G: Disability Skills*.)

PITFALL	PREVENTION
Difficulty identifying fractures	• Recognize the limitations of radiographs in identifying injuries, especially at growth plates. • Use the patient's history, behavior, mechanism of injury, and physical examination findings to develop an index of suspicion.
Missed child maltreatment	• Be suspicious when the mechanism and injury are not aligned.

CHILD MALTREATMENT

Any child who sustains an intentional injury as the result of acts by caregivers is considered to be a battered or maltreated child. Homicide is the leading cause of intentional death in the first year of life. Children who suffer from nonaccidental trauma have significantly higher injury severity and a six-fold higher mortality rate than children who sustain accidental injuries. Therefore, a thorough history and careful evaluation of children in whom maltreatment is suspected is crucial to prevent eventual death, especially in children who are younger than 2 years of age. Clinicians should suspect child maltreatment in these situations:

- A discrepancy exists between the history and the degree of physical injury—for example, a young child loses consciousness or sustains significant injuries after falling from a bed or sofa, fractures an extremity during play with siblings or other children, or sustains a lower-extremity fracture even though he or she is too young to walk.

- A prolonged interval has passed between the time of the injury and presentation for medical care.

- The history includes repeated trauma, treated in the same or different EDs.

- The history of injury changes or is different between parents or other caregivers.

- There is a history of hospital or doctor "shopping."

- Parents respond inappropriately to or do not comply with medical advice—for example, leaving a child unattended in the emergency facility.

- The mechanism of injury is implausible based on the child's developmental stage (■ TABLE 10-7).

The following findings, on careful physical examination, suggest child maltreatment and warrant more intensive investigation:

- Multicolored bruises (i.e., bruises in different stages of healing)

- Evidence of frequent previous injuries, typified by old scars or healed fractures on x-ray examination

- Perioral injuries

- Injuries to the genital or perianal area

TABLE 10-7 BABY MILESTONES

AGE	TYPICAL SKILLS
1 month	• Lifts head when supine • Responds to sounds • Stares at faces
2 months	• Vocalizes • Follows objects across field of vision • Holds head up for short periods
3 months	• Recognizes familiar faces • Holds head steady • Visually tracks moving objects
4 months	• Smiles • Laughs • Can bear weight on legs • Vocalizes when spoken to
5 months	• Distinguishes between bold colors • Plays with hands and feet
6 months	• Turns toward sounds or voices • Imitates sounds • Rolls over in both directions
7 months	• Sits without support • Drags objects toward self
8 months	• Says "mama" or "dada" to parents • Passes objects from hand to hand
9 months	• Stands while holding on to things
10 months	• Picks things up with "pincer" grasp • Crawls well with belly off the ground
11 months	• Plays games like "patty cake" and "peek-a-boo" • Stands without support for a few seconds
12 months	• Imitates the actions of others • Indicates wants with gestures

- Fractures of long bones in children younger than 3 years of age

- Ruptured internal viscera without antecedent major blunt trauma

- Multiple subdural hematomas, especially without a fresh skull fracture

- Retinal hemorrhages

- Bizarre injuries, such as bites, cigarette burns, and rope marks

- Sharply demarcated second- and third-degree burns

- Skull fractures or rib fractures seen in children less than 24 months of age

In many nations, clinicians are bound by law to report incidents of child maltreatment to governmental authorities, even cases in which maltreatment is only suspected. Maltreated children are at increased risk for fatal injuries, so reporting is critically important. The system protects clinicians from legal liability for identifying confirmed or even suspicious cases of maltreatment.

Although reporting procedures vary, they are most commonly handled through local social service agencies or the state's health and human services department. The process of reporting child maltreatment assumes greater importance when one realizes that 33% of maltreated children who die from assault in the United States and United Kingdom were victims of previous episodes of maltreatment.

PREVENTION

The greatest pitfall related to pediatric trauma is failure to have prevented the child's injuries in the first place. Up to 80% of childhood injuries could have been prevented by the application of simple strategies in the home and community. The ABCDE's of injury prevention have been described, and warrant special attention in a population among whom the lifetime benefits of successful injury prevention are self-evident (■ BOX 10-1).

BOX 10-1 ABCDES OF INJURY PREVENTION

- **Analyze** injury data
  - Local injury surveillance
- **Build** local coalitions
  - Hospital community partnerships
- **Communicate** the problem
  - Injuries are preventable
- **Develop** prevention activities
  - Create safer environments
- **Evaluate** the interventions
  - Ongoing injury surveillance

Source: Pressley JC, Barlow B, Durkin M, et al. A national program for injury prevention in children and adolescents: the injury free coalition for kids. *J Urban Health* 2005; 82:389–401.

Not only can the social and familial disruption associated with childhood injury be avoided, but for every dollar invested in injury prevention, four dollars are saved in hospital care.

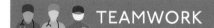 TEAMWORK

The care of severely injured children presents many challenges that require a coordinated team approach. Ideally, injured children are cared for in settings that have a pediatric trauma team composed of a physician with expertise in managing pediatric trauma, pediatric specialist physicians, and pediatric nurses and staff.

Team members should be assigned specific tasks and functions during the resuscitation to ensure an orderly transition of care.

The reality is that most injured children will initially be treated in a facility with limited pediatric specialty resources. An adult trauma team may be responsible for the care of injured children and must provide the following:

- A trauma team leader who has experience in the care of injured patients and is familiar with the local medical resources available to care for injured children

- A provider with basic airway management skills

- Access to providers with advanced pediatric airway skills

- Ability to provide pediatric vascular access via percutaneous or intraosseous routes

- Knowledge of pediatric fluid resuscitation

- Appropriate equipment sizes for a range of different ages

- Strict attention to drug doses

- Early involvement of a surgeon with pediatric expertise, preferably a pediatric surgeon

- Knowledge and access to available pediatric resources (pediatrician, family medicine) to help manage pediatric-specific comorbidities or issues

- Inclusion of the child's family during the emergency department resuscitation and throughout the child's hospital stay

- It is particularly important to debrief after a pediatric trauma case. Team members and others present in the resuscitation room may be deeply affected by poor outcomes for children. Appropriate mental health resources should be available.

CHAPTER SUMMARY

1. Unique characteristics of children include important differences in anatomy, body surface area, chest wall compliance, and skeletal maturity. Normal vital signs vary significantly with age. Initial assessment and management of severely injured children is guided by the ABCDE approach. Early involvement of a general surgeon or pediatric surgeon is imperative in managing injuries in a child.

2. Nonoperative management of abdominal visceral injuries should be performed only by surgeons in facilities equipped to handle any contingency in an expeditious manner.

3. Child maltreatment should be suspected if suggested by suspicious findings on history or physical examination. These include discrepant history, delayed presentation, frequent prior injuries, injuries incompatible with developmental stage, and perineal injuries.

4. Most childhood injuries are preventable. Doctors caring for injured children have a special responsibility to promote the adoption of effective injury prevention programs and practices within their hospitals and communities.

BIBLIOGRAPHY

1. American College of Surgeons Committee on Trauma, American College of Emergency Physicians, National Association of EMS Physicians, Pediatric Equipment Guidelines Committee—Emergency Medical Services for Children (EMSC) Partnership for Children Stakeholder Group and American Academy of Pediatrics Baby Center. Your Baby's Developmental Milestones. Milestone chart: 1 to 6 months and Milestone chart: 7 to 12 months. http://www.babycenter.com/baby-milestones. Accessed April 1, 2016.
2. American College of Surgeons Committee on Trauma, American College of Emergency Physicians Pediatric Emergency Medicine Committee, National Association of EMS Physicians and American Academy of Pediatrics Committee on Pediatric Emergency Medicine. Withholding Termination of Resuscitation in Pediatric Out of Hospital Traumatic Cardiopulmonary Arrest. *Pediatrics* 2014;133:e1104–e1116.
3. Berg MD, Schexnayder SM, Chameides L, et al. 2010 American Heart Association Guidelines for Cardiopulmonary Resuscitation and Emergency Cardiovascular Care Science. Part 13: Pediatric Basic Life Support. 2010 American Heart Association Guidelines for Cardiopulmonary Resuscitation and Emergency Cardiovascular Care.
4. Bratton SL, Chestnut RM, Ghajar J, et al. Guidelines for the management of severe traumatic brain injury. II. Hyperosmolar therapy. *J Neurotrauma* 2007; 24(Suppl 1):S14–20.
5. Brain Trauma Foundation; American Association of Neurological Surgeons; Congress of Neurological Surgeons; Joint Section on Neurotrauma and Critical Care, AANS/CNS. *Pediatrics* 2009; 124(1): e166–e171.
6. Brain Trauma Foundation. Guidelines for the Acute Medical Management of Severe Traumatic Brain Injury in Infants, Children, and Adolescents—Second Edition. *Pediatr Crit Med* 2012;13:S1–82.
7. Capizzani AR, Drognonowski R, Ehrlich PF. Assessment of termination of trauma resuscitation guidelines: are children small adults? *J Pediatr Surg* 2010;45:903–907.1.
8. Carcillo JA. Intravenous fluid choices in critically ill children. *Current Opinions in Critical Care* 2014;20:396–401.
9. Carney NA, Chestnut R, Kochanek PM, et al. Guidelines for the acute medical management of severe traumatic brain injury in infants, children, and adolescents. *J Trauma* 2003;54:S235–S310.
10. Chesnut RM, Marshall LF, Klauber MR, et al. The role of secondary brain injury in determining outcome from severe head injury. *J Trauma* 1993;43:216–222.
11. Chidester SJ, Williams N, Wang W, et al. A pediatric massive transfusion protocol. *J Trauma Acute Care Surg* 2012;73(5):1273–1277.
12. Chwals WJ, Robinson AV, Sivit CJ, et al. Computed tomography before transfer to a level I pediatric trauma center risks duplication with associated radiation exposure. *J Pediatr Surg* 2008;43:2268–2272.
13. Clements RS, Steel AG, Bates AT, et al. Cuffed endotracheal tube use in paediatric prehospital intubation: challenging the doctrine? *Emerg Med J* 2007;24(1):57–58.

14. Cloutier DR, Baird TB, Gormley P, et al. Pediatric splenic injuries with a contrast blush: successful nonoperative management without angiography and embolization. *J Pediatr Surg* 2004;39(6):969–971.

15. Cook SH, Fielding JR, Phillips JD. Repeat abdominal computed tomography scans after pediatric blunt abdominal trauma: missed injuries, extra costs, and unnecessary radiation exposure. *J Pediatr Surg* 2010;45:2019–2024.

16. Cooper A, Barlow B, DiScala C, et al. Mortality and truncal injury: the pediatric perspective. *J Pediatr Surg* 1994;29:33.

17. Cooper A, Barlow B, DiScala C. Vital signs and trauma mortality: the pediatric perspective. *Pediatr Emerg Care* 2000;16:66.

18. Corbett SW, Andrews HG, Baker EM, et al. ED evaluation of the pediatric trauma patient by ultrasonography. *Am J Emerg Med* 2000;18(3):244–249.

19. Davies DA, Ein SH, Pearl R, et al. What is the significance of contrast "blush" in pediatric blunt splenic trauma? *J Pediatr Surg* 2010;45:916–920.

20. Dehmer JJ, Adamson WT. Massive transfusion and blood product use in the pediatric trauma patient. *Semin Pediatr Surg* 2010;19(4):286–291.

21. DiScala C, Sage R, Li G, et al. Child maltreatment and unintentional injuries. *Arch Pediatr Adolesc Med* 2000;154:16–22.

22. Dressler AM, Finck CM, Carroll CL, et al. Use of a massive transfusion protocol with hemostatic resuscitation for severe intraoperative bleeding in a child. *J Pediatr Surg* 2010;45(7):1530–1533.

23. Emery KH, McAneney CM, Racadio JM, et al. Absent peritoneal fluid on screening trauma ultrasonography in children: a prospective comparison with computed tomography. *J Pediatr Surg* 2001;36(4):565–569.

24. Estroff JM, Foglia RP, Fuchs JR. A comparison of accidental and nonaccidental trauma: it is worse than you think. *J Emerg Med* 2015;48:274–270.

25. Fastle RK, Roback MG. Pediatric rapid sequence intubation: incidence of reflex bradycardia and effects of pretreatment with atropine. *Pediatr Emerg Care* 2004; 20(10): 651–655.

26. Global Burden of Diseases Pediatric Collaboration. Global and National Burden of Diseases and Injuries Among Children and Adolescents Between 1990 and 2013, Findings from the Global Burden of Disease 2013 Study. *JAMA Pediatrics* 2014;170:263–283.

27. Hannan E, Meaker P, Fawell L, et al. Predicting inpatient mortality for pediatric blunt trauma patients: a better alternative. *J Pediatr Surg* 2000; 35:155–159.

28. Haricharan RN, Griffin RL, Barnhart DC, et al. Injury patterns among obese children involved in motor vehicle collisions. *J Pediatr Surg* 2009;44:1218–1222.

29. Harris BH, Schwaitzberg SD, Seman TM, et al. The hidden morbidity of pediatric trauma. *J Pediatr Surg* 1989;24:103–106.

30. Harvey A, Towner E, Peden M, et al. Injury prevention and the attainment of child and adolescent health. *Bull World Health Organ* 2009;87(5):390–394.

31. Hendrickson JE, Shaz BH, Pereira G, et al. Coagulopathy is prevalent and associated with adverse outcomes in transfused pediatric trauma patients. *J Pediatr* 2012;160(2): 204–209.

32. Hendrickson JE, Shaz BH, Pereira G, et al. Implementation of a pediatric trauma massive transfusion protocol: one institution's experience. *Transfusion* 2012;52(6):1228–1236.

33. Herzenberg JE, Hensinger RN, Dedrick DE, et al. Emergency transport and positioning of young children who have an injury of the cervical spine. *J Bone Joint Surg Am* 1989;71:15–22.

34. Holmes JF, Brant WE, Bond WF, et al. Emergency department ultrasonography in the evaluation of hypotensive and normotensive children with blunt abdominal trauma. *J Pediatr Surg* 2001;36(7):968–973.

35. Holmes JF, Gladman A, Chang CH. Performance of abdominal ultrasonography in pediatric blunt trauma patients: a meta-analysis. *J Pediatr Surg* 2007;42:1588–1594.14.

36. Holmes J, Lillis K, Monroe D, et al. Identifying children at very low risk of intra-abdominal injuries undergoing acute intervention. *Acad Emerg Med* 2011;18:S161.

37. Holmes JF, London KL, Brant WE, et al. Isolated intraperitoneal fluid on abdominal computed tomography in children with blunt trauma. *Acad Emerg Med* 2000;7(4):335–341.

38. Kassam-Adams N, Marsac ML, Hildenbrand A, et al. Posttraumatic stress following pediatric injury; Update on diagnosis, risk factors, and intervention. *JAMA Peds* 2013;167:1158–1165.

39. Kharbanda AB, Flood A, Blumberg K, et al. Analysis of radiation exposure among pediatric patients at national trauma centers. *J Trauma* 2013;74: 907–911.

40. Kuppermann N, Holmes JF, Dayan PS, et al., for the Pediatric Emergency Care Applied Research Network (PECARN): Identification of children at very low risk of clinically important brain injuries

after head trauma: a prospective cohort study. *Lancet* 2009;374:1160–1170.

41. Leonard JC, Kuppermann N, Olsen C, et al., for the Pediatric Emergency Care Applied Research Network. Factors associated with cervical spine injury in children following blunt trauma. *Ann Emerg Med* 2011;58:145–155.

42. Lutz N, Nance ML, Kallan MJ, et al. Incidence and clinical significance of abdominal wall bruising in restrained children involved in motor vehicle crashes. *J Pediatr Surg* 2004;39(6): 972–975.

43. McAuliffe G, Bissonnette B, Boutin C. Should the routine use of atropine before succinylcholine in children be reconsidered? *Can J Anaesth* 1995;42(8):724–729.

44. McVay MR, Kokoska ER, Jackson RJ, et al. Throwing out the "grade" book: management of isolated spleen and liver injury based on hemodynamic status. *J Pediatr Surg* 2008;43: 1072–1076.

45. Murphy JT, Jaiswal K, Sabella J, et al. Prehospital cardiopulmonary resuscitation in the pediatric trauma patient. *J Pediatr Surg* 2010 Jul;45(7):1413–1419.

46. National Safety Council. Injury Facts. Itasca, IL: National Safety Council; 2016.

47. Neal MD, Sippey M, Gaines BA, et al. Presence of pneumomediastinum after blunt trauma in children: what does it really mean? *J Pediatr Surg* 2009;44(7):1322–1327.

48. Neff NP, Cannon JW, Morrison JJ, et al. Clearly defining pediatric mass transfusion: cutting through the fog and friction using combat data. 2014;78:21–28.

49. Paddock HN, Tepas JJ, Ramenofsky ML. Management of blunt pediatric hepatic and splenic injury: similar process, different outcome. *Am Surg* 2004;70:1068–1072.

50. Palusci VJ, Covington TM: Child maltreatment deaths in the U.S. National Child Death Review Case Reporting System. *Child Abuse & Neglect* 2014;38:25–36.

51. Paris C, Brindamour M, Ouimet A, et al. Predictive indicators for bowel injury in pediatric patients who present with a positive seat belt sign after motor vehicle collision. *J Pediatr Surg* 2010;45:921–924.

52. Patel JC, Tepas JJ. The efficacy of focused abdominal sonography for trauma (FAST) as a screening tool in the assessment of injured children. *J Pediatr Surg* 1999;34:44–47.

53. Patregnani JT, Borgman MA, Maegele M, et al. Coagulopathy and shock on admission is associated with mortality for children with traumatic injuries at combat support hospitals. *Pediatr Crit Care Med* 2012;13(3):1–5.

54. Pershad J, Gilmore B. Serial bedside emergency ultrasound in a case of pediatric blunt abdominal trauma with severe abdominal pain. *Pediatr Emerg Care* 2000;16(5):375–376.

55. Pieretti-Vanmarcke R, Vehmahos GC, Nance ML, et al. Clinical clearance of the cervical spine in blunt trauma patients younger than 3 years: a multi-center study of the American Association for the Surgery of Trauma. *J Trauma* 2009;67:543–550.

56. Pigula FA, Wald SL, Shackford SR, et al. The effect of hypotension and hypoxia on children with severe head injuries. *J Pediatr Surg* 1993;28:310–316.

57. Pressley J, Barlow B, Durkin M, et al. A national program for injury prevention in children and adolescents: the Injury Free Coalition for Kids. *J Urban Health* 2005;82:389–402.

58. Puntnam-Hornstein E: Report of maltreatment as a risk factor for injury death: a prospective birth cohort. *Child Maltreatment* 2011;16:163–174.

59. Rana AR, Drogonowski R, Breckner G, et al. Traumatic cervical spine injuries: characteristics of missed injuries. *J Pediatr Surg* 2009;44: 151–155.

60. Retzlaff T, Hirsch W, Till H, et al. Is sonography reliable for the diagnosis of pediatric blunt abdominal trauma? *J Pediatr Surg* 2010;45(5):912–915.

61. Rice HE, Frush DP, Farmer D, et al., APSA Education Committee. Review of radiation risks from computed tomography: essentials for the pediatric surgeon. *J Pediatr Surg* 2007;42:603–607.

62. Rogers CG, Knight V, MacUra KJ. High-grade renal injuries in children—is conservative management possible? *Urology* 2004;64: 574–579.

63. Rothrock SG, Pagane J. Pediatric rapid sequence intubation incidence of reflex bradycardia and effects of pretreatment with atropine. *Pediatr Emerg Care* 2005;21(9):637–638.

64. Sasser SM, Hunt RC, Faul M, et al. Guidelines for field triage of injured patients: recommendations of the National Expert Panel on Field Triage. *Morb Mortal Wkly Rep* 2012;61(RR-1): 1–21.

65. Scaife ER, Rollins MD, Barnhart D, et al. The role of focused abdominal sonography for trauma (FAST) in pediatric trauma evaluation. *J Ped Surg* 2013;48:1377–1383.

66. Schwaitzberg SD, Bergman KS, Harris BW. A pediatric trauma model of continuous hemorrhage. *J Pediatr Surg* 1988;23:605–609.

67. Soudack M, Epelman M, Maor R, et al. Experience with focused abdominal sonography for trauma (FAST) in 313 pediatric patients. *J Clin Ultrasound* 2004;32(2):53–61.

68. Soundappan SV, Holland AJ, Cass DT, et al. Diagnostic accuracy of surgeon-performed focused abdominal sonography (FAST) in blunt paediatric trauma. *Injury* 2005;36(8): 970–975.

69. Stylianos S. Compliance with evidence-based guidelines in children with isolated spleen or liver injury: a prospective study. *J Pediatr Surg* 2002;37:453–456.

70. Tepas JJ, DiScala C, Ramenofsky ML, et al. Mortality and head injury: the pediatric perspective. *J Pediatr Surg* 1990;25:92–96.

71. Tepas JJ, Ramenofsky ML, Mollitt DL, et al. The Pediatric Trauma Score as a predictor of injury severity: an objective assessment. *J Trauma* 1988;28:425–429.

72. Tollefsen WW, Chapman J, Frakes M, et al. Endotracheal tube cuff pressures in pediatric patients intubated before aeromedical transport. *Pediatr Emerg Care* 2010 May;26(5):361–363.

73. Tourtier JP, Auroy Y, Borne M, et al. Focused assessment with sonography in trauma as a triage tool. *J Pediatr Surg* 2010;45(4):849; author reply 849.

74. Van der Sluis CK, Kingma J, Eisma WH, et al. Pediatric polytrauma: short-term and long-term outcomes. *J Trauma* 1997;43(3):501–506.

75. Weiss M, Dullenkopf A, Fischer JE, et al., European Paediatric Endotracheal Intubation Study Group. Prospective randomized controlled multi-centre trial of cuffed or uncuffed endotracheal tubes in small children. *Br J Anaesth* 2009;103(6):867–873.

11 GERIATRIC TRAUMA

When managing geriatric patients with trauma, the effects of aging on physiological function and the impact of preexisting conditions and medications cannot be overemphasized.

CHAPTER 11 OUTLINE

OBJECTIVES

After reading this chapter and comprehending the knowledge components of the ATLS provider course, you will be able to:

1. Explain the physiological changes that occur with aging and how they affect geriatric injury and the patient's response to trauma.

2. Identify mechanisms of injury commonly encountered in older adult patients.

3. Describe the primary survey with resuscitation and management of critical injuries in geriatric patients by using the ABCDE principles of ATLS.

4. Discuss the unique features of specific types of injury seen in the elderly, such as rib fractures, traumatic brain injury, and pelvic fractures.

5. Identify common causes and signs of elder maltreatment, and formulate a strategy for managing situations of elder maltreatment.

early every country in the world is experiencing a growth in the proportion of older people in their population. Older adults comprise the fastest-growing segment of the United States' population. In fact, by 2050 almost one-half of the world's population will live in a country where at least 20% of the population is older than 60 years, and one-fourth will live in a country where older people comprise more than 30% of the population.

Aging of the population is expected to be one of the most significant social transformations of the 21st century. This generation will live longer than the preceding one and will have access to high-quality health care. In addition, the ever-increasing mobility and active lifestyles of today's elderly individuals places them at increased risk for serious injury. Injury is now the fifth leading cause of death in the elderly population.

Geriatric trauma patients pose a unique challenge to trauma teams. Although the mechanisms of injury may be similar to those for the younger population, well-established data demonstrates increased mortality with similar severity of injury in older adults. Failure to properly triage elderly trauma patients, even those with critical injuries, may be responsible in part for the attributable mortality. Of course, failure to triage is just one factor that impacts mortality from geriatric trauma. Senescence of organ systems, both anatomically and physiologically, preexisting disease states, and frailty all play a part in placing older adults at higher risk from trauma. Depression, substance abuse, and maltreatment are additional factors to consider, and screening can be accomplished through several different tools. Acceptable outcomes depend upon proper identification of the elderly patient at risk for death and a well-coordinated, frequently multidisciplinary, aggressive therapeutic approach. For these reasons, thorough evaluation of geriatric patients at a trauma center improves their outcomes.

EFFECTS OF AGING AND IMPACT OF PREEXISTING CONDITIONS

Declining cellular function, eventually leading to organ failure, is part of the aging process. Therefore, aging is characterized by impaired adaptive and homeostatic mechanisms that cause an increased susceptibility to the stress of injury. This condition is commonly described as decreased physiologic reserve. Insults commonly tolerated by younger patients can lead to devastating results in elderly patients.

There is a large body of evidence documenting that preexisting conditions (PECs) impact morbidity and mortality. In a recent study, investigators identified five PECs that appeared to influence outcomes in trauma patients: cirrhosis, coagulopathy, chronic obstructive pulmonary disease (COPD), ischemic heart disease, and diabetes mellitus. In the study of more than 3,000 patients, one-fourth of individuals over the age of 65 years had one of these five PECs. Patients with one or more of these conditions were nearly two times more likely to die than those without PECs. The same researchers reported on the interaction between injury and host factors, which included age, gender, and PECs (■ FIGURE 11-1). Although injury severity was the primary

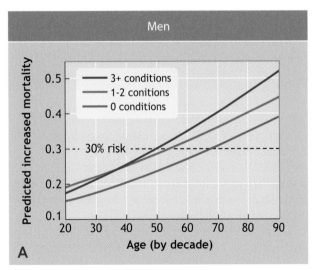
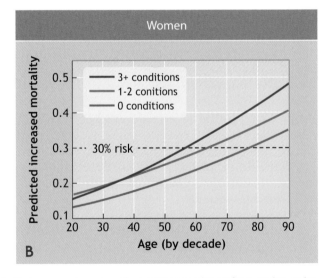

■ FIGURE 11-1 Risk of mortality-associated geriatric complications or death, by age and number of preexisting conditions for **A.** Males, and **B.** Females. Note the risk of death increases with an increasing number of preexisting conditions and age. Source: Adapted with permission from Min L, Burruss, S, Morley E, et al. A simple clinical risk nomogram to predict mortality-associated geriatric complications in severely injured geriatric patients. *J Trauma Acute Care Surg* 2013;74(4):1125–1132. Copyright © 2013 Lippincott Williams & Wilkins.

determinant of mortality, host factors also played a significant role.

MECHANISM OF INJURY

Common mechanisms of injury encountered in older patients include falls, motor vehicle crashes, burns, and penetrating injuries.

FALLS

The risk of falling increases with age, and falls are the most common mechanism of fatal injury in the elderly population. Nonfatal falls are more common in women, and fractures are more common in women who fall. Falls are the most common cause of traumatic brain injury (TBI) in the elderly. Nearly one-half of deaths associated with ground-level falls are a result of TBI. One-half of elderly patients suffering a hip fracture will no longer be able to live independently. Risk factors for falls include advanced age, physical impairments, history of a previous fall, medication use, dementia, unsteady gait, and visual, cognitive, and neurological impairments. Environmental factors, such as loose rugs, poor lighting, and slippery or uneven surfaces, play an additional role in fall risk.

MOTOR VEHICLE CRASHES

In general, older people drive fewer total miles, on more familiar roads, and at lower speeds than younger drivers. They also tend to drive during the day. Thus most of the elderly traffic fatalities occur in the daytime and on weekends, and they typically involve other vehicles. Contributing risk factors in the elderly for motor vehicle crashes include slower reaction times, a larger blind spot, limited cervical mobility, decreased hearing, and cognitive impairment. Additionally, medical problems such as myocardial infarction, stroke, and dysrhythmias can result in conditions that precipitate a collision.

BURNS

Burn injury can be particularly devastating in elderly patients. The impact of age on burn mortality has long been recognized; however, despite significant declining mortality in younger age groups, the mortality associated with small- to moderate-sized burns in older adults remains high. In examining deaths

from structural fires, researchers find the elderly are particularly at risk because of decreased reaction times, impaired hearing and vision, and the inability to escape the burning structure. Spilled hot liquids on the leg, which in a younger patient may re-epithelialize due to an adequate number of hair follicles, will result in a full-thickness burn in older patients with a paucity of follicles. Their aging organ systems have a major impact on the outcomes of elderly burn patients; changes in the skin are obvious, but the patient's inability to meet the physiological demands associated with burn injury likely has the most influence on outcome and survival.

PENETRATING INJURIES

By far, blunt trauma is the predominant mechanism of injury in older adults; however, a significant number of people over the age of 65 years are victims of penetrating injury. In fact, penetrating injury is the fourth most common cause of traumatic death in individuals 65 years and older. Many deaths associated with gunshot wounds are related to intentional self-harm or suicide.

PRIMARY SURVEY WITH RESUSCITATION

As with all trauma patients, the application of ATLS principles in assessment and management of older adults follows the ABCDE methodology. Clinicians must take into consideration the effects of aging on organ systems and their implications for care, as outlined in ■ TABLE 11-1. (Also see *Effects of Aging on MyATLS mobile app.*)

AIRWAY

The elderly airway poses specific challenges for providers. Given that older adults have significant loss of protective airway reflexes, timely decision making for establishing a definitive airway can be lifesaving. Patients may have dentures that may loosen and obstruct the airway. If the dentures are not obstructing the airway, leave them in place during bag-mask ventilation, as this improves mask fit. Some elderly patients are edentulous, which makes intubating easier but bag-mask ventilation more difficult. Arthritic changes may make mouth opening and cervical spine management difficult (■ FIGURE 11-2). When performing rapid sequence intubation, reduce

TABLE II-I EFFECTS OF AGING ON ORGAN SYSTEMS AND IMPLICATIONS FOR CARE

ORGAN SYSTEM	FUNCTIONAL CHANGES	IMPLICATIONS FOR CARE
Cardiac	• Declining function • Decreased sensitivity to catecholamines • Decreased myocyte mass • Atherosclerosis of coronary vessels • Increased afterload • Fixed cardiac output • Fixed heart rate (β-blockers)	• Lack of "classic" response to hypovolemia • Risk for cardiac ischemia • Increased risk of dysrythmias • Elevated baseline blood pressure
Pulmonary	• Thoracic kyphoscoliosis • Decreased transverse thoracic diameter • Decreased elastic recoil • Reduced functional residual capacity • Decreased gas exchange • Decreased cough reflex • Decreased mucociliary function • Increased oropharyngeal colonization	• Increased risk for respiratory failure • Increased risk for pneumonia • Poor tolerance to rib fractures
Renal	• Loss of renal mass • Decreased glomerular filtration rate (GFR) • Decreased sensitivity to antidiuretic hormone (ADH) and aldosterone	• Routine renal labs will be normal (not reflective of dysfunction) • Drug dosing for renal insufficiency • Decreased ability to concentrate urine • Urine flow may be normal with hypovolemia • Increased risk for acute kidney injury
Skin/Soft Tissue/ Musculoskeletal	• Loss of lean body mass • Osteoporosis • Changes in joints and cartilages • Degenerative changes (including c-spine) • Loss of skin elastin and subcutaneous fat	• Increased risk for fractures • Decreased mobility • Difficulty for oral intubation • Risk of skin injury due to immobility • Increased risk for hypothermia • Challenges in rehabilitation
Endocrine	• Decreased production and response to thyroxin • Decreased dehydroepiandrosterone (DHEA)	• Occult hypothyroidism • Relative hypercortisone state • Increased risk of infection

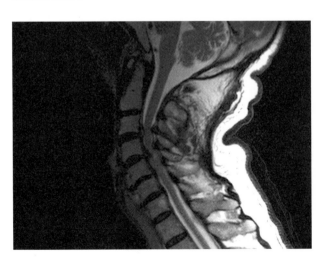

■ FIGURE 11-2 Arthritic changes can complicate airway and cervical spine management. This sagittal T2-weighted image shows severe multilevel degenerative changes affecting disk spaces and posterior elements, associated with severe central canal stenosis, cord compression, and small foci of myelomalacia at the C4-C5 level.

the doses of barbiturates, benzodiazepines, and other sedatives to between 20% and 40% to minimize the risk of cardiovascular depression.

Key physiological changes and management considerations of concern to airway assessment and management are listed in ■ TABLE 11-2.

BREATHING

Changes in the compliance of the lungs and chest wall result in increased work of breathing with aging. This alteration places the elderly trauma patient at high risk for respiratory failure. Because aging causes a suppressed heart rate response to hypoxia, respiratory failure may present insidiously in older adults. Interpreting clinical and laboratory information can be difficult in the face of preexisting respiratory disease or non-pathological changes in ventilation associated with age. Frequently, decisions to secure a patient's airway and provide mechanical ventilation may be made before fully appreciating underlying premorbid respiratory conditions.

Key physiological changes and management considerations in assessing and managing of breathing and ventilation are listed in ■ TABLE 11-3.

CIRCULATION

Age-related changes in the cardiovascular system place the elderly trauma patient at significant risk for

being inaccurately categorized as hemodynamically normal. Since the elderly patient may have a fixed heart rate and cardiac output, response to hypovolemia will involve increasing systemic vascular resistance. Furthermore, since many elderly patients have preexisting hypertension, a seemingly acceptable blood pressure may truly reflect a relative hypotensive state. Recent research identifies a systolic blood pressure of 110 mm Hg to be utilized as threshold for identifying hypotension in adults over 65 years of age.

It is critical to identify patients with significant tissue hypoperfusion. Several methodologies have been and continue to be used in making this diagnosis. These include base deficit, serum lactate, shock index, and tissue-specific end points. Resuscitation of geriatric patients with hypoperfusion is the same as for all other patients and is based on appropriate fluid and blood administration.

The elderly trauma patient with evidence of circulatory failure should be assumed to be bleeding. Consider the early use of advanced monitoring (e.g., central venous pressure [CVP], echocardiography and ultrasonography) to guide optimal resuscitation, given the potential for preexisting cardiovascular disease. In addition, clinicians need to recognize that a physiological event (e.g., stroke, myocardial infarction, dysrhythmia) may have triggered the incident leading to injury.

Key physiological changes and management considerations in the assessment and management of circulation are listed in ■ TABLE 11-4.

TABLE 11-2 PHYSIOLOGICAL CHANGES AND MANAGEMENT CONSIDERATIONS: AIRWAY

PHYSIOLOGICAL CHANGES WITH AGING	MANAGEMENT CONSIDERATIONS
• Arthritic changes in mouth and cervical spine • Macroglossia • Decreased protective reflexes	• Edentulousness • Use appropriately sized laryngoscope and tubes. • Place gauze between gums and cheek to achieve seal when using bag-mask ventilation. • Ensure appropriate dosing of rapid sequence intubation medications.

TABLE 11-3 PHYSIOLOGICAL CHANGES AND MANAGEMENT CONSIDERATIONS: BREATHING

PHYSIOLOGICAL CHANGES WITH AGING	MANAGEMENT CONSIDERATIONS
• Increased kyphoscoliosis • Decreased functional residual capacity (FRC) • Decreased gas exchange • Decreased cough reflex • Decreased mucociliary clearance from airways	• Limited respiratory reserve; identify respiratory failure early. • Manage rib fractures expeditiously. • Ensure appropriate application of mechanical ventilation.

TABLE II-4 PHYSIOLOGICAL CHANGES AND MANAGEMENT CONSIDERATIONS: CIRCULATION

PHYSIOLOGICAL CHANGES WITH AGING	MANAGEMENT CONSIDERATIONS
• Preexisting cardiac disease or hypertension • Lack of a "classic response" to hypovolemia • Likelihood of cardiac medications	• Look for evidence of tissue hypoperfusion. • Administer balanced resuscitation and blood transfusion early for obvious shock. • Use advanced monitoring as necessary and on a timely basis.

PITFALL	PREVENTION
Failure to recognize shock	• Do not equate blood pressure with shock. • Recognize the likelihood of preexisting hypertension and, when possible, obtain medical history. • Use serum markers such as lactate and base deficit to evaluate for evidence of shock. • Use noninvasive studies such as echocardiography to assess global function and volume status. • Recognize the potential for increased blood loss from soft-tissue injuries and pelvic and long-bone fractures.

DISABILITY

Traumatic brain injury (TBI) is a problem of epidemic proportion in the elderly population. Aging causes the dura to become more adherent to the skull, thereby increasing the risk of epidural hematoma with injury. Additionally, older patients are more commonly prescribed anticoagulant and antiplatelet medications for preexisting medical conditions. These two factors place the elderly individual at high risk for intracranial hemorrhage. Atherosclerotic disease is common with aging and may contribute to primary or secondary brain injury. Moderate cerebral atrophy may permit intracranial pathology to initially present with a normal neurological examination. Degenerative disease of the spine places elderly patients at risk for fractures and spinal cord injury with low kinetic ground-level falls. The early identification and timely, appropriate support—including correction of therapeutic anticoagulation—can improve outcomes in elderly patients.

Key physiological changes and management considerations of concern to assessment and management of disability are listed in ■ TABLE 11-5.

EXPOSURE AND ENVIRONMENT

Musculoskeletal changes associated with the aging process present unique concerns during this aspect of the initial assessment of the elderly trauma patient. Loss of subcutaneous fat, nutritional deficiencies, chronic medical conditions, and preexisting medical therapies place elderly patients at risk for hypothermia and the complications of immobility (pressure injuries and delirium). Rapid evaluation and, when possible, early liberation from spine boards and cervical collars will minimize the complications.

Key physiological changes and management considerations concerning exposure and environment are listed in ■ TABLE 11-6.

SPECIFIC INJURIES

Specific injuries common in the elderly population include rib fractures, traumatic brain injury, and pelvic fractures.

TABLE II-5 PHYSIOLOGICAL CHANGES AND MANAGEMENT CONSIDERATIONS: DISABILITY

PHYSIOLOGICAL CHANGES WITH AGING	MANAGEMENT CONSIDERATIONS
• Cerebral atrophy • Degenerative spine disease • Presence of preexisting neurological or psychiatric disease	• Liberally use CT imaging to identify brain and spine injuries. • Ensure early reversal of anticoagulant and/or antiplatelet therapy.

TABLE 11-6 PHYSIOLOGICAL CHANGES AND MANAGEMENT CONSIDERATIONS: EXPOSURE AND ENVIRONMENT	
PHYSIOLOGICAL CHANGES WITH AGING	**MANAGEMENT CONSIDERATIONS**
• Loss of subcutaneous fat • Loss of skin elasticity • Arthritic skeletal changes • Nutritional deficiencies	• Perform early evaluation and liberate patients from spine boards and cervical collars as soon as possible. • Pad bony prominences when needed. • Prevent hypothermia.

RIB FRACTURES

Elderly patients are at increased risk for rib fractures due to anatomical changes of the chest wall and loss of bone density. The most common cause of rib fractures is a ground-level fall, followed by motor vehicle crashes. The primary complication in elderly patients with rib fractures is pneumonia. In the elderly population, the incidence of pneumonia can be as high as 30%. Mortality risk increases with each additional rib fractured.

The main objectives of treatment are pain control and pulmonary hygiene. Pain management can include oral medication, intravenous medications, transdermal

PITFALL	PREVENTION
Respiratory failure develops following fall with rib fractures.	• Recognize the potential for pulmonary deterioration in elderly patients with rib fractures. • Provide effective analgesia. • Ensure adequate pulmonary toilet. • Recognize the patient's comorbid conditions and their impact on the response to injury and medications.
Patient develops delirium after receiving long-acting narcotic dose.	• Obtain medication history and note potential interactions. • Use smaller doses of shorter-acting narcotics when needed. • Consider non-narcotic alternatives. • Use transdermal local anesthetics, blocks, or epidurals when possible.

medications, or regional anesthetics. Narcotic administration in elderly patients must be undertaken cautiously and only in the proper environment for close patient monitoring. Avoiding untoward effects, particularly respiratory depression and delirium, is of paramount importance.

TRAUMATIC BRAIN INJURY

There is overwhelming evidence to suggest that the geriatric population is at highest risk for TBI-associated morbidity and mortality. This increased mortality is not necessarily related to the magnitude of the injury, but rather to the elderly patient's inability to recover. To date there are few recommendations on age-specific management of TBI. Delirium, dementia, and depression can be difficult to distinguish from the signs of brain injury. Management of elderly patients with TBI who are undergoing anticoagulant and/or antiplatelet therapy is particularly challenging, and the mortality of these patients is higher.

Liberal use of CT scan for diagnosis is particularly important in elderly patients, as preexisting cerebral atrophy, dementia, and cerebral vascular accidents make the clinical diagnosis of traumatic brain injury difficult. Additionally, aggressive and early reversal of anticoagulant therapy may improve outcome. This result may be accomplished rapidly with the use of prothrombin complex concentrate (PCC), plasma, and vitamin K. Standard measures of coagulation status may not be abnormal in patients taking newer anticoagulants. Unfortunately, specific reversal agents are not yet available for many of the newer direct thrombin and anti-Xa inhibitors, and a normal coagulation status may be difficult to achieve. (See Table 6-5 Anticoagulant Management in *Chapter 6*.)

PELVIC FRACTURES

Pelvic fractures in the elderly population most commonly result from ground-level falls. As patients age, the incidence of osteoporosis increases linearly; most individuals over the age of 60 have some degree of osteoporosis. Mortality from pelvic fracture is four times higher in older patients than in a younger cohort. The need for blood transfusion, even for seemingly stable fractures, is significantly higher than that seen in a younger population. Older adults also have a much longer hospital stay and are less likely to return to an independent lifestyle following discharge. Fall prevention is the mainstay of reducing the mortality associated with pelvic fractures.

SPECIAL CIRCUMSTANCES

Special circumstances that require consideration in the treatment of elderly trauma patients include medications, maltreatment, and establishing goals of care.

MEDICATIONS

Beta blockers are used in approximately 20% of elderly patients with coronary artery disease and 10% of patients with hypertension. The inherent physiological blockade of the expected response to hypovolemia may provide triage and treatment obstacles. Anticoagulation therapy, antiplatelet therapy, and use of direct thrombin inhibitors pose significant problems for the bleeding patient. Rapidly identifying the type of drug and then instituting a reversal agent (if one is available) may save the patient's life.

ELDER MALTREATMENT

When evaluating an injured elderly patient, team members should consider the possibility of maltreatment. Maltreatment is defined as any willful infliction of injury, unreasonable confinement, intimidation, or cruel punishment that results in physical harm, pain, mental anguish, or other willful deprivation by a caretaker of goods or services that are necessary to avoid physical harm, mental anguish, or mental illness. Maltreatment of the elderly may be as common as child maltreatment.

Elder maltreatment can be divided into six categories:

1. Physical maltreatment
2. Sexual maltreatment
3. Neglect
4. Psychological maltreatment
5. Financial and material exploitation
6. Violation of rights

Often, several types of maltreatment occur simultaneously. Multifaceted in cause, elder maltreatment often is unrecognized and underreported. Signs of maltreatment can be subtle (e.g., poor hygiene and dehydration) and go undetected. Physical maltreatment occurs in up to 14% of geriatric trauma admissions, resulting in a higher mortality than in younger patients.

Physical findings suggesting elder maltreatment are listed in ■ BOX 11-1.

The presence of physical findings suggesting maltreatment should prompt a detailed history. If the history conflicts with the physical findings or reveals an intentional delay in treatment, immediately report the findings to appropriate authorities for further investigation. If maltreatment is suspected or confirmed, take appropriate action, including removal of the elderly patient from the abusive situation. According to the National Center on Elder Abuse, more than 1 in 10 older adults may experience some type of maltreatment, but only 1 in 5 or fewer of those cases are reported. A multidisciplinary approach is required to address the components of care for victims of elder maltreatment.

ESTABLISHING GOALS OF CARE

Trauma is the fifth leading cause of death in patients over the age of 65. Among trauma patients, the elderly

---

BOX II-I PHYSICAL FINDINGS SUGGESTIVE OF ELDER MALTREATMENT

- Contusions affecting the inner arms, inner thighs, palms, soles, scalp, ear (pinna), mastoid area, buttocks
- Multiple and clustered contusions
- Abrasions to the axillary area (from restraints) or the wrist and ankles (from ligatures)
- Nasal bridge and temple injury (from being struck while wearing eyeglasses)
- Periorbital ecchymoses
- Oral injury
- Unusual alopecia pattern
- Untreated pressure injuries or ulcers in non-lumbosacral areas
- Untreated fractures
- Fractures not involving the hip, humerus, or vertebra
- Injuries in various stages of evolution
- Injuries to the eyes or nose
- Contact burns and scalds
- Scalp hemorrhage or hematoma

comprise only 12% of the overall population; but strikingly, they account for nearly 30% of deaths due to trauma. Without question, advancing age contributes to increased morbidity and mortality. Preexisting medical diseases may accompany the aging physiology. A patient-centered approach to care should include early discussion with the patient and family regarding goals of care and treatment decisions. In the trauma setting, it is important to have early and open dialogue to encourage communication. Many patients have already discussed their wishes regarding life-sustaining therapies before the acute event occurs. Early consultation with palliative care services may be helpful in determining limitations in care, as well as effective palliative approaches to ease the patient's symptoms.

TEAMWORK

- Trauma teams are increasingly managing trauma in the elderly population.

- Because of preexisting medical conditions and the potential complications of anticoagulant and antiplatelet drug therapy, successful management of geriatric trauma remains challenging. A trauma team with an understanding of the unique anatomical and physiological changes related to aging can have a positive impact on patient outcome.

- Early activation of the trauma team may be required for elderly patients who do not meet traditional criteria for activation. A simple injury, such as an open tibia fracture, in a frail elderly person may quickly become life-threatening.

- The effect of cardiac drugs, such as beta blockers, may blunt the typical physiological response to hemorrhage, making interpretation of traditional vital signs difficult. The team member responsible for managing circulation must ensure that the team leader is made aware of even minor changes in physiological parameters, and he or she should assess for perfusion status to promptly identify and manage catastrophic hemorrhage.

- The outcomes for elderly trauma patients are often poor. The team leader must consider patients' advanced directives and recognize the patient's goals of care. Often, members of the team provide opinions or

suggestions that may be helpful in caring for patients in these difficult situations.

CHAPTER SUMMARY

1. Older adults are the fastest growing segment of the population. Trauma providers will see an increasing number of elderly injured.

2. The elderly patient presents unique challenges for the trauma team. The influence of changes in anatomy and physiology, as well as the impact of pre-existing medical conditions, will influence outcomes.

3. Common mechanisms of injury include falls, motor vehicle crashes, burns, and penetrating injuries.

4. The primary survey sequence and resuscitation are the same as for younger adults; however, the unique anatomy and physiology of older patients will influence timing, magnitude, and end-points.

5. Common injuries in the elderly include rib fractures, traumatic brain injury, and pelvic fractures. Understanding the impact of aging and the influences on pitfalls seen with these injuries will result in better outcomes.

6. The impact of medications, elderly maltreatment, and understanding the goals of care are unique features of trauma care of the elderly patient. Early identification will influence care and outcomes.

BIBLIOGRAPHY

1. American College of Surgeons, Committee on Trauma, National Trauma Data Bank (NTDB). http://www.facs.org/trauma/ntdb. Accessed May 12, 2016.
2. Braver ER, Trempel RE. Are older drivers actually at higher risk of involvement in collisions resulting in deaths or nonfatal injuries among their passengers and other road users? *Inj Prev* 2004;10:27–29.
3. Bulger EM, Arenson MA, Mock CN, et al. Rib fractures in the elderly. *J Trauma* 2000;48: 1040–1046.
4. Li C, Friedman B, Conwell Y, et al. Validity of the Patient Health Questionnaire-2 (PHQ-2) in

identifying major depression in older people. *J Am Geriatr Soc* 2007 April;55(4):596–602.

5. Milzman DP, Rothenhaus TC. Resuscitation of the geriatric patient. *Emerg Med Clin of NA*. 1996; 14:233–244.

6. Min L, Burruss S, Morley E, et al. A simple clinical risk nomogram to predict mortality-associated geriatric complications in severely injured geriatric patients *J Trauma* 74(4):1125–1132. Copyright © 2013 Lippincott Williams & Wilkins.

7. Oyetunji TA, Chang DC, et al. Redefining hypotension in the elderly: normotension is not reassuring. *Arch Surg*. 2011 Jul ;146(7):865-9.

8. Romanowski KS, Barsun A, Pamlieri TL, et al. Frailty score on admission predicts outcomes in elderly burn injury. *J Burn Care Res* 2015;36:1–6.

9. Stevens JA. Fatalities and injuries from falls among older adults—United States 1993-2003 and 2001–2005. *MMWR Morb Mortal Wkly Rep* 2006; 55:1221–1224.

10. Sussman M, DiRusso SM, Sullivan T, et al. Traumatic brain injury in the elderly: increased mortality and worse functional outcome at discharge despite lower injury severity. *J Trauma* 2002; 53:219–224.

11. United Nations, Department of Economic and Social Affairs, Population Division (2015). World Population Ageing.

12. United States Census: http://www.census.gov/ prod/1/pop/p25-1130.pdf . Accessed June 2016.

13. Yelon JA. Geriatric trauma. In Moore EE, Feliciano DV, and Mattox K, eds. *Trauma* 7th ed. McGraw Hill, 2012.

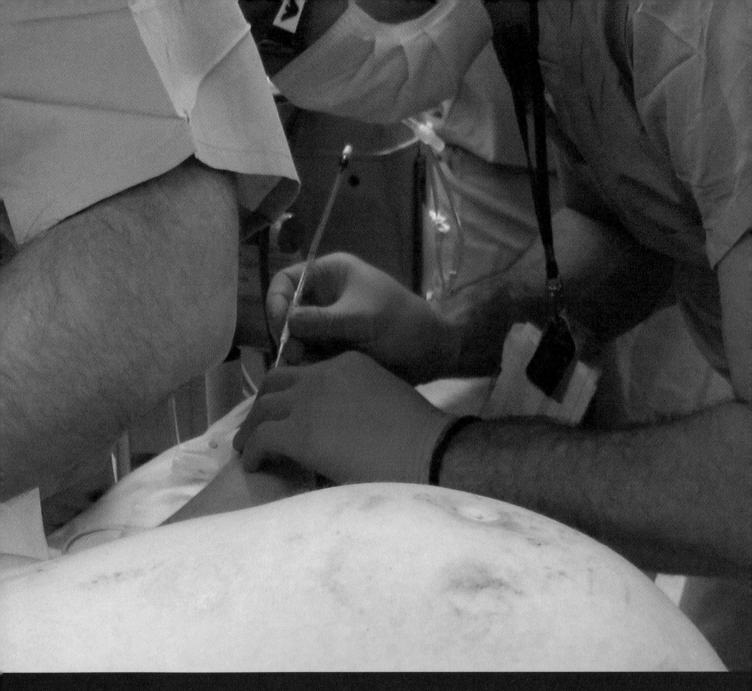

12 TRAUMA IN PREGNANCY AND INTIMATE PARTNER VIOLENCE

Although pregnancy causes alterations in normal physiology and responses to injury and resuscitation, the sequence of the initial assessment and management of pregnant patients remains the same as for all trauma patients.

CHAPTER 12 OUTLINE

OBJECTIVES

After reading this chapter and comprehending the knowledge components of the ATLS provider course, you will be able to:

1. Describe the anatomical and physiological alterations of pregnancy and their impact on patient treatment.

2. Identify common mechanisms of injury in pregnant patients and their fetuses.

3. Outline the treatment priorities and assessment methods for pregnant patients and their fetuses during the primary and secondary surveys, including use of adjuncts.

4. State the indications for operative intervention that are unique to injured pregnant patients.

5. Explain the potential for isoimmunization and the need for immunoglobulin therapy in pregnant trauma patients.

6. Identify patterns of intimate partner violence.

Pregnancy causes major physiological changes and altered anatomical relationships involving nearly every organ system of the body. These changes in structure and function can influence the evaluation of injured pregnant patients by altering the signs and symptoms of injury, approach and responses to resuscitation, and results of diagnostic tests. Pregnancy also can affect the patterns and severity of injury.

Clinicians who treat pregnant trauma patients must remember that there are two patients: mother and fetus. Nevertheless, initial treatment priorities for an injured pregnant patient remain the same as for the nonpregnant patient. The best initial treatment for the fetus is to provide optimal resuscitation of the mother. Every female of reproductive age with significant injuries should be considered pregnant until proven otherwise by a definitive pregnancy test or pelvic ultrasound. Monitoring and evaluation techniques are available to assess the mother and fetus. If x-ray examination is indicated during the pregnant patient's treatment, it should not be withheld because of the pregnancy. A qualified surgeon and an obstetrician should be consulted early in the evaluation of pregnant trauma patients; if not available, early transfer to a trauma center should be considered.

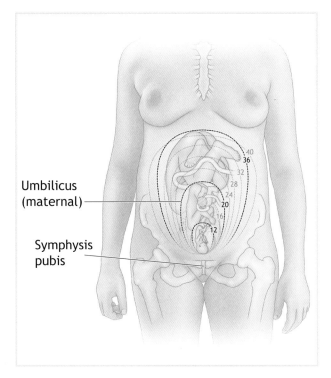

■ FIGURE 12-1 Changes in Fundal Height in Pregnancy. As the uterus enlarges, the bowel is pushed cephalad, so that it lies mostly in the upper abdomen. As a result, the bowel is somewhat protected in blunt abdominal trauma, whereas the uterus and its contents (fetus and placenta) become more vulnerable.

ANATOMICAL AND PHYSIOLOGICAL ALTERATIONS OF PREGNANCY

An understanding of the anatomical and physiological alterations of pregnancy and the physiological relationship between a pregnant patient and her fetus is essential to providing appropriate and effective care to both patients. Such alterations include differences in anatomy, blood volume and composition, and hemodynamics, as well as changes in the respiratory, gastrointestinal, urinary, musculoskeletal, and neurological systems.

ANATOMICAL DIFFERENCES

The uterus remains an intrapelvic organ until approximately the 12th week of gestation, when it begins to rise out of the pelvis. By 20 weeks, the uterus is at the umbilicus, and at 34 to 36 weeks, it reaches the costal margin (■ FIGURE 12-1; also see *Changes in Fundal Height in Pregnancy on MyATLS mobile app*). During the last 2 weeks of gestation, the fundus frequently descends as the fetal head engages the pelvis.

As the uterus enlarges, the intestines are pushed cephalad, so that they lie mostly in the upper abdomen.

As a result, the bowel is somewhat protected in blunt abdominal trauma, whereas the uterus and its contents (fetus and placenta) become more vulnerable. However, penetrating trauma to the upper abdomen during late gestation can result in complex intestinal injury because of this cephalad displacement. Clinical signs of peritoneal irritation are less evident in pregnant women; therefore, physical examination may be less informative. When major injury is suspected, further investigation is warranted.

During the first trimester, the uterus is a thick-walled structure of limited size, confined within the bony pelvis. During the second trimester, it enlarges beyond its protected intrapelvic location, but the small fetus remains mobile and cushioned by a generous amount of amniotic fluid. The amniotic fluid can cause amniotic fluid embolism and disseminated intravascular coagulation following trauma if the fluid enters the maternal intravascular space. By the third trimester, the uterus is large and thin-walled. In the vertex presentation, the fetal head is usually in the pelvis, and the remainder of the fetus is exposed above the pelvic brim. Pelvic fracture(s) in late gestation can result in skull fracture or serious intracranial injury to the fetus. Unlike the elastic myometrium, the placenta has little elasticity. This lack of placental

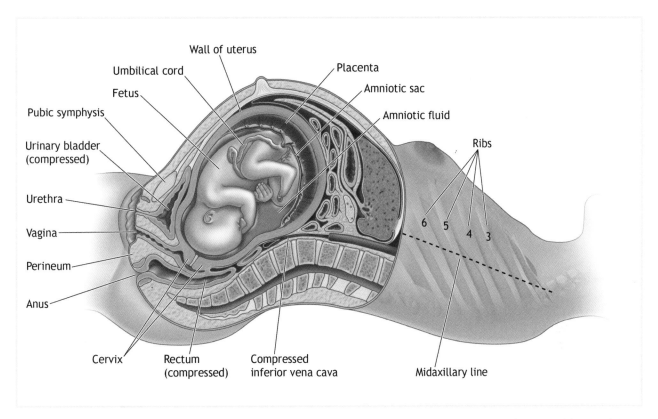

■ **FIGURE 12-2 Full-Term Fetus in Vertex Presentation.** The abdominal viscera are displaced and compressed into the upper abdomen. This results in their relative protection from blunt injury, but increased risk for complex intestinal injury from upper abdominal penetrating injury. Elevation of the diaphragm may require placement of chest tubes through a higher intercostal space.

elastic tissue results in vulnerability to shear forces at the uteroplacental interface, which may lead to abruptio placentae (■ FIGURE 12-2).

The placental vasculature is maximally dilated throughout gestation, yet it is exquisitely sensitive to catecholamine stimulation. An abrupt decrease in maternal intravascular volume can result in a profound increase in uterine vascular resistance, reducing fetal oxygenation despite reasonably normal maternal vital signs.

BLOOD VOLUME AND COMPOSITION

Plasma volume increases steadily throughout pregnancy and plateaus at 34 weeks of gestation. A smaller increase in red blood cell (RBC) volume occurs, resulting in a decreased hematocrit level (i.e., physiological anemia of pregnancy). In late pregnancy, a hematocrit level of 31% to 35% is normal. Healthy pregnant patients can lose 1,200 to 1,500 mL of blood before exhibiting signs and symptoms of hypovolemia. However, this amount of hemorrhage may be reflected by fetal distress, as evidenced by an abnormal fetal heart rate.

The white blood cell (WBC) count increases during pregnancy. It is not unusual to see WBC counts of 12,000/mm³ during pregnancy or as high as 25,000/ mm³ during labor. Levels of serum fibrinogen and other clotting factors are mildly elevated. Prothrombin and partial thromboplastin times may be shortened, but bleeding and clotting times are unchanged. ■ TABLE 12-1 compares normal laboratory values during pregnancy with those for nonpregnant patients. (Also see *Normal Lab Values during Pregnancy on MyATLS mobile app.*)

HEMODYNAMICS

Important hemodynamic factors to consider in pregnant trauma patients include cardiac output, heart rate, blood pressure, venous pressure, and electrocardiographic changes.

Cardiac Output

After the 10th week of pregnancy, cardiac output can increase by 1.0 to 1.5 L/min because of the increase in plasma volume and decrease in vascular resistance of the uterus and placenta, which receive 20% of the patient's cardiac output during the third trimester

TABLE 12-1 NORMAL LABORATORY VALUES: PREGNANT VS. NONPREGNANT

VALUE	PREGNANT	NONPREGNANT
Hematocrit	32%–42%	36%–47%
WBC count	5,000–12,000 μL	4,000–10,000 μL
Arterial pH	7.40–7.45*	7.35–7.45
Bicarbonate	17–22 mEq/L	22–28 mEq/L
$PaCO_2$	25–30 mm Hg (3.3–4.0 kPa)	30–40 mm Hg (4.0–5.33 kPa)
Fibrinogen	400–450 mg/dL (3rd trimester)	150–400 mg/dL
PaO_2	100–108 mm Hg	95–100 mm Hg

* Compensated respiratory alkalosis and diminished pulmonary reserve

of pregnancy. This increased output may be greatly influenced by the mother's position during the second half of pregnancy. In the supine position, vena cava compression can decrease cardiac output by 30% because of decreased venous return from the lower extremities.

Heart Rate

During pregnancy, the heart rate gradually increases to a maximum of 10–15 beats per minute over baseline by the third trimester. This change in heart rate must be considered when interpreting a tachycardic response to hypovolemia.

Blood Pressure

Pregnancy results in a fall of 5 to 15 mm Hg in systolic and diastolic pressures during the second trimester, although blood pressure returns to near-normal levels at term. Some pregnant women exhibit hypotension when placed in the supine position, due to compression of the inferior vena cava. This condition can be corrected by relieving uterine pressure on the inferior vena cava, as described later in this chapter. Hypertension in the pregnant patient may represent preeclampsia if accompanied by proteinuria.

Venous Pressure

The resting central venous pressure (CVP) is variable with pregnancy, but the response to volume is the same as in the nonpregnant state. Venous hypertension in the lower extremities is present during the third trimester.

Electrocardiographic Changes

The axis may shift leftward by approximately 15 degrees. Flattened or inverted T waves in leads III and AVF and the precordial leads may be normal. Ectopic beats are increased during pregnancy.

PITFALL	PREVENTION
Not recognizing the anatomical and physiological changes that occur during pregnancy	• Review physiology in pregnancy during the pretrauma team time-out.

RESPIRATORY SYSTEM

Minute ventilation increases primarily due to an increase in tidal volume. Hypocapnia ($PaCO_2$ of 30 mm Hg) is therefore common in late pregnancy. A $PaCO_2$ of 35 to 40 mm Hg may indicate impending respiratory failure during pregnancy. Anatomical alterations in the thoracic cavity seem to account for the decreased residual volume associated with diaphragmatic elevation, and a chest x-ray reveals increased lung markings and prominence of the pulmonary vessels. Oxygen consumption increases during pregnancy. Thus it is important to maintain and ensure adequate arterial oxygenation when resuscitating injured pregnant patients.

PITFALL	PREVENTION
Failure to recognize that a normal $PaCO_2$ may indicate impending respiratory failure during pregnancy	• Predict the changes in ventilation that occur during pregnancy. • Monitor ventilation in late pregnancy with arterial blood gas values. • Recognize that pregnant patients should be hypocapneic.

In patients with advanced pregnancy, when chest tube placement is required it should be positioned higher to avoid intraabdominal placement given the elevation of the diaphragm. Administer supplemental oxygen to maintain a saturation of 95%. The fetus is very sensitive to maternal hypoxia, and maternal basal oxygen consumption is elevated at baseline.

GASTROINTESTINAL SYSTEM

Gastric emptying is delayed during pregnancy, so early gastric tube decompression may be particularly important to prevent aspiration of gastric contents. The mother's intestines are relocated to the upper part of the abdomen and may be shielded by the uterus. The solid viscera remain essentially in their usual anatomic positions.

URINARY SYSTEM

The glomerular filtration rate and renal blood flow increase during pregnancy, whereas levels of serum creatinine and urea nitrogen fall to approximately one-half of normal pre-pregnancy levels. Glycosuria is common during pregnancy.

MUSCULOSKELETAL SYSTEM

The symphysis pubis widens to 4 to 8 mm, and the sacroiliac joint spaces increase by the seventh month of gestation. These factors must be considered in interpreting x-ray films of the pelvis (■ FIGURE 12-3).

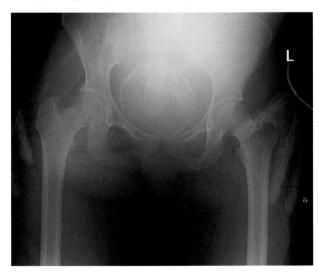

■ **FIGURE 12-3** Radiograph demonstrating fetal head engaged in the pelvis with a normal symphysis pubis and mildly widened right sacroiliac joint.

The large, engorged pelvic vessels surrounding the gravid uterus can contribute to massive retroperitoneal bleeding after blunt trauma with associated pelvic fractures.

NEUROLOGICAL SYSTEM

Eclampsia is a complication of late pregnancy that can mimic head injury. It may be present if seizures occur with associated hypertension, hyperreflexia, proteinuria, and peripheral edema. Expert neurological and obstetrical consultation frequently is helpful in differentiating among eclampsia and other causes of seizures.

PITFALL	PREVENTION
Mistaking eclampsia for head injury	• Obtain a CT of the head to exclude intracranial bleeding. • Maintain a high index of suspicion for eclampsia when seizures are accompanied by hypertension, proteinuria, hyperreflexia, and peripheral edema in pregnant trauma patients.

▶ MECHANISMS OF INJURY

■ **TABLE 12-2** outlines the distribution of mechanisms of injury in pregnancy. Most mechanisms of injury

TABLE 12-2 DISTRIBUTION OF MECHANISMS OF INJURY IN PREGNANCY	
MECHANISM	**PERCENTAGE**
Motor vehicle collision	49
Fall	25
Assault	18
Gunshot wound	4
Burn	1

Source: Chames MC, Pearlman MD. Trauma during pregnancy: outcomes and clinical management. *Clin Obstet Gynecol,* 2008;51:398

TABLE 12-3 DISTRIBUTION OF BLUNT AND PENETRATING ABDOMINAL INJURY IN PREGNANCY

MECHANISM	PERCENTAGE
Blunt	91
Penetrating	9
Gunshot wound	73
Stab wound	23
Shotgun wound	4

Source: Data from Petrone P, Talving P, Browder T, et al. Abdominal injuries in pregnancy: a 155-month study at two level I trauma centers. *Injury*, 2011;42(1):47–49.

are similar to those sustained by nonpregnant patients, but certain differences must be recognized in pregnant patients who sustain blunt or penetrating injury. The distribution of blunt and penetrating abdominal injury in pregnancy is shown in ■ TABLE 12-3.

BLUNT INJURY

The abdominal wall, uterine myometrium, and amniotic fluid act as buffers to direct fetal injury from blunt trauma. The presence of external contusions and abrasions of the abdominal wall, as demonstrated in ■ FIGURE 12-4, are signs of possible blunt uterine injury. Nonetheless, fetal injuries may occur when the abdominal wall strikes an object, such as the dashboard or steering wheel, or when a pregnant patient is struck by a blunt instrument. Indirect injury to the fetus may occur from rapid compression, deceleration, the contrecoup effect, or a shearing force resulting in abruptio placentae.

Compared with restrained pregnant women involved in collisions, unrestrained pregnant women have a higher risk of premature delivery and fetal death. The type of restraint system affects the frequency of uterine rupture and fetal death. Using a lap belt alone allows forward flexion and uterine compression with possible uterine rupture or abruptio placentae. A lap belt worn too high over the uterus may produce uterine rupture because it transmits direct force to the uterus on impact. Using shoulder restraints in conjunction with a lap belt reduces the likelihood of direct and indirect fetal injury, presumably because the shoulder belt dissipates deceleration force over a greater surface area and helps prevent the mother from flexing forward over the gravid uterus. Therefore, in the overall assessment it is important to determine the type of restraint device worn by the pregnant patient, if any. The deployment of airbags in motor vehicles does not appear to increase pregnancy-specific risks.

PENETRATING INJURY

As the gravid uterus grows larger, the other viscera are relatively protected from penetrating injury. However, the likelihood of uterine injury increases. The dense uterine musculature in early pregnancy can absorb a significant amount of energy from penetrating objects, decreasing their velocity and lowering the risk of injury to other viscera. The amniotic fluid and fetus also absorb energy and contribute to slowing of the penetrating object. The resulting low incidence of associated maternal visceral injuries accounts for the generally excellent maternal outcome in cases of penetrating wounds of the gravid uterus. However, fetal outcome is generally poor when there is a penetrating injury to the uterus.

SEVERITY OF INJURY

The severity of maternal injuries determines maternal and fetal outcome. Therefore, treatment methods also depend on the severity of maternal injuries. All pregnant patients with major injuries require admission to a facility with trauma and obstetrical capabilities. Carefully observe pregnant patients with even minor injuries, since occasionally minor injuries are associated with abruptio placentae and fetal loss.

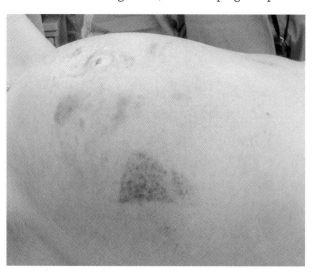

■ FIGURE 12-4 External contusions and abrasions of the abdominal wall are signs of possible blunt uterine trauma.

ASSESSMENT AND TREATMENT

To optimize outcomes for the mother and fetus, clinicians must assess and resuscitate the mother first and then assess the fetus before conducting a secondary survey of the mother.

PRIMARY SURVEY WITH RESUSCITATION

Mother

Ensure a patent airway, adequate ventilation and oxygenation, and effective circulatory volume. If ventilatory support is required, intubate pregnant patients, and consider maintaining the appropriate PCO_2 for her stage of pregnancy (e.g., approximately 30 mm Hg in late pregnancy).

Uterine compression of the vena cava may reduce venous return to the heart, thus decreasing cardiac output and aggravating the shock state. Manually displace the uterus to the left side to relieve pressure on the inferior vena cava. If the patient requires spinal motion restriction in the supine position, logroll her to the left 15–30 degrees (i.e., elevate the right side 4–6 inches), and support with a bolstering device, thus maintaining spinal motion restriction and decompressing the vena cava (■ FIGURE 12-5; also see *Proper Immobilization of a Pregnant Patient on MyATLS mobile app.*)

Because of their increased intravascular volume, pregnant patients can lose a significant amount of blood before tachycardia, hypotension, and other signs of hypovolemia occur. Thus, the fetus may be in

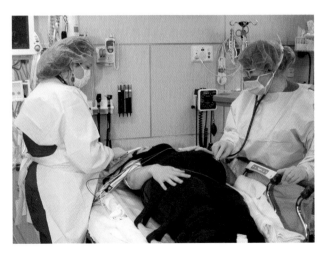

■ FIGURE 12-5 Proper Immobilization of a Pregnant Patient. If the patient requires immobilization in the supine position, the patient or spine board can be logrolled 4 to 6 inches to the left and supported with a bolstering device, thus maintaining spinal precautions and decompressing the vena cava.

distress and the placenta deprived of vital perfusion while the mother's condition and vital signs appear stable. Administer crystalloid fluid resuscitation and early type-specific blood to support the physiological hypervolemia of pregnancy. Vasopressors should be an absolute last resort in restoring maternal blood pressure because these agents further reduce uterine blood flow, resulting in fetal hypoxia. Baseline laboratory evaluation in the trauma patient should include a fibrinogen level, as this may double in late pregnancy; a normal fibrinogen level may indicate early disseminated intravascular coagulation.

PITFALL	PREVENTION
Failure to displace the uterus to the left side in a hypotensive pregnant patient	• Logroll all patients appearing clinically pregnant (i.e., second and third trimesters) to the left 15–30 degrees (elevate the right side 4–6 inches).

Fetus

Abdominal examination during pregnancy is critically important in rapidly identifying serious maternal injuries and evaluating fetal well-being. The main cause of fetal death is maternal shock and maternal death. The second most common cause of fetal death is placental abruption. Abruptio placentae is suggested by vaginal bleeding (70% of cases), uterine tenderness, frequent uterine contractions, uterine tetany, and uterine irritability (uterus contracts when touched; ■ FIGURE 12-6A). In 30% of abruptions following trauma, vaginal bleeding may not occur. Uterine ultrasonography may be helpful in the diagnosis, but it is not definitive. CT scan may also demonstrate abruptio placenta (■ FIGURE 12-6A and C) Late in pregnancy, abruption may occur following relatively minor injuries.

Uterine rupture, a rare injury, is suggested by findings of abdominal tenderness, guarding, rigidity, or rebound tenderness, especially if there is profound shock. Frequently, peritoneal signs are difficult to appreciate in advanced gestation because of expansion and attenuation of the abdominal wall musculature. Other abnormal findings suggestive of uterine rupture include abdominal fetal lie (e.g., oblique or transverse lie), easy palpation of fetal parts because of their extrauterine location, and inability to readily palpate the uterine fundus when there is fundal rupture. X-ray evidence of rupture includes extended fetal extremities, abnormal fetal position, and free intraperitoneal air. Operative exploration may be necessary to diagnose uterine rupture.

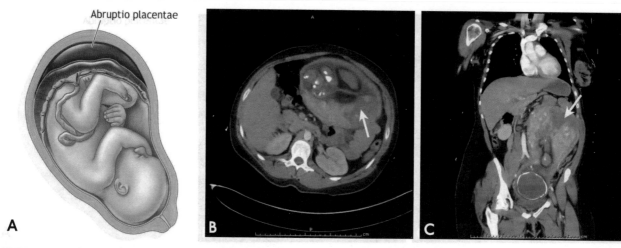

■ FIGURE 12-6 **Abruptio placentae. A.** In abruptio placentae, the placenta detaches from the uterus. **B.** Axial and **C.** Coronal sections of the abdomen and pelvis, demonstrating abruptio placentae.

In most cases of abruptio placentae and uterine rupture, the patient reports abdominal pain or cramping. Signs of hypovolemia can accompany each of these injuries.

Initial fetal heart tones can be auscultated with Doppler ultrasound by 10 weeks of gestation. Perform continuous fetal monitoring with a tocodynamometer beyond 20 to 24 weeks of gestation. Patients with no risk factors for fetal loss should have continuous monitoring for 6 hours, whereas patients with risk factors for fetal loss or placental abruption should be monitored for 24 hours. The risk factors are maternal heart rate > 110, an Injury Severity Score (ISS) > 9, evidence of placental abruption, fetal heart rate > 160 or < 120, ejection during a motor vehicle crash, and motorcycle or pedestrian collisions.

ADJUNCTS TO PRIMARY SURVEY WITH RESUSCITATION

Mother

If possible, the patient should be monitored on her left side after physical examination. Monitor the patient's fluid status to maintain the relative hypervolemia required in pregnancy, as well as pulse oximetry and arterial blood gas determinations. Recognize that maternal bicarbonate normally is low during pregnancy to compensate for respiratory alkalosis.

Fetus

Obtain obstetrical consultation, since fetal distress can occur at any time and without warning. Fetal heart rate is a sensitive indicator of both maternal blood volume status and fetal well-being. Fetal heart tones should be monitored in every injured pregnant woman. The normal range for fetal heart rate is 120 to 160 beats per minute. An abnormal fetal heart rate, repetitive decelerations, absence of accelerations or beat-to-beat variability, and frequent uterine activity can be signs of impending maternal and/or fetal decompensation (e.g., hypoxia and/or acidosis) and should prompt immediate obstetrical consultation. If obstetrical services are not available, arrange transfer to a trauma center with obstetrical capability.

Perform any indicated radiographic studies because the benefits certainly outweigh the potential risk to the fetus.

SECONDARY SURVEY

During the maternal secondary survey, follow the same pattern as for nonpregnant patients, as outlined in Chapter 1: Initial Assessment and Management. Indications for abdominal computed tomography, focused assessment with sonography for trauma (FAST), and diagnostic peritoneal lavage (DPL) are also the same. However, if DPL is performed, place the catheter above the umbilicus using the open technique. Be alert to the presence of uterine contractions, which suggest early labor, and tetanic contractions, which suggest placental abruption.

Evaluation of the perineum includes a formal pelvic examination, ideally performed by a clinician skilled in obstetrical care. The presence of amniotic fluid in the vagina, evidenced by a pH of greater than 4.5, suggests ruptured chorioamniotic membranes. Note the cervical effacement and dilation, fetal presentation, and relationship of the fetal presenting part to the ischial spines.

Because vaginal bleeding in the third trimester may indicate disruption of the placenta and impending death of the fetus, a vaginal examination is vital. However, repeated vaginal examinations should be avoided. The decision regarding an emergency cesarean section should be made in consultation with an obstetrician.

CT scans can be used for pregnant trauma patients if there is significant concern for intra-abdominal injury. An abdomen/pelvis CT scan radiation dose approaches 25 mGy, and fetal radiation doses less than 50 mGy are not associated with fetal anomalies or higher risk for fetal loss.

Admission to the hospital is mandatory for pregnant patients with vaginal bleeding, uterine irritability, abdominal tenderness, pain or cramping, evidence of hypovolemia, changes in or absence of fetal heart tones, and/or leakage of amniotic fluid. Care should be provided at a facility with appropriate fetal and maternal monitoring and treatment capabilities. The fetus may be in jeopardy, even with apparently minor maternal injury.

DEFINITIVE CARE

Obtain obstetrical consultation whenever specific uterine problems exist or are suspected. With extensive placental separation or amniotic fluid embolization, widespread intravascular clotting may develop, causing depletion of fibrinogen, other clotting factors, and platelets. This consumptive coagulopathy can emerge rapidly. In the presence of life-threatening amniotic fluid embolism and/or disseminated intravascular coagulation, immediately perform uterine evacuation and replace platelets, fibrinogen, and other clotting factors, if necessary.

As little as 0.01 mL of Rh-positive blood will sensitize 70% of Rh-negative patients. Although a positive Kleihauer-Betke test (a maternal blood smear allowing detection of fetal RBCs in the maternal circulation) indicates fetomaternal hemorrhage, a negative test does not exclude minor degrees of fetomaternal hemorrhage that are capable of isoimmunizing the Rh-negative mother. All pregnant Rh-negative trauma patients

should receive Rh immunoglobulin therapy unless the injury is remote from the uterus (e.g., isolated distal extremity injury). Immunoglobulin therapy should be instituted within 72 hours of injury.

■ TABLE 12-4 summarizes care of injured pregnant patients.

PERIMORTEM CESAREAN SECTION

Limited data exists to support perimortem cesarean section in pregnant trauma patients who experience hypovolemic cardiac arrest. Remember, fetal distress can be present when the mother has no hemodynamic abnormalities, and progressive maternal instability compromises fetal survival. At the time of maternal hypovolemic cardiac arrest, the fetus already has suffered prolonged hypoxia. For other causes of maternal cardiac arrest, perimortem cesarean section occasionally may be successful if performed within 4 to 5 minutes of the arrest.

INTIMATE PARTNER VIOLENCE

Intimate partner violence is a major cause of injury to women during cohabitation, marriage, and pregnancy, regardless of ethnic background, cultural influences, or socioeconomic status. Seventeen percent of injured pregnant patients experience trauma inflicted by another person, and 60% of these patients experience repeated episodes of intimate partner violence. According to estimates from the U.S. Department of Justice, 2 million to 4 million incidents of intimate partner violence occur per year, and almost one-half of all women over their lifetimes are physically and/or psychologically abused in some manner. Worldwide, 10% to 69% of women report having been assaulted by an intimate partner.

Document and report any suspicion of intimate partner violence. These attacks, which represent an increasing number of ED visits, can result in death and disability. Although most victims of intimate partner violence are women, men make up approximately 40% of all reported cases in the United States. Indicators that suggest the presence of intimate partner violence include:

- Injuries inconsistent with the stated history

- Diminished self-image, depression, and/or suicide attempts

PITFALL	PREVENTION
Failure to recognize the need for Rh immunoglobulin therapy in an Rh-negative mother	• Administer Rh immunoglobulin therapy to all injured Rh-negative mothers unless the injury is remote from the uterus (e.g., isolated distal extremity).

TABLE 12-4 TRAUMA IN THE OBSTETRICAL PATIENT: A BEDSIDE TOOL

VITAL SIGNS

Position	Hypotension treatment and prophylaxis > 20 weeks, left lateral decubitus.		
Hypotension	See "Treatments," below.	IV fluids	Transfusion
Hypertension	Criteria: ≥140 systolic, >90 diastolic		Treat: >160 systolic, >110 diastolic
Fetal Uterine Monitoring	>20 weeks; initiate as soon as possible.		
	If unable to offer OB intervention, stabilize and arrange prompt transfer.		
Vaginal Bleeding	Treat hypotension as above, OB consultation, Rh negative gets RhIG.		

LAB (IN ADDITION TO USUAL TRAUMA STUDIES)

CBC	Low hematocrit
Type screen Kleihauer-Betke	Rh-negative
Coagulation Profile	INR, PTT, fibrin degradation, fibrinogen, i-Coombs

DIAGNOSTIC IMAGING

- Order for the same general indications as for nonpregnant patients.
- Coordinate with radiologist and consider ultrasound to replace x-ray when possible.
- Shield abdomen, pelvis, and neck when possible.

TREATMENTS (MEDICATIONS LISTED ARE COMMONLY RECOMMENDED)

IV Fluids	Patients require larger fluid requirements when hypotensive; avoid dextrose (D5) loads.	
Oxygen	To avoid fetal hypoxia, administer high-concentration oxygen.	
Intubation and rapid sequence induction	Indications for procedures are generally similar to nonpregnancy.	
Analgesia	Use as needed, and inform OB of doses and times if fetal delivery is anticipated.	
Antiemetics	metoclopramide	5–10 mg IV or IM
	ondansetron	4–8 mg IV
Antibiotics	Ceftriaxone	1 g IV
	(if penicillin allergy) clindamycin	600 mg IV
Transfusion	CMV antibody—neg	leukocyte—reduced

Continued

TABLE 12-4 TRAUMA IN THE OBSTETRICAL PATIENT: A BEDSIDE TOOL *(continued)*

TREATMENTS (MEDICATIONS LISTED ARE COMMONLY RECOMMENDED)

Rh-negative	RhIG I ampule (300 g) IM	
Tetanus	Td safe	
BP >160 s, >110 d Hypertension	labetalol 10–20 mg IV bolus	
Seizures	Eclamptic	magnesium sulfate 4–6 Gm IV load over 15–20 minutes
	Non-eclamptic	lorazepam 1–2 mg/min IV
CPR ACLS >20 wks	Patient should be in left lateral decubitus position. If no return of spontaneously circulation after 4 minutes of CPR, consider cesarean delivery of viable fetus.	

DISPOSITION

Admission and Monitoring	4 hours fetal monitoring of potentially viable fetus
Discharge	Prompt follow up with OB

Adapted with permission from the American College of Emergency Physicians. Clinical and Practice Management Resources. *Trauma in the Obstetric Patient: A Bedside Tool*, http://www.acep.org. Accessed May 16, 2016.

BOX 12-1 ASSESSMENT OF IMMEDIATE SAFETY SCREENING QUESTIONS

1. Are you in immediate danger?
2. Is your partner at the health facility now?
3. Do you want to (or have to) go home with your partner?
4. Do you have somewhere safe to go?
5. Have there been threats of direct abuse of the children (if s/he has children)?
6. Are you afraid your life may be in danger?
7. Has the violence gotten worse or is it getting scarier? Is it happening more often?
8. Has your partner used weapons, alcohol, or drugs?
9. Has your partner ever held you or your children against your will?
10. Does your partner ever watch you closely, follow you or stalk you?
11. Has your partner ever threatened to kill you, him/herself or your children?

Reprinted with permission from Family Violence Prevention Fund, San Francisco, CA. Copyright 2002.

- Self-abuse and/or self-blame for injuries
- Frequent ED or doctor's office visits
- Symptoms suggestive of substance abuse
- Isolated injuries to the gravid abdomen
- Partner insists on being present for interview and examination and monopolizes discussion

These indicators raise suspicion about the potential for intimate partner violence and should serve to initiate further investigation. The screening questions in ■ BOX 12-1, when asked in a nonjudgmental manner and without the patient's partner being present, can identify many victims of intimate partner violence. Suspected cases of intimate partner violence should be handled through local social service agencies or the state health and human services department.

 TEAMWORK

- The team leader should remind the team of the major anatomical and physiological changes associated with pregnancy that may affect evaluation of the pregnant injured patient.

- The team must remember that, although there are two patients, the team's primary mission is to ensure optimal resuscitation of the mother.

- The team leader should notify the on-call obstetrician and the obstetrics unit of the impending arrival of an injured pregnant patient as soon as possible while continuing to direct the overall resuscitation.

- The team must maintain an appropriately high index of suspicion for the presence of intimate partner violence, carefully documenting all injuries.

CHAPTER SUMMARY

1. Important and predictable anatomical and physiological changes occur during pregnancy and can influence the assessment and treatment of injured pregnant patients. Attention also must be directed toward the fetus, the second patient of this unique duo, after its environment is stabilized. A qualified surgeon and an obstetrician should be consulted early in the evaluation of pregnant trauma patients. If obstetric services are not available, consider early transfer to a trauma center with obstetrical services. agree with edit.

2. The abdominal wall, uterine myometrium, and amniotic fluid act as buffers to direct fetal injury from blunt trauma. As the gravid uterus increases in size, other abdominal viscera are relatively protected from penetrating injury, whereas the likelihood of uterine injury increases.

3. Appropriate volume resuscitation should be given to correct and prevent maternal and fetal hypovolemic shock. Assess and resuscitate the mother first, and then assess the fetus before conducting a secondary survey of the mother.

4. A search should be made for conditions unique to the injured pregnant patient, such as blunt or penetrating uterine trauma, abruptio placentae, amniotic fluid embolism, isoimmunization, and premature rupture of membranes.

5. Minor degrees of fetomaternal hemorrhage are capable of sensitizing the Rh-negative mother. All pregnant Rh-negative trauma patients should receive Rh immunoglobulin therapy unless the injury is remote from the uterus.

6. Presence of indicators that suggest intimate partner violence should serve to initiate further investigation and protection of the victim.

ADDITIONAL RESOURCES CONCERNING INTIMATE PARTNER VIOLENCE

National Coalition Against Domestic Violence, PO Box 18749, Denver, CO 80218-0749; 303-839-1852

https://www.ted.com/talks/leslie_morgan_steiner_why_domestic_violence_victims_don_t_leave

http://phpa.dhmh.maryland.gov/mch/Pages/IPV.aspx

http://www.cdc.gov/violenceprevention/intimate partnerviolence/

http://www.cdc.gov/violenceprevention/pdf/ipv-nisvs-factsheet-v5-a.pdf</arul>

BIBLIOGRAPHY

1. ACEP Clinical Policies Committee and Clinical Policies Subcommittee on Early Pregnancy. American College of Emergency Physicians. Clinical policy: critical issues in the initial evaluation and management of patients presenting to the emergency department in early pregnancy. *Ann Emerg Med* 2003;41:122–133.
2. Adler G, Duchinski T, Jasinska A, et al. Fibrinogen fractions in the third trimester of pregnancy and in puerperium. *Thromb Res* 2000;97:405–410.
3. American College of Emergency Physicians. Clinical and Practice Management Resources. *Trauma in the Obstetric Patient: A Bedside Tool.* http://www.acep.org. Accessed May 16, 2016.
4. American College of Radiology. Practice Parameter. http://www.acr.org/~/media/9e2ed55531fc4b4fa53ef3b6d3b25df8.pdf. Accessed May 17, 2016.
5. Berry MJ, McMurray RG, Katz VL. Pulmonary and ventilatory responses to pregnancy, immersion, and exercise. *J Appl Physiol* 1989;66(2):857–862.
6. Chames MC, Perlman MD. Trauma during pregnancy: outcomes and clinical

management. *Clin Obstet Gynecol* 2008; 51:398.

7. Curet MJ, Schermer CR, Demarest GB, et al. Predictors of outcome in trauma during pregnancy: identification of patients who can be monitored for less than 6 h. *J Trauma* 2000;49:18–25.

8. Eisenstat SA, Sancroft L. Domestic violence. *N Engl J Med* 1999;341:886–892.

9. Family Violence Prevention Fund. (2002). National consensus guidelines on identifying and responding to domestic violence victimization in health care settings. San Francisco, CA: Author. www. endabuse.org/programs/healthcare/files/ Consensus.pdf

10. Feldhaus KM, Koziol-McLain J, Amsbury HL, et al. Accuracy of 3 brief screening questions for detecting partner violence in the emergency department. *JAMA* 1997;277:1357–1361.

11. Goodwin T, Breen M. Pregnancy outcome and fetomaternal hemorrhage after noncatastrophic trauma. *Am J Obstet Gynecol* 1990;162:665–671.

12. Grisso JA, Schwarz DF, Hirschinger N, et al. Violent injuries among women in an urban area. *N Engl J Med* 1999;341:1899–1905.

13. Hamburger KL, Saunders DG, Hovey M. Prevalence of domestic violence in community practice and rate of physician inquiry. *Fam Med* 1992;24:283–287.

14. Hellgren M. Hemostasis during normal pregnancy and puerperium. *Semin Thromb Hemost* 2003;29(2):125–130.

15. Hyde LK, Cook LJ, Olson LM, et al. Effect of motor vehicle crashes on adverse fetal outcomes. *Obstet Gynecol* 2003;102:279–286.

16. Ikossi DG, Lazar AA, Morabito D, et al. Profile of mothers at risk: an analysis of injury and pregnancy loss in 1,195 trauma patients. *J Am Coll Surg* 2005;200:49–56.

17. Intimate Partner Violence Facts. www.who.int/ violence_injury_prevention/violence/world_ report/factsheets/en/ipvfacts.pdf. Accessed May 17, 2016.

18. Jain V, Chari Radha, Maslovitz S, et al. Guidelines for the management of a pregnant trauma patient. *J Obstet Gynaecol Can* 2015;37(6):553–571.

19. Kissinger DP, Rozycki GS, Morris JA, et al. Trauma in pregnancy—predicting pregnancy outcome. *Arch Surg* 1991;125:1079–1086.

20. Klinich KD, Schneider LW, Moore JL et al. Investigations of crashes involving pregnant occupants. *Annu Proc Assoc Adv Automot Med* 2000;44:37–55.

21. Kyriacou DN, Anglin D, Taliaferro E, et al. Risk factors for injury to women from domestic violence. *N Engl J Med* 1999;341: 1892–1898.

22. Lee D, Contreras M, Robson SC, et al. Recommendations for the use of anti-D immunoglobulin for Rh prophylaxis. British Blood Transfusion Society and Royal College of Obstetricians and Gynaecologists. *Transfus Med* 1999;9:93–97.

23. Mattox KL, Goetzl L. Trauma in pregnancy. *Crit Care Med* 2005;33:S385–S389.

24. Metz TD, Abbott JT. Uterine trauma in pregnancy after motor vehicle crashes with airbag deployment: a 30-case series. *J Trauma* 2006;61: 658–661.

25. Minow M. Violence against women—a challenge to the Supreme Court. *N Engl J Med* 1999;341:1927–1929.

26. Pearlman MD, Tintinalli JE, Lorenz RP. Blunt trauma during pregnancy. *N Engl J Med* 1991; 323:1606–1613.

27. Pearlman M, Tintinalli J, Lorenz R. A prospective controlled study of outcome after trauma during pregnancy. *Am J Obstet Gynecol* 1990; 162:1502–1510.

28. Petrone P, Talving P, Browder T, et al. Abdominal injuries in pregnancy: a 155-month study at two level 1 trauma centers. *Injury* 2011;42(1):47–49.

29. Schoenfeld A, Ziv E, Stein L, et al. Seat belts in pregnancy and the obstetrician. *Obstet Gynecol Surv* 1987;42:275–282.

30. Scorpio R, Esposito T, Smith G, et al. Blunt trauma during pregnancy: factors affecting fetal outcome. *J Trauma* 1992;32:213–216.

31. Sela HY, Weiniger, CF, Hersch M, et al. The pregnant motor vehicle accident casualty. Adherence to basic workup and admission guidelines. *Ann Surg* 2011;254(2).

32. Shah AJ, Kilcline BA. Trauma in pregnancy. *Emerg Med Clin North Am* 2003;21:615–629.

33. Sims CJ, Boardman CH, Fuller SJ. Airbag deployment following a motor vehicle accident in pregnancy. *Obstet Gynecol* 1996;88:726.

34. Sisley A, Jacobs LM, Poole G, et al. Violence in America: a public health crisis—domestic violence. *J Trauma* 1999;46:1105–1113.

35. Statement on Domestic Violence. *Bull Am Coll Surg* 2000;85:26.

36. Towery RA, English TP, Wisner DW. Evaluation of pregnant women after blunt injury. *J Trauma* 1992;35:731–736.

37. Tsuei BJ. Assessment of the pregnant trauma patient. *Injury* 2006;37:367–373.

38. Weinberg L, Steele RG, Pugh R, et al. The pregnant trauma patient. *Anaesth Int Care* 2005;33: 167–180.

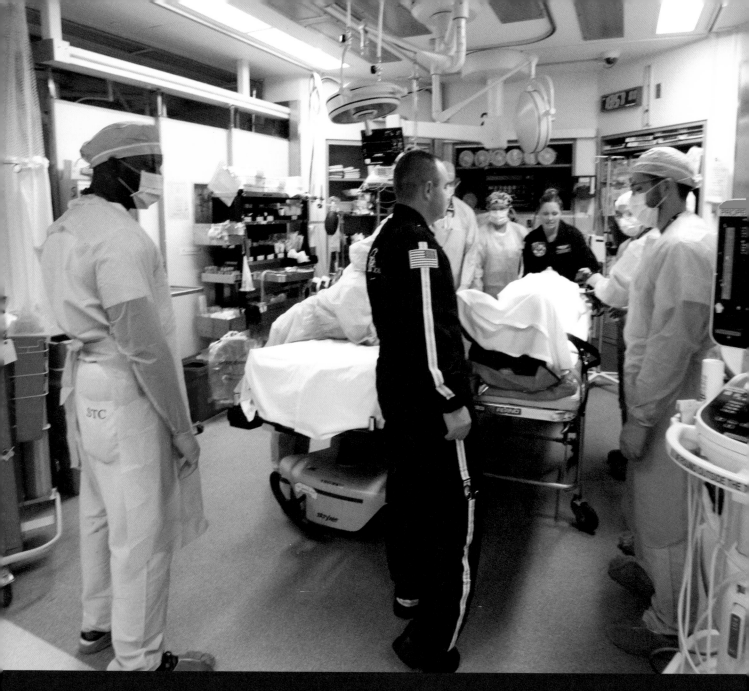

13 TRANSFER TO DEFINITIVE CARE

The decision to transfer a patient to another facility for definitive care is influenced by the identified and suspected injuries, the expected progression of these injuries, and the capabilities on hand to expeditiously diagnose and treat them, especially the potentially life-threatening injuries.

CHAPTER 13 OUTLINE

OBJECTIVES

After reading this chapter and comprehending the knowledge components of the ATLS provider course, you will be able to:

1. Identify injured patients who require transfer from a local receiving hospital to a facility capable of providing the necessary level of trauma care.

2. Describe the responsibilities of the referring and receiving doctors during the process of timely transfer to a higher level of care, to include physician-to-physician communication, documentation, and determination of mode of transport.

3. Identify patients who require further timely imaging and/or stabilization before transfer.

4. Recognize the need to provide ongoing care during transfer to ensure the patient arrives at the receiving hospital in the best possible condition.

The Advanced Trauma Life Support® course is designed to train clinicians to be proficient in assessing, stabilizing, and preparing trauma patients for definitive care. Definitive trauma care, whether support and monitoring in an intensive care unit (ICU), admission to an unmonitored unit, or operative intervention, requires the presence and active involvement of a team of providers with the skills and knowledge to manage the injuries sustained by the trauma patient. If definitive care cannot be provided at a local hospital, transfer the patient to the closest appropriate hospital that has the resources and capabilities to care for the patient. Ideally, this facility should be a verified trauma center at a level that is appropriate to the patient's needs.

The decision to transfer a patient to another facility depends on the patient's injuries and the local resources. Decisions about which patients need to be transferred and when and how the transfer will occur are based on medical judgment. Evidence supports the view that trauma outcome is enhanced if critically injured patients are treated in trauma centers. See *ACS COT Resources for Optimal Care of the Injured Patient*; *Guidelines for Trauma System Development* and *Trauma Center Verification Processes and Standards*.

The major principle of trauma management is to do no further harm. Indeed, the level of care of trauma patients should consistently improve with each step, from the scene of the incident to the facility that offers the patient necessary and proper definitive treatment.

DETERMINING THE NEED FOR PATIENT TRANSFER

The vast majority of patients receive their total care in a local hospital, and movement beyond that point is not necessary. It is essential that clinicians assess their own capabilities and limitations, as well as those of their institution, to allow for early differentiation between patients who may be safely cared for in the local hospital and those who require transfer for definitive care.

TRANSFER FACTORS

Patients who require prompt transfer can be identified on the basis of physiologic measurements, specific identifiable injuries, and mechanism of injury. Patients with severe head injury (GCS score of 8 or less) and hypotension are easily recognized and warrant urgent transfer. However, the need to transfer patients with multiple injuries without obvious

hemodynamic abnormalities may be less obvious. Therefore, diligence in recognizing the need for early transfer is critical.

To assist clinicians in determining which patients require care at a higher-level facility, the ACS Committee on Trauma recommends using certain physiological indices, injury mechanisms and patterns, and historical information. These factors also help clinicians decide which stable patients might benefit from transfer. Suggested guidelines for interhospital transfer when a patient's needs exceed available resources are outlined in ■ TABLE 13-1. It is important to note that these guidelines are flexible and must take into account local circumstances.

Certain clinical measurements of physiologic status are useful in determining the need for transfer to an institution that provides a higher level of care. Patients who exhibit evidence of shock, significant physiologic deterioration, or progressive deterioration in neurologic status require the highest level of care and will likely benefit from timely transfer (■ FIGURE 13-1).

Stable patients with blunt abdominal trauma and documented liver or spleen injuries may be candidates for nonoperative management, requiring the immediate availability of an operating room and a qualified surgical team. A general or trauma surgeon should supervise nonoperative management, regardless of the patient's age. If the facility is not prepared for urgent operative intervention, these patients should be transferred to a trauma center.

Patients with specific injuries, combinations of injuries (particularly those involving the brain), and/or a history indicating high-energy-transfer injury may be at risk for death and are candidates for early transfer to a trauma center. Elderly patients should be considered for transfer for less severe injuries (e.g., multiple rib fractures and patients on anticoagula-

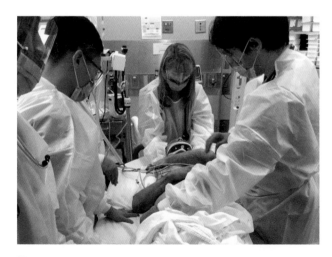

■ **FIGURE 13-1** Trauma teams rapidly assess patients to determine the need for transfer to a higher level of care.

TABLE 13-1 RAPID TRIAGE AND TRANSPORT GUIDELINES

PRIMARY SURVEY	FINDING	INTERVENTIONS AND ADJUNCTS TO BE PERFORMED AT LOCAL FACILITY	CONSIDER TRANSFER?
Airway	Airway compromise	Intubate, end-tidal CO_2, pulse oximeter, EKG, chest x-ray	Y
	High risk for airway loss	Monitor EKG, pulse oximeter, ABG	Y
Breathing	Tension pneumothorax	Needle, finger, chest tube	Y
	Hemothorax, open pneumothorax	Chest x-ray, chest tube	Y
	Hypoxia/hypoventilation	Intubate	Y
Circulation	Hypotension	Reliable IV/IO access, warm IV fluids, control external hemorrhage using pressure, topical hemostatics, or tourniquets	Y
	Pelvic fracture	Pelvic x-ray, pelvic binder, or sheet	Y
	Vascular injury (hard signs, such as expanding hematoma and active bleeding)	Reliable IV/IO access, warm IV fluids, control external hemorrhage using pressure, topical hemostatics, or tourniquets	Y
	Open fracture	Reduce and splint and dress	Y
	Abdominal distention/peritonitis	FAST[a]	Y
Disability	GCS < 13	Intubate when GCS < 9[b]	Y
	Intoxicated patient who cannot be evaluated	Sedate, intubate	Y
	Evidence of paralysis	Restrict spinal motion; monitor for neurogenic shock	Y
Exposure	Severe hypothermia	External warming	Y
SECONDARY SURVEY	FINDING	INTERVENTIONS AND ADJUNCTS TO BE PERFORMED AT LOCAL FACILITY	CONSIDER TRANSFER?
Head and Skull	Depressed skull fracture or penetrating injury	CT scan[c]	Y
Maxillofacial	Eye injury, open fractures, complex laceration, ongoing nasopharyngeal bleeding	CT scan[c]	Y

Note: Evaluate and make the decision to transfer within first 15–30 minutes of trauma team leader arrival.
a. Perform only if it affects the decision to transfer.
b. Patients with GCS scores 9–13 may require intubation, depending on clinical circumstances and discussion with accepting doctor.
c. Perform only in hemodynamically stable patients for whom the results will affect the decision to transfer or the care provided before transfer.

Continued

	TABLE 13-1 RAPID TRIAGE AND TRANSPORT GUIDELINES *(continued)*		
SECONDARY SURVEY	**FINDING**	**INTERVENTIONS AND ADJUNCTS TO BE PERFORMED AT LOCAL FACILITY**	**CONSIDER TRANSFER?**
Neck	Hematoma, crepitus, midline tenderness or deformity	CT scan[c]	Y
Chest	Multiple rib fractures, flail chest, pulmonary contusion, widened mediastinum, mediastinal air	CXR, FAST[c], CT scan[c]	Y
Abdomen	Rebound, guarding	FAST, DPL[a], CT scan[c]	Y
Perineum/ Rectum/Vagina	Laceration	Proctosigmoidoscopy[c], speculum examination[c]	Y
Neurologic	Deficit	Plain films[c], CT scan[c], MRI[c]	Y
Musculoskeletal	Complex or multiple fractures or dislocations or bony spine injuries	Extremity xrays[c], spine xrays[c], or CT scan[c]	Y
Other Factors	Age, multiple comorbidities, pregnancy, burn		

Note: Evaluate and make the decision to transfer within first 15–30 minutes of trauma team leader arrival.
a. Perform only if it affects the decision to transfer.
b. Patients with GCS scores 9-13 may require intubation, depending on clinical circumstances and discussion with accepting doctor.
c. Perform only in hemodynamically stable patients for whom the results will affect the decision to transfer or the care provided before transfer.

tion therapy) because of their limited physiologic reserve and potential for comorbid illnesses.

Obese patients rarely require transfer specifically because of their weight except in extreme cases in which CT scans cannot be obtained due to the patient's size or special equipment is required for an operative procedure. The difficult airway often associated with obesity may warrant early intubation before transfer when there is a risk that mental status or respiratory status may deteriorate during transport.

Abuse of alcohol and/or other drugs is common to all forms of trauma and is particularly important to identify, because these substances can alter pain perception and mask significant physical findings. Alterations in the patient's responsiveness can be related to alcohol and/or drugs, but cerebral injury should never be excluded as a potential cause of mental status change, even in the presence of alcohol or drugs. If the examining doctor is unsure, transfer to a higher-level facility may be appropriate.

Death of another individual involved in the traumatic incident suggests the possibility of severe, occult injury in survivors. In these cases, a thorough and careful evaluation of the patient is mandatory, even when there are no obvious signs of severe injury.

TIMELINESS OF TRANSFER

Patient outcome is directly related to the time elapsed between injury and properly delivered definitive care. In institutions without full-time, in-house emergency department (ED) coverage, the timeliness of transfer depends partly on how quickly the doctor on call can reach the ED. Consequently, trauma teams should develop effective communication with the prehospital system to identify patients who require a doctor to be present in the ED at the time of arrival (■ FIGURE 13-2). In addition, the attending doctor must be committed to respond to the ED before the arrival of critically injured patients.

The timing of interhospital transfer varies based on transfer distance, available skill levels of transferring personnel, circumstances of the local institution, and the interventions required before safely transferring the patient. If resources are available and the necessary

to provide definitive care. Frequently, CT scans done before transfer to definitive care are repeated upon arrival to the trauma center, making the necessity of a pre-transfer CT questionable. Multiple scans result in increased radiation exposure and additional hospital costs as well as a delay in transfer to definitive care.

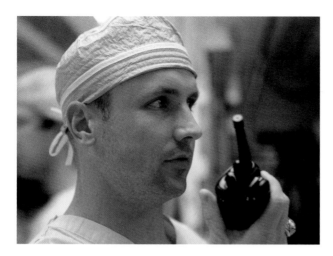

■ **FIGURE 13-2** Effective communication with the prehospital system should be developed to identify patients who require the presence of a doctor in the ED at the time of arrival.

procedures can be performed expeditiously, life-threatening injuries should be treated before patient transport. This treatment may require operative intervention to ensure that the patient is in the best possible condition for transfer. Intervention before transfer requires judgment.

After recognizing the need for transfer, expedite the arrangements. Do not perform diagnostic procedures (e.g., diagnostic peritoneal lavage [DPL] or CT scan) that do not change the plan of care. However, procedures that treat or stabilize an immediately life-threatening condition should be rapidly performed.

Despite the principle that transfer should not be delayed for diagnostic procedures, a significant portion of trauma patients transferred to regional trauma centers undergo CT scanning at the primary hospital, thus leading to an increased length of stay before transfer. In fact, research has shown that much of the time delay between injury and transfer is related to diagnostic studies performed despite lack of a surgeon

PITFALL	PREVENTION
Delay in transfer of a patient to definitive care	• Consider transfer early in the assessment process. • Quickly determine the needs of the patient and the capabilities of the institution. • Order only tests that will identify life-threatening injuries that can be treated or stabilized before transfer.

TREATMENT BEFORE TRANSFER

Patients should be resuscitated and attempts made to stabilize their conditions as completely as possible based on the following suggested procedure:

1. Airway

   a. Insert an airway or endotracheal tube, if needed. Establish a low threshold to intubate patients with altered GCS, even above 8, when there is concern for potential deterioration, and discuss this decision with the receiving doctor.

   b. Provide suction.

   c. Place a gastric tube in all intubated patients and in non-intubated patients with evidence of gastric distention. Use judgment when patients are agitated or intoxicated, as this procedure can induce vomiting, risking aspiration.

2. Breathing

   a. Determine rate and administer supplementary oxygen.

   b. Provide mechanical ventilation when needed.

   c. Insert a chest tube if needed. Patients with known or suspected pneumothorax should have a chest tube placed when they are being moved by air transport.

3. Circulation

   a. Control external bleeding, noting time of placement when tourniquet is used.

   b. Establish two large-caliber intravenous lines and begin crystalloid solution infusion.

   c. Restore blood volume losses using crystalloid fluid and blood to achieve balanced resuscitation (see *Chapter 3: Shock*) and continue replacement during transfer.

   d. Insert an indwelling catheter to monitor urinary output.

   e. Monitor the patient's cardiac rhythm and rate.

   f. Transport patients in late pregnancy, tilted to the left side to improve venous return.

Restrict spinal motion if indicated. Ensure the receiving facility is capable of treating both the mother and baby.

4. Central nervous system

   a. Assist respiration in unconscious patients.

   b. Administer mannitol or hypertonic saline, if needed, when advised by the receiving doctor.

   c. Restrict spinal motion in patients who have or are suspected of having spine injuries.

5. Perform appropriate diagnostic studies (sophisticated diagnostic studies, such as CT and aortography, are usually not indicated; when indicated, obtaining these studies should not delay transfer).

   a. Obtain x-rays of chest, pelvis, and extremities.

   b. Obtain necessary blood work.

   c. Determine cardiac rhythm and hemoglobin saturation (electrocardiograph [ECG] and pulse oximetry).

6. Wounds (Note: Do not delay transfer to carry out these procedures.)

   a. Clean and dress wounds after controlling external hemorrhage.

   b. Administer tetanus prophylaxis.

   c. Administer antibiotics, when indicated.

7. Fractures

   a. Apply appropriate splinting and traction.

The flurry of activity surrounding initial evaluation, resuscitation, and preparations for transfer of trauma patients often overrides other logistic details. This situation may result in failure to include certain information sent with the patient, such as x-ray films, laboratory reports, and narrative descriptions of the evaluation process and treatment rendered at the local hospital. To ensure that all important components of care have been addressed, use a checklist. Checklists can be printed or stamped on an x-ray jacket or the patient's medical record to remind the referring doctor to include all pertinent information. (See *Transfer Checklist on MyATLS mobile app.*)

Treatment of combative and uncooperative patients with an altered level of consciousness is difficult and potentially hazardous. These patients often require restriction of spinal motion and are placed in the supine position with wrist/leg restraints. If sedation is required, the patient should be intubated. Therefore, before administering any sedation, the treating doctor must: ensure that the patient's ABCDEs are

PITFALL	PREVENTION
Inadequate handover between treatment and transferring teams	• Use a transfer checklist to ensure that all key aspects of care rendered are properly communicated to the transfer team. • Verify that copies of medical records and x-rays are prepared and provided to the transfer team.
Inadequate preparation for transport, increasing the likelihood of patient deterioration during transfer	• Identify and initiate resuscitative efforts for all life-threatening conditions. • Ensure that transfer agreements are in place to enable rapid determination of the best receiving facility based on the patient's injuries. • Confirm that all patient transport equipment is pre-staged and ready to go at all times.

appropriately managed; relieve the patient's pain if possible (e.g., splint fractures and administer small doses of narcotics intravenously); and attempt to calm and reassure the patient.

Remember, benzodiazepines, fentanyl (Sublimaze), propofol (Diprivan), and ketamine (Ketaset) are all hazardous in patients with hypovolemia, patients who are intoxicated, and patients with head injuries. Pain management, sedation, and intubation should be accomplished by the individual most skilled in these procedures. (See *Chapter 2: Airway and Ventilatory Management.*)

TRANSFER RESPONSIBILITIES

The referring doctor and the receiving doctor hold specific transfer responsibilities.

REFERRING DOCTOR

The referring doctor is responsible for initiating transfer of the patient to the receiving institution and selecting the appropriate mode of transportation and level of care required for the patient's optimal treatment en route. The referring doctor should consult with the receiving doctor and be thoroughly familiar with the transporting agencies, their capabilities, and the arrangements for patient treatment during transport. Within the capabilities of his or her institution, the referring doctor must stabilize the patient's condition before transfer to another facility. The transfer process is initiated while resuscitative efforts are in progress.

Transfer between hospitals is expedited by establishing transfer agreements. They provide for consistent, efficient movement of patients between institutions. Additionally these agreements allow for feedback to the referring hospital and enhance the efficiency and quality of the patient's treatment during transfer.

Providing a complete and succinct patient summary using a standardized template is useful to ensure vital information is communicated. Omission of information can delay the identification and care of injuries, which can influence patient outcome. SBAR (Situation, Background, Assessment, and Recommendation) is a commonly used handover tool developed to improve patient safety by facilitating the communication of patient-specific information. ■ TABLE 13-2 outlines a sample ABC-SBAR template for transfer of trauma patients.

When adequately trained emergency medical personnel are not available, ensure that a nurse or doctor accompanies the patient. All monitoring and management rendered en route is carefully documented.

Pediatric patients require special expertise, and transfer to a designated pediatric treatment facility is often indicated. Depending on local circumstances this may be an adult trauma center with pediatric

TABLE 13-2 SAMPLE ABC-SBAR TEMPLATE FOR TRANSFER OF TRAUMA PATIENTS

ACRONYM	MEANING	INFORMATION TO PROVIDE
A	Airway	
B	Breathing	All airway, breathing, and circulation problems identified and interventions performed
C	Circulation	
S	Situation	Patient Name Age Referring Facility Referring physician name Reporting nurse name Indication for transfer IV access site IV fluid and rate Other interventions completed
B	Background	Event history AMPLE assessment Blood products Medications given (date and time) Imaging performed Splinting
A	Assessment	Vital signs Pertinent physical exam findings Patient response to treatment
R	Recommendation	Transport mode Level of transport care Medication intervention during transport Needed assessments and interventions

PITFALL	PREVENTION
Inadequate or inappropriate communication between referring and receiving providers, resulting in loss of information critical to the patient's care	• Initiate call early in treatment process, that is, upon identifying the need to transfer to definitive care. • Specify all injuries identified, emphasizing life-threatening conditions. • Provide all pertinent information regarding the patient's injuries, care received, patient's response to care, and reason for transfer.

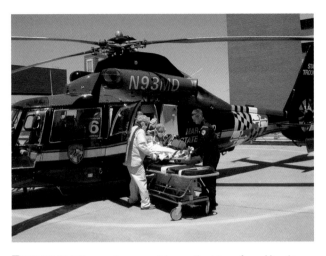

■ **FIGURE 13-3** Trauma team receiving patient transferred by air.

capabilities. Transport teams should be familiar with the safe transport of pediatric patients, including the need for airway management, medication dosing, and resuscitative adjuncts.

RECEIVING DOCTOR

The receiving doctor must be consulted to ensure that the proposed receiving institution is qualified, able, and willing to accept the patient and agrees with the intent to transfer. The receiving doctor assists the referring doctor in arranging for the appropriate mode and level of care during transport. If the proposed receiving doctor and facility are unable to accept the patient, they can assist in finding an alternative placement for the patient.

The quality of care rendered en route is vital to the patient's outcome. Only by directly communicating can the referring and receiving doctors clearly outline the details of patient transfer.

▶ MODES OF TRANSPORTATION

When choosing the mode of patient transportation, the most important principle is to do no further harm. Ground, water, and air transportation can be safe and effective in fulfilling this principle, and no one form is intrinsically superior to the others (■ FIGURE 13-3). Local factors such as availability, geography, cost, and weather are the main factors determining which mode to use in a given circumstance. ■ BOX 13-1 lists general questions to ask in determining appropriate transportation mode.

Interhospital transfer of a critically injured patient is potentially hazardous; therefore, it is optimal to

BOX 13-1 QUESTIONS THAT CAN ASSIST IN DETERMINING APPROPRIATE TRANSPORT MODE

• Does the patient's clinical condition require minimization of time spent out of the hospital environment during the transport?

• Does the patient require specific or time-sensitive evaluation or treatment that is not available at the referring facility?

• Is the patient located in an area that is inaccessible to ground transport?

• What are the current and predicted weather situations along the transport route?

• Is the weight of the patient (plus the weight of required equipment and transport personnel) within allowable ranges for air transport?

• For interhospital transports, is there a helipad and/or airport near the referring hospital?

• Does the patient require critical care life support (e.g., monitoring personnel, specific medications, specific equipment) during transport, which is not available with ground transport options?

• Would use of local ground transport leave the local area without adequate emergency medical services coverage?

• If local ground transport is not an option, can the needs of the patient (and the system) be met by an available regional ground critical care transport service (i.e., specialized surface transport systems operated by hospitals and/or air medical programs)?

Reprinted with permission from Thomson DP, Thomas SH. Guidelines for Air Medical Dispatch. *Prehospital Emergency Care* 2003; Apr–Jun;7(2):265–71.

stabilize the patient's condition before transport, ensure transfer personnel are properly trained, and make provisions for managing unexpected crises during transport. To ensure safe transfers, trauma surgeons must be involved in training, continuing education, and quality improvement programs designed for transfer personnel and procedures. Surgeons also should be actively involved in developing and maintaining systems of trauma care. See *"Appropriate use of Helicopter Emergency Medical Services for transport of trauma patients: Guidelines from the Emergency Medical System Subcommittee, Committee on Trauma, American College of Surgeons."*

TRANSFER PROTOCOLS

When protocols for patient transfer do not exist, the following guidelines regarding information from the referring doctor, information to transferring personnel, documentation, and treatment during transport are suggested.

INFORMATION FROM REFERRING DOCTOR

The doctor who determines that patient transfer is necessary should speak directly to the physician accepting the patient at the receiving hospital. The ABC-SBAR (refer to ■ TABLE 13-2) can serve as a checklist for the telephone report between physicians and the verbal report to transporting personnel.

INFORMATION TO TRANSFERRING PERSONNEL

Information regarding the patient's condition and needs during transfer should be communicated to the transporting personnel (refer to the ABC-SBAR template in ■ TABLE 13-2).

DOCUMENTATION

A written record of the problem, treatment given, and patient status at the time of transfer, as well as certain physical items (e.g., disks that contain radiologic images), must accompany the patient (■ FIGURE 13-4). Digital media may be transmitted to the referring facility to expedite the transfer of information and make imaging available for review at a distance; when electronic transmission is not possible, facsimile transmission of reports may be used to avoid delay in transfer. The most acceptable IT (information technology) enhanced communication medium may be used to avoid delay in transfer.

TREATMENT DURING TRANSPORT

Trained personnel should transfer the patient, based on the patient's condition and potential problems. Treatment during transport typically includes:

- Monitoring vital signs and pulse oximetry
- Continuing support of cardiorespiratory system

PITFALL	PREVENTION
Dislodged or mal-positioned endotracheal tubes and intravenous lines during transport	• Ensure that necessary equipment for reintubation and line placement accompanies the patient. • Verify that transfer personnel are capable of performing the procedure and managing any potential complications that occur. • Ensure tubes and lines are adequately secured.
Failure to anticipate deterioration in the patient's neurologic condition or hemodynamic status during transport	• For elderly patients, intoxicated patients, and patients with head injuries, there is often no way to predict if neurological status will change; thus, airway protection during transport is sometimes indicated for individuals with GCS scores >8. • The transporting physician should consider the possibility of potential neurological change and airway compromise when deciding to intubate before transport. • The receiving surgeon should offer advice if the decision to intubate is not clear based on consideration of the injury pattern and transport time.

UNIVERSAL INTERHOSPITAL HAND-OFF TRANSFER FORM
(Optional Use)

Patient Identification Label

TIME-SPECIFIC	TREATMENTS	PATIENT ASSESSMENT (most recent) SYSTEMS ASSESSMENT & PAST MEDICAL HISTORY PERTINENT TO TRANSFER	PATIENT INFORMATION

PATIENT INFORMATION

TRANSFER DATE: _____ TRANSFER TIME: _____ TRANSFER FROM: _____ TRANSFER TO: _____

TRANSPORT MODE: _____ ETA: _____ REASON FOR TRANSFER: □Higher Level of Care; □Cardiac Intervention

DIAGNOSIS RELATED TO TRANSFER: _____

□Stroke Intervention □Adult Trauma □Pediatric Trauma □Specialty Referral; □Hand □Eye □Adult Burn □Pediatric Burn □Other _____

PATIENT NAME: LAST _____ FIRST _____ DOB: _____ AGE: _____ □M □F Pregnant? □Y □N LMP _____

MEDICAL ORDERS for LIFE SUSTAINING TREATMENT (MOLST): Documents □Y □N; Attached □Y □N

CONTACT PERSON: LAST NAME _____ FIRST _____ RELATIONSHIP _____ PHONE: Day _____ Night _____ Cellular _____

Contact with Patient? □Y □N, Contact Notified of Transfer? □Y □N (Date _____ Time _____) □N, Contact Enroute to Receiving Hospital? □Y □N

INFORMATION GIVEN TO CONTACT PERSON: _____

Healthcare Representative/Proxy/Legal Guardian: □Y □N LAST NAME _____ FIRST _____

PATIENT ASSESSMENT (most recent) SYSTEMS ASSESSMENT & PAST MEDICAL HISTORY PERTINENT TO TRANSFER

DATE _____ TIME _____ HT _____ WT _____ Kg. T _____ P _____ R _____ BP _____ Pulse Ox _____ □O2/N Cannula _____ L. Pain Score _____ □Numbers □Faces

Airway: □Natural □LMA □King □ ETT; Size _____ On Vent □Y □N, Vent Setting _____ Tolerating □Y □N. OG Tube □Y □N. CPR □Y □N

GCS: Eye _____ Motor _____ Verbal = _____ Total _____ Pupil size: (mm) R _____ Depth _____ L _____ EKG: □Y □N; Abnormal Rhythm _____

ALLERGIES: _____ IMMUNIZATIONS/SCREENING DATES: Flu _____ Tetanus _____ Pneumonia _____ PPD _____ □Pos □Neg

Abnormal Assessment Findings Past Medical History

Cardiovascular: _____ □CABG □CAD □AICD □MI □Pacemaker □Stent □Other

Gastrointestinal: _____

Genitourinary: _____ □Renal Failure

HEENT: _____

Integumentary: _____

Musculoskeletal: _____

Nervous/Neurological: _____ □TIA □Stroke □Shunt □AVM □Hemorrhage □ Other

Thorax/Lungs 'Respiratory': _____ □Trach

PRE-EXISTING MEDICATION: Anticoagulants □Y □N; Name: _____

ISOLATION PRECAUTIONS: □None □MRSA □VRE □ESBL □C-Diff □Colonized □Other, specify _____ Other: _____ Site _____

TREATMENTS

TOTAL INTAKE: _____ Blood Products Given: PRBC/ _____ units, FFP/ _____ units, Platelets/ _____ units, Other _____

TOTAL OUTPUT: _____ □Voided □Foley □Gastric □Chest Tube _____ □Estimated Blood Loss _____ For Burns: Total Crystalloids Given _____ units

LAB TESTS: CBC _____ Coags _____ CMP _____ Trop _____ Myo _____ Other _____ IMAGING: Films Sent □Y □N; X-Rays _____ CT _____ MRI _____

OPERATIVE PROCEDURES: _____ OTHERS: _____

MEDICATIONS GIVEN PRIOR TO TRANSFER AT HOSPITAL: Antibiotics, Resuscitative, Sedative/Paralytic, Thrombolytics/TPA, Others

Medication	Dosage	Date	Time	Medication	Dosage	Date	Time

TIME-SPECIFIC

TRAUMA: Date of Injury _____ Time of Injury _____ Death in same incident □Y □N, Family Member □Y □N, Was patient notified? □Y □N

Mechanism of Injury □ MVC □MCC □Ped □ATV □Bicycle □Beating □Cut/Pierce □Firearm □Burn □Fall □Drowning □Blast □Other

Spinal Protection: □Backboard □C-Collar □Pelvic □Extremity: _____ RU _____ LU _____ RL _____ LL _____ □Towel Roll/Bolster □Other _____

Social Concern: □Domestic Violence Suspicion. □Child/Elder. □ Suspicion □Neglect □Abuse. Reported? □Y □N. To Whom? _____

Sending Physician Name: _____ Receiving Physician Name: _____

Sending Facility Contact Name: _____ Receiving Facility Contact Name: _____

Form Completed By Name: _____ Date: _____ Time: _____

■ FIGURE 13-4 Sample Transfer Form. This form includes all the information that should be sent with the patient to the receiving doctor and facility.

- Continued balanced fluid resuscitation
- Using medications as ordered by a doctor or as allowed by written protocol
- Maintaining communication with a doctor or institution during transfer
- Maintaining accurate records during transfer

When preparing for transport and while it is underway, remember that during air transport, changes in altitude lead to changes in air pressure. Because this can increase the size of pneumothoraces and worsen gastric distention, clinicians should carefully consider placing a chest tube or gastric tube. Similar cautions pertain to any air-filled device. For example, during prolonged flights, it may be necessary to decrease the pressure in air splints or endotracheal tube balloons. When transporting pediatric patients, pay special attention to equipment sizes and the expertise of personnel before transport.

TRANSFER DATA

The information accompanying the patient should include both demographic and historical information pertinent to the patient's injury. Uniform transmission of information is enhanced by the use of an established transfer form, such as the example shown in Figure 13-4. In addition to the information already outlined, provide space for recording data in an organized, sequential fashion—vital signs, central nervous system (CNS) function, and urinary output—during the initial resuscitation and transport period.

TEAMWORK

- When the level of care exceeds the capabilities of the treating facility, the trauma team leader must work quickly and efficiently to initiate and complete transfer to definitive care.
- Other team members can assist the team leader by communicating with the receiving facility while the trauma team leader remains focused on the patient.
- The team leader ensures rapid preparation for transfer by limiting tests (particularly CT scans) to those needed to treat immediately life-threatening conditions that can be managed by specialists and facilities at hand.

- Upon accepting a patient for transfer to definitive care, team members will collaborate to prepare records for transfer, including documentation of diagnoses, treatment, medications given, and x-rays performed.

CHAPTER SUMMARY

1. Patients whose injuries exceed an institution's capabilities for definitive care should be identified early during assessment and resuscitation. Individual capabilities of the treating doctor, institutional capabilities, and guidelines for transfer should be familiar. Transfer agreements and protocols can expedite the process.

2. Life-threatening injuries should be identified and treated to the extent possible at the referring (local) facility. Procedures and tests that are not required to stabilize the patient should not be performed.

3. Clear communication between the referring and receiving physician and transporting personnel must occur. ABC-SBAR is a useful template to ensure key information about the patient is communicated.

4. Transfer personnel should be adequately skilled to administer the required patient care en route to ensure that the level of care the patient receives does not decrease.

5. Special patient group considerations should be made when deciding who to transfer. Pre-defined transfer agreements can speed the process.

BIBLIOGRAPHY

1. American College of Surgeons Committee on Trauma. *Resources for Optimal Care of the Injured Patient*. Chicago, IL: American College of Surgeons; 2006.
2. Bledsoe BE, Wesley AK, Eckstein M, et al. Helicopter scene transport of trauma patients with nonlife-threatening injuries: a meta-analysis. *J Trauma* 2006;60: 1257–1266.
3. Borst GM, Davies SW, Waibel BH et al. When birds can't fly: an analysis of interfacility ground transport using advanced life support

when helicopter emergency medical service is unavailable. *J Trauma* 77(2):331–336.

4. Brown JB, Stassen NA, Bankey PE et al. Helicopters improve survival in seriously injured patients requiring interfacility transfer for definitive care. *J Trauma* 70(2):310–314.

5. Champion HR, Sacco WJ, Copes WS, et al. A revision of the trauma score. *J Trauma* 1989; 29:623–629.

6. Compton J, Copeland K, Flanders S, et al. Implementing SBAR across a large multihospital health system. *Joint Commission J Quality and Patient Safety* 2012;38:261–268.

7. Doucet J, Bulger E, Sanddal N, et al.; endorsed by the National Association of EMS Physicians (NAEMSP). Appropriate use of helicopter emergency medical services for transport of trauma patients: guidelines from the Emergency Medical System Subcommittee, Committee on Trauma, American College of Surgeons. *J Trauma* 2013 Oct 75(4):734–741.

8. Edwards C, Woodard, E. SBAR for maternal transports: going the extra mile. *Nursing for Women's Health* 2009;12:516–520.

9. Harrington DT, Connolly M, Biffl WL, et al. Transfer times to definitive care facilities are too long: a consequence of an immature trauma system. *Ann Surg* 241(6):961–968.

10. McCrum ML, McKee J, Lai M, et al. ATLS adherence in the transfer of rural trauma patients to a level I facility. *Injury* 44(9):1241–1245.

11. Mullins PJ, Veum-Stone J, Helfand M, et al. Outcome of hospitalized injured patients after institution of a trauma system in an urban area. *JAMA* 1994;271:1919–1924.

12. Onzuka J, Worster A, McCreadie B. Is computerized tomography of trauma patients associated with a transfer delay to a regional trauma centre? *CJEM*:10(3):205–208.

13. Quick JA, Bartels AN, Coughenour JP, et al. Trauma transfers and definitive imaging: patient benefit but at what cost? *Am Surg* 79(3):301–304.

14. Scarpio RJ, Wesson DE. Splenic trauma. In: Eichelberger MR, ed. *Pediatric Trauma: Prevention, Acute Care, Rehabilitation*. St. Louis, MO: Mosby Yearbook 1993; 456–463.

15. Schoettker P, D'Amours S, Nocera N, et al. Reduction of time to definitive care in trauma patients: effectiveness of a new checklist system. *Injury* 2003;34:187–190.

16. Sharar SR, Luna GK, Rice CL, et al. Air transport following surgical stabilization: an extension of regionalized trauma care. *J Trauma* 1988;28:794–798.

17. Thomson DP, Thomas SH. Guidelines for Air Medical Dispatch. *Prehospital Emergency Care* 2003; Apr–Jun;7(2):265–71.

APPENDICES

Appendix A
OCULAR TRAUMA

OBJECTIVES

1. Understand basic orbital and ocular anatomy.

2. Describe a focused history for ocular trauma.

3. Describe a systematic examination of the orbit and its contents.

4. Explain how to assess intraocular pressure.

5. Understand the characteristics of lid lacerations that require referral to a specialist.

6. Describe the fluorescein dye test and its utility.

7. Identify signs of retrobulbar hemorrhage and explain the necessity for immediate treatment and referral.

8. Describe the treatment of eye injuries that result from chemical exposure.

9. Identify signs of a ruptured-globe injury and describe its initial management before referral to an ophthalmologist.

10. Understand the characteristics of eye injuries that require referral to an ophthalmologist.

In military medicine, doctors and support personnel have long cited the mantra "life, limb, or eyesight" to describe what constitutes a true medical emergency. Although emergent medical care has changed with time, this concept still holds true. The eye is important indeed, but it is typically not evaluated until after the patient is deemed medically stable.

Minor abrasions and lacerations to the eye and eyelids are common in polytrauma patients. This appendix focuses on the few ocular injuries that can blind a patient if not treated within the first few hours after onset. Understanding the fundamentals of the eye exam after injury, begins with a review of basic eye anatomy.

ANATOMY REVIEW

The cornea is the transparent layer that forms the anterior boundary of the space known as the anterior chamber, and it is contiguous with the sclera. The interior of the globe is divided into anterior and posterior segments by the lens. The anterior segment includes the cornea, sclera, conjunctiva, iris, and lens. The space between the cornea and iris is called the anterior chamber and is filled with aqueous humor—a solution of sodium, chloride, and other ions. The posterior segment of the globe is between the lens and the retina, and it is filled with vitreous humor—a clear, jelly-like substance. The optic nerve is at the back of the eye; it travels through the muscle cone, through the orbit, and then into the brain. ■ FIGURE A-1 provides a review a anatomy of the eye.

The globe includes the attachments of the extraocular muscles to the sclera. The sclera and muscles are covered by an epithelium called the conjunctiva, which extends from the cornea-sclera junction over the sclera and then turns to cover the inside of the eyelids. The extraocular muscles join together to make a "cone," which is covered in a fascia-like sheath called Tenon's capsule. This minimally distensible fascial covering limits the ability of these muscles to expand; thus, hemorrhage in this area may produce a compartment syndrome.

The globe–muscle cone complex sits in the orbit of the eye, which is a pear-shaped cavity formed by bones that separate the orbital compartment from the sinus and brain tissue. The eyelids have tendinous attachments (canthal tendons) medially and temporally on the bony orbit, which keep the globe from moving forward. This arrangement

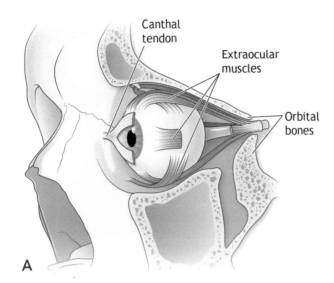
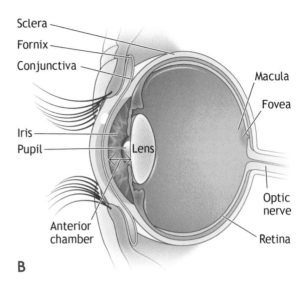

■ **FIGURE A-1** anterior and posterior anatomy <AU: Please write an explanatory legend once the illustration is final.>

creates another space with limited expansion where compartment syndrome can also occur.

ASSESSMENT

Like all others evaluations, assessment of ocular trauma includes a focused history and physical examination. The patient's pre-injury comorbidities and vision history may be pertinent. Accurately assessing ocular trauma can change the patient's disposition, especially in a setting in which emergent ophthalmic care is not available.

HISTORY

Obtaining the history necessary to treat ocular trauma is the same as for any other trauma. It includes a complete review of systems and the patient's past medical history. Make sure to ask the time and mechanism of injury. Further specific historical information to obtain is described within the physical exam section that follows.

PHYSICAL EXAMINATION

When possible, every eye exam should document the three "vital signs" of the eye: vision, pupils, and intraocular pressure. These functions will give the provider key information about the basic health of the eye. In addition, physical examination includes the anterior and posterior segment of the eye.

Vision

A vision exam can be as simple as holding up a near vision test card or any reading material at the appropriate distance and recording the vision in each eye. Always note if the patient normally wears glasses or contact lenses, and if so, whether for distance or near (reading) vision. If a refractive error is known, but the patient does not have glasses, ask the patient to look through a pinhole, which minimizes the refractive error, and recheck the vision. To make a pinhole, take a piece of paper or cardboard and use a ballpoint pen or paper clip to make a hole of about 0.2 mm in the center of it. If a professional pinhole occluder is available, use it to obtain slightly more accurate results.

Pupils

If the patient is wearing contact lenses, they should be removed. Pupils should be equal, round, reactive and without an afferent pupillary defect. A sluggish or poorly reactive pupil indicates a possible brain abnormality such as stroke or herniation. Be aware that these findings do not typically indicate ocular pathology. However, it is important to note that a pupil can become enlarged due to blunt trauma (e.g., pupillary sphincter tear), past surgery, and other ocular disease processes. When an abnormal pupillary exam results from an ocular cause alone, the pupil often retains some reactivity to light, even though it is a different size. The patient's medical history should reflect a positive past ocular history; if it does not, further investigation and examination is necessary to evaluate for intracranial pathology.

In checking for optic nerve dysfunction, use the "swinging flashlight test" to look for an afferent pupillary defect. When there is concern for optic nerve dysfunction related to trauma, consult an ophthalmologist for a detailed examination.

Intraocular Pressure

Handheld tonometry devices, such as the Tono-pen, are now available in many emergency rooms. These gauges have improved the clinician's ability to check eye pressures in diverse patient situations.

When using handheld tonometry devices, open the eyelid while being careful not to push on the globe, because doing so can falsely elevate the eye pressure. Make sure the fingers retracting the eyelids are resting on the bony orbit, not the globe. Always obtain 2–3 measurements of each eye, at the highest percentage of reliability on the Tono-pen (normal eye pressure is between 8 and 21 mmHg). The "data" or "%" reading on the pen indicates the likelihood that this reading is accurate. It is important to note that readings can vary with mechanical ventilation, Valsalva maneuvers, and accidental pressure on the globe during eye opening. When possible, anesthetize the eye with topical anesthetic ophthalmic drops (i.e., proparacaine) if the patient is not fully sedated. Otherwise, the patient may blink excessively or squeeze the eyelids shut when the tip of the instrument touches the eye.

Without a tonometer, you can roughly estimate eye pressure by gently pressing with two index fingers on each side of the eye with the eyelids closed. If you are unsure what normal is, press your own eye or the patient's unaffected eye in the same manner and compare. Most importantly, evaluate whether the patient has a firmer eye on the injured side.

If an open globe is suspected, do *not* check the eye pressure, because you might drive more intraocular contents from the eye. In such cases, check visual acuity and conduct a visual inspection only.

Anterior Exam

The anterior exam addresses several aspects of eye anatomy: the periorbita, extraocular muscles, lids, lashes, lacrimal sacs, conjunctiva, sclera, cornea, iris, anterior chamber, and lens.

Periorbita: Note any ecchymosis and lacerations around the eye. Evaluate the forward extent of the globes. This can be done with eyelids open or closed, by looking down the face while the patient is supine and determining if one eye is farther forward than the other. This can also be evaluated radiographically by using the axial cut of a CT head scan through the orbits, measuring from the lateral wall of the orbit to the nose on each side, and then determining how much of the globe protrudes beyond this imaginary line.

On a normal exam, when you gently push on the eye through the eyelid, you will feel the globe give a little and move backward. When this does not occur, there is resistance to retropulsion, indicating the possibility of increased pressure behind the eye, as with a retrobulbar hemorrhage. Another sign of retrobulbar hemorrhage is when the globe pushes against the eyelids, creating such pressure that the eyelid is taut and cannot be pulled away from the globe. Lastly, when evaluating wounds of the periorbita, always inspect lacerations to ensure they are not full thickness and eliminate the possibility of a concealed foreign body. Even if the globe seems unaffected, any foreign bodies penetrating the orbit require immediate ophthalmic examination to determine if the globe is open.

Extraocular muscles: For patients able to follow instructions, ask them to follow your finger up, down, and side to side. Restricted ocular movement may be from high pressure inside the orbit, from orbital fractures, or from muscle or nerve injury.

Lids, lashes, and lacrimal sac: Examine the eyelids to look for lacerations, and note whether they are full or partial thickness. The nasal portion of the upper and lower eyelids contains the superior and inferior puncta and canaliculi, which drain tears from the ocular surface. Tears flow through the puncta, then through the canaliculi into the lacrimal sac and then down the nasolacrimal duct into the nose.

Full-thickness lid lacerations require surgical repair by a surgeon familiar with eyelid and lacrimal drainage anatomy. Although this procedure need not happen immediately, repair within 72 hours of injury increases the likelihood of success. If the nasolacrimal duct system is involved, it is most ideal to repair before onset of tissue edema, so consult a specialist as soon as you identify the issue. Be especially aware of eyelid lacerations that align with conjunctival or corneal lacerations, because these are often associated with occult open globes.

Conjunctiva, sclera, and cornea: Note any subconjunctival hemorrhages and their extent; the more extensive they are, the more likely the globe itself has sustained substantial injuries. If the conjunctiva is lacerated, pay close attention to the underlying sclera, which may also be lacerated. Again, an injury like this could indicate an occult open globe.

Also check for lacerations or abrasions of the conjunctiva, sclera, and cornea, noting their relationship to any eyelid lacerations. To check for subtle injuries of the conjunctiva and cornea, conduct the fluorescein dye test:

1. Anesthetize the eye with topical drops.
2. Using a moistened fluorescein strip, place a few drops of fluorescein in the eye. (The patient may need to blink to fully distribute the dye.)
3. Shine a blue light (Wood's lamp or ophthalmoscope) on the eye.
4. The dye will fluoresce in the green spectrum and highlight the area of epithelium that has been disrupted.

Abrasions of the cornea or conjunctiva can be treated with simple ophthalmic ointment. Lacerations of the cornea or sclera are of greater concern because when full thickness, they indicate an open globe. This injury requires immediate consultation with an ophthalmologist for further evaluation. Lastly, if you note that the patient is wearing contact lenses; remove them, as wearing contact lenses for an extended period of time greatly increases the risk of infectious corneal ulcers. The fluorescein dye test may also be helpful in identifying infectious corneal ulcers and occult open globes.

Iris: The iris is a spongy, distensible muscle that is generally round and reactive to light. If the pupil is round and reactive to light, but slightly larger than the pupil of the unaffected eye, the patient likely has a pupillary sphincter tear. This injury commonly occurs with blunt trauma to the globe. However, if the pupil is not round, further examination is warranted. With smaller globe injuries, the globe may remain formed, but the pupil will have an irregular "peaked" appearance. Look for the iris plugging the hole in the globe or poking out of the sclera or cornea in the direction in which the peaked pupil is pointing: This is where the full-thickness cornea or scleral laceration should be.

Anterior chamber: The anterior chamber should be relatively deep; i.e., the iris should be flat with an approximately 45-degree angle between the iris plane and the curve of the cornea, and be full of clear, aqueous humor. When the iris is close to the cornea, or the anterior chamber is "shallow," aqueous humor may be leaking out due to an open globe. Look closely for clouding of this fluid, which may indicate the presence of red blood cells. Blood in the anterior chamber, known as a hyphema, has two forms: (1) dispersed, with red blood cells floating in the aqueous humor and thus making the patient's vision and your view into the eye hazy; (2) layered, with blood on top of the iris; or layered, with blood inferiorly if gravity has shifted the blood cells down. A hyphema may cause

dramatically elevated intraocular pressure and can indicate significant trauma to the globe. It is important to consult an ophthalmologist immediately if this diagnosis is made.

Lens: The lens is typically clear in young people or appears varying shades of yellow in patients older than 40 years (e.g., indicating a cataract). The lens is encased in a clear, taut capsule. If the capsule is violated, the lens turns white, often swelling with time. This injury can induce significant intraocular inflammation and elevated intraocular pressure, unless there is a concomitant large globe injury. If the examination indicates a violated lens capsule, the globe is most likely open, and the eye may contain a foreign body.

Posterior Exam

The posterior segment eye exam can be difficult, especially if the pupil is small due to sedatives or pain medications. You can usually observe the presence of a red reflex (i.e., reddish orange reflection of light from the retina) at a minimum. If the pupil is larger, you can use an ophthalmoscope to visualize the optic nerve and/or posterior retina, but this is still not a complete exam. If you cannot view the back of the eye, you cannot exclude the possibility of vitreous hemorrhage, retinal detachment, or other pathology. Unlike spontaneous retinal detachments, traumatic retinal detachments or other posterior pathology is not usually treated with emergent surgery. Nevertheless, be sure to notify the ophthalmologist on call of your findings because vitreous hemorrhage from trauma is usually a result of significant force and the eye is at risk for more serious injuries.

SPECIFIC OCULAR INJURIES

Polytrauma patients are at high risk for many ocular injuries. This section describes some of the most time sensitive, vision-threatening injuries that trauma team members may encounter.

ORBIT FRACTURES AND RETROBULBAR HEMORRHAGES

Fractures of the orbit may cause bleeding in the muscle cone or around it. These compartments are limited by the insertion of the eyelid tendons to the bony attachments of the medial and lateral canthi. If the bleeding is significant enough, a compartment syndrome can develop that obstructs the blood supply to the optic nerve and globe. Signs of a retrobulbar hemorrhage with compartment syndrome include decreased vision, elevated eye pressure, asymmetrical proptosis (eye bulge), resistance to retropulsion, and tight eyelids against the globe ("rock-hard eye").

A CT scan can reveal retrobulbar hemorrhage, but only a clinical exam will determine whether this bleeding is causing a compartment syndrome and requires treatment. Vision loss can occur after about 1.5 hours of impaired blood supply, so immediate treatment is imperative. If you are concerned about a retrobulbar hemorrhage causing a compartment syndrome, immediately contact a provider who has the ability to perform canthotomy and cantholysis. Canthotomy alone (i.e., cutting dermis only) does *not* improve retrobulbar compartment syndrome. It is the cantholysis that increases the size of the orbital compartment, which is equivalent to a performing a fasciotomy.

Do not delay treatment with canthotomy and cantholysis by obtaining a CT scan for further proof of hemorrhage.

Orbital fractures can also result in entrapment of extraocular muscles within the bony fracture site. Repair within 48 hours of onset is recommended to avoid muscle ischemia and permanent damage; thus, consult an ophthalmic specialist to evaluate for this condition. Larger fractures with significant bony displacement are less likely to cause muscle belly impingement and ischemia. Larger fractures usually occur in adults; entrapment and smaller fractures are more common in children, whose bones are less brittle.

CHEMICAL BURNS

Chemical burns are true ocular emergencies and must be treated as soon as the patient arrives. Initial treatment involves copious irrigation of the affected eye and requires little equipment. Ideally, a liter of normal saline or lactated ringers (use tap water only when sterile solutions are not available) is connected to a Morgan lens. Place the lens in the eye, and tilt the patient's head so that the fluid runs out toward the temple (not into the other eye). If a Morgan lens is not available, cut a length of IV tubing bluntly to maximize flow. When possible, the patient can hold the tip of the tubing on the nasal aspect of the eye so the water runs out of the eye. When both eyes require irrigation, you can connect a nasal cannula to fluid and place it over the bridge of the nose so it drains into both eyes. Be sure to call the ophthalmic specialist at this time to notify him or her of the situation.

While flushing the patient's eye, obtain details about the chemical. For example, is it acid or base, and is it a liquid, powder, or other solid material? Alkaline solutions are usually more damaging to the eye and often require more flushing to normalize the pH (~ 7.0). Powders have small granules that can easily get stuck in the superior and inferior fornices of the eye. This situation sometimes requires inverting the eyelids and directly flushing with saline through a 10-cc syringe to dislodge the granules.

After each liter of solution, or about every 30 minutes, stop the fluid, wait 5 to 10 minutes, and check the pH of the tears. While you are waiting, it is ideal to start the eye exam. When the pH is neutral (~ 7.0) you may stop irrigating the eye. If the pH is not neutral, continue this cycle of irrigation, flushes to the fornix, and pH checking until the tears are neutral. This process may require hours of time and liters of saline, so patience and perseverance are crucial. If you are in doubt about whether all chemical has been cleared from the eye, continue to flush until the ophthalmologist arrives to examine the patient. Based on the ophthalmic exam, treatment will likely include antibiotic ointments, oral pain medications, and possible drops for inflammation and elevated eye pressure.

OPEN GLOBES

Open globes include eye injuries that have full-thickness penetration through the sclera or cornea. The size and extent of penetrating injuries varies considerably. Some injuries are so small that a microscope is required for diagnosis; others involve visible foreign bodies still lodged in the eye. Signs of an open globe include a peaked pupil, shallow anterior chamber, corneal or scleral laceration, abnormal pigmented tissue pushing through the sclera or cornea, and the presence of many floating red or white blood cells (seen on slit lamp examination) in the aqueous humor fluid.

A Seidel test can locate small leaks of aqueous fluid from the anterior chamber. To perform a Seidel test, anesthetize the eye, wet the fluorescein strip, and wipe the strip over the area of concern while keeping the patient from blinking. The undiluted fluorescein appears dark orange in normal light; but if a leak is present, it becomes light orange or green when viewed under blue light.

Although many ocular trauma scores have been developed to determine the degree and prognosis of globe injury, initial treatment of all open globes is the same. Once the condition is identified, immediately consult an ophthalmic specialist and describe the situation. Prepare the patient for surgery or transfer, because open globes are surgical emergencies that require immediate intervention in hemodynamically stable patients. While awaiting patient transfer or specialist consultation, follow this procedure:

1. Cover the affected eye with a rigid shield. If a foreign body is sticking out of the eye, cut a foam or paper cup to accommodate the foreign body. Never place a pressure dressing, gauze, or other soft material under the rigid shield because pressure may force contents out of the eye. Furthermore, gauze or soft eye pads can stick to extruding iris or other ocular contents, which might then be pulled out of the eye when removing the pad.

2. Provide an IV antibiotic. Fluoroquinolones are the only class of antibiotics that penetrate the vitreous at therapeutic concentrations when given by an intravenous or oral route. Gatifloxacin and levofloxacin are preferred over older fluoroquinolones due to higher vitreous concentrations from oral dosing. IV formulations are preferred for patients with oral restrictions awaiting surgery. If fluoroquinolones are unavailable, give IV broad-spectrum antibiotics to cover both gram-negative and gram-positive bacteria. Be sure the patient is up to date with tetanus immunization.

3. Explain to the patient the importance of minimizing eye movement if possible. Extraocular muscle movement can cause further extrusion of intraocular contents. Eye movements are linked in the brain, so moving the good eye causes the injured eye to move as well.

4. Treat pain, nausea, and coughing. Valsalva maneuvers can increase pressure on the back of the eye (through the venous system), so reduce these activities to help keep intraocular contents inside of the eye. If the patient is intubated or has an airway in place, ensure that he or she is not getting excessive positive pressure or coughing.

5. Minimize manipulation of the eye. Do not perform any examination beyond visual acuity and observation. This is the extent of evaluation necessary before the ophthalmologist arrives.

6. Order a CT scan (only if the patient will be treated in your facility) with fine cuts through the orbits to look for a foreign body or other ocular injuries. Each hospital has a slightly different orbital protocol for this, but generally the cuts are 1 mm or less. IV contrast is not required.

When you suspect there is an open globe, call the ophthalmologist for immediate examination to make a definitive diagnosis. These injuries should be treated promptly once diagnosed.

SUMMARY

1. A thorough ocular exam in the secondary survey can identify subtle ocular injuries that may threaten loss of sight if not treated right away. In such cases, immediately consult an ophthalmologist.

2. Other ocular concerns can often wait until the hospital ophthalmologist is available during the day for further exam and consultation.

3. When you are in doubt, consult immediately, and the consulting ophthalmologist will determine the timing of the eye exam.

BIBLIOGRAPHY

1. Bagheri N, Wajda B, Calvo C, et al. *The Wills Eye Manual*. 7th ed. Philadelphia, PA: Lippincott Williams & Wilkins, 2016.
2. Hariprasad SM, Mieler WF, Holz ER. Vitreous and aqueous penetration of orally administered gatifloxacin in humans. *Arch Ophthalmol* 2003;121(3):345–350.
3. Hayreh SS, Jonas JB. Optic disk and retinal nerve fiber layer damage after transient central retinal artery occlusion: an experimental study in rhesus monkeys. *Am J Ophthalmol* 2000;129(6),786–795.
4. Herbert EN, Pearce IA, McGalliard J, et al. Vitreous penetration of levofloxacin in the uninflamed phakic human eye. *Br J Ophthalmol* 2002;86:387–389.
5. Yung CW, Moorthy RS, Lindley D, et al. Efficacy of lateral canthotomy and cantholysis in orbital hemorrhage. *Ophthal Plast. Reconstr Surg* 1994;10(2),137–141.

Appendix B
HYPOTHERMIA AND HEAT INJURIES

OBJECTIVES

1. Identify the problems encountered with injuries due to exposure.

2. Explain the mechanism and risks posed by hypothermia and heat injury in injured patients.

3. Define the three levels of hypothermia.

4. Define the two levels of heat injury.

5. Describe treatment approaches for hypothermia and heat injury.

The body strives to maintain a constant temperature between 36.4°C (97.5°F) and 37.5°C (99.5°F). Exposure to extreme temperatures can override normal thermoregulation, raising or lowering the core body temperature. Significant alterations in core body temperature result in life-threatening systemic effects. Environmental exposure may be the only injury, or the exposure can complicate other traumatic injuries.

COLD INJURY: SYSTEMIC HYPOTHERMIA

Hypothermia is defined as a core body temperature below 35°C (95°F). In the absence of concomitant traumatic injury, hypothermia may be classified as mild (35°C to 32°C, or 95°F to 89.6°F), moderate (32°C to 30°C, or 89.6°F to 86°F), or severe (below 30°C, or 86°F). Hypothermia in the presence of traumatic injury can be particularly troubling. It occurs in 10% of injured patients and as many as one-third of severely injured patients (Injury Severity Score > or equal to 16). The synergy of hypothermia and injury can lead to increased organ failure and mortality. Therefore in the presence of injury, different thresholds for classification are recommended: mild hypothermia is 36° C (96.8° F), moderate hypothermia is <36° C to 32° C (< 96.8° F to 89.6° F), and severe hypothermia is < 32° C (89.6° F). Hypothermia also can be staged clinically, based on clinical signs, by using the Swiss staging system (■ TABLE B-1). This system is favored over the traditional

method when the patient's core temperature cannot easily be measured. Thermometers that are calibrated to read low temperatures are required to detect severe hypothermia, and the temperature measured can vary with body site, perfusion, and ambient temperature.

Acute hypothermia occurs rapidly with sudden cold exposure, as in immersion in cold water or in an avalanche. The rapid exposure to low temperatures overwhelms the body's capacity to maintain normothermia, even when heat production is maximal. Hypothermia takes about 30 minutes to be established.

Subacute hypothermia occurs in concert with depletion of the body's energy reserves. It is accompanied by hypovolemia, and its treatment requires clinicians to administer fluid along with rewarming the patient's body. *Subchronic hypothermia* occurs when there is prolonged exposure to slight cold and the regulatory response is inadequate to counter it. A classic example of subchronic hypothermia occurs after an older individual falls, sustains a hip fracture, and lies immobile on the ground.

Cold and wet environments offer the greatest risk of producing hypothermia. Disasters and wars are common settings for hypothermia, but it also happens in urban settings among the homeless, in association with alcohol or drug use, and when young, fit individuals participate in outdoor activities or work.

Older adults are particularly susceptible to hypothermia because of their impaired ability to increase heat production and decrease heat loss by vasoconstriction. In the United States, 50% of deaths

TABLE B-1 STAGING AND MANAGEMENT OF ACCIDENTAL HYPOTHERMIA

STAGE	CLINICAL SYMPTOMS	TYPICAL CORE TEMPERATURE [a]	TREATMENT
1	Conscious shivering	35°C to 32°C (95-89.6 F)	Warm environment and clothing, warm sweet drinks, and active movement (if possible)
2	Impaired consciousness, not shivering	< 32°C to 28°C (< 89.6- 82.4 F)	Cardiac monitoring, minimal and cautious movements to avoid arrhythmias, horizontal position and immobilization, full-body insulation, active external rewarming
3	Unconscious and not shivering; vital signs present	< 28°C to 24°C (<82.4-75.2 F)	Stage 2 management plus airway management ECMO or CPB in cases with cardiac instability that is refractory to medical management
4	No vital signs	< 24°C (<75.2 F)	Stage 2 and 3 management plus CPR and up to three doses of epinephrine (1 mg) and defibrillation, with further dosing guided by clinical response; rewarming with ECMO or CPB (if available) or CPR with active eternal and alternative internal rewarming

CPB = cardiopulmonary bypass.

CPR = cardiopulmonary resuscitation.

ECMO = extracorporeal membrane oxygenation.

[a] Risk of cardiac arrest increases with temperature below 32° C and increases substantially with temperature < 28° C.

Adapted with permission from: Brown DJA, Brugger H, Boyd J, Paal P. Accidental hypothermia. *New England Journal of Medicine* 2012; 367: 1930-8.

due to hypothermia occur in adults over the age of 65 years. Children also are more susceptible because of their relatively increased body surface area (BSA) and limited energy sources. Both of these populations may also be susceptible because of limited ability to remove themselves from the cold environment due to limitations in stamina and mobility.

The risk of hypothermia is of special concern in trauma patients because they are exposed for examinations, may be given room-temperature fluid boluses, and may be given medication that affects their ability to maintain core body temperature, such as paralytics.

Hypothermia is present in up to one-third of patients with severe injury. Healthcare providers can limit further loss of core temperature by administering warmed intravenous fluids and blood, judiciously exposing the patient, and maintaining a warm environment. Because it is essential to determine core temperature (i.e., esophageal, rectal, or bladder temperature) in diagnosing systemic hypothermia, special thermometers capable of registering low temperatures are required in patients suspected of moderate to severe hypothermia.

SIGNS

Shivering is present in mildly hypothermic patients. The skin is cool to the touch because of vasoconstriction. Moderate hypothermia results in mental confusion, amnesia, apathy, slurred speech, and loss of fine motor skills. Severely hypothermic patients may have fixed and dilated pupils, bradycardia, hypotension, pulmonary edema, apnea, or cardiac arrest.

Heart rate and blood pressure are all variable, and the absence of respiratory or cardiac activity is not uncommon in patients who eventually recover. Because hypothermia can severely depress the respiratory rate and heart rate, carefully assess patients to avoid missing signs of respiratory and cardiac activity.

PHYSIOLOGICAL EFFECTS

Cardiac output falls in proportion to the degree of hypothermia, and cardiac irritability begins at approximately 33°C (91.4°F). ECG findings are nonspecific but may include J (Osborn) waves. These appear as an upward deflection after the QRS complex.

Ventricular fibrillation becomes increasingly common as the temperature falls below 28°C (82.4°F) and at temperatures below 25°C (77°F), asystole can occur. Cardiac drugs and defibrillation are not usually effective in the presence of acidosis, hypoxia, and hypothermia. In general, postpone these treatment methods until the patient is warmed to at least 28°C (82.4°F). Given the high potential for cardiac irritability, large-bore peripheral IVs—or if necessary, femoral central lines—are preferred for access. When subclavian or internal jugular routes are used, do not advance the wire into the heart. Administer 100% oxygen while the patient is being rewarmed. Do not let attempts to actively rewarm the patient delay his or her transfer to a critical care setting.

MANAGEMENT

The trauma teams' immediate attention should be focused on addressing the ABCDEs, including initiating cardiopulmonary resuscitation (CPR) and establishing intravenous access if the patient is in cardiopulmonary arrest. Prevent heat loss by removing the patient from the cold environment and replacing wet, cold clothing with warm blankets. Administer oxygen via a bag-reservoir device. Use the proper rewarming technique as determined by the core temperature, clinical condition of the patient, available techniques, and experience of the trauma team (■ TABLE B-2).

Mild hypothermia is usually treated with noninvasive, passive external rewarming. Repeat temperature measurements to identify falling temperatures that may require escalation of the warming technique. Moderate hypothermia can be treated with passive external rewarming in a warm room using warm blankets, ambient overhead heaters, warmed forced-air blankets, and warmed intravenous fluids. Severe hypothermia may require active core rewarming methods. Provide humidified and warmed air through mechanical ventilation. Warm fluid lavage through a bladder catheter, thoracostomy tube, or peritoneal dialysis catheter may be effective. Use extracorporeal-assisted rewarming in cases of severe hypothermia. Rapid rewarming is possible with this technique; rewarming rates of 1.5 to 10 degrees per hour have been reported. Special equipment and expertise is required. These patients require close monitoring of their organ function during the warming process.

■ FIGURE B-1 presents an algorithm for warming strategies for trauma patients after arrival to the hospital. Warming strategies are escalated based on degree of hypothermia.

Care must be taken to identify the presence of an organized cardiac rhythm; if one exists, sufficient

circulation in patients with markedly reduced metabolism is likely present, and vigorous chest compressions can convert this rhythm to fibrillation. In the absence of an organized rhythm, CPR should be instituted and continued until the patient is rewarmed or there are other indications to discontinue CPR. However, the exact role of CPR as an adjunct to rewarming remains controversial.

TABLE B-2 REWARMING TECHNIQUES

REWARMING TECHNIQUE	LEVEL OF HYPOTHERMIA
PASSIVE REWARMING	
• Dry patient • Warm environment • Shivering • Blankets or clothing • Cover head	Mild (HTI) hypothermia 35°C to 32° C (95-89.6 F)
ACTIVE REWARMING	
External • Heating pad • Warm water, blankets, and warm water bottles • Warm water immersion • External convection heaters (lamps and radiant warmers)	Mild (HT I) (35°C to 32° C [95-89.6 F]) and moderate (HT II) hypothermia < 32°C to 28° C (< 89.6-82.4 F)
Internal • Heated intravenous fluids • Gastric or colonic lavage • Peritoneal lavage • Mediastinal lavage • Warmed inhalational air or oxygen	Moderate (HT II) < 32°C to 28° C (< 89.6-82.4 F) and severe hypothermia (HT III and IV) < 28°C to < 24°C (<82.4-<75.2 F)
Extracorporeal Rewarming • Hemodialysis • Continuous arteriovenous rewarming (CAVR) • Continuous venovenous rewarming (CVVR) • Cardiopulmonary bypass	Severe hypothermia (HT III and IV) < 28°C to < 24°C (<82.4-<75.2 F)

Adapted with permission from Spence R. Cold Injury. In Cameron JL, editor. *Current Surgical Therapy*, 7th ed. St. Louis, MO: Mosby, 2001.

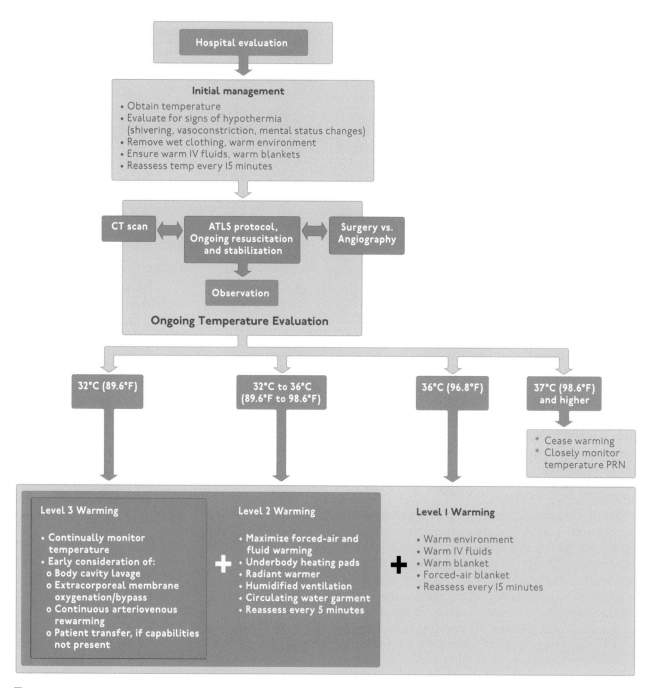

■ **FIGURE B-1 Warming Strategies in Trauma.** An algorithm for early, goal-directed therapy for hypothermia in trauma.
Adapted with permission from Perlman R, Callum J, Laflammel C, Tien H, Nascimento B, Beckett A, & Alam A. (2016). A recommended early goal-directed management guideline for the prevention of hypothermia-related transfusion, morbidity, and mortality in severely injured trauma patients. *Critical Care*, 20:107

Treat the patient in a critical care setting whenever possible, and continuously monitor cardiac activity. Do a careful search for associated disorders (e.g., diabetes, sepsis, and drug or alcohol ingestion) and occult injuries, and treat the disorders promptly. Obtain blood samples for complete blood count (CBC), coagulation profile, fibrinogen, electrolytes, blood glucose, alcohol, toxins, creatinine, amylase, liver function tests, and blood cultures. Treat any abnormalities accordingly;

for example, hypoglycemia requires intravenous glucose administration.

Determining death can be difficult in patients with severe hypothermia. In patients who appear to have suffered a cardiac arrest or death as a result of hypothermia, do not pronounce them dead until having made full efforts to rewarm. Remember the axiom: "You are not dead until you are warm and dead." An exception to this rule is a patient with hypothermia who has sustained an anoxic event while still normothermic and who has no pulse or respiration, or one who has a serum potassium level greater than 10 mmol/L. Another exception is a patient who presents with an otherwise fatal wound (transcerebral gunshot wound, complete exsanguination, etc.) and hypothermia.

HEAT INJURIES

Illnesses related to heat are common worldwide. In the United States, on average over 600 deaths each year result from heat overexposure. Heat exhaustion and heat stroke, the most serious forms of heat injury, are common and preventable conditions. Excessive core temperature initiates a cascade of inflammatory pathologic events that leads to mild heat exhaustion and, if untreated, eventually to multi-organ failure and death. The severity of heat stroke correlates with the duration of hyperthermia. Rapid reduction of body temperature is associated with improved survival. Be sure to assess patients with hyperthermia for use of psychotropic drugs or a history of exposure to anesthetics.

TYPES OF HEAT INJURIES

Heat exhaustion is a common disorder caused by excessive loss of body water, electrolyte depletion, or both. It represents an ill-defined spectrum of symptoms, including headache, nausea, vomiting, light-headedness, malaise, and myalgia. It is distinguished from heat stroke by having intact mental function and a core temperature less than 39°C (102.2°F). Without treatment, heat exhaustion can potentially lead to heat stroke.

Heat stroke is a life-threatening systemic condition that includes (1) elevated core body temperature ≥ 40°C (104°F); (2) involvement of the central nervous system in the form of dizziness, confusion, irritability, aggressiveness, apathy, disorientation, seizures, or coma; and (3) systemic inflammatory response with multiple organ failure that may include encephalopathy, rhabdomyolysis, acute renal failure, acute respiratory distress syndrome, myocardial injury, hepatocellular injury, intestinal ischemia or infarction, and hemotologic complications such as disseminated intravascular coagulation (DIC) and thrombocytopenia. ■ TABLE B-3 compares the physical findings of patients with heat exhaustion and heat stroke.

There are two forms of heat stroke. *Classic*, or *nonexertional heat stroke*, frequently occurs during environmental heat waves and involves passive exposure to the environment. Individuals primarily affected are young children, the elderly, and the physically or mentally ill. A child left in a poorly ventilated automobile parked in the sun is a classic form of nonexertional heat stroke. Homeostatic mechanisms fail under the high ambient temperature.

Exertional heat stroke usually occurs in healthy, young, and physically active people who are engaged in strenuous exercise or work in hot and humid environments. Heat stroke occurs when the core body temperature rises and the thermoregulatory system fails to respond adequately.

The mortality of heat stroke varies from 10% to as high as 33% in patients with classic heat stroke. Those individuals who do survive may sustain permanent neurological damage. Patients with heat stroke will often be tachycardic and tachypnic. They may be hypotensive or normotensive with a wide pulse pressure. Core body temperature is ≥ 40°C (104°F). Skin is usually warm and dry or clammy and diaphoretic. Liver and muscle enzymes level will be elevated in

PHYSICAL FINDINGS	HEAT EXHAUSTION	HEAT STROKE
Symptoms	Headache, nausea, vomiting, dizziness, malaise and myalgias	Headache, nausea, vomiting, dizziness, malaise and myalgias, mental confusion, irritability, disorientation, seizure, coma
Temperature	< 39° C (102.2° F)	≥ 40° C (104° F)
Systemic Signs	Syncope, low blood pressure	Encephalopathy, hepatocellular injury, disseminated intravascular coagulation (DIC), acute kidney injury, tachypnea, acute respiratory distress syndrome, arrythmias

TABLE B-3 PHYSICAL FINDINGS IN PATIENTS WITH HEAT EXHAUSTION AND HEAT STROKE

virtually all cases. Dehydration, low physical fitness, lack of acclimation, sleep deprivation, and obesity increase the likelihood of developing exertional heat stroke.

PATHOPHYSIOLOGY

Through multiple physiological responses that help balance heat production and dissipation, the human body is able to maintain a core body temperature of about 37°C (98.6°F) despite being exposed to a wide range of environmental conditions. Heat is both generated by metabolic processes and gained from the environment.

The first response to an elevated core temperature is peripheral vasodilation, increasing loss through radiation. However, if the ambient air temperature is greater than the body temperature, hyperthermia is exacerbated. Sweating is required to dissipate heat when the ambient temperature exceeds 37°C (98.6°F). Ambient temperature and relative humidity can affect the efficiency of heat dissipation. The average person can produce 1.5 L of sweat per hour, increasing to 2.5 L in well-trained athletes. Cutaneous vasodilatation may increase peripheral blood flow from 5% to up to 20% of total cardiac output.

The efferent information sent to the temperature-sensitive neurons in the preoptic anterior hypothalamus results in a thermoregulatory response. This response includes not only autonomic changes, such as an increase in skin blood flow and sweating, but also behavioral changes such as removing clothing or moving to a cooler area. Proper thermoregulation depends on adequate hydration. The normal cardiovascular adaptation to severe heat stress is to increase cardiac output up to 20 L/min. This response can be impaired by salt and water depletion, cardiovascular disease, or medication that interferes with cardiac function (like beta blockers), resulting in increased susceptibility to heat stroke. When the normal physiological response fails to dissipate heat, the core body temperature increases steadily until it reaches 41°C to 42°C (105.8°F to 107.6°F), or critical maximum temperature.

At the cellular level, exposure to excessive heat can lead to denaturation of proteins, phospholipids, and lipoprotein, and liquefaction of membrane lipids. This results in cardiovascular collapse, multi-organ failure, and ultimately death. A coordinated inflammatory reaction to heat stress involves endothelial cells, leukocytes, and epithelial cells in an attempt to protect against tissue injury and promote healing. A variety of cytokines are produced in response to endogenous or environmental heat. Cytokines mediate fever and leukocytosis, and they increase synthesis of acute phase proteins. Endothelial cell injury and diffuse microvascular thrombosis are prominent features of heat stroke, leading to DIC. Fibrinolysis is also highly activated. Normalization of the core body temperature inhibits fibrinolysis, but not the activation of coagulation. This pattern resembles that seen in sepsis.

Heat stroke and its progression to multi-organ dysfunction are due to a complex interplay among the acute physiological alterations associated with hyperthermia (e.g., circulatory failure, hypoxia, and increased metabolic demand), the direct cytotoxicity of heat, and the inflammatory and coagulation responses of the host.

MANAGEMENT

In treating heat injuries, pay special attention to airway protection, adequate ventilation, and fluid resuscitation because pulmonary aspiration and hypoxia are important causes of death. Initially, administer 100% oxygen; after cooling, use arterial blood gas results to guide further oxygen delivery.

Patients with an altered level of consciousness, significant hypercapnia, or persistent hypoxia should be intubated and mechanically ventilated. Obtain arterial blood gas, electrolytes, creatinine, and blood urea nitrogen levels as early as possible. Renal failure and rhabdomyolysis are frequently seen in patients with heat stroke. Have a chest x-ray performed. Use standard methods to treat hypoglycemia, hyperkalemia, and acidosis. Hypokalemia may become apparent and necessitate potassium replacement, particularly as acidemia is corrected. Seizures may be treated with benzodiazepines.

Prompt correction of hyperthermia by immediate cooling and support of organ-system function are the two main therapeutic objectives in patients with heat stroke.

Rapid cooling improves survival. The goal is to decrease body temperature to < 39°C within 30 minutes. Start cooling measures as soon as practical at the scene and continue en route to the emergency department. Water spray and airflow over the patient is ideal in the prehospital setting. Alternatively, apply ice packs to areas of high blood flow (e.g., groin, neck, axilla). Although experts generally agree on the need for rapid and effective cooling of hyperthermic patients with heat stroke, there is debate about the best method to achieve it. The cooling method based on conduction—namely, immersion in iced water started within minutes of the onset of exertional heat stroke—is fast, safe and effective in young, healthy, and well-trained military personnel or athletes. Do not use this method in elderly patients because it can increase rather than decrease mortality. Alternatively, use a commercial cooling device.

In mass casualty events with classic heat stroke, the body-cooling unit (BCU) can achieve excellent cooling rates with improved survival. The BCU involves spraying patients with water at 15°C (59°F) and circulating warm air that reaches the skin at 30°C to 35°C (86°F to 95°F). This technique is well tolerated and allows for optimal monitoring and resuscitation of unconscious and hemodynamically unstable patients. Noninvasive and well-tolerated cooling modalities such as ice packs, wet gauze sheets, and fans—alone or in combination—could represent reasonable alternatives because they are easily applied and readily accessible. Survival and outcomes in heat stroke are directly related to the time required to initiate therapy and cool patients to ≤ 39°C (102.2°F).

PHARMACOLOGY

In the case of malignant hyperthermia related to anesthetic agents or neuroleptic malignant syndrome, dantrolene (Dantrium, Revonto) reduces muscle excitation and contraction and decreases core body temperature. Dantrolene has not been shown to decrease body temperature when used to treat heat stroke.

Medications can potentially increase risk of exertional heat stroke. Examples include but are not limited to alcohol, any prescription or over-the-counter stimulant, caffeine or energy drinks, diuretics, angiotensin converting enzyme converting inhibitors (especially combined with diuretic), antihistamines, and anticholinergics. Amphetamines and salicylates in large doses can elevate the hypothalamic set point. Antipsychotic medication and antidepressant medications such as lithium (Lithobid, Lithane) and selective serotonin reuptake inhibitors can interfere with thermoregulatory mechanisms. When possible, obtain a medication history from patient, family, and/or prehospital personnel. ■ BOX B-1 lists some medications and drugs that may worsen heat illnesses.

PROGNOSIS

Factors associated with poor prognosis include hypotension, the need for endotracheal intubation, altered coagulation, old age, temperature > 41°C (105.8°F), long duration of hyperthermia, prolonged coma, hyperkalemia, and oliguric renal failure.

BOX B-1 MEDICATIONS AND DRUGS THAT MAY EXACERBATE HEAT ILLNESSES

- Alcohol
- Alpha adrenergics
- Amphetamines
- Anticholinergics
- Antihistamines
- Antipsychotics
- Benzodiazepines
- Beta blockers
- Calcium channel blockers
- Clopidogrel (Plavix)
- Cocaine
- Diuretics
- Ecstasy
- Laxatives
- Lithium (Lithobid, Lithane)
- Neuroleptics
- Phenothiazines
- Thyroid agonist
- Tricyclic antidepressants

SUMMARY

The injuries due to heat and cold exposure are not only burns or frostbite, but can result in systemic alterations in temperature regulation and homeostasis. It is important to understand the etiology and treatment of exposure injuries.

BIBLIOGRAPHY

Cold Injuries

1. Avellanasa ML, Ricart A, Botella J, et al. Management of severe accidental hypothermia. *Med Intensiva* 2012;36:200–212.
2. Brown DJA, Brugger H, Boyd J, Paal P. Accidental hypothermia. *New England Journal of Medicine* 2012; 367: 193-8.
3. Castellani JW, Young AJ, Ducharme MB, et al. American College of Sports Medicine position stand: prevention of cold injuries during exercise. [Review]. *Med Sci Sports Exer* 2006;38(11):2012–2029.
4. Dunne B, Christou E, Duff O, et al. Extracorporeal-assisted rewarming in the management of accidental deep hypothermic cardiac arrest: a systematic review of the

literature. *Heart, Lung and Circul* 2014;23(11): 1029–1035.

5. Guly H. History of accidental hypothermia. *Resuscitation* 2011;82:122–125.

6. Hildebrand F, Giannoudis PV, van Griensven M, et al. Pathophysiologic changes and effects of hypothermia on outcome in elective surgery and trauma patients. *Am J Surg* 2004;187(3):363–371.

7. Konstantinidis A, Inaba K, Dubose J, et al. The impact of nontherapeutic hypothermia on outcomes after severe traumatic brain injury. *J Trauma* 2011;71(6):1627–1631.

8. Larach MG. Accidental hypothermia. *Lancet* 1995;345(8948):493–498.

9. Mallett ML. Accidental hypothermia. *QJM* 2002;95(12):775–785.

10. Perlman R, Callum J, Laflammel C, Tien H, Nascimento B, Beckett A, & Alam A. A recommended early goal-directed management guideline for the prevention of hypothermia-related transfusion, morbidity, and mortality in severely injured trauma patients. *Critical Care* 2016;20:107.

11. Petrone P, Asensio JA, Marini CP. Management of accidental hypothermia and cold injury. *Current Prob Surg* 2014;51:417–431.

Heat Injuries

1. Glazer JL. Management of heatstroke and heat exhaustion. *Am Fam Physician* 2005;71 (11):2133–2140.

2. Yeo TP. Heat stroke: a comprehensive review. *AACN Clin Issues* 2004;15(2):280–293.

Heat Stroke

1. Casa DJ, Armstrong LE, Kenny GP, et al. Exertional heat stroke: new concepts regarding cause and care. *Curr Sports Med Reports* 2012;11:115–123.

2. Hadad E, Rav-Acha M, Heled Y, et al. A review of cooling methods. *Sports Med* 2004;34(8):501–511.

3. Lipman GS, Eifling KP, Ellis MA, et al. Wilderness Medical Society practice guidelines for the prevention and treatment of heat-related illness: 2014 update. *Wilderness & Environ Med* 2013;24(4):351–361.

4. Raukar N, Lemieux R, Finn G, et al. Heat illness—a practical primer. *Rhode Island Med J* 2015;98(7):28–31.

5. Sharyn Ireland, Ruth Endacott, Peter Cameron, Mark Fitzgerald, Eldho Paul. The incidence and significance of accidental hypothermia in major trauma—A prospective observational study. *Resuscitation* 2001;82(3):300–306.

6. Søreide K. Clinical and translational effects of hypothermia in major trauma patients: From pathophysiology to prevention, prognosis and potential preservation. *Injury, Int. J. Care Injured* 2014;45:647–654.

7. Spence R. Cold Injury. In Cameron JL, editor. *Current Surgical Therapy*, 7th St. Louis, MO: Mosby, 2001.

Appendix C
TRAUMA CARE IN MASS-CASUALTY, AUSTERE, AND OPERATIONAL ENVIRONMENTS (OPTIONAL LECTURE)

OBJECTIVES

1. Describe how mass-casualty events create a population-based standard of care.

2. Describe tools for effective mass-casualty care.

3. List the priorities for care of an individual in mass-casualty situations.

4. Discuss challenges for mass-casualty care.

5. Identify challenges of providing trauma care in operational, austere, and resource-constrained environments.

6. Review the principles of Tactical Combat Casualty Care (TCCC).

7. Outline the concept of the Advanced Trauma Life Support® in the Operational Environment (ATLS-OE) supplemental curriculum.

8. Define the principles for management of intentional mass-casualty and active shooter events.

The ability to provide quality trauma care in any resource-constrained environment, including areas of conflict, disaster, and other austere settings, may be highly variable. In the worst-case scenario, adequate care may be available only through delivery of external resources to the battlespace or site of disaster. The many challenges associated with functioning within the disaster or austere environment will affect every echelon or level of care, from the point of injury to the evacuation of the casualty to a modern tertiary care center (when possible). All healthcare providers in these environments must understand these limitations and how they will critically impact trauma care, as well as of the strategies available to mitigate these disadvantages. Enhanced situational awareness is of paramount importance in these settings.

Disasters occur globally due to natural and technological phenomena as well as human conflict. No community is immune. Even the most sophisticated hospitals can become austere facilities after a disaster, due to limitation of available resources and/or overwhelming numbers of casualties. Effective disaster management is not business as usual; it requires a unique mind-set that recognizes the need for a population-based standard of care and healthcare worker safety. "Adapt and overcome" is the slogan for readiness.

Advanced Trauma Life Support (ATLS) had its origins in a Nebraska cornfield following a plane crash in which the injured received inadequate care in an austere environment. Although commonly seen through the lens of plentiful resources, ATLS provides an initial framework for all trauma patients and is applicable in mass-casualty events and austere or conflict-ridden environments with limited resources. Further depth can be found in the American College of Surgeons Disaster Management and Emergency Preparedness (DMEP) course and the U.S. Military's Advanced Trauma Life Support® for the Operational Environment (ATLS-OE).

MASS-CASUALTY CARE

A mass-casualty event exists when casualties exceed the resources to provide complete individual care, typically in the setting of limited information and uncertainty about event evolution. During a mass casualty event, the care paradigm shifts from the greatest good for the individual to the greatest good for the greatest number of casualties. This population-based standard of care is different from everyday trauma care, in which all resources are mobilized for the good of an individual injured patient. In the disaster setting, decisions made for one casualty can affect decisions for other casualties because of resource limitations and circumstances. Increased mortality can result from faulty decision making.

Casualty disposition in the aftermath of disaster relates to the intersection of casualty, resource, and situational considerations. Casualty characteristics include immediately life-threatening injuries, complexity of interventions to manage threats to life, injury severity, and survivability. Inability to survive is both absolute (e.g., 100% third-degree body-surface area burns) and relative (e.g., extensive injuries consume resources for one casualty that could be used to save more than one casualty).

Resource considerations include what is available (e.g., space, staff, supplies, systems) for care and evacuation (transportation, roads), as well as the timeline for resupply and casualty evacuation.

The *situation* involves event progression, secondary events (i.e., additional events relating to the inciting event, such as secondary bombs, structural collapse after an explosion, and flooding after levees break), and environmental conditions (i.e., time of day, weather, and geography).

PITFALL	PREVENTION
Key resources are depleted during the care of only a few casualties.	• Recognize and communicate priorities of care to all team members. • Maintain situational awareness by communication through the command structure to know numbers of potential causalities and available resources.

TOOLS FOR EFFECTIVE MASS-CASUALTY CARE

Incident command and triage are essential tools for effective mass-casualty care. The **Incident Command System (ICS)** is a management tool that transforms existing organizations across planning, operations, logistics, and finance/administration functions for integrated and coordinated response. An incident commander has responsibility for the overall response to ensure the safety of responders, save lives, stabilize the incident, and preserve property and the environment. Medical care falls under the Operations element of ICS. Casualties in a disaster require more basic care than specialty care; thus, health care functions in a more general role in disaster response. Specialty physicians, for example, may be part of the workforce pool for logistics and casualty transport.

Triage is a system decision tool used to sort casualties for treatment priority, given casualty needs, resources, and the situation. The triage goal is to do the best for most, rather than everything for everyone. Effective triage is an iterative process done across all settings of casualty care. At each setting, an experienced acute care professional with knowledge of the health system should serve as the triage officer. Triage is not a one-time decision; it is a dynamic sequence of decisions. Casualties, resources, and situations change, leading to refined triage decisions. The ICS can provide information about expected numbers and types of patients and resources to enable triage decision making.

The triage decision at the incident scene by first responders identifies who is alive and moves these casualties to a safe area away from the scene to a casualty collection point. The next triage decision determines who is critically injured (i.e., who has immediately life-threatening injuries). Use of a scene triage system is helpful. A common system is SALT (Sort, Assess, Lifesaving Interventions, Treatment/Transport), which quickly "sifts the injured using response to verbal command, presence of breathing, and presence of uncontrolled bleeding. This initial triage allows tagging of injured individuals with a color-coded category that identifies the necessary urgency of care required (■ BOX C-1). This approach helps to rapidly separate the critically injured. The casualties who can walk to another collection point or who can wave an extremity purposefully are less likely to have life-threatening injuries, while those who do not move are likely critically injured or dead. Among the critically

BOX C-I SALT TRIAGE CATEGORIES

1. **Immediate:** immediately life-threatening injuries.
2. **Delayed:** injuries requiring treatment within 6 hours
3. **Minimal:** walking wounded and psychiatric
4. **Expectant:** severe injuries unlikely to survive with current resources
5. **Dead**

injured, some may survive and some may not. Triage is a dynamic process and must be repeated with greater focus and discrimination as casualties move away from the scene to other settings and healthcare facilities.

Each casualty category should have a defined area for collection and management. Immediate casualties should gain entrance to the emergency room. Delayed casualties can be initially managed in outpatient clinic–type settings. Minimal casualties can be kept outside of hospital main treatment areas in adjacent buildings. Expectant patients must have their own area. Although not expected to survive, these patients should not be labeled as dead, since resources and situations may improve and allow for later attempts at salvage without harm to other patients.

MANAGEMENT PRIORITIES

The ATLS primary survey provides the framework for initial casualty assessment and intervention by receiving providers. Simple clinical assessments and interventions are paramount in austere and operational environments. Creative solutions involve improvisation of materials to address life-threatening physiology. For example, an initial airway intervention might stop at side positioning and placing an oral airway in an unconscious patient when endotracheal tubes and the resources to manage the casualty after intubation are not available. Surgical airways might be considered, using tubes that are readily available, such as a hollow pen casing. Restriction of cervical spine motion can be accomplished with rolled blankets or the patient/casualty's shoes. Supplemental oxygen is likely to be unavailable. Absent stethoscopes and sphygmomanometers, assessment for tension pneumothorax might be performed with ear to chest and blood pressure estimated with a pulse check (carotid 60 torr; femoral 70 torr; radial 80 torr). Needle decompression requires longer needles in muscular or obese individuals. Field chest tubes can be managed with a "Heimlich valve," constructed as the cut finger of a rubber glove over a tube.

Circulation is addressed by stopping the bleeding. Commercial tourniquets are a useful investment for hospital and emergency medical services (EMS) disaster supplies. Although somewhat less effective than commercial devices, tourniquets may also be fashioned from belts, clothing, or cables and used to manage bleeding from mangled or amputated extremities. This frees the hands of responders to manage additional casualties. Vascular access and volume are secondary considerations to rapid cessation of bleeding. In conscious casualties, oral fluids might be appropriate for management of hypovolemia. Scalp lacerations

can be managed with rapid whipstitch closure. Long-bone extremity fractures can be reduced and splinted with improvised materials to reduce hemorrhage and limit pain.

Typical trauma patient care moves quickly from primary survey with resuscitation to secondary survey and definitive care. However, providers may need to defer the secondary survey and definitive care in favor of identifying and managing as many casualties as possible with life-threatening injuries. That is, the secondary survey and definitive care may be delayed from the primary survey and resuscitation. Beyond the focused assessment with sonography for trauma (FAST) exam, there is little role for extensive radiological imaging and laboratory studies in the first phases of mass-casualty response—a single radiology tech and x-ray machine can perform conventional trauma x-ray studies on only about six patients per hour.

CHALLENGES

Communication is the dominant challenge in disaster response across all environments. Normal communication systems are often nonfunctional, and multiple agencies and organizations, each with its own procedures and taxonomies, are brought together under stress with equipment and protocols having limited interoperability. Even the trauma team itself may be comprised of members who do not normally work together. Application of the National Incident Management System's - Incident Command System (ICS)can improve response and communication. Communication plans should be rehearsed regularly with disaster exercises. Good communication will also provide valuable information about outside events, available plans, and resources, thus reducing fear and rumors.

Transportation options are often limited; any vehicle can be used to move casualties, including buses, cars, and boats. *Safety and security* are challenged due to environmental and conflict conditions. These conditions should be emphasized, planned for, and practiced in drills. Protection of the facility is a key function of the operations chief in ICS. Logistics is challenged by the just-in-time supply systems of many hospitals, and this function can be facilitated by regional mutual supply caches and prearranged supply orders. State and federal government agencies can supply resources; however, delays of 96 hours or more before full mobilization have been experienced in past incidents.

Mass volunteerism and *self-deployment* can swamp a facility or scene with well-meaning providers who have undetermined credentialing and skills. They must be managed by a plan that controls access until they are acceptably vetted. Joining medical assistance teams in advance of events prevents this difficulty.

Special and vulnerable populations include children, the elderly, the obese, those with psychiatric illnesses, and patients on home dialysis or ventilators. Declaration of a disaster or emergency by a responsible official suspends many healthcare regulations. Facilities must plan to accept trauma patients in disasters even if they are not a trauma center. Similarly, burn or pediatric patients may have to be initially treated in nonspecialized centers. Loss of utilities or evacuations may place extra demands on dialysis units, ventilators, and pharmacy units. Evacuation sleds and disaster litters must be able to cope with obese patients.

Multidimensional injuries are complex injuries not normally seen in daily practice that can occur in disaster. Such injuries may result from high-energy firearms and high-energy explosives. High-energy gunshot wounds, such as those from assault rifles, are created by the linear and cavitating (radial) energy of the missile and cause tissue devitalization and destruction outside the actual path of the missile. High-energy explosives, such as those using military or commercial grade explosives in improvised explosive devices (IEDs), cause multidimensional blast injuries across four mechanisms: primary blast from the supersonic pressure wave; secondary blast from fragments; tertiary blast from blunt or penetrating impact with objects in the environment; and quaternary blast as in burns, crushing, or infections.

A prominent injury pattern includes multiple traumatic amputations and traumatic brain injury. Low-energy explosives, such as gunpowder in pipe bombs or pressure cookers, tend to produce secondary blast injuries from fragments for a smaller radius; however, individuals close to such explosions may have extensive penetrations and amputations. Wound management includes hemorrhage control and debridement of devitalized tissue. Energy tracks along tissue planes and strips soft tissue from bone. There may be skip areas of viable tissue with more proximal devitalized tissue.

Loss of infrastructure and austere environments can lead to dehydration, disordered body temperature regulation, and heat injury including heat cramps, exhaustion, and stroke in both staff and patients. Prevention of heat casualties includes acclimation for 3–5 days, alternating work and rest cycles, and emphasis on regular fluid and electrolyte replacement (see Chapter 9: Thermal Injuries). Decontamination and security teams are especially vulnerable.

Psychosocial issues dominate in long-term recovery from disasters and can be more pressing in austere and conflict environments. Healthcare providers are at risk for psychosocial stress disorders from a disaster; such stress can be attenuated through awareness, good communications, and debriefings. Healthy behaviors and organizational practice can improve personnel resiliency before disaster occurs. Monitoring your team and yourself for signs of acute stress reactions is important; appropriate good humor, breaks, and reassurance can boost morale.

CHALLENGES OF OPERATIONAL, AUSTERE, AND RESOURCE-CONSTRAINED ENVIRONMENTS

While ATLS has formed the critical foundation of care for the injured patient in modern civilian and military environments, the experience during prolonged conflicts in Iraq and Afghanistan has also dictated military-specific modifications to standard ATLS principles and practice due to the multiple unique and challenging aspects of providing trauma care in this severely resource-poor environment. Additional factors include operating in an environment with the continuous threat of hostile action, limited basic equipment and personnel capabilities, limitations in the supply and resupply chains, lack of the full range of modern diagnostic and therapeutic technology (e.g., CT scanners, MRI, angiography), and a significantly degraded or even nonexistent local healthcare infrastructure.

The operational or austere environment presents a wide variation in threats, injuries, human resources, and medical materiel availability that all must be considered when planning and executing trauma and other healthcare operations. Additionally, many of these same challenges may be applicable to civilian trauma care in the remote environment, although typically to a lesser degree. ■ TABLE C-1 compares the factors that impact trauma care in the civilian urban, civilian rural, and operational/disaster environments.

SECURITY AND COMMUNICATION

The tactical situation in any constrained environment is highly dynamic, resulting in varying degrees of threat. Both internal and external security concerns must be considered for the protection of both staff and patients. Measures may need to include increased physical plant security with armed personnel or police presence depending on the environment and situation, as well as restrictions in facility access, screening, and identity verification of staff, patients, and visitors, and the searching of vehicles and personnel for weapons.

TABLE C-I COMPARISON OF FACTORS IMPACTING TRAUMA CARE IN THE CIVILIAN URBAN, CIVILIAN RURAL, AND OPERATIONAL/DISASTER ENVIRONMENTS

	CIVILIAN URBAN	CIVILIAN RURAL	OPERATIONAL/DISASTER
Threat level	none	none	high
Resources	readily available	may be limited	severely limited
Personnel	excess	limited but expandable	fixed and limited
Supplies/Equipment	fully equipped, resupply readily available	adequately equipped, delay to resupply	limited supplies, resupply significantly delayed
Available expertise	full subspecialty services	limited specialties locally available	no subspecialty services immediately available
Transfer Availability	immediately available	available but longer transport times	highly variable, may be no option for transfer
Multiple or Mass Casualty Events	uncommon	rare	common

Depending on the environment, key infrastructure considerations, such as electrical power, lighting, and communications, can also dramatically influence a facility's security posture. Although these security needs are most apparent in times of armed conflict, care must be taken to ensure that every treatment facility's operational plans fully address other scenarios, such as when a local facility is overwhelmed or incapacitated by natural disaster, riot, or intentional mass-casualty event.

Likewise, reliable internal and external communication remains a vexing problem. Lack of system interoperability and reliance on native infrastructure, such as vulnerable telephone landline, computer networks, and cell phone systems, are frequent communication limitations. Unfortunately, failed and disrupted communications remain common issues in operational, disaster, and rural environments; therefore, contingency plans must be established in advance.

WAR WOUNDS

Healthcare providers in operational environments must consider the unique wounding patterns associated with war wounds, including the potential for significant tissue devitalization and destruction from the increased ballistic effects of high-velocity ammunition compared with wounds typically encountered in civilian centers.

Although improvised explosive devices are most often encountered in theaters of war, they are also increasingly used as a weapon of choice for intentional mass-casualty events at home and abroad. These highly morbid and highly lethal weapons produce complex multidimensional wounding that may include components of penetrating injury, blunt injury, primary blast overpressure, crushing, and burning. Morbidity depends on the distance from the device, extent of cover, and any protective gear that may have been in place. Trauma teams must exercise vigilance in search of internal damage including vascular injuries, since patients often present a complex combination of wounds, ranging from devastating traumatic amputation to multiple small penetrating wounds with highly variable penetration and wound trajectories that are extremely difficult to assess without adjunct imaging.

MILITARY TRAUMA CARE

TACTICAL COMBAT CASUALTY CARE

A precedent for the modification of civilian trauma training courses to incorporate military-specific needs can be found in the example of Prehospital Trauma Life Support (PHTLS) and Tactical Combat Casualty

Care (TCCC). Initially developed as a curriculum for U.S. Special Operations Command, TCCC has now been implemented across the battlefield and is the standard for combat prehospital care. A military edition of the *Prehospital Trauma Life Support* textbook was developed to support this curriculum.

The widespread implementation and training of all combat personnel as competent initial responders has resulted in demonstrable reductions in preventable death on the battlefield. Today, the TCCC and PHTLS curricula represent a highly successful collaborative effort between the U.S. Department of Defense Committee on Tactical Combat Casualty Care, the American College of Surgeons Committee on Trauma, and the National Association of Emergency Medical Technicians.

TCCC divides point-of-injury care into three distinct phases: (1) Care Under Fire, (2) Tactical Field Care, and (3) Tactical Evacuation.

Care Under Fire

The Care Under Fire phase involves the care rendered by fellow soldiers ("buddy aid") or the unit medic or corpsman at the scene of the injury while the immediate responder and the casualty are still under effective direct or indirect hostile fire. The primary focus for this phase of field medical care is fire superiority and suppression of the source of ongoing attacks. The only medical intervention conducted in this phase is rapid control of ongoing hemorrhage, typically by applying a tourniquet and/or hemostatic dressing. These supplies can be self-administered or applied by a fellow combatant or a combat medic.

Tactical Field Care

In the second phase, care is provided by the medic or corpsman once no longer under effective hostile fire. Tactical Field Care can be highly variable depending on the setting, but all efforts should be expended to minimize the time from injury to arrival at a forward medical treatment facility (MTF) with surgical capabilities. In addition, reengagement with the enemy remains a possibility and must always be anticipated.

In this phase of care, the standard critical prehospital trauma assessments and interventions are conducted. In contrast to the ordered ABCDE approach emphasized in standard ATLS teachings, TCCC emphasizes hemorrhage control (or "C") first, followed by airway and breathing. This approach is based on consistent findings that the most common cause of potentially preventable deaths on the modern battlefield (up to 90%) is due to uncontrolled hemorrhage. Other interventions emphasized in this phase include establishing a secure airway if needed, decompression of tension pneumothorax, judicious resuscitation using permissive hypotension, pain control, antibiotic administration if indicated, and preparation for transport to the next phase of care.

Tactical Evacuation Care

Tactical Evacuation care is rendered once the casualty has been placed in the **medical evacuation (MEDEVAC) platform**. It includes care provided from the point of injury and during transport to the most appropriate higher-level medical facility. Care during this phase focuses on continuing the initial interventions performed in the Tactical Field Care phase, assessment and intervention for any additional life- or limb-threatening injuries, and initiating fluid resuscitation, pain control, and antibiotic therapy if not already begun. More detailed evaluation and greater options for intervention are indicated in this phase of care. The primary philosophy involves minimizing unnecessary or nonurgent interventions and focusing on rapid transportation to a higher level of care.

ATLS IN THE OPERATIONAL ENVIRONMENT (ATLS-OE)

Just as TCCC is to PHTLS, ATLS in the Operational Environment (ATLS-OE) is a course of instruction that emphasizes the importance of maintaining situational awareness while providing care in a potentially hostile, resource-constrained, and manpower-limited environment. The unique situational and environmental factors in the operational setting often include severely constrained resources or supply chains, variable communication capabilities, limited evacuation and transport options, extremes of weather, and a dynamically changing security or tactical environment. In addition, the numbers of casualties, severity and types of injuries, and wounding mechanisms seen with modern combat or even large-scale disasters may be considerably different when compared with standard civilian trauma patterns.

The operational or combat environment involves various unique challenges that require providers to be ever cognizant. These challenges rarely present an issue in the stable civilian environment, although some of these same concepts are also applicable to the rural environment. Providers who render trauma care in an austere environment will be required not only to deliver high-quality modern trauma care, but to do so without the benefit of the plentiful personnel, supplies, and technology that are routinely available in civilian settings. ATLS-OE emphasizes the unique challenges as described earlier and provides students with information that is critical to success in these difficult environments.

ATLS-OE incorporates this additional subject matter in two ways; (1) through addition/supplementation of military relevant information to key ATLS lectures or skills stations and (2) through the addition of several unique and military-specific lectures to the curriculum. For example, new topics such as situational awareness, damage control, and team dynamics have been added.

While the standard ATLS course teaches the primary and secondary surveys, ATLS-OE also stresses the importance of the *tertiary survey*. Once a patient has reached definitive care, the tertiary survey is performed to ensure that all injuries have been identified and none have been overlooked.

A key foundation of ATLS-OE involves the addition of two additional components that must be incorporated into the trauma assessment; the *zero survey* and *quaternary survey*. Initial trauma care in the austere environment requires careful consideration of internal capabilities and external factors (**zero survey**). Additionally, patients are often rapidly transported across multiple facilities and require careful attention to preparation for safe evacuation to the next higher

echelon of care (**quaternary survey**). ■ FIGURE C-1 diagrams the components of ATLS-OE.

Zero Survey

The standard ATLS course briefly addresses preparation to receive trauma patients as they flow from the prehospital environment to the hospital. The zero survey is implied, but it is not specifically characterized or formalized as a separately named survey. ATLS-OE formalizes this prearrival preparation as a critical concept for the student. While this preparation is important to the care of any severely wounded patient, it is absolutely critical as the first step in making appropriate triage decisions in the setting of multiple casualties. The process emphasizes the importance of an accurate inventory of local resources, staffing, expertise, environmental and operational conditions, and any other anticipated or potential challenges in preparation for the arrival of one or more injured patients.

The zero survey identifies provider and/or systems issues that may not yet have been identified or mitigated and that may significantly affect decisions made during the initial evaluation. These are factors and issues that the student never may have considered, but they may be equally or even more important than the actual patient injuries or required interventions. The zero survey

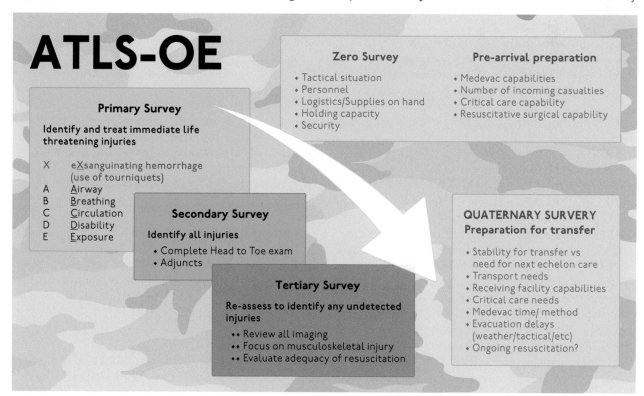

■ **FIGURE C-1** Expanded ATLS-OE Trauma Survey incorporates tourniquet use into Primary survey (X) and the new Zero and Quaternary surveys.

dictates how patients are triaged and prioritized, what injury types or patterns exceed the local capabilities or available expertise, and which resources are in short supply or unavailable.

These factors will include the following:

- How many and what type of medical personnel are available?

- What medical and surgical expertise or specialties are available?

- What is the amount and type of blood products available?

- What are the critical supply shortages, if any?

- Is resupply on short notice available, including blood products?

- Is there a need to initiate a fresh whole-blood drive?

- What is the available source of oxygen, and how much supply is currently available?

- Is direct communication with the next phase of care available if a transfer is required?

- What is the tactical situation, and is security adequate?

The fluidity and potential chaos inherent to the austere environment dictate the importance of the zero survey in practice.

Triage decisions and initial care priorities may change rapidly as situational factors and care capacity of the facility evolve over time and between events. In this environment, as personnel and supply resources become more limited, triage decisions become increasingly difficult.

Quaternary Survey

Although the standard ATLS course emphasizes preparation of the injured patient for transfer from the initial facility to a trauma center, this is typically a single transfer over a relatively short distance by a fully equipped medical team. In contrast, a patient in the operational environment may undergo multiple sequential transfers over prolonged distances while initial resuscitation is ongoing. It is not uncommon for a patient to undergo a major damage control surgery and then be placed into the medical evacuation continuum within minutes to hours of surgery and/or injury. These transfers are often by helicopter in an environment that makes continuous care exceedingly challenging. Therefore, to minimize the likelihood of problems or complications arising during transport, strict attention must be paid to completely preparing the patient for safe transportation.

The quaternary survey formalizes this preparation for transfer. It should be repeated for each successive transfer in the medical evacuation chain. In the operational setting, the time in transit may be a matter of minutes—or it may be many hours. This unknown must be considered not only in preparation for transport but also in deciding readiness for transport. En route care capabilities must also be considered because of potential variation in transportation facilities, available en route care providers, equipment, supplies and medications, environment, and the potential for external threats.

Assessing the patient's response to resuscitation is critical. The potential of meeting desirable end points of resuscitation versus the local resources available to meet these end points are real and important considerations. Although it is certainly desirable to ensure that a severely injured patient is clinically "stable," has had a complete and thorough evaluation with identification of all injuries, and has been fully resuscitated to standard end points, this is often not practical or possible in the operational environment. The limited supply of critical resources such as blood products and the limited holding capacity of the most forward treatment facilities (such as the Forward Surgical Team) make prolonged care and sustained massive transfusions logistically impossible. Thus, often the better of two suboptimal choices must be made, and the patient is placed into the transport system much sooner or in a more tenuous phase of resuscitation than is frequently done in the civilian setting.

The following are additional considerations as patients are prepared for movement within the operational environment:

- Will weather or hostile action prevent movement of casualties?

- What supportive treatments must accompany the patient (ventilator, suction, etc.), and what potential en route problems or malfunctions could occur?

- Will the evacuation team have the skills to manage a critically ill patient and the supportive equipment accompanying the patient?

- What medications, fluids, blood products, and other resuscitative or supportive treatments can be realistically and reliably administered during the transport?

- What protective equipment is needed to prevent hypothermia, eye injury, and ear/hearing injury during transport?

Implementation of ATLS-OE

ATLS-OE is currently offered for all new military medical officer accessions, through the Defense Medical Readiness Training Institute and the Uniformed Service University, and will soon be made available to all military ATLS programs.

IMPROVING SURVIVAL FROM ACTIVE SHOOTER AND INTENTIONAL MASS-CASUALTY EVENTS

From 2000 to 2013, there were 160 active shooter events with 1,043 casualties and 486 deaths in the United States. Similarly, during the period from 1983 to 2002, there were more than 36,000 explosive incidents in the United States with 6,000 injuries and nearly 700 deaths. Most concerning is that the incidence of active shooter events has risen in recent years, and the extreme lethality of these events cannot be ignored.

THE HARTFORD CONSENSUS

With these events in mind, in the aftermath of the tragic shootings at Sandy Hook Elementary School in Connecticut in 2012 and the Boston Marathon bombing in 2013, the Joint Committee to Develop a National Policy to Increase Survival from Active Shooter and Intentional Mass Casualty Events was established by the American College of Surgeons in collaboration with leaders from the various federal institutions including the National Security Council; U.S. military and federal law enforcement agencies; police, fire and emergency medical organizations; and several key healthcare organizations. The committee's efforts have been a national call to action to address survivability of these events and to train first responders and the lay public in the control of hemorrhage. The committee's recommendations are referred to as the Hartford Consensus, and currently consist of four reports:

- Hartford Consensus I: Improving Survival from Active Shooter Events (June 1, 2013)

- Hartford Consensus II: Active Shooter and Intentional Mass-Casualty Events (September 1, 2013)
- The Hartford Consensus III: Implementation of Bleeding Control (July 1, 2015)
- The Hartford Consensus IV: A Call for Increased National Resilience March 1, 2016

Given the high volatility of an active shooter event, the most important initial step is threat suppression by law enforcement personnel. However, the immediate priorities of rapid extremity hemorrhage control by trained first responders and expeditious transport of those with potentially noncompressible internal hemorrhage must be considered.

Critical events in an integrated response to an active shooter event are represented by the acronym THREAT:

- **T**hreat suppression
- **H**emorrhage control
- **R**apid **E**xtrication
- **A**ssessment by medical providers
- **T**ransport to definitive care

Using lessons learned from the military's experience with TCCC, early external hemorrhage control must be the responsibility of the earliest person on scene, and law enforcement personnel should be trained and equipped to control bleeding with tourniquets and hemostatic agents. Similarly, EMS and fire personnel must shift operational tactics and develop new paradigms of emergency management coordination to push forward in support of rapid casualty evacuation.

STOP THE BLEED CAMPAIGN

In response to these recommendations, the White House launched the "Stop the Bleed" initiative in October 2015, with the goal to provide bystanders of emergency situations with the tools and knowledge to stop life-threatening bleeding. In a public health mandate similar to the widespread teaching of cardiopulmonary resuscitation (CPR) and the Heimlich maneuver, the lay public should be trained in immediate bleeding control, or "buddy aid." Appropriate bleeding control equipment (gloves, tourniquets, hemostatic dressings) should be readily available to all emergency personnel and in publicly accessible "hemorrhage control kits" that are as readily accessible and as identifiable as automatic external defibrillators. Lastly, the training alone is not

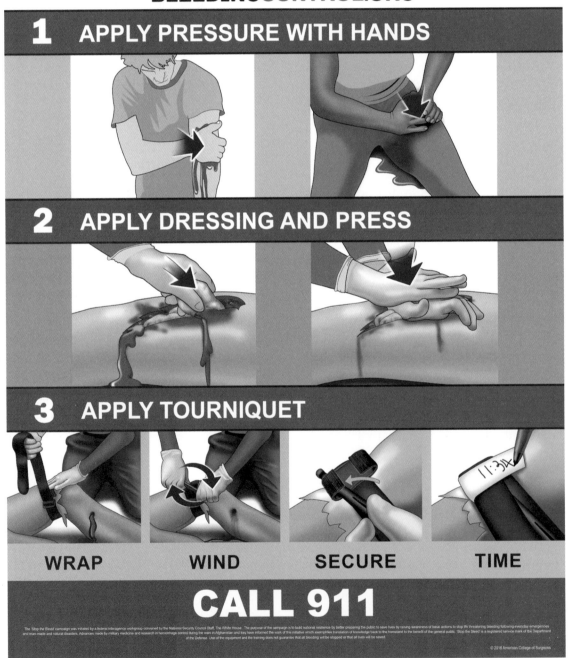

■ FIGURE C-2 The Stop the Bleed Campaign empowers the lay responder to act.

enough; the lay bystander must be empowered to act in time of emergency (■ **FIGURE C-2**).

BLEEDING CONTROL FOR THE INJURED

Bleeding Control for the Injured (B-Con), a short modular course developed by the National Association of Emergency Medical Technicians and co-sponsored by the American College of Surgeons Committee on Trauma in support of the national "Stop the Bleed" campaign. It is designed to instruct either the layperson immediate responder with no medical training or the professional responder, adapted from TCCC/PHTLS principles, this course introduces the concepts of external pressure, tourniquets, hemostatic dressings, and basic airway maneuvers. An additional module for professional responders includes an introduction to THREAT principles. For more information on the B-Con course, visit www.bleedingcontrol.org or contact your ATLS state chair or international region chief.

SUMMARY

1. Mass-casualty incidents change the fundamental treatment paradigm from maximizing the outcomes for an individual to maximizing outcomes for the largest number of people.

2. Tools for improving mass-casualty care include establishment and communication of triage categories and use of the Incident Command System.

3. Challenges after a mass-casualty incident are both immediate (overwhelming numbers and types of patients, security, supplies, communication, transportation), and long term (fatigue, dehydration, psychological).

4. The principles of ATLS provide a framework for evaluating and treating life-threatening injuries in all situations and environments; however, these principles must be adapted to the situation based on available resources.

5. Austere and operational environments require increased situational awareness and detailed prearrival and pretransfer assessments due to resource constraints.

6. The Stop the Bleed Campaign provides for hemorrhage control training for the public and empowers the immediate bystander to act.

ADDITIONAL RESOURCES

Incident Command System
https://www.fema.gov/incident-command-system-resources

Blast injuries
https://emergency.cdc.gov/masscasualties/blastinjury-mobile-app.asp

Chemical and Radiation Hazards
https://www.remm.nlm.gov/
https://chemm.nlm.nih.gov/

Stop the Bleed/Hartford consensus/Bleeding Control for the Injured course
https://www.facs.org/about-acs/hartford-consensus
https://bleedingcontrol.org

ATLS for the Operational Environment
For more information about ATLS-OE, the Region XIII (Military) Chief may be contacted via the ATLS Program Office.

BIBLIOGRAPHY

1. Auf der Heide E. *Disaster Response: Principles of Preparation and Coordination*. St. Louis, MO: C.V. Mosby Company; July 1989.
2. Beninati W, Meyer MT, Carter TE. The critical care air transport program. *Crit Care Med* 2008;36(7 Suppl):S370–376.
3. Blair JP, Schweit KW. *A Study of Active Shooter Incidents*, 2000–2013. Texas State University and Federal Bureau of Investigation. Washington, DC: U.S. Department of Justice; 2014.
4. Bulger E, Snyder D, Schoelles K, et al. An evidence-based prehospital guideline for external hemorrhage control. American College of Surgeons Committee on Trauma. *Prehosp Emerg Care* 2014;18(2): 163–173.
5. Butler FK, Blackbourne LH. Battlefield trauma care then and now: a decade of Tactical Combat Casualty Care. *J Trauma* 2012;73(6 Suppl 5):S395–S402.
6. Butler FK, Giebner SD, McSwain N, et al., eds. *Prehospital Trauma Life Support Manual*. 8th ed., military version. Burlington, MA: Jones and Bartlett Learning; 2014.

7. Butler FK, Hagmann J, Butler EG. Tactical combat casualty care in special operations. *Milit Med* 1996;161(Suppl):3–16.

8. Disaster and Mass Casualty Subcommittee, American College of Surgeons' Committee on Trauma. *Disaster Management and Emergency Preparedness Manual (DMEP®)*. Chicago, IL: American College of Surgeons; 2016.

9. Eastridge BJ, Mabry RL, Seguin P, et al. Prehospital death on the battlefield (2001–2011): implications for the future of combat casualty care. *J Trauma* 2012;73(6 Suppl 5):S431–S437.

10. Jacobs LM Jr. Joint Committee to Create a National Policy to Enhance Survivability from Mass Casualty Shooting Events: Hartford Consensus II. *JACS* 2014;218(3):476–478.

11. Jacobs LM, Joint Committee to Create a National Policy to Enhance Survivability from Intentional Mass Casualty and Active Shooter Events. The Hartford Consensus III: implementation of bleeding control—if you see something, do something. *Bull Am Coll Surg* 2015;100(7): 20–26.

12. Jacobs LM, Wade DS, McSwain NE, et al. The Hartford consensus: THREAT, a medical disaster preparedness concept. *JACS* 2013;217(5): 947–953.

13. Joint Trauma System. TCCC Guidelines and Resources. http://www.usaisr.amedd.army. mil/10_jts.html. Accessed September 17, 2015.

14. Kapur GB, Hutson HR, Davis MA, Rice PL. The United States twenty-year experience with bombing incidents: implications for terrorism preparedness and medical response. *J Trauma* 2005; Dec;59(6):1436-44.

15. Kotwal RS, Montgomery HR, Kotwal BM, et al. Eliminating preventable death on the battlefield. *Arch Surgery* 2011;146(12):1350–1358.

16. Kragh JF Jr, Walters TJ, Baer DG, et al. Practical use of emergency tourniquets to stop bleeding in major limb trauma. *J Trauma* 2008;64(Suppl 2):S38–S50.

17. Kragh JF Jr, Walters TJ, Baer DG, et al. Survival with emergency tourniquet use to stop bleeding in major limb trauma. *Ann Surg* 2009;249(1):1–7.

18. Morrison JJ, Oh J, Dubose, JJ, et al. En route care capability from point of injury impacts mortality after severe wartime injury. *Ann Surg* 2013;257(2):330–334.

19. National Association of Emergency Medical Technicians. TCCC-MP Guidelines and Curriculum. http://www.naemt.org/education/ TCCC/guidelines_curriculum. Accessed September 17, 2015.

20. SALT mass casualty triage: concept endorsed by the American College of Emergency Physicians, American College of Surgeons Committee on Trauma, American Trauma Society, National Association of EMS Physicians, National Disaster Life Support Education Consortium, and State and Territorial Injury Prevention Directors Association. *Disaster Med Public Health Prep* 2008 Dec;2(4):245–246.

21. Walters TJ, Wenke JC, Kauvar DS, et al. Effectiveness of self-applied tourniquets in human volunteers. *Prehosp Emerg Care* 2005;9(4):416–422.

Appendix D
DISASTER PREPAREDNESS AND RESPONSE (OPTIONAL LECTURE)

OBJECTIVES

1. Define the terms *multiple casualty incident (MCI)* and *mass-casualty event (MCE)*.

2. Explain the differences between MCIs and MCEs.

3. Describe the "all hazards" approach and its importance in disaster management.

4. Identify the four phases of disaster management, and describe the key elements of each phase, including challenges for trauma teams.

5. Describe the structure and key principles of the Incident Command System (ICS) and its integration into specific practice areas.

6. Describe the role of ATLS principles in disaster management.

Contemporary disasters follow no rules. Management of the medical effects of today's disasters, whether natural or human-made, is one of the most significant challenges facing trauma teams today. Disaster trauma care is *not* the same as conventional trauma care. Disaster care requires a fundamental change in the care provided to disaster victims to achieve the objective of providing the greatest good for the greatest number of individuals; crisis management care takes precedence over traditional standards of care. The demands of disaster trauma care have changed over the past decade, in the scope of trauma care, the types of threats, and the field of operations. The ATLS course offers a structural approach to the challenges of disaster medicine.

Disaster preparedness is the readiness for and anticipation of the contingencies that follow in the aftermath of disasters; it enhances the ability of the healthcare system to respond to the challenges imposed. Such preparedness is the institutional and personal responsibility of every healthcare facility and professional. The best guideline for developing disaster plans is adherence to the highest standards of medical practice consistent with the available medical resources. The ability to respond to disaster situations is commonly compromised by the excessive demands placed on resources, capabilities, and organizational structures.

Multi-casualty incidents (MCIs) are situations in which medical resources (i.e., prehospital and hospital assets) are strained but not overwhelmed. **Mass-casualty events (MCEs)** result when casualty numbers are large enough to disrupt the healthcare services in the affected community or region. Demand for resources always exceeds the supply of resources in an MCE. It is important to determine the balance between what is needed versus what is available in terms of human and material resources. Any given hospital must determine its own thresholds, recognizing that its disaster plan must address both MCIs and MCEs. ATLS priorities are the same for both MCIs and MCEs.

As in most disciplines, experts in disaster management have developed a nomenclature unique to their field and regions throughout the world (■ BOX D-1). The basic principles are the same, just as the principles of ATLS are applicable in all organizations and countries.

THE NEED

Disaster management (preparedness and response) constitutes key knowledge areas that prepare trauma

BOX D-1 KEY TERMINOLOGY USED IN DISASTER MANAGEMENT

Acute Care The early care of disaster victims that is provided in the field and/or in the hospital by multidisciplinary trauma teams.

Area of Operations The geographic subdivision established around a disaster site; only qualified disaster response personnel are permitted entrance.

Casualty Collection Point (CCP) A safe location within the external perimeter of the area of operations where patients undergo triage and, if possible, initial resuscitation.

CBRNE Acronym for Chemical, Biological, Radiological, Nuclear, and Explosive (including incendiary) agents.

Decontamination Corridor A fixed or deployable facility for decontamination of contaminated patients. The decontamination site is arranged in three zones: the hot zone, the warm zone, and the cold zone.

Disaster A natural or human-made incident, whether internal (originating inside the hospital) or external (originating outside the hospital) in which the needs of patients overwhelm the resources needed to care for them.

Emergency Medical Services (EMS) Emergency medical responders, including emergency medical technicians and paramedics, who provide prehospital care under medical direction as part of an organized response to medical emergencies.

Emergency Operations Center (EOC) Headquarters of the Unified Command (UC), a coordinating center for the multiple agencies/organizations or jurisdictions that are involved in the disaster response. The EOC is established in a safe location outside the area of operations, usually at a fixed site, and staffed by representatives of the key organizations involved in the disaster response.

Hazardous Materials (HAZMATs) Any materials (chemical, biological, radioactive, or explosive agents) that pose potential risks to human life, health, welfare, and safety.

Hazard Vulnerability Analysis (HVA) An analysis of the probability and severity of the risks posed to a community's health and safety by various hazardous materials (industrial mishaps, natural disasters, and weather systems).

Hospital Incident Command System (HICS) A modification of the ICS for hospitals. (Hospitals typically adopt their own versions of this system.)

Incident Command or Incident Commander (IC) The final authority that sets objectives and priorities for the disaster response and maintains overall responsibility for the incident.

Incident Command Post Headquarters for incident command at the disaster site, established in safe locations within the area of operations.

Incident Command System (ICS) An organizational structure that provides overall direction for management of the disaster response.

Mass-casualty Event (MCE) An event causing numbers of casualties large enough to disrupt the healthcare services of the affected community/region.

Multiple-casualty Incident (MCI) A circumstance in which patient care resources are overextended but not overwhelmed.

Minimally Acceptable Care The lowest appropriate level of lifesaving medical and surgical interventions (crisis management care) delivered in the acute phase of the disaster.

Mitigation Activities that healthcare facilities and professionals undertake in an attempt to lessen the severity and impact of a potential disaster. These include establishing alternative sites for the care of mass casualties, triage sites outside the hospital, and procedures in advance of a disaster for the transfer of stable patients to other medical facilities to allow for care of incoming disaster victims.

Personal Protective Equipment (PPE) Special clothing and equipment worn by disaster response personnel to avoid self-contamination by HAZMATs.

Preparedness Activities that healthcare facilities and providers undertake to build capacity and identify resources that may be used if a disaster occurs.

Recovery Activities designed to assist health care facilities and professionals resume normal operations after a disaster situation is resolved.

Response Activities that healthcare facilities and professionals undertake in providing crisis management care to patients in the acute phase of the disaster.

Search and Rescue (SAR) Teams of medical and nonmedical experts trained to locate, rescue, and perform initial medical stabilization of disaster victims trapped in confined spaces.

Surge Capability The extra assets (personnel and equipment) that can be deployed in a disaster (e.g., ventilators with adequate critical care staff to care for patients).

Surge Capacity Extra assets (personnel and equipment) that potentially can be used in mass-casualty event without consideration of the essential supporting assets (e.g., excess ventilators without adequate staff to actually care for patients).

Unified Command (UC) A single coordinated incident command structure that allows all organizations responding to the disaster to work under a single command structure.

Weapons of Mass Destruction (WMDs) Hazardous materials used, or intended to be used, for the explicit purpose of harming or destroying human life.

teams to apply ATLS principles during natural and human-made disasters. Successful application of these principles during the chaos that typically comes in the aftermath of such catastrophes requires both familiarity with the disaster response and knowledge of the medical conditions likely to be encountered.

Disasters involving weapons of mass destruction and terrorist events are particular challenges for trauma teams. Seventy percent of terrorist attacks involve the use of explosive weapons with the potential to cause multidimensional injuries. Explosions produce blast injuries which are complex because of the multiple mechanisms of injury that result (e.g., primary, secondary, tertiary, and quaternary blast injuries). The ATLS course focuses on initial management of the traumatic injuries encountered in such complex disasters by providing a framework of order to evaluate multifaceted injury.

THE APPROACH

The key concept in contemporary disaster management is the "all hazards" approach to disaster preparedness. This approach is based on a single plan for all disasters that is flexible and includes branch points that lead to specific actions depending on the type of disaster encountered. Similar to the ABCs of trauma care, disaster response includes basic public health and medical concerns that are similar in all disasters regardless of etiology. The ABCs of the medical response to disasters include (1) search and rescue; (2) triage; (3) definitive care; and (4) evacuation. Unique to disasters is the degree to which certain capabilities are needed in specific disasters and the degree to which outside assistance (i.e., local, regional, national) is needed. Rapid assessment will determine which of these elements are needed in the acute phase of the disaster. Trauma teams are uniquely qualified to participate in all four aspects of the disaster medical response given their expertise in triage, emergency surgery, care of critically injured patients, and rapid decision making.

PHASES OF DISASTER MANAGEMENT

The public health approach to disaster management consists of four distinct phases:

1. Preparedness (Planning–Training)
2. Mitigation–Hazard Vulnerability
3. Response–Emergency Phase
4. Recovery–Restoration

In most nations, local and regional disaster response plans are developed in accordance with national response plans. Multidisciplinary medical experts must be involved in all four phases of management with respect to the medical components of the operational plan.

Trauma team members must be prepared to participate in all aspects of the medical response to disasters, and they are uniquely qualified to do so. ATLS principles are applicable both to prehospital and hospital disaster care, and all providers should be familiar with the ATLS course content. Ensuring scene safety and determining the necessity for decontamination of affected disaster victims are among the first priorities of disaster response before initiating medical care both at the disaster site and in the hospital.

THE INCIDENT COMMAND/ INCIDENT MANAGEMENT SYSTEM

Medical providers cannot use traditional command structures when participating in a disaster response. The **Incident Command System (ICS)** is a key structure to be used in all four phases of disaster management to ensure coordination among all organizations potentially responding to the disaster. ICS is a modular and adaptable system for all incidents and facilities and is the accepted standard for all disaster response. **The Hospital Incident Command System (HICS)** is an adaptation of the ICS for hospital use. It allows for effective coordination in disaster preparedness and response activities with prehospital, public health, public safety, and other response organizations. The trauma system is an important component of the ICS. Various organizations and countries have modified the structure of the ICS to meet their specific organizational needs.

Functional requirements, not titles, determine the ICS hierarchy. The ICS is organized into five major management activities (Incident Command, Operations, Planning, Logistics, and Finance/Administration). Key activities of these categories are listed in ■ BOX D-2.

The structure of the ICS is the same regardless of the disaster. The difference is in the particular expertise of key personnel. An important part of hospital disaster planning is to identify the incident commander and other key positions *before* a disaster occurs. The positions should be staffed 24 hours a day, 7 days a week. Each person in the command structure should supervise *only* 3–7 persons. This approach is significantly different from conventional

BOX D-2 INCIDENT COMMAND SYSTEM, STAFF, AND ACTIVITIES

Incident Commander (IC)
+ Sets objectives and priorities and maintains overall responsibility for the disaster.
+ The IC is assisted by the Liaison Officer, Public Information Officer, and Safety Officer.

Operations
+ Conduct operations to carry out the Incident Action Plan (IAP).
+ Direct all disaster resources, including medical personnel.

Planning
+ Develop Incident Action Plan(s).
+ Collect and evaluate information.
+ Maintain resource status.

Logistics
+ Provide resources and support to meet incident needs, including responder needs.

Finance/Administration
+ Monitor costs, execute contracts, provide legal advice.
+ Maintain records of personnel.

hospital command structures. All medical providers must adhere to the ICS structure to ensure that they integrate successfully into the disaster response.

PREPAREDNESS

Community Preparedness

Disaster planning, whether at the local, regional, or national level, involves a wide range of individuals and resources. All plans should involve key medical and public health organizations in the community as well as public safety officials (e.g., fire, police, etc.).

Special needs populations pose unique challenges in emergency preparedness at all levels, including the hospitals. Children, the elderly, long-term care facility populations, the disabled (both physically and mentally), the poor, and the homeless have special needs in both disaster preparedness and response activities. All disaster plans must take into account these groups, which are often neglected in disaster management.

Although a regional approach to planning is ideal for managing MCEs, circumstances may require each hospital to function with little or no outside support.

Earthquakes, floods, riots, radioactive contamination, and incidents involving infrastructure may require an individual hospital to operate in isolation. Situations may exist that disrupt the community's infrastructure and prevent access to the medical facility. For this reason, it is vital that each hospital develop a disaster plan that accurately reflects its hazard vulnerability analysis (HVA).

Hospitals should be able to deploy sufficient staff, equipment, and resources to care for an increase, or "surge," in patient volume that is approximately 20% higher than its baseline. The term *surge capacity* is used in disaster plans more often than *surge capability*, but the ATLS course uses the latter term because it is more inclusive. Too often, hospital disaster plans use surge capacity *only* in referring to the number of additional personnel, beds, or assets (e.g., ventilators and monitors) that might be pressed into service on the occasion of an MCE. By contrast, surge capability refers to the number of additional beds that can be staffed, or to the number of ventilators and monitors with qualified personnel who can operate the equipment in caring for patients.

Hospital Preparedness

Hospital preparedness for disasters includes both planning and training. Preparedness involves the activities a hospital undertakes to identify risks, build capacity, and identify resources that may be used if an internal or external disaster occurs. These activities include doing a risk assessment of the area, developing an all hazards disaster plan that is regularly reviewed and revised as necessary, and providing disaster training that is necessary to allow these plans to be implemented when indicated. All plans must include training in emergency preparedness appropriate to the skills of the individuals being trained and to the specific functions they will be asked to perform in a disaster. It is important for individuals to do what they are familiar with, if at all possible. Cross-training of functional capabilities is also important in disaster response.

Hospital preparedness should include the following steps:

- Provide for a means of communication, considering all contingencies such as loss of telephone landlines and cellular circuits.

- Provide for storage of equipment, supplies, and any special resources that may be necessary based on local hazard vulnerability analysis (HVA).

- Identify priorities in all four phases of the disaster cycle.

- Execute pre-disaster agreements for transporting casualties and/or inpatients to other facilities should the local facility become saturated or unusable.

- Plan for mobilization of surge capabilities to care for patients already in the hospital as well as incoming disaster victims.

- Provide training in nonmedical and medical disaster management.

Planning must also anticipate the elements needed in the actual disaster situation, and include these procedures:

- Institute security precautions, including hospital lockdown if necessary.

- Mobilize incident command staff to the predesignated incident command center.

- Notify on-duty and off-duty personnel.

- Activate the hospital disaster plan.

- Prepare decontamination, triage, and treatment areas.

- Activate previously identified hospital disaster teams based on functional capacities.

- Develop plans to ensure feasibility of unidirectional flow of patients from the emergency department to inpatient units. This includes making emergency department beds available for later-arriving patients. Often the least-injured patients arrive at the hospital first; triage them to areas outside the emergency department to allow for the arrival of more critical patients.

- Evaluate in-hospital patient needs to determine whether additional resources can be acquired to care for them or whether they must be discharged or transferred.

- Check supplies (e.g., blood, fluids, medication) and other materials (food, water, power, and communications) essential to sustain hospital operations, preferably for a minimum of 72 hours.

- Establish a public information center and provide regular briefings to hospital personnel and families.

There are several types of disaster drills and exercises. *Tabletop exercises* use written and verbal scenarios to evaluate the effectiveness of a facility's overall disaster plan and coordination. *Field exercise practical drills* employ real people and equipment and may involve specific hospital departments/organizations. Field exercises may be limited in scope (i.e., test of decontamination facility or emergency department) or involve the entire organization(s). Disaster preparedness must include practical drills to ascertain the true magnitude of system problems.

Mass-casualty drills must include three phases: preparation, exercise management, and patient treatment. During the preparation phase, functional areas of responsibility are clearly defined so they can be evaluated objectively. The exercise management phase involves an objective evaluation of all key functional roles in the ICS. The patient treatment phase involves the objective evaluation of well-defined functional capacities such as triage and initial resuscitation.

Personal Planning

Family disaster planning is a vital part of pre-event hospital disaster preparation for both the hospital and its employees. Most healthcare providers have family responsibilities, and if they are worried about their family's health and safety, they may be uncomfortable—or even unable—to meet their employment responsibilities during a disaster event. Hospitals need to plan a number of ways to assist healthcare providers in meeting their responsibilities both to the hospital and to their families. Among these needs are assistance in identifying alternative resources for the care of dependent children and adults and ensuring that all employees develop family disaster plans. All hospital-specific response plans depend on mobilization of additional staff, whose first duty in any disaster will be to ensure the health and safety of themselves and their families.

SEARCH AND RESCUE

Many disasters, both natural and human-made, involve large numbers of victims in collapsed structures. Many countries, including the United States, have developed specialized search and rescue teams as an integral part of their national disaster plans. Local emergency medical services (EMS) systems also have search and rescue assets as part of their teams and often use hospital personnel to assist with resuscitation and field amputations. Members of search and rescue (SAR) teams receive specialized training in confined-space and other environments and generally include the following personnel:

- Acute care medical specialists
- Technical specialists knowledgeable in hazardous materials, structural engineering, heavy equipment operation, and technical search and rescue methodology
- Trained canines and their handlers

▶ TRIAGE OF DISASTER VICTIMS

Triage is one of the most important and psychologically challenging aspects of the disaster medical response, both during the prehospital and hospital phases of disaster response. This is especially true for disasters occurring in austere environments where resources and evacuation assets are limited.

Disaster triage is significantly different from conventional triage. The objective of conventional trauma triage is to do the greatest good for the individual patient. Severity of injury/disease is the major determinant of triage category when adequate resources are available for the care of the patient. In contrast, the objective of disaster triage is to do the "greatest good for the greatest number of patients." In a mass-casualty event, critical patients who have the greatest chance of survival with the least expenditure of time and resources (i.e., equipment, supplies, and personnel) are treated first. ATLS principles, although modified in disasters, still guide trauma teams in triaging victims with the blunt and penetrating injuries seen in disasters.

LEVELS OF DISASTER TRIAGE

Triage is a dynamic and redundant decision-making process of matching patients' needs with available resources. Triage occurs at many different levels as patients move from the disaster scene to definitive medical care.

Field Medical Triage—Level I

Field medical triage involves rapidly categorizing disaster victims who potentially need immediate medical care "where they are lying" or at a casualty collection center. Patients are designated as acute (non-ambulatory) or non-acute (ambulatory). Color coding may be used.

Medical Triage—Level 2

Medical triage is the rapid categorization of patients by experienced medical providers at a casualty collection site or at the hospital (fixed or mobile medical facility). Medical personnel who perform triage must have knowledge of various disaster injuries/illnesses. Many hospitals use disaster triage in their emergency departments to better familiarize medical providers with the triage categories.

- **Red (urgent)**—Lifesaving interventions (airway, breathing, circulation) are required.
- **Yellow (delayed)**—Immediate lifesaving interventions are not required.
- **Green (minor)**—Minimal or no medical care is needed, or the patient has psychogenic casualties.
- **Black**—Patient is deceased.

Evacuation Triage—Level 3

Evacuation triage assigns priorities to disaster victims for transfer to medical facilities. The goal is appropriate evacuation (by land or air) of victims according to severity of injury, likelihood of survival, and available resources.

A category of triage, the expectant or palliative category, is unique to mass-casualty events. Patients are classified as "expectant" if they are not expected to survive due to the severity of injuries (massive crush injuries or extensive body-surface burns) or underlying diseases and/or limited resources. The expectant category of triage was first developed given the threat of chemical warfare during military conflicts.

Traditionally this category of disaster casualties has been classified as yellow, or delayed. Currently most EMS and hospital systems classify expectant patients as a separate triage category with a different color designation and administer palliative care. Classification of the expectant category of disaster victims remains controversial and must be decided at the time of the disaster.

TRIAGE ERRORS

Triage errors, in the form of over-triage and under-triage, are always present in the chaos of disasters. *Over-triage* occurs when non-critical patients with no life-threatening injuries are assigned to immediate urgent care. The higher the incidence of over-triaged patients, the more the medical system is overwhelmed. *Under-triage* occurs when critically injured patients requiring immediate medical care are assigned to a delayed category. Under-triage leads to delays in medical treatment as well as increased mortality and morbidity.

PITFALL	PREVENTION
Medical providers over-triage children and pregnant women.	Base triage on severity of injury and likelihood of survival, not emotional considerations of age and gender.
Blast injury victims are over-triaged due to mechanism of injury.	Although the mortality of blasts is significant, base the triage of surviving victims on ATLS principles and severity of injury, not etiology of the disaster.

DEFINITIVE MEDICAL CARE

Definitive medical care refers to care that will improve rather than simply stabilize a casualty's condition. Maximally acceptable care for all disaster victims is not possible in the early stages of the disaster given the large number of patients in a mass-casualty event. In the initial stages of the disaster, minimally acceptable trauma care (i.e., crisis management care) to provide lifesaving interventions is necessary to provide the greatest good for the greatest number of individuals. Damage control surgery is an important component of crisis management care. In many disasters, hospitals are destroyed and transportation to medical facilities may not be feasible, or the environment may be contaminated. To ensure surge capacity, many hospitals use mobile facilities that can provide a graded, flexible response for trauma care.

EVACUATION

Evacuation is often necessary in disasters, both at the disaster scene and to facilitate transfer of patients to other hospitals. Acute care providers, in addition to their medical knowledge, must be aware of physiological changes due to the hypobaric environment and decreased partial pressure of oxygen that can occur during air evacuation.

DECONTAMINATION

Decontamination is the removal of hazardous materials from contaminated persons or equipment without further contaminating the patient and the environment, including hospitals and rescuers. Decontamination may be necessary following both natural and human-made disasters.

Prehospital and hospital personnel must rapidly determine the likelihood of contaminated victims in a disaster and proceed accordingly. Decontamination must be performed before patients enter the emergency department. Failure to do so can result in contamination and subsequent quarantine of the entire facility. Hospital security and local police may be required to lockdown a facility to prevent contaminated patients from entering the hospital. Events such as the terrorist attack using the nerve agent sarin in Tokyo in 1995 have shown that up to 85% of the patients arrive at the healthcare facility without prehospital decontamination.

The basic principles in response to any hazardous material incident are the same regardless of the agents involved. Removal of clothing and jewelry may reduce contamination by up to 85%, especially with biological and radioactive agents. To protect themselves during decontamination, medical providers must wear the appropriate level of personal protective equipment.

The site for decontamination is arranged in three zones: the hot zone, the warm zone, and the cold zone.

- The hot zone is the area of contamination. The area should be isolated immediately to avoid further contamination and casualties.

- The warm zone is the area where decontamination takes place. The warm zone should be "upwind" and "uphill" from the hot zone. Intramuscular (IM) antidotes and simple life-saving medical procedures, such as controlling hemorrhage, can be administered to patients before decontamination by medical personnel wearing appropriate protective gear.

- The cold zone is the area where the decontaminated patient is taken for definitive care, if needed, and disposition (transfer to other facilities or discharge).

The choice of decontamination technique (gross decontamination versus full decontamination) depends on the number of casualties, severity of contamination, severity of injuries, and available resources. There are two types of decontamination:

- Gross decontamination consists of removing the patient's clothing and jewelry and, if possible, irrigating the patient's entire body with water. Casualties may be rinsed off with water hoses and sprays. This type of decontamination is often used in mass-casualty events.

- Full decontamination (ambulatory or non-ambulatory) is more time-consuming and expensive. Many hospitals use portable decontamination tents for this purpose.

PITFALL	PREVENTION
Contamination of facility, leading to quarantine	• Identify patients that require decontamination. • Decontaminate patients that require it before admission to the facility. • Ensure that providers performing decontamination are properly trained and wearing appropriate PPE for the agent involved. • Assign security personnel to protect entrances to prevent unintended admission of contaminated patients.

SPECIFIC INJURY TYPES

The following are descriptions of the key features, special considerations, and treatment guidelines for blast, chemical, and radioactive injuries and illnesses.

BLAST INJURIES

Blast injuries are multisystem life-threatening injuries that are caused by explosions. The blast wave is a supersonic overpressure shock wave created by high-order explosives. This wave can produce injury at air fluid interfaces so potentially can result in lung and gastrointestinal injury. Improvised explosive devices (IEDs) are homemade bombs and/or destructive devices designed to kill or incapacitate people and are a particular challenge for trauma team members. These devices are sometimes packed with projectiles that result in multiple penetrating injuries. The blast wind is capable of tossing the victim into stationary objects. Blast injuries thereby involve both blunt and penetrating trauma. Lastly, structural collapse can result in crush injuries, significant debris inducing airway and breathing problems, and fire which can result in thermal injury. Knowledge of ATLS guidelines for managing traumatic injuries is essential for providers in treatment of such complex injuries.

Mechanisms of blast injury include:

- *Primary Blast Injury*—Injuries that result from the direct effects of the blast wave and affect mainly gas-containing organs: the gastrointestinal tract, the lung, and the middle ear.

- *Secondary Blast Injury*—Injuries resulting from patients being struck by objects and debris that have been accelerated by the explosion. IEDs and other explosive devices are often packed with screws, bolts, or other sharp objects.

- *Tertiary Blast Injury*—Injuries resulting from the victims being thrown by the high winds produced by the blast waves.

- *Quaternary Blast Injury*—All other injuries caused by explosives such as burns, crush injuries, and toxic inhalations (carbon monoxide, dust, hot gases).

Prognostic factors that affect mortality and morbidity include victim orientation to the blast, magnitude of the blast, environment of the blast (outdoor vs. indoor vs. underwater), structural collapse, triage accuracy, and available medical resources.

CHEMICAL INJURIES AND ILLNESSES

There are several special considerations in the care of chemical injuries and illnesses, whether nerve agents, asphyxiant agents, pulmonary agents, or vesicant agents.

Nerve agents (e.g., Tabun [GA], Sarin [GB], Soman [GD], and VX) enter the body either percutaneously (through the skin) or by inhalation (through the lungs). They affect the cholinergic nervous system, both the muscarinic system (smooth muscles and exocrine glands) and nicotinic system (skeletal muscles, pre-ganglionic nerves, adrenal medulla).

Nerve agents disrupt the normal mechanisms by which nerves communicate with muscles, glands and other nerves.

Symptoms of nerve agent exposure following large liquid or vapor exposure include loss of consciousness, convulsions, apnea, and flaccid paralysis.

Asphyxiants are chemicals that interfere with the body's ability to perform aerobic metabolism. An example is hydrogen cyanide, a deadly poison that causes death within minutes. Symptoms of a large exposure to an asphyxiant include loss of consciousness, convulsions, apnea, and cardiac arrest.

Pulmonary agents are substances that cause pulmonary edema, such as phosgene and chlorine.

Vesicant agents are substances that cause erythema (redness) and vesicles (blisters) on the skin as well as injury to the eyes, airways and other organs. Sulfur mustard and Lewisite are examples of vesicant agents.

Symptoms of exposure to vesicant agents include erythema and vesicles, conjunctivitis, pain, and upper respiratory distress.

Riot control agents, such as chloroacetophenone (CN) and chlorobenzalmalononitrile (CS), are tear gases or lacrimators. Symptoms of exposure include burning eyes and skin, respiratory discomfort, and bronchospasm.

Special considerations in the care of chemical injuries are outlined in ■ BOXES D-3 AND D-4.

RADIOACTIVE INJURIES AND ILLNESSES

There are two major types of ionizing radiation:

1. Electromagnetic radiation (external radiation: gamma rays and x-rays)—Passes through

---

BOX D-3 SPECIAL CONSIDERATIONS IN THE CARE OF CHEMICAL INJURIES

Nerve Agents
- Ventilation with oxygen
- Suction of copious secretions from airways
- Atropine (antidote)—affects muscarinic system symptoms
- Pralidoxime (2-PAM) (antidote)—affects nicotinic system symptoms. Timing of 2-PAM administration is critical because the binding of the nerve agents to cholinesterase (enzyme responsible for breaking down the neurotransmitter acetylcholine) can become irreversible with time.
- Diazepam—auto-injector for convulsions
- DuoDote—single auto injector (atropine+ pralidoxime)
- Mark I Kit—atropine + pralidoxime chloride auto-injectors

Asphyxiant Agents
- Ventilation with oxygen
- Cyanide antidote kit or hydroxocobalamin IV (preferred)

Pulmonary Agents
- Termination of exposure
- Oxygen/ventilation as needed
- No physical activity!

Vesicant Agents
- Decontamination
- Symptomatic management of lesions

Riot Control Agents (tear gasses/lacrimators)
- Generally not life-threatening
- Symptomatic management of lesions
- Normal saline irrigation to eyes or cool water and liquid skin detergent to affected areas of body.
- CN (Chloroacetophenone) and CS (chlorobenzyliden malononitrile) most common.

BOX D-4 CLASSIC TOXIDROMES

Exposure to Nerve Agents (Muscarinic System)		Exposure to Nerve Agent Symptoms (Nicotinic System)
SLUDGE*	DUMBELS*	MTW(t)HF^
Salivation,	Diarrhea	• Mydriasis
Lacrimation	Urination	• Tachycardia
Urination	Miosis	• Weakness (muscle)
Defecation	Bradycardia, Bronchorrhea, Bronchospasm	• (t)Hypertension, hyperglycemia
Gastroenteritis	Emesis	• Fasciculations
Emesis	Lacrimation	
	Salivation, Secretions, Sweating	^ Nicotinic effects

* Muscarinic effects treated with atropine

tissue, irradiating casualties but leaving no radioactivity behind.

2. Particle radiation (alpha and beta particles)— Does not easily penetrate tissue. (The amount of radiation absorbed by cells is measured in Grays (Gy) or new international standard of radiation dose the rad 1 Gy = 100 rad.)

Radiation exposure can consist of external contamination, localized or whole body, or internal contamination. With external contamination, radioactive debris is deposited on the body and clothing. With internal contamination, radioactive debris is inhaled, ingested or absorbed. Assume both external and internal contamination when responding to disasters involving radioactive agents.

Emergency Management of Radiation Victims

The medical effects of radiation include focal tissue damage and necrosis, acute radiation syndrome (ARS, ■ BOX D-5), and long-term effects that can persist for weeks to decades, such as thyroid cancer, leukemia, and cataracts.

Principles of the emergency management of radiation victims include:

- Adhere to conventional trauma triage principles, because radiation effects are delayed.

- Perform decontamination before, during, or after initial stabilization, depending on the severity of injury.

- Recognize that radiation detectors have specific limitations, and many detectors measure only beta and gamma radiation.

- Emergency surgery and closure of surgical wounds should be performed early in victims of radiation exposure.

- Nuclear reactors contain a specific mixture of radioactive elements. Iodine tablets are effective *only* against the effects of radioactive iodine on the thyroid.

■ BOX D-6 outlines key features of several radiation threat scenarios.

BOX D-5 ACUTE RADIATION SYNDROME (ARS)

- Group of clinical sub-syndromes that develop acutely (within several seconds to several days) after exposure to penetrating ionizing radiation above whole-body doses of 1 Gy (100 rads).
- ARS affects different systems, depending on the total dose of radiation received.
- Lower doses predominantly damage the hematopoietic system.
- Increasing doses damage the gastrointestinal system, the cardiovascular system, and the central nervous system, in that order.
- The higher the exposure, the earlier symptoms will appear and the worse the prognosis.

Prodromal Phase
- Symptoms—nausea, vomiting, diarrhea, fatigue

Latent Phase
- Length of phase variable depending on the exposure level
- Symptoms and signs—relatively asymptomatic, fatigue, bone marrow depression
- A reduced lymphocyte count can occur within 48 hours and is a clinical indicator of the radiation severity.

Manifest Illness
- Symptoms—Clinical symptoms associated with major organ system injury (marrow, intestinal, neurovascular)

Death or Recovery

BOX D-6 RADIATION THREAT SCENARIOS

Nuclear Detonations
Three types of injuries result from nuclear detonations:
- Blast injuries—overpressure waves
- Thermal injuries—flash and flame burns
- Radiation injuries—irradiation by gamma waves and neutrons and radioactive debris (fallout)

Meltdown of a Nuclear Reactor
- Core must overheat, causing nuclear fuel to melt
- Containment failure must occur, releasing radioactive materials into environment

Radiation Dispersal Device (dirty bomb)
- Conventional explosive designed to spread radioactive material
- No nuclear explosion

Simple Radiological Dispersion
- Simple radioactive device that emits radioactivity without an explosion

---

PITFALLS

The four common pitfalls in disaster medical response are always the same—security, communications, triage

PITFALL	PREVENTION
Inadequate security	• Include security provisions in disaster plans. • Be prepared to reroute/limit flow into the hospital. • Be mindful of surroundings (situational awareness).
Failed communication	• Don't assume landlines and cell phones will function. • Have backup such as runners and walkie-talkie radios available for use.
Over-triage	• Take available resources into account. • Use minimally acceptable care (crisis management care).
Under-triage	• Use personnel trained in rapid triage to perform this task. • Apply the ABCDs within the framework of doing the greatest good for the greatest number of patients.
Inadequate capacity to manage influx of patients	• Remember that capacity does not equal capabilities. • Make provisions for the obtaining the personnel and equipment necessary to align capability and capacity.

errors, and surge capabilities. The lessons learned from previous disasters are invaluable in teaching us how to better prepare for them.

SUMMARY

A consistent approach to disasters by all organizations, including hospitals, based on an understanding of their common features and the response they require, is becoming the accepted practice throughout the world. The primary objective in a mass casualty event is to reduce the mortality and morbidity caused by the disaster. The ATLS course is an important asset in accomplishing these goals.

ATLS guidelines for managing traumatic injuries are applicable to all disaster situations. All medical providers need to incorporate the key principles of the

MCE response in their training, given the complexity of today's disasters.

The goal of the disaster medical response, both pre-hospital and hospital, is to reduce the critical mortality associated with a disaster. Critical mortality rate is defined as the percentage of critically injured survivors who subsequently die. Numerous factors influence the critical mortality rate, including:

- Triage accuracy, particularly the incidence of over-triage of victims
- Rapid movement of patients to definitive care
- Implementation of damage control procedures
- Coordinated regional and local disaster preparedness.

BIBLIOGRAPHY

1. Ahmed H, Ahmed M, et al. Syrian revolution: a field hospital under attack. *Am J Disaster Med* 2013;8(4); 259–265.
2. American Academy of Pediatrics (Foltin GL, Schonfeld DJ, Shannon MW, eds.). *Pediatric Terrorism and Disaster Preparedness: A Resource for Pediatricians.* AHRQ Publication No. 06-0056-EF. Rockville, MD: Agency for Healthcare Research and Quality; 2006. http://www.ahrq.org/research/pedprep/resource.htm. Accessed February 26, 2008.
3. Bartal C, Zeller L, Miskin I, et al. Crush syndrome: saving more lives in disasters, lessons learned from the early-response phase in Haiti. *Arch Intern Med* 2011;171(7):694–696.
4. Born C, Briggs SM, Ciraulo DL, et al. Disasters and mass casualties: II. Explosive, biologic, chemical, and nuclear agents. *J Am Acad of Orthop Surg* 2007;15:8:461–473.
5. Briggs, SM. *Advanced Disaster Medical Response, Manual for Providers.* 2nd ed. Woodbury, CT: Cine-Med; 2014.
6. Committee on Trauma, American College of Surgeons. *Disaster Management and Emergency Preparedness Course.* Chicago, IL: American College of Surgeons; 2009.
7. Gutierrez de Ceballos JP, Turegano-Fuentes F, Perez-Diaz D, et al. 11 March 2004: the terrorist bomb explosions in Madrid, Spain—an analysis of the logistics, injuries sustained and clinical management of casualties treated at the closest hospital. *Crit Care* 2005;9: 104–111.

8. Holden, PJ. Perspective: the London attacks—a chronicle. *N Engl J Med* 2005;353:541–550.

9. Kales SN, Christiani DC. Acute chemical emergencies. *N Engl J Med* 2004;350(8):800–808.

10. Kearns, R, Skarote, MB, Peterson, J, et al. Deployable, portable and temporary hospitals; one state's experiences through the years, *Am J Disaster Med* 2014;9(3):195–207.

11. Latifi, R, Tilley, E. Telemedicine for disaster management: can it transform chaos into an organized, structured care from the distance? *Am J Dis Medicine* 2014;9(1):25–37.

12. Lin G, Lavon H, Gelfond R, et al. Hard times call for creative solutions: medical improvisations at the Israel Defense Forces Field Hospital in Haiti. *Am J Disaster Med* 2010 May–June;5(3):188–192.

13. Mettler FA, Voelz GL. Major radiation exposure—what to expect and how to respond. *N Engl J Med* 2002;346(20):1554–1561.

14. Musolino SV, Harper FT. Emergency response guidance for the first 48 hours after the outdoor detonation of an explosive radiological dispersal device. *Health Phys* 2006;90(4):377–385.

15. Pediatric Task Force, Centers for Bioterrorism Preparedness Planning, New York City Department of Health and Mental Hygiene (Arquilla B, Foltin G, Uraneck K, eds.). *Children in Disasters: Hospital Guidelines for Pediatric Preparedness.* 3rd ed. New York: New York City Department of Health and Mental Hygiene; 2008. https://www1.nyc.gov/assets/doh/downloads/pdf/bhpp/hepp-peds-childrenindisasters-010709.pdf. Accessed January 4, 2017.

16. Sechriest, VF, Wing V, et al. Healthcare delivery aboard US Navy hospital ships following earthquake disasters: implications for future disaster relief missions. *Am J of Disaster Med* 2012;7(4):281–294.

17. Sever MS, Vanholder R, Lameire N. Management of crush-related injuries after disasters. *N Engl J Med* 2006;354(10):1052–1063.

18. Weiner DL, Manzi SF, Briggs SM, et al. Response to challenges and lessons learned from hurricanes Katrina and Rita: a national perspective. *Pediatrics* 2011;128:S31.

Appendix E

ATLS AND TRAUMA TEAM RESOURCE MANAGEMENT

OBJECTIVES

1. Describe the configuration of a trauma team.

2. Identify the team leader's roles and responsibilities.

3. Discuss the qualities of effective leadership.

4. List the roles and responsibilities of team members.

5. Describe how a team can work effectively to deliver ATLS.

6. Describe best communication practices among team members.

7. Describe areas of potential conflict within a trauma team and general principles for managing conflict.

Despite advances in trauma care, primary threats to patient safety have been attributed to teamwork failures and communication breakdown. In the dynamic and unique emergency department (ED) environment, complex trauma care requires strong interprofessional teamwork and resource management. Success requires not only individual competence in Advanced Trauma Life Support (ATLS®) but also a well-coordinated ATLS® trauma team.

This appendix describes team resource management principles intended to make best use of available personnel, resources, and information. Team resource management is a set of strategies and plans for making the best use of available resources, information, equipment, and people. Historically ATLS® has concentrated on the best-practice assessment and management skills for an individual physician managing victims of major trauma. In fact, teams often provide trauma care; therefore, teamwork is a fundamental part of ATLS® provision.

To function well as part of a team, an individual must be familiar with all the individual steps required to attain the best possible outcome. This appendix demonstrates how a clinician trained in ATLS® techniques can function with others to deliver excellent team care with a common goal. In today's healthcare world, many teams have little chance to prepare or practice together; however, knowledge of team resource management gives every member of the trauma team ways to optimize team performance.

This appendix also addresses how the ATLS® model fits comfortably with trauma team resource management, describes the qualities of an effective team leader, suggests ways to integrate trauma team members into new teams, and describes effective communication in this setting. For the purposes of this appendix, "leader" in an ATLS context is understood to represent the person managing, leading, or taking the dominant or directive role in resuscitating a victim of major trauma.

TRAUMA TEAM CONFIGURATION

Trauma teams ideally are composed of a group of people who have no other commitment than to receive trauma patients. However in most institutions this is not possible, so teams need to be flexible and adapt to the resources available.

A trauma team should at minimum consist of:

- Team leader (senior doctor experienced in trauma management)

- Airway manager (provider skilled in airway management), referred to as Doctor A
- Airway assistant
- Second provider, referred to as Doctor B
- Two nurses, referred to as Assistant A and Assistant B

Additional staff should include, where possible:

- A scribe/coordinator
- Transporters/technicians/nursing assistants
- Radiology support
- Specialist (e.g., neurosurgeon, orthopedic surgeon, vascular surgeon)

The team should have access to other areas of the hospital, including the CT scanner, angiography suite, operating rooms, and intensive care facilities.

Composition of the team and backup resources vary from country to country and among institutions. However, the team composition and standard operating procedures — including protocols for transfer to other facilities — should always be agreed upon and in place in advance of receiving patients.

CHARACTERISTICS OF A SUCCESSFUL ATLS® TEAM

A successful and effective trauma team requires a good leader with experience not just in managing clinical cases but also in leading and directing the team. Trauma team leaders may not necessarily be the most senior clinicians available. Of more importance is their experience in providing care according to ATLS® principles, particularly their exposure to a wide spectrum of clinical scenarios. They require broad knowledge concerning how to handle challenging situations and the ability to direct the team while making crucial decisions. They must be prepared to take ultimate responsibility for team actions.

Regardless of their clinical background, team leaders and their team members share a common goal: to strive for the best possible outcome for the patient.

Principles of communication can be challenged in stressful situations with critically ill or injured patients. However, communication between the team leader and team members is vital and a key

factor of a successful trauma team. Communication encompasses information about the patient's physical state (according to the ABCDEs) and directions from the team leader in response to this information. Frequently, additional members join the team after resuscitation has begun. The team leader must then communicate to incoming team members the roles they will perform and what their contributions should be. (Additional information about communication within a trauma team is provided later in this appendix.)

Many trauma teams have no opportunity to train or work as a consistent team, so cohesion and mutual respect may be more difficult to foster. ATLS® gives team members a common language for understanding each other's actions and thought processes, particularly when prioritizing interactions during the primary survey.

Feedback—"after-action" review or debriefing once the patient has been transferred to definitive care—can be valuable in reinforcing effective team behavior and highlighting areas of excellence. Equally, it can provide individuals with opportunities to share opinions and discuss management.

ROLES AND RESPONSIBILITIES OF THE TEAM LEADER

The team leader is ultimately responsible for the team and its work. Several elements of team leadership can affect the team's efficacy as well as the clinical outcome. These include preparing the team, receiving the handover, directing the team, responding to information, debriefing the team, and talking with the patient's family/friends. A checklist for the trauma team leader is presented in ■ BOX E-1.

PREPARING THE TEAM

Preparation is one of the team leader's most important roles. ■ BOX E-2 summarizes the process for briefing the trauma team.

RECEIVING THE HANDOVER

The act of handover involves relinquishing authority (or property) from one control agency to another. In medicine, this often means the transfer of professional responsibility and accountability. In managing victims of major trauma, the central handover is usually between the prehospital care staff and the trauma team leader in the emergency department (ED). It is critical to relay important and relevant

BOX E-I CHECKLIST FOR THE TRAUMA TEAM LEADER

- Introduce the team and assign roles.

- Identify the scribe.

- Explain how the team will communicate and use time-outs.

- Ensure that all team members adhere to universal precautions.

- Ensure assistants are available to help team members.

- Prioritize patient management during the primary survey.

- Order appropriate diagnostic interventions and clinical procedures, and ensure that they are carried out rapidly and accurately.

- Check results of investigations once performed (e.g., review CT scan report).

- Make sure relatives are aware of what is happening.

- Call additional specialist team members when needed.

- Arrange for definitive care and communicate with receiving physician, when appropriate.

- Check that documentation is inclusive.

- Debrief the team.

BOX E-2 TEAM LEADER BRIEFING THE TRAUMA TEAM

- Introduce yourself, and ensure all team members know you are the team leader.

- Ask team members to introduce themselves to you and other members as they arrive.

- Establish the skill levels of team members, especially their competency to perform practical procedures, and assign roles appropriately. Establish that nurse assistants are familiar with the environment, particularly the location of equipment.

- Allocate the role of scribe to a suitable member of the team and ensure that documentation is timely.

- Ensure that team members use universal precautions to appropriately protect themselves from infectious hazards.

- Explain the procedure for taking handover of the patient.

- Ensure that team members know how to communicate important positive and negative findings during the primary survey, especially when the patient's condition deteriorates.

- Emphasize that important information about the primary survey must be communicated *directly* to you, the team leader.

- Give clear instructions for any lifesaving procedures required during the primary survey, and establish the priority of these procedures.

- Explain that "time-outs" occur at approximately 2, 5, and 10 minutes. These give the opportunity to review the condition of the patient and plan further resuscitation.

- Emphasize that team members who need additional support, equipment, drugs, or resources must communicate directly to you, the team leader.

- Greet any additional providers who arrive to assist the team, although their help may not be immediately required. Assign roles and responsibilities when appropriate. For example, a neurosurgical consultant may not be required during the primary survey, but may be necessary when deciding if a patient requires craniotomy or intracranial pressure monitoring.

information to the team taking over without delay or prolonged discussion.

The MIST mnemonic is an excellent handover tool that can be used in a time-pressured environment to ensure safe transfer of information without loss of important details:

- Mechanism

- Injuries sustained

- Signs

- Treatment and travel

Handover processes may vary by country and among healthcare institutions and municipalities; however, there are two main options:

1. The prehospital team hands over to the team leader while the trauma team transfers the patient to the ED setting and continues resuscitation. The team leader then relates the important information to his or her team during the primary survey.

2. The prehospital team hands over to the entire team on arrival in the ED. This process necessitates a brief period of silence as the team listens to the information.

Either option is acceptable as long as information is handed over clearly and concisely (■ BOX E-3). It can be helpful for the prehospital team to record the history of injury on a whiteboard to which the team and its leader can refer. This information may include an AMPLE history (see Chapter 1: Initial Assessment and Management).

DIRECTING THE TEAM AND RESPONDING TO INFORMATION

The team leader is responsible for directing the team and responding to information during patient care. Because he or she must maintain overall supervision at all times and respond rapidly to information from the team, the team leader does not become involved in performing clinical procedures.

BOX E-3 TAKING HANDOVER FROM THE PREHOSPITAL TEAM

- Ask for silence from the team.

- Direct one person to speak at a time.

- Ensure that an immediate lifesaving procedure is not needed (e.g., management of obstructed airway).

- Use tools such as MIST and AMPLE to ensure complete information is gathered.

- Focus on the ABCDEs, and establish which interventions have been performed and how the patient has responded.

- Make note of critical time intervals, such as time for extrication and transport.

- Record contact information for the patient's family/friends.

The leader gives clear instructions regarding procedures, ensures that they are performed safely and according to ATLS® principles. He or she makes decisions regarding adjuncts to the primary survey, directs reevaluation when appropriate, and determines how to respond to any unexpected complications, such as failed intubation or vascular access, by advising team members what to do next or calling in additional resources. The team leader also arranges appropriate definitive care, ensures that transfer is carried out safely and promptly, and oversees patient handover to the doctor providing definitive care. The SBAR acronym provides a standard template to ensure inclusion of all pertinent information when communicating with referring or receiving facilities (see Chapter 13 Transfer to Definitive Care).

DEBRIEFING THE TEAM

The team debriefing offers an opportunity for team members to reflect on the care provided to the patient. Areas of success and areas that require improvement can be identified that may improve future team performance. Ideally, the team debriefing occurs immediately or as soon as possible after the event and includes all team members. Follow a recognized protocol that includes questions such as:

- What went well?

- What could we have done differently?

- What have we learned for next time?

- Are there any actions we need to take before next time (e.g., receiving special training, requesting additional resources or equipment?

TALKING WITH THE PATIENT'S FAMILY/FRIENDS

The trauma team leader is responsible for communicating with the patient's family/friends about the patient's injuries and immediate care. Therefore, the team leader should be an individual who is experienced in talking to patients and relatives about difficult situations. If necessary, team leaders can seek further training in these skills. Resuscitation of patients with major trauma is one of the most difficult areas of communication between doctors and families. The team leader should ensure that communication lines with the relatives are maintained at all times while continuing to lead the team and ensure the best possible trauma care. This work can be one of the most challenging aspects of being a trauma team leader. ■ BOX E-4 provides tips for effectively communicating in such situations.

If the team leader needs to leave the patient to speak with the family/friends, he or she must wait until the patient's condition is adequately stabilized and appoint another team member to continue the resuscitation. If early communication with the patient's family/friends is required before the team leader can leave the patient, a member of the nursing staff may be called on to speak with the relatives and keep them updated until the team leader arrives. This approach can also provide an opportunity for the team to start developing a relationship with the family. An early discussion with family/friends may also yield important information about the patient's medical history or comorbidities that can be communicated back to the team during the resuscitation process.

Advance directives or do not resuscitate (DNR) orders should be discussed with the relatives if appropriate. When difficult information and decisions need to be

■ FIGURE E-1 Communication with family and friends occurs in a quiet, private space. Ideally the team leader, a nurse, and specialty consultants, and faith leaders, may be included when appropriate.

discussed with the relatives, it generally is advisable to give the family time and space for thought by moving them briefly to a room adjacent to the resuscitation room (■ FIGURE E-1). However, some people prefer to remain with their injured loved one at all times, and their wishes should be respected whenever possible. Although guidelines vary by institution, following are general guidelines related to family/friends being present in the resuscitation room:

- Dedicate a staff member *solely* to stay with the family/friends and explain what is happening.

- Allow the family/friends to leave and return at any stage.

- Ensure the family/friends knows they can choose *not* to witness their relative undergoing invasive procedures.

- Allow the family/friends to ask questions and remain close to their injured relative if this does not hinder the trauma team's work.

While remaining sensitive to the family/friends' concerns, the team leader must remember that the team's ultimate responsibility is to do its best for the patient.

EFFECTIVE LEADERSHIP

Strong leadership skills can enhance team performance and effectiveness even in challenging situations. Medical practice requires competence as well as

BOX E-4 TIPS FOR COMMUNICATING WITH THE PATIENT'S FAMILY/FRIENDS

- Try to find a quiet room where everyone (including yourself) can be seated.

- Always have another staff member with you. If you have to leave suddenly, he or she can stay with the family.

- Introduce yourself and establish who the family members or friends are and what they know already.

- Reassure the family/friends that other team members are continuing to care for the patient.

- Explain things clearly, and repeat important facts.

- Allow time for questions, and be honest if you do not know the answers.

- Do not offer platitudes or false hopes.

- If appropriate, emphasize that the patient is not in pain or suffering.

- Be prepared for different reactions, including anger, frustration, and guilt.

- Before leaving the family, explain what will happen next and when they will be updated again.

proficiency in teamwork and leadership skills. Review of the literature reveals that, across a multitude of publications on the subject, there is no consensus on the definition of leadership. Theories and research into leadership are far from complete, and ideas have changed over time reflecting social, political, economic, and technological influences. However, considerable research evidence suggests that team leadership affects team performance.

The work of leadership theorists has broadened the view of leadership, and good leaders are acknowledged to be people who have a wide range of skills, personal qualities, and organizational understanding. Leadership is a relational and shared process, and it is the interactions of people working in collaboration that creates leadership, irrespective of the role they occupy.

QUALITIES AND BEHAVIORS OF AN EFFECTIVE TEAM LEADER

Three major qualities of outstanding leadership have been identified from interviews with leaders. Outstanding leaders:

1. Think systematically, seeing the whole picture with a keen sense of purpose.

2. Perceive relationships to be the route to performance and therefore attend to their team members as partners.

3. Display a self-confident humility that acknowledges their inability to achieve everything and their need to rely on others in the team.

Emotional intelligence is considered a prerequisite for effective leadership. Studies on authentic leadership claim that leadership is positively affected by "the extent to which a leader is aware of and exhibits patterns of openness and clarity in his/her behavior toward others by sharing the information needed to make decisions, accepting others' inputs, and disclosing his or her personal values, motives, and sentiments in a manner that enables followers to more accurately assess the competence and morality of the leader's actions." ■ **BOX E-5** lists behaviors that are consistent with effective leadership.

CULTURE AND CLIMATE

A key attribute of an effective leader is the ability to create the most appropriate culture for the work to be

---

BOX E-5 BEHAVIORS CONSISTENT WITH EFFECTIVE LEADERSHIP

+ Showing genuine concern

+ Being accessible

+ Enabling and encouraging change

+ Supporting a developmental culture

+ Focusing on the team effort, inspiring others

+ Acting decisively

+ Building a shared vision

+ Networking

+ Resolving complex problems

+ Facilitating change sensitively

---

carried out. The leader must have sufficient knowledge about the culture in which the work is to be done and the capability to foster a culture that encourages, facilitates, and sustains a favorable level of innovation, exploitation of ideas, and collective learning within the team.

Climate is a common theme in much of the research into leadership and teamwork. Highly functioning teams have an atmosphere that supports individual contribution and effectively distributes activity across the team. A clear common goal, sufficient composition of the team, and a sense of satisfaction with team achievements are linked to a strong team climate.

ROLES AND RESPONSIBILITIES OF TEAM MEMBERS

Although all team members need to understand the team leader's roles and responsibilities, the concept of "followership" emphasizes the importance of each team member in contributing to trauma care. This section addresses the ways in which trauma team members can best prepare for and contribute to optimal patient care as part of the team.

Entering into a trauma team for the first time, or even subsequent experiences as a relatively junior doctor or provider, can be daunting. A good team leader will facilitate the integration of team members into the team, but there are ways for individuals to assist. Everyone concerned with trauma care can help ensure that ATLS® newcomers are integrated into the team as positively as possible, not only for optimal patient care but also to contribute to the ongoing development of care provision through ATLS® teamwork.

THE ATLS® TEAM MEMBER

It is important for ATLS® team members to understand what an ATLS® team does, the role of the team leader, roles of team members, structure of the team approach, application of ATLS® in the team, effective communication strategies, and common pitfalls of teamwork.

General guidelines for ATLS® team members include:

1. Team members do not act in isolation. However brief the preparation time is, each person should be introduced by name and role on the team. For example, "Hello, my name is Sanya. I work for the on-call surgical team. I can help with the primary survey, but especially with circulation problems." Suddenly arriving and joining the team without an introduction can confuse and even alienate other team members.

2. Be aware and honest about your competencies, and never hesitate to ask for help. If the team leader asks you to perform a procedure that you feel uncomfortable doing, speak up and ask for assistance.

3. Understand the impact of your behavior on other members of the team. Arguing about a clinical decision will negatively affect team functioning.

4. When you do not agree with what is happening, calmly and reasonably voice your concerns. Everyone is entitled to an opinion, and a good team leader listens to everyone in the team before making important clinical decisions.

5. Trust the team leader and other team members. Everyone is working in a stressful situation and wants what is best for the patient. Every team member deserves respect, regardless of role.

Trust is an essential factor in the efficacy of a team, although it may be more difficult to establish in teams that do not regularly work together. Furthermore, early clinical experiences affect identity development, which in turn can affect social participation in teams. Emotional responses and the meanings we attribute to

highly stressful experiences can play a role in forming a provider's identity and determining how he or she functions in future teamwork. Adverse effects can result from novices' experiences in new teams, so the whole team benefits from ensuring that newcomers are well integrated into the team.

RESPONSIBILITIES OF TEAM MEMBERS

Individual team members are responsible for being available to respond to a request for a trauma team. Key responsibilities of ATLS® team members include preparation, receiving the handover, assessing and managing the patient, and participating in the after-action review.

Preparing for the Patient

As a team member, ensure you are aware of your roles, responsibilities, and resources. Become familiar with the layout of the resuscitation room and the location of resources. Recognize that you are responsible for your own safety and ensure you are always protected against infection hazard by using universal precautions.

Receiving the Handover

Typically, the prehospital team will hand over to the team leader, who ensures that information is rapidly accessible to all team members. When directed to do so by the team leader, team members may begin assessing the patient during handover. When the prehospital team is handing over to the entire team, it is vital for team members to listen to this handover and keep noise level to a minimum so everyone can clearly hear the prehospital team.

Assessing and Managing the Patient

All team members should promptly and effectively perform their assigned roles. Assess the patient in accordance with ATLS® principles and communicate your findings directly to the team leader, ensuring that the team leader has heard the information. Team members may be asked to perform certain procedures by the team leader or may be directed to further assess the patient. Team members who are performing interventions should keep the team leader aware of their progress and inform the team leader immediately of any difficulties encountered.

Team members should communicate *all* information to the team leader. Communication or discussion between team members that does not involve the team leader can lead to confusion and conflicting decisions about next steps.

Participating in the Debriefing

Feedback has been shown to correlate with overall team performance outcomes. Team member should remain for debriefing in nearly all circumstances. Debriefing gives team members a chance to discuss how the patient was managed and particularly to identify areas of good practices as well as any actions that should be undertaken before they are part of the team next time. Debriefing also gives the whole team opportunities to consider different or alternative courses of action or management.

DELIVERING ATLS® WITHIN A TEAM

Specific patient management strategies are outlined in the ATLS® Student Manual. This section describes the specific roles trauma team members assume while delivering care according to those principles.

PATIENT ARRIVAL

▪ **TABLE E-1** presents examples of criteria for trauma team activation, although these will vary by institution.

The team leader receives the handover, ensures that all important information is transferred swiftly to the team members, and establishes the most important aspects of the handover using the ABCDE approach to prioritize the injuries identified by prehospital providers. At some point an AMPLE history must be taken, although complete information about the patient may not be available at handover.

AIRWAY CONTROL AND RESTRICTION OF CERVICAL SPINE MOTION

Securing an airway is often the role of the anesthetist/anesthesiologist or an emergency room physician trained in airway techniques (Doctor A). Doctor A should as a minimum have basic airway skills and understand the indications for definitive airway management. Ideally, Doctor A is familiar with and competent to place a laryngeal mask airway (LMA)

TABLE E-1 CRITERIA FOR TRAUMA TEAM ACTIVATION

CATEGORY	CRITERIA
Mechanism of Injury	• Falls > 5 meters (16.5 feet) • High-speed motor vehicle accident • Ejection from vehicle • High-speed motor vehicle collision • Pedestrian, bicyclist, or motorcyclist vs. vehicle > 30 kph (18 mph) • Fatality in same vehicle
Specific Injuries	• Injury to more than two body regions • Penetrating injury to the head, neck, torso, or proximal limb • Amputation • Burn > 15% BSA adults, 10% BSA children or involving airway • Airway obstruction
Physiological Derangement	• Systolic < 90 mm Hg • Pulse > 130 • RR < 10 or > 30 • GCS score < 14/15 • Chest injury in patient older than 70 years • Pregnancy > 24 weeks with torso injury

or endotracheal tube using appropriate drugs when required for the patient.

When cervical spine injury is suspected, the doctor will establish the airway while restricting cervical spine motion. This procedure requires an airway assistant to stabilize the neck and restrict spinal motion during intubation. The anesthetic assistant supports doctor A by providing appropriate equipment, intubation drugs, and assistance.

Doctor A, who is in charge of the airway, informs the team leader at regular intervals of the steps being taken to secure the airway. If at any point the airway becomes difficult to establish, Doctor A should inform the team leader immediately.

BREATHING WITH VENTILATION

The first responsibility of Doctor B is to quickly assess breathing and establish that ventilation is satisfactory using the standard, safe ATLS® approach. Doctor B reports his or her findings to the team leader and ensures that the team leader has heard them clearly. If a patient has life-threatening chest injuries, Doctor B may be required to urgently perform a needle, finger, or tube thoracostomy.

CIRCULATION WITH HEMORRHAGE CONTROL

If Doctor B identifies no life-threatening problems when examining the patient's chest, he or she may then move on to assess circulation, again by standard ATLS® techniques. However, if Doctor B is needed to perform interventions to establish breathing and ventilation, a third provider may be required to assess and assist with circulation. Areas of potential hemorrhage should be identified and intravenous access established with appropriate fluid resuscitation.

Team members who are assisting the doctors in assessing breathing and circulation should be well acquainted with the emergency room layout, particularly the location of equipment such as central venous lines, intraosseous needles, and rapid transfuser sets. They should be competent in setting up and using these adjuncts.

If a pelvic binder is required limit pelvic bleeding, two doctors may be needed to apply it. A specialty doctor arriving to join the team may be helpful in this role, particularly one trained in trauma and orthopedics. All doctors who are qualified as ATLS® providers should be able to safely apply a pelvic binder.

DISABILITY

Doctor A, who is establishing the airway, can usually determine the patient's Glasgow Coma Scale (GCS) score and assess pupil size while positioned at the head of the patient. For a patient requiring immediate or urgent intubation, the doctor establishing the airway should note GCS score and pupil size before administering any drugs.

EXPOSURE AND ENVIRONMENT

It is vital to fully expose the patient, cutting off garments to fully expose the patient for examination. During exposure a full visual inspection of the patient can be undertaken, and any immediately obvious injuries should be reported to the team leader. This procedure can be performed by nurse assistants or by medical staff if appropriate. At this stage, a secondary survey is not

■ **FIGURE E-2** Dedicated scribes are trained to document all information accurately and completely.

performed. Following exposure, cover the patient with warm blankets to maintain body temperature.

RECORD KEEPING

Record keeping is an important role and in some jurisdictions is performed by a dedicated scribe who has been trained to document all information in an appropriate fashion (■ **FIGURE E-2**). When scribes are not available documentation follows patient care. It is the team leader's responsibility to ensure that the scribe is aware of all important information and findings. The team leader should also ensure documentation includes any significant decisions regarding definitive care or urgent investigations. Many trauma charts use the ABCDE system, so important information can be recorded as the team relates its findings to the team leader.

ENSURING EFFECTIVE TEAM COMMUNICATION

It matters little how competent the clinical care is if the trauma team does not communicate effectively and efficiently. Communication is not just a set of skills to be performed; it involves a shared experiential context and a collective understanding of the purpose of the team's activity.

Research studies in primary healthcare teams found that structured time for decision making, team building, and team cohesiveness influenced communication within teams. Failure to set aside time for regular meetings to clarify roles, set goals, allocate tasks, develop and encourage participation, and manage change were inhibitors to good communication within teams. Variation in status, power, education, and assertiveness within a team can contribute to poor communication. Joint professional training and regular team meetings facilitate communication for multi-professional teams.

In addition, different clinical professions may have issues in communicating related to variations in how information is processed analytically vs intuitively. Furthermore, there is greater valuing of information among those of the same clinical group, and stereotyping may occur between members of different clinical professions. To reduce such biases, clear expectations should be set for the trauma team.

In the context of a team managing major trauma:

- Communication between a team member and team leader should be direct and only two way.

- The team member should relay information, and the team leader should confirm that he or she heard and understood the information.

- Time-outs at 2, 5, and 10 minutes may allow for discussion or review of findings.

- All communication should take place at normal voice level.

- Communication should not become extended discussions over the patient. Complex decisions may require discussion between team members but should always be conducted calmly and professionally. Hold discussions a short distance away from the patient, especially if he or she is conscious.

MANAGING CONFLICT

The trauma team should function as a cohesive unit that manages the patient to the best possible outcome. In the majority of cases, all members of the team manage the patient to the best of their ability. Unfortunately, as in any field of medical care, controversy and conflict do arise. Examples of sources of conflict include:

- Making a difficult decision about whether a patient requires an urgent CT or immediate laparotomy.

- Determining the best treatment for bleeding from a pelvic fracture: interventional radiology or pre-peritoneal pelvic packing.

- Deciding the appropriate use of balanced resuscitation versus the standard use of resuscitative fluids and blood.

- Determining the end points of resuscitation.

- Deciding whether to activate the massive transfusion protocol.

- Determining when to stop resuscitating a trauma patient because further resuscitative measures may be futile.

These are all difficult situations to address while managing a severely injured trauma victim, and the ways in which they are handled will vary depending on local standards and resources. It is impossible to provide a single solution for each of these examples, but general guidelines for addressing conflict are helpful.

Remember that all team members should have the opportunity to voice suggestions about patient management (during time-outs). Yet the team leader has ultimate responsibility for patient management. All actions affecting the patient should be made in his or her best interests.

Many conflicts and confrontations about the management of trauma patients arise because doctors are unsure of their own competencies and unwilling or reluctant to say so. If doctors do not have the experience to manage a trauma patient and find themselves in disagreement, they should immediately involve a more senior physician who may be in a position to resolve the situation with a positive outcome for both the patient and the team. Trauma team leaders tend to be senior doctors but, depending on resources, more junior doctors may be acting as trauma team leaders. In this situation, it is vital to have a senior doctor available for support in making challenging decisions.

Discussions between doctors may become more difficult to resolve when doctors strongly believe that their system of doing things is the one that should be followed. In such cases it can be helpful to involve a senior clinician, such as a trauma medical director. They may be in a position to help with decisions, particularly where hospital protocols or guidelines are available.

Ethical dilemmas may also cause conflict among members of the trauma team. Examples might include the decision to end resuscitation of a severely injured patient or to resuscitate patients with blood or blood products when the patient's religious views do not permit such action. Remember that expert advice is available on these matters. The trauma team leader or a designated deputy can seek further information or support that can identify the best decision for the patient.

The vast majority of trauma teams work well together and achieve positive outcomes for their patients. When controversies do arise, they are dealt with professionally and calmly, if possible away from the patient being resuscitated. Much can be learned from discussions about the challenges of managing trauma victims. The more patients the team treats, the more experienced the members become and the more clearcut these situations are to address. Trauma team members can prepare for their role by learning ATLS® principles as well as the basics of performance within the medical team.

SUMMARY

Where resources allow, the best management of a trauma victim is by a trained trauma team with a competent and skilled trauma team leader. ATLS® principles are fundamental to the function of the trauma team. All trauma team members should be ATLS® providers with experience in the resuscitation room. Trauma team leaders require specific skills and competencies as well as considerable experience in the delivery of trauma care according to ATLS® standards. Trauma team members can prepare for their part in the treatment of trauma and learn from their experiences in different trauma teams.

BIBLIOGRAPHY

1. Alimo-Metcalfe B. A critical review of leadership theory. In: Lewis R, Leonard S, Freedman A, eds. *The Psychology of Organizational Development, Leadership and Change*. London, UK: Wiley Blackwell; 2013.
2. Avery GC. *Understanding Leadership*. London, UK: Sage Publications; 2004.
3. Avolio BJ, Sosik JJ, Jung DI, et al. Leadership models, methods, and applications. *Handbook of Psychology: Industrial and Organizational Psychology* (Vol. 12). Hoboken, NJ: John Wiley & Sons; 2003:277–307.
4. Blakar RM. *Communication: A Social Perspective on Clinical Issues*. Oxford, UK: Oxford University Press; 1985.
5. Brewer N, Wilson C, Beck K. Supervisory behavior and team performance among police patrol sergeants. *J Occup Organ Psych* 1994:67; 69–78.
6. Burford B. Group processes in medical education: learning from social identity theory. *Med Educ* 2012;46:143–152.
7. Burke CS, Stagl KC, Klein C, et al. What type of leadership behaviors are functional in teams? A meta-analysis. *Leadership Q* 2006;17:288–307.
8. Cant S, Killoran A. Team tactics: a study of nurse collaboration in general practice. *Health Ed J* 1993;52(4):203–208.
9. Chowdhury S. The role of affect- and cognition-based trust in complex knowledge sharing. *J Managerial Issues* 2005;17(3):310–327.
10. Collins J. *Good to Great*. London, UK: Random House; 2001.
11. Dreachslin JL, Hunt PL, Sprainer E. Conceptualizing diversity and leadership: evidence from 10 cases. *Educ Management Admin & Leadership* 2006 April;34:151–165.
12. Fernandez R, Nozenilek JA, Hegerty CB, et al. Developing expert medical teams: towards an evidence based approach. *Acad Emerg Med* 2008 Nov;15:11:1025–1036.
13. Field R, West MA. Teamwork in primary health care, 2: Perspectives from practices. *J Interprofessional Care* 1995;9(2):123–130.
14. Goleman D, Boyatzis R, McKee A. *Primal Leadership: Unleashing the Power of Emotional Intelligence*. Boston, MA: Harvard Business Press; 2013.
15. Helmich E, Bolhuis S, Laan R, et al. Entering medical practice for the very first time: emotional talk, meaning and identity development. *Med Educ* 2012;46:1074–1087.
16. Komaki JL, Desselles ML, Bowman ED. Definitely not a breeze: extending an operant model of effective supervision to teams. *J Appl Psychol* 1989;74:522–529.
17. Kozlowski SW, Gully SM, Salas E, et al. Team leadership and development: theory, principles and guidelines for training leaders and teams. In: Beyerlein MM, Johnson DA, Beyerlein ST, eds. *Advances in Interdisciplinary Studies of Work Teams: Team Leadership* (Vol 3). Greenwich, CT: Elsevier Science/JAI Press; 1996: 253–291.
18. Lim B-C, Ployhart RE. Transformational leadership: relations to the five-factor model and team performance in typical and maximum contexts. *J Appl Psychol* 2004 Aug;89(4): 610–621.
19. Micklan MS, Rodger SS. Effective health care teams: a model of six characteristics developed from shared perceptions *J Interprofessional Care* 2005;19(4):358–370.
20. Newell S, David G, Chand D. An analysis of trust among globally distributed work teams in an organizational setting. *Knowledge and Process Management* 2007;14(3):158–168.

21. Ostrom TM, Carpenter, SL, Sedikides C, et al. Differential processing of in-group and out-group information. *J Pers Soc Psychol* 1993;64:21–34.

22. Politis J. The connection between trust and knowledge management; what are its implications for team performance? *J Knowledge Management* 2003;7(5):55–67.

23. Rath T, Conchie B. *Strengths Based Leadership.* New York, NY: Gallup Press; 2008.

24. Riggio RE, Chaleff I, Blumen-Lipman J. *The Art of Followership: How Great Followers Create Great Leaders and Organizations.* San Francisco, CA: Jossey-Bass; 2008.

25. Salas E, Rosen MA, King H. Managing teams managing crises: principles of teamwork to improve patient safety in the emergency room and beyond. *Theor Issues Ergon Sci* 2007;8:381–394.

26. Schein EH. *Organizational Culture and Leadership.* 3rd ed. San Francisco, CA: Jossey-Bass; 2004.

27. Thylefors I, Persson O, Hellstrom D. Team types, perceived efficiency and team climate in Swedish cross-professional teamwork. *J Interprofessional Care* 2005;19(2):102–114.

28. Tonkin TH. *Authentic Leadership: A Literature Review.* Virginia Beach, VA: Regent University, School of Leadership Studies; 2010.

29. Walumbwa FO, Wang P, Wang H, et al. Psychological processes linking authentic leadership to follower behaviors. *Leadership Quarterly* 2010; 21:901–914.

30. Weick K. The collapse of sense making in organizations: The Mann Gulch Disaster. *Adm Sci Quarterly* 1993;38:628–652.

31. West MA, Field R. Teamwork in primary health care, 1: perspectives from organizational psychology. *J Interprofessional Care* 1995;9(2): 117–122.

32. Wilder DA. Some determinants of the persuasive power of in-groups and out-groups: organization of information and attribution of independence. *J Pers Soc Psychol* 1990;59:1202–1213.

33. Yukl G. *Leadership in Organizations.* 7th ed. Upper Saddle River, NJ: Prentice Hall; 2009.

Appendix F
TRIAGE SCENARIOS

OBJECTIVES

1. Define triage.

2. Explain the general principles of triage and the factors that must be considered during the triage process.

3. Apply the principles of triage to actual scenarios.

This is a self-assessment exercise, to be completed *before* you arrive for the course. Please read through the introductory information on the following pages before reading the individual scenarios and answering the related questions. This content is presented in a group discussion format during the course, and your active participation is expected. At the end of this session, your instructor will review the correct answers.

The goal of this exercise is to understand how to apply trauma triage principles in multiple-patient scenarios.

DEFINITION OF TRIAGE

Triage is the process of prioritizing patient treatment during mass-casualty events.

PRINCIPLES OF TRIAGE

The general principles of triage include:

- Recognize that rescuer safety is the first priority.
- Do the most good for the most patients using available resources.
- Make timely decisions.
- Prepare for triage to occur at multiple levels.
- Know and understand the resources available.

- Plan and rehearse responses with practice drills.
- Determine triage category types in advance.
- Triage is continuous at each level.

SAFETY COMES FIRST

By rushing into a scene that is hazardous, responders can risk creating even more casualties—themselves. The goal of rescue is to rapidly extricate individuals from the scene, and generating more injured persons is certainly counterproductive. Triage should only begin when providers will not be injured. Responders must be aware of the possibility of a "second hit" (e.g., further structural collapse, perpetrators, fires, earthquake aftershocks, additional explosions, and additional vehicle collisions). Some scenes may need to be made safe by firemen, search and rescue teams, or law enforcement before medical personnel can enter.

DO THE MOST GOOD FOR THE MOST PATIENTS USING AVAILABLE RESOURCES

The central, guiding principle underlying all other triage principles, rules, and strategies is to do the most good for the most patients, using available resources. Multiple-casualty incidents, by definition, do not exceed the resources available. Mass-casualty events, however, do exceed available medical resources and require triage; the care provider, site, system, and/or facility is unable to manage the number of casualties using standard methods. Standard of care

317

interventions, evacuations, and procedures cannot be completed for each injury for every patient within the usual time frame. Responders apply the principles of triage when the number of casualties exceeds the medical capabilities that are immediately available to provide usual and customary care.

MAKE TIMELY DECISIONS

Time is of the essence during triage. The most difficult aspect of this process is making medical decisions without complete data. The triage decision maker (or triage officer) must be able to rapidly assess the scene and the numbers of casualties, focus on individual patients for short periods of time, and make immediate triage determinations for each patient. Triage decisions are typically made by deciding which injuries constitute the greatest immediate threat to life. Thus the airway, breathing, circulation, and disability priorities of ATLS are the same priorities used in making triage decisions. In general, airway problems are more rapidly lethal than breathing problems, which are more rapidly lethal than circulation problems, which are more rapidly lethal than neurologic injuries. Trauma team members use all available information, including vital signs when available, to make each triage decision.

TRIAGE OCCURS AT MULTIPLE LEVELS

Triage is not a one-time, one-place event or decision. Triage first occurs at the scene or site of the event as decisions are made regarding which patients to treat first and the sequence in which patients will be evacuated. Triage also typically occurs just outside the hospital to determine where patients will be seen in the facility (e.g., emergency department, operating room, intensive care unit, ward, or clinic). Triage occurs again in the pre-operative area as decisions are made regarding the sequence in which patients are taken for operation. Because patients' conditions may improve or worsen with interventions and time, they may be triaged several times.

KNOW AND UNDERSTAND THE RESOURCES AVAILABLE

Optimal triage decisions are made with knowledge and understanding of the available resources at each level or stage of patient care. The triage officer must be knowledgeable and kept abreast of changes in resources.

A surgeon with sound knowledge of the local health system may be the ideal triage officer for in-hospital triage positions because he or she understands all components of hospital function, including the operating rooms. This arrangement will not work in situations with limited numbers of surgeons and does not apply to the incident site. As responders arrive at the scene, they will be directed by the incident commander at the scene. For mass-casualty events, a hospital incident commander is responsible for directing the response at the hospital.

PLANNING AND REHEARSAL

Triage must be planned and rehearsed, to the extent possible. Events likely to occur in the local area are a good starting point for mass-casualty planning and rehearsal. For example, simulate a mass-casualty event from an airplane crash if the facility is near a major airport, a chemical spill if near a busy railroad, or an earthquake if in an earthquake zone. Specific rehearsal for each type of disaster is not possible, but broad planning and fine-tuning of facility responses based on practice drills are possible and necessary.

DETERMINE TRIAGE CATEGORY TYPES

The title and color markings for each triage category should be determined at a system-wide level as part of planning and rehearsal. Many options are used around the world. One common, simple method is to use tags with the colors of a stoplight: red, yellow, and green. Red implies life-threatening injury that requires immediate intervention and/or operation. Yellow implies injuries that may become life- or limb-threatening if care is delayed beyond several hours. Green patients are the walking wounded who have suffered only minor injuries. These patients can sometimes be used to assist with their own care and the care of others. Black is frequently used to mark deceased patients.

Many systems add another color, such as blue or gray, for "expectant" patients—those who are so severely injured that, given the current number of casualties requiring care, the decision is made to simply give palliative treatment while first caring for red (and perhaps some yellow) patients. Patients who are classified as expectant due to the severity of their injuries would typically be the first priority in situations in which only two or three casualties require immediate care. However, the rules, protocols, and standards of care change in the face of a mass-casualty event in which providers must "do the most good for the most patients using available resources." (Also see triage information in Appendix C: Trauma Care in Mass-Casualty, Austere, and Operational Environments and Appendix D: Disaster Preparedness and Response.)

TRIAGE IS CONTINUOUS

Triage should be continuous and repetitive at each level or site where it is required. Constant vigilance and reassessment will identify patients whose circumstances have changed with alterations in either physiological status or resource availability. As the mass-casualty event continues to unfold, the need for retriage becomes apparent. The physiology of injured patients is not constant or predictable, especially considering the limited rapid assessment required during triage. Some patients will unexpectedly deteriorate and require an "upgrade" in their triage category, perhaps from yellow to red. In others, an open fracture may be discovered after initial triage has been completed, mandating an "upgrade" in triage category from green to yellow.

An important group that requires retriage is the expectant category. Although an initial triage categorization decision may label a patient as having nonsurvivable injuries, this decision may change after all red (or perhaps red and some yellow) patients have been cared for or evacuated or if additional resources become available. For example, a young patient with 90% burns may survive if burn center care becomes available.

TRIAGE SCENARIO I
Mass Shooting at a Shopping Mall

SCENARIO

You are summoned to a safe triage area at a shopping mall where 6 people are injured in a mass shooting. The shooter has killed himself. You quickly survey the situation and determine that the patients' conditions are as follows:

PATIENT A—A young male is screaming, "Please help me, my leg is killing me!"
PATIENT B—A young female has cyanosis and tachypnea and is breathing noisily.
PATIENT C—An older male is lying in a pool of blood with his left pant leg soaked in blood.
PATIENT D—A young male is lying facedown and not moving.
PATIENT E—A young male is swearing and shouting that someone should help him or he will call his lawyer.
PATIENT F—A teenage girl is lying on the ground crying and holding her abdomen.

QUESTIONS FOR RESPONSE

1. For each patient, what is the primary problem requiring treatment?

PATIENT A—is a young male screaming, "Please help me, my leg is killing me!"
*Possible Injury/Problem:*_____

_____

PATIENT B—appears to have cyanosis and tachypnea and is breathing noisily.
*Possible Injury/Problem:*_____

_____

PATIENT C—is an older male lying in a pool of blood with his left pant leg soaked in blood.
*Possible Injury/Problem:*_____

_____

PATIENT D—is lying facedown and not moving.
*Possible Injury/Problem:*_____

_____

PATIENT E—is swearing and shouting that someone should help him or he will call his lawyer.
*Possible Injury/Problem:*_____

_____

(continued)

TRIAGE SCENARIO I (CONTINUED)

PATIENT F—A teenaged girl is lying on the ground crying and holding her abdomen.
Possible Injury/Problem:_____
_____

2. Establish the patient priorities for further evaluation by placing a number (I through 6, where I is the highest priority and 6 is the lowest) in the space next to each patient letter.

_____ Patient A
_____ Patient B
_____ Patient C
_____ Patient D
_____ Patient E
_____ Patient F

3. Briefly outline your rationale for prioritizing the patients in this manner.

PRIORITY	PATIENT	RATIONALE
I		
2		
3		
4		
5		
6		

4. Briefly describe the basic life support maneuvers and/or additional assessment techniques you would use to further evaluate the problem(s).

PRIORITY	PATIENT	BASIC LIFE SUPPORT MANEUVERS AND/OR ADDITIONAL ASSESSMENT TECHNIQUES
I		
2		
3		
4		
5		
6		

TRIAGE SCENARIO II
Mass Shooting at a Shopping Mall (cont'd)

CONTINUATION OF TRIAGE SCENARIO I

1. Characterize the patients according to who receives basic life support (BLS) and/or advanced life support (ALS) care, and describe what that care would be. (Patients are listed in priority order as identified in Triage Scenario I.)

PATIENT	BLS OR ALS		DESCRIPTION OF CARE
	BLS	ALS	
	BLS	ALS	
	BLS	ALS	
	BLS	ALS	
	BLS	ALS	
	BLS	ALS	

2. Prioritize patient transfers and identify destinations. Provide a brief rationale for your destination choice.

PRIORITY	PATIENT	DESTINATION		RATIONALE
		TRAUMA CENTER	NEAREST HOSPITAL	
1				
2				
3				
4				
5				
6				

3. In situations involving multiple patients, what criteria would you use to identify and prioritize the treatment of these patients?

_____
_____
_____
_____

(continued)

TRIAGE SCENARIO II (CONTINUED)

4. What cues can you elicit from any patient that could be of assistance in triage?

_____
_____
_____
_____

5. Which patient injuries or symptoms should receive treatment at the scene before prehospital personnel arrive?

_____
_____
_____
_____

6. After prehospital personnel arrive, what treatment should be instituted, and what principles govern the order of initiating such treatment?

_____
_____
_____
_____

7. In multiple-patient situations, which patients should be transported? Which should be transported early?

_____
_____
_____
_____

8. Which patients may have treatment delayed and be transported later?

_____
_____
_____
_____

TRIAGE SCENARIO III
Trailer Home Explosion and Fire

SCENARIO

The police were conducting a raid of a mobile home suspected of being an illicit methamphetamine lab when an explosion occurred and the trailer was engulfed in flames. You receive notification that 2 ambulances are inbound with 5 patients from the scene: one police officer and 4 people who were in the trailer, including a child. They are brought to your small hospital emergency department with spinal motion restricted on long spine boards and with cervical collars in place.

The injured patients are as follows.

PATIENT A

A 45-year-old male police officer, who entered the trailer to bring out the child, is coughing and expectorating carbonaceous material. Hairs on his face and head are singed. His voice is clear, and he reports pain in his hands, which have erythema and early blister formation. Vital signs are: BP 120 mm Hg systolic, HR 100 beats per minute, and RR 30 breaths per minute.

PATIENT B

A 6-year-old female who was carried out of the trailer by Patient A appears frightened and is crying. She reports pain from burns (erythema/blisters) over her back, buttocks, and both legs posteriorly. Vital signs are: BP 110/70 mm Hg, HR 100 beats per minute, and RR 25 breaths per minute.

PATIENT C

A 62-year-old male is coughing, wheezing, and expectorating carbonaceous material. His voice is hoarse, and he responds only to painful stimuli. There are erythema, blisters, and charred skin on the face and neck, anterior chest and abdominal wall, and circumferential burns of all four extremities with sparing of the groin creases and genitals. Vital signs are: BP 80/40 mm Hg, HR 140 beats per minute, and RR 35 breaths per minute.

PATIENT D

A 23-year-old female is obtunded but responds to pain when her right humerus and leg are moved. There is no obvious deformity of the arm, and the thigh is swollen while in a traction splint. Vital signs are: BP 140/90 mm Hg, HR 110 beats per minute, and RR 32 breaths per minute.

PATIENT E

A 30-year-old male is alert, pale, and reports pain in his pelvis. There is evidence of fracture with abdominal distention and tenderness to palpation. There is erythema and blistering of the anterior chest, abdominal wall, and thighs. He also has a laceration to the forehead. Vital signs are: BP 130/90 mm Hg, HR 90 beats per minute, and RR 25 breaths per minute. He has a pungent, oily liquid over his arms and chest.

(continued)

TRIAGE SCENARIO III (CONTINUED)

Management priorities in this scenario can be based on information obtained by surveying the injured patients at a distance. Although there may be doubt as to which patient is more severely injured, based on the available information, a decision must be made to proceed with the best information available at the time.

1. Which patient(s) has associated trauma and/or inhalation injury in addition to body-surface burns?

   _____

   _____

2. Using the table provided below:

   a. Establish priorities of care in your hospital emergency department by placing a number (1 through 5, where 1 is the highest priority and 5 is the lowest) in the space next to each patient letter in the Treatment Priority column.
   b. Identify which patient(s) has associated trauma and/or an airway injury, and write "yes" or "no" in the appropriate Associated Injuries columns.
   c. Estimate the percentage of body surface area (BSA) burned for each patient, and enter the percentage for each patient letter in the % BSA column.
   d. Identify which patient(s) should be transferred to a burn center and/or a trauma center, and write "yes" or "no" in the Transfer column.
   e. Establish the priorities for transfer, and enter the priority number in the Transfer Priority column.

PATIENT	TREATMENT PRIORITY (1–5)	ASSOCIATED INJURIES (YES/NO)			% BSA	TRANSFER (YES/NO)	TRANSFER PRIORITY (1–5)
		AIRWAY INJURY	TRAUMA	BURN			
A							
B							
C							
D							
E							

3. Describe any necessary precautions staff members need to take in evaluating and treating these patients in light of the methamphetamine production.

   _____

   _____

   _____

   _____

   _____

TRIAGE SCENARIO IV
Cold Injury

SCENARIO

While in your hospital, you receive a call that five members of a doctor's family were snowmobiling on a lake when the ice broke. Four family members fell into the lake water. The doctor was able to stop his snowmobile in time and left to seek help. The response time of basic and advanced life support assistance was 15 minutes. By the time prehospital care providers arrived, one individual had crawled out of the lake and removed another victim from the water. Two individuals remained submerged; they were found by rescue divers and removed from the lake. Rescuers from the scene provided the following information:

PATIENT A—The doctor's 10-year-old grandson was removed from the lake by rescuers. His ECG monitor shows asystole.

PATIENT B—The doctor's 65-year-old wife was removed from the lake by rescuers. Her ECG monitor shows asystole.

PATIENT C—The doctor's 35-year-old daughter, who was removed from the water by her sister-in-law, has bruises to her anterior chest wall. Her blood pressure is 90 mm Hg systolic.

PATIENT D—The doctor's 35-year-old daughter-in-law, who had been submerged and crawled out of the lake, has no obvious signs of trauma. Her blood pressure is 110 mm Hg systolic.

PATIENT E—The 76-year-old retired doctor, who never went into the water, reports only cold hands and feet.

1. Establish the priorities for transport from the scene to your emergency department, and explain your rationale.

TRANSPORT PRIORITY	PATIENT	RATIONALE
1		
2		
3		
4		
5		

2. In the emergency department, all patients should have their core temperature measured. Core temperatures for these patients are as follows:

PATIENT A: 29°C (84.2°F)
PATIENT B: 34°C (93.2°F)
PATIENT C: 33°C (91.4°F)
PATIENT D: 35°C (95°F)
PATIENT E: 36°C (96.8°F)

(continued)

TRIAGE SCENARIO IV (CONTINUED)

Briefly outline your rationale for the remainder of the primary assessment, resuscitation, and secondary survey.

PRIORITY	PATIENT	RATIONALE FOR REMAINDER OF PRIMARY ASSESSMENT, RESUSCITATION, AND SECONDARY SURVEY
1		
2		
3		
4		
5		

TRIAGE SCENARIO V
Bus Crash

SCENARIO

You are the only doctor available in a 100-bed community emergency department. One nurse and a nurse assistant are available to assist you. Ten minutes ago you were notified by radio that ambulances would be arriving with patients from a single- passenger bus crash. The bus apparently lost control, exited the highway, and rolled over several times. The bus was reportedly traveling at 65 mph (104 kph) before it crashed. No further report is received other than that two of the bus passengers were dead at the scene. Two ambulances arrive at your facility carrying five patients who were occupants in the bus. The surviving injured patients are as follows.

PATIENT A

A 57-year-old male was the driver of the bus. He apparently experienced chest pain just before the crash and slumped over against the steering wheel. Upon impact, he was thrown against the windshield. On admission, he is notably in severe respiratory distress. Injuries include apparent brain matter in his hair overlying a palpable skull fracture, an angulated deformity of the left forearm, and multiple abrasions over the anterior chest wall. Vital signs are: BP 88/60 mm Hg, HR 150 beats per minute, RR 40 breaths per minute, and Glasgow Coma Scale (GCS) score 4.

PATIENT B

A 45-year-old woman was a passenger on the bus. She was not wearing a seat belt. Upon impact, she was ejected from the bus. On admission, she is notably in severe respiratory distress. Prehospital personnel supply the following information to you after preliminary assessment: Injuries include (1) severe maxillofacial trauma with bleeding from the nose and mouth, (2) an angulated deformity of the left upper arm, and (3) multiple abrasions over the anterior chest wall. Vital signs are: BP 150/80 mm Hg, HR 120 beats per minute, RR 40 breaths per minute, and GCS score 8.

PATIENT C

A 48-year-old male passenger was found under the bus. At admission he is confused and responds slowly to verbal stimuli. Injuries include multiple abrasions to his face, chest, and abdomen. Breath sounds are absent on the left, and his abdomen is tender to palpation. Vital signs are: BP 90/50 mm Hg, HR 140 beats per minute, RR 35 breaths per minute, and GCS score 12.

PATIENT D

A 25-year-old female was extricated from the rear of the bus. She is 8 months pregnant, behaving hysterically, and reporting abdominal pain. Injuries include multiple abrasions to her face and anterior abdominal wall. Her abdomen is tender to palpation. She is in active labor. Vital signs are: BP 120/80 mm Hg, HR 100 beats per minute, and RR 25 breaths per minute.

(continued)

TRIAGE SCENARIO V (CONTINUED)

PATIENT E

A 6-year-old boy was extricated from the rear seats. At the scene, he was alert and talking. He now responds to painful stimuli only by crying out. Injuries include multiple abrasions and an angulated deformity of the right lower leg. There is dried blood around his nose and mouth. Vital signs are: BP 110/70 mm Hg, HR 180 beats per minute, and RR 35 breaths per minute.

1. Describe the steps you would take to triage these five patients.

    _____

    _____

2. Establish the patient priorities for further evaluation by placing a number (1 through 5, where 1 is the highest priority and 5 is the lowest) in the space next to each patient letter.

    _____ Patient A   _____ Patient D
    _____ Patient B   _____ Patient E
    _____ Patient C

3. Briefly outline your rationale for prioritizing these patients in this manner.

PRIORITY	PATIENT	RATIONALE
1		
2		
3		
4		
5		

4. Briefly describe the basic life support maneuvers and/or additional assessment techniques you would use to further evaluate the problem(s).

PRIORITY	PATIENT	BASIC LIFE SUPPORT MANEUVERS AND/OR ADDITIONAL ASSESSMENT TECHNIQUES
1		
2		
3		
4		
5		

TRIAGE SCENARIO VI
Earthquake and Tsunami

SCENARIO

A coastal city of 15,000 people is struck by a magnitude 7.2 earthquake, followed by a tsunami that travels 2.5 miles (4 km) inland. In the aftermath, there is an explosion and fire at a seaside nuclear power reactor. Many structures have collapsed, and some victims are trapped inside. Others may have been swept out to sea. Some of the roads leading out of the region are blocked by flooding and landslides. Local utilities, including electricity and water, have failed. The temperature currently is 13°C (55°F), and it is beginning to rain; the sun sets in 2 hours. Upon responding to the event, firefighters and paramedics find the following scene:

INJURED

Two technicians are brought from the nuclear power plant:

- The first technician has 40% BSA second- and third-degree burns. A survey with a Geiger counter shows he has radioactive materials on him.
- The second technician has no burns, but she is confused and repeatedly vomiting. She also has radioactivity on her clothing.

Paramedics have triaged 47 injured residents of the surrounding area:

- 12 category Red patients
  - 8 with extensive (20% to 50% BSA) second- and third-degree burns
- 8 category Yellow patients
  - 3 with focal (< 10% BSA) second-degree burns
- 23 category Green patients
  - 10 with painful extremity deformities
- 5 category Blue or Expectant patients
  - 3 with catastrophic (> 75% BSA) second- and third-degree burns

DECEASED

At least six nuclear plant technicians and five residents are dead, including one infant with a fatal head injury. Many other people are missing

Two fire companies and two additional ambulances have been called. The local community hospital has 26 open beds, 5 primary care providers, and 2 surgeons, 1 of whom is on vacation. The nearest surviving trauma center is 75 miles (120 km) away, and the nearest designated burn center is more than 200 miles (320 km) away.

1. Should community disaster plans be invoked? Why, or why not?

   _____

   _____

2. If a mass-casualty event is declared, who should be designated the incident commander?

   _____

   _____

(continued)

TRIAGE SCENARIO VI (CONTINUED)

3. What is the first consideration of the incident commander at the scene?

_____

_____

4. What is the second consideration of the incident commander at the scene?

_____

_____

5. What considerations should be taken into account in medical operations at the scene?

_____

_____

6. How does the presence of radiological contamination change triage, treatment, and evacuation?

_____

_____

7. What is the meaning of the red, yellow, green, blue, and black triage categories?

_____

_____

8. Given the categories in Question 7, which patients should be evacuated to the hospital, by what transport methods, and in what order?

_____

_____

9. What efforts should the incident commander make to assist with response and recovery?

_____

_____

TRIAGE SCENARIO VII
Suicide Bomber Blast at a Political Rally

SCENARIO

A suicide bomber blast has been reported at an evening political rally. The area is 30 minutes away from your level II trauma center. You are summoned to the scene as one of the triage officers. Initial report reveals 12 deaths and 40 injured. Many rescue teams are busy with search and rescue.

You arrive at an area where you find 3 dead bodies and 6 injured patients. The conditions of the 6 injured patients are as follows:

PATIENT A

A young male, conscious and alert, has a small penetrating wound in the lower neck just to the left side of the trachea, with mild neck swelling, hoarse voice, and no active bleeding.

PATIENT B

A young male is soaked in blood, pale, and lethargic, yet responding to verbal commands. Both legs are deformed and attached only by thin muscular tissue and skin below the knees bilaterally.

PATIENT C

A young female is complaining of shortness of breath. She has tachypnea, cyanosis, and multiple small penetrating wounds to the left side of her chest.

PATIENT D

A middle-aged male has multiple penetrating wounds to the left side of the abdomen and left flank. He is pale and complaining of severe abdominal pain. Second- and third-degree burns are visible over the lower abdomen.

PATIENT E

An elderly male is breathless and coughing up bloodstained sputum. He is disoriented and has multiple bruises and lacerations over his upper torso.

PATIENT F

A young male has a large wound on the anterior aspect of the right lower leg with visible bone ends projecting from wound. He is complaining of severe pain. There is no active bleeding.

(continued)

TRIAGE SCENARIO VII (CONTINUED)

QUESTIONS FOR RESPONSE

1. Based on the information, describe the potential A, B, and C problems for each patient:

PATIENT	POTENTIAL AIRWAY PROBLEMS	POTENTIAL BREATHING PROBLEMS	POTENTIAL CIRCULATION PROBLEMS
A			
B			
C			
D			
E			
F			

2. What initial life support maneuvers can be offered before transport to a trauma center (assuming that typical prehospital equipment is available at this time)?

PATIENT A—*Initial life support measures:*_____

_____

PATIENT B—*Initial life support measures:*_____

_____

PATIENT C—*Initial life support measures:*_____

_____

PATIENT D—*Initial life support measures:*_____

_____

PATIENT E—*Initial life support measures:*_____

_____

PATIENT F—*Initial life support measures:*_____

_____

3. What other considerations do you keep in mind during triage at the scene of this incident?

_____

_____

_____

_____

4. Describe the transfer to the trauma center of each patient in order of priority with your rationale (I is the highest and 6 is the lowest).

TRANSFER PRIORITY	PATIENT	RATIONALE
I		
2		
3		
4		
5		
6		

5. What should be your primary management considerations when the patients arrive at the trauma center?

_____

_____

_____

_____

Appendix G
SKILLS

Skill Station A
AIRWAY

PART 1: BASIC AIRWAY SKILLS

- Insertion of Nasopharyngeal Airway
- Safe Use of Suction
- Insertion of Oropharyngeal Airway
- One-Person Bag-Mask Ventilation
- Two-Person Bag-Mask Ventilation

PART 2: ADVANCED AIRWAY MANAGEMENT

- Insertion of Laryngeal Mask Airway (LMA)
- Insertion of Laryngeal Tube Airway (LTA)
- Oral Endotracheal Intubation

PART 3: PEDIATRIC AIRWAY AND CRICOTHYROTOMY

- Infant Endotracheal Intubation
- Needle Cricothyrotomy
- Surgical Cricothyrotomy

LEARNING OBJECTIVES

Part 1: Basic Airway Skills

1. Assess airway patency in a simulated trauma patient scenario.

2. Apply a non-rebreathing mask to maximize oxygenation.

3. Apply a pulse oximeter.

4. Perform a jaw thrust on a manikin to provide an adequate airway.

5. Demonstrate airway suctioning on a manikin.

6. Insert a nasopharyngeal airway and oropharyngeal airway on a manikin.

7. Perform one-person and two-person bag-mask ventilation of a manikin.

Part 2: Advanced Airway Management

1. Insert a supraglottic or extraglottic device on a manikin.

2. State the indications for a definitive airway.

3. Attempt oral endotracheal intubation on a manikin.

Part 3: Pediatric Airway and Cricothyrotomy

1. Review basic management of the pediatric airway.

2. Attempt infant endotracheal intubation on a manikin.

3. Identify the anatomic landmarks for cricothyroidotomy.

4. Perform a needle cricothyrotomy and describe the options for oxygenation.

5. Perform a surgical cricothyrotomy on a model.

PART I: BASIC AIRWAY SKILLS

SKILLS INCLUDED IN THIS SKILL STATION

- Insertion of Nasopharyngeal Airway (NPA)
- Safe Use of Suction
- Insertion of Oropharyngeal Airway and Reassessment
- One-Person Bag-Mask Ventilation
- Two-Person Bag-Mask Ventilation

INSERTION OF NASOPHARYNGEAL AIRWAY (NPA)

Note: Do not use a nasopharygeal airway in a patient with midface fractures or suspected basilar skull fracture.

STEP 1. Assess the nasal passages for any apparent obstruction (e.g., polyps, fractures, or hemorrhage).

STEP 2. Select the proper size of airway. Look at the nostril diameter to determine the greatest size that will pass easily through the nostril.

STEP 3. Lubricate the nasopharyngeal airway with a water-soluble lubricant or tap water.

STEP 4. With the patient's head in neutral position, stand to the side of the patient. Holding the NPA like a pencil, gently insert the tip of the airway into the nostril and direct it posteriorly and toward the ear.

STEP 5. Gently insert the nasopharyngeal airway through the nostril into the hypopharynx with a slight rotating motion, until the flange rests against the nostril. If during insertion the NPA meets any resistance, remove the NPA and attempt insertion on the other side. If the NPA causes the patient to cough or gag, slightly withdraw the NPA to relieve the cough or gag and then proceed.

STEP 6. Reassess the patient to ensure that the airway is now patent.

SAFE USE OF SUCTION

STEP 1. Turn on the vacuum, selecting a midpoint (150 mm Hg) rather than full vacuum (300 mm Hg).

STEP 2. Gently open the mouth, inspecting for bleeding, lacerations or broken teeth. Look for the presence of visible fluid, blood, or debris.

STEP 3. Gently place the suction catheter in the oropharynx and nasopharynx, keeping the suction device (Yankauer) tip in view at all times.

INSERTION OF OROPHARYNGEAL AIRWAY (OPA) (AIRWAY CLEAR)

STEP 1. Select the proper size of airway. A correctly sized OPA device extends from the corner of the patient's mouth to the earlobe.

STEP 2. Open the patient's mouth with the crossed-finger (scissors) technique.

STEP 3. Insert a tongue blade on top of the patient's tongue and far enough back to depress the tongue adequately. Be careful not to cause the patient to gag.

STEP 4. Insert the airway posteriorly, gently sliding the airway over the curvature of the tongue until the device's flange rests on top of the patient's lips. The device must not push the tongue backward and block the airway. An alternate technique for insertion, termed the rotation method, involves inserting the OPA upside down so its tip is facing the roof of the patient's mouth. As the airway is inserted, it is rotated 180 degrees until the flange comes to rest on the patient's lips and/or teeth. *This maneuver should not be used in children.*

STEP 5. Remove the tongue blade.

STEP 6. Reassess the patient to ensure that the airway is now patent.

ONE-PERSON BAG-MASK VENTILATION

STEP 1. Select the proper size of mask to fit the patient's face. The mask should extend from the proximal half of the nose to the chin.

STEP 2. Connect the oxygen tubing to the bag-mask device and adjust the flow of oxygen to 15 L/min.

STEP 3. Ensure that the patient's airway is patent (an oropharyngeal airway will prevent obstruction from the tongue).

STEP 4. Apply the mask over the patient's nose and mouth with the dominant hand, ensuring a good seal. This is done by creating a 'C' with the thumb and index finger while lifting the mandible into the mask with other three fingers of the dominant hand.

STEP 5. Initiate ventilation by squeezing the bag with the non-dominant hand.

STEP 6. Assess the adequacy of ventilation by observing the patient's chest movement.

STEP 7. Ventilate the patient in this manner every 5 seconds.

TWO-PERSON BAG-MASK VENTILATION

STEP 1. Select the proper size of mask to fit the patient's face.

STEP 2. Connect the oxygen tubing to the bag-mask device and adjust the flow of oxygen to 15 L/min.

STEP 3. Ensure that the patient's airway is patent (an oropharyngeal airway will prevent obstruction from the tongue).

STEP 4. The first person applies the mask to the patient's face, performing a jaw-thrust maneuver. Using the thenar eminence (or thumbs-down) technique may be easier for novice providers. Ensure a tight seal with both hands.

STEP 5. The second person initiates ventilation by squeezing the bag with both hands.

STEP 6. Assess the adequacy of ventilation by observing the patient's chest movement.

STEP 7. Ventilate the patient in this manner every 5 seconds.

PART 2: ADVANCED AIRWAY MANAGEMENT

SKILLS INCLUDED IN THIS SKILL STATION

- Insertion of Laryngeal Mask Airway (LMA)
- Insertion of Laryngeal Tube Airway (LTA)
- Oral Endotracheal Intubation

INSERTION OF LARYNGEAL MASK AIRWAY (LMA)

STEP 1. Ensure that adequate ventilation and oxygenation are in progress and that suctioning equipment is immediately available in case the patient vomits.

STEP 2. Choose the correct size of LMA: 3 for a small female, 4 for a large female or small male, and 5 for a large male.

STEP 3. Inspect the LMA to ensure it is sterile and has no visible damage; check that the lumen is clear.

STEP 4. Inflate the cuff of the LMA to check that it does not leak.

STEP 5. Completely deflate the LMA cuff by pressing it firmly onto a flat surface. Lubricate it.

STEP 6. Have an assistant restrict motion of the patient's cervical spine.

STEP 7. Hold the LMA with the dominant hand, as you would hold a pen, placing the index finger at the junction of the cuff and the shaft and orienting the LMA opening over the patient's tongue.

STEP 8. Pass the LMA behind the upper incisors, keeping the shaft parallel to the patient's chest and the index finger pointing toward the intubator.

STEP 9. Push the lubricated LMA into position along the palatopharyngeal arch while using the index finger to maintain pressure on the tube and guide the LMA into final position.

STEP 10. Inflate the cuff with the correct volume of air (indicated on the shaft of the LMA).

STEP 11. Check placement of the LMA by applying bag ventilation.

STEP 12. Confirm proper position by auscultation, chest movement, and ideally verification of CO_2 by capnography.

INSERTION OF LARYNGEAL TUBE AIRWAY (LTA)

STEP 1. Ensure that adequate ventilation and oxygenation are in progress and that suctioning equipment is immediately available in case the patient vomits.

STEP 2. Choose the correct size of LTA.

STEP 3. Inspect the LTA device to ensure it is sterile and the lumen is clear and has no visible damage.

STEP 4. Inflate the cuff of the LTA to check that it does not leak. Then fully deflate the cuff.

STEP 5. Apply a water-soluble lubricant to the beveled distal tip and posterior aspect of the tube, taking care to avoid introducing lubricant into or near the ventilatory openings.

STEP 6. Have an assistant restrict motion of the patient's cervical spine.

STEP 7. Hold the LTA at the connector with the dominant hand. With the nondominant hand, open the mouth.

STEP 8. With the LTA rotated laterally 45 to 90 degrees, introduce the tip into the mouth and advance it behind the base of the tongue.

STEP 9. Rotate the tube back to the midline as the tip reaches the posterior wall of the pharynx.

STEP 10. Without excessive force, advance the LTA until the base of the connector is aligned with the patient's teeth or gums.

STEP 11. Inflate the LTA cuffs to the minimum volume necessary to seal the airway at the peak ventilatory pressure used (just seal volume).

STEP 12. While gently bagging the patient to assess ventilation, simultaneously withdraw the airway until ventilation is easy and free flowing (large tidal volume with minimal airway pressure).

STEP 13. Reference marks are provided at the proximal end of the LTA; when aligned with the upper teeth, these marks indicate the depth of insertion.

STEP 14. Confirm proper position by auscultation, chest movement, and ideally verification of CO_2 by capnography.

STEP 15. Readjust cuff inflation to seal volume.

STEP 16. Secure LTA to patient using tape or other accepted means. A bite block can also be used, if desired.

ORAL ENDOTRACHEAL INTUBATION

STEP 1. Ensure that adequate ventilation and oxygenation are in progress and that suctioning equipment is immediately available in case the patient vomits.

STEP 2. Choose the correctly sized endotracheal tube (ETT).

STEP 3. Inspect the ETT to ensure it is sterile and has no visible damage. Check that the lumen is clear.

STEP 4. Inflate the cuff of the ETT to check that it does not leak.

STEP 5. Connect the laryngoscope blade to the handle, and check the light bulb for brightness.

STEP 6. Assess the patient's airway for ease of intubation, using the LEMON mnemonic.

STEP 7. Direct an assistant to restrict cervical motion. The patient's neck must not be hyperextended or hyperflexed during the procedure.

STEP 8. Hold the laryngoscope in the left hand. (regardless of the operator's dominant hand).

STEP 9. Insert the laryngoscope into the right side of the patient's mouth, displacing the tongue to the left.

STEP 10. Visually identify the epiglottis and then the vocal cords. External laryngeal manipulation with backward, upward, and rightward pressure (BURP) may help to improve visualization.

STEP 11. Gently insert the ETT through the vocal cords into the trachea to the correct depth without applying pressure on the teeth, oral tissues or lips.

STEP 12. If endotracheal intubation is not accomplished before the SpO_2 drops below 90%, ventilate with a bag-mask device and change the approach [equipment, i.e., gum elastic bougie (GEB) or personnel].

STEP 13. Once successful intubation has occurred, apply bag ventilation. Inflate the cuff with enough air to provide an adequate seal. Do not overinflate the cuff.

STEP 14. Visually observe chest excursions with ventilation.

STEP 15. Auscultate the chest and abdomen with a stethoscope to ascertain tube position.

STEP 16. Confirm correct placement of the tube by the presence of CO_2. A chest x-ray exam is helpful to assess the depth of insertion of the tube (i.e., mainstem intubation), but it does not exclude esophageal intubation.

STEP 17. Secure the tube. If the patient is moved, reassess the tube placement.

STEP 18. If not already done, attach a pulse oximeter to one of the patient's fingers (intact peripheral perfusion must exist) to measure and monitor the patient's oxygen saturation levels and provide immediate assessment of therapeutic interventions.

PART 3: PEDIATRIC AIRWAY AND CRICOTHYROTOMY

SKILLS INCLUDED IN THIS SKILL STATION

- Infant Endotracheal Intubation
- Needle Cricothyrotomy
- Surgical Cricothyrotomy with Jet Insufflation

INFANT ENDOTRACHEAL INTUBATION

STEP 1. Ensure that adequate ventilation and oxygenation are in progress and that suctioning equipment is immediately available in case the patient vomits.

STEP 2. Select the proper-size tube, which should be the same size as the infant's nostril or little finger, or use a pediatric resuscitation tape to determine the correct tube size. Connect the laryngoscope blade and handle; check the light bulb for brightness.

STEP 3. Direct an assistant to restrict cervical spine motion. The patient's neck must not be hyperextended or hyperflexed during the procedure.

STEP 4. Hold the laryngoscope in the left hand (regardless of the operator's dominant hand).

STEP 5. Insert the laryngoscope blade into the right side of the mouth, moving the tongue to the left.

STEP 6. Observe the epiglottis and then the vocal cords. External laryngeal manipulation with backward, upward, and rightward pressure (BURP) may be helpful for better visualization.

STEP 7. Insert the endotracheal tube not more than 2 cm (1 inch) past the cords.

STEP 8. Carefully check placement of the tube by bag ventilation, observing lung inflations, and auscultating the chest and abdomen with a stethoscope. Confirm correct placement of the tube by the presence of CO_2. A chest x-ray exam is helpful to assess the depth of insertion of the tube (i.e., mainstem intubation), but it does not exclude esophageal intubation.

STEP 9. If endotracheal intubation is not accomplished within 30 seconds or in the same time required to hold your breath before exhaling, discontinue attempts, ventilate the patient with a bag-mask device, and try again.

STEP 10. Secure the tube. If the patient is moved, tube placement should be reassessed.

STEP 11. Attach a CO_2 detector to the secured endotracheal tube between the adapter and the ventilating device to confirm the position of the endotracheal tube in the trachea.

STEP 12. If not already done, attach a pulse oximeter to one of the patient's fingers (intact peripheral perfusion must exist) to measure and monitor the patient's oxygen saturation levels and provide an immediate assessment of therapeutic interventions.

NEEDLE CRICOTHYROTOMY

STEP 1. Assemble and prepare oxygen tubing by cutting a hole toward one end of the tubing. Connect the other end of the oxygen tubing to an oxygen source capable of delivering 50 psi or greater at the nipple, and ensure the free flow of oxygen through the tubing. Alternatively, connect a bag mask by introducing a 7.5 mm endotracheal tube connector to a 3 cc syringe wtih the plunger removed.

STEP 2. Place the patient in a supine position. Have an assistant restrict the patient's cervical motion.

STEP 3. Attach a 12- or 14-gauge over-the-needle cannula to a 5-ml syringe (16-18 gauge for infants and young children).

STEP 4. Surgically prepare the neck, using antiseptic swabs.

STEP 5. Palpate the cricothyroid membrane anteriorly between the thyroid cartilage and the cricoid cartilage. Stabilize the trachea with the thumb and forefinger of the nondominant hand to prevent lateral movement of the trachea during the procedure.

STEP 6. Puncture the skin in the midline with the cannula attached to a syringe, directly over the cricothyroid membrane.

STEP 7. Direct the cannula at a 45-degree angle caudally, while applying negative pressure to the syringe.

STEP 8. Carefully insert the cannula through the lower half of the cricothyroid membrane, aspirating as the needle is advanced. The addition of 2-3 cc of saline to the syringe will aid in detecting air.

STEP 9. Note the aspiration of air, which signifies entry into the tracheal lumen.

STEP 10. Remove the syringe and withdraw the needle while gently advancing the cannula downward into position, taking care not to perforate the posterior wall of the trachea.

STEP 11. Attach the jet insufflation equipment to the cannula, or attach the oxygen tubing or 3 mL syringe (7.5) endotracheal tube connector combination over the catheter needle hub, and secure the catheter to the patient's neck.

STEP 12. Apply intermittent ventilation either by using the jet insufflation equipment, or using your thumb to cover the open hole cut into the oxygen tubing or inflating with an ambu bag. Deliver oxygen for 1 second and allow passive expiration for 4 seconds. *Note: Adequate PaO_2 can be maintained for only around 30 to 45 minutes, and CO_2 accumulation can occur more rapidly.*

STEP 13. Continue to observe lung inflation, and auscultate the chest for adequate ventilation. To avoid barotrauma, which can lead to pneumothorax, pay special attention to lung deflation. If lung deflation is not observed, in the absence of serious chest injury it may be possible to support expiration by using gentle pressure on the chest.

SURGICAL CRICOTHYROTOMY

STEP 1. Place the patient in a supine position with the neck in a neutral position. Have an assistant restrict the patient's cervical motion.

STEP 2. Palpate the thyroid notch, cricothyroid cartilage, and sternal notch for orientation.

STEP 3. Assemble the necessary equipment.

STEP 4. Surgically prepare and anesthetize the area locally, if the patient is conscious.

STEP 5. Stabilize the thyroid cartilage with the non-dominant hand, and maintain stabilization until the trachea is intubated.

STEP 6. Make a 2- to 3-cm vertical skin incision over the cricothyroid membrane and, using the nondominant hand from a cranial direction, spread the skin edges to reduce bleeding. Reidentify the cricothyroid membrane and then incise through the base of the membrane transversely. **Caution:** *To avoid unnecessary injury, do not cut or remove the cricoid and/or thyroid cartilages.*

STEP 7. Insert hemostat or tracheal spreader or back handle of scalpel into the incision, and rotate it 90 degrees to open the airway.

STEP 8. Insert a properly sized, cuffed endotracheal tube or tracheostomy tube (usually a size 5–6) through the cricothyroid membrane incision, directing the tube distally into the trachea. If an endotracheal tube is used, advance only until the cuff is no longer visible to avoid mainstem intubation.

STEP 9. Inflate the cuff and ventilate.

STEP 10. Observe lung inflation and auscultate the chest for adequate ventilation. Confirm the presence of CO_2 and obtain a chest x-ray.

STEP 11. Secure the endotracheal or tracheostomy tube to the patient, to prevent dislodgement.

LINKS TO FUTURE LEARNING

Airway and breathing problems can be confused. The ability to rapidly assess the airway to determine if airway or ventilation compromise is present is of vital importance. Oxygen supplementation is one of the first steps to be performed in the management of trauma patients. The assessment of the airway is the first step of the primary survey and requires reassessment frequently and in conjunction with any patient deterioration. Failure of basic skills to produce adequate oxygenation and ventilation usually indicates the need to use more advanced airway skills. Failure to obtain an airway using advanced skills may require creation of a needle or surgical airway.

Post ATLS—Each student has different experience with the skills taught in the airway skill station. It is important for all students to practice these skills under appropriated supervision after returning to the workplace. The ability to identify patients with obstructed airways and to use simple maneuvers to assist with ventilation are important skills that can be lifesaving. The student should find opportunities in their clinical environment to practice these skills and develop more comfort with using them. Gaining more experience and expertise, particularly with advanced airway skills, is important if these skills are likely to be performed clinically.

Mace SE and Khan N. Needle cricothyrotomy. *Emerg Med Clin North Am.* 2008;26(4):1085.

Gaufberg SV and Workman TP. Needle crico-thyroidotomy set up. *Am J Emerg Med.* 2004; 22(1): 37–39.

Note: Skills videos are available on the MyATLS mobile app.

Skill Station B
BREATHING

LEARNING OBJECTIVES

1. Assess and recognize adequate ventilation and oxygenation in a simulated trauma patient.

2. Identify trauma patients in respiratory distress.

3. Practice systematically reading chest x-rays of trauma patients.

4. Recognize the radiographic signs of potentially life-threatening traumatic injuries.

5. Identify appropriate landmarks for needle decompression and thoracostomy tube placement.

6. Demonstrate how to perform a needle decompression of the pleural space on a simulator, task trainer, live anesthetized animal, or cadaver.

7. Perform a finger thoracostomy using a simulator, task trainer, live anesthetized animal, or cadaver.

8. Insert a thoracostomy tube using a simulator, task trainer, live anesthetized animal, or cadaver.

9. Discuss the basic differences between pediatric chest injury and adult chest injury.

10. Explain the importance of adequate pain control following chest trauma.

11. List the steps required to safely transfer a trauma patient with a breathing problem.

SKILLS INCLUDED IN THIS SKILL STATION

- Breathing Assessment
- Interpretation of Chest X-ray
- Finger and Tube Thoracostomy
- Needle Decompression
- Use of Pediatric Resuscitation Tape

BREATHING ASSESSMENT

STEP 1. Listen for signs of partial airway obstruction or compromise.

- Asymmetrical or absent breath sounds
- Additional sounds (e.g., sounds indicative of hemothorax)

STEP 2. Look for evidence of respiratory distress.

- Tachypnea
- Use of accessory muscles of respiration
- Abnormal/asymmetrical chest wall movement
- Cyanosis (late finding)

STEP 3. Feel for air or fluid.

- Hyperresonance to percussion
- Dullness to percussion
- Crepitance

INTERPRETATION OF CHEST X-RAY

The DRSABCDE mnemonic is helpful for interpreting chest x-rays in the trauma care environment:

STEP 1. **D**—**D**etails (name, demographics, type of film, date, and time)

STEP 2. **R**—**R**IPE (assess image quality)

- Rotation
- Inspiration—5–6 ribs anterior in midclavicular line or 8–10 ribs above diaphragm, poor inspiration, or hyperexpanded
- Picture (are entire lung fields seen?)
- Exposure penetration

STEP 3. **S**—**S**oft tissues and bones. Look for subcutaneous air and assess for fractures of the clavicles, scapulae, ribs (1st and 2nd rib fractures may signal aortic injury), and sternum.

STEP 4. **A**—**A**irway and mediastinum. Look for signs of aortic rupture: widened mediastinum, obliteration of the aortic knob, deviation of the trachea to the right, pleural cap, elevation and right shift of the right mainstem bronchus, loss of the aortopulmonary window, depression of the left mainstem bronchus, and deviation of the esophagus to the right. Look for air in the mediastinum.

STEP 5. **B**—**B**reathing, lung fields, pneumothoraces, consolidation (pulmonary contusion), cavitary lesions

STEP 6. **C**—**C**irculation, heart size, position borders shape, aortic stripe

STEP 7. **D**—**D**iaphragm shape, angles, gastric bubble, subdiaphragmatic air

STEP 8. **E**—**E**xtras: endotracheal tube, central venous pressure monitor, nasogastric tube, ECG electrodes, chest tube, pacemakers

NEEDLE DECOMPRESSION

STEP 1. Assess the patient's chest and respiratory status.

STEP 2. Administer high-flow oxygen and ventilate as necessary.

STEP 3. Surgically prepare the site chosen for insertion. (For pediatric patients, the 2nd intercostal space midclavicular line is appropriate.) For adults (especially with thicker subcutaneous tissue), use the fourth or fifth intercostal space anterior to the midaxillary line.

STEP 4. Anesthetize the area if time and physiology permit.

STEP 5. Insert an over-the-needle catheter 3 in. (5 cm for smaller adults; 8 cm for large adult) with a Luer-Lok 10 cc syringe attached into the skin. Direct the needle just over the rib into the intercostal space , aspirating the syringe while advancing. (Adding 3 cc of saline may aid the identification of aspirated air.)

STEP 6. Puncture the pleura.

STEP 7. Remove the syringe and listen for the escape of air when the needle enters the pleural space to indicate relief of the tension pneumothorax. Advance the catheter into the pleural space.

STEP 8. Stabilize the catheter and prepare for chest tube insertion.

FINGER AND TUBE THORACOSTOMY

STEP 1. Gather supplies, sterile drapes, and antiseptic, tube thoracostomy kit (tray) and appropriately sized chest tube (28-32 F). Prepare the underwater seal and collection device.

STEP 2. Position the patient with the ipsilateral arm extended overhead and flexed at the elbow (unless precluded by other injuries). Use an assistant to maintain the arm in this position.

STEP 3. Widely prep and drape the lateral chest wall, include the nipple, in the operative field.

STEP 4. Identify the site for insertion of the chest tube in the 4th or 5th intercostal space. This site corresponds to the level of the nipple or inframammary fold. The insertion site should be between the anterior and midaxillary lines.

STEP 5. Inject the site liberally with local anesthesia to include the skin, subcutaneous tissue, rib periosteum, and pleura. While the local anesthetic takes effect, use the thoracostomy tube to measure the depth of insertion. Premeasure the estimated depth of chest tube by placing the tip near the clavicle with a gentle curve of chest tube toward incision. Evaluate the marking on the chest tube that correlates to incision, ensuring the sentinel hole is in the pleural space. Often the chest tube markings will be at 10–14 at the skin, depending on the amount of subcutaneous tissue (e.g., obese patients).

STEP 6. Make a 2- to 3-cm incision parallel to the ribs at the predetermined site, and bluntly dissect through the subcutaneous tissues just above the rib.

STEP 7. Puncture the parietal pleura with the tip of the clamp while holding the instrument near the tip to prevent sudden deep insertion of the instrument and injury to underlying structures. Advance the clamp over the rib and spread to widen the pleural opening. Take care not to bury the clamp in the thoracic cavity, as spreading will be ineffective. Air or fluid will be evacuated. With a sterile gloved finger, perform a finger sweep to clear any adhesions and clots (i.e., perform a finger thoracostomy).

STEP 8. Place a clamp on the distal end of the tube. Using either another clamp at the proximal end of the thoracostomy tube or a finger as a guide, advance the tube into the pleural space to the desired depth.

STEP 9. Look and listen for air movement and bloody drainage; "fogging" of the chest tube with expiration may also indicate tube is in the pleural space.

STEP 10. Remove the distal clamp and connect the tube thoracostomy to an underwater seal apparatus with a collection chamber. Zip ties can be used to secure the connection between the thoracostomy tube and the underwater seal apparatus.

STEP 11. Secure the tube to the skin with heavy, nonabsorbable suture.

STEP 12. Apply a sterile dressing and secure it with wide tape.

STEP 13. Obtain a chest x-ray.

STEP 14. Reassess the patient.

USE OF PEDIATRIC RESUSCITATION TAPE

STEP 1. Unfold the pediatric resuscitation tape.

STEP 2. Place the tape along the side of the chest tube task trainer to estimate the weight and note color zone.

STEP 3. Read the size of equipment to be used with patient, noting chest tube size.

LINKS TO FUTURE LEARNING

Reassess breathing frequently during the primary survey and resuscitation. Review the MyATLS mobile app for video demonstrations of procedures. In addition, www.trauma.org provides descriptions of the management of a variety of thoracic injuries in trauma patients.

Post ATLS—Practice using a structured approach to reading chest x-rays before looking at the radiologist's interpretation to improve your proficiency. Review the MyATLS video demonstration of chest tube insertion prior to performing the procedure to reinforce procedural steps.

Skill Station C
CIRCULATION

LEARNING OBJECTIVES

1. Diagnose the presence of shock, both compensated and uncompensated.

2. Determine the type of shock present.

3. Choose the appropriate fluid resuscitation.

4. Demonstrate on a model the application of a staged approach to control external hemorrhage by using direct pressure, wound packing, and application of a tourniquet.

5. Demonstrate on a model placement of intraosseous access, and discuss other options for vascular access and their indications.

6. Demonstrate the application of a pelvic stabilization device for pelvic fractures and understand the indications and contraindications for the use of traction devices for femur fractures.

7. Recognize the need for patient reassessment and additional resuscitation based on the patient's response to treatment.

8. Recognize which patients require definitive hemorrhage control (i.e., operative and/or catheter based) and/or transfer to a higher level of care.

9. Describe and demonstrate (optional) the indications and techniques of central intravenous access, peripheral venous cutdown, diagnostic peritoneal lavage (DPL), and pericardiocentesis.

SKILLS INCLUDED IN THIS SKILL STATION

- Wound Packing
- Application of Combat Application Tourniquet
- Application of Traction Splint (Demonstration)
- Placement of Intraosseous Device, Humeral Insertion
- Placement of Intraosseous Device, Proximal Tibial Insertion
- Application of Pelvic Binder or Other Pelvic Stabilization Device
- Diagnostic Peritoneal Lavage (DPL) —Optional Skill
- Femoral Venipuncture: Seldinger Technique— Optional Skill
- Subclavian Venipuncture: Infraclavicular Approach—Optional Skill
- Venous Cutdown—Optional Skill
- Pericardiocentesis Using Ultrasound—Optional Skill

WOUND PACKING

STEP 1. Fully expose the wound and cut clothing, if not previously done.

STEP 2. Use gauze pads to mop bleeding and identify the general area that is bleeding.

STEP 3. Place a stack of gauze pads over that area and press down firmly. Hold for 5-10 minutes if using gauze or 3 minutes if using hemostatic gauze.

STEP 4. If bleeding is controlled, secure the gauze pads with roll gauze, an elastic bandage, or self-adhering wrap (3M Coban™). Consult trauma, vascular, or orthopedic surgeon, based on injury type.

STEP 5. If bleeding is not controlled and there is a cavity, use gloved finger or forceps to place gauze into wound, ensuring that the gauze reaches the base of the wound. Place more gauze until the wound is tightly packed. Hold pressure for an additional 3 minutes, and reassess. Gauze impregnated with a topical hemostatic agent can be used, if available. Gauze without a hemostatic agent may be just as effective for wound packing as gauze treated with a hemostatic agent. Large wounds may require multiple gauze dressings to fully pack the wound. Pack in as much gauze as will fit into the wound, and push in even more if you can. If these steps fail to control the bleeding, proceed with placing tourniquet while awaiting surgical consultation.

APPLICATION OF COMBAT APPLICATION TOURNIQUET

STEP 1. Insert the wounded extremity (arm or leg) through the combat application tourniquet (CAT).

STEP 2. Place the tourniquet proximal to the bleeding site, as distal as possible. Do not place at a joint.

STEP 3. Pull the self-adhering band tight, and securely fasten it back on itself. *Be sure to remove all slack.*

STEP 4. Adhere the band around the extremity. Do not adhere the band past the clip.

STEP 5. Twist the windlass rod until the bleeding has stopped.

STEP 6. Ensure arterial bleeding is arrested. Tourniquet should be tight and painful if the patient is conscious.

STEP 7. Lock the windlass rod in place in the windlass clip. Bleeding is now controlled.

STEP 8. Adhere the remaining self-adhering band over the rod, through the windlass clip, and continue around the patient's arm or leg as far as it will go.

STEP 9. Secure the rod and the band with the windlass strap. Grasp the strap, pull it tight, and adhere it to the opposite hook on the windlass clip.

STEP 10. Note the time the tourniquet was applied. If you have a marker, you can write it directly on the tourniquet.

STEP 11. If the bleeding is not stopped with one tourniquet and it is as tight as you can get it, place a second one, if available, just above the first. Tighten it as before.

APPLICATION OF TRACTION SPLINT

STEP 1. Consider need for analgesia before applying a traction splint, and select the appropriate splint to use.

STEP 2. Measure splint to the patient's unaffected leg for length.

STEP 3. Ensure that the upper cushioned ring is placed under the buttocks and adjacent to the ischial tuberosity. The distal end of the splint should extend beyond the ankle by approximately 6 inches (15 cm).

STEP 4. Align the femur by manually applying traction though the ankle.

STEP 5. After achieving realignment, gently elevate the leg to allow the assistant to slide the splint under the extremity so that the padded portion of the splint rests against the ischial tuberosity.

STEP 6. Reassess the neurovascular status of the injured extremity after applying traction.

STEP 7. Ensure that the splint straps are positioned to support the thigh and calf.

STEP 8. Position the ankle hitch around the patient's ankle and foot while an assistant maintains manual traction on the leg. The bottom strap should be slightly shorter than, or at least the same length as, the two upper crossing straps.

STEP 9. Attach the ankle hitch to the traction hook while an assistant maintains manual traction and support. Apply traction in increments, using the windlass knob until the extremity appears stable or until pain and muscle spasm are relieved.

STEP 10. Recheck the pulse after applying the traction splint. If perfusion of the extremity distal to the injury appears worse after applying traction, gradually release it.

STEP 11. Secure the remaining straps.

STEP 12. Frequently reevaluate the neurovascular status of the extremity. Document the patient's neurovascular status after every manipulation of the extremity.

PLACEMENT OF INTRAOSSEOUS DEVICE, HUMERAL INSERTION

STEP 1. Flex the patient's elbow and internally rotate the arm, placing the patient's hand on the abdomen with the elbow close to the body and the hand pronated. The insertion site is the most prominent aspect of the greater tubercle.

STEP 2. Use your thumb(s) to slide up the anterior shaft of the humerus until you can feel the greater tubercle, about 1 cm (1/3 in.) above the surgical neck.

STEP 3. Prepare the site by using an antiseptic solution.

STEP 4. Remove the needle cap and aim the needle tip downward at a 45-degree angle to the horizontal plane. The correct angle will result in the needle hub lying perpendicular to the skin. Push the needle tip through the skin until the tip rests against the bone. The 5-mm mark must be visible above the skin for confirmation of adequate needle length.

STEP 5. Gently drill into the humerus 2 cm (3/4 in.) or until the hub reaches the skin in an adult.

Stop when you feel the "pop" or "give" in infants. (When using a needle not attached to a drill, orient the needle perpendicular to the entry site and apply pressure in conjunction with a twisting motion until a "loss of resistance" is felt as the needle enters the marrow cavity.)

STEP 6. Hold the hub in place and pull the driver straight off. Continue to hold the hub while twisting the stylet off the hub with counterclockwise rotations. The needle should feel firmly seated in the bone (first confirmation of placement). Place the stylet in a sharps container.

STEP 7. Place the EZ-Stabilizer dressing over the hub. Attach a primed EZ-Connect™ extension set to the hub, firmly secure by twisting clockwise. Pull the tabs off the EZ-Stabilizer dressing to expose the adhesive and apply it to the skin.

STEP 8. Aspirate for blood/bone marrow (second confirmation of placement).

STEP 9. Secure the arm in place across the abdomen.

STEP 10. Attach a syringe with saline to the needle and flush, looking for swelling locally or difficulty flushing. Inject with lidocaine if the patient is alert and experiences pain with infusion.

PLACEMENT OF INTRAOSSEOUS DEVICE, PROXIMAL TIBIAL INSERTION

STEP 1. Place the patient in the supine position. Select an uninjured lower extremity, place sufficient padding under the knee to effect approximate 30-degree flexion of the knee, and allow the patient's heel to rest comfortably on the gurney or stretcher.

STEP 2. Identify the puncture site—the anteromedial surface of the proximal tibia, approximately one fingerbreadth (1 to 3 cm) below the tubercle.

STEP 3. Cleanse the skin around the puncture site well and drape the area.

STEP 4.   If the patient is awake, use a local anesthetic at the puncture site.

STEP 5.   Initially at a 90-degree angle, introduce a short (threaded or smooth), large-caliber, bone-marrow aspiration needle (or a short, 18-gauge spinal needle with stylet) into the skin and periosteum, with the needle bevel directed toward the foot and away from the epiphyseal plate.

STEP 6.   After gaining purchase in the bone, direct the needle 45 to 60 degrees away from the epiphyseal plate. Using a gentle twisting or boring motion, advance the needle through the bone cortex and into the bone marrow.

STEP 7.   Remove the stylet and attach to the needle a 10-mL syringe with approximately 6 mL of sterile saline. Gently draw on the plunger of the syringe. Aspiration of bone marrow into the syringe signifies entrance into the medullary cavity.

STEP 8.   Inject the saline into the needle to expel any clot that can occlude the needle. If the saline flushes through the needle easily and there is no evidence of swelling, the needle is likely located in the appropriate place. If bone marrow was not aspirated as outlined in Step 7, but the needle flushes easily when injecting the saline and there is no evidence of swelling, the needle is likely in the appropriate place. In addition, proper placement of the needle is indicated if the needle remains upright without support and intravenous solution flows freely without evidence of subcutaneous infiltration.

STEP 9.   Connect the needle to the large-caliber intravenous tubing and begin fluid infusion. Carefully screw the needle further into the medullary cavity until the needle hub rests on the patient's skin and free flow continues. If a smooth needle is used, it should be stabilized at a 45- to 60-degree angle to the anteromedial surface of the patient's leg.

STEP 10. Apply sterile dressing. Secure the needle and tubing in place.

STEP 11. Routinely reevaluate the placement of the intraosseous needle, ensuring that it remains through the bone cortex and in the medullary canal. Remember, intraosseous infusion should be limited to emergency resuscitation of the patient and discontinued as soon as other venous access has been obtained.

APPLICATION OF PELVIC BINDER OR OTHER PELVIC STABILIZATION DEVICE

STEP 1.   Select the appropriate pelvic stabilization device.

STEP 2.   Identify the landmarks for application, focusing on the greater trochanters.

STEP 3.   Internally rotate and oppose the ankles, feet, or great toes using tape or roll gauze.

STEP 4.   Slide the device from caudal to cephalad, centering it over the greater trochanters. Two people on opposite sides grasp the device at bottom and top and shimmy it proximally into position. Alternatively, or place the device under the patient while restricting spinal motion and with minimal manipulation of the pelvis by rotating the patient laterally. Place folded device beneath patient, reaching as far beneath patient as possible. Rotate the other direction and pull the end of the device through. If using a sheet, cross the limbs of the sheet and secure with clamps or towel clamp.

STEP 5.   Roll the patient back to supine and secure the device anteriorly. Ensure that the device is adequately secured with appropriate tension, observing internal rotation of lower limbs, which indicates pelvic closure.

DIAGNOSTIC PERITONEAL LAVAGE (DPL)—OPTIONAL SKILL

STEP 1.   Obtain informed consent, if time permits.

STEP 2.   Decompress the stomach and urinary bladder by inserting a gastric tube and urinary catheter.

STEP 3. After donning a mask, sterile gown, and gloves, surgically prepare the abdomen (costal margin to the pubic area and flank to flank, anteriorly).

STEP 4. Inject local anesthetic containing epinephrine in the midline just below the umbilicus, down to the level of the fascia. Allow time to take affect.

STEP 5. Vertically incise the skin and subcutaneous tissues to the fascia.

STEP 6. Grasp the fascial edges with clamps, and elevate and incise the fascia down to the peritoneum. Make a small nick in the peritoneum, entering the peritoneal cavity.

STEP 7. Insert a peritoneal dialysis catheter into the peritoneal cavity.

STEP 8. Advance the catheter into the pelvis.

STEP 9. Connect the dialysis catheter to a syringe and aspirate.

STEP 10. If gross blood or organic matter is aspirated, the patient should be taken for laparotomy. If gross blood is not obtained, instill 1 L of warmed isotonic crystalloid solution (10 mL/kg in a child) into the peritoneum through the intravenous tubing attached to the dialysis catheter.

STEP 11. Gently agitate the abdomen to distribute the fluid throughout the peritoneal cavity and increase mixing with the blood.

STEP 12. If the patient's condition is stable, allow the fluid to remain a few minutes before placing the intravenous fluid bag on the floor and allowing the peritoneal fluid to drain from the abdomen. Adequate fluid return is > 20% of the infused volume.

STEP 13. After the fluid returns, send a sample to the laboratory for Gram stain and erythrocyte and leukocyte counts (unspun). A positive test and thus the need for surgical intervention is indicated by 100,000 red blood cells (RBCs)/mm³ or more, greater than 500 white blood cells (WBCs)/mm³, or a positive Gram stain for food fibers or bacteria. A negative lavage does not exclude

retroperitoneal injuries such as pancreatic and duodenal injuries.

FEMORAL VENIPUNCTURE: SELDINGER TECHNIQUE— OPTIONAL SKILL

Note: Sterile technique should be used when performing this procedure.

STEP 1. Place the patient in the supine position.

STEP 2. Cleanse the skin around the venipuncture site well and drape the area.

STEP 3. Locate the femoral vein by palpating the femoral artery. The vein lies directly medial to the femoral artery (remember the mnemonic NAVEL, from lateral to medial: nerve, artery, vein, empty space, lymphatic). Keep a finger on the artery to facilitate anatomical location and avoid insertion of the catheter into the artery. Use ultrasound to identify the femoral artery and visualize placement of needle into the vein.

STEP 4. If the patient is awake, use a local anesthetic at the venipuncture site.

STEP 5. Introduce a large-caliber needle attached to a 10-mL syringe with 0.5 to 1 mL of saline. Direct the needle toward the patient's head, entering the skin directly over the femoral vein. Hold the needle and syringe parallel to the frontal plane.

STEP 6. Directing the needle cephalad and posteriorly, slowly advance it while gently withdrawing the plunger of the syringe.

STEP 7. When a free flow of blood appears in the syringe, remove the syringe and occlude the needle with a finger to prevent air embolism. If the vein is not entered, withdraw the needle and redirect it. If two attempts are unsuccessful, a more experienced clinician should attempt the procedure, if available.

STEP 8. Insert the guidewire and remove the needle.

STEP 9. Make a small skin incision at the entry point of wire, pass the dilator (or dilator introducer combination) over the wire and remove the dilator holding pressure at the exit site of the wire (or remove dilator if introducer combination is used).

STEP 10. Insert the catheter over the guidewire aspirate to assure free blood flow. If using an introducer, aspirate it.

STEP 11. Flush the catheter or introducer with saline and cap or begin fluid infusion.

STEP 12. Affix the catheter in place (with a suture), dress the area according to local protocol.

STEP 13. Tape the intravenous tubing in place.

STEP 14. Change the catheter location as soon as it is practical.

SUBCLAVIAN VENIPUNCTURE: INFRACLAVICULAR APPROACH—OPTIONAL SKILL

Note: Sterile technique should be used when performing this procedure.

STEP 1. Place the patient in the supine position, with the head at least 15 degrees down to distend the neck veins and prevent air embolism. Only if a cervical spine injury has been excluded can the patient's head be turned away from the venipuncture site.

STEP 2. Cleanse the skin around the venipuncture site well, and drape the area.

STEP 3. If the patient is awake, use a local anesthetic at the venipuncture site.

STEP 4. Introduce a large-caliber needle, attached to a 10-mL syringe with 0.5 to 1 mL of saline, 1 cm below the junction of the middle and medial one-third of the clavicle.

STEP 5. After the skin has been punctured, with the bevel of the needle upward, expel the skin plug that can occlude the needle.

STEP 6. Hold the needle and syringe parallel to the frontal plane.

STEP 7. Direct the needle medially, slightly cephalad, and posteriorly behind the clavicle toward the posterior, superior angle of the sternal end of the clavicle (toward the finger placed in the suprasternal notch).

STEP 8. Slowly advance the needle while gently withdrawing the plunger of the syringe.

STEP 9. When a free flow of blood appears in the syringe, rotate the bevel of the needle, caudally remove the syringe, and occlude the needle with a finger to prevent air embolism. If the vein is not entered, withdraw the needle and redirect it. If two attempts are unsuccessful, a more experienced clinician (if available) should attempt the procedure.

STEP 10. Insert the guidewire while monitoring the electrocardiogram for rhythm abnormalities.

STEP 11. Remove the needle while holding the guidewire in place.

STEP 12. Use an 11 blade to incise the skin around the exit site of the guidewire. Insert the dilator over the guidewire to dilate the area under the clavicle. Remove the dilator, leaving the wire in place. Thread the catheter over the wire to a predetermined depth (the tip of the catheter should be above the right atrium for fluid administration).

STEP 13. Connect the catheter to the intravenous tubing.

STEP 14. Affix the catheter securely to the skin (with a suture), dress the area according to local protocol.

STEP 15. Tape the intravenous tubing in place.

STEP 16. Obtain a chest x-ray film to confirm the position of the intravenous line and identify a possible pneumothorax.

VENOUS CUTDOWN OPTIONAL SKILL

STEP 1. Cleanse the skin around the site chosen for cutdown, and drape the area.

STEP 2. If the patient is awake, use a local anesthetic at the venipuncture site.

STEP 3. Make a full-thickness, transverse skin incision through the anesthetized area to a length of 1 inch (2.5 cm).

STEP 4. By blunt dissection, using a curved hemostat, identify the vein and dissect it free from any accompanying structures.

STEP 5. Elevate and dissect the vein for a distance of approximately 3/4 inch (2 cm) to free it from its bed.

STEP 6. Ligate the distal mobilized vein, leaving the suture in place for traction.

STEP 7. Pass a tie around the vein in a cephalad direction.

STEP 8. Make a small, transverse venotomy and gently dilate the venotomy with the tip of a closed hemostat.

STEP 9. Introduce a plastic cannula through the venotomy and secure it in place by tying the upper ligature around the vein and cannula. To prevent dislodging, insert the cannula an adequate distance from the venotomy.

STEP 10. Attach the intravenous tubing to the cannula, and close the incision with interrupted sutures.

STEP 11. Apply a sterile dressing.

PERICARDIOCENTESIS USING ULTRASOUND—OPTIONAL SKILL

STEP 1. Monitor the patient's vital signs and electrocardiogram (ECG) before, during, and after the procedure.

STEP 2. Use ultrasound to identify the effusion.

STEP 3. Surgically prepare the xiphoid and subxiphoid areas, if time allows.

STEP 4. Locally anesthetize the puncture site, if necessary.

STEP 5. Using a 16- to 18-gauge, 6-in. (15-cm) or longer over-the-needle catheter, attach a 35-mL empty syringe with a three-way stopcock.

STEP 6. Assess the patient for any mediastinal shift that may have caused the heart to shift significantly.

STEP 7. Puncture the skin 1 to 2 cm inferior to the left of the xiphochondral junction, at a 45-degree angle to the skin.

STEP 8. Carefully advance the needle cephalad and aim toward the tip of the left scapula. Follow the needle with the ultrasound.

STEP 9. Advance the catheter over the needle. Remove the needle.

STEP 10. When the catheter tip enters the blood-filled pericardial sac, withdraw as much nonclotted blood as possible.

STEP 11. After aspiration is completed, remove the syringe and attach a three-way stopcock, leaving the stopcock closed. The plastic pericardiocentesis catheter can be sutured or taped in place and covered with a small dressing to allow for continued decompression en route to surgery or transfer to another care facility.

STEP 12. If cardiac tamponade symptoms persist, the stopcock may be opened and the pericardial sac reaspirated. This process may be repeated as the symptoms of tamponade recur, before definitive treatment.

LINKS TO FUTURE LEARNING

Shock can develop over time, so frequent reassessment is necessary. Hemorrhage is the most common cause of shock in the trauma patient, but other causes can occur and should be investigated. The MyATLS mobile app provides video demonstrations of most procedures. Also visit www.bleedingcontrol.org for more information regarding external hemorrhage control. Visit https://www.youtube.com/watch?v=Wu-KVibUGNM to view a video demonstrating the humeral intraosseous approach, and https://www.youtube.com/watch?v=OwLoAHrdpJA to view video of the ultrasound-guided approach to pericardiocentesis.

Skill Station D
DISABILITY

LEARNING OBJECTIVES

1. Perform a brief neurological examination, including calculating the Glasgow Coma Scale (GCS) score, performing a pupillary examination, and examining the patient for lateralizing signs.

2. Identify the utility and limitations of CT head decision tools.

3. Identify the utility and limitations of cervical spine imaging decision tools.

4. Perform proper evaluation of the spine while restricting spinal motion, including evaluating the spine, logrolling the patient, removing the backboard, and reviewing cervical spine and head CT images.

5. Identify the signs, symptoms, and treatment of neurogenic shock.

6. Demonstrate proper helmet removal technique.

7. Identify the signs and symptoms of spinal cord injury in a simulated patient.

8. Demonstrate the hand-over of a neurotrauma patient to another facility or practitioner.

SKILLS INCLUDED IN THIS SKILL STATION

- Brief or Focused Neurological Examination
- Evaluation of Cervical Spine
- Transfer Communication
- Helmet Removal
- Detailed Neurological Exam
- Removal of Spine Board
- Evaluation of Head CT Scans
- Evaluation of Cervical Spine Images

BRIEF OR FOCUSED NEUROLOGICAL EXAMINATION

EXAMINE PUPILS

STEP 1. Note size and shape of pupil.

STEP 2. Shine light into eyes and note pupillary response.

DETERMINE NEW GCS SCORE

STEP 3. Assess eye opening.

    A. Note factors interfering with communication, ability to respond, and other injuries.

    B. Observe eye opening.

    C. If response is not spontaneous, stimulate patient by speaking or shouting.

    D. If no response, apply pressure on fingertip, trapezius, or supraorbital notch.

    E. Rate the response on a scale of not testable (NT), 1–4.

STEP 4. Assess verbal response.

A. Note factors interfering with communication, ability to respond, and other injuries.

B. Observe content of speech.

C. If not spontaneous, stimulate by speaking or shouting.

D. If no response, apply pressure on fingertip, trapezius, or supraorbital notch.

E. Rate the response on a scale of NT, 1–5.

STEP 5. Assess motor response.

A. Note factors interfering with communication, ability to respond, and other injuries.

B. Observe movements of the right and left sides of body.

C. If response is not spontaneous, stimulate patient by speaking or shouting.

D. If no response, apply pressure on fingertip, trapezius, or supraorbital notch (if not contraindicated by injury).

E. Rate the response on a scale of NT, 1–6.

STEP 6. Calculate total GCS score and record its individual components.

EVALUATE FOR ANY EVIDENCE OF LATERALIZING SIGNS

STEP 7. Assess for movement of upper extremities.

STEP 8. Determine upper extremity strength bilaterally, and compare side to side.

STEP 9. Assess for movement of the lower extremities.

STEP 10. Determine lower extremity strength bilaterally, and compare side to side.

EVALUATION OF CERVICAL SPINE

STEP 1. Remove the front of the cervical collar, if present, while a second person restricts patient's cervical spinal motion.

STEP 2. Inform the patient that you are going to examine him or her. The patient should answer verbally rather than nodding the head.

STEP 3. Palpate the posterior cervical spine for deformity, swelling, and tenderness. Note the level of any abnormality. Look for any penetrating wounds or contusions. If the cervical spine is nontender and the patient has no neurological deficits, proceed to Step 4. If not, stop, replace the cervical collar, and obtain imaging.

STEP 4. Ask the patient to carefully turn his or her head from side to side. Note if there is pain, or any paresthesia develops. If not, proceed to Step 5. If yes, stop, reapply the cervical collar, and obtain imaging.

STEP 5. Ask the patient to extend and flex his or her neck (i.e., say, "Look behind you and then touch your chin to your chest."). Note if there is pain or any paresthesia develops. If not, and the patient is not impaired, head injured, or in other high-risk category as defined by NEXUS Criteria or the Canadian C-Spine Rule (CCR), discontinue using the cervical collar. If yes, reapply the cervical collar and obtain imaging.

TRANSFER COMMUNICATION

STEP 1. Use the ABC SBAR method of ensuring complete communication.

A. Airway

B. Breathing

C. Circulation

D. Situation

- Patient name
- Age
- Referring facility
- Referring physician name
- Reporting nurse name
- Indication for transfer
- IV access site

- IV fluid and rate
- Other interventions completed

E. Background

- Event history
- AMPLE assessment
- Blood products
- Medications given (date and time)
- Imaging performed
- Splinting

F. Assessment

- Vital signs
- Pertinent physical exam findings
- Patient response to treatment

G. Recommendation

- Transport mode
- Level of transport care
- Meds intervention during transport
- Needed assessments and interventions

HELMET REMOVAL

STEP 1. One person stabilizes the patient's head and neck by placing one hand on either side of the helmet with the fingers on the patient's mandible. This position prevents slippage if the strap is loose.

STEP 2. The second person cuts or loosens the helmet strap at the D-rings.

STEP 3. The second person then places one hand on the mandible at the angle, positioning the thumb on one side and the fingers on the other. The other hand applies pressure from under the head at the occipital region. This maneuver transfers the responsibility for restricting cervical motion to the second person.

STEP 4. The first person then expands the helmet laterally to clear the ears and carefully removes the helmet. If the helmet has a face cover, remove this device first. If the helmet

provides full facial coverage, the patient's nose will impede helmet removal. To clear the nose, tilt the helmet backward and raise it over the patient's nose.

STEP 5. During this process, the second person must restrict cervical spine motion from below to prevent head tilt.

STEP 6. After removing the helmet, continue restriction of cervical spine motion from above, apply a cervical collar.

STEP 7. If attempts to remove the helmet result in pain and paresthesia, remove the helmet with a cast cutter. Also use a cast cutter to remove the helmet if there is evidence of a cervical spine injury on x-ray film or by examination. Stabilize the head and neck during this procedure; this is accomplished by dividing the helmet in the coronal plane through the ears. The outer, rigid layer is removed easily, and the inside layer is then incised and removed anteriorly. Maintaining neutral alignment of the head and neck, remove the posterior portions of the helmet.

DETAILED NEUROLOGICAL EXAM

STEP 1. Examine the pupils for size, shape, and light reactivity.

STEP 2. Reassess the new GCS score.

STEP 3. Perform a cranial nerve exam by having patient open and close eyes; move eyes to the right, left, up, and down; smile widely; stick out the tongue; and shrug the shoulders.

STEP 4. Examine the dermatomes for sensation to light touch, noting areas where there is sensory loss. Examine those areas for sensation to pinprick, noting the lowest level where there is sensation.

STEP 5. Examine the myotomes for active movement and assess strength (0–5) of movement, noting if limited by pain.

- Raises elbow to level of shoulder—deltoid, C5

- Flexes forearm—biceps, C6
- Extends forearm—triceps, C7
- Flexes wrist and fingers, C8
- Spreads fingers, T1
- Flexes hip—iliopsoas, L2
- Extends knee—quadriceps, L3–L4
- Flexes knee—hamstrings, L4–L5 to S1
- Dorsiflexes big toe—extensor hallucis longus, L5
- Plantar flexes ankle—gastrocnemius, S1

STEP 6. Ideally, test patient's reflexes at elbows, knees, and ankles (this step is least informative in the emergency setting).

▶ REMOVAL OF SPINE BOARD

Note: Properly securing the patient to a long spine board is the basic technique for splinting the spine. In general, this is done in the prehospital setting; the patient arrives at the hospital with spinal motion already restricted by being secured to a long spine board with cervical collar in place and head secured to the long spine board. The long spine board provides an effective splint and permits safe transfers of the patient with a minimal number of assistants. However, unpadded spine boards can soon become uncomfortable for conscious patients and pose a significant risk for pressure sores on posterior bony prominences (occiput, scapulae, sacrum, and heels). Therefore, the patient should be transferred from the spine board to a firm, well-padded gurney or equivalent surface as soon as it can be done safely. Continue to restrict spinal motion until appropriate imaging and examination have excluded spinal injury.

STEP 1. Assemble four people and assign roles: one to manage the patient's head and neck and lead the movement; one to manage the torso; and one to manage the hips and legs. The fourth person will examine the spine, perform the rectal exam, if indicated, and remove the board.

STEP 2. Inform the patient that he or she will be turned to the side to remove the board and examine the back. Instruct the patient to place his or her hands across the chest if able and to respond verbally if he or she experiences pain during examination of the back.

STEP 3. Remove any blocks, tapes, and straps securing the patient to the board, if not already done. The lower limbs can be temporarily secured together with roll gauze or tape to facilitate movement.

STEP 4. All personnel assume their roles: The head and neck manager places his or her hands under the patient's shoulders, palms up, with elbows and forearms parallel to the neck to prevent cervical spinal motion. The torso manager places his or her hands on the patient's shoulder and upper pelvis, reaching across the patient. The third person crosses the second person's hand, placing one hand at the pelvis and the other at the lower extremities. (Note: If the patient has fractures, a fifth person may need to be assigned to that limb.)

STEP 5. The head and neck manager ensures the team is ready to move, and then the team moves the patient as a single unit onto his or her side.

STEP 6. Examine the back.

STEP 7. Perform rectal examination, if indicated.

STEP 8. On the direction of the head and neck manager, return the patient to the supine position. If the extremities were tied or taped, remove the ties.

▶ EVALUATION OF HEAD CT SCANS

Note: The steps outlined here for evaluating a head CT scan provide one approach to assessing for significant, life-threatening pathology

STEP 1. Confirm the images are of the correct patient and that the scan was performed without intravenous contrast.

STEP 2. Assess the scalp component for contusion or swelling that can indicate a site of external trauma.

STEP 3. Assess for skull fractures. Remember that suture lines can be mistaken for fractures. Missile tracts may appear as linear areas of low attenuation.

STEP 4. Assess the gyri and sulci for symmetry. Look for subdural hematomas and epidural hematomas.

STEP 5. Assess the cerebral and cerebellar hemispheres. Compare side to side for density and symmetry. Look for areas of high attenuation that may represent contusion or shearing injury.

STEP 6. Assess the ventricles. Look for symmetry or distortion. Increased density represents intraventricular hemorrhage.

STEP 7. Determine shifts. Hematoma or swelling can cause midline shift. A shift of more than 5 mm is considered indicative of the need for surgery.

STEP 8. Assess the maxillofacial structures. Look for fractures and fluid in the sinuses. Remember the four things that cause increased density: contrast, clot, cellularity (tumor), and calcification.

EVALUATION OF CERVICAL SPINE IMAGES

Note: Before interpreting the x-ray, confirm the patient name and date of examination.

STEP 1. Assess adequacy and alignment.

A. Identify the presence of all 7 cervical vertebrae and the superior aspect of T1.

B. Identify the

- Anterior vertebral line
- Anterior spinal line
- Posterior spinal line
- Spinous processes

STEP 2. Assess the bone.

A. Examine all vertebrae for preservation of height and integrity of the bony cortex.

B. Examine facets.

C. Examine spinous processes.

STEP 3. Assess the cartilage, including examining the cartilaginous disk spaces for narrowing or widening.

STEP 4. Assess the dens.

A. Examine the outline of the dens.

B. Examine the predental space (3 mm).

C. Examine the clivus; it should point to the dens.

STEP 5. Assess the extraaxial soft tissues.

A. Examine the extraaxial space and soft tissues:

- 7 mm at C3
- 3 cm at C7

LINKS TO FUTURE LEARNING

"New" Glasgow Coma Scale: www.glasgowcomascale.org

Brain Trauma Foundation Guidelines: Carney M, Totten AM, Reilly C, Ullman JS et al. "Guidelines for the Management of Severe Traumatic Brain Injury, 4th Edition" 2016: Brain Trauma Foundation. www.braintrauma.org

"New Orleans Criteria" for CT scanning in minor head injury: Haydel MJ, Preston CA, Mills TJ, Luber S, Blaudeau E, DeBlieux PMC. Indications for computed tomography in patients with minor head injury. *N Engl J Med*. 2000;343:100-105

"Canadian Head CT rules":

- Stiell IG, Lesiuk H, Wells GA, et al. The Canadian CT Head Rule Study for patients with minor head injury: rationale, objectives, and methodology for phase I (derivation). Ann Emerg Med. 2001;38:160-169. 25. Stiell IG, Lesiuk H, Wells GA, et al. Canadian CT Head Rule Study for patients with minor head injury: methodology for phase II (validation and economic analysis). *Ann Emerg Med*. 2001;38:317-322.

- NEXUS criteria: Hoffman JR, Wolfson AB, Todd K, Mower WR (1998). "Selective cervical spine radiography in blunt trauma: methodology of the National Emergency X-Radiography

Utilization Study (NEXUS).". *Ann Emerg Med*. 32 (4): 461–9.

Canadian C-spine rules:

- Stiell IG, Wells GA, Vandemheen KL, Clement CM, Lesiuk H, De Maio VJ, et al. The Canadian C-spine rule for radiography in alert and stable trauma patients. *JAMA*. 2001 Oct 17. 286(15):1841-8.

- Stiell IG, Clement CM, O'Connor A, Davies B, Leclair C, Sheehan P, et al. Multicentre prospective validation of use of the Canadian C-Spine Rule by triage nurses in the emergency department. *CMAJ*. 2010 Aug 10. 182(11):1173-9.

Post-ATLS—Evaluate what procedures exist in your practice setting for rapidly evaluating patients for traumatic brain injury (TBI). Does your practice setting have a protocol for prevention of secondary brain injury once TBI is diagnosed? Also evaluate what procedures exist in your practice setting for spine immobilization. Are all staff members who deal with trauma patients adequately educated in these procedures? Evaluate your practice setting regarding how the cervical spine is evaluated and cleared (if appropriate). Are all staff members who evaluate trauma patients adequately educated in the existing, evidence-based criteria for evaluation and clearance of the cervical spine?

Skill Station E
ADJUNCTS

LEARNING OBJECTIVES

1. Identify the appropriate positioning of an ultrasound probe for FAST and eFAST exams.

2. Identify fluid on still images or video of FAST exam.

3. Identify ultrasound evidence of pneumothorax on video images of an eFAST exam.

4. Use a structured approach to interpret a chest x-ray and identify injuries present (see Skill Station B: Breathing).

5. Explain the value of the anteroposterior (AP) pelvic x-ray examination to identify the potential for massive blood loss, and describe the maneuvers that can be used to reduce pelvic volume and control bleeding.

6. Use a structured approach to interpreting a plain x-ray of the spine or CT (based on course director's preference).

7. Use a structured approach to evaluating a pelvic x-ray.

SKILLS INCLUDED IN THIS SKILL STATION

- Perform a FAST Exam and Properly Position Probes

- Perform an eFAST Exam and Properly Position Probes

- Identify Abnormal eFAST on Still or Video Images

- Identify Fluid on FAST Video or Still Images of FAST

- Evaluate Thoracic and Lumbar Spine Images

- Interpret a Pelvic X-Ray

■ FIGURE G-1

PERFORM A FAST EXAM AND PROPERLY POSITION PROBES

STEP 1. Use a low-frequency probe (3.5 mHz). Start with the heart to ensure the gain is set appropriately. Fluid within the heart will appear black. Place the probe in the subxyoid space, with the probe marker to the right (■ FIGURE G-1). The probe angle is shallow, and the liver is used as an acoustic window.

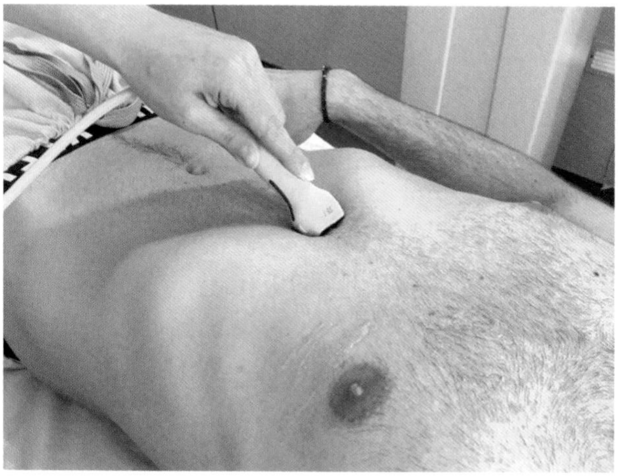

STEP 2. Move to the right upper quadrant view. Place the probe marker toward the head in the coronal plane in the anterior axillary line (■ FIGURE G-2). Rotate the probe obliquely and scan from cephalad to caudad to visualize the diaphragm, liver, and kidney.

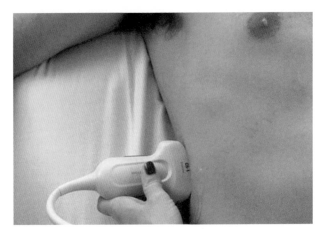

■ FIGURE G-2

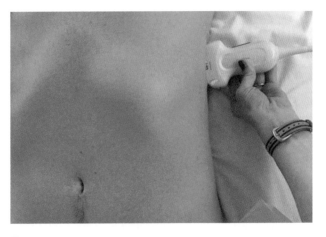

■ FIGURE G-3

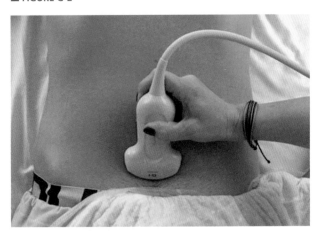

■ FIGURE G-4

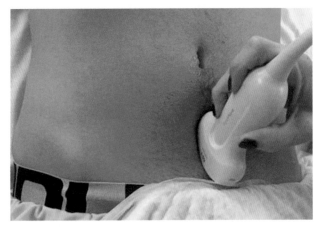

■ FIGURE G-5

STEP 3. Scan the left upper quadrant. Position the probe marker toward the head in the coronal plane (■ FIGURE G-3). Begin scan more cephalad than on the right and more posterior. Begin in the midaxillary line. Rotate the probe obliquely and visualize the diaphragm, spleen, and kidney.

STEP 4. (Ideally, the bladder is full.) Place the probe above the pubic bone with the probe marker pointing to the right (■ FIGURE G-4). Scan for fluid, which appears as a dark stripe. Rotate the probe 90 degrees so the probe marker points to the head (■ FIGURE G-5). Scan for fluid.

PERFORM AN EFAST EXAM AND DEMONSTRATE PROPER PROBE POSITIONING

STEP 1. Place the probe in the second or third intercostal space in the mid clavicular line in a sagittal orientation (■ FIGURE G-6), and slide the probe caudally (■ FIGURE G-7). Examine 2 or 3 interspaces. Including more interspaces increases the sensitivity

STEP 2. Evaluate the right and left diaphragms using the same probe position as for evaluation of the perihepatic and perisplenic space (■ FIGURE G-8), sliding the probe one rib space cephalad (■ FIGURE G-9).

IDENTIFY ABNORMAL eFAST ON STILL OR VIDEO IMAGES

STEP 1. Look for lung sliding. If you see none, look for lung pulse.

STEP 2. Look for comet tails.

STEP 3. Look for seashore, bar code, or stratosphere sign in M mode. Bar code and stratosphere signs indicate pneumothorax.

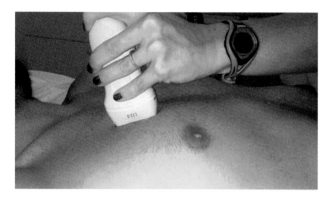

■ FIGURE G-6

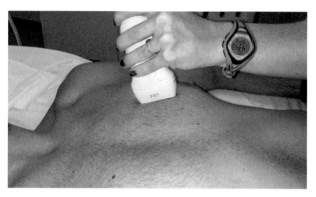

■ FIGURE G-7

■ FIGURE G-8

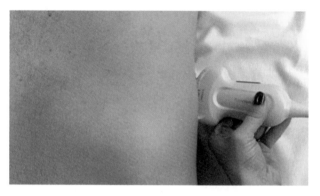

■ FIGURE G-9

STEP 4. Look for black or anechoid areas above the diaphragm.

IDENTIFY FLUID ON FAST VIDEO OR STILL IMAGES OF FAST

STEP 1. On the pericardial view, look for a black stripe of fluid separating the hyperechoic pericardium from the gray myocardium. This stripe represents fluid.

STEP 2. Look at the hepatorenal space. Intraperitoneal fluid has a black hypoechoic or anechoic appearance.

STEP 3. Look at the splenorenal space. Blood will appear as a hypoechoic or anechoic strip in this area.

STEP 4. Look around the bladder for an area of hypoechogenicity.

STEP 5. Be sure you have thoroughly visualized all spaces before declaring an examination negative.

EVALUATE THORACIC AND LUMBAR SPINE IMAGES (OPTIONAL)

Note: Before interpreting the x-ray, confirm the patient name and date of examination.

STEP 1. Assess for alignment of vertebral bodies/ angulation of spine.

STEP 2. Assess the contour of the vertebral bodies.

STEP 3. Assess the disk spaces.

STEP 4. Assess for encroachment of vertebral body on the canal.

INTERPRET A PELVIC X-RAY

Note: Before interpreting the x-ray, confirm the patient name and date of examination.

STEP 1. Check for interruption of the arcuate and ilioischial lines, including the pubic symphysis. The pubic symphysis should be less than 1 cm in pregnancy and less than 0.5 cm in nonpregnant adults.

STEP 2. Check for widening or displacement of the sacroiliac joints. Check the transverse processes of L-5 because they may fracture with sacroiliac disruption.

STEP 3. Check the sacrum for evidence of fracture. The arcs of the foramina may be interrupted with sacral fractures.

STEP 4. Check the acetabulum bilaterally for interruption and femoral dislocation. Check the femoral head and neck for disruption bilaterally.

LINKS TO FUTURE LEARNING

Post ATLS—Review the FAST performance video on the MyATLS mobile app. After this course, take the opportunity to perform FAST and eFAST on your patients to improve your comfort with use of this technology. In addition, make an effort to read pelvic x rays on your own before looking at the radiologist interpretation.

SECONDARY SURVEY

LEARNING OBJECTIVES

1. Assess a simulated multiply injured patient by using the correct sequence of priorities and management techniques for the secondary survey assessment of the patient.

2. Reevaluate a patient who is not responding appropriately to resuscitation and management.

3. Demonstrate fracture reduction in a simulated trauma patient scenario.

4. Demonstrate splinting a fracture in a simulated trauma patient scenario.

5. Evaluate a simulated trauma patient for evidence of compartment syndrome.

6. Recognize the patient who will require transfer to definitive care.

7. Apply a cervical collar.

SKILLS INCLUDED IN THIS SKILL STATION

- Perform a Secondary Survey in a Simulated Trauma Patient

- Reduce and Splint a Fracture in a Simulated Trauma Patient

- Apply a Cervical Collar in a Simulated Trauma Patient

- Evaluate for the Presence of Compartment Syndrome

PERFORM SECONDARY SURVEY IN A SIMULATED TRAUMA PATIENT

STEP 1. Obtain AMPLE history from patient, family, or prehospital personnel.

- A—allergies

- M—medications

- P—past history, illnesses, and pregnancies

- L—last meal

- E—environment and exposure

STEP 2. Obtain history of injury-producing event and identify injury mechanisms.

HEAD AND MAXILLOFACIAL

STEP 3. Assess the head and maxillofacial area.

A. Inspect and palpate entire head and face for lacerations, contusions, fractures, and thermal injury.

B. Reevaluate pupils.

C. Reevaluate level of consciousness and Glasgow Coma Scale (GCS) score.

D. Assess eyes for hemorrhage, penetrating injury, visual acuity, dislocation of lens, and presence of contact lenses.

E. Evaluate cranial nerve function.

F. Inspect ears and nose for cerebrospinal fluid leakage.

G. Inspect mouth for evidence of bleeding and cerebrospinal fluid, soft-tissue lacerations, and loose teeth.

CERVICAL SPINE AND NECK

STEP 4. Assess the cervical spine and neck.

A. Inspect for signs of blunt and penetrating injury, tracheal deviation, and use of accessory respiratory muscles.

B. Palpate for tenderness, deformity, swelling, subcutaneous emphysema, tracheal deviation, and symmetry of pulses.

C. Auscultate the carotid arteries for bruits.

D. Restrict cervical spinal motion when injury is possible.

CHEST

STEP 5. Assess the chest.

A. Inspect the anterior, lateral, and posterior chest wall for signs of blunt and penetrating injury, use of accessory breathing muscles, and bilateral respiratory excursions.

B. Auscultate the anterior chest wall and posterior bases for bilateral breath sounds and heart sounds.

C. Palpate the entire chest wall for evidence of blunt and penetrating injury, subcutaneous emphysema, tenderness, and crepitation.

D. Percuss for evidence of hyperresonance or dullness.

ABDOMEN

STEP 6. Assess the abdomen.

A. Inspect the anterior and posterior abdomen for signs of blunt and penetrating injury and internal bleeding.

B. Auscultate for the presence of bowel sounds.

C. Percuss the abdomen to elicit subtle rebound tenderness.

D. Palpate the abdomen for tenderness, involuntary muscle guarding, unequivocal rebound tenderness, and a gravid uterus.

PERINEUM/RECTUM/VAGINA

STEP 7. Assess the perineum. Look for:

- Contusions and hematomas
- Lacerations
- Urethral bleeding

STEP 8. Perform a rectal assessment in selected patients to identify the presence of rectal blood. This includes checking for:

- Anal sphincter tone
- Bowel wall integrity
- Bony fragments

STEP 9. Perform a vaginal assessment in selected patients. Look for:

- Presence of blood in vaginal vault
- Vaginal lacerations

MUSCULOSKELETAL

STEP 10. Perform a musculoskeletal assessment.

A. Inspect the upper and lower extremities for evidence of blunt and penetrating injury, including contusions, lacerations, and deformity.

B. Palpate the upper and lower extremities for tenderness, crepitation, abnormal movement, and sensation.

C. Palpate all peripheral pulses for presence, absence, and equality.

D. Assess the pelvis for evidence of fracture and associated hemorrhage.

E. Inspect and palpate the thoracic and lumbar spines for evidence of blunt and penetrating injury, including contusions, lacerations, tenderness, deformity, and sensation (while restricting spinal motion in patients with possible spinal injury).

NEUROLOGICAL

STEP 11. Perform a neurological assessment.

    A. Reevaluate the pupils and level of consciousness.

    B. Determine the GCS score.

    C. Evaluate the upper and lower extremities for motor and sensory functions.

    D. Observe for lateralizing signs.

REDUCE AND SPLINT A FRACTURE IN A SIMULATED TRAUMA PATIENT

STEP 1. Ensure that the ABCDEs have been assessed and life-threatening problems have been addressed.

STEP 2. Completely expose the extremity and remove all clothing.

STEP 3. Clean and cover any open wounds.

STEP 4. Perform a neurovascular examination of the extremity.

STEP 5. Provide analgesia.

STEP 6. Select the appropriate size and type of splint. Include the joint above and below the injury.

STEP 7. Pad the bony prominences that will be covered by the splint.

STEP 8. Manually support the fractured area and apply distal traction below the fracture and counter traction just above the joint.

STEP 9. Reevaluate the neurovascular status of the extremity.

STEP 10. Place the extremity in the splint and secure.

STEP 11. Obtain orthopedic consultation.

APPLY A CERVICAL COLLAR IN A SIMULATED TRAUMA PATIENT

STEP 1. Place the patient in the supine position.

STEP 2. Place your extended fingers against the patient's neck. Your little finger should almost be touching the patient's shoulder. Count how many of your fingers it takes to reach the jawline. Remember, sizing a cervical collar is not an exact science; the available sizes are limited, so make your best estimate.

STEP 3. Find the appropriately sized collar or use an adjustable one, if available.

STEP 4. Have another provider restrict the patient's cervical spinal motion by standing at head of bed and holding either side of the head.

STEP 5. Slide the posterior portion of the collar behind the patient's neck, taking care not to move the neck.

STEP 6. Place the anterior portion of the collar on while making sure to place the patient's chin in the chin holder.

STEP 7. Secure the collar with the hook and loop fasteners, making it snug enough to prevent flexion but allowing the patient to open his or her mouth.

EVALUATE FOR PRESENCE OF COMPARTMENT SYNDROME

STEP 1. Assess the degree of pain — is it greater than expected and out of proportion to the stimulus or injury?

STEP 2. Determine if there is pain on passive stretch of the affected muscle.

STEP 3. Determine if there is altered sensation or paresthesia distal to the affected compartment.

STEP 4. Determine if there is tense swelling of the affected compartment.

STEP 5. Palpate the muscular compartments of the extremity and compare the tension in the injured extremity with that in the noninjured extremity. Asymmetry may be an important finding.

STEP 6. Compartment pressures may be measured, but the diagnosis is clinical. Pressure measurements may be useful in unconscious or neurologically impaired patients.

STEP 7. Frequently reevaluate the patient, because compartment syndrome can develop over time.

STEP 8. Obtain surgical or orthopedic consultation early.

▶ LINKS TO FUTURE LEARNING

Review the secondary survey video on the MyATLS mobile app.

Post ATLS—Recognize that the secondary survey is similar to the comprehensive physical examination learned in medical school. It incorporates the AMPLE history and takes into account the mechanism of traumatic injury. It is easy therefore to find opportunities in one's practice setting to continue to practice the skills learned in the secondary survey skill station.

INDEX